THE

CLASSIC *f*M

GUIDE TO

CLASSICAL
MUSIC

THE

CLASSIC *f*M

GUIDE TO

CLASSICAL MUSIC

THE ESSENTIAL
COMPANION TO
COMPOSERS AND
THEIR MUSIC

CONSULTANT EDITOR ROBIN RAY
INTRODUCED BY HUMPHREY BURTON
JEREMY NICHOLAS

PAVILION

To the three women in my life:
the one who had the piano,
the one who listens with me
and the one for whom I wrote this book,
with love

First published in Great Britain in 1996 by
Pavilion Books Ltd
26 Upper Ground
London SE1 9PD

Text copyright © Jeremy Nicholas
Foreword copyright © Humphrey Burton
Cartoons copyright © James Browne
Photographs copyright © Hulton Deutsch Collection
Bernstein photograph copyright © Christina Burton

The moral right of the author has been asserted

Designed by Castle House Press, Llantrisant, South Wales
Picture Research: Lynda Marshall

A CIP catalogue record for this book is available from the British Library.

ISBN 1-85793-760-0

Printed and bound in Great Britain by Butler & Tanner Ltd

2 4 6 8 10 9 7 5 3 1

This book may be ordered by post direct from the publisher.
Please contact the Marketing Department.
But try your bookshop first.

CONTENTS

ACKNOWLEDGMENTS

A number of friends and colleagues have been of immense assistance during the planning and writing of this book. I should like to thank in particular Rowena Webb; John Spearman and Robert O'Dowd (Classic fM); Colin Webb, Trevor Dolby and my editors Rosanna Dickinson and Emma Lawson (Pavilion Books); Stephen Jackson, who made many useful observations on the first draft; Alison Waggitt for a superb index; and Eileen Townsend Jones (Castle House Press) and Kay Sayce (Sayce Publishing) for editing and designing the book with such care and precision.

Peter Robinson of Curtis Brown has offered advice and assistance beyond the call of duty. Throughout the project I have had the support and encouragement of Robin Ray, whose shared aims in matters musical have been both reassuring and stimulating. Finally, but most importantly, I want to record my gratitude to Jill, my wife, for providing the perfect conditons in which to write.

PREFACE

A few years ago, I was in the back of a taxi being driven to one of the concerts marking the bicentenary of Mozart's death. The driver asked me where I was going. 'This Mozart – he was a bit special then, was he?' 'Yes, he was,' I replied. 'To lots of people he's not only a musical genius but the greatest composer who's ever lived.' 'Yeah, but when was he around?' asked the driver. 'Towards the end of the eighteenth century,' I told him. 'Well, he *would* be a bit of a genius then, wouldn't he? I mean there was no one else around doing it, was there?' 'No one else?' I began. 'Well,' he said, 'I mean the Irish had their drums and things but that was about all....'

I've puzzled over that ever since. The gap was too wide to bridge, the time too short. How to explain Mozart and the history of classical music in a matter of minutes to someone who had not been fortunate enough ever to have come into contact with it?

To someone like me, who has listened to classical music all his life and derived more pleasure from it more consistently than almost anything else, it is easy to forget how many people have never given it a moment's thought. Some have an inbuilt resistance to it and say things like 'it's too difficult' or 'you have to be educated' or 'there's too much to learn' or 'I don't know what to listen to.' I think I would feel rather the same if I were beginning to learn to paint or fish, or starting up as a market gardener – there's so much to learn, the language is so different and vast that the prospect is too daunting, and so, especially after our formal education has finished, we don't bother. It takes too much time and effort to assimilate a new language. We want everything on a plate.

Well, here is the restaurant. The menu is enormous. What do you choose to eat? You certainly won't like all the dishes; you'll have to experiment. Some of the dishes you try, you will want to spit out; others you'll want to gorge on. Some will taste so delicious that you may not feel like sampling anything else. But for a true enjoyment of food, a balanced and varied diet is best (so say the experts). It's also a good idea to try everything at least once (so say our mothers).

Bite-sized chunks are a good way of starting. I remember a conductor, the late Norman Del Mar, telling me that his love of music and an intimate knowledge of Wagner's vast operas were acquired almost incidentally as a child by listening to four-minute sections over and over again, working his way slowly through twenty sides of *Das Rheingold*. He grew up thinking that that was how Wagner had written the music, in little four- or five-minute bits. Before he knew it, he had absorbed one of the lengthiest and most complex works of music ever written.

That, for what it's worth, is how I became interested in classical music. Like most people, my parents loved music but were not in any way knowledgeable about it. They bought records of the popular classics infrequently, chosen because they had heard and liked them on the radio or at a concert. I grew up towards the end of the

78-r.p.m. era, and the length of those discs suited my attention span perfectly. Rather less precocious than Norman Del Mar and with Wagner distinctly absent from our house, I remember a record with Sousa's marches *Washington Post* on one side and *Liberty Bell* on the other as being the first music to 'get to me' and I played it constantly, until my father sat on it. There were also classical singles, 45-r.p.m. discs with a one-inch-diameter hole in the middle, which meant you had to have a special insertable spindle to play them.

Some choices were not for me. Marion Anderson, the American contralto, singing Schubert's *Death and the Maiden* put me off German *Lieder* until I was much older. But Weber's *Invitation to the Dance* in Berlioz's orchestration and, above all, Vladimir Horowitz, the great piano virtuoso, playing Liszt's Hungarian Rhapsody No.6 were the keys to the door. At the same time, the first LPs appeared on the market. I've still got them: Strauss waltzes, Tchaikowsky's *Nutcracker,* Gilbert and Sullivan operas, the Handel-Harty *Water Music,* Schubert's 'Unfinished' Symphony, Beethoven's 'Pastoral' Symphony and his Piano Concerto No.4 – goodness knows how many times I listened to them as a child.

That was my way in, and it was the beginning of a lifelong love affair. From then on, every time I heard a new piece of music that I liked, I would make every effort to find out its name and who composed it, then save up enough pocket money to buy the record, or tape it (illegally) from the radio. Very quickly, I knew what sort of music appealed to me most and who the composers and artists were with whom I had an affinity.

The endless pleasure of discovery continued from there, for one of the greatest joys of classical music is its bottomless treasure chest. Hardly a day – and certainly not a week – goes by without my hearing a piece I have never encountered before and wondering why it has taken so long for me to come across it. Only today I have been introduced to the plaintive opening Adagio of Mozart's Piano Sonata in E flat (K282) and listened enraptured to an aria from Stravinsky's *A Rake's Progress.* Yesterday – a confession, this – I heard for the first time the music to one of the world's most popular ballets, *Giselle.* The journey continues.

There were some good books, too, to serve as maps. Choosing them was also very much trial and error. Some were too technical, some were too schoolmasterly, some were written in a dry, stuffy manner that made the subject unattractive. Two of the best I've ever read were by the distinguished American critic Harold Schonberg: *Lives of the Great Composers* (full of gossip, tittle-tattle and sound advice and judgments) and *The Great Pianists,* which in my early teens brought me to the realization that, in my particular case, the piano was the area of music I most loved.

If this book proves half as stimulating as Mr Schonberg's, I shall be a happy man. If you know a great deal about classical music, I hope I have tempted you to try some as-yet-unsampled composers and works; if you know a little and listen a lot, I trust that I have provided enough signposts, encouragement and information to enhance your enjoyment still further; and for anyone who, like my taxi driver, finds everything about classical music except 'Nessun dorma' to be a bit of a mystery, I offer this as a key to the locked door.

Jeremy Nicholas
Barley Fen
March 1996

FOREWORD

Music has always played a very important part in my life. I enjoy running through piano duets and singing in choirs (or even going solo for an after-supper sing-song of Gershwin and Cole Porter) even more than I do listening to music – and I've done a great deal of *that!* For a fair proportion of the past forty years I've also had the good fortune to earn my living through music in an active way: by directing and introducing radio and television programmes on a wide assortment of musical subjects, ranging from Wagner's *The Golden Ring* (1964) to Bernstein's *The Making of West Side Story* (1984), by way of *Young Musician of the Year*, *Cardiff Singer of the World* and any number of televised Proms and opera relays.

So I've picked up a good deal of my knowledge of music, such as it is, on the job. But one has to start one's musical education somewhere and I was pretty well self-taught. Indeed, I am appalled to remember that I sat my School Certificate examination, aged sixteen, having read only two music books: a primer on theory (by a certain Macpherson, if memory serves aright) and the slightly less ancient but still pre-war *Musical Companion* edited by Bacharach. Another pre-war primer, bravely entitled *A Key to the Art of Music*, was enormously influential on my later teens. Soon I was a voracious reader about matters musical.

When I joined the BBC, back in the distant 1950s, I learnt from my years of working with my editor, Huw Wheldon, that there was nothing to be ashamed about in consulting encyclopaedias, biographies and other learned tomes as part of the preparation for the making of the arts documentaries that were often my concern on *Monitor*. When we were making our centenary film about Sir Edward Elgar, Ken Russell and I had to produce printed evidence for the ever-sceptical Wheldon that Elgar really did like flying kites with his daughter, or sliding down the Malvern Hills on a tea tray, or carrying out chemical experiments in his backyard.

I've always been one of those people who positively enjoys doing homework. I do my own research for my films and radio productions; I even like reading programme notes at concerts. I believe that the more information you have in advance about a subject, the more likely you are to understand it and thus to get the most out of it; music is no exception to that rule. Some of the most enthralling hours of my life were the mornings I spent in Bayreuth reading Ernest Newman's *Wagner Nights* in preparation for my first exposure to the complete *Ring* in the theatre.

Inevitably, I've accumulated a fair number of musical encyclopaedias and lexicons, as well as biographies of the great composers and interpreters and innumerable cardboard boxes of opera and concert programmes – my study is close to bursting. I'm very partial to reference books but I don't recommend my squirrel instincts, particularly if your shelf space is at a premium.

So if you have room for only one reference book concerned with the composers of classical music, then it seems to me that this *Classic fM Guide* is the one you should possess, since Jeremy Nicholas has achieved in it the remarkable feat of producing concise text without sacrificing an ounce of human interest or readability. Placed handily next to your FM receiver or your CD player, it will surely add a great deal to your listening pleasure. Its layout has evidently been designed for swift and effective consultation, the illustrations are remarkably fresh and I'm sure I shall be turning to it frequently, for instance on those rather madcap weeks when I'm asked to stand in for Henry Kelly on his famous morning music shows for Classic fM.

In my work as a broadcaster I have been an unashamed elitist, by which I mean not that I wish to exclude anybody from music but that only the best will do. The successful development of the Classic fM radio station in recent years has borne out my long-held assertion that in this country there is a large public, running into many millions, that appreciates good, so-called 'classical' music. Some of these music-lovers may not know much about the nuts and bolts of the art, but they recognize its power, they are grateful for the pick-me-up it provides on a cold winter's morning and they can be deeply moved by its profound message, which, as Mendelssohn once observed, sometimes goes too deep for mere words to explain. But we can all do with a helping hand, which is what Jeremy Nicholas is offering us in this exemplary guide. To take but one example, the Chronology of Music at the beginning of the book is a truly helpful summary of a thousand years of musical history.

May I conclude by commending to you one of the definitions given by the good Dr Samuel Johnson? 'Sir,' he wrote, 'a desire of knowledge is the natural feeling of mankind; and every human being, whose mind is not debauched, will be willing to give all that he has to get knowledge.' There's enough knowledge enshrined in these pages for me to wish you many hours of undebauched but engrossing study – and happy listening!

Humphrey Burton
London
March 1996

ABOUT THIS BOOK

This book is about Western classical music, 'Western' for these purposes embracing Russia and the Americas, as well as Scandinavia and Europe. Almost all the music discussed here was written by white males; only a handful of entries even refer to female composers. It is a strange and sad fact that even in this enlightened century, great male composers heavily outnumber those of the opposite sex. Similarly, few coloured writers have made their mark internationally in the field of classical music. The reasons for this are numerous – but this area of human expression seems to remain the domain of those who developed the concept in the first place.

For many people, music in one form or another is a basic necessity of life. Most have broad, middle-of-the-road tastes. They will tackle anything from the popular classics and Broadway musicals to jazz and pop. Those who run the classical music business in broadcasting, concerts and records can never quite believe this. It is, however, a fact that the majority of their audience has reserved tastes and very little specialized knowledge. The musical arbiters assume that the average listener can share their specialist interests, musical erudition, innate curiosity and enthusiasm for the latest, the oldest or the most obscure. Writers and programme-makers who find an opera by Janáček to be the most accessible of works cannot understand that it may present a difficult challenge to ears more attuned to the melodies, harmonies and rhythms of an opera by Puccini or Mozart. Classical music is a minority interest. It is not as central to the lives of most people as the taste-makers would like to think.

Yet – and yet – those same people with ordinary likes and dislikes who love listening to a wide variety of music are capable of being contradictory. There are those who look blank at the mention of Anton Webern, and, if taken to the Royal Festival Hall for a concert of his works, would make a run for it after five minutes. Yet they will happily tolerate the background music of a TV or movie thriller, not noticing that it is frequently as atonal and dissonant as anything written by the most ardent Serialist composer of concert works.

Chronology of music and composers

To be able to place a work of art in its historical context can be a revealing and rewarding exercise. The sound world, the musical texture that a composer conjures up, reflects the age in which he lived, and echoes other contemporary areas of creative endeavour.

The CHRONOLOGY OF MUSIC not only lists the dates of all the composers mentioned in the main text but juxtaposes them with interesting or important world events, musical era by musical era. The significance of each of these eras is explained in the accompanying essay.

The CHRONOLOGY OF COMPOSERS allows the reader to see at a glance the dates of all the most significant composers of Western classical music and who their immediate contemporaries were, as well as providing something about the life and most notable works of 250 other composers who are not included in the COMPOSERS A TO Z.

Composers A to Z

The main part of the book is devoted to the lives and music of the most significant composers. To know something of a composer's life and character enhances the enjoyment of his music immeasurably. In the foreword to his book *The Lure of Music,* the eminent American critic Olin Downes (1886–1955) relates the story of a friend who '"wasn't musical but knew what he liked"'! Reading, by chance, a paragraph about one of the compositions he liked, he suddenly realized that this composition told the story of an episode in the life of another man, a human being who lived, struggled, rejoiced, and narrated his experiences in the language of music. Having read the story, he played the record over again, and discovered that it meant far more to him than it ever had before.'

If you are using this book as an introduction to classical music, you could justifiably ask, 'How have the composers earned their entry? Who says that those included are the most important or wrote the best music?' History has dictated the choice. The composers whose names have survived produced music that has stood the test of time – music that speaks to us today with the same power as it did when first written, or has changed fashions and forced progress. There are undoubtedly some good composers who have been forgotten for various reasons and who wrote worthwhile, rewarding music. But they are very few, and there are certainly no undiscovered Beethovens. The pantheon of the Great Composers has been established for us. By and large, the amount of space devoted to each composer in this book reflects their importance.

With any book such as this, a cut-off point has to be fixed. My not-quite-arbitrary decision is that the composer, to qualify for inclusion, has to have been born at least fifty years ago. I take the view that half a century needs to elapse before a composer's music can be properly evaluated or viewed in its historical context; by then it will have been judged to have stayed the course or be worthy of revival after years of neglect. Or not.

Several music directories on my shelf bear witness to the folly of eagerly bunging in every new name that appeared on a concert programme. One otherwise-excellent book devotes much space to Antheil, Joio, Diamond, Gilbert, Lopatnikoff, Mignone, Pizzetti, and a dozen more. Although highly rated at the time the book was published, they have vanished from public view and references to them consequently mean little. I have, with only a few exceptions, concentrated on those names established indubitably in the Hall of Fame.

Necessarily, a book of this size cannot hope to cover every composer and, inevitably, personal taste and experience have also coloured the contents a little. It won't take an Inspector Morse to discover where my sympathies lie: with melody, rhythm and harmony, with music that edifies, elucidates, entertains and enriches. Like Sir Thomas Beecham, I am 'not interested in music – or in any work of art – that fails to stimulate enjoyment of life and, what is more, pride of life'.

'One-hit wonders' and other lesser composers

Some composers, (sometimes unfairly) remembered today for a single work, feature in this book as 'one-hit wonders'. I have also chosen to include a number of other minor composers, such as Gottschalk, MacDowell and Kreisler. The reason for this is that, while their aims might not have been Olympian, the pleasure that their music gives and the sheer craft with which it was written are celebrated too rarely.

Type of music, influences, contemporaries

The entries for all but the minor composers begin by summarizing the forms in which they wrote, together with the notable influences on their work. This has been done to encourage the reader to investigate and compare their work, and to trace the development of a particular school or musical train of thought. Those born immediately before or after the composer are listed on either side in chronological order of birth (composers with their own main entry are listed in SMALL CAPITALS; all the rest are in A CHRONOLOGY OF COMPOSERS). To hear how differently two contemporaries wrote can be stimulating; likewise, the frequent similarity of styles between contemporaries might lead the listener to sample the music of a composer whose works may be new territory but which complements those that are already familiar.

Essential works

The most famous, important and popular works of a particular composer are listed as Essential Works. These represent the composer at his best and are an excellent introduction to his particular style and language. Space does not permit the listing of a composer's complete works, but I trust that my comments will be enough to tempt the curious to investigate further. In the case of Puccini, for instance, the operas are the obvious starting points. If they particularly appeal to you then you'll want to find out more about the rest of his music. You'll see the mention of his *Missa di Gloria* – an uneven, early work and by no means 'essential' Puccini – but I guarantee that parts of this little-known piece will enrapture you.

You may ask: 'Who decides which are a composer's "best" and "worst" compositions?' Two criteria apply: first, the historical, whereby time has shown that the music in question stands out from its contemporaries or among the main body of a composer's work; second, from a purely musical viewpoint, if the piece is widely considered to be well written, and has been of some influence on others. 'By general agreement' is the deciding factor. A composer's 'Greatest Hits' will, I hope, all have been listed, whether trifles or works of some consequence. Where a composer's works have been designated Opus numbers, I have given them, along with their dates of composition. This helps their precise identification.

Glossary

In the course of each entry you may come across musical terms you haven't encountered before – contrapuntal, sonata, polytonal, and so on. Explanations will be found either in the GLOSSARY at the end of the book, or in the immediate text. It is important not to be put off by the vocabulary of classical music, which can, at first glance, make the subject seem difficult and inaccessible. Yet it is genuinely no more complicated than learning the basic rules of football. Familiarity and repetition make a strange language friendly. If I were to go to a football match for the first time, I could easily see what was going on and what the aim was of the whole exercise; but I'd need someone to explain the rules, the idiosyncrasies of teams and players, the terminology which, to a novice, is a closed book.

Recordings

Very occasionally I have mentioned specific recordings, but only when there is an indisputably great and unsurpassed interpretation that has survived the test of time. In this I acknowledge my inconsistency in not including every such recording: time and space preclude that. As far as recommended recordings in general are concerned, so many different pieces are referred to that to have listed a recording for each would have needed a whole companion volume. For detailed comparative reviews, refer to the excellent guides published by Penguin and *Gramophone*. These also cover budget-price discs. If you want to amass a working knowledge of the basic classical repertoire, this is undoubtedly the path to choose.

Finding your way

- **By cross-references:** wherever a composer's name appears in SMALL CAPITALS, it signals that the composer has a main entry in the COMPOSERS A TO Z. Sections of the book are also cross-referred in this way.
- **By date:** through the CHRONOLOGY OF COMPOSERS, or through the time charts in the CHRONOLOGY OF MUSIC.
- **Alphabetically:** main composers through the COMPOSERS A TO Z; everything else through the comprehensive INDEX.

Index

The title of every piece of music mentioned in the book is indexed. Most foreign titles (arias from operas, for instance) are also listed in the English translations used in the main text. Thus 'Che gelida manina' ('Your tiny hand is frozen') from *La Bohème* appears under both 'C' and 'Y'. As the essential works of a particular composer are listed in the A to Z entry, they are not duplicated here.

The main aim of the book has not been mentioned – one that I trust the above elements of the book will inspire: to browse. Dip into it, skip about, look up something at random. May you pass many happy hours doing so.

A CHRONOLOGY OF MUSIC

In the last century, musicologists divided the art of music into different periods corresponding to the outlines of cultural history that had already been identified. The debate continues, however, as to exactly when, for example, the Baroque era began and finished. The labels that have been given to each of these periods are convenient approximations, and they inevitably overlap. These periods span a thousand years.

So far, no generic term for the music of the twentieth century has emerged that adequately covers Serialism, neo-classicism and all the other -isms and fragmentations of the past hundred years.

Major musical terms used in this chapter are explained in the GLOSSARY.

Early music (1000–1200)	Method of notating music invented Simple vocal harmony develops
Medieval (1200–1450)	Start of polyphony in church music Minstrels, troubadours and *Trouvères* Establishment of instrumental music
Renaissance (1450–1600)	The golden age of polyphonic church music Madrigals, chansons and similar forms become popular Slow development of instrumental music
Baroque (1600–1750)	Beginnings of opera and oratorio The first orchestras Rise in experimentation with instrumental music Introduction of sonatas, concertos, suites and symphonies Polyphonic writing reaches its peak
Classical (1750–1820)	Concert symphony and concerto become popular Introduction of string quartets Decline of church music Major developments in opera
Early Romantic (1800–50)	Symphonic and concerto forms mature Development of Romantic opera The age of the piano virtuoso Introduction of nocturnes and symphonic poems Establishment of *Lieder* as an art form Beginnings of nationalism

High Romantic (1850–1910)	Emergence of music drama
	Nationalism becomes prominent
	Heyday of the symphonic or tone-poem
	Verismo opera
Modern (1900 to present)	Impressionism
	Post-Romanticism
	Neo-classicism
	Expressionism
	Gigantism
	Atonal and dissonant music
	Serial ('twelve-note') music
	Jazz, rock, pop etc.
	Electronic and computer music
	Minimalism

In the chronological lists that follow, composers are placed within their historical period alongside notable contemporary events. The sometimes unexpected juxtaposition of political and social affairs and artistic achievements helps to put the composer's life into context and gives a perspective to the kind of musical sound produced in their day.

Music-making as a means of expression has always been part of mankind's pleasure; it is an art form as ancient and as necessary as dance and painting. The cave paintings of 40,000 years ago depict man dancing, and there are representations of musical instruments dated to about 4000 BC. The earliest composer whose name we know is Mery, an Egyptian who lived c.2450 BC; the earliest musical notation, discovered in present-day Iraq, dates back before 1800 BC; and one of the first accounts of a public concert is in the Book of Daniel 3:15 (sixth century BC):

> *Now if ye be ready that at what time ye hear the sound of the cornet, flute, harp, sackbut, psaltery and dulcimer, and all kinds of musick, ye fall down and worship the image which I have made; well: but if ye worship not, ye shall be cast the same hour into the midst of a burning fiery furnace; and who is that God that shall deliver you out of my hands?*

The Ancient Egyptians and Babylonians appear to have stolen a march on us. It seems strange that the form of music now familiar to us took so long to mature – much longer than any other art. Not until the sixteenth century did Western music blossom with any certainty – then it flowered with some rapidity, stimulated by the introduction of printing and the development of an agreed formula for writing it down. It has taken the best part of six hundred years to iron out most of the difficulties presented in the scoring of music.

The events in the first table show how energetically the West produced architecture, painting, sculpture and literature, and how comparatively late and very sluggish was the progression from simple plainsong to polyphony. Yet the leap from there to the development of the symphony, sonata and other musical forms was made extraordinarily quickly, in the space of about one hundred years.

Early music

A convenient starting point for the beginnings of modern Western music is 1000 AD, for it was at about this time that composition was first introduced. 'Composition' at first meant the provision of accompanying contrapuntal parts for a plainsong tenor part. **Plainsong**, a translation of *Cantus planus*, is the traditional ritual melody of the Western Christian Church. It was derived from Greek songs and the chants of the Jewish synagogue, with its rhythm based on the free rhythm of speech.

At the end of the fourth century, the plainsong repertory of the early Christian church was set in order by Ambrose, Bishop of Milan, and two centuries later Pope Gregory reviewed the subject further. For the first millennium of the Christian era its music consisted of single-line chants without any instrumental accompaniment.

Guido d'Arezzo, an eleventh-century Benedictine monk, teacher and musical theorist, is generally credited with the introduction of a stave of horizontal lines by which the pitch of notes could be accurately recorded. He also devised what is now known as the tonic sol-fa system used by singers – in which notes are named according to their position in the scale, as opposed to being named after letters of the alphabet (a practice derived from the ancient Greeks).

Still, there was no method of indicating the length of a note. Without this, it is difficult to see how any sense of rhythm could be measured. Some scholars say that this was defined by the natural accentuation and emphasis of speech patterns and that therefore no special device was needed – the singers (without a conductor, of course) provided their own 'flow' and expression.

With two of the three main elements of music – **melody** and **rhythm** – in the process of being codified, the concept of **harmony** was introduced. Naturally, not all the singers in a choir would have the same vocal range, a problem for the comfortable unison-singing of the psalms. So voices began to be divided according to natural range, chanting the plainsong in parallel lines at two pitches, four or five notes apart (C⇨G, for instance). The gap between the two notes is called an interval (see GLOSSARY), thus the singers sang the interval of a perfect fifth. From this apparently simple concept the idea grew that while one line sang the plainsong (the 'tenor' or 'holding' part), others could weave another tune around it.

Rules were drawn up as to which part of the service could use which type of intervals. Gradually, the interval of a third (C⇨E, for instance), long considered to be a discord, was allowed. Within the relatively short time-scale of a century, Pérotin of Notre-Dame was writing music for three and four voices; he was one of the early masters of polyphony.

Parallel to the development of liturgical or church music ran that of the secular music of the **troubadours** – poet-musicians who sang of beautiful ladies, chivalry and spring. The troubadours were the successors to the court minstrels, employed to sing the great sagas and legends, and who, in turn, had their less-educated counterparts in the *jongleurs*, itinerant singers and instrumentalists. Of noble birth for the most part, the troubadours came from Provence and Aquitaine; the *trouvères*, their northern counterparts, and the *Minnesingers* of Germany were almost contemporary. Only about sixty manuscripts of troubadour and *trouvère* poetry survive today; few use musical notation, and they contain indications of pitch but not of note length.

These two hundred years witnessed the invention of composition, the birth of harmony, of modern musical notation, the dance and song craze that pervaded

Significant composers	Musical events	Other events
	EARLY MUSIC 1000–1200	
1000 Guido d'Arezzo, Italian (c.997–c.1050) Hildegard of Bingen, German (1098–1179)	Beginnings of modern musical notation Use of clef signs	**1066** Norman Conquest **1086** Doomsday Book **1086–97** Construction of White Tower (Tower of London) **1093–1274** Building of Durham cathedral
1100 Pérotin, French (fl. 1180)	Troubadours, minstrels of France	**1163–c.1250** Notre-Dame, Paris, constructed **1170** Murder of Thomas à Becket

Europe during the time of the crusades and the complex structure of the troubadours' poetry. All this was more than enough to ignite the imagination of Renaissance man.

Music in medieval Europe

The study and use of chords is called harmony. **Diaphony** – meaning 'two-voiced' music – dominated musical composition until the thirteenth century; the application of this two-part singing to plainchant was also called *organum*. Voices would sing an octave (C⇨C), a perfect fifth (C⇨G), a perfect fourth (C⇨F) or a major third (C⇨E) apart.

Polyphony – meaning 'many-sounds' or 'many-voiced' – is also concerned with the sounding of more than one note, but through melody. The addition of three, four or more independent musical lines sung or sounded together was the next obvious development, and it was Philippe de Vitry, a French bishop, composer, musical theorist, poet and diplomat who showed the way forward in his famous book *The New Art – Ars nova*, as opposed to the *Ars antiqua* of Guido d'Arezzo. **Time signatures** indicated a rhythm for the music; **notation** was developed to symbolize note lengths, using the ancestors of our minim, breve and semibreve. Guillaume de Machaut, a French priest, poet and composer, took de Vitry's ideas a stage further and wrote both secular songs and settings of the Mass (1364 – the earliest known complete setting by one composer) with three and four polyphonic voices.

Although France was the musical centre of Europe at this time, Italy was developing its own *ars nova* independently, with music that reflected the warmth and sensuality of the country, in contrast to the more intellectual Gallic writing. England, less affected by *ars nova*, made no significant contribution to musical development until the arrival of John Dunstable. Living in France as court composer to the Duke of Burgundy, the younger brother of Henry V, Dunstable utilized rhythmic phrases and traditional plainchant and added other free parts, combining them to create a flowing style. Nearly sixty pieces of his music still survive.

Dunstable in turn influenced the Burgundian composers Guillaume Dufay and Gilles Binchois, whose music can be said to be the stylistic bridge between *ars nova* and the fully developed polyphony of the fifteenth century. The technical aspects of

Significant composers	Musical events	Other events
	MEDIEVAL 1200–1450	
1200		
Adam de la Halle, French (c.1240–c.1286)	**1200** Peak of German *Minnesingers*	**1215** Magna Carta **1220** Amiens and Salisbury
Philippe de Vitry, French (1291–1361)	**1200–1300** Introduction of treble clef	cathedrals begun **1246** Sainte-Chapelle, Paris **1248** Cologne cathedral begun **1261–1324** York Minster begun **1265–1321** Dante **c.1266–1337** Giotto
1300		
Guillaume de Machaut, French (1300–77)	**1310** *Ars antiqua* develops into *Ars nova*	**1304–74** Petrarch **1313–1375** Boccaccio
Francesco Landini, Italian (1325–97)	**1340 onwards** Increase in secular and instrumental	**c.1340–c.1400** Geoffrey Chaucer
John Dunstable, English (c.1390–1453)	music **1370** German *Meistersingers*	**1370–1441** Jan van Eyck
1400		
Gilles Binchois, French (c.1400–60)		**1415** Battle of Agincourt **1426** First printed books
Guillaume Dufay, French (c.1400–74)		**1431** Joan of Arc died **1446–1515** King's College,
Johannes Ockeghem, Flemish (c.1430–c.1495)		Cambridge built
Josquin des Prés, Flemish (c.1440–1521)		

composition and the almost mathematical fascination with note combination began to open the door to the reflection of the composer's personality in his music.

By the middle of the fifteenth century, royal and aristocratic patronage had usurped the Church as the most important influence on the course of music. In 1416, for example, Henry V of England employed over thirty voices in the Chapel Royal while the Papal Chapel had only nine. One by-product was the closer relationship between secular music and church music, a cross-pollination that benefited the development of both. The musicians who passed through the Burgundian court spread its style and learning to all points of the European compass.

A new sense of adventure

The most noticeable advances during this period were the increased freedom given by composers to their vocal lines and the difference in the treatment of the texts they set. Previously, words had to fit the music; now the reverse was the case, no better illustrated than by the work of one of the next generation of composers – Josquin des Prés. His music incorporates a greater variety of expression – even flashes of humour – and includes attempts at **symbolism**, where the musical ideas match those of the text. With various voices singing in polyphony, it is difficult to follow the words; where the subject called for the text to be heard clearly, he wrote music that had the voices singing different notes but the same words at the same time – chordal music. Not surprisingly, he has been called 'the first composer whose music appeals to our modern sense of art.' After him, it is easy for our ears to follow the development of music into the language of the great classical works of two centuries later.

The high Renaissance

The sixteenth century witnessed four major musical phenomena: the polyphonic school reached its peak, the tradition of instrumental music was established, the first opera was produced and music began to be printed. For most people, the opportunity to see and read music had simply not been there; now, musicians could stand around a printed score and sing or play their part. Limited and expensive though it was, music in a fixed form was now widely available. No wonder it flourished.

It is hard today to conceive of the central importance of the Christian Church at that time. The splendid and confident buildings erected symbolized the age of 're-birth' and the music rose to fill the naves of the magnificent European cathedrals. Palestrina in Italy, Lassus in the Netherlands and Byrd in England extended Josquin's legacy; they produced complex and richly expressive works, taking the art of polyphonic writing for the voice to new heights and imbuing man's ability to express his faith with a glory and fervour that no previous century had matched.

How is this rich cloth of musical gold woven? One distinguished writer on music, Percy Scholes, drew an illuminating analogy with the weaving of musical 'fabric' when discussing the music of Palestrina.

> The music consists of the intertwining of a fixed number of strands. And as [the composer] weaves he is producing a 'woof' as well as a 'warp'. Looked at as warp the composition is a horizontal combination of melodies; looked at as woof it is a perpendicular collection of chords. The composer necessarily has both aspects in his mind as he pens his piece, but the horizontal (or 'warp') aspect is probably uppermost with him. Such music as this we speak of as 'Contrapuntal' or as 'in Counterpoint'. The 'woof' [= perpendicular, i.e. 'Harmonic'] element is there, but is less observable than the 'warp' [= horizontal, i.e. 'Contrapuntal']. A moment's thought will show that all Contrapuntal music must also be Harmonic, and a second moment's thought that not all Harmonic music need be Counterpoint.

New musical developments have always caused controversy. As early as 1581, Vincenzo Galilei wrote: 'Why cause words to be sung by four or five voices so that they cannot be distinguished when the Ancients aroused the strongest passions by means of a single voice supported by a lyre? We must renounce counterpoint and different kinds of instruments and return to primitive simplicity.' It had taken a thousand years from the earliest plainsong for the tradition to develop into a highly sophisticated art form, which produced such masterpieces as Palestrina's *Stabat mater*, Victoria's *Ave verum corpus* and Byrd's *O quam gloriosum*.

A fusion of styles

New preoccupations now challenged composers. The reverent, lush choral works of the Church, mainly from northern Europe, were influenced by the sunny dances

Significant composers	Musical events	Other events
	RENAISSANCE 1450–1600	
1450 John Taverner, English (**c.1490–1545**) Thomas Tallis, English (**c.1505–85**) Giovanni da Palestrina, Italian (**c.1525–94**) Orlando de Lassus, Netherlandish (**1532–94**) Andrea Gabrieli, Italian (**c.1533–85**) William Byrd, English (**1543–1623**) Tomás Luis de Victoria, Spanish (**c.1548–1611**)	**1527** Singing school founded in Venice	**1452–1519** Leonardo da Vinci **1453** Fall of Constantinople **c.1460–1516** Hieronymus Bosch **c.1466–1536** Erasmus **1469–1527** Machiavelli **1471–1528** Dürer **1475–1564** Michelangelo **c.1477–1576** Titian **1483–1520** Raphael **1485** Battle of Bosworth and start of Tudor dynasty **c.1494–c.1553** Rabelais **c.1503** *Mona Lisa* (da Vinci) **1509** Henry VIII **1509** Michelangelo begins Sistine Chapel ceiling **1515** Hampton Court palace built **1518–94** Tintoretto **1519** Circumnavigation of the world by Magellan **1527** Sack of Rome **1537–1619** Hilliard **1541–1614** El Greco **1547–1616** Cervantes **1547** Ivan the Terrible **1548** English *Book of Common Prayer*
1550 Giovanni Gabrieli, Italian (**1554–1612**) Thomas Morley, English (**1557–1602**) Giles Farnaby, English (**c.1560–1640**) John Bull, English (**c.1562–1628**) Jan Sweelinck, Dutch (**1562–1621**) John Dowland, English (**1563–1626**) Claudio Monteverdi, Italian (**1567–1643**) Orlando Gibbons, English (**1583–1625**) Girolamo Frescobaldi, Italian (**1583–1643**)	**1554** Palestrina's first book of masses **1597** Peri's opera *Dafne*	**1558** Elizabeth I **1564–93** Christopher Marlowe **1564–1616** William Shakespeare **1564–1642** Galileo **1572–1631** John Donne **1573–1610** Caravaggio **1573–1637** Ben Jonson **1573–1652** Inigo Jones **1577–1640** Rubens **1590** Spenser's *Faerie Queene* **1594–1665** Poussin **1598–1680** Bernini **1599–1641** Van Dyck **1599–1660** Velazquez

and songs of the south. The secular counterparts to the church musicians began to compose **madrigals,** contrapuntal settings of poems, of about twelve lines long, usually on an amorous or pastoral subject. The emphasis was on the quality of word-setting. The form proved to be remarkably popular (if short-lived), especially in England where Gibbons, Weelkes and Morley were its finest exponents.

Madrigals, like liturgical **motets** and settings of the Mass, were all written for unaccompanied voices – a quality that characterized most of the music produced up to this time. It was not until the end of the fourteenth century that **instrumental music** began to emerge as an art form in its own right. The recorder, lute, viol and spinet had played their part in dance music and in accompanying voices, and occasionally replaced them. Now, composers such as Byrd, Gibbons, Farnaby and Frescobaldi began to write for specific instruments, although this form of composition did not truly flourish until the Baroque era. Musicians would join together to play a series of varying dance pieces, forming a loosely constructed suite, a player might improvise his own theme round another's – a 'fancy' or 'fantasia' – or they might compose variations on a tune played over the same repeating bass line – 'variations on a ground' as it is called. Other innovations were made by the Italians Andrea Gabrieli (c.1510–86), the first to combine voices with brass instruments, and his nephew Giovanni (1557–1612), whose 'antiphonal' effects for choirs of brass instruments might have been written for our modern stereo systems.

Emergence of opera

It was from Italy that the next important step in musical history was taken. Indeed, Italy was the country – actually a collection of small independent states at the time, ruled by a number of affluent and cultured families – that would dominate the musical world for a century and a half from 1600. Such was the influence of Italy at this time that music adopted the Italian language as its *lingua franca*. To this day, composers almost universally write their performance directions in Italian. The word **opera**, itself, described a new art form that combined drama and music.

In the late sixteenth century, artists, writers and architects became interested in the ancient cultures of Greece and Rome. In Florence, a group of the artistic intelligentsia became interested in how the ancient Greek dramas had been performed. Experimenting with declaiming the more poetic passages and using a few chords of instrumental music to accompany other passages in natural speech rhythm, the idea of music reflecting, supporting and commenting upon dramatic action was born: *dramma per musica* ('drama by means of music') – a play with a musical setting.

Into the ring then came one of the supreme musicians of history, Claudio Monteverdi. He did not write the first opera – that honour goes to Jacopo Peri and his *Dafne*, now lost, of 1597 – but with one work, *Orfeo* (1607), he suggested the future possibilities of the medium. Solo singers were given a dramatic character to portray and florid songs to sing; there were choruses, dances, orchestral interludes and scenery. Opera was a markedly different kind of entertainment but, more importantly, it was a completely new way of using music.

Monteverdi's successors, such as Pier Cavalli and Marc'Antonio Cesti, developed a type of flowing, lyrical song inspired by spoken Italian – *bel canto* ('beautiful singing') – which, in turn, brought about the prominence of the singer. Dramatic truth soon went out of the window in favour of the elaborate vocal displays of the opera soloists; composers were only too happy to provide what their new public wanted – and no class of singer was more favoured than the *castrato*. Feted wherever they appeared, the *castrati*, who had had their testicles removed as young boys, to preserve their high voices, were highly paid and immensely popular, a not dissimilar phenomenon to the Three Tenors of today (with two small differences). The

Significant composers	Musical events	Other events
	BAROQUE 1600–1750	

1600

Significant composers	Musical events	Other events
Jean-Baptiste Lully, French (1632–87)	**c.1600** Violin, viola, cello, double bass, trombone and harp introduced	**1606–69** Rembrandt
Dietrich Buxtehude, German (1637–1707)	**1607** Timpani and kettle drum introduced	**1608–74** John Milton
Arcangelo Corelli, Italian (1653–1713)	**1609–19** *Fitzwilliam Virginal Book* compiled	**1611** King James Authorized Version of *The Bible*
Giuseppe Torelli, Italian (1658–1709)	**c.1619** Bassoon introduced	**1615** Cervantes' *Don Quixote*
Henry Purcell, English (1659–95)	**1627** First German opera (*Dafne* by Schütz) produced	**1616–84** Corneille
Tommaso Albinoni, Italian (1671–1751)	**1637** First public opera house opened (Teatro di San Cassiano, Venice)	**1620** Mayflower sets sail
Antonio Vivaldi, Italian (1678–1741)	**1639** French horn introduced	**1622–73** Molière
Georg Philipp Telemann, German (1681–1767)	**1642** Monteverdi's *L' incoronazione di Poppea*	**1628–88** John Bunyan
Jean-Philippe Rameau, French (1683–1764)	**1653** Lully appointed director of Louis XIV's orchestra	**1632–75** Vermeer
Johann Sebastian Bach, German (1685–1750)	**1657** Oboe introduced	**1632–1723** Christopher Wren
Domenico Scarlatti, Italian (1685–1757)	**1671** First French opera house opens in Paris	**1634** Milton's *Comus*
George Frideric Handel, German/English (1685–1759)	**1672** Flute introduced	**1639–99** Racine
Francesco Geminiani, Italian (1687–1762)	**1678** First German opera house opens in Hamburg	**1642–46** English Civil War
Giuseppe Tartini, Italian (1692–1770)	**1687** Lully died	**1642–1727** Isaac Newton
Pietro Locatelli, Italian (1695–1764)	**1689** Purcell's *Dido and Aeneas*	**1649** Charles I executed
	1692 Purcell's *The Fairy Queen*	**1658** Death of Oliver Cromwell
		1660 Pepys begins his diaries
		1660 Charles II
		1665–66 Great Plague and Fire of London
		1667 Milton's *Paradise Lost*
		1670–1729 William Congreve
		1672 Newton's law of gravitation
		1675–1710 Wren rebuilds St Paul's cathedral
		1684 Bunyan's *Pilgrim's Progress*
		1689 William and Mary
		1694–1778 Voltaire
		1694 Bank of England established
		1697–1764 Hogarth
		1697–1768 Canaletto

1700

Significant composers	Musical events	Other events
Thomas Arne, English (1710–78)	**1704** J.S. Bach writes his first cantata	**1709–84** Dr. Johnson
Christoph Willibald von Gluck, German (1714–87)	**c.1700** Cristofori builds the first pianoforte	**1714** Death of Queen Anne
Carl Philipp Emanuel Bach, German (1714–88)	**1709** First violin concerto written by Giuseppe Torelli	**1719** Defoe's *Robinson Crusoe*
	1716 Couperin's *L'art de toucher le clavecin*	**1723–92** Sir Joshua Reynolds
	1717 Handel's *Water Music*	**1726** Swift's *Gulliver's Travels*
	1717 Piccolo introduced	**1727–88** Gainsborough
	1721 J.S. Bach's 'Brandenburg' Concertos	**1728–92** Robert Adam
	1722 Bach's *Well-tempered Clavier* Bk.1	**1730–95** Josiah Wedgwood
	1726 Clarinet introduced	
	1728 Gay's *The Beggar's Opera*	
	1730 Guarneri violins made in Cremona	

practice of castration to produce an entertainer, an extraordinarily barbaric concept, was halted only in the early nineteenth century. The last *castrato*, Alessandro Moreschi, survived until as late as 1922 and made a dozen or so recordings in 1902.

St Paul had written that women should keep silent in church. They were therefore not available for the taxing high lines in church music. If the origins of the *castrati* could be laid firmly at the door of the Church, similar dogma can also be held responsible for the slow progress of instrumental composition. From the earliest times the Church had voiced its disapproval of the practice. St Jerome had said that no Christian maiden should know what a lyre or flute looked like, let alone hear one. The weakening of the Church's authority after the Reformation encouraged composers to write instrumental music for groups, music moreover that took into account the strengths and colours of the different instruments, another new concept.

Sonatas and soloists

The same change of emphasis led to a flood of accomplished **soloists**. Among them was a brilliant Italian-born violinist Jean-Baptiste Lully, who went to France in 1646. Here he worked for Louis XIV, the extravagant builder of Versailles, who employed 120 musicians in various ensembles. A celebrated orchestra of 'Twenty-four violins' provided music at the French court; with Lully's addition of flutes, oboes, bassoons, trumpets and timpani, the modern **orchestra** began to take shape.

Another significant by-product of the Italian opera was the introduction of the **sonata** – the term originally meant a piece to be sounded, or played, as opposed to sung (cantata). Although it quickly took on a variety of forms, the sonata began with the Italian violinists imitating the vocal displays of opera – a single melody played against a harmonized background or accompanied by chords. This differed considerably from the choral works of a century earlier, driven by their polyphonic interweavings. Now there was music to which, even without a background accompaniment, the listener's ears could supply the harmony mentally – one could tell where the tune was going to resolve, could sense its shape and destination.

With the musical emphasis on harmony – a key feature of the coming century and a half – **rhythm** began to take an increasingly important part. Chordal patterns naturally fall in sequences, in regular measures or bars. Listen to a **chaconne** by Purcell or Handel and you realize that the theme is not a tune but a sequence of chords. Measuring the beats in a bar (*one*-two or *one*-two-three or *one*-two-three-four, the emphasis always on the first beat) gives the music a sense of form and helps it to progress. Phrases lead the ear to the next sequence like the dialogue between two people, exchanging thoughts in single words, short sentences or long paragraphs. Singing a simple hymn tune such as 'All people that on earth do dwell', one is aware of what music had now acquired – a strong **tonal** centre.

Makers of musical instruments responded by adapting and improving their products. Celebrated makers from this time include the great Italian violinmakers Stradivari, Amati and Guarneri, the Ruckers family of Antwerp with their harpsichords and the organ-building Harris family of England.

Italian opera made a final contribution to this period. The use of the orchestra in opera naturally led to the expression of dramatic musical ideas – one reason why the Italian orchestra developed faster than elsewhere. Towards the beginning of the eighteenth century, composers began to write **overtures** in three sections (fast, slow, fast), providing the model for the classical sonata form used in instrumental pieces, concertos and symphonies for the following two hundred years and more. Thus this '**homophonic**' period, featuring music with a single melody and harmonic accompaniment, melted seamlessly during the seventeenth century into the Baroque era of Vivaldi, Bach and Handel.

The **sonata** developed from the dance suites and their vocal equivalent, the *Canzoni* cantatas, popular in Italy at the beginning of the seventeenth century, known as the *Sonata da camera* (chamber sonata) as opposed to the *Sonata da chiesa* (church sonata) with its more abstract movements. Likewise, there were two types of **concerto**, the *Concerto da chiesa* and the *Concerto da camera*. Originally a composition that contrasted two groups of instrumentalists with each other, these forms developed into the **concerto grosso** ('great concerto'), of which the first leading exponent was Arcangelo Corelli. Here a group of solo string instrumentalists alternate with the main body of strings in a work usually of three or four movements. Geminiani, Albinoni, Torelli, Handel and others contributed to the form. It was but a short step from here to the solo concerto in which a soloist is contrasted with, then pitted against, the orchestra. No concerto of this period has achieved the popularity of Vivaldi's, whose 500 essays in the genre (mainly for strings but sometimes for wind instruments) are the product of one of the most remarkable masters of the early eighteenth century. His concerto *The Four Seasons*, among the best known and most frequently played pieces of classical music, illustrates the new concept.

Northern Europe provided the springboard for the rapid development of keyboard music: the North German school of organ music, founded by Frescobaldi and Sweelinck a century earlier, with its interest in contrapuntal writing, laid the way for the likes of Pachelbel and Buxtehude whose line reached its climax in the great works of Johann Sebastian Bach; Rameau and Couperin in France were producing short descriptive harpsichord pieces (as well as operas) in a style called '**rococo**' – from the French *rocaille*, a term originally alluding to fancy shell- and scroll-work in art. It was predominantly diverting rather than elevating work and rococo usefully defines the character of lighter music written in the **Baroque** period, especially when contrasted with the works of the two musical heavyweights of the time, J.S. Bach and George Frideric Handel.

Bach and Handel

In his own time Bach was considered old-fashioned, a provincial composer from central Germany. But his music is among the noblest and most sublime expressions of the human spirit and, with him, the art of contrapuntal writing reached its zenith. The forty-eight Preludes and Fugues in *The Well-tempered Clavier* explore the permutations of fugal writing in all the major and minor keys; his final work, *The Art of Fugue* (left unfinished at his death), takes a mathematical delight in the interweaving of contrapuntal variations on the same theme. Yet the technical brilliance of Bach's music is subsumed in the expressive power of his compositions, in particular his organ music, church cantatas and the great *St Matthew Passion* and *Mass in B minor*. His instrumental works are evidence that he was by no means always the stern God-fearing Lutheran – the exuberant six 'Brandenburg' Concertos show that he was well acquainted with the sunny Italian way of doing things, and many of his most beautiful and deepest thoughts are reserved for the concertos and orchestral suites. Bach's influence on composers and musicians down the years has been immeasurable and, for many, this composer remains the foundation stone of their art.

Bach's contemporary, Handel, also came from Germany but in contrast was a widely-travelled man of the world who settled in England and became a shrewd entrepreneur and manipulator of musical affairs. In instrumental forms such as the concerto grosso, Handel was equally at home writing in homophonic or polyphonic style and introduced a variety of wind-and-string combinations in his colourful scoring. He developed the typical seventeenth-century dance suite into such famous occasional works as the *Water Music* and *Music for the Royal Fireworks*.

Opera was a field into which Bach never ventured but, between 1711 and 1729, Handel produced nearly thirty operas in the Italian style until the public tired of these when, ever the pragmatist, he turned to oratorio. An **oratorio** is an extended setting of a (usually) religious text in dramatic form, which does not require scenery or stage action. Handel's oratorios have an immense dramatic and emotional range and often employ daring harmonies, glorious melodies and uplifting choruses.

Bach was the last great composer to be employed by the Church, fittingly, for the Church had been the mainspring for the progress of polyphonic music and Bach was the *ne plus ultra* of the style. Henceforth, musical patronage came from the nobility and the nobility preferred music that was elegant, entertaining and definitely not smacking of anything too 'churchy'. Following the example of the French court and Italian principalities in the seventeenth century, every European duke of any substance aspired to having his own orchestra and music director. One such patron was at the court of Mannheim, where an orchestra under the direction of Johann Stamitz raised orchestral playing to an exceptional standard. A new era, breaking away from the contrapuntal writing of the late Baroque, was ushered in.

What is classical music?

The term 'classical music' has two meanings: it describes any music that is supposedly 'serious' (as opposed to pop or jazz, and as in 'I can't stand classical music'). It also defines a certain period in the development of music: the **Classical** era. This can be characterized as music notable for its masterly economy of form and resources, and for its lack of overt emotionalism. If Bach and Handel dominated the first half of the seventeenth century, Haydn and Mozart are their counterparts for the latter half, and epitomize the virtues of the Classical style.

This can be traced back to a generation or so before Haydn's birth to the rococo style of Couperin and Rameau and, more powerfully, to the invigorating keyboard works of Domenico Scarlatti, whose over five hundred short sonatas composed in his sixties demonstrate a brilliance only Bach equalled. Scarlatti, though, writing on a smaller scale, had the specific intent of delighting and instructing his pupil, the Queen of Spain. His near-contemporary, Georg Philipp Telemann, brought the rococo style to Germany. Lighter and even more fecund than Bach, Telemann was held in far greater esteem in his lifetime. Despite his stated credo – 'He who writes for the many does better work than he who writes only for the few...I have always aimed at facility. Music ought not to be an effort, an occult science' – the two men greatly admired each other, to such an extent that Bach named his third son Carl Philipp Emanuel after Telemann, and chose him as the boy's godfather.

A changing sound-world

C.P.E. Bach's music represents a crossroads between the Franco-Italian rococo and the emerging Classical schools – indeed, in some of his keyboard music he seems to anticipate Beethoven. His piano sonatas, making use of the expressive powers of the newly invented pianoforte, necessitate a redefinition of the term 'sonata' as used previously. It now becomes a formalized structure with related keys and themes. These Bach developed into extended movements, as opposed to the short movements of the Baroque form. Listening to his works, written by perhaps the most original and daring composer of the mid-eighteenth century, one is aware of the serious and comical, the inspired and routine, lying side by side with engaging unpredictability.

Parallel to this was the music of Johann Stamitz. His work is rarely heard today, yet he and his son Carl (1746–1801) were pioneers in the development of the **symphony**. This form had grown out of the short quick-slow-quick one-movement overtures or *sinfonias* of Italian opera. The symphonies that Johann Stamitz wrote at Mannheim were to be the pattern for those of Haydn and Mozart. In them we can see, as in C.P.E. Bach's sonatas, the use of related keys, two contrasted first-movement subjects, or themes, and the graceful development of material. He was the first to introduce the clarinet into the orchestra and was probably the first to write a concerto for the instrument, also giving the brass and woodwind greater prominence. His orchestral crescendos, a novel effect at this time, were said 'to have excited audiences to rise from their seats'.

Italy had dominated the musical world of the seventeenth and early eighteenth centuries with its operas and great violinists. From the middle of the eighteenth century, the centre of musical pre-eminence moved to Vienna, a position the city would retain until the end of the Hapsburg empire in the early years of the twentieth century. The Hapsburgs loved music and imported the best foreign musicians to their court; the imperial chapel became a second centre of musical excellence. Equally important was Vienna's location in Europe. With the court as its focus, all kinds of influences met and mingled from nearby Germany, Bohemia and Italy.

Less than half a century separates the death of Handel (1759) from the first performance of Beethoven's *Fidelio* (1809). Bach and Handel were still composing when Haydn was a teenager. To compare the individual 'sound-world' of any of these four composers is to chart the rapid progress in musical thinking. Without doubt, the most important element of this was the advancement of the **sonata** and **symphonic forms**. During this period, a typical example followed a basic structure of four movements: 1) the longest, sometimes with a slow introduction, 2) slow movement, 3) minuet, 4) fast, short and light in character. Each movement in turn had its own internal structure and order of progress. Most of Haydn and Mozart's sonatas, symphonies and chamber music are written in accordance with this framework and three-quarters of Beethoven's music conforms to 'sonata form'.

Haydn and Mozart

Haydn's contribution to musical history is immense; nicknamed 'the father of the symphony' despite Stamitz's prior claim, he was also the progenitor of the **string quartet**. Like his well-trained contemporaries, Haydn had a thorough knowledge of polyphony and counterpoint and, indeed, was not averse to using it, but his music

Significant composers	Musical events	Other events
	CLASSICAL 1750–1820	
1730	**1733** Bach's B minor Mass	**1732** First Covent Garden
Joseph Haydn, Austrian	**1742** Handel's *Messiah*	theatre completed
(**1732–1809**)	**1750** Bach's *The Art of Fugue*	**1732–99** Beaumarchais
Luigi Boccherini, Italian	**1750** J.S. Bach died	**1746–1828** Goya
(**1743–1805**)	**1755** Haydn writes his first	**1749–1832** Goethe
Muzio Clementi, Italian	string quartet	**1749** Fielding's *Tom Jones*
(**1752–1832**)	**1759** Handel died	**1751–1816** Sheridan
Wolfgang Amadeus Mozart,	**1760** Cor anglais introduced	**1757–1827** William Blake
Austrian (**1756–91**)	**1762** Gluck's *Orfeo ed*	**1759–96** Robert Burns
Luigi Cherubini, Italian	*Eurydice*	**1759–1805** Horatio Nelson
(**1760–1842**)	**1776** First concerto for piano	**1759** Voltaire's *Candide*
Ludwig van Beethoven,	written by J.C. Bach	**1760** George III
German (**1770–1827**)		**1762–1835** John Nash
Johann Nepomuk Hummel,		**1769–1821** Napoleon
Hungarian (**1778–1837**)		Bonaparte
		1770–1850 William
		Wordsworth
		1771–1832 Sir Walter Scott
		1775–1817 Jane Austen
		1775–1851 J.M.W. Turner
		1776–88 Gibbon's *Decline and*
		Fall of the Roman Empire
		1776–1837 Constable
		1776 American Declaration of
		Independence
		1777 Sheridan's *The School*
		for Scandal
1780	**1782** Mozart begins his	**1780** Rowlandson's caricatures
John Field, Irish (**1782–1837**)	'Haydn' Quartets	**1788–1824** Byron
Daniel Auber, French	**1785** Mozart's *The Marriage of*	**1789** French Revolution
(**1782–1871**)	*Figaro*	**1791** Boswell's *Life of Jonson*
Niccolò Paganini, Italian	**1787** Gluck died	**1792–1822** Percy Bysshe
(**1782–1840**)	**1787** Mozart's *Don Giovanni*	Shelley
Carl Maria von Weber, German	**1788** C.P.E. Bach died	**1795–1821** John Keats
(**1786–1826**)	**1791** Mozart's *The Magic Flute*	**1796–1875** Corot
Ferdinand Hérold, French	**1791** Mozart died	**1798–1863** Delacroix
(**1791–1833**)	**1799** Haydn's *The Creation*	**1799–1837** Pushkin
Giacomo Meyerbeer, German		**1799–1850** Balzac
(**1791–1864**)		
Gioachino Rossini, Italian		
(**1792–1868**)		
Franz Schubert, Austrian		
(**1797–1828**)		
Gaetano Donizetti, Italian		
(**1797–1848**)		

is predominantly homophonic. His 104 symphonies cover a wide range of expression and harmonic ingenuity; the same is true of the string quartets. With its perfect balance of string sound (two violins, viola and cello), the implicit economy in the scoring and the precision and elegance in the handling of the medium, the string quartet is the quintessential Classical art form.

Mozart composed forty-one symphonies and in the later ones enters a realm beyond Haydn's – searching, moving and profound (try the famous opening of

No.40 in G minor). This is even more true of the **piano concertos**, among music's most exalted creations, where the writing becomes deeply involved – the slow movement of the Concerto in A (K488) is grief-stricken, anticipating the writing of a future generation. It was Mozart, too, who raised opera to new heights. Gluck had singlehandedly broken away from the ossified, singer-dominated Italian opera and shown in works such as *Orfeo ed Euridice* (1762) that music could correspond to the mood and style of the piece, could colour and complement the stage action; arias became part of the continuous action and not merely inserted to display the singer's vocal talents. Mozart went further, and in his four masterpieces *The Marriage of Figaro*, *Così Fan Tutte*, *Don Giovanni* and *The Magic Flute* revealed more realistic characters, truer emotions and incomparably greater music than anything that had gone before. For the first time, opera reflected the foibles and aspirations of mankind, themes on which the **Romantic** composers were to dwell at length.

Beethoven and his successors

'The Old Order Changeth': for the first half of the nineteenth century, Europe, taking its cue from the French Revolution and American War of Independence, was imbued with a spirit of general political unrest, culminating in the 1848 uprisings. Nationalism and the struggle for individual freedom and self-expression were reflected in and inspired by the arts – the one fed off the other. The neat, well-ordered regime of the periwig and minuet gave way to the impetuous, passionate world of the tousle-haired revolutionary.

Ludwig van Beethoven coupled his genius for music with deeply-held political beliefs and an almost religious certainty about his purpose. With the possible exception of Wagner, no other composer has changed the course of music so dramat-ically and continued to develop and experiment throughout his career. His early music, built on the Classical paths trod by Haydn and Mozart, demonstrates his individuality in taking established musical structures and re-shaping them to his own ends. Unusual keys and harmonic relationships are explored while, as early as the Third Symphony ('Eroica'), the music is more visionary than anything Mozart achieved, even in a late masterpiece such as the 'Jupiter'. Six more symphonies followed, all different in character, all reaching new heights of musical expression, culminating in the great 'Choral' Symphony No.9 with its ecstatic final choral movement celebrating man's existence. No wonder so many composers felt daunted by the symphonic form after Beethoven and that few ever attempted more than the magical Beethovenian number of nine.

His chamber music tells a similar story, building on the Classical form of the string quartet, gradually making it his own, as in the middle-period 'Razumovsky' quartets, right up to the final group of late quartets, which contain music of profound spirituality and unequivocal personal statements. The cycle of thirty-two piano sonatas again is a portrait of his life's journey; the final three of his five piano concertos and the sublime Violin Concerto are on a par with the symphonies and quartets. His single opera *Fidelio*, while not a success as a piece of theatre, seems to express all the themes that Beethoven held most dear – his belief in the brotherhood of man, his disgust at revolutionaries-turned-dictators and the redeeming strength of human love. All this was achieved, romantically enough, while he himself struggled with profound deafness. Beethoven's unquenchable spirit and his ability

A CHRONOLOGY OF MUSIC

Significant composers	Musical events	Other events
	EARLY ROMANTIC 1800–50	
1800 Vincenzo Bellini, Italian (**1801–35**) Hector Berlioz, French (**1803–69**) Mikhail Glinka, Russian (**1804–57**) Felix Mendelssohn, German (**1809–47**) Frédéric Chopin, Polish (**1810–49**) Robert Schumann, German (**1810–56**) Franz Liszt, Hungarian (**1811–86**) Richard Wagner, German (**1813–83**) Giuseppe Verdi, Italian (**1813–1901**) Charles Gounod, French (**1818–93**) Jacques Offenbach, German/French (**1819–80**) Franz von Suppé, Austrian (**1819–95**) César Franck, Franco-Belgian (**1822–90**) Bedřich Smetana, Czech (**1824–84**) Anton Bruckner, Austrian (**1824–96**)	**1800** Beethoven's Symphony No.1 **c.1800** Valved trumpet introduced **1803** Beethoven's 'Eroica' Symphony **1805** Beethoven's *Fidelio* **1806** Beethoven's Violin Concerto **1809** Haydn died **1814** Field's Nocturnes **1815** Schubert's *Erl King* **1816** Rossini's *The Barber of Seville* **1819** Schubert's 'Trout' Quintet **1821** Weber's *Der Freischütz* **1822** Schubert's 'Unfinished' Symphony **1823** Beethoven's Diabelli Variations	**1802–85** Victor Hugo **1802–73** Edwin Landseer **1805** Battle of Trafalgar **1806–59** Isambard Kingdom Brunel **1808 and 1832** Goethe's *Faust* **1809–82** Charles Darwin **1809–49** Edgar Allan Poe **1811–25** Nash: Regent St. and Regent's Park, London **1812–15** Grimm's *Fairy Tales* **1812–70** Charles Dickens **1812–89** Robert Browning **1813** Jane Austen's *Pride and Prejudice* **1815** Battle of Waterloo **1816–55** Charlotte Brontë **1816** Constable's *Flatford Mill* **1818–48** Emily Brontë **1818–83** Turgenev **1819–91** Hermann Melville **1819–92** Walt Whitman **1820–1910** Florence Nightingale **1821–81** Dostoyevsky **1821** Constable's *The Haywain* **1822–95** Louis Pasteur
1825 Johann Strauss II, Austrian (**1825–99**) Louis Moreau Gottschalk, American (**1829–69**) Anton Rubinstein, Russian (**1829–94**) Alexander Borodin, Russian (**1833–87**) Johannes Brahms, German (**1833–97**) Camille Saint-Saëns, French (**1835–1921**) Léo Delibes, French (**1836–91**) Mily Balakirev, Russian (**1837–1910**) Georges Bizet, French (**1838–75**) Max Bruch, German (**1838–1920**) Modest Mussorgsky, Russian (**1839–81**) Peter Ilyich Tchaikowsky, Russian (**1840–93**)	**1826** Weber's *Oberon* **1826** Mendelssohn's Overture to *A Midsummer Night's Dream* **1827** Beethoven died **1827** Schubert's 'Wintemeise' **1828** Schubert's C Major Quintet and final piano sonatas **1828** Schubert died **1829** Rossini's *William Tell* **1829** Mendelssohn conducts Bach's *St Matthew Passion* **1829** Tuba introduced **1830** Berlioz's *Symphonie fantastique* **1831** Bellini's *Norma* **1834** Schumann's Carnaval **1835** Donizetti's *Lucia di Lammermoor* **1836** Glinka's *A Life for the Tsar* **1839** Chopin's Twenty-four Preludes	**1828–1906** Ibsen **1828–1910** Tolstoy **1829–96** Millais **1830–1903** Pissarro **1832–83** Manet **1834–1917** Degas **1835–1910** Mark Twain **1836** Dickens' *Pickwick Papers* **1837** Accession of Queen Victoria **1839–1906** Cézanne **1840–1917** Rodin **1840–1926** Monet **1840–1928** Thomas Hardy **1841–1919** Renoir **1843–1916** Henry James **1847** Charlotte Brontë's *Jane Eyre* **1847** Emily Brontë's *Wuthering Heights* **1847–1931** Thomas Edison **1848** Year of European political upheaval

Significant composers	Musical events	Other events
	EARLY ROMANTIC 1800–50	
1825 (contd)		
Emmanuel Chabrier, French (**1841–94**)	**1840** Adolphe Sax invents the saxophone	**1848** Marx & Engels: Communist manifesto
Antonin Dvořák, Czech (**1841–1904**)	**1841** Adam's *Giselle*	**1848–1903** Gaugin
Sir Arthur Sullivan, English (**1842–1900**)	**1842** Verdi's *Nabucco*	**1849–1912** Strindberg
Jules Massenet, French (**1842–1912**)	**1843** Donizetti's *Don Pasquale*	
Edvard Grieg, Norwegian (**1843–1907**)	**1844** Mendelssohn's Violin Concerto	
Nikolai Rimsky-Korsakov, Russian (**1844–1908**)	**1845** Wagner's *Tannhäuser*	
Gabriel Fauré, French (**1845–1924**)	**1845** Completion of Schumann's Piano Concerto	
	1846 Mendelssohn's *Elijah*	
	1849 Chopin died	

to use music as a means of self-expression place his works at the forefront of man's creative achievements. 'Come the man, come the moment' – Beethoven's lifespan helpfully encompasses the late Classical period and the early Romantics. His music is the titanic span between the two.

Many who followed revered him as a god. Schubert, the next great Viennese master, twenty-seven years younger but who survived him by only eighteen months, was in awe of Beethoven. He did not advance the symphonic or sonata forms, there was no revolutionary zeal in his make-up. What he possessed was the gift of melody. His other merits apart, Schubert is arguably the most wondrous tunesmith the world has ever known and, with over six hundred songs, he established the German song, or **Lied**, tradition. From his *Erl King* (1815) on, Schubert unerringly caught the heart of a poem's meaning and reflected it in its setting. For the first time, too, the piano assumed equal importance with the vocal part, painting a tone-picture or catching the mood of the piece in its accompaniment.

The new iron-string pianos came to be the favoured instrument of the first part of the Romantic era. A bewildering number of composer-pianists were born just after the turn of the century, the most prominent of whom were Liszt, Chopin, Schumann and Mendelssohn. Of these, Mendelssohn relied on the elegant, traditional structures of Classicism in which to wrap his refined poetic and melodic talents. Many of his piano works (his *Songs Without Words*, for example) and orchestral pieces (*Hebrides* Overture and 'Italian' Symphony) describe nature, places and emotions. Schumann, too, favoured such short musical essays with titles such as *Träumerei* ('Dreaming') and *Des Abends* ('In the evening') to evoke a mood or an occasion – 'characteristic pieces' they were called and, later on, '**programme music**'.

The undisputed master of the Romantic keyboard style was Frédéric Chopin. Almost his entire *oeuvre* is devoted to the piano, in a string of highly individual and expressive works composed in the short period of twenty years. Fifty years after his early death in 1849, composers were still writing pieces heavily influenced by him. Chopin rarely used descriptive titles for his work beyond such labels as Nocturne, Berceuse or Barcarolle. The technical and lyrical possibilities of the instrument were raised to new heights in such masterpieces as the Four Ballades, the final two (of three) piano sonatas and the numerous short, dance-based compositions. A large number of these were inspired by Poland, his homeland, and, as a self-imposed exile living in Paris, Chopin was naturally drawn to expressing his love of his country. Nationalism of a much more fervent kind was to be a key factor in the music of composers writing later in the Romantic tradition. Chopin himself disliked being labelled 'a Romantic'.

To define the Romantic era in music, we have to look at the three composers who dominated the musical world for the second and third quarters of the nineteenth century and pushed music towards the dawn of the next: Liszt, Berlioz and Wagner.

Rebellion and freedom of expression lie at the heart of the Romantic movement in the fields of music, literature, painting and architecture. There was a self-conscious breaking of the bonds and a belief in the right of the artist. Liszt – Byronic in both looks and temperament – was the greatest pianist of the day, and gave us the **solo piano recital**, the '**symphonic poem**' (the extended orchestral equivalent of Schumann's 'characteristic pieces') and a bewildering variety of music in all shapes and forms. The B minor Piano Sonata, in which all the elements of traditional sonata form are subsumed into an organic whole, is one of the cornerstones of the repertory; his final piano works anticipate the harmonies of Debussy, Bartók and beyond. While his music is not always profound – there is a great deal of gloss and glitter – his adventurous scores and his patronage and encouragement of young composers made Liszt one of the most influential musical geniuses of the entire century.

Berlioz was not a pianist. Perhaps that is why he is held to be the era's most important composer for orchestra. He based his music on 'the direct reaction of feeling' and could summon up with extraordinary vividness such notions as 'the supernatural' or 'the countryside' or 'ardent lovers'. Like Liszt, he never wrote a formal symphony: Liszt's *Faust Symphony* and Berlioz's *Symphonie fantastique* are 'programmatic' and rely on literary inspiration for their structure. Berlioz wrote on an epic scale, employing huge forces to convey his vision: the *Grande messe des morts*, for example, requires a tenor solo, brass bands and a massive chorus as well as an expanded orchestra.

Technical improvements in the manufacture of orchestral instruments – the brass and woodwind especially – helped composers like Berlioz achieve their ends, by providing a wider range and variety of sound. This additional colour in the composer's orchestral palette encouraged more extended, and sometimes seemingly formless, works. The prop of the symphonic structure was considered to be less essential – although, at the close of the twentieth century, it is evident, even today, that many still enjoy the challenge of writing in that form.

Wagner

The third titan of the Romantics was the most written- and talked-about composer of all time: Richard Wagner. As intelligent and industrious as he was ruthless and egocentric, Wagner produced a mighty achievement – *Der Ring des Nibelungen*, a cycle of four operas that transported the form from the realm of entertainment to a quasi-religious experience. Influenced by Beethoven, Mozart (whom he held to be the first truly German operatic composer), and Meyerbeer (whose sense of epic theatre, design and orchestration impressed him), Wagner's vision was to create a work that was a fusion of all the arts. He called his vision '**music-drama**'.

Some of his ideas had been anticipated forty years earlier by Carl Maria von Weber, one of the first composers to insist on total control of all aspects of the production of his work; as early as 1817 he wrote of his desire to fuse all art forms into one great new form. Weber's opera *Der Freischütz*, the first German Romantic opera, was a milestone in the development of these ideas, using German mythology as its subject.

Wagner felt that the music must grow from the libretto, so he supplied his own; there must be no display arias for their own sake. The music, like the opera's narrative flow, must never cease, for it held the two equally important roles of the telling of the story and commenting on the action and characters. Short musical phrases *(leitmotivs)* associated with different characters and moods, would recur throughout the score to underpin and bind the work. The orchestral contribution was at least as important as the vocal element.

But Wagner was more than just an operatic reformer. He opened up a new harmonic language, especially in the use of **chromaticism** (*see* below). This had not only a profound influence on succeeding generations of composers but led logically to the atonal music of the twentieth century.

Other directions

Not all composers fell under Wagner's spell. Brahms was the epitome of traditional musical thought. His four symphonies are nearer the style of Beethoven than of Mendelssohn or Schumann, and the first was not finished until 1875, when Wagner had all but completed *The Ring*. Indeed, Brahms is by far the most Classical of the German Romantics. He wrote little programme music and no operas. He distinguished himself in the musical forms that Wagner chose to ignore – chamber music, concertos, variation writing and symphonies.

It was only in old age that Giuseppe Verdi adopted some of Wagner's musical ideas. Verdi represents the culmination of a different school of opera. Wagner's operas are the descendents of Beethoven and Weber; Verdi's developed from the comic masterpieces of Rossini and the romantic dramas of Bellini and Donizetti. With the famous trilogy of *Rigoletto* (1851), *Il trovatore* (1853) and *La traviata* (1853), Verdi combined his mastery of drama with a flow of unforgettable lyrical melodies, masterpieces that have never fallen from public favour. His *Don Carlos* (1867), *Aida* (1871), *Otello* (1887) and *Falstaff* (1893) show the development of a tirelessly searching mind, and remain among the great miracles of music.

One thing that Wagner and Verdi had in common was their fierce patriotism. In his own lifetime, Verdi was held as a potent symbol of Italian independence, while Wagner espoused the dubious theories that later made him such a hero of the Third Reich. During the course of the nineteenth century, Western music, now dominated by German tradition and forms, began to be influenced more and more by the rise of nationalism. Composers wanted to reflect the character and cultural identity of their native lands by using material and forms that derived from their own country.

Russia was the foremost in the surge of **nationalism** that now became a feature of the late Romantic era. Glinka was the first important Russian composer to use Russian subjects and folk tunes, in his opera *A Life for the Tsar*. Although it had been influenced by the Italian tradition, this work succeeded in conveying typical Russian song and harmony, and it had a profound effect on Borodin, Balakirev, Cui, Mussorgsky and Rimsky-Korsakov – the group known as the Mighty Five or **the**

Significant composers	Musical events	Other events
	HIGH ROMANTIC 1850–1910	
1850 Leos Janáček, Czech (**1854–1928**) John Philip Sousa, American (**1854–1932**) Ruggiero Leoncavallo, Italian (**1857–1919**) Edward Elgar, English (**1857–1934**) Giacomo Puccini, Italian (**1858–1924**) Isaac Albéniz, Spanish (**1860–1909**) Gustave Charpentier, French (**1860–1956**) Gustav Mahler, Austro- Bohemian (**1860–1911**) Hugo Wolf, Austrian (**1860–1903**) Edward MacDowell, American (**1860–1908**) Claude Debussy, French (**1862–1918**) Frederick Delius, English (**1862–1934**) Pietro Mascagni, Italian (**1863–1945**) Richard Strauss, German (**1864–1949**) Alexander Glazunov, Russian (**1865–1936**) Jean Sibelius, Finnish (**1865–1957**) Carl Nielsen, Danish (**1865–1931**) Ferrucio Busoni, Italian (**1866–1924**) Erik Satie, French (**1866–1925**) Enrique Granados, Spanish (**1867–1916**) Franz Lehár, Hungarian (**1870–1948**) Alexander Scriabin, Russian (**1872–1915**) Ralph Vaughan Williams, English (**1872–1958**) Sergei Rachmaninov, Russian (**1873–1943**) Gustav Holst, English (**1874–1934**) Arnold Schoenberg, Austrian (**1874–1951**) Charles Ives, American (**1874–1954**)	**1850** Wagner's *Lohengrin* **1851** Verdi's *Rigoletto* **1856** Schumann died **1857** Glinka died **1859** Wagner's *Tristan und* *Isolde* **1859** Gounod's *Faust* **1866** Smetana's *The Bartered* *Bride* **1867** Wagner's *Die* *Meistersinger* **1867** J. Strauss' *Blue Danube* Waltz **1868** Grieg's Piano Concerto **1869** Tchaikowsky's *Romeo* *and Juliet* Overture **1869** Wagner's *Das Rheingold* performed **1870** Delibes' *Coppélia* **1871** Verdi's *Aida* **1872–1929** Diaghilev, creator of Ballets Russes **1873–1921** Caruso **1874** J. Strauss' *Die* *Fledermaus* **1876** Completion of Brahms' First Symphony	**1850** Dickens' *David* *Copperfield* **1850–94** R.L. Stevenson **1853–90** Van Gogh **1854–56** Crimean War **1854–1900** Oscar Wilde **1856–1939** Sigmund Freud **1856–1950** G.B. Shaw **1857** Trollope's *Barchester* *Towers* **1860–1904** Chekhov **1860** Abraham Lincoln becomes US President **1862** Hugo's *Les Misérables* **1864–1901** Toulouse-Lautrec **1865** Lewis Carroll's *Alice's* *Adventures in Wonderland* **1865–1936** Rudyard Kipling **1866–1946** H.G. Wells **1867** Ibsen's *Peer Gynt* **1869–1944** Edwin Lutyens **1869–1948** Mahatma Gandhi **1869–1954** Matisse **1869–1960** Frank Lloyd Wright **1870–1924** Lenin **1871** William I of Prussia becomes first German emperor (Kaiser) **1871–1922** Proust **1872** George Eliot's *Middlemarch* **1874–1965** Winston Churchill

Significant composers	Musical events	Other events
	HIGH ROMANTIC 1850–1910	
1875 Maurice Ravel, French (1875–1937) Manuel de Falla, Spanish (1876–1946) Ottorino Respighi, Italian (1879–1936) Béla Bartók, Hungarian (1881–1945) Karol Szymanowski, Polish (1882–1937) Percy Grainger, Australian/American (1882–1961) Zoltán Kodály, Hungarian (1882–1967) Igor Stravinsky, Russian (1882–1971) Anton Webern, Austrian (1883–1945) Alban Berg, Austrian (1885–1935) Heitor Villa-Lobos, Brazilian (1887–1959) Sergei Prokofiev, Russian (1891–1953) Arthur Honegger, Franco-Swiss (1892–1955) Darius Milhaud, French (1892–1974) Paul Hindemith, German (1895–1963) Carl Orff, German (1895–1982) Erich Wolfgang Korngold, Austrian (1897–1957) George Gershwin, American (1898–1937) Francis Poulenc, French (1899–1963)	**1875** Bizet's *Carmen* **1879** Tchaikowsky's *Eugene Onegin* **1879** Sullivan's *The Pirates of Penzance* **1880** Celesta invented **1882** Brahms' Piano Concerto No.2 **1883** Wagner died **1884** Smetana died **1885** Franck's *Symphonic Variations* **1887** Verdi's *Otello* **1887** Bruckner's Eighth Symphony **1888** First recording of serious music on Edison cylinder (pianist Josef Hofmann) **1888** Berliner invents gramophone **1893** Verdi's *Falstaff* **1893** Tchaikowsky's 'Pathétique' Symphony **1893** Gounod and Tchaikowsky died **1895** First Promenade Concert, conducted by Henry Wood **1897** Brahms died **1897** First recording studio and retail record shop **1899** Elgar's *Enigma Variations*	**1876** Mark Twain's *Tom Sawyer* **1877** Edison invents phonograph **1877** Tolstoy's *Anna Karenina* **1879** Ibsen's *The Doll's House* **1881–1973** Picasso **1882–1941** James Joyce **1883** R.L. Stevenson's *Treasure Island* **1883** Nietzsche's *Also Sprach Zarathustra* **1888–1965** T.S. Eliot **1889** Eiffel Tower built **1892** Conan Doyle's *The Adventures of Sherlock Holmes* **1895** Hardy's *Jude the Obscure* **1898–1986** Henry Moore **1899** Boer War **1899–1973** Noël Coward
1900 Aaron Copland, American (1900–90) Joaquín Rodrigo, Spanish (b.1901) William Walton, English (1902–83) Aram Khachaturian, Russian (1903–78) Sir Michael Tippett, English (b.1905) Dmitri Shostakovich, Russian (1906–75) Olivier Messiaen, French (1908–92) Samuel Barber, American (1910–81)	**1900** Elgar's *The Dream of Gerontius* **1901** Verdi died **1901** Rachmaninov's Piano Concerto No.2 **1902** Debussy's *Pelléas et Mélisande* **1903** First 12-inch record **1903** Schoenberg's *Verklärte Nacht* **1904** Dvořák died **1907** Grieg died **1909** Strauss' *Elektra* **1910** Vaughan Williams' Fantasy on a Theme by Thomas Tallis **1910** Stravinsky's *The Firebird*	**1901–04** Picasso's Blue Period **1903–66** Evelyn Waugh **1904–89** Salvador Dalí **1907–73** W.H. Auden **1908–14** Cubism **1913** Shaw's *Pygmalion*

Mighty Handful (although Cui's contribution to the history of music is hardly 'mighty' compared to the genius of his peers).

Tchaikowsky, the most accomplished of all his Russian contemporaries, paid lip-service to the nationalists but composed largely in the German tradition. Elsewhere in Europe, nationalist schools of music arose: in Bohemia there were Smetana, Dvořák and Janáček; in Scandanavia, Nielsen, Grieg and Sinding; in Finland, Sibelius, whose symphonies developed the medium in a highly individual way; in Spain, Albéniz, Granados and Manuel de Falla. Britain and the United States were slow in taking up the cause: Parry and Elgar wrote firmly in the German manner and it was not until the later arrival of Vaughan Williams and Holst that a 'British' (or, at any rate, 'English') sound began to emerge. America was a curious case. Its first native composer of any note, Gottschalk, used indigenous native rhythms for his (mainly) piano compositions as early as the 1850s – South American, New Orleans and Cuban elements are boldly to the fore in his work. It took another half century before any music directly derived from indigenous American material began to assert itself.

Decline of Romanticism

The dates for each period of music, as we have seen, must be viewed as being flexible. The Romantic period embraces a wide divergence of personal styles and represents a long and eventful period in Western music's development. In common with every aspect of life, the art of music developed at an ever-increasing pace. Parallel to the growth of nationalism, came the Italian *verismo* style of opera, the school of realism or naturalism epitomized by the works of Puccini, Leoncavallo and Mascagni, who drew their subjects from contemporary life and presented them with heightened violence and emotions. During the closing years of the Romantic period, emerging under the influence of Wagner, came the **neo-Romantics**, whose use of massive symphonic structures and elaborate orchestration is heard in the music of Bruckner, Mahler, Scriabin and the early works of Richard Strauss.

Towards the end of the nineteenth century, there was a reaction against the excesses of the Romantics – the too obvious, heart-on-sleeve approach, the emotional over-indulgence, the extra-musical programmes and philosophies began to pall. The Baroque period had melted into the Classical, and the Classical drifted into the early Romantic era, but the close of the nineteenth century saw a tendency toward bold experimentation in new styles and techniques. Coinciding with the French **Impressionist** movement in painting and poetry, came Impressionist music, epitomized by the daring (at the time), personal, harmonic idiom of Claude Debussy. Here emphasis was laid not on the subject but on an emotion or sensation aroused by the subject. His music is just as closely organized as anything in the Classical German manner but, using the **whole-tone scale** and fresh harmonies, Debussy conjures up a sensuous, atmospheric spell in his piano music and orchestral works. The fastidious Maurice Ravel followed; his work rang with exotic evocations of light and colour, later tinged with **jazz** references.

On the other hand, composers such as Camille Saint-Saëns and Max Bruch (both of whom survived into the 1920s) continued to produce work in the well-crafted, melodious tradition of Mendelssohn, oblivious to – or, at least, aloof from – the musical revolution raging around them.

By the turn of the century, it was no longer possible to define a dominant general musical trend. With its many fragmented sub-divisions, the successor of the Classical and Romantic periods has as yet no better label than 'Modern' music.

Stravinsky and Schoenberg

Igor Stravinsky studied with one of music's great orchestrators, Rimsky-Korsakov. He orchestrated some of Beethoven's piano sonatas as an exercise; he worked at counterpoint and learned about classical forms – in other words, he had a sound, traditional conservatory training. Yet in less than a decade, he was writing music a world away from that of his mentor. His ballet masterpieces *The Firebird* (1909), *Petrushka* (1911) and *The Rite of Spring* (1913) showed progressive adventurousness: in *Petrushka*, there are **bitonal** passages (written in two keys simultaneously), **dissonant** chords, a new rhythmic freedom and a percussive orchestral quality; in *The Rite of Spring*, a score that provoked a riot at its premiere, Stravinsky pared down the elements of music to reinforce rhythm. As Debussy and Schoenberg, in certain of their works, reduced music to the vertical effect of simultaneously sounding notes, so Stravinsky reduced melody and harmony to rhythm. This was a new element in music. As Alec Harman and Wilfred Mellers put it in their *Man and His Music*:

> *Harmony without melody and rhythm, rhythm without melody and harmony, are static. Both the pandemonium of Stravinsky's* Rite of Spring *and Debussy's* Voiles *deprive music of the sense of motion from one point to another. Though they started from diametrically opposed points, both composers mark a radical departure from the traditions of European music since the Renaissance.*

Stravinsky went on to write in a number of other styles and dominated the musical world for fifty years in the same way that his almost exact contemporary Pablo Picasso did in his own field. Arguably, no other composer this century has exercised a greater influence than Stravinsky – Debussy and Ravel were less wide-ranging, Sibelius and Bartók less daring and Schoenberg and Webern less accessible.

Arnold Schoenberg is Stravinsky's only rival to the title of 'musical colossus of the age'. To some, he opened the door into a whole new world of musical thought that is as exciting as it is challenging; to others he is the bogeyman of music, who sent it spiralling out of the reach of the ordinary man in the street. Nearly a hundred years later, many feel that Schoenberg's new path has proved to be a *cul de sac*.

Since the Renaissance, all music had had a tonal centre. No matter how far away from the tonic (the basic key) the music wandered, the listener was always conscious of the inevitability of a final return to that centre. Increasingly, towards the end of the nineteenth century, music began to incorporate intervals outside the prevailing diatonic scale, with the result that a work might feature an extraordinary amount of modulation. This is known as **chromatic** writing, since intervals from the chromatic scale (not the diatonic scale) are used to harmonize a piece.

Listen to Wagner's later works and to those of Mahler and Richard Strauss that followed soon afterwards. It becomes less clear which key the piece is written in, and its tonal centre is less obvious. Schoenberg followed logically on from this and asked: 'If I can introduce these chromatic notes into my music, can a particular key be said

Significant composers	Musical events	Other events
	MODERN 1900 to present	

1900
Benjamin Britten, English
(1913–76)
Witold Lutosławski, Polish
(1913–94)
Leonard Bernstein, American
(1918–90)
Malcolm Arnold, English
(b.1921)
György Ligeti, Hungarian
(b.1923)

1911 Mahler died
1912 Ravel's *Daphnis et Chloë*
1912 Schoenberg's *Pierrot Lunaire*
1913 Stravinsky's *The Rite of Spring*
1913 Vaughan Williams' *A London Symphony*
1915 Sibelius' Fifth Symphony
1916 Jazz begins to excite interest in USA
1917 Prokofiev's 'Classical' Symphony
1918 Bartók's *Bluebeard's Castle*
1918 Debussy died
1919 Elgar's Cello Concerto
1923 Maria Callas born
1923 Honegger's *Pacific 231*
1924 Gershwin's *Rhapsody in Blue*

1912–56 Jackson Pollock
1913 D.H. Lawrence's *Sons and Lovers*
1914 Joyce's *Dubliners*
1914–18 World War I
1914–53 Dylan Thomas
1915 Arthur Miller
1917 Russian Revolution
1919 Paderewski becomes President of Poland
1920 First British public broadcasting station (Chelmsford)
1922 T.S. Eliot's 'The Waste Land'
1924 First commercial electrical recording

1925
Pierre Boulez, French (b.1925)
Hans Werner Henze, German
(b.1926)
Karlheinz Stockhausen,
German (b.1928)
Malcolm Williamson, Australian
(b.1931)
Henryk Mikołaj Górecki, Polish
(b.1933)
Harrison Birtwistle, English
(b.1934)
Peter Maxwell Davies, English
(b.1934)
Arvo Pärt, Estonian (b.1935)
Steve Reich, American
(b.1936)
Philip Glass, American
(b.1937)
John Tavener, English (b.1944)

1925 Berg's *Wozzeck*
1928 Brecht/Weill *The Threepenny Opera*
1928 Ravel's *Boléro*
1931 Walton's *Belshazzar's Feast*
1934 Vibraphone introduced
1934 Delius, Holst, Elgar died
1935 Pavarotti born
1935 Gershwin's *Porgy and Bess*
1935 Swing music developing from jazz
1936 Barber's Adagio for Strings
1937 Orff's *Carmina burana*
1937 Shostakovich's Fifth Symphony
1937 Berg's *Lulu*
1939 Rodrigo's *Concierto de Aranjuez*
1943 Bartók's *Concerto for Orchestra*
1943 Rachmaninov died
1945 Charlie Parker in forefront of transitional jazz
1945 Britten's *Peter Grimes*
1945 Webern died
1947 Messiaen's *Turangalîla Symphony*
1948 First LP microgroove discs
1948 R. Strauss' *Four Last Songs*

1927 First cinema 'talkie'
1927 Establishment of BBC
1929 Wall Street Crash
1932 F.D. Roosevelt US President
1933 Hitler becomes German Chancellor
1936 Spanish Civil War
1937 Coronation of George VI
1939–45 World War II
1940 Walt Disney's Fantasia
1942 T.S. Eliot's 'The Four Quartets'
1945 German and Japanese surrender
1945 George Orwell's *Animal Farm*
1946 Nuremberg trials
1946 Picasso, Matisse and Henry Moore active
1949 George Orwell's *1984*

Significant composers	Musical events	Other events
	MODERN 1900 to present	
1950 Oliver Knussen, English (b.1952) James MacMillan, Scottish (b.1959) George Benjamin, English (b.1960) Mark-Anthony Turnage, English (b.1960)	**1951** Schoenberg died **1952** John Cage's *4'3"* **1953** Prokofiev died **1956** Rock'n'roll craze arrives **1957** Bernstein's *West Side Story* **1957** Sibelius died **1957** First stereo discs appear **1958** Vaughan Williams died **1958** Stereo broadcasting developed by BBC **1960** Shostakovich's Eighth Quartet **1960** Stockhausen's *Kontakte* **1961** Britten's *War Requiem* **1962** Shostakovich's 'Babi Yar' Symphony **1969** Carter's Concerto for Orchestra **1971** Stravinsky died **1972** Birtwistle's *The Triumph of Time* **1975** Shostakovich died **1976** Britten died **1976** Górecki's Third Symphony **1983** Commercial launch of compact disc **1983** Walton died **1990** Bernstein died **1992** Messiaen died **1994** Lutosławski died	**1951** Festival of Britain **1952** Agatha Christie's *The Mousetrap* opens **1953** Coronation of Elizabeth II **1954** Kingsley Amis' *Lucky Jim* **1955** Samuel Beckett's *Waiting for Godot* **1956** John Osborne's *Look Back In Anger* **1958** Last steam locomotive manufactured at Crewe **1959** Shelagh Delaney's *A Taste of Honey* **1960** J.F. Kennedy elected US President **1960** Film: *Saturday Night and Sunday Morning* **1961** First man in space **1963** J.F. Kennedy assassinated **1969** First man on the moon **1973** Picasso, Casals and W.H. Auden died **1977** Maria Callas died **1978** *Evita* opens **1982** Falklands War **1985** Live Aid Concert **1989** Collapse of Communism in Eastern Europe

to exist at all? Why should any note be foreign to any given key? Harmony is simply the sounding together of notes, so why shouldn't the twelve semitones of the chromatic scale be accorded equal significance?'

A summary of the 'twelve-note' (also known as **serial** or **dodecaphonic**) technique appears in the entries on Schoenberg and his disciples Berg and Webern. The theories and music of the so-called Second Viennese School – in succession to the First Viennese School of Haydn, Mozart *et al* – put the listener's expectations on a wrong footing. This music has none of the familiar features of chords we can recognize, tunes we can hum or rhythms we can tap our feet to. On the score, all that remained was the traditional manner of indicating the individual notes, time signatures and expression marks. And because tonal music forms the basis of our musical acquaintance, it is fairly easy to assimilate a Beethoven symphony on a first hearing. But serial music is written in a foreign language for which most of us have no immediate reference points – so its effect is like listening to a Scandinavian epic poem spoken in Japanese. We have to understand the language – the technique of the composition – before it can be appreciated. There are comparatively few who have the time to study Scandinavian poetry in Japanese translation....

Not all composers were attracted to the new technique but dissonance, **atonality** and the abandonment of melody are strong features of many twentieth-century works. Little serial or atonal music has established itself in the regular concert repertoire, still less has found its way into the hearts of the music-loving public. This is especially true of music written since the Second World War. A list of works by famous contemporary composers will elicit a blank response from most people. The avant-garde of today is taking far longer to become assimilated than the avant-garde of previous centuries. Opinions are deeply divided over the merits of a composer such as Charles Ives, for example, whose **polyrhythmic, polytonal** works are too complex for them to become widely popular; Stockhausen, Birtwistle, Cage, Carter, Berio (the list is endless) will remain a closed book for most people. Yet each has a devoted following. Musical development will, it is to be hoped, always have daring, fantastical innovators, examining new possibilities, expressing themselves in original ways. Whether they will find a broad, responsive and appreciative audience, only time will tell. Most new commissions have a premiere, a broadcast (if they're lucky) and are then consigned to oblivion – in *whatever* musical language they are written.

The legacy of Romanticism

The other path taken this century is that which retains music's link with tonality and, increasingly, with melody. Harsh and acid though some of Prokofiev's music may be, his style is a tangible descendant of the Romantics. Shostakovich too, sharing Prokofiev's love of the spiky, humorous and satirical, as well as the sombre and introspective, follows on from this tradition. Rachmaninov to an even greater degree wrote in the late-Romantic vein, producing some of the most popular symphonies and concertos written this century. In France, the most important composers after Ravel and Debussy were Honegger, Milhaud and Poulenc, three dissimilar composers unhelpfully grouped together as **Les Six** (the other three made negligible contributions) and all influenced by the whimsical and eccentric Satie.

From the next generation was Olivier Messaien, the most significant French composer since the Impressionists; he used elements of Indian music and birdsong in his music. Pierre Boulez, whose complex works are often based on mathematical relationships, and Karlheinz Stockhausen, whose scores for his innovative electronic music are represented by charts and diagrams, were both pupils of Messiaen.

Looking towards the future

No longer does one school of musical thought prevail. There seems little to link the **socio-political** operas of Kurt Weill and their brittle, haunting melodies, with his contemporary, Paul Hindemith and his dense, contrapuntal, **neo-Classical** idiom. Far less does Aaron Copland, born in 1900, only five years later than Hindemith, have any connection with either. The first conspicuously great American-born composer Copland established an authentic American school utilizing a combination of folk material, the sixth and seventh intervals of the **blues**, echoes of cowboy songs, jazz and the memory of Jewish synagogues.

And what has happened to British music? The Purcell bicentenary of 1895 stimulated interest in the great heritage of England's musical past; the English Folk

Song Society was founded in 1898; the London Promenade Concerts were inaugurated in 1895 and suddenly, 'the land without music' found itself in the midst of a musical renaissance. No one deserves more credit for this revival than Ralph Vaughan Williams and Gustav Holst. Vaughan Williams took as his creed the belief that 'The Art of Music above all other arts is the expression of the soul of the nation.' He was attracted by the music of Tudor England, by medieval tonalities and folk song, and he composed in what might loosely be called a Romantic neo-Classical style, using counterpoint, Classical forms (such as the symphony and the fugue) and modern harmony. Holst was inspired similarly, but he also was influenced by the East – his most famous piece, *The Planets*, evolved from ideas of Chaldean astrology.

Of the succeeding generation, the most important British composers have been Benjamin Britten, Michael Tippett and William Walton. Britten, with his many dramatic works, was especially significant; he established English music on the international stage, writing for a wide variety of media including an opera for television (*Owen Wingrave*). The list of his works composed since the Second World War and still actively in the regular concert repertoire is remarkably high: *Peter Grimes*, *Billy Budd*, his War Requiem, the Nocturne for tenor horn and orchestra, *The Young Person's Guide to the Orchestra*. William Walton's most outstanding contributions were made before the war, with *Façade*, *Belshazzar's Feast,* the Viola Concerto and the First Symphony. Tippett has had less of a lasting success than his two contemporaries, but *A Child of Our Time* (1941), the Concerto for double string orchestra (1939) and the *Fantasia concertante on a Theme of Corelli* (1953) will undoubtedly stay the course.

Of the more recent generations of composers, it is still too early to say with any certainty who and what will be remembered fifty years hence. The Manchester School of Peter Maxwell Davies, Harrison Birtwistle and Alexander Goehr has its champions; add to these the disparate voices of Richard Rodney Bennett, Malcolm Arnold and George Lloyd and the younger generation of Oliver Knussen, Steve Martland and Mark-Anthony Turnage (to name only those who currently enjoy the highest public profiles) and you have a fair representation of where classical music is going at present: it is more eclectic, more unpredictable in its form and inspiration than ever before.

The Minimalist, the Atonalist, the Serialist and those still using the musical language of the nineteenth century exist, not always comfortably, side by side. 'Serious' music has never been open to so many outside influences: jazz, pop, heavy rock, country and western, Third World music, the Broadway musical – all have had their effect on the composition of contemporary classical music. Indeed, at the close of the twentieth century it is difficult to sustain any longer a single definition of 'classical music'.

To the rock guitarist Jimi Hendrix, music was 'a safe kind of high', which is succinct and all-encompassing. But for me, it is most powerfully defined in the words of an anonymous writer: 'Servant and master am I: servant of those dead, and master of those living. Through my spirit immortals speak the message that makes the world weep and laugh, and wonder and worship.... For I am the instrument of God. I am Music.'

A CHRONOLOGY
OF COMPOSERS

Composers whose name appears in SMALL CAPITALS in this chronology are given a full entry in the COMPOSERS A TO Z.

flor. c.1000: Guido d'Arezzo
Developed the stave (lines on which music is written) and the sol-fa system, still taught to some children today as a means of learning to read music.

1098–1179: Abbess HILDEGARD OF BINGEN

flor. c.1180: Pérotin
French composer, among the first to notate music in a measured, rhythmical style and to write in canon.

c.1300–77: Guillaume de Machaut
French composer, poet and priest, the chief exponent of *Ars nova* in France, whose music (still preserved in thirty-two manuscripts) includes ballades, rondeaux, motets and the earliest surviving polyphonic (for four voices) setting of the Mass by a single composer.

c.1390–1453: John Dunstable
The most important English composer of the early fifteenth century. A writer of mainly church music, his most important contribution was to allow the rhythm of the spoken word to influence that of the music.

c.1400–74: Guillaume Dufay
French composer of motets and masses, a chorister in the Vatican choir and teacher of Okeghem.

c.1430–c.1495: Johannes Okeghem
Flemish composer and teacher, possibly of Josquin, noted for his mastery of counterpoint.

c.1440–1521: JOSQUIN DES PRÉS

1483–1546: Martin Luther
The German Protestant leader, a skilled flutist, lutenist, singer and composer of many hymns such as 'A Stronghold Sure'.

c.1490–1545: John Taverner
Highly esteemed English organist and composer of mainly church music.

1494–1576: Hans Sachs
Immortalized in Wagner's opera *Die Meistersinger von Nürnberg* (*The Mastersingers of Nuremburg*), Sachs was the most famous of the German mastersingers (members of guilds founded in 1311 to preserve the art of the troubadours) and also a prolific composer.

c.1505–85: Thomas TALLIS

c.1510–c.1557: Jacobus Clemens non Papa
Flemish composer of tuneful and likeable masses and motets.

1510–66: Antonio de Cabezón
Spanish composer who became blind in infancy. As organist to the Emperor Charles V, his compositions greatly influenced other keyboard composers in Europe. His sets of variations are particularly distinguished.

c.1525–94: Giovanni da PALESTRINA

1532–94: Roland de Lassus
Known in Italy as Orlando di Lasso, de Lassus was born in the Netherlands. One of the finest contrapuntal writers of the Renaissance, he was astonishingly prolific, writing more than 2,000 works. He stayed in the same post in Munich for nearly forty years, as musician to Albert V, Duke of Bavaria, producing madrigals in three different languages, and masses and motets of great skill and vision. More vivacious and vital than that of his contemporary, Palestrina, de Lassus' music looks forward to the Baroque period. Try *The Seven Penitential Psalms of David* (1563) and the motets 'Adoremus te, Christe', 'Tristis est anima mea' and 'In hora ultima'.

c.1533–85: Andrea Gabrieli
An Italian organist and composer, one of the first to write for a new instrument called the violin. His numerous madrigals and motets are notable for the response of the music to the text.

1543–88: Alfonso Ferrabosco
Highly competent Italian composer of madrigals, motets and other pieces, who was making a good living by the age of

nineteen in the court of Elizabeth I in
London. Rumoured variously to be a
French double-agent and murderer, he left
for Paris, then Italy in 1578.

1543–1623: William BYRD

c.1548–1611: Tomás Luis de Victoria

Sometimes called Vittoria, the Italian form
of this Spanish composer's name, for he
worked in Rome for twenty years. Although
influenced by his friend Giovanni
Palestrina, Victoria's music is more
dramatic and richly textured, full of
religious fervour. Worth investigating are
his motet *O quam gloriosum* and his
masterpiece, a Requiem Mass for the
Spanish Dowager Empress.

c.1554–1612: Giovanni Gabrieli

The first composer to indicate at what
volume music should be performed. He
transformed St Mark's, Venice into the
musical capital of Europe. Look out for his
Sonata pian' e forte alla quarta bassa from
Book 1 of *Sacrae symphoniae*.

1557–1602: Thomas Morley

A student of Byrd, he is remembered today
for his madrigals 'It was a Lover and his
Lass' and 'Now is the Month of Maying'.

c.1560–1613: Don Carlo Gesualdo

Italian composer and nobleman, Prince of
Venosa, as famous for murdering his
unfaithful first wife as for his fascinating
and lurid madrigals, which are musically
adventurous in the extreme.

c.1560–1640: Giles Farnaby

English composer of madrigals, motets and
other vocal works, which include many
original, even eccentric touches. His
keyboard miniatures, such as *Tower Hill*
and *His Dreame*, are his chief bequest. Fifty
of them appeared in the *Fitzwilliam
Virginal Book*.

1561–1633: Jacopo Peri

The Italian who is credited with writing
the first opera, *Dafne* (1597), now lost, and
Euridice (1600), the earliest still-surviving
opera.

1562–1621: Jan Sweelinck

Dutch composer whose fugal writing for
the keyboard was to have a huge influence
on J.S. Bach.

c.1562–1628: John Bull

English, of course, and the greatest
keyboard composer of the day. He wrote
over 200 works for virginals and organ that
made unprecedented demands on the
performer.

c.1563–1626: John Dowland

Famous English lutenist and songwriter
whose best-known works are *Lachrimae,*

or Seaven Teares and his three *Books of
Songs or Aires*.

1567–1643: Claudio MONTEVERDI

1572–1656: Thomas Tomkins

A pupil of William Byrd, composer of
church music and, particularly, madrigals,
among which are the most inspired
examples of the period.

c.1575–1623: Thomas Weelkes

English composer of sacred music and
madrigals, many of which are still
performed today, including his most
famous, 'As Vesta was from Latmos
Hill descending', from the collection
The Triumphes of Oriana.

1582–1652: Gregorio ALLEGRI

1583–1625: Orlando GIBBONS

1583–1643: Girolamo Frescobaldi

Italian organist whose compositions had a
far-reaching influence on succeeding
generations of musicians, including
Froberger and J.S. Bach.

1585–1672: Heinrich Schütz

The greatest German composer prior to
J.S. Bach was the Kapellmeister of the
Chapel Royal in Dresden under the
autocratic Elector of Saxony. Schütz stayed
there for the rest of his life. Influenced by
Monteverdi after a trip to Italy, he wrote the
first German opera in 1627 (*Dafne*, now
lost). His masterpieces are the St Matthew,
St Luke and St John Passions.

1602–76: Pietro Francesco Cavalli

Italian pupil of Monteverdi, who developed
opera in a variety of forms and wrote over
forty-five of them.

1632–87: Jean-Baptiste LULLY

c.1637–1707: Dietrich BUXTEHUDE

1644–82: Alessandro Stradella

He forged a huge reputation in his short
life (he was murdered in Genoa), with
many operas and cantatas. His oratorio *San
Giovanni Battista* (1675) is worth a listen.

1645–1704: Marc-Antoine Charpentier

Not to be confused with his namesake
Gustave, the composer of the opera *Louise*,
Marc-Antoine had the bad luck to be
working in Paris at the same time as Lully,
who opposed his advancement in musical
circles. But the trumpet tune from his
Te Deum (a great favourite at weddings) is
played today more often than all of Lully's
works put together.

1647–74: Pelham Humfrey

Precocious English composer who studied
in Italy and France (probably with Lully)
under the patronage of Charles II. His
anthems, songs and incidental music for
plays had a decisive effect on English

music and, not least, on Purcell, whose teacher he was. Especially effective are his anthems 'By the Waters of Babylon' and 'O Lord my God' and the music for Shakespeare's *The Tempest*. He died aged twenty-seven.

1649–1708: John Blow

A pupil of Gibbons and teacher of Purcell, he wrote *Venus and Adonis* in the 1680s, considered to be the first English opera.

1653–1706: Johann PACHELBEL

1653–1713: Arcangelo CORELLI

1654–1728: Agostino Steffani

Cleric, diplomat and composer, he was the first to take the novelty of Italian opera to the courts of Munich and Hanover. Handel succeeded him as Kapellmeister to the Elector of Hanover.

1657–1726: Michel-Richard Delalande

French composer and keyboard virtuoso whose career was spent in the service of the French court. Many of his fine settings of Latin sacred texts have been recorded.

c.1659–95: Henry PURCELL

1660–1725: Alessandro Scarlatti

Leading Italian opera composer of his day, with 114 to his credit and more than 500 chamber cantatas, and father of the more famous Domenico.

c.1665–c.1750: Tommaso Antonio Vitali

Italian violinist and composer, remembered today for his much-played Chaconne for violin and keyboard accompaniment; Respighi's arrangement of the piece for violin and organ opened Jascha Heifetz's legendary 1917 Carnegie Hall debut.

1667–1752: Johann Christoph Pepusch

German-born, English by adoption; John Gay's collaborator on *The Beggar's Opera*.

1668–1733: François COUPERIN

1670–1747: Giovanni Bononcini

The lifelong rival of Handel in Berlin and London, his career was eventually ruined by accusations of plagiarism. 'Mio caro ben' from *Ascanto*, one of his twenty-nine operas, is worth tracking down.

1671–1751: Tomaso ALBINONI

c.1673–1707: Jeremiah Clarke

Famous for his *Trumpet Voluntary*, long attributed to Purcell, originally written for the harpsichord and called 'The Prince of Denmark's March'. Shot himself when rejected by a suitor.

1678–1727: William Croft

Composed in the style of Purcell. Sections of his setting of the Anglican funeral service are still used today, but he is best known for the hymn tune to 'O God Our Help in Ages Past'.

1678–1741: Antonio VIVALDI

1681–1767: Georg Philipp TELEMANN

c.1682–1738: Jean-François Dandrieu

His harpsichord and organ pieces are still occasionally heard today.

1683–1764: Jean-Philippe RAMEAU

1685–1750: Johann Sebastian BACH

1685–1757: DOMENICO SCARLATTI

1685–1759: George Frideric HANDEL

1686–1739: Benedetto Marcello

Violinist, singer, poet, translator and civil servant, whose *Paraphrase of the Psalms* is a complex and original choral work. He is principally remembered for his D minor Oboe Concerto, one of the loveliest in the repertoire. The pope ordered an official day of mourning when he died.

1686–1768: Niccolò Antonio Porpora

One of the most famous singing teachers of the century. He wrote about fifty operas, which rivalled Handel's in popularity. He employed the young Haydn as his valet in Vienna while giving him lessons.

c.1687–1730: Jean-Baptiste Senaillé

French composer and violinist; one of his sonatas contains the 'Allegro spiritoso' transcribed as a popular encore for the bassoon, in a celebrated old recording by Archie Camden.

c.1687–1749: John Ernest Galliard

Minor German-born composer who settled in London; his wide variety of works included one for twenty-four bassoons and four double-basses.

1687–1762: Francesco Geminiani

Italian violinist and composer, a pupil of Corelli, who lived in England after 1714 and died in Dublin. Though his many works for the instrument fall short of those by Corelli, he made advances to violin technique and, most importantly, published the first violin method *The Art of Playing on the Violin* (1730), codifying principles many of which are still in common use.

1690–1768: Francesco Veracini

Veracini, a violinistic rival to Tartini, performed all over Europe. While in Dresden he threw himself out of a window in a fit of depression and was maimed for life. He died in poverty. His violin sonatas are well worth hearing.

1692–1770: Guiseppe TARTINI

1694–1772: Louis-Claude Daquin

An infant prodigy, he was only twelve when he became organist of the Sainte-Chapelle in Paris. His harpsichord piece *Le coucou* is still popular, as is his *Noël* No.10 in G minor for organ.

1695–1750: Giuseppe Sammartini
Composer and virtuoso oboist whose First
Symphony (1734) was among the earliest
of the form, and influential in its day. He
was also the teacher of Gluck. Try his
Sonata for strings in A major, Op.1 No.4.

1695–1764: Pietro Locatelli
Italian composer and violinist who studied
with Corelli. He became the leading
virtuoso of his day and left behind some
attractive concertos designed to
demonstrate his brilliant technique.

1697–1773: Johann Joachim Quantz
The first 'star' flute player, a German
whose works for the instrument have the
same purpose as Locatelli's for the violin.

1706–84: Giambattista Martini
Known as 'Padre' Martini after he took
holy orders in 1729, this Italian teacher,
scholar and composer was among the
most respected musicians of his day. His
pupils included J.C. Bach, Gluck and
Grétry – and Mozart.

1706–85: Baldassare Galuppi
A composer of operas and keyboard works,
he was a popular figure in London,
St Petersburg and his native Venice. He is
commemorated in Robert Browning's
poem 'A Toccata of Galuppi's'.

1710–36: Giovanni Pergolesi
His brief life contributed the opera *La serva
padrona*, which was at the centre of the
notorious *guerre des bouffons* (war of the
comedians), a musical and journalistic
squabble in Paris over the relative merits of
Italian and French opera. But his claim to
fame is the exquisite *Stabat mater*. Sir John
Barbirolli fashioned a delightful oboe
concerto from movements of this and other
Pergolesi works.

1710–78: Thomas ARNE
c.1710–79: William Boyce
English organist and composer of much
church and stage music, eight symphonies,
and songs, including 'Heart of Oak'.

1710–84: Wilhelm Friedemann Bach
The eldest son of J.S. and reckoned to be
the most gifted of his children. Alas,
success eluded him and he died embittered
and impoverished in Berlin.

1712–86: John Stanley
The blind English composer and organist
was at London's Temple Church for more
than fifty years and succeeded Boyce as
Master of the King's Musick in 1779. His
organ voluntaries are still played, especially
the stately Trumpet Voluntary in D.

1714–74: Niccolò Jomelli
Known as the 'Italian Gluck' (curiously, he

too died of 'an apoplectic fit'), he was a
pioneer in the use of orchestral crescendo.

1714–87: Christoph Willibald GLUCK
1714–88: Carl Philipp Emanuel BACH
1717–57: Johann Wenzel Stamitz
Czech composer and conductor. Regarded
as one of the founders of modern orchestral
sound and father of the 'Mannheim
School', which cultivated the birth of the
classical symphony and refined orchestral
technique.

1729–83: Antonio Soler
A Spanish monk, pupil of Domenico
Scarlatti, composer, harpsichordist and
organist at the monastery of Escurial in
Madrid.

1731–98: Gaetano Pugnani
Italian violinist and composer in the style
of Giuseppe Tartini. 'His' most popular
work is in fact a pastiche by Fritz Kreisler,
'attributed to Pugnani' and entitled
Prelude and Allegro.

1732–1809: Joseph HAYDN
1734–1829: François Gossec
Belgian composer and pioneer of orchestral
technique in Paris, where he succeeded his
mentor Jean-Philippe Rameau. James
Galway made his Tambourin briefly
popular.

1735–82: J.C. Bach
Johann Christian Bach was the eighteenth
child of Johann Sebastian, known as 'the
English' or 'London Bach' after moving to
London in 1762 and remaining there until
his death. Interesting historically because
his numerous keyboard concertos and
sonatas emphasize the brilliance of
instrumental display. This was a feature of
the Classical era exemplified by the works
of Mozart, a composer whom J.C. had
befriended as a child when Mozart visited
London in 1764.

1736–1809: Johann Georg Albrechtsberger
Austrian composer chiefly remembered
today as the distinguished teacher of
Beethoven; Hummel was also a pupil. His
Harp Concerto in C and Organ Concerto
in B flat are worth a listen.

1743–1805: Luigi BOCCHERINI
1745–1814: Charles Dibdin
Self-taught English composer, singer,
theatrical manager and author of novels
who, in 1789, instituted 'table
entertainments' at which he narrated, sang
and accompanied. Among his many
once-popular songs, 'Tom Bowling' can
still bring a tear to the eye.

1749–1801: Domenico Cimarosa
Italian composer of sixty operas and holder

of court posts in St Petersburg and Vienna. *Il matrimonio segreto* (*The Secret Marriage*) (1792) was a huge success, and there is a pleasant Oboe Concerto fashioned from his sonatas by Arthur Benjamin. Banished from Naples for supposed pro-French sentiments, he was rumoured to have been poisoned.

1750–1825: Antonio Salieri
Italian composer, protégé of Gluck and teacher of Beethoven and Schubert. Served the Hapsburg court for more than half a century and wrote dull, worthy music with occasional flashes of real inspiration. Intriguer, yes, but not a poisoner.

1752–1832: Muzio Clementi
Born in Rome, died in Evesham, Worcestershire, a piano virtuoso, piano manufacturer and teacher. His *Gradus ad Parnassum* (*Steps to Parnassus* – the mountain sacred to the Muses) is a collection of piano studies tackled by generations of students. Vladimir Horowitz went some way to reclaiming his sonatas from neglect.

1755–1824: Giovanni Battista Viotti
Italian composer and violinist from a poor family, a pupil of Pugnani, who became the greatest virtuoso of the day. A handful of his twenty-nine violin concertos are still played. Died impoverished in London.

1756–91: Wolfgang Amadeus MOZART

1757–1831: Ignaz Pleyel
An Austrian composer and piano manufacturer who settled in Paris (Chopin made his debut in his rooms). His Sinfonie concertante in B flat, Op.29 is an agreeable Haydnesque work.

1760–1812: Jan Ladislav Dussek
Czech composer and pianist of great originality, a pupil of C.P.E. Bach, who toured all over Europe, ending up as *maître de chapelle* to Prince Talleyrand.

1760–1842: Luigi Cherubini
Italian resident in Paris from 1788 and head of the Paris Conservatoire from 1822. Beethoven's vocal music was influenced by him, but his own music is very ordinary.

1766–1837: Samuel Wesley
English organist and composer, father of S.S. Wesley, pupil of William Boyce, brother of Charles and nephew of John Wesley, the founder of Methodism. His Air and Gavotte for organ is a charming example of his work. A skull injury in his youth resulted in later mental instability.

1770–1827: Ludwig van BEETHOVEN

1774–1851: Gaspare Spontini
Italian opera composer of wide influence and huge popularity in his day but who was nevertheless unable to equal the success of *La Vestale* (1807), written in his early thirties. Esteemed as a conductor, he was musical director to the court in Berlin from 1820–42. Became deaf, and left his entire fortune to the poor.

1775–1834: François-Adrien Boïeldieu
French opera composer, whose secure middle-class background did not prevent him from prospering after the Revolution. *La dame blanche* and *The Caliph of Baghdad* were his biggest successes, and the overtures are occasionally heard today.

1775–1838: Bernhard Henrik Crusell
Finnish clarinettist and composer whose attractive Clarinet Concerto in F minor, Op.5 was rescued from oblivion by the young Emma Johnson, winner of the 1983 BBC Young Musician of the Year award.

1778–1837: Johann Nepomuk HUMMEL

1782–1837: John FIELD

1782–1840: Niccolò PAGANINI

1782–1871: Daniel-François-Esprit AUBER

1784–1859: Louis Spohr
German composer of operas, oratorios and seventeen violin concertos (No.8 in the form of a song-scena is worth tracking down, as is his attractive Nonet). One of the first composers to use a baton when conducting.

1786–1826: Carl Maria Freiherr von WEBER

1786–1855: Henry Bishop
Bishop was the first musician to be knighted by a British sovereign (1842). His opera *Clari, or The Maid of Milan* (1823), includes 'Home, Sweet Home' as a recurrent theme, anticipating the device of *leitmotif* by several decades. This, plus Bishop's 'Echo Song', 'Pretty Mocking-Bird' and, particularly, 'Lo, hear the Gentle Lark' were favourites of the great coloratura soprano Amelita Galli-Curci, who recorded them.

1791–1833: Ferdinand HÉROLD

1791–1857: Carl Czerny
Viennese teacher, pianist and composer who numbered Liszt among his pupils; he himself a pupil of Beethoven, Clementi and Hummel. His studies have been the basis for many a career.His many pedagogic works have obscured some compositions of real musical interest: his *Nonet*, for instance, and Piano Concerto in A minor.

1791–1864: Giacomo MEYERBEER

1792–1868: Gioachino ROSSINI

1794–1870: Ignaz Moscheles
Much-revered pianist, teacher of Mendelssohn among others, and composer;

he lived in London from 1826 to 1846. His Piano Concerto in G minor and his once-popular piano études are well worth hearing.

1795–1870: Saverio Mercadante
Italian composer, church musician and director of the Naples Conservatory. His sixty operas are only rarely performed, but his orchestral works are highly attractive and deserve to be better known. The Flute Concerto in E minor (1819), Clarinet Concerto in B flat, Op.101 (1819), and the Concerto for horn in F are fine examples.

1796–1868: Franz Berwald
The only Swedish composer of any significance, whose highly appealing Symphony No.3 in C, 'Singulière' is still in the repertoire. His Grand Septet in B flat is a one-off, marvellous entertainment, supremely well written and unaccountably rarely heard in the concert hall.

1797–1828: Franz SCHUBERT
1797–1848: Gaetano DONIZETTI
1799–1862: Jacques-François-Fromenthal-Elie Halévy
French composer of over thirty operas. His finest hour came with his melodramatic twelfth opera La Juive (The Jewess), in which the lady is revealed to be a cardinal's daughter moments before her execution. Halévy's daughter married Bizet, who was his former pupil.

1801–35: Vincenzo BELLINI
1801–43: Josef Lanner
Austrian violinist and composer of 200 waltzes. He was as responsible for the Viennese waltz craze as Johann Strauss I, his chief rival.

1801–51: Albert Lortzing
German librettist and composer of operettas. His Zar und Zimmermann (Tsar and Carpenter) is still in the German repertoire.

1803–56: Adolphe ADAM
1803–69: Hector BERLIOZ
1804–47: Mikhail GLINKA
1804–85: Julius Benedict
German-born composer and conductor who settled in England in 1835. Queen Victoria knighted him in 1871. His opera The Lily of Killarney was enormously popular in Britain for many years.

1805–1900: Johan Peter Hartmann
Long-lived Danish composer of operas (The Raven and Little Christina had libretti by Hans Christian Andersen), whose Symphony in G minor is the first Romantic symphony of the Danish school.

1808–70: Michael William Balfe
Irish singer and composer remembered today for his opera The Bohemian Girl (1843) with its once-popular aria 'I Dreamt I dwelt in Marble Halls'. Balfe's most enduring legacy is that most celebrated of Victorian drawing-room ballads 'Come into the Garden, Maud'.

1809–47: Felix MENDELSSOHN
1810–49: Frédéric CHOPIN
1810–49: Otto Nicolai
German composer and conductor, founder of the Vienna Philharmonic Orchestra. He died of a stroke just before his fortieth birthday and two months after the première of his greatest success, the opera The Merry Wives of Windsor. The overture from this remains a concert favourite.

1810–56: Robert SCHUMANN
1810–76: Félicien David
French composer whose 1844 symphonic poem Le Désert, written after a protracted journey to the Near East, although forgotten today, was highly acclaimed.

1810–76: Samuel Sebastian Wesley
English composer of organ and choral works, and the illegitimate son of Samuel Wesley. He did more than anyone else to raise the standards of Anglican church music in the nineteenth century. The anthem 'Blessed be the God and Father' is still performed often, as are many of his hymn tunes, including 'The Church's One Foundation', and organ pieces Holsworthy Church Bells and Choral Song and Fugue.

1811–86: Franz LISZT
1811–96: Ambroise Thomas
Director of the Paris Conservatoire and once-popular composer of lightweight operas such as Mignon, Raymond and Hamlet. At one time every coloratura soprano had the aria 'Io son Titania' from Mignon in her repertoire.

1812–65: Vincent Wallace
Irish opera composer who found success at his first attempt with Maritana (1845), from which come the once-modish arias 'Scenes that are Brightest' and 'Let me like a Soldier fall'.

1812–71: Sigismund Thalberg
Liszt's only rival as a pianist in the 1830s and the composer of opera fantasies. Many feature the pianistic device he invented of playing a melody in the middle of the keyboard with alternate hands, the free hand to supply the bass/harmony or decorations, giving the impression of three hands playing.

1812–83: Friedrich von Flotow
German composer of noble birth who had an enormous success with his opera *Martha* (1847), still performed occasionally. It contains the tenor favourite M'apparei (and 'The Last Rose of Summer', which Flotow 'lifted' and interpolated into the score).

1813–69: Alexander Dargomizhsky
Russian nationalist composer, associated with (though not a member of) the Mighty Handful. His operas *The Stone Guest* and *Russalka* contain some splendid music; 'Danse Slave' and 'Tzigane' from the latter are occasionally played, while both works remain under-rated.

1813–83: Richard WAGNER

1813–88: Charles-Valentin ALKAN

1813–1901: Giuseppe VERDI

1814–88: Stephen Heller
Hungarian composer and pianist, resident in Paris, now unfairly known only for his keyboard exercises but whose études, sonatas and preludes are subtle and individual. He was an influence on the following generation of French composers such as Fauré.

1814–89: Adolf von Henselt
Bavarian pianist and composer (a student of Hummel) who composed one master-piece, his Piano Concerto in F minor, Op.16, which was *de rigeur* for all pianists until the advent of Tchaikowsky's Piano Concerto No.1. Among his two sets of piano studies, Opp.2 & 5 is *Si oiseau j'étais* (*If I were a bird*), an exacting étude once recorded by Rachmaninov, whose father studied with Henselt.

1816–75: Sir William Sterndale Bennett
English composer and friend of Mendelssohn and Schumann (whose works strongly influenced him), later Principal of the Royal Academy of Music. His Fourth Piano Concerto – particularly the Barcarolle movement – was very much in vogue at one time.

1817–90: Niels Gade
Danish-born, German-trained and much influenced by Mendelssohn, but whose Danish 'national' traits exist even in early works.

1818–91: Henry Charles LITOLFF

1818–93: Charles François GOUNOD

1818–97: Antonio Bazzini
Italian composer remembered today solely for his pyrotechnical showpiece for violin and piano *La Ronde des Lutins* (*The Dance of the Goblins*).

1819–80: Jacques OFFENBACH

1819–95: Franz von SUPPÉ

1820–81: Henri Vieuxtemps
Famed Belgian violinist and composer who toured from the age of seven. Two of his seven violin concertos are extremely fine: No.4 in D minor and No.5 in A minor.

1822–82: Joachim Raff
Swiss composer of well-crafted and wonderfully melodic works; the inconsistency of his inspiration have brought him a poorer reputation than he deserves. Still heard occasionally are his celebrated *Cavatina* (recorded by Itzhak Perlman), *Rigaudon*, Op.204 No.3, *La polka de la reine* and *La fileuse*, all pretty piano pieces once much played. But these are pot-boilers beside his magnificent Piano Concerto in C minor (1873), Cello Concerto in D, the three String Quartets and the Piano Suite in D minor.

1822–90: César FRANCK

1823–92: Édouard LALO

1824–1910: Carl Reinecke
German composer, pianist and conductor. His Piano Concerto No.1 in F sharp minor Op.72 (1879), Introduction and Allegro appassionato in C minor for clarinet and piano, Op.256 (c.1900), Wind Octet, Op.216 (c.1892) and Piano Sonata for the left hand alone, Op.179 are all worth tracking down.

1824–84: Bedřich SMETANA

1824–96: Anton BRUCKNER

1825–99: JOHANN STRAUSS II

1826–64: Stephen Collins Foster
The son of a wealthy Pennsylvania businessman, self-taught composer of 200 songs including 'Old Folks at Home', 'Camptown Races', 'Jeanie with the Light Brown Hair', 'My Old Kentucky Home', 'Beautiful Dreamer' and 'Oh! Susanna'. He earned a fortune, spent it all and died (possibly by suicide) an impoverished alcoholic aged thirty-eight.

1829–69: Louis Moreau GOTTSCHALK

1829–94: Anton RUBINSTEIN

1830–1915: Karl Goldmark
Austro-Hungarian composer, a brilliant orchestrator whose *Rustic Wedding* Symphony was once a favourite; less understandable is the neglect of his romantic, lyrical Violin Concerto No.1 in A minor, a magnificent work.

1831–1907: Joseph Joachim
Famed Hungarian violinist and composer, the dedicatee of Brahms' Violin Concerto and founder of the celebrated 'Joachim' Quartet. His Violin Concerto in the Hungarian manner, Op.11 has been recorded, as have some concert overtures;

in 1903 he recorded pieces by himself, Bach and his friend Brahms.

1833–87: Alexander BORODIN

1833–97: Johannes BRAHMS

1834–58: Julius Reubke

Every organist knows his Sonata on the 94th Psalm, a cornerstone of the repertoire; his Piano Sonata is also very powerful – two extraordinary works from a mere handful produced in his all-too-brief life.

1834–86: Amilcare PONCHIELLI

1835–80: Henryk Wieniawski

Polish violinist-composer and, after Paganini, the most important of the nineteenth century. His Concerto No.2 in D minor is one of the great works of the fiddle-player's literature and is a must for any collection. His touching *Légende*, Concerto No.1 in F sharp minor, *Souvenir de Moscou*, Polonaise in D, Op.14, Fantasy on Gounod's *Faust* and *Scherzo-tarantelle* are still widely played.

1835–1918: César Cui

Cui was by far the least significant member of the group of Russian composers known as the Mighty Handful, and was the son of a soldier in Napoleon's army. His less-than-mighty contribution to musical history can be heard in such attractive miniatures as *Orientale* from the *Kaleidoscope* Suite.

1835–1921: Camille SAINT-SAËNS

1836–91: Léo DELIBES

1837–1910: Mily BALAKIREV

1837–1915: Emile Waldteufel

Alsatian composer, pianist to the Empress Eugénie of France and immortalized by one composition, *The Skaters' Waltz*. His *Les Grenadiers* and *Estudiantina* waltzes are equally catchy.

1838–75: Georges BIZET

1838–1920: Max BRUCH

1839–81: Modest MUSSORGSKY

1839–1901: Josef Rheinberger

A German composer, Rheinberger was a child prodigy who held a post as church organist at the age of seven. Some of his many works for the instrument are on the stodgy side; not so the two magnificent Organ Concertos (No.1 in F, Op.137 and No.2 in G minor, Op.177). The latter, composed in 1894, has a first movement theme reminiscent of Elgar's 'Nimrod' from the *Enigma Variations*.

1840–1901: Sir John Stainer

An immensely influential English composer in his day, who ended up as Principal of what is now the Royal College of Music. Among his works that are still

performed are the 1887 oratorio *The Crucifixion* and his many hymn tunes, which include 'Love Divine, all Loves Excelling' and 'There's a Friend for Little Children'.

1840–93: Peter Ilyich TCHAIKOWSKY

1840–1911: Johann Svendsen

Norwegian composer whose attractive Romance in G for violin and orchestra is a concert favourite. His orchestral *Carnival in Paris*, Op.9 and four *Norwegian Rhapsodies* (1872–78) are well worth hearing.

1841–94: Emmanuel CHABRIER

1841–1904: Antonin DVOŘÁK

1842–1900: Sir Arthur SULLIVAN

1842–1912: Jules MASSENET

1842–1918: Arrigo Boito

The son of an Italian painter and Polish countess, he became both a librettist (notably for Verdi's *Otello* and *Falstaff*) and composer. His opera *Mefistofele* (1868) has remained on the fringe of the repertoire.

1843–1907: Edvard GRIEG

1844–1908: Nicolai RIMSKY-KORSAKOV

1844–1908: Pablo de Sarasate

Spanish violin virtuoso, among the most acclaimed figures in the instrument's history, whose *Zigeunerweisen* (*Gypsy Airs*) is still much played. He lived long enough to record some of his own pieces. Bruch, Lalo and Saint-Saëns were among those who dedicated works to him.

1844–1913: Stephen Adams

The pen-name of the baritone Michael Maybrick, English composer of such songs as 'The Holy City', 'The Star of Bethlehem' and 'Nirvana'.

1844–1937: Charles-Marie WIDOR

1845–1924: Gabriel-Urbain FAURÉ

1848–1918: Hubert PARRY

1850–1924: Xaver Scharwenka

German pianist and composer, whose *Polish Dance*, Op.3 No.1 became his calling-card. But it is his four piano concertos that earn his entry here, as interesting and exciting as many of the standard Romantic concertos we hear today and, until the advent of Rachmaninov's, widely played. Especially notable are the First Concerto (in B flat, Op.32, recorded by Earl Wild) and the Fourth (in E minor, Op.82, championed on disc by the remarkable Stephen Hough).

1851–1931: Vincent d'Indy

Inspired by Franck, whose pupil he was, and Wagner, d'Indy became an important influence on French music after he co-founded the Schola Cantorum Paris (1894). The one work of his still heard regularly is the invigorating *Symphony on a French Mountain Song*, Op.25 for piano and orchestra, based on a simple folk melody.

1852–1924: Charles Villiers STANFORD
1854–1921: Engelbert HUMPERDINCK
1854–1925: Moritz MOSZKOWSKI
1854–1928: Leos JANÁČEK
1854–1932: John Philip SOUSA
1855–99: Ernest CHAUSSON
1855–1914: Anatoli Liadov

Russian pupil of Rimsky-Korsakov whose small output is represented today by his symphonic tone-poems *Kikimora* and *The Enchanted Lake*, both fine works well worth tracking down, as well as his Polonaise in C, Op.49 and the piano miniature *The Music Box*.

1856–1941: Christian SINDING
1857–1934: Edward ELGAR
1857–1919: Ruggiero LEONCAVALLO
1857–1944: Cécile Chaminade

French pianist and composer whose concert study 'Automne' was once in every piano stool in the land. Fluent, melodic charmers like her *Concertstück* for piano and orchestra, and solos such as 'The Flatterer' and 'Scarf Dance', receive the occasional revival.

1858–1924: Giacomo PUCCINI
1858–1944: Dame Ethel Smyth

Redoubtable German-trained English composer, whose compositions, now beginning to receive belated attention, are uneven but at their best highly impressive. *The Wreckers* and *Mass in D* are her two best-known works. A militant suffragette, she was jailed in 1911; deafness and distorted hearing put an end to her composing career.

1859–1924: Sergei Liapunov

Pupil of Tchaikowsky and Sergei Taneyev, his legacies are the terrifyingly difficult Twelve Transcendental Études, Op.11, inspired by Liszt's trail-blazing set of the same title; there are also the flashy and highly entertaining Piano Concerto No.2 in E and the *Rhapsody on Ukrainian themes*.

1859–1935: Mikhail Ippolitov-Ivanov

Russian composer greatly influenced by folk music, whose *Caucasian Sketches* are still played. He ended up as Director of the Moscow Conservatoire.

1860–1903: Hugo WOLF
1860–1908: Edward Alexander MACDOWELL
1860–1909: Isaac ALBÉNIZ
1860–1911: Gustav MAHLER
1860–1941: Ignacy Jan Paderewski

The most celebrated and highly paid pianist of his day, a great Polish patriot who became prime minister of his country in 1919. His compositions include the ubiquitous Minuet in G, a lushly romantic Piano Concerto in A minor and *Fantaisie polonaise* for piano and orchestra, the latter two well worth hearing in recordings by Earl Wild.

1860–1945: Emil Nikolaus von Reznicek

Austrian composer whose one hit is the lively Overture to his comic opera *Donna Diana*.

1860–1956: Gustave CHARPENTIER
1861–1906: Anton ARENSKY
1861–1925: Enrico Bossi

A minor Italian composer and organist, whose *Giga* and *Étude symphonique* are idiomatic and effective.

1862–97: Leon Boëllmann

A short-lived French organist and composer whose *Suite gothique* is part of every organist's repertoire; *Prière àNotre Dame*, its reflective third movement, precedes a scintillating, typically French Toccata.

1862–1918: Claude DEBUSSY
1862–1934: Frederick DELIUS
1862–1936: Edward German

German was as English as they come (born in Shropshire), as were the titles of his most successful works: the operetta *Merrie England*, his song 'Glorious Devon' and the stage music for *Nell Gwynn* and *Henry VIII*. His *Welsh Rhapsody* is good light music, a genre of which he was a master.

1863–1919: Horatio Parker

American composer and teacher of Charles Ives; his oratorio *Hora Novissima* is a significant American choral work.

1863–1937: Gabriel Pierné

French composer and organist, now remembered for his once-popular light music favourite *March of the Little Lead Soldiers*.

1863–1945: Pietro MASCAGNI
1864–1932: Eugen d'Albert

Glasgow-born composer, pianist and pupil of Liszt. His two piano concertos have recently been recorded, but the opera *Tiefland* is still his best-known piece. Married seven times, including the thrice-married pianist Teresa Carreño.

1864–1935: Johann Halvorsen

A Norwegian, married to Grieg's niece. His *Norwegian Air* is an enchanting little piece for violin.

1864–1949: RICHARD STRAUSS
1864–1956: Alexander Grechaninov

Russian pupil of Rimsky-Korsakov, writing in traditional Russian idiom. There is a famous and much-requested old recording of his *Creed* by the Russian Metropolitan Church Choir.

1865–1931: Carl NIELSEN

1865–1934: Edwin Lemare

English organist and composer whose transcriptions of orchestral works are among the most ingenious and effective for the organ; after many years, these and his original compositions (like his Rondo capriccio Op.64 No.9) are coming back into fashion. His most famous piece is the Andantino in D flat (1888), adapted into the popular song 'Moonlight and Roses'.

1865–1935: Paul DUKAS

1865–1936: Alexander GLAZUNOV

1865–1957: Jean SIBELIUS

1866–1924: Ferruccio BUSONI

1866–1925: Erik SATIE

1866–1950: Francesco Cilèa

Italian opera composer in the style of Puccini, remembered for his *Adriana Lecouvreur* (1902) and *L'arlesiana*, the work in which Caruso made his name.

1867–1916: Enrique GRANADOS

1868–1916: Hamish MacCunn

Scottish composer of the popular overture *The Land of the Mountain and the Flood*, and other tartan music.

1868–1917: Scott Joplin

American ragtime composer whose forgotten name was revived by the inclusion of his music in the film *The Sting*. We have had to endure *The Entertainer* ever since, but the best of Joplin's piano rags are the American equivalent of Mozart's minuets and Chopin's mazurkas.

1868–1946: Sir Granville Bantock

His orchestral work *Fifine at the Fair* was a favourite of Beecham's, while his *Celtic*, *Pagan* and *Hebridean* Symphonies deserve to be far better known. Oriental culture features in many of his 250 songs.

1869–1937: Albert Roussel

After a naval career, he studied with d'Indy and composed works with an Eastern influence, later turning to neo-classicism. His Second Symphony and Suite in F are representative of his work.

1869–1941: Sir Henry Walford Davies

Musical educator and composer who was made Master of the King's Musick in 1934; his *Solemn Melody* is much used at funerals, State and otherwise.

1869–1949: Hans Pfitzner

Musical descendant of Wagner and worshipped as such in Germany; his opera *Palestrina* is considered a masterpiece. As an ardent supporter of the Third Reich

(Pfitzner even dedicated a piece to the murderous Gauleiter of Poland, Hans Frank), he faced the DeNazification Court in 1948, but was exonerated because of his poor physical condition.

1869–1958: Armas Järnefelt

Finnish composer of the once well-known *Praeludium*. Married to Sibelius' sister.

1870–1894: Guillaume Lekeu

Belgian composer who died at twenty-four; his Violin Sonata is a magnificent and under-valued work.

1870–1937: Louis Vierne

Blind French organist and composer (pupil of Franck and Widor), who died at the organ of Notre-Dame. Organ fanciers will know his Symphonies Nos.1 and 2 for the instrument as well as his thrilling evocation of Big Ben, *Carillon de Westminster*.

1870–1938: Leopold Godowsky

Polish-born American composer and pianist whose contrapuntal mastery led to some of the most prodigiously difficult piano works ever, including Fifty-three Studies on Chopin's Études and a Passacaglia on the opening bars of Schubert's 'Unfinished' Symphony. His reputation is on the increase.

1870–1948: Franz LEHÁR

1872–1915: Alexander SCRIABIN

1872–1958: Ralph VAUGHAN WILLIAMS

1872–1960: Hugo Alfvén

Swedish composer of *Midsummer Vigil*, Op.19, otherwise known as the *Swedish Rhapsody*; little else of his music is known, though the Elegy from his *Gustav II Adolf Suite*, Op.49 is appealing.

1873–1916: Max Reger

German pianist, organist, pianist, teacher and composer working in thick contrapuntal textures, much influenced by Bach and Beethoven; mainly stodgy, occasionally inspired (Variations on a Theme of Mozart, for example). His organ works are (like it or not) part of the repertory.

1873–1943: Sergei RACHMANINOV

1873–1953: Joseph Jongen

Belgian composer and director of the Brussels Conservatory from 1920–39. Among his many compositions, the spectacular *Symphonie concertante* for organ and orchestra stands out, not least for its thrilling final movement, a noisy toccata given full measure in a recording by the American virtuoso Virgil Fox.

1874–1934: Gustav HOLST

1874–1947: Reynaldo Hahn

Venezuelan French-born conductor and

composer of elegant, graceful music. Of his many fine songs, 'Si mes vers avaient des ailes' ('If my songs only had wings') is the most famous. His opera based on Shakespeare's *The Merchant of Venice* and his Piano Concerto No.1 in E minor (recorded by him in 1937) are representative of his other works.

1874–1951: Arnold SCHOENBERG

1874–1954: Charles IVES

1875–1912: Samuel Coleridge-Taylor

The first black composer to achieve recognition (his father was a doctor from Sierra Leone, his English mother was from Croydon) he achieved fame at twenty-three with his cantata *Hiawatha's Wedding Feast* – 'Onaway, awake, beloved' was once a concert favourite of tenors. Other works include some attractive chamber music, a Violin Concerto in G minor and his *Petite suite de concert*.

1875–1937: Maurice RAVEL

1875–1956: Reinhold Glière

Russian pupil of Arensky and Ippolitov-Ivanov, his Third Symphony 'Ilya Murometz' is conceived on an epic scale; another popular nationalistic work is his ballet *The Red Poppy*. Try also his Concerto for coloratura soprano and orchestra and his Horn Concerto, both conventional but lyrical and melodic.

1875–1959: Albert Ketèlbey

English light music composer, the perpetrator of *In a Monastery Garden* and *In a Persian Market*, also of a pretty *Concertstück* for piano and orchestra and an orchestral *Suite de ballet*.

1875–1962: Fritz KREISLER

1876–1906: William Hurlstone

English composer whose early death deprived us of a major talent exhibited in his *Fantasy-Variations on a Swedish Air*, Piano Trio in G and, especially, the superb Piano Concerto in D.

1876–1946: Manuel de FALLA

1876–1948: Ermanno Wolf-Ferrari

German-Italian pupil of Rheinberger, whose light touch and assured style brought him much acclaim for his comic operas, such as *The Jewels of the Madonna* and *Susanna's Secret*; the overtures to both are high-spirited, while the Act 2 Intermezzo of the former is one of those hauntingly familiar tunes that are so hard to name.

1876–1972: Havergal Brian

Long-lived legend, mainly self-taught, Staffordshire-born composer who had composed thirty-two symphonies by the time he died, twenty-two of them after reaching the age of 80 and seven after the age of ninety. Performances of these were few during his lifetime, but a devoted band of admirers has ensured the slow acceptance of some of his grandiose conceptions, some of which have now been recorded.

1877–1952: Sergei Bortkiewicz

A minor Russian composer and pianist. His Piano Concerto in B flat, Op.16 is popular with Classic fM listeners: a lush, romantic work that could have been written for a Bette Davis movie.

1877–1953: Roger Quilter

English composer noted for his fine settings of Shakespeare's songs, his *Children's Overture* on nursery rhyme tunes, and the music to the play *Where the Rainbow Ends*.

1877–1960: Ernst von DOHNÁNYI

1878–1951: Selim Palmgren

Finnish composer whose Piano Concerto No.2 'The River' is worth investigating; his brief *En route* is a dazzling piano encore.

1878–1958: Joseph Holbrooke

English composer of the Wagner-like operatic trilogy *The Cauldron of Annwen*, comprising *The Children of Don* (1911), *Dylan* (1914) and *Bronwen* (1929). Though his Piano Concerto, Piano Quartet in G minor and orchestral *Variations on Three Blind Mice* (1900) have their moments (the latter was recorded by Sir Henry Wood), Holbrooke has yet to have his day.

1878–1960: Rutland Boughton

English composer who is famed for his once-popular opera *The Immortal Hour* and who hoped to emulate Wagner's Bayreuth by his festival operatic centre in Glastonbury (1914–25).

1879–1936: Ottorino RESPIGHI

1879–1941: Frank Bridge

Better known as the teacher of Benjamin Britten than for his music, but his suite *The Sea* and *There is a Willow grows aslant a Brook* are fine and characteristic works.

1879–1957: Joseph CANTELOUBE

1879–1962: John Ireland

English composer whose setting of John Masefield's 'Sea Fever' is his best-known work, but his *Comedy* Overture, Piano Concerto in E flat and (especially) his motet *Greater Love hath no Man* are worth adding to any collection.

1879–1970: Cyril Scott

Nicknamed rather unfairly 'the English Debussy', his songs and piano pieces, such as *Lotus Land*, are particularly effective. Try also his two Piano Concertos and Variations on 'Early One Morning'.

1880–1951: Nicolai Medtner

Russian of German descent who settled in England in 1936, he composed almost exclusively for the piano. Unkindly called 'a poor man's Rachmaninov' in some quarters; quite a number of his concertos and sonatas are far better than that – but you have to pick and choose.

1880–1959: Ernest Bloch

Swiss-born American, notable for his work with specific Jewish associations, especially his *Schelomo* for cello and orchestra and the *Baal Shem* Suite for violin and orchestra.

1881–1945: Béla BARTÓK

1881–1950: Nicolai Miaskovsky

A Russian pupil of Rimsky-Korsakov, teacher of Dmitry Kabalevsky and Aram Khachaturian, and prolific composer of twenty-seven symphonies written under the artistic restraints of the Communist regime; denounced in 1948 for 'formalism', along with Prokofiev, Shostakovich and others. His 1945 Cello Concerto is a distinguished work.

1881–1955: Georges Enescu

Romania's most distinguished composer, violinist and teacher of Yehudi Menuhin, among others. His two *Romanian Rhapsodies* are especially good, using folk influence but with more traditional harmonies than Bartók.

1882–1937: Karol SZYMANOWSKY

1882–1948: Manuel Ponce

Mexican composer whose many guitar works include *Concierto del sur* (*Southern Concerto*), written for Segovia, and his popular song 'Estrellita'; still something of a hero in his own country.

1882–1949: Joaquín Turina

Fellow Spanish composer Albéniz taught him to 'fight for the national music of our country', and in such works as the symphonic poem *La procesión del Rocio* and his symphonic Rhapsody for piano and orchestra he does just that; a major influence on Spanish music.

1882–1961: Percy GRAINGER

1882–1967: Zoltán KODÁLY

1882–1971: Igor STRAVINSKY

1883–1945: Anton von WEBERN

1883–1947: Alfredo Casella

Italian student of Fauré who abandoned his early Romantic style for atonality, renouncing that for Stravinskian neo-classicism. His *La giara*, Partita and *Scarlattiana* were his most notable successes in this idiom.

1883–1950: Lord Berners

English composer, painter, diplomat and author, born Gerald Hugh Tyrwhitt-Wilson, under which name his first works appeared. Eccentric, gifted, self-taught and a skilled parodist, his greatest triumph was the ballet *The Triumph of Neptune* (1926).

1883–1953: Arnold BAX

1883–1964: Sir George Dyson

His choral works, especially *The Canterbury Pilgrims*, kept the English tradition going in fine form. Became director of the Royal College of Music and, during World War I, wrote the official *Manual of Grenade Fighting*.

1883–1965: Edgard Varèse

Studied with d'Indy, Widor and Roussel, and settled in the USA in 1915. His music avoids any reference to previous forms or logic to produce works of extreme dissonance, unusual instrumentation and abstract titles (e.g., *Density 21.5*, *Octandre* and *Ionisation*). A significant influence on some composers.

1884–1920: Charles Griffes

American pupil of Humperdinck, but much influenced by French Impressionism, as can be heard in his alluring orchestral pieces *The Pleasure Dome of Kubla Khan* (after Coleridge's poem) and *The White Peacock* (originally for piano).

1885–1916: George Butterworth

A collector of English folk songs, which inspired his much-loved *The Banks of Green Willow* and *A Shropshire Lad* (settings of A.E. Housman's poems). Awarded the Military Cross in World War I but killed in action a month later.

1885–1935: Alban BERG

1886–1957: Eric Coates

The quintessential English light music composer, many of whose works have become familiar through their use as radio and television signature tunes: the march *Knightsbridge* from his *London* Suite No.1 (for *In Town Tonight*), *By a Sleepy Lagoon* (for *Desert Island Discs*), and *Calling All Workers* (for *Music While You Work*). His *Dambusters March* is a firm favourite. Worth trying are his many songs, the *Saxophone Rhapsody*, and his orchestral suites: *Summer Days*, *From Meadow to May Fair*, *The Three Bears* and *The Three Elizabeths*.

1886–1971: Marcel Dupré

French composer and organist (a pupil of Widor), whose Organ Concerto in E minor, Symphony for organ in G minor and Prelude and Fugue in G minor, Op.7 No.3 are among his most striking works.

1887–1959: Heitor VILLA-LOBOS

1890–1959: Bohuslav Martinů

Prolific Czech composer, sometimes referred to as 'the twentieth-century Smetana', whose works are bewilderingly varied in quality and interest. At his best, with the Double Concerto for two string orchestras, piano and timpani, and *Sinfonietta giocosa*, Martinů is inspired; at his worst, you may find your attention wandering.

1890–1962: Jacques Ibert

Witty, tuneful and highly coloured scores are the hallmarks of this felicitous French composer, whose *Divertissement*, arranged from the music he wrote for the play *The Italian Straw Hat*, shows him at his best. His orchestral suite *Escales*, *Concerto da Camera* for alto saxophone, and his piano piece *Le petit âne blanc* from the suite *Histoires* are also most enjoyable.

1890–1974: Frank Martin

Swiss composer whose Schoenbergian modernism was tempered by a strong lyrical gift. His *Petite symphonie concertante* and catchy (if sometimes lugubrious) *Harpsichord Concerto* are excellent.

1891–1953: Sergei PROKOFIEV

1891–1975: Sir Arthur Bliss

Master of the Queen's Musick from 1953 and composer of the ballets *Checkmate* and *Miracle in the Gorbals*, as well as a titanic Piano Concerto, *A Colour Symphony*, and one of the first important film scores – *The Shape of Things to Come* (1935).

1892–1955: Arthur HONEGGER

1892–1972: Ferde Grofé

Famous as the man who orchestrated Gershwin's *Rhapsody in Blue* (he was the arranger for bandleader Paul Whiteman). His *Grand Canyon* Suite was popularized by Toscanini, but his *Mississippi*, *Aviation* and *Hudson River* Suites are also quintessential American light music.

1892–1974: Darius MILHAUD

1892–1983: Herbert Howells

Pupil of Charles Villiers Stanford; his works, which have frequent religious and pastoral allusions, include *Pastoral Rhapsody*, *Sine Nomine* and *Hymnus Paradisi*.

1892–1988: Kaikhosru Sorabji

Extraordinary English composer of Parsi-Spanish-Sicilian background, baptised Leon Dudley, responsible for the longest piano work ever, *Opus clavicembalisticum*, which takes about five hours to play.

Sorabji forbade performances of his work in 1936 and only lifted the ban in 1975. Complex individual Euro-Asian textures.

1893–1960: Arthur Benjamin

Australian-born composer now indelibly linked with his popular *Jamaican Rumba*. His *Overture to an Italian Comedy* is well worth a try.

1894–1930: Peter Warlock

The pseudonym used as a composer by the writer Philip Heseltine. Influenced by Delius and by Elizabethan music, his settings of Old English verse and the song-cycle 'The Curlew' (settings of Yeats' verse) are especially notable, as is his string suite *Capriol*. He committed suicide.

1894–1950: E.J. Moeran

English pastoral composer of Symphony in G minor, Violin Concerto and Cello Concerto, influenced by folk-songs and Delius.

1894–1976: Walter Piston

American composer (pupil of Nadia Boulanger) and teacher (of Shapero and Bernstein). His eight symphonies are the basis of his output, written in a modern but always tonal idiom (except for Symphony No.8). His most popular work is the orchestral suite from the ballet *The Incredible Flutist*.

1894–1979: Dimitri Tiomkin

Russian-born pupil of Glazunov and Busoni, he was a piano virtuoso and avant-garde composer before arriving in the USA, where he changed course and started writing for films. He won four Oscars, two of them for *High Noon*.

1895–1963: Paul HINDEMITH

1895–1968: Mario Castelnuovo-Tedesco

Italian composer whose Guitar Concerto was popularized by Segovia.

1895–1982: Carl ORFF

1896–1970: Roberto Gerhard

Spanish-born composer and pupil of Granados and Pedrell, who then adopted the twelve-tone system after studies with Schoenberg; his opera *The Duenna* uses both tonal and atonal styles. Resident in Britain from 1938.

1896–1985: Roger Sessions

Uncompromising American composer who studied with Bloch. His music appeals more to critics and other composers than to the public; his compositions, in his dense polytonal style, include eight symphonies.

1896–1989: Virgil Thomson

American composer and a distinguished and acerbic critic for the *New York Times*, whose works, influenced by Satie and revivalist hymn-tunes, include *Four Saints in Three Acts* (opera) and *The Plow that Broke the Plains* (film score).

1897–1957: Erich KORNGOLD

1898–1937: George GERSHWIN

1898–1979: Roy Harris

American pupil of Nadia Boulanger; his Symphony No.3, one of eleven, is the most-played work in the genre by an American.

1899–1963: Francis POULENC

1899–1978: Carlos Chávez

European- and American-trained Mexican composer of the ballet 'H.P.' (horse-power), as well as six symphonies and many atonal works using Mexican rhythms and folk idioms.

1899–1983: Georges Auric

The youngest member of Les Six, whose undemanding and attractive music has some of the wit and grace of Poulenc, in particular his ballet scores for Diaghilev, *Les fâcheux* (1924) and *Les matelots* (1925); also a prolific film composer.

1900–50: Kurt WEILL

1900–59: George Antheil

Unorthodox American composer whose *Ballet mécanique* (1925) requires aeroplane propellers, bells, motor-horns and eight pianos. He later turned to film scores.

1900–90: Aaron COPLAND

1900–91: Ernst Krenek

Austrian-born composer, married at one time to Mahler's daughter, Anna; wrote in an austere, atonal style, later softening his approach with jazz. His opera *Jonny spielt auf*, the story of a black jazz violinist, was a huge success.

1901–56: Gerald Finzi

An unmistakably English composer, influenced by Elgar and Vaughan Williams; his Clarinet Concerto and Five Bagatelles for clarinet and piano are among the masterpieces for the instrument. No one should miss his choral and vocal works, especially the song-cycle 'Let us Garlands Bring' (settings of Shakespeare), 'Dies Natalis', 'Lo, the full, final Sacrifice' and 'Intimations of Immortality'. Finzi's Eclogue for piano and strings is another moving and beautifully-wrought work.

1901–86: Edmund Rubbra

English composer, journalist and a student of Holst and Vaughan Williams. His ten symphonies are worshipped by Rubbra-ites; other numerous works for all combinations tend to the exotic and spiritual.

1901– : Joaquín RODRIGO

1902–83: Sir William WALTON

1902–86: Maurice Duruflé

Leading French organist and composer whose Requiem, a child of Fauré's, is quite exquisite.

1903–75: Boris Blacher

Part-Jewish, German composer born of Russian parents in China, who was for many years the director of the Berlin Hochschule für Musik. He evolved a system of 'variable metres' in which the number of beats in the bar is planned according to mathematical relationships. His orchestral Variations on a theme of Paganini (the same theme used by Rachmaninov and Brahms) has been frequently broadcast.

1903–78: Aram KHACHATURIAN

1904–75: Luigi Dallapiccola

Italian serial composer, teacher and pianist, whose works include a one-act opera based on Antoine de Saint-Exupéry's *Vol de nuit*.

1904–77: Richard Addinsell

English composer famous for *The Warsaw Concerto*, which featured in his film score for the 1941 film *Dangerous Moonlight*.

1904–87: Dmitri KABALEVSKY

1905–51: Constant Lambert

English composer, conductor and writer on music, who was still a student and only twenty when Diaghilev commissioned him to write a ballet, *Romeo and Juliet*. The jazz elements in his *Elegiac Blues* (1927) and, especially, the unmissable *Rio Grande* (1927), based on a poem by Sacheverell Sitwell, combined to make him one of the great hopes of English music. However, booze and high living got the better of him, and after his ballet *Horoscope* (1937) he composed little.

1905–64: Marc Blitzstein

American pupil of Nadia Boulanger and Arnold Schoenberg, who wrote socially conscious music. His opera *The Cradle will Rock* (1937) made him famous, and his ambitious *Airborne Symphony* (1944) concerns the evolution of flying.

1905–71: Alan Rawsthorne

Began as a dentist before turning to music, composing mainly instrumental works influenced by Hindemith; generally atonal yet rarely unsettling, his overture *Street Corner* (1944) is his best-known work.

1905–86: Dag Wirén

Swedish composer influenced by Honegger, whose works, little known in the UK, include four symphonies, concertos, stage and film music.

1905– : Sir Michael TIPPETT

1906–75: Dmitri SHOSTAKOVICH
1906–83: Elisabeth Lutyens
English serial composer and the daughter of the architect Sir Edwin Lutyens, her works include concertos, quartets, songs and an unaccompanied motet on a German philosophical text by Wittgenstein.
1906–85: Paul Creston
A self-taught American composer and organist (real name, Giuseppe Guttoveggio) who wrote for every musical medium. His powerful orchestral work *Invocation and Dance* was used for the ballet *Time out of Mind*.
1908–92: Oliver MESSIAEN
1908– : Elliott Carter
Another distinguished and important American contemporary composer, who uses serial techniques, the results of which have yet to be welcomed by the general music-loving public. His finest achievements are, perhaps, Variations for Orchestra (1955) and the String Quartet No.2 (1959).
1910–81: Samuel BARBER
1910–92: William Schuman
American composer, educator and, from 1945–61, head of the Juillard School of Music; his Violin Concerto and *American Festival* Overture are among his cosmopolitan and approachable works.
1911–75: Bernard Herrmann
Outstanding American film composer whose sixty-one scores include *Citizen Kane* and a succession of Hitchcock thrillers. His other works include the operas *Wuthering Heights*, *A Christmas Carol* and *A Child Is Born*, a symphony and a violin concerto.
1911– : Gian Carlo Menotti
Italian composer celebrated for his television opera *Amahl and the Night Visitors*, but others, such as *Amelia goes to the Ball*, *The Medium*, *The Telephone* and *The Consul*, have also made their mark.
1912–92: John Cage
Extreme avant-garde American composer and authority on mushrooms; his most famous piece, called *4' 33"*, consists of a pianist sitting at the piano for exactly four minutes and thirty-three seconds – in silence. On being told of this 'composition', Igor Stravinsky said: 'I look forward to hearing his longer works.' His Sonatas and Interludes (1946–48) exploits Cage's most celebrated addition to twentieth-century music: the 'prepared' piano, which involves inserting bits of wood, screws and other objects onto the strings. Sir Thomas

Beecham was asked if he'd ever played any of Cage's music. 'No,' replied Sir Thomas, 'but I've trod in some.'
1912– : Jean Françaix
Minor but highly enjoyable French composer following in the footsteps of Ibert and Poulenc; his Piano Concertino is a charmer.
1913–76: Benjamin BRITTEN
1913–94: Witold LUTOSŁAWSKI
1913– : Tikhon Khrennikov
Soviet composer best remembered for his role in denouncing Prokofiev and others for 'formalism' in 1948, rather than for his ballets, film music, symphonies, concertos, operas and piano pieces.
1913– : George LLOYD
1914–91: Andrzej Panufnik
Polish-born of an English mother, he became a British citizen in 1961; with Lutosławski, the leading Polish post-war composer, writing strongly dissonant works like *Sinfonia sacra* and *Sinfonia rustica*.
1915–82: Humphrey Searle
Impenetrable English composer and pupil of Webern; also the author of a useful study of Liszt.
1916–83: Alberto Ginastera
Interesting Argentinian composer who wrote ballet, orchestral and piano pieces, mainly in a nationalistic vein.
1916– : Milton Babbitt
American serial composer, the first to write a piece for live performer and synthesizer (1961).
1918–90: Leonard BERNSTEIN
1920–90: Peter Racine Fricker
Highly dissonant English composer, who began as a dance band orchestrator and moved to the University of California in 1965; his Symphonies Nos.1 and 4 met with some success.
1920– : Harold Shapero
American pupil of Hindemith, Piston and Boulanger, best known for his *Nine-minute Overture*; prefers to write in neo-classical forms.
1921– : Malcolm ARNOLD
1922– : Lukas Foss
German-born Foss (originally Fuchs) settled in the United States in 1937, since when he has built up a formidable reputation as pianist, conductor and composer. His early works are conservative ('The Prairie', a cantata; *The Jumping Frog*, an opera). Later he was more avant-garde: the soloist in his Cello Concerto is allowed a free choice of accompaniment. His 'Baroque' Variations for orchestra are fun.

1923– : György Ligeti

Avant-garde Hungarian composer whose works include *Atmosphères* for orchestra, *Articulation* for recorded tape, and the demanding Cello Concerto; the *Kyrie* from his Requiem (1965) was featured in the film *2001: A Space Odyssey*.

1923– : Ned Rorem

American composer particularly noted for his song settings, strongly influenced by Satie and Poulenc. His three symphonies, the Organ Suite 'A Quaker Reader' and three piano concertos are among a host of Rorem works rarely heard in the UK.

1925– : Luciano Berio

Italian composer of the extreme avant-garde using serial and aleatory techniques; a keen proponent of electronic music since the 1950s. Many of his early vocal works were written for his then wife, the soprano Cathy Berberian.

1925– : Pierre Boulez

French conductor and now, arguably, his country's leading composer. A pupil of Messiaen, Boulez once declared: 'Since the discoveries made by the [Second Viennese School], all composition other than twelve-tone is useless.' 'Le marteau sans maître' ('The hammer without a master') for contralto and chamber group (1954, rev. 1957) and 'Pli selon pli' ('Fold upon fold') are still his best-known works.

1926– : Hans Werner Henze

German composer influenced by Schoenberg, Stravinsky, Blacher and by his teacher Wolfgang Fortner. His seven symphonies inhabit a sound world of their own, but opera and ballet have also been preoccupations. These include *Boulevard Solitude* (1951), *King Stag* (1955), *Undine* (1959) and *The Bassarids* (1966).

1928– : Karlheinz Stockhausen

German whose name has become a synonym for any advanced music. The first composer to have an electronic score/diagram published (1956), he has been a pioneer of music that allows a free choice for the performer and the medium's spatial possibilities: *Carré* (1960) with its four orchestras and four choruses provides a demonstration.

1929– : George Crumb

American avant-garde composer whose *Echoes of Time and the River* won the Pulitzer Prize for music in 1968; it requires the players to whisper and shout, and instructions to the percussionist include lowering a gong into a bucket containing nine inches of water.

1929– : Alun Hoddinott

Welsh composer of serious tastes, with flashes of wit and tunefulness, as in his 'Welsh Dances'. Try his *Variants for Orchestra* and Horn Concerto of 1969.

1931– : Malcolm WILLIAMSON

1932– : Alexander Goehr

Son of the conductor Walter Goehr and a disciple of Schoenberg and Messiaen, Goehr is not the most accessible of composers, but the *Little Symphony*, Piano Trio (1966) and the opera *Arden Must Die* have their champions.

1932– : Hugh Wood

A serialist whose music is far more amiable than most. His Cello and Violin Concertos have passages of sonorous beauty, while his recent Piano Concerto attracted much attention (the central movement is a set of variations on Nat King Cole's 1957 hit 'Sweet Lorraine').

1933– : Henryk GÓRECKI

1933– : Krzysztof Penderecki

Eminent Polish composer who first became known through his *Threnody for the Victims of Hiroshima*, a composition for fifty-two string instruments, which are tapped and slapped as much as they are bowed. Try also his telling *St Luke Passion* – among the first avant-garde works to be accepted by a wider public – and *Dies irae*, dedicated to those who died in Auschwitz.

1934– : Harrison BIRTWISTLE

1934– : Sir Peter Maxwell DAVIES

1935– : Nicholas Maw

His titanic *Odyssey*, considered the longest continuous orchestral work yet written, lasting one hour and forty minutes, took fifteen years to complete; the slow movement alone lasts half an hour.

1935– : Arvo PÄRT

1936–81: Cornelius Cardew

Extreme, avant-garde Marxist English composer, assistant to Stockhausen in Cologne, whose compositions often relied on improvisation and chance. His famous Scratch Orchestra performed his work.

1936– : Richard Rodney BENNETT

1936– : Steve Reich

Among the three foremost minimalist composers, with Philip Glass and John Adams. The American Reich is considered the prime mover in the evolution of minimalist music, which relies on weaving a tapestry of repeated patterns and additional short phrases to hypnotic effect.

1937– : Philip Glass

American minimalist composer. Studied in Paris with Nadia Boulanger and Indian sitarist and composer Ravi Shankar. Assembled his own electronic ensemble to perform his works, and has collaborated with such pop gurus as David Bowie and Brian Eno.

1939– : John McCabe

Liverpool-born pianist and composer of symphonies, concertos, chamber and choral works, including *Aspects of Whiteness* (1969), a setting of words from Herman Melville's novel *Moby Dick*.

1943– : Gavin Bryars

Minimalist composer who had a surprise success with his curiously touching *Jesus' Blood Never Failed Me*, which uses a repeated tape loop of a London tramp singing against a slowly growing orchestral accompaniment.

1944– : John Tavener

British spiritual minimalist. Moved on from his early modernist works like *The Celtic Requiem* to music that reflects his Russian Orthodox beliefs. His *The Protecting Veil* has achieved enormous popularity.

1946– : Colin Matthews

Less well known than his slightly younger counterpart Oliver Knussen. Both grew up under the influence of Benjamin Britten, the then dominant voice in British music. His Cello Concerto, baritone song cycle *The Great Journey* and orchestral *Landscape* are well worth trying.

1947– : John Adams

Leading minimalist, with the distinction of having written the most played work by a living American composer: *Short Ride in a Fast Machine*. He also composed the operas *The Death of Klinghoffer* and *Nixon in China*.

1948– : Michael Nyman

Best known for the film score for *The Piano*. Currently undergoing the difficult metamorphosis from film composer to composer of serious concert works.

1952– : Oliver Knussen

Influenced by Benjamin Britten. Best known are his three one-act operas *Higglety Pigglety Pop!* and *Where the Wild Things Are*. His *Ophelia Dances*, Symphony No.2 and Symphony No.3 have been much praised as the work of a meticulous and original craftsman.

1954– : Judith Weir

British composer. Try *Ascending into Heaven* (anthem) and *Airs from Another Planet* (wind quintet and piano).

1959– : Steve Martland

Danceworks (1993) is irresistibly hypnotic. His *Shoulder to Shoulder*, *Principia* and *Patrol* (string quartet) are also worth investigating.

1960– : George Benjamin

British child prodigy, a pupil of Messiaen and Goehr, and friend of Boulez. Representative works are *Ringed by the Flat Horizon*, *At First Light* and *Antara* (featuring the panpipes), all of which have been recorded.

1960– : Mark-Anthony Turnage

During his period as Composer in Association with the City of Birmingham Symphony Orchestra (1989–93), Turnage composed *Kai* (for the Birmingham Contemporary Music Group), *Momentum* (for the opening of Birmingham's Symphony Hall), *Leaving* (a choral work) and *Drowned Out* (1993). His best-known work remains *Three Screaming Popes* (cf. Francis Bacon's disturbing triptych).

COMPOSERS
A TO Z

Adolphe ADAM

(1803–56)

Giselle, ballet, 1841

Adam devoted his career to music for the theatre and was astonishingly prolific: he wrote one opera for every year of his life (he died just short of his fifty-third birthday), composing as many as three per season at the height of his powers. Among them is the once-popular *Si j'étais roi*, but he is remembered mainly for his appealing ballet *Giselle*.

Two other pieces by Adam receive an occasional airing: 'Cantique de Noël' is revived each Christmas (it was featured in the film *Home Alone*), and his 'Variations on "Ah, vous dirai-je maman?"' (we know the tune as 'Twinkle, twinkle little star'), from his 1849 opera *Le Toréador*, remains a sensational, if silly, test of soprano coloratura agility.

One of France's great melodists, Adam enjoyed immense success, but was no business-man. In the revolution of 1848 he lost all his savings and incurred so many debts that he spent the rest of his life in poverty.

Isaac ALBÉNIZ

Born: 29 May 1860, Camprodon, near Gerona, Spain
Died: 18 May 1909, Cambo-les-Bains (French Pyrénées)
Full name: Isaac Manuel Francisco Albéniz
Type of music: Spanish nationalist, Romantic-Impressionist; mainly piano
Influences: folk music, Liszt, Debussy, Fauré, Dukas and Spanish musicologist Felipe Pedrell
Contemporaries: Mikhail Ippolitov-Ivanov, WOLF, MACDOWELL, **ALBÉNIZ**, MAHLER, Ignacy Paderewski, Emil von Reznicek, CHARPENTIER, ARENSKY

HIS LIFE

Albéniz's eventful early life is one of the most extraordinary of any musician. In fact his whole life was something of an adventure. When he was just one year old he was taught the elements of piano playing by his sister and made his debut at the age of four, improvising at a public concert. His father, a tax inspector with an eye to producing some extra revenue, exploited him as a child prodigy before his mother took him to Paris in 1867 to study privately under the great Jean-François Marmontel, teacher of Bizet and Debussy.

Albéniz returned to Spain but soon ran away from home, living rough and support-ing himself by playing the piano as a vaudeville stunt: standing with the keyboard behind him, he would play with the *backs* of his fingers, palms up, dressed as a musketeer with

a rapier at his side. After many more incidents, at the age of twelve he stowed away in a ship bound for Buenos Aires. Thereafter he made his way via Cuba to the United States, giving concerts in New York and San Francisco before re-crossing The Pond and performing in Liverpool, London and Leipzig.

When he was fifteen, Albéniz decided to take himself more seriously but he did not have the self-discipline that was necessary for systematic study. At different times he came into contact with Liszt (in Budapest), d'Indy and Dukas (in Paris) and, more importantly, Felipe Pedrell (1841–1922), the Spanish composer and musicologist (see also GRANADOS).

Pedrell's passionate belief in Spanish folk music and dance motivated Albéniz to become a composer, turning to Spanish idioms for inspiration. It took him some time to find that the piano suited him best. In 1893, he moved to Paris, writing unsuccessful *zarzuelas* (a Spanish form of light opera) before meeting the wealthy English banker, Francis Money-Coutts. Albéniz was paid an annual stipend of $5,000 to set to music the appalling librettos that Money-Coutts wrote in his spare time under the pseudonym Mountjoy. This led to an (abandoned) Arthurian trilogy and such bizarre productions as his opera *Enrico Clifford* (1895), a romance set in the time of the Wars of the Roses, sung in Italian and given its first performance in Barcelona in 1895.

However, it was his piano music, with its Spanish flavour, that made Albéniz famous, and after 1896 he moved between Paris, Barcelona and Nice, composing and teaching. His last years were marred by tragedy: his daughter died, his wife became sick with an incurable illness, and his own health deteriorated as he developed Bright's disease.

HIS MUSIC

Very little classical music emerged from Spain in the nineteenth century. Many composers from Glinka and Chabrier to Rimsky-Korsakov had evoked Spanish rhythms and melodies, but these were impressions. Albéniz was the first to attempt to create an authentic Spanish school, followed by Granados, Falla and Turina. Though Albéniz's piano idiom is clearly in the debt of Liszt, its inspiration is Spanish: here are the guitars, flamenco dancers, exuberant rhythms, sensuous textures and catchy melodies of the Spanish folk idiom – Andalusia in particular – transmuted into virtuoso keyboard works.

Essential works

Iberia, piano (1906–09): Albéniz's masterpieces, twelve tonal portraits of Spain, are rich in impressionistic imagery and are immensely difficult to play – so difficult that at one time Albéniz came close to burning the manuscript. Only by borrowing the manuscript, committing the pieces to memory and then playing them did the pianist Blanche de Selva (who gave the first performance) convince him that they were playable. Many of the pieces have been effectively orchestrated by Leopold Stokowski, Enrique Arbós and others. *Triana* is perhaps the best-known piece of the cycle.

Navarra: left unfinished at Albéniz's death (and completed by Granados) this is a brilliant pendant to *Iberia*, a bravura piano solo of passion and flamboyance.

Suite Española, Op.47 (1886): originally three pieces but expanded posthumously by a publisher to include pieces from *Cantos de España*, Op.232 and other sources to make eight short Spanish pictures; *Sevillanas, Asturias* and *Segudillas* are better known in versions for guitar solo.

Tango in D, Op.165 No.2: of the remainder of Albéniz's 250 piano works (most of which are very slight and which he disowned) the Tango in D is by far his most popular work; there is a highly-scented arrangement of it by Leopold Godowsky.

Tomaso ALBINONI
(1671–1751)

Adagio for organ and strings in G minor (arr. Giazotto)

Albinoni was a prolific and much-admired composer; he produced fifty-three operas, all long since forgotten. J.S. Bach not only transcribed a number of his works but also borrowed some of his tunes. However, Albinoni is remembered now for just one piece. The trouble is, he didn't write it.

In 1958, a distinguished Albinoni scholar, Remo Giazotto, revealed that the Adagio was all that remained of a Trio Sonata in G minor. Of that fragment only the bass and some scribbled ideas for violin had survived. In 1945, Giazotto had put the two together and, feeling that the music had a mystic quality and was therefore probably intended as a church sonata, decided that there should be an organ accompaniment, rather than a harpsichord. That is the story behind this classical 'pop'. Scholars describe it as 'vulgar' and 'a pastiche', but who cares? It's beautiful music.

There are many other works by Albinoni and none more attractive than the Oboe Concerto in D minor, Op.9 No.2 (the slow movement is utterly beguiling); try also the Trumpet Concerto in D, Op.7 No.6 and the Double Oboe Concerto Op.9 No.3.

Charles-Valentin ALKAN

'The Berlioz of the piano' (Hans von Bülow)

Born: 30 November 1813, Paris
Died: 29 March 1888, Paris
Original name: Charles-Valentin Morhange
Type of music: Romantic; concerto, chamber, piano
Influences: Mendelssohn, Weber, Chopin, Liszt
Contemporaries: Friedrich von Flotow, Alexander Dargomizhsky, WAGNER, **ALKAN**, VERDI, Stephen Heller, Adolf von Henselt, Sterndale Bennett, Niels Gade

HIS LIFE AND MUSIC

Alkan (his father's first name, which he adopted as his surname) is one of the most puzzling cases of 'composer neglect'. His piano music, which contains many novel concepts, is the equal of anything by his contemporaries such as Chopin, Schumann and Liszt, and sometimes even outstrips them. Yet he was all but forgotten until a few decades ago. Since then, the advocacy of a few pianists has persuaded many that he was a genius.

He was a strange, bitter man, a misanthrope with two houses in Paris (one in the Square d'Orléans, near Chopin and George Sand) so that he could avoid visitors. His illegitimate son, the wondrously named Elie Miriam Delaborde, shared his home with two apes and 121 cockatoos. He was a formidable pianist – Liszt declared that Alkan had the greatest technique he had ever known – but seldom played in public. Passed over for a major position at the Paris Conservatoire, ignored and – as he saw it – humiliated, he withdrew from public life. Today, it is the nature of his death, rather than his music, that evokes a reaction at the mention of his name: he was crushed to death by a falling bookcase. The legend of Alkan reaching up for a copy of the Talmud which, miraculously, remained clutched in his hand, is possibly a romanticized version of the event.

It is easy to see why Alkan's music dropped out of sight: it was advanced for its day; it is ferociously difficult to play; he did little to promote it; and he had few champions. By the time this 'Berlioz of the piano' had been rediscovered, tastes had changed and

Debussy, Bartók and Schoenberg had set new fashions. Yet for anyone remotely interested in the piano, Alkan will provide an exciting, not to say jaw-dropping, experience.

Essential works

Twelve Études in all the minor keys, Op.39 (1857): these are not études on the miniature scale of Chopin, and they exceed even Liszt's Transcendental études in scope and language. **Nos.4, 5, 6 & 7** form the Symphony for solo piano, **Nos.8, 9 & 10** the Concerto for solo piano. **No.8** alone lasts for nearly half an hour, and in the hands of artists such as Ronald Smith or Marc-Andre Hamelin will impress even the most piano-shy listener. **No.12** is Alkan's best-known work, entitled *Le festin d'Esope (The Feast of Aesop)*, comprising twenty-five variations on a theme and as entertaining to hear as it is challenging to play.

Grande Sonata, Op.33 (1848): subtitled 'Les quatre âges'. Alkan takes us through four stages of a man's life, aged twenty, thirty, forty and fifty; this means that, unusually, the fast movements come first, the slow ones last.

Trois grandes études, Op.76 (c.1838): few pianists can play these extraordinary pieces because of the technical demands, but the musical content gives them an equal interest: the first étude is a Fantasie in A flat for the left hand, the second a lengthy *Introduction and Variations* for the right hand (to which few pieces have ever been devoted), and the third a *Perpetual Motion* whirlwind for both hands.

Also worth investigating

Le chemin de fer, Op.27 (1844): the first attempt to transfer the sound and speed of a steam train to the keyboard.

The impressionistic **La chanson de la folle au bord de la mer** ('Song of the Mad Woman on the Seashore').

Le tambour bat aux champs ('The Drumbeats in the Fields').

Grand duo concertant, Op.21 for violin and piano.

Gregorio ALLEGRI
(1582–1652)

Miserere

Miserere mei Deus (Have mercy upon me, O God) is Psalm 50 in the Roman Catholic enumeration. It is sung on the Thursday, Friday and Saturday of Holy Week as part of the *Tenebrae (The Darkness)* service and has become a classical favourite, largely because of the celebrated recording by boy soprano Roy Goodman, the King's College Choir and Sir David Willcocks. Allegri, a priest, tenor singer and composer, entered the musical service of the Pope in about 1629 and wrote this setting for the Sistine Chapel choir.

The music for the Chapel was jealously guarded; at one time, excommunication was the penalty for infringing its copyright. Legend has it that the young Mozart, visiting Rome for Holy Week with his father, heard the *Miserere* and afterwards scribbled down the entire score from memory – an incredible feat, though he almost certainly knew the work beforehand and returned later to check his accuracy at a second performance.

Anton ARENSKY

Born: 12 July 1861, Novgorod, Russia
Died: 25 February 1906, Terioki, Finland
Full name: Anton Stepanovich Arensky
Type of music: Romantic; piano, chamber; also symphony, opera
Influences: Chopin, Liszt, Tchaikowsky
Contemporaries: Emil Nikolaus von Reznicek, CHARPENTIER, **ARENSKY**, Enrico Bossi, Leon Boëllmann, DEBUSSY, DELIUS, Edward German

HIS LIFE AND MUSIC

Though a minor composer, Arensky wins his place in this book with his Piano Trio, among the most appealing works in the chamber music repertoire. A composition pupil of Rimsky-Korsakov, Arensky eschewed current nationalistic tendencies and was championed by his friend Tchaikowsky. Arensky taught at the Moscow Conservatory, where Rachmaninov, Scriabin and Gretchaninov were among his students, before succeeding Balakirev as director of the Imperial Court Chapel in 1894.

The most puzzling thing about Arensky is the contradiction between the genial, attractive lyricism of his music and his austere, mysterious private life. Through it there ran a dark, troubled streak: he was an alcoholic from a early age and an inveterate gambler. He never married and chose to receive few visitors. He died of consumption in a Finnish sanatorium.

Essential works

Piano Trio in D minor, Op.32: composed in 1894 and dedicated to the memory of the great Russian cellist Carl Davidov (1838–89); the four movements are well contrasted, with memorable themes, especially the third with its elegiac cello solo.

Piano Concerto in F minor, Op.2: a youthful, tuneful confection, indebted to Chopin, Liszt and Mendelssohn. The last movement has the unusual time signature of 5/4, and threatens, at times, to break into Grieg's Piano Concerto.

Suite No.1 for two pianos, Op.15: Arensky wrote four suites for this medium, all of which deserve to be better known, but the Waltz from No.1 is a good example of graceful, high-class *salon* music.

Thomas ARNE

'Doctor Arne'

Born: 12 March 1710, Covent Garden, London
Died: 5 March 1778, Covent Garden, London
Full name: Thomas Augustine Arne
Type of music: Baroque; opera, masque, theatre music
Influences: Purcell, Handel
Contemporaries: Baldassare Galuppi, Giovanni Pergolesi, **ARNE**, William Boyce, Wilhelm Friedemann Bach, John Stanley, Niccolò Jomelli

HIS LIFE AND MUSIC

Arne was the Eton-educated son of an upholsterer and coffin-maker. Like most of his contemporaries, his music resembles Handel's while retaining its own distinctive voice. Some of his best work was for the theatre – masques, operas and incidental music for plays. Despite numerous alternatives by other composers, his settings of Shakespeare songs remain the only versions generally known (for example 'Where the Bee Sucks' from *The Tempest* and 'When Daisies Pied' from *Love's Labours Lost*).

However, it is as the composer of 'Rule Britannia' that his name survives. The song was first heard on 1 August 1740, at Clivedon, the Prince of Wales' residence in Buckinghamshire. It comes from the masque *Alfred*, which was written to commemorate the succession of the House of Hanover to the throne, and concludes with the patriotic 'Ode in honour of Great Britain'. 'Rule Britannia / Britannia rules the waves' (or 'rule the waves' as it was originally, giving it an entirely different meaning) has been a national anthem ever since, an immovable part of the Last Night Of The Proms. More than 250 years on, the song still manages to warm the cockles. Perhaps Wagner was right when he said that the first eight notes sum up the whole British character.

Also worth investigating
Overtures 1–8
Six Favourite Concertos for keyboard and strings (c.1787)

Four Symphonies (1767)
'The Soldier Tir'd' (from *Artaxerxes*) (1762)
'The Glitt'ring Sun' (from *The Morning*)

Malcolm ARNOLD

Born: 21 October 1921, Northampton
Type of music: opera, symphony, orchestral, ballet, concerto, chamber, film
Influences: Berlioz, the English tradition, Gordon Jacob, jazz
Contemporaries: BERNSTEIN, Peter Racine Fricker, Harold Shapero, **ARNOLD**, Lukas Foss, György Ligeti, Ned Rorem, Luciano Berio, Pierre Boulez

HIS LIFE AND MUSIC

Is there another contemporary composer whose music is as accessible as it is rewarding, as entertaining as it is thought-provoking? Of course, Arnold has his detractors because his writing is resolutely tonal and actually contains tunes – not fashionable at all. ('Dash it, the fellow writes film music. How can we possibly take him seriously?')

Arnold was born into a musical family, but it was Louis Armstrong who inspired him to take up the trumpet at the age of twelve. By twenty-one he was principal trumpet of the London Philharmonic, a post he held on and off between 1942 and 1948. He then abandoned orchestral life in order to devote himself to composition. His versatility has led him to write for almost every medium, most notably for the cinema, where his scores include *The Inn of the Sixth Happiness, The Sound Barrier, Whistle Down the Wind, The Angry Silence, Tunes of Glory, The Heroes of Telemark* and, most memorably, *The Bridge on the River Kwai.* The latter, which won him an Academy Award, revitalized Kenneth Alford's 1914 march *Colonel Bogey.*

Arnold has had his personal problems – his frankly autobiographical Eighth Symphony depicts a suicide attempt – but the range of his work, its superb craftsmanship (he studied with Gordon Jacob and is one of the most skilful of living orchestrators), coupled with his gift for melody and pungent rhythms, ensures that more of his work will survive than that of many of his contemporaries.

Essential works

Beckus the Dandipratt (1943): one of Arnold's earliest works, this lively overture has much in common with Richard Strauss' *Till Eulenspiegel;* 'dandipratt' is an old word for an urchin.

Tam O'Shanter (1955): another spirited concert piece, depicting the night ride of Robert Burns' hero.

Eight English Dances in two sets (1950–51): **No.5** is widely known as the signature tune for television's *What the Papers Say.*

Four Scottish Dances (1957) and **Four Cornish Dances** (1966): also worth a try – inimitable Arnold.

Peterloo (1968): written to commemorate the centenary of the Trades Union Congress, the title refers to the 1819 massacre in St Peter's Fields, Manchester, when the cavalry was sent in to quell a political reform meeting, a moment that Arnold captures vividly with an onslaught of percussion.

Concerto for two pianos (1969): also known as the Concerto for Three Hands, this piece was composed for Phyllis Sellick and her husband Cyril Smith, who had lost the use of his left hand after a stroke in 1956; the piece was premiered at the Proms; the last movement is a riot.

A Grand, Grand Overture (1956): scored for orchestra, this piece also calls for virtuoso performances on three vacuum cleaners, one floor polisher and four rifles; it was written for a 1956 Hoffnung concert. Forget the jolly japes, the big tune is terrific.

Also worth investigating
Three Shanties for wind quintet (1944)
Serenade for guitar and strings (1955)

Daniel-François-Esprit AUBER

Born: 29 January 1782, Caen, Normandy
Died: 12 May 1871, Paris
Type of music: opera
Influences: Cherubini, Boïeldieu, Rossini
Contemporaries: Bernhard Henrik Crusell, HUMMEL, FIELD, PAGANINI, **AUBER**, Louis Spohr, WEBER, Henry Bishop, HÉROLD, Carl Czerny, MEYERBEER

HIS LIFE AND MUSIC

Auber was fabulously successful in his lifetime, but little of his work has survived into this century beyond the performance of some of his opera overtures. He was so modest and timid a person that it is said he never heard a note of his music in performance. He certainly never conducted it, saying, 'If I ever listened to one of my own works I would probably never write another note.'

Of his nearly fifty comic operas, thirty-seven had libretti by Eugène Scribe, one of the best theatre writers of the day. Rossini was a fan ('although Auber's music is light, his art is profound') and even the notoriously scabrous Wagner admired his one serious opera, *La muette de Portici* (The Blind Girl of Portici), also known as *Masaniello*, but dismissed Auber's lighter side as 'the work of a barber who lathers but forgets to shave'. The fact is that Auber laid the foundations of French grand opera, for *Masaniello* led directly to Meyerbeer's *Robert le Diable* and Rossini's *William Tell*.

Worth investigating
Overtures to:
Fra Diavolo (1830)
Le cheval de bronze (1835)
Les diamants de la couronne (1841)
Le domino noir (1837)

La muette de Portici (1828): the political libretto and stirring airs of this piece provoked an anti-Dutch riot after its 1830 Brussels premiere, the catalyst that eventually led to Belgium's independence from Holland.

Carl Philipp Emanuel BACH

The 'Hamburg' or 'Berlin' Bach

Born: 8 March 1714, Weimar
Died: 14 December 1788, Hamburg
Type of music: Baroque-Classical; concerto, symphony, chamber, oratorio, song and (especially) keyboard
Influenced by: J.S. Bach, Telemann, Stamitz
Contemporaries: John Stanley, Niccolò Jomelli, GLUCK, **C.P.E. BACH**, Johann Wenzel Stamitz, Antonio Soler, Gaetano Pugnani, HAYDN, François Gossec

HIS LIFE AND MUSIC

'C.P.E.' – referred to mischievously as 'the great Bach' by some who regard him as a more inventive composer than his father – was the third son of Johann Sebastian. Having been his father's pupil and assistant, he studied law before turning to music. The flute-playing Crown Prince of Prussia hired him as a keyboard player, and, on becoming King Frederick the Great in 1740, appointed him as chamber musician to the court at Berlin. He remained there for the next twenty-eight years, composing a vast amount of varied music. He also wrote *Essay on the True Art of Keyboard Playing*, one of the most informative testimonies on how music was performed in the eighteenth century. In 1767, he succeeded his godfather, Georg Philipp Telemann, as music director of Hamburg's five main churches. Here he remained till his death.

C.P.E. Bach's importance rests mainly on his pioneering of the sonata-symphony (*see* GLOSSARY), the impact of which reached down the centuries, from those of Haydn, Mozart and Beethoven to Brahms and Elgar. Instead of the musically disconnected, separate movements, or suites, until then fashionable, his works contrast different moods and develop the thematic material in certain ways, heightening the drama in the music.

He is a transitional composer: his earliest works appeared when his father was still alive, and he led the way into the new Classical period, even presaging the later Romantic school with works of clear personal, emotional involvement. His music is eminently endearing: full of quirky, angular themes that swoop in unexpectedly, virile, bustling allegros and pensive, yearning movements of surprising candour. There are exacting passages for the soloist in his concertos, witty and exuberant and far more interesting than the made-to-measure work of his brother Johann Christian, the 'English' Bach.

Essential works

C.P.E. Bach's works are known by their Wq numbers after Alfred Wotquenne (1867–1939), pronounced *Vot'*-ken, who compiled the thematic catalogue of his work.

Six Symphonies, Wq182 (1773) and **Four Symphonies, Wq183** (1775–76): composed in Hamburg after leaving the service of Frederick the Great, when Bach was free to write in the style he wanted, rather than in the lighter Italian manner that had been demanded by his erstwhile employer.

Harpsichord Concerto in D minor, Wq23 (1748): an arresting work written some forty years before Mozart's great D minor Piano Concerto; compare this with:

Double Concerto for harpsichord and fortepiano in E flat, Wq47 (1788): written forty years later, while Mozart was producing his great series of piano concertos. An adventurous work for an unusual combination.

Magnificat, Wq215 (1749): the opening chorus is guaranteed to make the hairs on the back of your neck stand on end.

Also worth investigating

There are numerous other symphonies, the **Cello Concerto in A, Wq172**, fourteen more **keyboard concertos** (for harpsichord, including two for harpsichord or organ) and five **flute concertos**, as well as the tiny **Solfeggio in C minor, Wq 117** (1766) – every fledgling pianist likes to see how fast it can be played!

Johann Sebastian BACH

'He is the father, and we his children' (Mozart)

Born: 21 March 1685, Eisenach, Thuringia
Died: 28 July 1750, Leipzig
Type of music: orchestral, church and secular choral works, chamber, instrumental (especially organ and other keyboards), lute
Influences: Palestrina, Frescobaldi, Vivaldi, Pachelbel, Buxtehude
Contemporaries: TELEMANN, Jean-François Dandrieu, RAMEAU, **J.S. BACH**, DOMENICO SCARLATTI, HANDEL, Benedetto Marcello, Niccolò Antonio Porpora

HIS LIFE

Seven generations of Bachs were professional musicians, and their north German
dynasty can be traced back to the early
sixteenth century. None earned more than
a local reputation and, surprising as it may
seem, 'the supreme arbiter and law-giver
of music', Johann Sebastian Bach,
achieved only limited fame during his
lifetime. Music was in the blood, his
musical talents taken for granted by the
composer and his family. He never saw
himself as exceptional, just as a pious
Lutheran artisan doing his best with a gift
that was as much a part of him as his
unquestioning religious belief.

1694 Bach had little systematic training
in his youth. It is said that, at nine, he
almost ruined his eyesight from secretly
copying out by moonlight an entire library
of instrumental music to which he had been denied access. In this year both his parents
died (his father was a respected violinist) and he was sent to live with his older brother,
Johann Christoph. None too happy at having an extra mouth to feed, Johann Christoph
treated his new charge with little sympathy, although grudgingly giving him lessons on
the harpsichord.

1700 At fifteen, Johann Sebastian gained a position in the choir at Lüneberg, where he
was able at last to indulge in every possible musical pursuit, immersing himself in scores,
composing and studying the organ, clavichord and violin. Several times he tramped the
thirty miles to Hamburg to hear the acclaimed organist Johann Adam Reinken, and he
travelled the sixty miles to Celle for his first encounter with French music in performance. Although Bach led an unadventurous and parochial life, his thirst for every new
musical experience open to him, his curiosity and his willingness to absorb what other
practitioners of the art were producing, played an important part in the extraordinary
diversity of music he was to write.

1704 Bach was appointed as organist at Arnstadt, aged just nineteen. He obtained leave
of absence and, so legend has it, walked to Lübeck (a distance of 213 miles), where the
celebrated organist Dietrich Buxtehude gave recitals and a once-weekly instrumental
concert. Scholars have calculated that he must have walked an average of twenty miles a
day, in inclement weather, and got through three or four pairs of boots, concluding, not
unreasonably, that he probably hired a coach and valet to accomplish the trip – but such
are the legends surrounding the deeds of great men. The outcome, anyway, was a
prolonged absence of four months, which did not endear him to the burghers of Arnstadt;
neither did the strange music that young Bach returned with, for, perhaps recalling
Buxtehude's playing, he began interpolating elaborate cadenzas and variations into the
staid chorales.

1707 In June he moved to Mühlhausen as organist, and four months later, at the age of
twenty-two, married his cousin Maria Barbara.

1708–17 The following year (1708) saw the first publication of a piece of his music, the
cantata *Gott ist mein König;* at the same time he left Mühlhausen to become court
organist to Duke Wilhelm Ernst of Weimar. Here he stayed more or less contentedly for
nine years, was made Konzertmeister (conductor) of the court orchestra in 1714, and
composed some of his finest organ works, including the Passacaglia and Fugue in C
minor and many of the great preludes and fugues. Here, too, the future King Frederick I

of Sweden heard him, recording that Bach's feet 'flew over the pedalboard as if they had wings'.

1717   Further advancement came when he accepted the position of music director to Prince Leopold of Anhalt in Cöthen. Duke Wilhelm at first refused to allow Bach to take up this new post and held him under arrest for a month. When at last Bach arrived in Cöthen, it was the beginning of one of his most fruitful periods as a composer, which saw the appearance of the *Brandenburg Concertos* and the first book of the *Well-tempered Clavier.*

1720   Bach accompanied the prince on a visit to Karlsbad, and it was there that he learnt of his wife's death. He lived as a widower for a year with his seven children before marrying his second wife, Anna Magdalena Wilcken, a daughter of the court trumpeter at Weissenfels, now immortalized in *The Little Clavier Book of Anna Magdalena*, a collection of short pieces Bach wrote for her study of the harpsichord. During their happy married life, she bore him a further thirteen children, although six of Bach's twenty children did not survive into adulthood.

1722   The Cantor at the Thomasschule, Leipzig died and Bach applied for this prestigious post. The authorities first offered it to Telemann, who declined it, and then to Christoph Graupner, who was unable to take up the appointment.

1723   The third choice, Bach succeeded to the title in April. He retained this job for the rest of his life. The arduous duties of the cantor involved playing the organ, teaching Latin and music in the St Thomasschule, writing music for the church services of both the Nicolaikirche and the Thomaskirche, and directing the music and training the musicians of a further two churches. The living conditions were cold and damp, the salary parsimonious, and Bach found himself fighting a running battle with the church authorities over financial matters. Yet the music that flowed from his pen – and there was a significant amount – is some of the greatest spiritual music ever written, including the Mass in B minor, the *St John* and *St Matthew Passions*, the *Christmas Oratorio* and nearly 300 church cantatas. From this period, too, come the *Goldberg Variations*, the *Italian Concerto*, the Partitas and the second book of the *Well-tempered Clavier.*

1747   Bach's third son, Carl Philipp Emanuel, was Kapellmeister to Frederick the Great, and the composer visited him in Potsdam. Allegedly, when Bach arrived, Frederick broke off the music-making and exclaimed, 'Old Bach is here!' and, without permitting him to change his clothes, plonked Bach down at the keyboard. Later, Bach composed a six-part fugue on a theme of Frederick the Great's – this was *The Musical Offering* written in gratitude for his welcome.

1749   By the end of his life, Bach's eyesight was failing due to cataracts. He was persuaded to have an operation performed by the same British optician, John Taylor, who had earlier treated Handel unsuccessfully for the same affliction. It left Bach almost completely blind. His sight then miraculously returned (the cataract may have receded spontaneously), allowing him to copy and revise feverishly what was to be his final work, *The Art of Fugue*. Ten days later he died of a cerebral haemorrhage. He was sixty-five years old. Bach was buried in the churchyard of St John in Leipzig. No identification marked the spot.

1895   His body was exhumed and photographs taken of his skeleton. On 28 July 1949, the 199th anniversary of his death, Bach's coffin was transferred to the choir room of the Thomaskirche.

HIS MUSIC

Bach is to music what Leonardo da Vinci is to art and Aristotle is to philosophy, one of the supreme creative geniuses of history. Amazingly, he was, in essence, a self-taught, provincial musician; he did not write music in a fever of inspiration like Beethoven, nor was he motivated by the same holy dedication to art as Wagner. Bach wrote 'For the glory of the most high God alone,' he said. 'Whoever is equally industrious will succeed just as well.' He wasn't considered to be special in his day. His son, Carl Philipp Emanuel, referred to him as 'old peruke'; he was an old fogey, writing in the Baroque polyphonic style that was already going out of fashion. He made little impression in the way of developing existing forms or inventing new ones. Little of his music was published or performed after his death and although it was by no means completely ignored as is often stated – Haydn, Mozart and Beethoven, for instance, all played his keyboard works – it was not until Mendelssohn's revival of the *St Matthew Passion* in Berlin in 1829 that Bach's worth started to be reassessed.

He wasn't a sophisticated intellectual either; far from it. His letters and notes betray an uneducated hand and mind – his German is littered with grammatical mistakes, he knew little of the other arts, and read mainly theological books. It is one of the most extraordinary paradoxes in musical history that a mind of such low culture could produce music of such unparalleled assurance, beauty and complexity. As the critic Ernest Newman observed, 'Truly, we have as yet barely the glimmer of an understanding of what the musical faculty is, and how it works.'

What makes Bach the great composer that he unarguably is? If it is assumed that the Baroque era began in 1600 with Monteverdi and ended in 1750, then Johann Sebastian represented the inevitable culmination of all Baroque styles: the contrapuntal German school, the melodic, singing Italian school and the elegant, dance-based French school. As a young man he had absorbed the works of Palestrina and Frescobaldi, knew the more recent works of Vivaldi and Albinoni, of Froberger, Pachelbel and Buxtehude, and made strenuous efforts to acquaint himself with the German musicians of the day. His command of counterpoint – the combined ingenuity and unforced complexity of which are unique – and his superior harmonic sense set him apart. A Vivaldi concerto bowls along on fairly predictable lines; Bach was daring – he took the music into unexpected areas. It made people complain, so curious did it sound to contemporary ears.

One wonders if he ever smiled. The music answers: 'Yes, but not often.' He wrote no operas or ballets (far too frivolous for a stern Lutheran like Bach). But he positively excludes bonhomie in the bursts of joy and exhilaration in some of the organ works and the sunny 'Brandenburg' Concertos; the finger-twisting (and foot-twisting) passages of his keyboard and organ sonatas; the contrast of mood and character from one prelude and fugue to the next in the great 'Forty-eight' (the two books of the *Well-tempered Clavier*); and the playful interplay between soloist and orchestra in the concertos.

The word 'Bach' means 'stream' in German; hence Beethoven's famous saying: 'Nicht Bach aber Meer haben wir hier' ('Not a stream but a whole ocean'). Two further curiosities: Bach's name is a musical theme. Our note B natural is the note H in German nomenclature; our note B flat is known as B. Thus, the composer's surname produces its own four-note *motif*: B flat, A, C, B natural. In *The Art of Fugue*, Bach produced an encyclopaedic work using every contrapuntal device imaginable based on a single theme. It was calculated to appeal to the visual senses as well as the aural, and it is a moot point whether Bach intended the cycle to be performed. The work remained unfinished at his death. On the very last page, Bach had begun a fugue adding his name as one of the themes. It was the final piece he wrote.

His lifelong love of mathematics meant that the cardinal numbers corresponding to the letters of his name were of some significance. The number 14 was important to him: B=2, A=1, C=3, H=8 (2+1+3+8=14). A chorale he wrote shortly before his death has a theme of 14 notes; 14 is 41 inverted and the theme of the whole melody numbers 41 notes, which is also the sum of the cardinal numbers of J.S. BACH (9+18+14). The principal melody of the choral prelude *Wenn wir in höchsten Nöten sein* has 166 notes, the same as the numbers relating to JOHANN SEBASTIAN BACH.

Unlike Handel, who wrote for patrons and public, Bach was motivated only by a need to express *himself*. His is deeply personal music, and yet it speaks to mankind, and the amount he wrote is staggering. When the task of gathering together and publishing all his music was undertaken, the project took forty-six years to complete. It has been calculated that if today a copyist was to write out all of Bach's music (including all the parts, as Bach did), it would take seventy years. How he did it, with all his other duties of conducting, teaching, playing the organ and (an old but pertinent chestnut) fathering twenty children, he explained with characteristic modesty: 'I worked hard.'

Essential works

J.S. Bach's works are known by their BWV numbers, an abbreviation of *Bach Werke-Verzeichnis* (Catalogue of Bach's Works). This catalogue was made in 1950 by Wolfgang Schmieder, so some people confuse things by calling them S numbers. They are not chronological, but grouped by genre. Space does not permit comment on each work, but from over 1,000 compositions it is hoped that the choice below represents the best from each category.

Keyboard: organ

The organ was Bach's favourite instrument, and his compositions are the basis of today's repertoire. 'Here all the earlier tendencies in organ music were swept to their ultimate destiny, both as to style and structure,' wrote one critic. 'Here a new world of effect, nuance, and techniques was explored.' The six works listed below are his greatest.

Prelude and Fugue in D BWV532
Fantasia and Fugue in C minor BWV537
Fantasia and Fugue in G minor, 'The Great' BWV542
Prelude and Fugue in A minor BWV543
Toccata, Adagio and Fugue in C BWV564
Passacaglia and Fugue in C minor BWV582
Toccata and Fugue in D minor BWV565: one of the most popular pieces of classical music, with its thunderous, dramatic introduction and the cumulative excitement of the fugue. Probably not by Bach, probably not originally an organ piece, probably written for the violin ... and the moon isn't made of cheese. It has been arranged for orchestra by the likes of Leopold Stokowski and Sir Henry Wood.

Prelude and Fugue in G BWV541: not as well known as others in this form, but perky, exuberant and a good one to start with.

Fugue in G (à la gigue) BWV577: a dance for the organist.

Fugue in G minor 'The Little' BWV578: so called to distinguish it from BWV542. The unusually expansive opening theme is joined by two others, and all three are brought together in the most ingenious counterpoint.

Keyboard: Clavier and harpsichord

The Well-tempered Clavier BWV846–893: in two books, with twenty-four preludes and fugues in all the major and minor keys in each, Bach lays out his system of 'equal temperament'; hence the title, which has nothing to do with having a nicely-behaved keyboard. Before Bach's time, the tuning of keyboard instruments had not been standard: in fact it was chaotic. Bach divided the octave up into twelve equal semitones. This made it possible for the first time to modulate and transpose into any key. Prelude No.1 is a well-known piece – every aspiring piano student has had a crack at it – given extra swing in the popular jazz version by Jacques Loussier. Gounod used this as the basis for his famous *Ave Maria*.

Partita No.1 in B flat BWV825
Italian Concerto BWV971

The *Clavierübung* is the name of the collection of Bach's keyboard music published between 1726 and 1742. The first part of the anthology contains the six clavier partitas. The second has the lively *Italian Concerto* – a solo work, despite its title. Bach's aim was to emulate a concerto in the style of earlier Italian masters.

Goldberg Variations BWV988: from the fourth part of the *Clavierübung*, this extraordinary work was written for one of Bach's pupils, Johann Gottlieb Goldberg, whose employer, Count Kaiserling, had trouble sleeping. He asked Bach to write some music for Goldberg to entertain him when he couldn't sleep; hence these thirty complex but beautiful variations on a tune Bach had written for Anna Magdalena. The pianist Glenn Gould made two illuminating recordings of the work.

Instrumental and orchestral

Harpsichord Concerto No.1 in D minor BWV1052
Harpsichord Concerto No.4 in A BWV1055
Harpsichord Concerto No.5 in F minor BWV1056

Of the seven concertos Bach wrote for the clavier – the first significant examples of the form – these are the finest. Many were transcribed from his violin concertos or other works; today the keyboard versions are heard on the harpsichord or the piano. The aria-like Largo of the Fifth Concerto is one of the great slow movements. For many years the performances by the Swiss pianist Edward Fischer were the touchstones for others.

Concerto No.1 in A minor for violin BWV1041
Concerto No.2 in E for violin BWV1042
Concerto in D minor for two violins BWV1043
Concerto in D minor for violin and oboe BWV1060

The two solo concertos were composed in Cöthen in the concerto grosso style. Albert Schweitzer thought 'the beauty of the A minor

Concerto was severe, that of the E major Concerto full of unconquerable joy of life that sings its song of triumph in the first and last movements.' The double Concerto is among the finest two-violin works, a supreme example of Baroque music; the slow movement is surely one of the most spiritual and serene pieces of music ever composed. The Violin and Oboe Concerto is a reconstruction of Bach's lost original, from his own transcription, as a Concerto for two harpsichords.

Chaconne (from Violin Partita No.2 in D minor) BWV1004: Bach wrote several partitas and suites for the solo violin and solo cello in which he demonstrates his mastery of the polyphonic possibilities of the instruments. From one of these comes the towering Chaconne, made even more effective, some think, in the monumental piano version by Busoni. It was also arranged by Brahms to be played on the piano by the left hand alone, and featured somewhat bizarrely in the camp horror film *The Beast With Five Fingers*.

'Brandenburg' Concertos Nos.1–6 BWV1046 –51: commissioned by the Margrave of Brandenburg in about 1720. Each concerto except No.3 features a different group of solo instruments, which Bach weaves into an invigorating contrapuntal network – the most sophisticated form of the Italian concerto grosso.

Suite No.2 in B minor BWV1067: a seven-movement orchestral dance suite, ending with the sparkling Badinerie for flute.

Suite No.3 in D BWV1068: a five-movement dance suite, the second of which is better known as the Air on a G String, a transcription for violin and piano by August Wilhelmj, now inextricably linked in the UK to a commercial for a certain brand of cigar.

Choral
St Matthew Passion BWV244
Mass in B minor BWV232
Two of the most exalted choral works ever written, though very different in character. The Passion is a dramatized version of Christ's crucifixion and resurrection, performed like an oratorio, except the congregation has chorales to sing; 'O Sacred Head, sore wounded' is the best known. The Mass, which many view as the summit of Bach's work, is a mammoth setting of the Latin Mass in twenty-four, mainly choral, sections. The *Gloria, Crucifixus, Sanctus* and *Credo* are awe-inspiring.

Also hat Gott die Welt geliebt, BWV68, Cantata No.68: from this comes the well-known soprano aria 'Mein gläubiges Herz' ('My heart ever faithful').

Ein' feste Burg ist unser Gott, BWV80b, Cantata No.80: based on the tune Martin Luther wrote for his setting of Psalm 46, in today's hymn book adapted as 'A safe stronghold our God is still'.

Wachet auf, BWV140, Cantata No.140: we know this as 'Sleepers awake!' with its majestic choral entry 'Zion hört die Wächter singen'. Bach used the music in an organ chorale prelude.

Herz und Mund und Tat und Leben, BWV147, Cantata No.147: the tenth part of this cantata is more familiarly known in a much-loved piano arrangement by Dame Myra Hess – *Jesu, joy of man's desiring*.

Was mir behagt, BWV208, Cantata No.208: a secular cantata from which comes the familiar 'Sheep shall safely graze'.

Amongst the many composers who have adapted or arranged Bach's music, of particular note are Busoni's piano transcriptions of organ and choral works, Liszt's piano transcriptions of organ works, the orchestral arrangements of instrumental works by Leopold Stokowski (unfashionable and overblown but great fun), Rachmaninov's masterly transcription for piano of the solo *Violin Partita No.3*, and Sir William Walton's ballet suite *The Wise Virgins*.

Mily BALAKIREV

'In time he will be a second Glinka' (Glinka)

Born: 2 January 1837, Nizny-Novgorod, Russia
Died: 29 May 1910, St Petersburg
Full name: Mily Alexeievitch Balakirev
Type of music: Nationalist, Romantic; symphony, orchestral, concerto, chamber, piano, vocal
Influences: German school, Glinka, Russian national music
Contemporaries: César Cui, SAINT-SAËNS, DELIBES, **BALAKIREV**, Emile Waldteufel, BIZET, BRUCH, MUSSORGSKY, Josef Rheinberger

HIS LIFE AND MUSIC

Balakirev (pronounced Ba-*lahk'*-i-reff) came, like his idol Glinka, from an affluent family. He began piano lessons with his mother and then, at the age of ten, came under the influence of the writer and musician Alexander Ulibischev (1795–1858). A country gentleman and authority on Mozart, Ulibischev ran his own private orchestra with which his protégé was allowed to experiment. On the whole, however, Balakirev the composer was self-taught. He had a good ear, absolute pitch and a huge amount of determination; how else could he have founded the Free School of Music at the age of twenty-five and been hailed as the heir to Glinka's new nationalistic outlook?

This stocky little man soon became the centre of a group of like-minded composers who looked to him as their teacher, adviser and leader. What the group advocated was: 'Look to Russian folk tunes for inspiration, look to the East, but don't look to the West and Germany; Russia can find her own cultural identity.' With Balakirev's encouragement, Rimsky-Korsakov, Borodin, Cui and Mussorgsky – all amateur musicians – began to make names for themselves. In May 1867, Balakirev organized a concert in Prague of work by himself, his four colleagues and Czech musicians. In response, a Russian critic wrote that his country now had its *moguchaya kuchka* – its 'mighty little company'. The phrase became a catchword, and musical history describes these composers as the Mighty Handful or The Five, who established Russia's musical identity. Cui's contribution to music was negligible, however, and the Mighty Four might have been more apt.

In the late 1860s Balakirev slowed down and for several years suffered bouts of severe depression and violent headaches. He had trouble completing scores: it took him thirty-three years (1864–97) to finish his First Symphony; he began his Second Piano Concerto in 1861 but put it aside until 1909; it took a mere eight years to complete his Second Symphony but many more to compose his masterpiece, *Tamara*. At the same time he sought employment far removed from the centre of the country's musical life. He took a clerical job on the Warsaw railway system in 1872 but then had a mental breakdown. In 1873, he was made an inspector for musical education in a women's college.

Although he returned to musical activities in 1881 and was appointed director of music to the Imperial Chapel in 1883, Balakirev became increasingly morose and isolated during his final years, a prey to religious mania and estranged from his former friends. He produced little of consequence in the last thirty years of his life; yet, from his few compositions and charismatic personality, his effect on Russian music was incalculable.

Essential works

Symphony No.1 in C (1864–97)
Symphony No.2 in D minor (1900–08)
If you haven't tracked down these two luscious works in which Balakirev's nationalistic ideas are put into practice, start with No.1. Many people were introduced to it by Sir Thomas Beecham's classic 1955 recording.
Tamara, symphonic poem (1867–82): this piece is the result of one of Balakirev's trips to the Caucasus in which the influence of quasi-

Oriental tunes and rhythms features strongly. It is a portrait of a temptress in *The Arabian Nights* and was doubtless the inspiration for Rimsky-Korsakov's *Scheherazade*.
Islamey, Oriental fantasy for piano (1869, revised 1902) – still considered to be among the most difficult pieces ever written for the instrument, and almost as exciting to watch as to hear! Alfredo Casella and Sergei Liapunov made orchestral arrangements of the work.

Samuel BARBER

(1910–81)

Adagio for strings

At the suggestion of Arturo Toscanini, Barber made an arrangement for orchestra of the slow movement of his String Quartet Op.11, which the great Italian conductor premiered in November 1938. Since then it has become one of the most popular pieces of American classical music, its solemn serenity rising to a pitch of grief before its hushed disappearance. It is impossible to forget the effect when it was played at the funeral of Princess Grace of Monaco in 1982. Or Oliver Stone's use of it as a moving commentary on the unspeakable horrors of the Vietnam War in his movie *Platoon*.

Of course, there is more to Barber than that. High on the list of his numerous other works are *Dover Beach* (1931), a setting of Matthew Arnold's poem, which the composer recorded himself in his mellifluous baritone; his Piano Sonata (1949), which Vladimir Horowitz introduced and recorded in electrifying fashion (start with the last movement), and the sophisticated, flamboyant and very difficult Piano Concerto (1962).

Barber is to America what Benjamin Britten is to Britain: they were contemporaries, both declining to adopt any form of fashionable modernism but carving their own distinctive, idiosyncratic styles.

Barber, incidentally, had two impressive teachers – he learned singing from his aunt, the famous operatic contralto Louise Homer, and conducting from Fritz Reiner.

Béla BARTÓK

'In the name of Nature, Art and Science' (Bartók)

Born: 25 March 1881, Nagyszentmiklos, Hungary (now Sinnicolau, Romania)
Died: 26 September 1945, New York
Type of music: Dissonant nationalist; orchestral, opera, chamber, concerto, piano
Influenced by: Richard Strauss, Liszt; in the early years Dohnányi, then Debussy, Stravinsky, Prokofiev and many elements of Hungarian folk music
Contemporaries: Cyril Scott, Nicolai Medtner, Ernest Bloch, **BARTÓK**, Nicolai Miaskovsky, Georges Enescu, SZYMANOWSKY, Manuel Ponce

HIS LIFE

Bartók's early years – like his last – were spent in economic hardship and poor health. His father, a director of the local agricultural college, was a good amateur pianist; his mother taught piano after her husband's death in 1888, trekking from school to school with her young son and daughter, eking out a living.

Bartók suffered from both bronchitis and pneumonia, and was treated, mistakenly, for curvature of the spine. He was shy and introverted, a small, retiring man who remained physically frail all his life. To make up for it, he had a cast-iron will that brushed aside rejection, incomprehension and failure. He began composing at the age of nine, and, at ten, gave his first concert as a 'pianist-composer'. In 1894, the family moved to Pressburg (Bratislava), where Bartók studied piano before enrolling at the Academy of Music in Budapest.

In 1904, a year after graduating, he made a discovery that changed his life. Until then his musical heroes had been Richard Strauss, Liszt and his slightly-older fellow countryman Dohnányi, but listening to Hungarian folk music galvanized his creative thinking.

With his friend Zoltán Kodály, Bartók went on lengthy trips armed with an Edison recording machine and a box of wax cylinders, systematically collecting folk tunes performed by the peasants of Hungary, Transylvania, Carpathia, even venturing as far as North Africa (1913) and Turkey (1936). Their work, catalogued and documented, was hailed as a major piece of ethnomusicology.

This music fed Bartók's soul and all his subsequent compositions are imbued with the varied character of native folk music. The Budapest Academy offered him a piano teaching post in 1907 (not composition, which Bartók always refused to teach), and he remained there until 1934.

The more he composed, the more his work became austere and experimental and, although it aroused strong opposition in his own country, outside Hungary his reputation grew steadily from a limited number of performances. Parallel to this was his burgeoning career as a pianist, predominantly in his own works.

After the *Anschluss* in March 1938, Bartók saw that it would be only a matter of time before Hungary fell to the Nazis. He was fifty-eight years old, supporting his mother, wife and family. What was he to do? His mother's death in 1939 decided him: he would go to the United States. He accepted a position at Columbia University, and he composed and played a few concerts, but the American public was indifferent. Though not as impoverished as legend has it, he certainly had very little money, and his health declined rapidly when leukaemia was diagnosed. He was isolated and somewhat embittered at the lack of recognition and, worst of all, in increasing pain.

Bartók's final completed score turned out to be his most popular, the Concerto for Orchestra. Before he died, leaving a handful of works unfinished, he lamented: 'The trouble is that I have to go with so much still to say.'

HIS MUSIC

Béla Bartók – the sounds of his two names are those of his music, one soft and romantic, the other hard and angular. Without doubt, he is one of the century's most important and individual composers, though his influence on others is more limited than has been claimed. Some of his work is easily accessible – Concerto for Orchestra and the Third Piano Concerto, for instance; more often than not it makes tremendous demands on the listener (try the Third String Quartet), and concert-goers have never taken much of it to their hearts. In 1912, after hearing some of his piano pieces, one writer reported that 'the composer was regarded with certain indulgence by the audience as, if not stark mad, certainly an eccentric person.'

However, musicians sing his praises for his intellectual rigour, his uncompromising individuality and the personal sound-world he dreamt up. They also like to rise to the particular technical demands Bartók makes on them. Connoisseurs of the genre are of the opinion that his six string quartets are the only original contribution to the medium since Beethoven's, qualities that are not immediately apparent to the casual listener. 'He not only never wears his heart on his sleeve,' wrote Colin Wilson, 'he seems to have deposited it in some bank vault.' Bartók, in a nutshell, is a composer who requires work before his muse is appreciated.

Essential works
Concerto for Orchestra (1943): this five-movement work is a concerto, Bartók explained, because of 'its tendency to treat the single instrument or instrument groups in concertante or soloistic manner'. It is a lugubrious work, though the witty second movement, with its parody of Shostakovich, and fiery finale stand out in sharp relief. It was commissioned by the conductor/publisher Serge Koussevitzky at the suggestion of the conductor Fritz Reiner and violinist Joseph Szigeti.
Music for Percussion, Strings and Celesta (1936): a rarefied, austere and impressionistic work in four movements for this unusual combination of instruments.
Piano Concerto No.2 (1931): the piano as percussive instrument, and the timpanists have their work cut out, too. The concerto (as one

writer put it) is 'characterized by a barbaric rhythmic force'.
Six String Quartets (1908–39): these works epitomize the evolution of Bartók's style, and have not been rivalled this century for their variety, resourcefulness and inventiveness. **No.1** was written after his first contact with folk music – 'the return to life of a man who has reached the shores of nothingness', wrote Kodály. **No.2** (1917) has abrupt changes of rhythm, violent and unexpected accents, and discordant, intense, brutal passages. **No.3** (1927) includes a variety of under-used effects for string instruments, including bowing close to the bridge, using the wooden box and snapping the strings so that they rebound against the fingerboard. **No.4** is more restrained, while the final two (**Nos.5 & 6**: 1934

and 1939) are simpler in scoring and intent.

The Miraculous Mandarin (1919): a one-act 'pantomime' or ballet now usually heard as an orchestral suite.

Duke Bluebeard's Castle (1911–18): Bartók's only opera, in a single act.

Also worth investigating

Violin Concerto No.2 (1938): lyrical, folk and jazz elements alternate in this, a suitable introduction to Bartók's world.

Contrasts (1938): for piano, violin and clarinet. It was written for the American jazz clarinettist Benny Goodman.

Piano Concerto No.3 (1945): a mellower, more amiable work than the Second Concerto. The slow movement, inspired by the birdsong of North Carolina, is one of his most lyrical.

Arnold BAX

Born: 8 November 1883, London
Died: 3 October 1953, Cork
Full name: Sir Arnold Edward Trevor Bax
Type of music: 'Celtic neo-Romantic' and Impressionist; symphony, symphonic poem, ballet, chamber, choral vocal, film
Influences: Irish folk-tunes, W.B. Yeats' poetry, Russian music, Impressionists
Contemporaries: STRAVINSKY, WEBERN, Alfredo Casella, Lord Berners, **BAX**, Sir George Dyson, Edgard Varèse, Charles Griffes, George Butterworth, BERG

HIS LIFE AND MUSIC

Only one work from Bax's prolific output is heard with any regularity in the concert hall today – his tone-poem *Tintagel*. A significant amount of his music is now on record (on the Chandos label, with conductor Bryden Thomson and pianist Eric Parkin leaving us in their debt), but few know his seven symphonies, the quintets and sonatas for various instrumental combinations; most have overlooked the music credits when enjoying films such as David Lean's *Oliver Twist* (1948).

Bax was a retiring man and didn't do himself any favours as far as self-promotion was concerned. His piano playing first attracted the attention of his teachers at the Royal Academy of Music – his sight-reading of full orchestral scores was legendary – but he refused to appear as a pianist in public, nor did he conduct his own works.

On completing his studies in 1905, all Bax wanted to do was compose. His interest in ancient Irish folklore and a visit to Russia in 1910 resulted in such titles as *May Night in the Ukraine*, *In a Vodka Shop*, his Irish fantasy *Moy Mell* and the tone-poem *The Wanderings of Usheen*, but the Celtic influences of mystery and fantasy dominate and colour most of his works, whatever their title.

By the end of his career, he had been awarded the prestigious Gold Medal of the Royal Philharmonic Society, been knighted by George VI in the coronation honours, and made Master of the King's Musick in 1941, succeeding Sir Walford Davies. He lived to contribute a march for the 1953 coronation.

Essential works

Tintagel, tone-poem (1917–19): 'the work', wrote Bax, 'is intended to evoke a tone-picture of the castle-crowned cliff of Tintagel, and more particularly, the wide distances of the Atlantic as seen from the cliffs of Cornwall on a sunny but not windless day'. The middle section depicts the legends associated with King Arthur, King Mark, Tristan and Isolde.

The Garden of Fand, tone-poem (1913–16),
and Bax's first international success, was premiered in Chicago in 1920. Fand, daughter of Macannan, Lord of the Ocean, lures the mythological Cuchulain to her garden, the sea.

Of the seven symphonies, **Symphony No.3** is a good one to start with, full of Baxian eloquence and with a wide emotional range.

The **Quintet for oboe and strings** (1923) is regarded as one of Bax's best chamber works.

Ludwig van BEETHOVEN

'A Titan, wrestling with the Gods' (Wagner)

Born: 15 or 16 December 1770, Bonn
Died: 26 March 1827, Vienna
Type of music: Early Romantic; symphony, orchestral, concerto, opera, oratorio, incidental music, vocal, chamber, instrumental, piano
Influences: Mozart, Haydn and his teachers Neefe, Albrechtsberger and Salieri
Contemporaries: Jan Ladislav Dussek, Samuel Wesley, **BEETHOVEN,** Gaspare Spontini, François-Adrien Boïeldieu, Bernhard Henrik Crusell, HUMMEL

HIS LIFE

Beethoven was convinced that the 'van' in his name indicated noble birth, and he allowed the rumour to circulate that he was the love child of Friedrich Wilhelm II, King of Prussia (or even – and more improbably – Frederick the Great). In fact, his family was of Dutch descent – Beethoven means 'beet garden'– and his grandfather had been a choir director in Louvain.

1770–82 Beethoven had a thoroughly miserable childhood thanks to his alcoholic brute of a father, a singer in the Electoral Chapel in Bonn. Fired by ambitions to transform his gifted son into a second Mozart, Johann van Beethoven would keep Ludwig slaving at the piano all night, raining blows on him whenever he made a mistake. The young Beethoven was an unprepossessing-looking child, he had no friends, he was clumsy and untidy in appearance, and the only warmth he knew came from his mother. Johann and fellow drinker Tobias Pfeiffer were his first teachers; various others contributed to his early musical study of the violin, organ, piano and French horn. His first published work was Nine Variations for piano on a March of Dressler, which he composed when he was twelve. His first significant lessons came from the court organist Christian Neefe, who recognized and nurtured Beethoven's talent. At fourteen, the Elector Maximilian Franz made him deputy court organist.

1787 Beethoven was sent to Vienna by the Elector. Legend has it that he played for Mozart, but it seems unlikely that they met. In any case, Beethoven returned to Bonn after a few weeks, when he received the news that his mother had died. Johann's alcoholism cost him his job, obliging Beethoven to earn enough money to keep the family (he had two younger brothers). This he did by playing the viola in a theatre orchestra and giving piano lessons to the wealthy widow of a court councillor. Among the affluent and influential admirers he met at this time was Count Ferdinand Waldstein, later immortalized by the dedication to him of one of Beethoven's sonatas.

1792 He studied briefly and unprofitably with Haydn in Vienna (which became his home for the rest of his life) before taking lessons in counterpoint from Johann Georg Albrechtsberger and vocal composition from Antonio Salieri. Haydn, it must be said, though as intolerant of Beethoven's crude manners as he was of his disregard for the normal rules of harmony, was moved to remark that Beethoven made the impression of 'a man who has several heads, several hearts and several souls'.

1795 Beethoven made his debut in Vienna (probably playing his Piano Concerto in B flat, Op.19), and his reputation as a virtuoso pianist and composer spread rapidly.

1796 Though it remained a secret between his doctor and himself for many years, Beethoven was aware of impending deafness as early as his twenty-sixth year. Oto-sclerosis (an abnormal growth of honeycomb bone in the inner ear) was certainly part of the cause, accompanied by tinnitus. A further contributory factor was congenital syphilis, the symptoms of which show up in the life mask made in 1812 and in the photograph taken of his skull in 1863 when the body was exhumed.

1802 In a document not discovered until after his death, Beethoven wrote poignantly of his condition, aware that the most important sense to him, that of hearing, was being taken away. This is the so-called 'Heiligenstadt Testament', written in the village of Heiligenstadt.

1803–08 His predicament spurred him to a furious spell of creativity and, in the circumstances, it is quite remarkable that he was able to compose such music – of every shape and form, embracing tragedy and joy – without apparent reference to his physical state; 'coolness under the fire of creative fantasy' was how Schubert summed up Beethoven's genius. During this period he presented his Third Piano Concerto and the 'Kreutzer' Sonata, his oratorio *Christus am Oelberge*, the 'Waldstein', 'Appassionata' and 'Moonlight' Sonatas, as well as his Symphony No.3 (the 'Eroica').

Another remarkable document, again discovered only after his death, was written around this time: the letter to the 'Immortal Beloved'. No one has positively identified which of the many women in Beethoven's life it refers to. Perhaps it was Giulietta Guicciardi, dedicatee of the 'Moonlight' Sonata, or her cousin Therese von Brunswick, the inspiration for the 'Appassionata', or any of a number of the other young, beautiful and unattainable ladies he fell for. It is quite possible the 'Immortal Beloved' is addressed to all womankind. Research into the identity of the 'Immortal Beloved' has exercised the detective skills of music scholars ever since, and there have been numerous other tenuously-held theories.

And still the music came pouring out: the first version of the opera *Fidelio* was given in 1805, followed by the 'Razumovsky' String Quartets, Symphonies 4, 5 and 6, the Violin Concerto, the Triple Concerto and a number of piano sonatas. Beethoven was offered the well-paid position of Kapellmeister of Kassel by King Jerome Bonaparte of Westphalia. However, despite the uncertainty of his income from various patrons, he decided to stay in Vienna.

1809–12 The inexorable progress of Beethoven's deafness made him increasingly irritable, over-sensitive, scornful and petulant, more inclined to retreat into himself and shun society. He exaggerated his poverty (he kept his shares and bonds locked up in a secret drawer) and assiduously studied the winning numbers in the Austrian national lottery in the hope of making a fortune.

Beethoven was also irredeemably untidy; his handwriting was all but indecipherable, and many manuscripts bear the circle made by using them as a cover for his soup or chamber pot. But his belief in himself and what he was doing was intense, and woe betide anyone who didn't acknowledge that. Many close friends were banished forever for trifling incidents; others had faith in him and were unsparingly supportive. Prince Lobkowitz, Countess Erdödy and especially the Archduke Rudolph all tolerated his foibles and stuck loyally by him. Beethoven knew that he was breaking new ground. 'With whom need I be afraid of measuring my strength?' he once boasted. To prove it, one masterpiece followed another – the Fifth Piano Concerto (the 'Emperor'), Symphonies 7 and 8, and the 'Les Adieux' Piano Sonata.

1812–17 The following five years saw a marked decline in the amount and adventurousness of music that Beethoven produced.

1818–27 The third and final phase of his development as a composer began in 1818 – and with a vengeance. It saw the appearance of the mammoth 'Hammerklavier' Piano Sonata, and it heralded the beginning of arguably his greatest and most productive period, which brought the Ninth 'Choral' Symphony, the *Missa Solemnis* and the late String Quartets. During this decade, deprived of a wife and family, Beethoven sought to find a surrogate son in the form of his nephew Karl, whose father had died in 1815. He regarded his sister-in-law, Karl's mother, as unfit to bring up the boy and engaged in a series of sordid and bitter court quarrels in an attempt to become Karl's guardian. Beethoven finally won the case in 1820 and for the following six years he stifled Karl with avuncular affection in a pathetic attempt to gain his love and reform his dissolute ways. Karl, in return, piled up enormous debts, regarded his uncle with some contempt and finally attempted suicide. At length, he joined the army and went on to enjoy a normal life.

Beethoven became totally deaf after 1818. His touching faith in every new 'hearing remedy' that came onto the market bears witness to his undying hope for a cure. His only means of communication was through conversation books; everything that anybody wanted to say to Beethoven was written down first and he would then answer orally. The most heart-rending demonstration of his affliction was in May 1824 at the premiere of the Ninth Symphony, which the composer insisted on conducting himself. It is said that as the Symphony ended, Beethoven was several bars adrift from the orchestra and chorus and continued to conduct even as a storm of enthusiastic applause broke out. The contralto soloist, Caroline Ungher, came over to him, and gently turned him round to face the audience. Only then did those present realize that Beethoven had not heard anything and, wrote Sir George Grove, '[it] acted like an electric shock on all present. A volcanic explosion of sympathy and admiration followed which was repeated again and again and again and seemed as if it would never end.'

1826 Beethoven caught a cold while visiting his brother; the cold developed into pneumonia, and jaundice and dropsy set in. His death on the afternoon of 26 March came in the middle of a violent thunderstorm, a coincidence that has appealed to his more romantically-inclined biographers. In fact, there *was* an electrical storm over Vienna that day, but the other legend, that of the dying Beethoven raising his fists to Heaven in a last defiant gesture, must be a fanciful invention, considering his feeble physical state. His last words were reported to have been: 'I shall hear in heaven.' For his funeral, schools closed, people stayed away from work and all Vienna mourned. Franz Schubert was one of the torch-bearers.

HIS MUSIC

There is a direct parallel between the political climate of the time and Beethoven's music. Just as the French Revolution overthrew established authority and spread a wave of rebellion throughout Europe, so Beethoven, with equal defiance and decisiveness, overthrew accepted musical form, traditional harmony and structure and the neat, well-ordered ways of the so-recent worlds of Haydn and Mozart. Beethoven's credo was the entirely new one expressed in the writings of the philosophers of the Enlightenment, such as Rousseau and Voltaire, which stated that the creative ego  has the right to express itself in its own way without fear or hindrance. As a devout republican, Beethoven – and his music – shouts from the rooftops: 'I, too, am King!'

'The first of Beethoven's compositions *are* music,' wrote the critic Eduard Hanslick. 'In his last compositions Beethoven *makes* music.' Scholars divide his work into three distinct periods. Up to about 1800, it is still clearly under the influence of the Classical period – listen to the first two piano concertos and sonatas and, *pace* Beethoven's personal colouring of the harmony and other effects, you are still in the world of Mozart and Haydn, the world of *Zopfmusik* – pigtail music. In the second period the pigtail is replaced by Beethoven's ruffled head of hair. Coinciding with his increasing deafness, the music becomes more adventurous in its breaking of accepted forms and harmonies; Beethoven is experimenting with his new-found, passionate need to express himself. To do this, he needed to invent additions to his musical vocabulary, increase the potential of what was there already and challenge all that had gone before. And here is a further distinction between the pigtails of Haydn and Mozart and the unkempt Beethoven: the former composed effortlessly, while the latter struggled to get what he had in his head down on paper. The music of the 'Eroica' Symphony and the 'Appassionata' Sonata, composed in 1803 when Haydn was still alive and only a decade after Mozart's death, is as remote from Haydn's music as Haydn's is from Bach's, composed seventy years earlier.

From 1818, Beethoven's music enters a clearly defined third and final phase. Here, he ventures into territory as distant from his second period as the abyss between the second period and the first. The daring modulations, harmonic progressions and unorthodox structures led many of his contemporaries to think he was 'quite ripe for the madhouse', as Weber put it. The brutality of some late Beethoven had never been experienced before; neither had the profound spiritual depths that he reached in other works – a clear reflection of his own torment, sometimes raging at the dying of the light, at other times serenely accepting his fate.

Essential works
The Nine Symphonies

Written over a span of twenty-three years, these masterpieces are the clearest, most concise way of seeing exactly how Beethoven's musical style developed. Curiously, the even-numbered symphonies are the slighter and less adventurous, while the odd-numbered pieces are more profound and challenging in their aims.

Symphony No.1 in C, Op.21 (1800)
Symphony No.2 in D, Op.36 (1802)
To our ears, the First Symphony is an easy, agreeable listen, but to the Viennese of Beethoven's day its very opening bars were considered shocking and dissonant. The traditional minuet of the third movement is turned into a scherzo – the formal court dance turned into a light-hearted, whimsical piece of music. Still, these two early symphonies are clearly derivative of Mozart and Haydn.

Symphony No.3 in E flat, 'Eroica' Op.55 (1804): the 'Eroica' has been described as 'one of the incomprehensible deeds of arts and letters, the greatest single step made by an individual composer in the history of the symphony and the history of music in general'. Its opening proclaims its epic scale and defiance of everything that has preceded it in symphonic terms, for nothing written previously compares with its sense of majestic grandeur, its drama and conflict. The second movement is a funeral march and the first to appear in a symphony, the third a bright and brisk scherzo; the finale returns to the emotional torment of the first, with a series of variations climaxing with a hymn for the hero who is being celebrated. The hero? Napoleon Bonaparte, whom Beethoven considered to be a champion of human freedom. When he heard that Napoleon had crowned himself Emperor, Beethoven saw that his hero was just as vain and ambitious as the rulers he had replaced and, disenchanted, scratched out the name

'Bonaparte' from the front page of the manuscript and replaced it with the one word 'Eroica', dedicating the symphony instead to 'the memory of a great man'.

Symphony No.4 in B flat, Op.60 (1806): a gentle, subdued experience after No.3, and typical of much of Beethoven's middle period in that he often relaxes from the intense concentration of his idealistic work; the comparatively genial Piano Concerto in G and the Violin Concerto are contemporary with this symphony.

Symphony No.5 in C minor, Op.67 (1808): perhaps the most familiar opening of any piece of music: three short notes, one long one, then repeated. 'Fate knocking at the door' is what it is said to represent. Beethoven specifically denied such an association, and it's possible it was inspired by the call of a particular songbird in the Viennese woods, but history has insisted that 'fate' is what it signifies, reinforced by the coincidence that three short dots and one long signifies 'V' in the Morse code. 'V' for 'Victory' and the four-note motif of Beethoven's Fifth became an effective call-sign for the Allied forces in the Second World War. The work is full of contrasts within and between each movement: conflict and turmoil in the opening, a beautiful song for the second movement, mystery coupled with a version of the opening theme dominate the third, while the fourth is an exultant, triumphal progression. Beethoven's Fifth is played to distraction and people return to it again and again for a reason: it is great and profound music.

Symphony No.6 in F, 'Pastoral' Op.68 (1808): inspired by Beethoven's love of nature, this is the only one of the symphonies with five movements instead of the traditional four; it is also the only one with a specific programme, for each section has its own descriptive title: *The Awakening of Joyful Feelings Upon Arrival in the Country, The Brook, Village Festival, The*

Storm and *The Shepherd's Thanksgiving*. To think of the symphony merely as 'programme music' is to do it a disservice: the whole work is a celebration of the spirit of nature.

Symphony No.7 in A, Op.92 (1812): Wagner described this work as 'the apotheosis of the dance' because of the emphasis on rhythmic power that pervades all four movements, culminating in an irresistible bacchanalian frenzy in the finale. The second movement Allegretto is one of Beethoven's most celebrated, and one that had a particular influence on the Romantic composers. Legend has it that Wagner once attempted to 'dance' the whole symphony to Liszt's piano accompaniment!

Symphony No.8 in F, Op.93 (1812): Beethoven takes (by his standards) a back seat in this charming, good-natured work, although the final movement is anything but lacking in vigour, and Ralph Hill has noted in its 'chattering opening' a 'touch of Rossinian burlesque'.

Symphony No.9 in D, 'Choral' Op.125 (1824): the idea of setting Schiller's *Ode to Joy* had been with Beethoven for a quarter of a century and, as early as 1817, he had considered incorporating it into a symphony. This work is a monumental achievement, encompassing and heightening all the familiar Beethovenian feelings of exaltation, spirituality and deep humanity. If the 'Pastoral' Symphony is a celebration of the spirit of nature, the 'Choral' is a celebration of the human spirit. In the famous choral finale, Beethoven used only about one third of Schiller's ode, arranging the stanzas in his own order. He writes for the human voice as though it were an orchestral instrument – much of it is scored ungratefully high, making the words difficult to distinguish. Yet that doesn't matter: the texture and emotional power of the whole score drives Beethoven's purpose into our consciousness.

Overtures

Leonore No.3, Op.72 (1806): the greatest of the four different overtures Beethoven wrote for his opera *Fidelio*, this was composed for its first revival in Vienna. As a result of their complicated gestation, *Leonore No.4* is now usually played as a prelude to the opera, while No.3 is performed between the first and second scenes of Act 2.

Coriolan, Op.62 (1807): composed not for a production of Shakespeare's play *Coriolanus*, but that by the German writer Heinrich von Collin.

Egmont, Op.84 (1809–10): the only part still played of the incidental music Beethoven wrote for Goethe's historical play about Lamoral, Count of Egmont (1522–68), the Flemish statesman who liberated the Netherlands from Spanish domination.

Concertos

Violin Concerto in D, Op.61 (1806): Beethoven's single essay in the genre is also one of the greatest. It is among his less combative works – the second movement is ethereal, with the lyrical soloist soaring over the orchestral chords – with a sprightly and buoyant finale. Also worth investigating are the two slightly earlier **Romances for violin and orchestra (No.1 in F and No.2 in G)**, mellifluous and heart-warming. Beethoven made a highly effective piano version of the Concerto, which is played all too rarely.

Piano Concerto No.1 in C, Op.15 (1795–98)
Piano Concerto No.2 in B flat, Op.19 (1793–98)
Piano Concerto No.3 in C minor, Op.37 (1800)
Triple Concerto for violin, cello and piano, Op.56 (1804)

The first three of Beethoven's five concertos for piano and orchestra are, like his first two symphonies, children of Mozart and Haydn – the opening of the darker Third Concerto is highly reminiscent of that to Mozart's C minor Concerto (No.24). Yet there are unmistakable hints of rebellion. The Triple Concerto, though not wholly satisfying, has an uplifting finale.

Piano Concerto No.4 in G, Op.58 (1806): the most lyrical of the five and one of the most beautiful of all piano concertos. The slow movement, in which the piano has an almost tangible spoken dialogue with the orchestra, is sublime – Liszt described it as 'Orpheus taming the wild beasts'. The concerto begins with the piano rather than the orchestra stating the theme, a device previously unheard of.

Piano Concerto No.5 in E flat, 'Emperor' Op.73 (1809): The 'Emperor' (not Beethoven's name) is a glorious work, the longest piano concerto ever written at that time. It is full of novel effects from the opening improvisatory flourish, the long orchestral exposition that follows, and the written (rather than improvized) first-movement cadenza. Its slow movement is introspective and serene, the finale a rumbustious, exuberant Rondo.

Piano sonatas

Just as a knowledge of Shakespeare is basic to an understanding of English, so Beethoven's thirty-two sonatas are central to the literature of the piano.

Sonata No.8 in C minor 'Pathétique' Op.13 (1797–98): the most famous of the early sonatas and, arguably, the first *piano* sonata proper, in that it uses the dynamics of the piano and could not work as music on the harpsichord or clavier; the middle movement is a love song.

Sonata No.14 in C sharp minor, 'Sonata quasi una Fantasia' 'Moonlight' Op.27 No.2

(1801): in the celebrated first movement we find Beethoven expressing emotions in a way that cannot compare with any previous work. Though anyone can play the notes, it takes a real musician to make it work to its full effect. Its nickname came from a Berlin critic who saw moonlight over the Lake of Lucerne when he first heard the opening. Incidentally, because of its immense popularity, everyone's forgotten about Op.27 No.1 (also subtitled 'a sonata somewhat like a fantasia') – it is a strong work, well worth investigating.

Sonata No.21 in C, 'Waldstein' Op.53 (1803–04): dedicated to one of Beethoven's patrons, Count Waldstein, a brilliant, questioning work whose second movement blends seamlessly into a defiant finale.

Sonata No.23 in F minor, 'Appassionata' Op.57 (1804–05): burning passion, contrasted with a lyrical andante, followed by an explosive and violent finale.

Sonata No.26 in E flat, 'Les Adieux' Op.81a (1809–10): one of Beethoven's rare examples of programme music. The sonata, subtitled 'Les adieux, l'absence et le retour', depicts the departure from Vienna of Beethoven's patron Archduke Rudolf from Vienna in the face of the advancing Napoleonic armies, and the joy at his return.

Sonata No.29 in B flat, 'Hammerklavier' Op.106 (1817–18): all of Beethoven's last sonatas are designated 'for the Hammerklavier' (the German word for the piano, as distinct from the harpsichord), but it seems particularly appropriate for the grim grandeur of this massive work, 'as long as a symphony, as difficult as a concerto': it lasts forty-five minutes. Most pianists consider the musical and technical demands of the colossal fugue finale a daunting prospect.

These are just a handful, and the more familiar, from this great cycle, but it is necessary to know all of them in order to know Beethoven; the piano was his principal instrument, and he was famed as an improviser. It seems invidious to pick out separate movements, but outstanding are the slow movements of **Sonata No.5 in C minor, Op.10 No.1** and **No.30 in E, Op.109**; the scampering scherzo of **No.18 in E flat, Op.31**, followed by the minuet (Saint-Saëns used the theme from its trio for his Variations on a theme of Beethoven); and the whole of the glorious **Sonata No.32 in C minor, Op.111**, to say nothing of the two early **Sonatas Nos.1 & 2** dedicated to Haydn.

Other keyboard works worth investigating

Andante in F, known as the 'Andante Favori' (1803)

Rondo a capriccio in G, 'Rage over a lost penny' Op.129
Variations in E flat, 'Eroica' Op.35
Bagatelle in A minor, 'Für Elise'
Thirty-two Variations in C minor (1806)

Chamber Music: String Quartets

Beethoven composed seventeen string quartets. The first six (Op.18) have the same stylistic proportions of Haydn's, with the occasional hint of Beethoven brusqueness. A comparison of the slow movements of Quartets No.1 and No.6 reveal how much more deeply expressive Beethoven has already made the medium.

'Razumovsky' Quartets, Op.59 (1805–06): From Beethoven's middle period, these three masterpieces were written for the violin-playing Count Razumovsky, the Russian ambassador to Austria. Volatile moods and a sense of struggle are contrasted with spiritual calm. The finale of Op.59 No.1 has a Russian theme, which Mussorgsky later used in the coronation scene of *Boris Godunov*. The third quartet of Op.59 is sometimes called the 'Hero' Quartet, because of its intense dramatic qualities. But the gem is, perhaps, the prayerful slow movement of the Quartet No.8 in E minor, Op.59 No.2.

Chamber music: the Late Quartets

No.12 in E flat, Op.127
No.13 in B flat, Op.130
No.14 in C sharp minor, Op.131
No.15 in A minor, Op.132
No.16 in F, Op.135

These mystical and frequently demanding works are considered by many to be Beethoven's greatest music in any form. Traditional ways of developing themes are abandoned; instead, there are fragments of ideas, sometimes repeated, interrupted or varied. The music is elevated to a spiritual plane that is not found in any of Beethoven's other works, conjuring 'a kind of peace such as we can never know'.

Other chamber works

Sonata for violin and piano No.5 in F, 'Spring', Op.24
Sonata for violin and piano No.9 in A, 'Kreutzer', Op.47

Bubbling with melodic warmth and rhythmic energy, these two are the best known of Beethoven's ten sonatas for violin and piano, some of which come with the injunction that they are 'for pianoforte with the accompaniment of the violin' in order to emphasize the important role of the piano.

Septet in E flat, Op.20 (1800): this is unbuttoned Beethoven, cheerful party music, influenced by Mozart's divertimentos and serenades, scored for clarinet, bassoon, horn and string quartet.

Vocal

Fidelio (begun in 1804, completed in 1814): Beethoven was less happy writing for the voice and the stage than for any other forms; hence the fact that he wrote only one opera. Its composition caused him agony; he rewrote one aria no less than eighteen times, and composed four alternative overtures (see above). The opera is based on a French play by Bouilly called *Leonore* (the name of the heroine and hence the title of Overtures 1, 2, 3 and 4). Yet here, as in the 'Choral' Symphony, he takes the listener well beyond the expectations of the medium into another realm. *Fidelio* is more a symphony-drama than an opera proper, and can be appreciated on record just as well as in the opera house.

Missa Solemnis, Op.123 (1818–23): this, with Bach's Mass in B minor and Mozart's C minor Mass 'Great', is the pinnacle of religious music composed since the Polyphonic era. It is in five large sections – one of the reasons why it is rarely performed – and, as one would expect from Beethoven, humility in the face of God does not feature largely. Rather, we hear the composer defiantly and proudly proclaiming that inside each man there is something of God.

Vincenzo BELLINI

'Long, long melodies, such as no one has ever written before' (Verdi)

Born: 3 November 1801, Catania, Sicily
Died: 23 September 1835, Puteaux, near Paris
Type of music: Romantic opera
Influences: Pergolesi, Jomelli, Paisiello, Cimarosa and his teacher Nicola Zingarelli
Contemporaries: SCHUBERT, DONIZETTI, Jacques Fromenthal Halévy, **BELLINI**, Josef Lanner, Albert Lortzing, ADAM, BERLIOZ, GLINKA, Julius Benedict

HIS LIFE AND MUSIC

Of the Famous Three of Italian opera (Rossini, Donizetti and Bellini), the latter did the most to develop the medium. Rossini and Donizetti could complete three or four operas a year; Bellini struggled with each one, shaping, structuring and experimenting.

What did he bring to the form that was new? One clue can be gained from a remark made to a friend after listening to Pergolesi's *Stabat Mater*: 'If I could write one melody as beautiful as this, I would not mind dying young like Pergolesi,' a hauntingly prescient comment. Bellini's operas are gloriously melodic, with arias of long-breathed, arching phrases: the epitome of the Italian *bel canto* style. Opera composers had written beautiful melodies before but they had never matched the intensity of Bellini's work. He achieved this by seriously reviewing the dramatic content of the libretto and writing music that reflected the emotion of the characters and their situation. This was a significant move away from the predominantly decorative vocal displays of the past and was one of the key developments in Italian opera.

Bellini made the most of writing for particular singers, and several of them, considered to be among the greatest of the century, frequently appeared together in his operas: Giuditta Pasta, Giulia Grisi, Antonio Tamburini, Luigi Lablache and, most electrifying of all, Giovanni Battista Rubini. He was the Pavarotti of his day, not much of an actor but in possession of a huge vocal range. On hearing Rubini and Pasta, Glinka wrote: '[They] sang with the most evident enthusiasm to support their favourite composer. In the second act, the singers themselves wept, and carried their audience along with them, so that ... tears were continually being wiped away in boxes and stalls alike ... I too shed tears of emotion and ecstasy.'

Although Bellini came from a family of musicians (both his father and grandfather were organists and *maestri di cappella*), a musical career was strongly opposed, but when the Duke and Duchess of San Martino offered to fund his studies at the Real Conservatorio di Musica in Naples, the family relented. Bellini proved to be a diligent student and wrote his first opera while in the final year of his studies. *Adelson e Salvini* (first performed by fellow students in 1825) was such a success that he was commissioned to write another for the following carnival season in Naples. Not every composer has such fairy-tale beginnings. For the following decade, Bellini produced an average of one opera per year for the major Italian houses. *Il pirata* (premiered at La Scala in 1827) set the seal on his fame and established the Bellini style. But it is the two masterpieces *La sonnambula* (1830) and *Norma* (1831) that have never lost their place in the international repertoire.

In 1833, Bellini paid a visit to London and then settled in Paris, where he befriended Chopin and Rossini, the latter living there already in early retirement. The two younger men had much in common – slim, aristocratic-looking, delicate, and highly appealing to members of the opposite sex. Their music reveals more interesting comparisons: Bellini's work is concerned with the voice and the vocal line – the orchestral accompaniment simply provides harmonic and rhythmic support; a Chopin nocturne has exactly the same qualities and, for example, the slow movement of the early Piano Concerto in E minor is like a Bellini aria for the keyboard. Each composer influenced the other. Perhaps more important was the influence of Bellini's music on the young Verdi in such early pieces as *Oberto* and *Nabucco*.

What might Bellini have achieved if he had lived longer? One feels that, by the time of his death, he was just getting into his stride, for each successive work is an advance on the previous one – but his career lasted just ten years. He was a few weeks short of his thirty-fourth birthday when he died in a house outside Paris from an acute inflammation of the large intestine and an abscess of the liver – a particularly unromantic way to go for this archetypal Romantic.

Essential works
La sonnambula, opera (1830): proof that lovers of opera don't go to the opera because of the plausibility of the plot, the highlights of 'The Sleepwalker' are the soprano arias 'Ah, non credea mirarti', 'Ah, no giunge' and 'Come per me sereno'. The great coloraturas have seized the role with relish.

Norma, opera (1831): set in Gaul during the Roman occupation, this is Bellini's masterpiece. 'A great score that speaks to the heart,' wrote Wagner, 'A work of genius'. Norma is one of the key soprano roles and among the most demanding. Lilli Lehmann (1848–1929) said she would rather sing three Brünnhildes than one Norma. 'Casta diva' has a claim to be the most popular of all soprano opera arias, 'Mira, O Norma' is certainly one of the finest

duets, while the final trio, 'Deh, non voleri vittime', provides a searing climax.

Other works
I puritani, opera (1835): has some of the most brilliant vocal writing of all Bellini's operas, in particular the sparkling Polonaise 'Son vergin vezzosa' and the exquisite 'Qui la voce'. The stirring bass/baritone duet 'Suoni la tromba' was the tune used by Liszt for his 'Hexameron' variations, to which Chopin and five other fashionable pianists of the day contributed.

Oboe Concerto in E flat: a short and charming work from Bellini's student days, an appendage to the long list of Italian oboe concertos by the likes of Albinoni, Marcello and Cimarosa.

Richard Rodney BENNETT

Born: 29 March 1936, Broadstairs, Kent
Type of music: Modern tonal and serial; symphony, opera, concerto, chamber, vocal, piano, film
Influences: Bartók, Boulez, jazz and popular song
Contemporaries: BIRTWISTLE, DAVIES, PÄRT, Cornelius Cardew, **BENNETT**, Steve Reich, Philip Glass, John McCabe, Gavin Bryars, John Tavener

HIS LIFE AND MUSIC

One of the very few contemporary composers who can straddle the worlds of serious and light music. Even fewer are as prolific and can also play brilliant jazz piano, do a neat cabaret turn and be equally highly-regarded in each of these different areas. He is, in fact, the complete musician.

Few familiar with his film scores for *Murder on the Orient Express*, *Nicholas and Alexandra*, *Far From the Madding Crowd*, *Equus* and *Yanks*, to name but a handful, would connect him with the opera *The Mines of Sulphur*, the advanced choral work *Spells* and the concertos he has written for an astonishing variety of instruments. He studied with Lennox Berkeley and Howard Ferguson in London before taking private lessons from Pierre Boulez in Paris. His Second Symphony, which was commissioned by Leonard Bernstein and the New York Philharmonic, made his reputation in the United States, where he now lives. He is underrated in his own country, of course.

Worth investigating

The Mines of Sulphur, opera (1963)
Aubade, orchestral (1964)
Guitar Concerto (1970): dedicated to Julian Bream, who has also made the definitive

recording; serialism in the first movement, Latin-American brio in the finale.
Four-Piece Suite, for two pianos (1974): samba, blues, ragtime and rock.

Alban BERG

'The best music always results from ecstasies of logic' (Berg)

Born: 9 February 1885, Vienna
Died: 24 December 1935, Vienna
Type of music: Serialist; opera, concerto, chamber, twelve-note
Influences: Mahler, Richard Strauss and (especially) Schoenberg
Contemporaries: Edgard Varèse, Charles Griffes, George Butterworth, **BERG**, Eric Coates, Marcel Dupré, VILLA-LOBOS, Bohuslav Martinů, Jacques Ibert

HIS LIFE AND MUSIC

For those who enjoy twelve-note music, Berg is the most expressive and accessible of the group of composers who use this technique. The best known are Arnold Schoenberg, Anton Webern and Berg – the so-called Second Viennese School. Very little of Berg's music is known to the general public, though his most important works have been much played and were composed sixty and more years ago. Conductors and programme planners have doggedly included them in concerts, and productions of his operatic masterpiece *Wozzeck* come and go, but the broad spectrum of music lovers remain impervious. However, there are some enriching pieces and, in most, behind the atonality are glimpses of the more conventional worlds of Mahler and Richard Strauss. All you need is perseverance.

Berg came from a musical family and, without any formal training, had written a group of songs by the age of fifteen. He worked as a clerk in the government and then, in 1904, met Schoenberg, an event that proved to be the turning point of his life. Over the following six years, their relationship developed from master and pupil into one of friend and colleague. Berg's move away from conventional harmony was gradual, but his music attracted fierce hostility. The first performance of his 'Altenberg' Songs in 1913 provoked a riot, and the premiere of *Wozzeck* – for which the conductor, Erich Kleiber, needed no less than 137 rehearsals – produced a storm of violent criticism. 'I had the sensation of having been not in a public theatre but in an insane asylum. On the stage, in the orchestra, in the stalls – plain madmen,' thundered the *Deutsche Zeitung*. Undeterred, Berg followed *Wozzeck* with the Chamber Concerto, dedicated to Schoenberg on his fiftieth birthday, and a second opera *Lulu*. With the Nazis' rise to power, Berg's music was labelled 'degenerate', and as performances of his work diminished, so did his income. Work on *Lulu* was interrupted by the composition of his Violin Concerto in the spring of 1935, and the opera was left incomplete. In September he was bitten by an insect, which caused an abscess on his back. Though this was treated, three months later the abscess burst internally, and he died, despite two operations, from blood poisoning at the age of fifty-one.

Essential works

Wozzeck, opera (1923): based the play by Georg Büchner, the opera compresses the twenty-five scenes of the original into fifteen, using traditional musical forms such as the passacaglia, sonata and fugue. The music is as tough and unedifying as the plot, which concerns the gradual destruction of a simple-minded soldier.

Violin Concerto (1935): Berg's most lyrical and accessible work is also one of the few modern masterpieces for the instrument. It is dedicated 'to the memory of an angel', inspired by the death of Manon Gropius, the eighteen-year-old daughter of Alma Mahler by her second marriage. There is a quite stunning moment at the end when Berg introduces Bach's chorale *Es ist Genug* (*It is enough*) into his own sound world.

Three movements from the Lyric Suite (1929): string arrangements of three of the six movements from the *Lyric Suite* for string quartet.

Piano Sonata, Op.1 (?1907–08): an early work written when Berg had begun studying with Schoenberg, before he had fully formed his own style; of interest for that fact alone.

Hector BERLIOZ

'A lark as great as an eagle' (Heine)

Born: 11 December 1803, La Côte-Saint-André, near Grenoble, Isère
Died: 8 March 1869, Paris
Full name: Louis-Hector Berlioz
Type of music: Romantic; symphony, orchestral, opera, choral, song
Influences: Beethoven, Lesueur, Goethe, literature and the fine arts
Contemporaries: BELLINI, Josef Lanner, Albert Lortzing, ADAM, **BERLIOZ**, GLINKA, Julius Benedict, Johan Peter Hartmann, Michael William Balfe

HIS LIFE

The life of Berlioz, the arch-Romantic composer, was all that you'd expect: turbulent, passionate, ecstatic and melancholic by turn, eccentric, excessive and egotistic. His influence on modern orchestral sound was profound; he propagated the idea of programme music (music that describes works of art or literature). It was a remarkable life and the best account of it is his own, which is arguably the finest autobiography of any composer.

1803 Berlioz's father, a country doctor practising near Grenoble, was musical enough to give his son his first lessons on the flute, but was against music as a career. Later, Berlioz took up the guitar but, unusually for a composer, never became proficient on any instrument.

1821 At his father's behest, he entered the school of medicine in Paris in order to become a doctor, while also taking private music lessons from Jean-François Lesueur. In 1824 he abandoned his medical studies in order to devote himself entirely to music and, aged twenty-two, enrolled at the Paris Conservatoire, where he learned composition from Lesueur and counterpoint and fugue from Anton Reicha.

1827–30 In September 1827, Berlioz became infatuated with the Irish actress Harriet Smithson after he'd seen her as Ophelia in a production of *Hamlet*. Berlioz knew no English, Miss Smithson knew no French, and his attempts to contact her met with no success: he bombarded her with love letters, which at first startled and then terrified her; he put on a concert of his works to impress her; he rented rooms near her – all to no avail. Instead, he transferred his affections to a young pianist, Camille Moke, who became a kind of surrogate Harriet.

Over the following three years, Berlioz worked on a symphony, a musical autobiography, a gigantic love letter to the real object of his affections, which became his most enduring masterpiece, *Symphonie fantastique*. It received its first performance at the Paris Conservatoire in December 1830, a date Berlioz timed to coincide with the return to Paris of his *grande passion*. The work was given to great acclaim, though Miss Smithson was not present at the occasion. 'Alas!' wrote Berlioz, "I learned afterwards that, absorbed in her own brilliant career, she never even heard of my name, my struggles, my concert, or my success!' What that astute critic Robert Schumann wrote of Berlioz the musician was equally true of Berlioz the man: 'Berlioz does not try to be pleasing and elegant; what he hates, he grasps fiercely by the hair; what he loves, he almost crushes in his fervour' – proof, if any were needed, of Berlioz's Romantic credentials, where the artist is as important as his art.

During this period, *père* Berlioz had become thoroughly disenchanted with his son's lack of progress and recognition, an attitude not unconnected with his son's inability to win the Prix de Rome, and withdrew all financial support, refusing to pay the enormous debts his son had run up.

The ultimate accolade for a student of music was to win this prestigious bursary, bestowed by the French Academy of Fine Arts since 1803. The recipient was entitled to study *gratis* in Rome for four years, living at the Villa Medici. No wonder it was fought for so competitively; students were locked up in a room for some days while they carried out the task of composing a cantata on a given subject. Berlioz's first effort was rejected in 1827; his next won second prize in 1828; he tried again in 1829, but no awards were given that year. Finally, at the fourth attempt, he won the prize with *La mort de Sardanapale*, though it was so poorly performed that Berlioz angrily threw the score at the musicians.

1830–33 Berlioz duly set off for Italy, but it proved to be a disaster. He did not take kindly to prescribed musical rules, and he disliked both the food and the music. When rumours reached him that Camille had taken a lover, he was incandescent with rage and left Rome for Paris, disguised as a lady's maid and with the intention of killing both Camille and her *amour*. While in Genoa, however, Berlioz mislaid his disguise, and the delay in finding a replacement gave him time to cool down. He returned meekly to Rome.

Back in Paris in 1832, he discovered Harriet was also in the city and arranged a second performance of the *Symphonie fantastique* for her. This time, the bewildered actress came,

heard and was conquered. After a feverish courtship, including an attempted suicide in her presence to prove the intensity of his feelings for her, Berlioz and Harriet Smithson were married in October 1833. 'We trust,' wrote the ungallant Court Journal, 'this marriage will ensure the happiness of an amiable young woman, as well as secure us against her reappearance on the English boards.'

1834–40 Predictably, the marriage was not a success. Before the wedding service, the bride broke her leg, and throughout their life together she suffered a series of debilitating illnesses. Alas for Berlioz, his wife turned out to be a shrew and, very soon afterwards, an alcoholic as well. After a volatile few years spent in poverty, they decided to live apart. Berlioz took up with a second-rate singer, Marie Recio, but never quite forgot Harriet, to whom he was solicitous and tender towards the end of her life when she had become an invalid. Harriet died in March 1853. A year later, Berlioz married Marie, a scarcely more successful partnership in which he again outlived his wife.

The concert that brought Harriet and Berlioz together introduced an important benefactor to the impoverished composer. Niccolò Paganini, then at the height of his considerable fame, commissioned from Berlioz a work for his newly acquired viola. The result was *Harold en Italie*, inspired by Byron's poem 'Childe Harold', but whereas Paganini had hoped for a virtuoso concerto for the unusual combination of viola and orchestra, Berlioz wrote a symphony with a viola obbligato – it did not produce the effect Paganini required, and he never played it. Throughout the following two decades, Berlioz composed industriously. His work was controversial (after all, he was the avant-garde of his day) and increasingly successful. He received commissions from the government, he became a music critic (from 1833 to 1863 he wrote for the influential *Journal des débats*), and he began his career as a conductor. In 1838, so legend has it, Paganini reappeared in Berlioz's life: after a performance of the rejected Viola Concerto on 16 December, the great violinist appeared on stage and knelt in homage to him, overwhelmed by hearing for the first time the work he had commissioned. The next day, he sent a message to Berlioz: 'Beethoven is dead and Berlioz alone can revive him.' With it came a cheque for 20,000 francs.

The money enabled Berlioz to write the ambitious work he had always dreamed of – the dramatic symphony, *Roméo et Juliette*, in which he relived his first feelings of love on seeing Harriet Smithson. The symphony was given its premiere in the following November and in the audience was the young, unknown composer, Richard Wagner. It took him by storm and 'impetuously fanned the flame of my personal feeling for music and poetry'.

1840–69 With another government commission for a large-scale work, *Grande symphonie funèbre et triomphale*, Berlioz's orchestral writing entered a period of unsurpassed grandeur and grandiloquence. The large numbers of musicians he employed to play his works, and those of others, had never been assembled before. It is said that he conducted the *Grande symphonie* with a drawn sword while marching through the streets of Paris. In 1844 he conducted a concert that included Beethoven's Fifth Symphony performed with thirty-six double basses, Weber's overture to *Der*

Freischütz with twenty-four French horns and *Moses' Prayer* (from Rossini's opera) with twenty-five harps – 1,022 performers in all. This was exceeded in 1855 by an orchestra, military band and chorus of 1,200 assembled for his celebratory *L'impériale*. How did he keep them all in time? By activating an 'electric metronome' in his left hand, with the signal being passed on to five sub-conductors, and holding the baton in his right hand. Such excesses prompted a barrage of ridicule from sceptical critics and caricaturists.

Tours of England and Russia ensued; a festival of his music at Weimar, produced by the ever-generous Liszt, was given in 1852; opera and stage compositions flowed from him; it looks like the portrait of a successful, admired composer. Yet, unlike Wagner and Liszt, Berlioz had no cult following; he wrote no solo works with which his name could appear regularly on concert programmes, and he had enormous difficulty in seeing his operas and stage works mounted regularly. The final years of Berlioz's life were miserable: he believed he was a failure as a composer and conductor in his own country, he knew his most productive days were over (a fact that deeply depressed him), his health began to give out, and his marriage was unhappy. The death, from yellow fever, of his only child, a son from his marriage to Harriet Smithson, came as a final blow.

At his funeral, his coffin was carried to its final resting place in Montmartre by Charles Gounod, Ambroise Thomas and other famous French musicians. The accompanying music was the funeral march from his *Grande symphonie funèbre et triomphale*.

HIS MUSIC

To read Berlioz's account of hearing music that he admired is to understand him as a musician and a man. 'My arteries quiver violently; tears … indicate only a condition which may be intensified. If the further stage is reached, muscles contract spasmodically; limbs tremble; feet and hands grow quite numb … I cannot see perfectly; I am giddy and half-fainting.' When Mendelssohn met him in Italy in 1832, he thought Berlioz 'a regular freak, without a vestige of talent', while Chopin was convinced 'he composes by splashing his pen over the manuscript and leaving the issue to chance.' Such a reaction from two such fastidious gentlemen is not a surprise. One has to turn to the poet Heinrich Heine to find someone who understood Berlioz's muse. In a wonderfully redolent phrase, he describes Berlioz as 'an immense nightingale, a lark as great as an eagle … the music causes me to dream of fabulous empires filled with fabulous sins.'

After Berlioz, the orchestra was never the same again. It wasn't just that he introduced at least two instruments as permanent members of the orchestral family (the cor anglais and the harp); he was also seduced by the potential sounds he could invent, the variety of colour that could be produced with a vast orchestral palette. Berlioz was constantly experimenting with different textures and instrumental combinations, the result, which he distilled in a famous treatise on orchestration, producing a wealth of innovations that influenced the whole course of music.

He was a pioneer, too, of programme music. His passion for Harriet Smithson was directly translated into sound, a tone-poem describing the artist's emotions. Liszt's symphonic poems are a direct result of Berlioz's, and Wagner's admiration for the *Symphonie fantastique* may well have influenced him in his use of *leitmotif* technique, for the whole piece is pinned together by a similar musical device, which Berlioz called the *idée fixe* – a recurrent musical theme, representing Harriet Smithson, which appears in all five movements.

It is true that Berlioz was not the most fecund melodist in the world; it might be claimed that his skill was greater than his inspiration, that the parts are greater than the whole. But who could deny the spine-tingling excitement of hearing the *Te Deum* or the *Grande messe des morts* for the first time; who could fail to fall under the spell of the *Symphonie fantastique* or *Roméo et Juliette;* who is not alert to the impending pleasures of a roller-coaster ride after the opening bars of *Le carnaval romain* or *Le corsaire* overtures – all vital, brilliant, bold, imperfect and original?

Essential works

Symphonie fantastique, Op.14 (1830): subtitled 'An Episode in the Life of an Artist', this five-movement symphony was Berlioz's first major work and remains his most popular. A young, sensitive musician with a vivid imagination has poisoned himself with opium in a fit of lovesick despair. The extraordinary visions he has form the programme of the symphony: *Artist's Reveries, The Ball, Scenes in the Country, The March to the Scaffold* and *Dream of the Witches' Sabbath*. It attracted its fair share of opprobrium; Schumann wrote, 'I believe that Berlioz, when a young student of medicine, never dissected the head of a handsome murderer with greater unwillingness than I feel in analysing his first movement,' while Rossini commented succinctly, 'What a good thing it isn't music.' The score was (later) dedicated, somewhat bizarrely, to the reactionary Tsar Nicholas I of Russia, perhaps because Berlioz had been welcomed to Russia in 1847.

Roméo et Juliette, Op.17 (1839): dramatic symphony for soloists, chorus and orchestra; the text is based on Shakespeare's play and is most usually encountered through orchestral excerpts such as the Love Music theme and the gossamer-like *Queen Mab* scherzo.

The Damnation of Faust, Op.24 (1845–46): performances of orchestral excerpts from Berlioz's 'dramatic legend' (as he described it) are far more frequent than of the whole opera. The most well-known are the *Will-o'the-Wisp* minuet, the *Dance of the Sylphs* (which Saint-Saëns caricatured in the *Carnival of the Animals* as *The Elephants*) and *Rákóczy March*; the latter, based on a Hungarian theme that had caught Berlioz's fancy, is a blazing orchestral showpiece.

Harold en Italie, Op.16 (1834): a successor to the *Symphonie fantastique*, the subtitle of the work is 'Symphony in G for viola and orchestra' and explains why Paganini was less than enthusiastic at seeing the work he had commissioned (see above). Berlioz was first inspired by his 'impressions recollected from wandering in the Abruzzi mountains'. The viola part is a kind of melancholy dreamer in the style of Byron's 'Childe Harold'.

Te Deum (1849): conceived on a vast scale, the score includes three choirs, and Berlioz directed that they should be placed at the opposite end of the church to the organ in order to maximise the antiphonal effect; the first performance in 1855, presented for the opening of the Universal Paris Exhibition, used 900 performers.

Grande messe des morts, Op.5 (1837): 'If I were threatened with the destruction of all my works but one, I would beg mercy for the *Messe des Morts*,' wrote the composer, who was a self-confessed agnostic. Its celebrated *Tuba Mirum* movement asks for four brass bands placed at the four points of the compass to conjure up the Day of Judgement. A work, in Berlioz's own words, of 'overwhelming and horrifying grandeur'.

Les Troyens (1856–58): this mammoth opera, inspired by Virgil's *Aeneid*, was not heard in its entirety in French until 1969. Berlioz divided it into two unequal parts: 'La prise de Troie' and 'Les troyens à Carthage'. He only lived to hear the second part; the first part was not given until 1890, and you are unlikely to hear a complete performance because the opera is simply too expensive to mount. Its most well-known passage is the *Royal Hunt and Storm*, after Act 1 (Part 2).

Les nuits d'été, Op.7 (1841): half a dozen settings of poems by Théophile Gautier for solo voice (generally sung by a soprano), these languid, serene songs constitute the first important song cycle in French, complementing the *Lieder* cycles of Schubert and Schumann.

La Marseillaise (1848): certainly not essential listening, but for an example of over-the-top kitsch, this bombastic setting of the French national anthem will almost persuade you to change nationality.

Overtures

Berlioz wrote some splendidly-rousing overtures. The three best known are:

Les francs-juges, Op.3 (1836): the intention was to write an opera about the *Vehmgerircht* or secret tribunal that flourished in Westphalia in the late medieval period; Berlioz abandoned the project after completing the overture. Its second theme served as the signature tune for the famous series of confrontational TV interviews in the early 1960s with John Freeman, *Face to Face*.

Le carnaval romain Overture, Op.9 (1844): originally the prelude to the second act of Berlioz's opera *Benvenuto Cellini* but composed half a dozen years after the opera's premiere in 1838. A dazzling display-piece for ensemble virtuosity.

Le corsaire Overture, Op.21 (1844): nothing to do with Byron's poem but inspired by James Fenimore Cooper's book, *The Red Rover*. The overture's original title was *Le corsaire rouge*, but while sketching it in Nice, Berlioz changed it to *Le tour de Nice*. He eventually reverted to a version of his original title, but it is essentially a sea piece.

Other overtures

Waverley, Op.1 (1828)
Le roi Lear, Op.4 (1831)
Rob Roy (1831)

Leonard BERNSTEIN

'A born entertainer of a superior sort' (D. Henehan, *New York Times*)

Born: 25 August 1918, Lawrence, Massachusetts
Died: 14 October 1990, New York
Original name: Louis Bernstein
Type of music: symphony, orchestral, opera, ballet, musical, chamber, film, song
Influences: Hindemith, Copland, Jewish music, jazz, twelve-note
Contemporaries: Humphrey Searle, Alberto Ginastera, **BERNSTEIN**,
Peter Fricker, Harold Shapero, ARNOLD, Lukas Foss, György Liget, Ned Rorem

HIS LIFE AND MUSIC

Has there been a more compelling, ebullient one-man band this century? 'One-man bridge' would be a more appropriate description, for, like no other musician of his age, he was able to straddle the extremes of the musical world – an intellectual, a composer who wrote complex symphonies and twelve-note music but who was equally happy playing the piano and writing Broadway musicals, he was able to take his adoring public

with him along most of the roads he chose to travel. His appetite for music and his zest for life, his passion to share his enthusiasms, his versatility and energy leave one quite breathless. As a conductor, composer, educator and pianist, 'Lenny' was to dominate American musical life for four decades.

He was born Louis, the son of Russian-Jewish immigrants, but changed his name by deed poll at the age of sixteen to avoid confusion with other Louis Bernsteins in the family. He had private piano lessons as a child before going to Harvard University, where a succession of distinguished mentors oversaw the development of a prodigious talent: Walter Piston and Edward Burlingame Hill for counterpoint, fugue and orchestration, followed,

at the Curtis Institute, by Fritz Reiner for conducting and Isabella Vengerova for piano. Scholarships enabled Bernstein to attend courses at the Berkshire Music Center at Tanglewood, Massachusetts in 1940 and 1941, where he received tuition under the renowned conductor, publisher and patron Serge Koussevitzky.

Bernstein became Koussevitzky's assistant at Tanglewood, before being made assistant to the legendary Artur Rodzinski at the New York Philharmonic. Fairy-tale stuff, and better was to come. In November 1943 Rodzinski was out of town and the young Bernstein was called upon at short notice to take over the conducting of a difficult programme for the indisposed Bruno Walter. Bernstein scored a huge personal triumph: he became famous overnight and the occasion heralded one of the most brilliant conducting careers in American history, crowned by his being made the first American-born conductor of the New York Philharmonic in 1958. He resigned in 1969, to give more time to composition, as 'conductor laureate'. His animal energy on the podium was compulsive, though the 'choreography' and histrionic mannerisms could become tedious, taking the focus from the music he was conducting. But few baton-wavers have ever crossed the footlights so effectively. Fewer still have managed to convey the rewards of classical music to those encountering it for the first time. In concerts, books, on radio and television, Bernstein was the supreme communicator, and the Young People's Concerts he presented from 1958 to 1973 introduced thousands to the music he so obviously loved.

Bernstein seemed to need little time before discovering his own distinctive style, strongly lyrical, jazz-slanted and redolent of his Jewish heritage. The forties and fifties saw the appearance of a bewildering variety of musical works in all shapes and forms, including his Symphonies 1 & 2, Clarinet Sonata, *Prelude, Fugue and Riffs*, his film score for *On The Waterfront* (1954), as well as a Broadway career. The latter developed as a result of his 1944 ballet *Fancy Free*, subsequently adapted into the musical comedy *On The Town;* that in turn led to another, *Wonderful Town*, and then, most spectacularly, to *West Side Story* (glumly dubbed by some commentators 'a social music drama'). Less commercially successful, but with interesting and delightful scores were the comedy operetta, *Candide*, and the one-act opera *Trouble In Tahiti*. He supplied his own text; his other writing talents included poetry. In the sixties came a series of religious works; his Symphony No.3 'Kaddish', the Chichester Psalms, commissioned by the Dean of Chichester in England and first performed in 1965, and a Mass, written for the opening of the John F. Kennedy Center for the Performing Arts in Washington, D.C. in 1971.

Bernstein married the Chilean actress Felicia Montealagre in 1951 (she died in 1978) but his sexual drive was devoted mainly to members of his own sex. The story goes that one young man was due to go to America to study with Bernstein. 'Be careful,' his father warned. 'Leonard Bernstein is gay.' The young man looked up in wonder. 'Is there *nothing* that man can't do?'

Essential works

Candide Overture (1956): arguably the best of Bernstein's work is his theatre music, although one could describe all his compositions as theatre music). The breathless four minutes of this tongue-in-cheek orchestral firework make it the theatrical curtain-raiser *par excellence.*

Symphony No.2 'The Age of Anxiety' (1949): as an introduction to Bernstein's serious side (as opposed to his West Side) you could do far worse than start with this reflection on the poem by W.H. Auden. The symphony makes a difficult first listen (although the jazzy scherzo is winningly on-Broadway) but is ultimately rewarding.

Musicals

Fancy Free (1944): ballet score, also an excellent orchestral suite.

On The Town (1944); **Wonderful Town** (1953); **Candide** (1956)

West Side Story (1957): the score was also converted into an effective suite.

Harrison BIRTWISTLE

Born: 15 July 1934, Accrington, Lancashire
Full title: Sir Harrison Birtwistle
Type of music: orchestral, opera, chamber
Influences: Stravinsky, Varèse, Greek drama
Contemporaries: Hugh Wood, GÓRECKI, Krzysztof Penderecki, **BIRTWISTLE**, DAVIES, PÄRT, Cornelius Cardew, BENNETT, Steve Reich, Philip Glass

HIS LIFE AND MUSIC

'Uncompromising', 'tough', 'hard-edged', 'violent' are just some of the reactions to the work of music's newest notable knight. You certainly don't go to him for a comfortable time. Tenderness, as with most of his contemporaries, is at a premium.

Birtwistle began his career in music as a clarinet player, one of the so-called Manchester School. Among his contemporaries at the Royal Manchester (now Northern) College of Music were Alexander Goehr and Peter Maxwell Davies, as well as the conductor Elgar Howarth and pianist John Ogdon. His Wind Quintet *Refrains and Choruses* first drew attention to his work in 1957, revealing a ready-formed and distinctive voice, but it wasn't until 1968 that he became internationally known with his controversial chamber opera *Punch and Judy*. Despite its being hailed variously as 'the first truly modern opera' and 'Britain's only modern opera', Benjamin Britten walked out of the premiere at Aldeburgh in 1968.

Since then: *The Triumph of Time, Secret Theatre*, held by some to be his finest achievement, the Trumpet Concerto *Endless Parade*, the mammoth opera *Gawain*, and the torrential work-out for saxophone *Panic* (1995) have put him in the vanguard of contemporary British music, some way from the pastoral idylls of Vaughan Williams.

Essential works

Punch and Judy, opera (1966–67)
The Triumph of Time for orchestra (1972): inspired by the Brueghel engraving.
Secret Theatre for orchestra (1984): the title is taken from a Robert Graves poem.

Gawain, opera (1991): there is also a suite, *Gawain's Journey*, drawn from the opera's salient passages.
Endless Parade (1987): trumpet concerto scored for vibraphone and strings.

Georges BIZET

'Let us have fantasy, boldness, unexpectedness, enchantment – above all tenderness, morbidezza!*'* (Bizet)

Born: 25 October 1838, Paris
Died: 3 June 1875, Bougival
Original name: Alexandre César Léopold Bizet
Type of music: symphony, orchestral, opera, piano
Influences: Mendelssohn, Rossini, Gounod, Verdi, Wagner
Contemporaries: SAINT-SAËNS, DELIBES, BALAKIREV, Emile Waldteufel, **BIZET**, BRUCH, MUSSORGSKY, Josef Rheinberger, Sir John Stainer, TCHAIKOWSKY

HIS LIFE

Mention Bizet and one thinks of *Carmen*; most people have to think hard to name another work. Perhaps it comes as a surprise to learn that he began his career as a child prodigy on the piano, entering the Paris Conservatoire when he was only nine. (He was the son of professional musicians, his father a singing teacher, his mother a fine pianist herself.) He wrote approximately 150 pieces for the piano; by the age of seventeen he had written his first symphony, quite the equal of anything Mozart or Mendelssohn wrote at the same age. He won the coveted Prix de Rome in 1857 and went to Italy to study, joined two years later by his lifelong friend Ernest Guiraud, the 1859 prize winner. It was a promising start and his natural talent soon attracted attention. Then it all went off course.

Bizet's problem was his inability to decide on any one project; those he did choose generally turned out to be failures. Throughout the 1860s, Bizet wrote a string of unsuccessful operas. He had an unerring eye for a weak libretto and unfailingly set them to uneven music, in such works as *The Pearl Fishers* and *The Fair Maid of Perth*. Ideas that initially filled him with enthusiasm were eventually abandoned and he found it difficult to focus his creative energies, happy to settle for an undemanding way of life. This included a relationship with the fantastic adventuress Céleste Mogador, his neighbour in Le Vésinet, the little village just outside Paris where Bizet lived in the cottage his father had built, overlooking the banks of the Seine. By the time he was thirty, he had little to show for all his early promise.

He was a plump young man with a short temper and an addiction to chocolate, cakes and *petits fours*, always to be seen elegantly dressed and invariably nibbling a bonbon. In 1869 he married the daughter of Jacques Halévy, his old professor at the Conservatoire and the composer of an immensely popular opera of the day, *La juive*. Incidentally, Geneviève Bizet was later to become the model for Proust's Princesse de Guermantes in *À la recherche du temps perdu*. More aborted schemes followed and then, slowly, things began to take shape. Bizet wrote the opera *Djamileh* in 1872. Although it was another disastrous failure – due in part to the miscasting of the title role – many discerned an originality and lyrical gift that hitherto had not been recognized (the opera later became a great favourite of Mahler's). Earlier in 1871, Bizet had written some delightful pieces for piano duet entitled *Jeux d'enfants*. At the same time he received a commission from the Opéra-Comique and was able to write to a friend of 'the absolute certainty of having found my path.' The libretto was by Henri Meilhac and Ludovic Halévy, a cousin of Bizet's wife, two experienced men of the theatre who had provided the libretti for some of Offenbach's successes. The opera was to be *Carmen*. Meanwhile, Bizet had produced the incidental music for Daudet's play *L'arlésienne*. In the theatre, the piece was a failure but, having rescored some of the music and formed it into a suite, Bizet found he had a success on his hands at last.

The struggle to mount *Carmen* and the reaction of the first night audience to the subject matter of the opera must, however, have disheartened Bizet even further. A low-life tale of passion and murder set against a background of gypsies, thieves and cigarette-makers, and the sight of girls smoking on the stage, to say nothing of the depraved character of Carmen herself, led to running battles with the opera management. It was not quite what the puritanical, middle-class Parisian audience was used to. 'A definite and hopeless flop,' Bizet pronounced after *Carmen*'s unenthusiastic reception. In fact, he had been paid a handsome 25,000 francs for the score of the opera by his publisher and had been made a Chevalier of the Légion d'honneur on the eve of the premiere of the opera, yet he was right in his initial assessment. Fate decreed that he should not live long enough to see his masterpiece widely acclaimed. On the evening of the

JIM

thirty-first performance of *Carmen*, Bizet died of a heart attack brought on by a throat affliction (probably cancer), from which he had suffered intermittently since his days in Rome. He was thirty-six years old. Had Bizet lived another few months he would have experienced *Carmen*'s total triumph; another three years and he would have seen it produced in almost every major opera house in Europe.

HIS MUSIC

It is one of musical history's cruellest blows that after so many doubts and set-backs, Bizet's life should be extinguished at the point when he had completed the first work of his maturity. Hampered by poor libretti, and uneven in invention, only his innate lyrical gift and melodic power shine through in the earlier operas. In *Carmen*, Bizet showed the way forward for French opera, aided by a strong libretto that inspired him to portray real life on stage, tackling complex emotions and powerful actions with truth and passion. In Meyerbeer's day, French opera had been concerned primarily with spectacle and melodrama. Gounod had refined the genre with economy and sensitivity and Bizet, adding a feeling for atmosphere and rich orchestration to his great melodic gifts, adopted the Wagnerian device of *leitmotif*, unifying the texture of the whole work. In his French way, Bizet was seeking to do what Mussorgsky was doing in his Russian way and what, shortly, the Italians would be doing with their *verismo* operas. What, one asks, might he have achieved had he been granted a longer life?

Essential works

Carmen, opera (1874): Brahms said 'I would go the ends of the earth to embrace the composer of *Carmen*.' The story of the bewitching dark-eyed gypsy girl who seduces the army corporal, Don José, and then rejects him in favour of the matador, Escamillo, has entranced audiences for nearly 125 years. With *Aida*, and *La bohème*, *Carmen* is the 'C' in the ABC of the world's most popular operas. It is a vibrant drama full of contrasting mood and emotion, colourfully scored, with exciting rhythms and exotic, melodic music. Bizet worked hard on the score to increase dramatic tension, cutting and rewriting sections; he had to revise the famous Habanera fourteen times to accommodate the first Carmen, Galli-Marié. The first complete recording of the opera was made in 1908 and covered thirty-six sides of 78-r.p.m. discs; it was filmed in the following year. There have been no less than fourteen screen versions, and a stage adaptation by Oscar Hammerstein II entitled *Carmen Jones* (1945), which was given a superb revival in London in 1991. Many composers have written works based on themes from the opera, most notably Pablo Sarasate and Franz Waxman for violin, and Ferruccio Busoni and Vladimir Horowitz for piano; there are also two *Carmen* Suites, which are purely orchestral arrangements of the music.

Among the string of well-known tunes from the opera are 'L'amour est un oiseau rebelle' ('Love is a bird that's hard to tame') – the Habanera, which Bizet mistakenly included, thinking that the melody was a folk song when it was in fact a song called 'El Arreglito' by the Spanish composer Yradier; 'Près des remparts de Séville' ('Near the ramparts of Seville'), also from Act 1; 'Les tringles des sistres tintaient' ('To the sound of tambourines') from Act 2 known as the 'Chanson bohème', Carmen's wild dance at the inn of Lillas Pastia; the 'Toreador's Song' (perhaps the best-known baritone aria in all opera) and 'La fleur que tu m'avais jetée' ('The flower that you threw me'), Don José's declaration of love for Carmen.

The Pearl Fishers (1863): much admired by Berlioz ('It does M. Bizet the greatest honour')

Les pêcheurs de perles is set on the island of Ceylon (Sri Lanka) in ancient times. From it comes the Act 1 duet for tenor and baritone, 'Au fond du temple saint' ('In the depths of the temple'), in which the fishermen Nadir and Zurga recall the love they both had for the same beautiful girl. Listeners to Classic fM and BBC Radio 2 have voted this their favourite piece of classical music, especially in the historic recording by Jussi Björling and Robert Merrill.

Symphony in C (1855): this student work remained completely unknown until 1933 when the composer Reynaldo Hahn handed it over to the Paris Conservatoire with a bundle of other manuscripts. Rossini, Mendelssohn and Gounod in particular loom large, but it is a remarkable work, composed in less than a month when Bizet was barely seventeen. There is also a contemporaneous but virtually unknown **Overture in A**, *à la* Rossini and great fun.

L'arlésienne Suite No.1 (1872): Bizet's most famous orchestral work was fashioned from the music written for Daudet's drama, set in the Provençal city of Arles. As in *Carmen* and *The Pearl Fishers*, Bizet shows an extraordinary ability to evoke the spirit of a particular country or region, here through the simulation of Provençal rhythms and folk songs. The opening Prelude is often heard separately. There is also a Suite No.2, adapted by Ernest Guiraud, which is not heard as frequently.

Jeux d'enfants (1871): these twelve piano duets are unmissable, innocent delights and conclude with the famous Galop – another of those pieces you can never put a name to. Five of them were orchestrated by Bizet.

Also worth investigating

The Fair Maid of Perth, opera (1866): loosely based on the novel by Sir Walter Scott, *La jolie fille de Perth* contains the celebrated Serenade in Act 2, made popular years ago in a recording by the British tenor, Heddle Nash.

Variations chromatiques (1868): for those who are interested in Bizet the pianist, this is an intriguing and revealing work.

Luigi BOCCHERINI
(1743–1805)

Minuet, c.1775

Who knows Boccherini's name today for any reason other than this celebrated minuet, used in films and television possibly more than any other piece as a shorthand way of conveying eighteenth-century elegance and refinement? Many will remember it being used with ironic effect in the 1955 Ealing comedy *The Ladykillers* with Peter Sellers, Herbert Lom *et al*.

The Minuet in A comes from the String Quintet in E Op.13 No.3, published in about 1775. It is always called 'Boccherini's Minuet', which is meaningless, because he wrote hundreds of *other* minuets – you might just as well say 'Schubert's Song' or 'Beethoven's Sonata'. He also wrote a further 124 string quintets, 102 string quartets and an enormous amount of other chamber music.

Boccherini was highly regarded during his life, so much so that he was referred to as 'the wife of Haydn', musically speaking, of course! Much of what he wrote is very fine and ought to be better-known – his piano quintets, for example, his eight surviving guitar quintets (No.4 in D has an infectiously-lively Fandango finale), and the once-popular Cello Sonata in A. Boccherini was a cello virtuoso, and of his eleven concertos for the instrument, the one in G major (G480 from 1770) is worth investigating. But the concerto that is most often heard today is in an arrangement by the nineteenth-century cellist Friedrich Grützmacher (Concerto in B flat, G482), a romantic conflation of two different works. It is the only Boccherini piece that is still played regularly, apart from 'the' minuet.

Alexander BORODIN

'Music… is a relaxation from more serious occupations' (Borodin)

Born: 12 November 1833, St Petersburg
Died: 27 February 1887, St Petersburg
Type of music: opera, symphony, chamber, piano, vocal
Influences: Schumann, Glinka, Mendelssohn, Balakirev and the Russian nationalist school, and Ekaterina Protopopova
Contemporaries: RUBINSTEIN, Karl Goldmark, Joseph Joachim, **BORODIN**, BRAHMS, Julius Reubke, PONCHIELLI, Henryk Wieniawski, César Cui

HIS LIFE AND MUSIC

Few people get two bites at the cherry, but Borodin is a rare example. No other great composer, with the arguable exception of Charles Ives, has achieved equal eminence in another, entirely different field of work. For a full-time, professional scientist to compose works of such originality and beauty as the Polovtzian Dances (from his opera, *Prince Igor*) and the String Quartet No.2 in D is a minor miracle. Borodin's first published work was not song or a sonata but a paper entitled 'On the Action of Ethyl Iodide on Hydrobenzamide and Amarine'; his first tour of Europe was not as a concert pianist but for scientific study.

Borodin's origins were as exceptional: he was the illegitimate son of a Georgian prince, Ghedeanov, and the wife of an army doctor. As was customary, he was registered as the lawful child of one of Ghedeanov's serfs, Porfiry Borodin. He learnt to speak several languages and was taught to play the flute, but it was his love of and natural bent for science and, in particular, chemistry, that dominated his professional life. He graduated with honours from the Academy of Medicine in St Petersburg in 1856 and by the mid-1860s was a Professor in the Academy of Physicians. No wonder that so much of his music was abandoned or left incomplete at his death – his public duties as an eminent scientist and research chemist left him little time for systematic composition, which, for Borodin, was, in any case, a slow process. Compared with Rimsky-Korsakov, his crafts-manship was modest, but his feeling for orchestral colour and rhythm, his melodic gift and innate evocative power were the equal of the other four Russian composers, the 'inspired dillettantes', who became known as the Mighty Handful – Balakirev, Cui, Mussorgsky and Rimsky-Korsakov. Borodin's meeting with the charismatic Balakirev in 1862 produced the same effect on him as it had on the others: a passionate desire to write music that evoked Russia and its people. Much of his music reflects the enchanting, unique mix of the sensuous East and the melancholic Russian; the exotic Oriental strain dominates, a characteristic that greatly appealed to the young Debussy.

Borodin's wife, Ekaterina (or Catherine) Protopopova, whom he married in 1863, was an excellent pianist and, as an admirer of Schumann and Wagner, exerted no little influence on her husband's music. Liszt, too, aided Borodin's growing reputation by championing a number of his works. Borodin was in Germany in 1877 for scientific purposes but found time to visit the Wizard of Weimar, and the two men quickly became firm friends. Throughout the 1870s Borodin worked fitfully on various compositions but during the last decade of his life produced very little – the two String Quartets, *In the Steppes of Central Asia* and a Suite for piano.

After his death (from a burst artery in the heart) Rimsky-Korsakov and Glazunov, ever the generous colleagues, prepared and completed much of Borodin's music for perfor-mance. In 1953, Robert Wright and George Forrest, two American songwriters, produced their musical *Kismet*. The themes are taken almost entirely from Borodin's work: 'Stranger in Paradise' derived from the Polovtzian Dances, 'And this is my beloved' and 'Baubles, bangles and beads' from the String Quartet in D, 'Fate' from the Second Symphony and 'Sands of time' from *In the Steppes of Central Asia*.

Essential works

Polovtzian Dances: from his opera *Prince Igor*, this work was begun in 1869, completed posthumously by Rimsky-Korsakov and Glaz-unov and not given its first performance until 1890. The Dances were premiered separately in St Petersburg in 1879 and have remained a favourite on concert programmes ever since. The opera, which concerns the capture of Prince Igor by a Tartar race, the Polovtzi in the twelfth century, is rarely heard today.

Symphony No.2 in B minor (1869–76): begun in 1869, it took Borodin six years to complete this symphony; the critics and public, however, were indifferent both to the music and the ideals of the nationalist school. It is a lavish *tour de force*, a kind of Oriental Tchaikowsky.

In the Steppes of Central Asia, a 'symphonic sketch', (1880): the archetypal Borodin juxta-position of folk-based Oriental and Russian characteristics, this is a musical picture of a caravan approaching, crossing the desert escorted by Russian soldiers and then dis-appearing into the distant horizon.

String Quartet No.2 in D (1881): the tender Nocturne (its third movement) is probably better known as 'And this is my beloved' from the musical *Kismet*, but the whole work, written in the unusually (for Borodin) short time of two months has a lyrical, amorous tone – it was dedicated to his wife to mark the twentieth anniversary of their first meeting.

Petite Suite for piano (1885)

Scherzo in A flat (1885)

Borodin was not primarily a piano composer but the *Au couvent* movement of the suite and the will-o'-the-wisp scherzo, recorded by Rachmaninov, are so distinctive that they should not be forgotten.

Johannes BRAHMS

'Bach the Father, Beethoven the Son, Brahms the Holy Ghost'

Born: 7 May 1833, Hamburg
Died: 3 April 1897, Vienna
Type of music: symphony, orchestral, chamber, choral, piano, vocal
Influences: Bach, Beethoven, Mendelssohn, Schumann
Contemporaries: Karl Goldmark, Joseph Joachim, BORODIN, **BRAHMS**, Julius Reubke, PONCHIELLI, Henryk Wieniawski, César Cui, SAINT-SAËNS

Eduard Marxsen, who taught the young Brahms, heard of Mendelssohn's death in 1847 and said: 'A master of the art is gone; a greater one arises in Brahms.' This was a remarkably accurate prediction to make about a fourteen-year-old student. The two remained friends for the rest of Marxsen's life, and Brahms dedicated his great Piano Concerto in B flat to him.

HIS LIFE

Johannes was the middle child of the family; he had an elder sister and a younger brother. Brahms' father was an impecunious double-bass player who eventually proved good enough for the Hamburg Philharmonic.

1839 At the age of six, Johannes was discovered to have perfect pitch and a natural talent for the piano.

1843 He made his first public appearance playing chamber music at the age of ten. A passing American impresario heard him, and offered the *Wunderkind* an American tour; however, this opportunity was forbidden by his teacher, Otto Cossel, wisely passing the boy over to Eduard Marxsen, who, incidentally, taught Brahms free of charge.

To supplement his income, the teenager played in taverns and, some say, bordellos. It remains debatable whether this period left its psychological scars. His parents were an ill-matched couple and, as a child, he frequently witnessed their violent arguments. Brahms never married – some have suggested impotence as the reason but, though he came close to it on several occasions, he could never quite take the plunge and seems to have resorted to prostitutes when the need arose. In the 1880s, so the story goes, Brahms entered a rather dubious establishment and was accosted by a well-known prostitute with the greeting 'Professor, play us some dance music,' whereupon the great composer sat down at the piano and entertained the assembled company. Brahms sublimated his love of and desire for women in his music. 'At least,' he said, recognizing his awkwardness with women, 'it has saved me from opera and marriage.'

1853 Brahms had been trying his hand at composition since 1848, but when he met up with the Hungarian violinist, Eduard Reményi, he leapt at the chance of becoming his accompanist and they went off on tour. It proved to be a fortuitous move. In Hanover, he was introduced to Reményi's old student friend, the violinist Joseph Joachim, who was only twenty-two years old but already held the position of Konzertmaster to the king. Brahms and Joachim formed a firm friendship, and Joachim, who was part of the Liszt circle, took Brahms with him to Weimar to meet the great man.

Of more significance was Joachim's introduction to Robert and Clara Schumann, who were then living in Düsseldorf. A brief note in Schumann's diary records the event; it reads simply: 'Brahms to see me (a genius).' In his last article for the *Neue Zeitschrift für Musik*, Schumann described Brahms as a young eagle and predicted great things from him. In fact, the Schumanns became so enamoured of the young man that they invited him to move into their house. Schumann introduced Brahms to his publishers, Breitkopf and Hartel, who published his early works. When Schumann tried to commit suicide, Brahms was there at Clara's side to help and comfort; he was there with her when

Schumann died in 1856. There is little doubt that Brahms was in love with Clara, but it seems unlikely that the relationship ever developed beyond a platonic friendship. They decided to go their separate ways after Robert's death, but Brahms' correspondence with her reveals a deep spiritual and artistic affinity – it is clear this was probably the most profound human relationship Brahms was ever to experience.

Only a few years later, he was castigated by his friends for compromising a young singer, Agathe von Siebold. She inspired many songs and attracted him immensely, but after becoming engaged to her, he wrote: 'I love you. I must see you again. But I cannot wear fetters....' Agathe naturally broke off the engagement.

1859 Meanwhile, Brahms had written his magnificent First Piano Concerto. It was hissed at its premiere, and the following year (1860) there was further disappointment when he was turned down for the conductorship of the Hamburg Philharmonic. Then, an invitation to conduct in Vienna, his mother's death in 1865 and his father's remarriage, all served to loosen his ties with Hamburg.

1872 Eventually, Brahms decided to make the Austrian capital his base. His German Requiem and Alto Rhapsody, composed in the late 1860s, made him famous, but it was the following two decades that saw the flowering of his genius. He was offered the conductorship of the famed *Gesellschaft der Musikfreunde* in 1872 but was so consumed with the need to compose that he resigned from this post in 1875. Within three years he had completed his Symphonies No.1 & 2 and the Violin Concerto, as well as the 'Academic Festival' and 'Tragic' Overtures. From the rigours of conducting and playing his music all over Europe, Brahms escaped every summer to the country, to stay in Baden-Baden, where Clara Schumann had a house, or in Ischl, where his good friend Johann Strauss II had a villa.

1878 A trip to Italy with a surgeon friend was the first of many visits to a country he came to love. Masterpiece followed masterpiece in the 1880s: the B flat Piano Concerto, the Third and Fourth Symphonies and the Concerto for violin and cello.

1890 onwards Brahms abandoned larger forms to concentrate on chamber music and more intimate, personal piano works, all tinged with nostalgia and a warm glow of autumnal romanticism. Perhaps they reflected a growing realization of life's transience: it seemed as though all those who mattered to him were dying, and the death of Clara Schumann in 1896 affected him deeply. His appearance deteriorated, his energy disappeared and he was persuaded to see a doctor. Only months after Clara's death, he too had died, like his father, from cancer of the liver.

Brahms had much in common with Beethoven. Both were short in stature and bad-tempered; neither was able or willing to have a lasting relationship with a woman; both were lovers of the countryside – they even walked about Vienna in the same way, with head forward and hands clasped behind the back. Like Beethoven, Brahms had an unhappy childhood and was a prickly, uncompromising man. He nevertheless had a wonderfully generous side to him, giving his help and encouragement to such young composers as Dvořák and Grieg. A sociable man who attracted many friends, Brahms could nevertheless be remarkably tactless on occasion; he could be blunt to the point of gruffness and was grumpy and cruelly sarcastic in later life. These characteristics did not help his relationships with other people. After one party in Vienna, Brahms is said to have left with the words, 'If there's anybody here I haven't insulted, I apologise.'

As a young man he was striking to look at, with fair hair and bright blue eyes, although his high-pitched voice annoyed him. The mental picture most people have of Brahms is of the successful and corpulent man with a long white beard, seen playing the piano or with an ever-present cigar in his mouth. Even when financially secure he enjoyed a humble lifestyle, eating at cheap restaurants and drinking a great deal of beer.

His one indulgence was music manuscripts. At one time he owned the score of Mozart's G minor Symphony and Wagner's *Tannhäuser*. (The latter was given to him by the pianist Carl Tausig but it turned out that it was not Tausig's to give and Wagner gently requested its return; Brahms did so and received an autographed copy of *Das Rheingold* instead.)

Brahms was always more the sturdy Prussian than the elegant Viennese. He dressed in loose-fitting clothes and was decidedly untidy in appearance – a contrast to his scores, which were models of clarity and legibility. His North German allegiance was shown most clearly in his desire to see a Europe dominated by Germany in both the military and the philosophical sense. In his workroom he kept a bust of Bismarck, the 'Iron Chancellor', crowned with a laurel wreath.

HIS MUSIC

The 'Three Bs' of classical music, according to Hans von Bülow, a champion of Brahms' work, were Bach, Beethoven and Brahms. The anecdote is now enshrined in music folklore but in fact, Bülow's *bon mot* came in reply to the question 'What is your favourite key?' He answered that it was E flat because this was the key of Beethoven's 'Eroica' Symphony, and because it had three Bs in the key signature – one for Bach, one for Beethoven, one for Brahms.

Other Bs have not been so laudatory: Benjamin Britten, for example, claimed that he played through 'the whole of Brahms' at intervals to see whether Brahms was really as bad as he thought and ended by discovering that he was actually much worse.

For a 'bad' composer, Brahms has an extraordinary amount of work still in the active repertoire – a huge proportion compared to that of Liszt and Schumann – and every branch of his art has at least one indispensible item. One of the giants of classical music, he appeared to arrive fully armed, for he found the style in which he was comfortable – the German idiom with traditional structures and tonality – and stuck to it throughout his life. He was no innovator, preferring the logic of the symphony, sonata, fugue and variation forms, and had no time for music that told stories or depicted events in literature or art. He wrote nothing for the stage, and showed no inclination to use such recent newcomers to the orchestra as the cor anglais or the tuba.

Wagner's methods of composing did not appeal. Nor did the music of most living composers; his favourite contemporary was Johann Strauss. In all this he was out of step with the time. Brahms did not care in the least. 'I let the world go the way it pleases,' he wrote. 'I am only too often reminded that I am a difficult person to get along with. I am growing accustomed to bearing the consequences of this.'

Bach introduced few developments in the way of structure, style or idiom, yet his work represents the culmination of the age of counterpoint; Brahms, likewise, added nothing, and he represents the culmination of the age of Romanticism.

Younger members of the New German School, the Liszt- and Wagnerites, sneered at Brahms' rock-like loyalty to classical thought and design. Some, such as Hugo Wolf (a follower of Wagner), bitterly attacked him. And Tchaikowsky had no time for him at all. 'I have played over the music of that scoundrel Brahms,' he confided in his diary. 'What a giftless bastard!' Schoenberg alone recognized Brahms as a visionary. There is one element lacking in his music – and that is wit. 'When Brahms is in extra good spirits,' quipped his friend, the violinist Hellmesberger, ' he sings "The grave is my joy".' It is all serious stuff, there's no superficial prettiness in his keyboard writing, and there are very few hints at empty virtuosity – it is all logically worked out by a meticulous, perfectionist craftsman. Some find Brahms a turgid Teutonic. Certainly some of his music, especially his later work, can sound thick-textured and plodding. But his many masterpieces have a confidence and ebullience, an irresistible lyricism and melodic charm that have no sign of losing their appeal a full century after his death.

Essential works
Orchestral

'Academic Festival' Overture, Op.80 (1880): written to mark his honorary degree of Doctor of Philosophy from the University of Bremen. The music is based on student songs, to acknowledge the academic life, and concludes with a powerful version of *Gaudeamus Igitur*.

'Tragic' Overture, Op.81 (1880): Brahms had no particular programme in mind, no hidden literary allusion, but the work has the nobility of a Greek tragedy and man's struggle with fate.

Symphony No.1 in C minor, Op.68 (1855–76): variously described as 'Beethoven's Tenth Symphony' (Bülow) and 'the greatest First Symphony in the history of music', this masterpiece was written when Brahms was in his mid-forties, finally confident in his ability to handle symphonic form. It is a work of intensity and epic proportions, which is why Brahms came to be hailed as Beethoven's successor in this genre. Indeed, the most famous theme of the work (the second subject of the finale) has a striking and celebrated similarity to the *Ode to Joy* in Beethoven's Ninth Symphony. 'Any fool can see that,' snapped Brahms when someone pointed it out.

Symphony No.2 in D, Op.73 (1877): the confidence gained from the success of Symphony No.1 led to a second symphony a year later, but written in a completely different character. No.2 is relaxed and pastoral in mood, and critics, taking the Beethoven comparisons further, dubbed it 'The Pastoral'.

Symphony No.3 in F, Op.90 (1883): the conductor Hans Richter liked to describe this as Brahms' 'Eroica': 'It repeats neither the poignant song of Fate of the First, nor the joyful idyll of the Second. Its fundamental note is proud strength that rejoices in deeds.' Some say this is the greatest of the four symphonies; the third movement is surely the loveliest.

Symphony No.4 in E minor, Op.98 (1885): Brahms, always whimsical about describing his music, liked to call this the 'Waltz and Polka Affair', the waltz being the last movement and the polka the third. But it was his own favourite orchestral work. Possibly inspired by his reading of *Oedipus* and other Greek tragedies, this is a towering work, tinged with melancholy. The last movement, far from being 'a waltz', is an exultant passacaglia on a theme derived

from Bach's Cantata No.150. Some critics cite Brahms as the greatest master of counterpoint since Bach. Here is the proof – the force of the music is irresistible.

Variations on a theme by Haydn (St Anthony Chorale), Op.56a (1873): Brahms was fond of the variation form, and this is the first example in musical history of an orchestral set of variations conceived as an independent work rather than part of a larger-scale piece. The composition has become one of his most frequently-played works. The theme, it has now been shown, is not by Haydn, but was found in a Haydn manuscript labelled *Chorale Antoni*.

Piano Concerto No.1 in D minor, Op.15 (1854–58): this passionate and turbulent work, one of the cornerstones of the concerto repertoire, was hissed at its premiere and did not become popular until the 1950s. The romantic second subject of the first movement was used in the film *The L-shaped Room*. The second movement, which was written in memory of his friend Robert Schumann, is a moving elegy, while the finale, a rondo modelled on Beethoven's Third Piano Concerto, provides a spirited contrast.

Piano Concerto No.2 in B flat, Op.83 (1878–81): one of the longest (about 45 minutes), most physically taxing of all piano concertos, more reflective than the youthful First Concerto but with passages of surging power; the solo cello, unusually, introduces the main theme of the beautiful third movement also used in Brahms' song 'Immer leiser wird mein Schlümmer'. The recordings of both piano concertos by Emil Gilels have never been out of the catalogue, and justifiably so.

Violin Concerto in D, Op.77 (1878): the long-promised concerto for Brahms' great friend Joachim, written with his expert advice on what was practicable for the instrument, received a lukewarm reception. The concerto is symphonic in character and was not the virtuoso vehicle expected by the audience, although there is plenty to keep the soloist occupied. It has gone on to become one of the most popular of all violin concertos; hear Jascha Heifetz, with the Chicago Symphony Orchestra conducted by Fritz Reiner, to experience it in full measure this 'song for the violin'.

Concerto for violin and cello in A minor, Op.102 (1887): known as the 'Double Concerto' or the 'Brahms Double', it is less inspired than the earlier concertos, yet full of memorable passages and mellifluous interplay between the two soloists. It was written for his friend Joachim as a peace-offering after Brahms had supported Joachim's wife in their acrimonious divorce.

Chamber

Quintet for clarinet and strings in B minor, Op.115 (1891): among the most cherished of all chamber works, the Quintet was written after Brahms visited the ducal court of Meiningen and heard Richard Mühlfeld, whom he considered one of the greatest woodwind players he had ever heard. It is a heartfelt work, and seems to sum up Brahms' life, with a mood of resignation-without-bitterness prevailing. This is one of Brahms' finest achievements.

Piano Quartet No.1 in G minor, Op.25 (1861)
Piano Quartet No.2 in A, Op.26 (1862)
When Brahms wrote works in pairs, which he did frequently, the first tends to be more fertile and inventive, the second less inspired melodically but better constructed. The piano writing in No.1 is over-cooked but the tunes come pouring out irresistibly; No.2 has a jolly Hungarian finale, but the second (*Poco adagio*) movement is the best.

Sonata for violin and piano No.3 in D minor, Op.108 (1888): the last of the three Sonatas for violin and piano, dedicated to Hans von Bülow, Brahms designated this a sonata 'for piano and violin' (not the other way round) to emphasise the equal importance of the two parts. The first movement has a particularly striking second subject, while the mood of the whole work contrasts violent passions and melancholic moods.

Keyboard

Piano Sonata No.3 in F minor, Op.5 (1853): as late as 1888, Brahms admitted to Clara Schumann that: 'It is quite a different approach to write for such instruments as one only knows from hearing as to write for an instrument that one knows thoroughly, as I know the piano, whereby I am entirely sure of what I write and why I write it in this way.' Even so, much of his early piano writing is awkward and laboured, especially the Piano Sonatas Nos.1 & 2. The five movements of his Third Sonata, written in his twentieth year, are a marked development. The second movement subject has more than a little in common with the theme from the film *Chariots of Fire*.

Four Ballades, Op.10 (1854)
Two Rhapsodies, Op.79 (1879)
Seven Piano pieces, Op.116 (1892)
Three Piano pieces, Op.117 (1892)

Six Piano pieces, Op.118 (1892)
Four Piano pieces, Op.119 (1892)
Brahms' richest contribution to the literature of his own instrument, the concertos excepted, is to be found in his many short works. Under their prosaic collective titles lurk some of the most beautiful gems for piano in the form of capriccios, intermezzos and rhapsodies. Most of them were written towards the end of Brahms' life and offer a kaleidoscopic portrait of his multi-faceted genius. All have something to offer, in their wide variety of moods and characters. The late Opus numbers represent his most personal music, best heard in a small room and not in a large concert hall.The **Rhapsody in E flat, Op.119 No.4**, the very last piano piece that Brahms wrote, has the defiant, all-conquering quality of his earliest works, and has a Schumannesque middle section: from the beginning to the end of his career, Brahms was true to Brahms.

Twenty-five Variations and Fugue on a theme of Handel, Op.24 (1861): taking his theme from Handel's Suite in B flat, where it is also the subject of variations, Brahms weaves his magisterial way through subtle and complex transformations to the climactic, sonorous fugue, offering further proof of his ability as a great contrapuntalist. One of the noblest examples of variation writing.

Twenty-eight Variations on a theme of Paganini, Op.35 (1863): while the Handel variations are an intellectual feat, these two sets of 'studies' are a virtuoso *tour de force*, the nearest Brahms came to producing piano music of Lisztian sparkle. The theme is the same one used by Rachmaninov, Lutosławski *et al* for their Paganini variations – the Caprice No.24 in A minor for solo violin.

Twenty-one Hungarian Dances (1852–69): these were originally written for two pianos, then adapted for solo piano, and then arranged for orchestra. They are based on Hungarian tunes introduced to Brahms by Eduard Reményi and then re-harmonized by him. Several will be instantly recognizable: **No.1 in G minor, No.4 in F minor, No.5 in F sharp minor, No.6 in D flat** and **No.7 in A** are the best known. All twenty-one were arranged for violin and piano by Joachim, and two or three of them remain effective and popular end-of-recital dazzlers.

Sixteen Waltzes, Op.39 (1865): here is Brahms the Viennese charmer. Intimate and short, some waltzes will remind you of Schubert; others have a gypsy flavour. **No.15 in A flat** is extremely famous.

Vocal and Choral

Alto Rhapsody, Op.53 (1869): the official designation for this piece is 'Rhapsody for alto voice, men's chorus and orchestra', and it is a setting of three of the eleven verses from Goethe's *Harzreise im Winter;* Brahms had just emerged from an unhappy love affair, and a mood of gloom prevails throughout, despite the optimism of the radiant ending.

Ein Deutsches Requiem, Op.45 (1857–68): a 'German Requiem' because Brahms set a text from the Lutheran Bible, rather than the more commonly used liturgical Latin. This was his first major success, the music full of a tenderness and sorrow prompted by the death of his mother in 1865.

Lieder

Brahms wrote about 200 songs in all throughout the forty-four years of his creative life, making him a worthy successor to Schubert. The first are his **Six Songs Op.3** (1852–54), the last the **Four Erbste Gesänge, Op.121**, completed in 1896. Love songs predominate,

some passionate, some wryly humorous, while many others are radiantly melancholic. Some of the poems he set are by the great Romantic poets such as Goethe, but a large proportion are by now-obscure poets whose names endure only through their connections with Brahms; a surprisingly sophisticated literary taste is revealed. The best-known are:

Die Mainacht, Op.43 No.2
Vergebliches Ständchen, Op.84 No.4
Feldeinsamkeit, Op.86 No.2
Sappische Ode, Op.94 No.4
Immer leiser wird mein Schlümmer, Op.105 No.2
Ständchen, Op.106 No.1
4 Erbste Gesänge, Op.121: especially fine in the recording by Kathleen Ferrier.
Wiegenlied ('Lullaby'), Op.49 No.4: the most celebrated lullaby of all.

Benjamin BRITTEN

'If wind and water could write music, it would sound like Ben's'
(Yehudi Menuhin)

Born: 22 November 1913, Lowestoft, Suffolk
Died: 4 December 1976, Aldeburgh, Suffolk
Full title: Lord Benjamin Britten
Type of music: symphony, orchestral, concerto, opera, choral, chamber, vocal
Influences: Mahler, Bridge, Ireland, Bartók, Berg, Schoenberg, W.H. Auden, Peter Pears
Contemporaries: Gian Carlo Menotti, John Cage, Jean Françaix, **BRITTEN**, LUTOSŁAWSKI, Tikhon Khrennikov, LLOYD, Andrzej Panufnik, Humphrey Searle

HIS LIFE

England's most significant composer in the middle years of the twentieth century was born on St Cecilia's Day. The patron saint of music indeed blessed Britten with precocious gifts: he began playing the piano at two and was reading symphony and opera scores in bed at the age of seven with the same alacrity with which most children read Enid Blyton. By his tenth birthday he had completed an oratorio and a string quartet; by sixteen he had produced a symphony, six quartets, ten piano sonatas and other smaller works – some of the material from these juvenile works were later incorporated into one of his first mature works, *Simple Symphony* (1934).

Britten's father was a dental surgeon and his mother was a fair amateur pianist. He had a good education, adding the viola to his sporting and musical accomplishments at school before studying with the major influence on his musical development, Frank Bridge. Later, at the Royal College of Music, John Ireland was his composition teacher, and Arthur Benjamin (of *Jamaican Rumba* fame) his piano teacher. Britten's unique voice was quickly established; soon after completing his studies he was commissioned to write the music for a number of innovative documentary films, most notably *Night Mail* for the GPO film unit. In this he collaborated with the second influential figure in his life, the poet W.H. Auden.

Auden not only provided the text for Britten's first song cycle *On this Island* but revealed to him the beauties of poetry and the full potential of setting words and music. He also enforced Britten's pacifist convictions. When Auden left for America in 1939, the composer, and his friend, the tenor Peter Pears, followed a few months later, feeling, in Britten's words, 'muddled, fed-up and looking for work, longing to be used'. Prior to this, the first performances of Variations on a theme of Frank Bridge had taken place at the Salzburg Festival (1937) and in London. Aaron Copland's review stated: 'The piece is what we would call a knock-out.' Not yet thirty, Britten was firmly on his way.

While in America he produced his first big orchestral work *Sinfonia da requiem* (1940) and his first dramatic work, the operetta *Paul Bunyan*, which was – as Britten put it – 'politely spat at'. In 1942, with the war going badly for Britain and feeling homesick, he decided to return home. Appearing before the Tribunal of Conscientious Objectors, Britten was exempted from military duty, but was prepared to do what he could for the war effort without sacrificing his pacifist ideals. He was allowed to continue composing as long as he took part in concerts promoted by CEMA (Council for the Encouragement of Music and the Arts). Apart from being a fine and exacting conductor of his own works, Britten was also an excellent pianist – he was the soloist in the first performance of his Piano Concerto in 1939.

Before the end of the war he had produced two of his most enduring works, *A Ceremony of Carols* and the *Serenade for tenor, horn and strings*, but the opera *Peter Grimes* made him internationally famous. This was the result of a commission from the Koussevitzky Foundation in America – the great Russian conductor and patron had already conducted Britten's earlier *Sinfonia da requiem*. The resumption of artistic activity after the war, and the re-opening of the Sadler's Wells theatre made the premiere of this work a keenly-anticipated event and produced one of the most memorable first nights in British music. *Peter Grimes* was hailed as a milestone in modern opera.

With only two opera companies in the country, Britten founded the English Opera Group. Then in 1948, with Eric Crozier and Peter Pears, he inaugurated the Aldeburgh Festival, which became a flagship of musical excellence. He and Pears had made their home in the Suffolk village and it was to remain so for the rest of their lives together.

A string of operas followed *Peter Grimes*, some with the traditional full orchestra, some scored for only twelve instruments, facilitating performances and showing the composer to be a master of inventiveness. *The Rape of Lucretia* (1946), *Albert Herring* (1947), *Billy Budd* (1951), *The Turn of the Screw* (1954), *A Midsummer Night's Dream* (1960) and *Death in Venice* (1973) have all, to a lesser or greater degree, established themselves in the repertoires of opera houses all over the world. (Britten is pictured above, at the piano, working with Ronald Duncan and Arthur Oldham in 1949 on *Billy Budd*.)

Britten was particularly adept at writing music for children that was accessible without being condescending. Works such as *Let's Make An Opera*, *Noye's Fludde* and *The Young Person's Guide to the Orchestra* have had a stimulating, not to say inspirational, effect on generations of young people. In 1961, he received a commission to celebrate the consecration of the newly-built Coventry Cathedral, replacing the building devastated during the war. The result was his powerful and profound *War Requiem*, which used words of the Latin Mass and the poems of the First World War poet, Wilfred Owen.

In 1967, the tiny Jubilee Hall in Aldeburgh was replaced by the Maltings at Snape, which had been converted into a larger concert and opera hall. Two years later the new building was destroyed by fire. The phoenix that rose from the ashes has proved to be among the most outstanding concert halls of Europe and it was here that Britten's last major composition, *Death in Venice*, was premiered in 1973. As with so much of his work, Britten's partner Peter Pears was the inspiration behind the opera, and it is as much a confessional as autobiographical piece. Whether or not you are a fan of Pears' voice, no one can deny his enormous influence on Britten's creative life during the course of their relationship. Few other composers' partners can claim such a positive contribution.

During work on *Death in Venice*, it became clear that Britten's heart condition was likely to be fatal and in the last few years of his life he was reduced to doing very little. He had been made a Companion of Honour as early as 1952 and was awarded the coveted Order of Merit in 1965. Less than six months before his death he was elevated to the peerage, the first composer to be honoured in this way.

HIS MUSIC

Britten wrote in a stunning variety of styles without ever losing his unmistakable sound. Hearing *Peter Grimes*, one would say that he is a modern, dissonant composer, yet there are pages of lush impressionism as well. In *A Ceremony of Carols* he recreates a medieval atmosphere, while in a *Simple Symphony* or *Let's Make An Opera*, he can be directness itself; *The Young Person's Guide to the Orchestra* introduces the listener to complex, polyphonic contemporary music without highlighting it. He can be romantic *(Spring Symphony)*, witty and satirical *(Albert Herring)* or, more frequently, tortured and solitary *(Peter Grimes, Billy Budd* and *Death in Venice)*. The angular vocal lines and sparse harmonies of some of his music can be an acquired taste. More memorable than the melodies he wrote are the haunting moods and atmospheres conjured up. The brooding flatness of the East Anglian landscape hovers round him. His friendships with some of the greatest artists of the day, including, most notably, the horn-player Dennis Brain, the cellist Mstislav Rostropovich and the pianist Sviatoslav Richter, encouraged music that delights in virtuosity. The sea, too, played a major part in his creative process. 'My parents' house directly faced the sea,' he wrote, 'and my childhood was coloured by the fierce storms that sometimes drove ships into our coast and ate away whole stretches of the neighbouring cliffs.' Britten came of age in 1934, the year in which Elgar, Holst and Delius died. He rapidly came to dominate British music in the succeeding era.

Essential works

Peter Grimes, opera (1945): the work that revitalized British opera – and, indeed, British music – after the Second World War was based on George Crabbe's poem 'The Borough'. Set in an East Anglian fishing village, the opera tells the story of Peter Grimes, a hard, solitary fisherman treated with distrust by the villagers after the death of an apprentice at sea. After a second boy dies, Grimes chooses to take his boat out to sea and drown. The theme of the outsider, of man's struggle against prejudice and intolerance, was a subject that strongly appealed to Britten, and it was one to which he returned frequently. The Four Sea Interludes are sometimes performed independently and are among the most powerful musical evocations of the sea, cleverly reflecting Grimes' own turmoil.

A Midsummer Night's Dream, opera (1960): premiered at Aldeburgh, this is a reduced version of Shakespeare's play, in which the three groups of protagonists (the Athenian lovers, the fairies and the mechanicals) each have their own style of music. Perhaps most memorable is the performance of *Pyramus and Thisbe* and its send-up of nineteenth-century grand opera.

War Requiem (1961): one of the century's choral masterworks interweaving the Latin Mass (soprano, chorus and orchestra) with the poems of Wilfred Owen (tenor and baritone soloists with chamber orchestra); to these are added a distant choir of boys' voices with organ accompaniment. Haunting and moving.

The Young Person's Guide to the Orchestra (1946): commissioned by the Ministry of Education for a film describing the various instruments of the orchestra, Britten decided to use a theme by Purcell (always close to his heart) and wrote a set of variations on the

Rondeau from the incidental music to *Abdelazar*. The piece culminates in a riotous fugue, all the instruments of the orchestra entering one by one until Purcell's theme is once again thundered out. It is sometimes performed with Eric Crozier's dry-as-dust linking commentary.

Spring Symphony (1949): fourteen English poems of springtime past and present, some sung by the chorus, some by soloists; inspired by the Suffolk countryside, Britten strives to evoke the mood of each poem in the character of Elizabethan madrigals, gathering them into four sections to simulate the four movements of a symphony.

Serenade for tenor, horn and strings (1943): written for Pears, this is Britten's finest song cycle; it takes the night as its subject, setting the poems of Tennyson, Blake, Jonson, Keats and Cotton to music. The first performance was given by Pears and the horn-player, Dennis Brain.

A Ceremony of Carols (1942): a setting of nine medieval lyrics for boys' voices and harp obbligato: plain chant in modern terminology, music that, in its simplicity and purity, radiates a poetic and spiritual feeling.

Also worth investigating
Variations on a theme of Frank Bridge, for string orchestra (1937)
Les illuminations, song cycle (1939)
Billy Budd, opera (1951)
Saint Nicholas, cantata (1948)

Max BRUCH

Born: 6 January 1838, Cologne
Died: 2 October 1920, Friedenau, near Berlin
Type of music: concerto, symphony, choral, chamber, instrumental
Influences: Mendelssohn, Schumann, Brahms
Contemporaries: DELIBES, BALAKIREV, Emile Waldteufel, BIZET, **BRUCH**, MUSSORGSKY, Josef Rheinberger, Sir John Stainer, TCHAIKOWSKY, Johann Svendsen

HIS LIFE AND MUSIC

Bruch is primarily known for just one work, his Violin Concerto No.1 in G minor, and in a recent poll, its *adagio* was voted the second most popular piece of all classical music. There's a little more to him than that. He wrote symphonies (his first at the age of fourteen), operas and oratorios; he was particularly adept at writing for large vocal forces and was regarded as a choral composer of genius during his time. By his mid-twenties he was famous, considered the equal of Brahms and a worthy successor to Mendelssohn.

Bruch had a peripatetic career teaching music in Cologne, conducting and composing all over Germany, moving from Berlin to Leipzig, Dresden and Munich. In 1867 he was made director of the court orchestra in Sonderhausen (his predecessors had been Spohr and Weber), returning to Berlin three years later. In 1880 he became conductor of the Liverpool Philharmonic Orchestra, marrying his German wife the week before he arrived in England. Three years later he went to America, then back to Germany in 1891 to become professor of composition at the *Hochschule für Musik* in Berlin. He was said to be self-centred and dictatorial – 'In personal appearance,' remarked a contemporary, 'Bruch is by no means as majestic as one would suppose from his works' – and not the sort of personality to adapt to the new world of Debussy and Stravinsky. His son's death in the First World War left him depressed; his choral music, as with other composers, fell out of fashion. No wonder this child of the nineteenth century died embittered, bewildered that his once considerable reputation had shrunk to nothing.

Essential works
Violin Concerto No.1 in G minor, Op.26 (1868): one of the best works of the Romantic period, written in the richly melodic style of Mendelssohn, with the same touch of genius, for the great violinist Joseph Joachim to whom Brahms was to dedicate *his* Violin Concerto.

Scottish Fantasy, Op.46 (1880): inspired by his love of Sir Walter Scott's novels, Bruch took the Scottish folk tunes *Auld Rob Morris, The Dusty Miller, I'm a doun for lack o' Johnny* and *Scots wha hae wi' Wallace bled* and wove them into this delightful and underrated work.

Kol nidrei, Op.47 (1881): still a favourite with cellists, this Adagio on a Hebrew melody, written for the Jewish community in Liverpool, has led people to assume that Bruch himself was Jewish. In fact, he came from a clerical Protestant family.

Anton BRUCKNER

'Bruckner! He is my man!' (Wagner)

Born: 4 September 1824, Ansfelden
Died: 11 October 1896, Vienna
Full name: Josef Anton Bruckner
Type of music: symphony, choral
Influences: Bach, Wagner, German choral and organ tradition
Contemporaries: FRANCK, LALO, Carl Reinecke, SMETANA, **BRUCKNER**, JOHANN STRAUSS II, Stephen Collins Foster, GOTTSCHALK, RUBINSTEIN

HIS LIFE

Quite how this unsophisticated, self-doubting and naive man came to write nine symphonies of such originality and epic splendour is one of music's contradictions. Bruckner was a complex personality: on one side there is the humble peasant, ill at ease in society, possessed of an almost childlike simplicity and devoutly religious – most of his works were inscribed *Omnia ad majorem Dei gloriam;* on the other there is the obsequious, obsessive perfectionist, hungry for recognition and honours. His worship of Wagner verged on the neurotic; the dedication to Wagner of his Third Symphony reads: 'To the eminent Excellency Richard Wagner the Unattainable, World-Famous, and Exalted Master of Poetry and Music, in Deepest Reverence Dedicated by Anton Bruckner' [sic]. Before the two men eventually met, Bruckner would sit and stare at his idol in silent admiration and after hearing *Parsifal* for the first time, fell on his knees in front of Wagner crying, 'Master – I worship you.' God, Wagner and Music were his three deities.

He was the son of a village schoolmaster whose duties included playing the organ in church and teaching music. When his father died in 1837, Bruckner enrolled as a chorister in the secluded monastery of St Florian where he studied organ, piano, violin and theory. He was thirty-one when he began studying with Sechter in Vienna and remained with him on and off until 1861. Up until his fortieth year, the story of his life was one of continual study, with an income derived from various meagre teaching and organ posts. Few major composers have waited so long before finding their voice. His lack

of confidence in his abilities as a composer led him onwards to more extended studies – this time of Italian and German polyphony, especially Bach – until, like Saul on the road to Damascus, the blinding light of Wagner hit him when he attended the first performance of *Tristan und Isolde* in Munich in 1865. All the rules and theories he had assiduously absorbed had to be abandoned – for that was what Wagner had done.

1868   The year 1868 saw the performance of his first important works, though one, the Mass in F minor, had been prefaced by depression and a nervous breakdown, which included a spell of numeromania (an obsession with counting). But if Wagner's music had opened the door, it had also put obstacles in the way of recognition. There was fierce opposition to Wagner in Vienna, orchestrated by the influential critic Eduard Hanslick whom Wagner caricatured as Beckmesser in his opera *Die Meistersinger von Nürnberg*. Anyone who was so clearly under the influence of this composer was also the subject of attack and Bruckner's Third Symphony was greeted with catcalls from the anti-Wagner, pro-Brahms faction of the audience at the premiere. Few remained in the hall to applaud. The Fourth Symphony, performed in Vienna under the great conductor Hans Richter, was better received and later Richter recalled the pathetic gesture of thanks that the tearful composer made after the first performance. 'Take it!' Bruckner said, squeezing a gulden into Richter's hand. 'Drink a pitcher of beer to my health.' Richter wore the coin on his watch chain for the rest of his life 'as a memento of the day on which I wept'.

1884   The tide finally turned. After conducting the premiere of Bruckner's Seventh Symphony, the charismatic Artur Nikisch wrote, 'since Beethoven there had been nothing that could even approach it.' During the last twenty-five years of his life, Bruckner combined composition with teaching and he held a number of prestigious appointments in Vienna, at the Conservatoire, the University and St Anna College.

He never ceased searching for a woman with whom to share his life. Bruckner was forty-three when he fell in love with a seventeen-year-old whose parents put an end to the relationship. He fell for another seventeen-year-old in his mid-fifties. Although the parents in this instance gave the relationship their blessing, the young girl tired of Bruckner and his passionate letters went unanswered. Later still, he became infatuated with the fourteen-year-old daughter of his first love; that came to nothing and at seventy he proposed to a young chambermaid. Her refusal to convert to Catholicism ended that. Piety and pubescent girls are not an attractive combination. Bruckner died a virgin and was buried under the organ at St Florian.

HIS MUSIC

Many argue that Bruckner was not a natural symphonist – in this most demanding of compositional structures, Bruckner seems frequently uneasy in his pursuit of coherence, the music is fragmented and its development abruptly curtailed or so overlaid with detail and ornamentation that one loses track of the original thought. The subject of Bruckner's revisions and the re-workings of his music by well-meaning friends or pupils could fill a book. His lack of confidence and naive willingness to be advised by others led to a complicated list of cuts, additions and substantially different versions of all but Symphonies Nos.0, 5, 6 & 7. (Symphony No.0 was so numbered by Bruckner – he abandoned the work, began on No.2, wrote what is now No.1 and relegated his first-born to No.0 when he decided to complete it. Clear?) Bruckner was not a proficient conductor, but he was a master organist – crowds flocked to hear him when he played in the Royal Albert Hall and the Crystal Palace, London – and it is the organ that makes its presence felt throughout his symphonies. Long passages devoted to one combination of sound, as an organist might dwell on a particular choice of registration; sudden changes of texture, as the organist changes manuals, and climactic sections of huge sonorities – are all indicative of Bruckner the church organist.

The influence of Wagner is pervasive. Bruckner's symphonies, someone said, are the symphonies that Wagner never wrote. They are on the same grand scale as Wagner's operas, 'Gothic cathedrals of sound', with the same sensuous, passionate emotions – Olympian and grandiose. Bruckner tried to emulate in the concert hall what Wagner did in the opera house. He also had Wagner's propensity for overstatement and long-windedness. What sets the symphonies apart, for all their faults, are their profound spirituality, the sheer magnificence of the orchestral sound, the massive scale of their conception and their unique 'Brucknerian' rhetoric. People love them or loathe them. Brahms described the symphonies as 'a swindle that will be forgotten in a few years' and 'greasy scraps from Wagner's table'; Hugo Wolf felt that, 'one single cymbal clash by Bruckner is worth all the four symphonies of Brahms with the serenades thrown in.'

Essential works

Symphony No.4 in E flat 'The Romantic': completed in its original form in 1874; usually heard today is the elaborately revised version with the extra 'hunting horn' scherzo, first performed in 1881. This is the best to start with and regarded as the most accessible.

Symphony No.7 in E (1883): this piece brought Bruckner the most success in his lifetime and contains perhaps his finest movement, in the Adagio, with its organ-like sonority, which was written in honour of his hero, Wagner, who died in 1883.

Te Deum (1881, revised 1883–84): much of Bruckner's symphonic style is encapsulated in this grand (four soloists, choir, organ and orchestra are requested) but brief (twenty minutes) devotional work, regarded by the composer as his finest. 'When God calls me to Him and asks me: 'What have you done with the talent I gave you?' Then I shall hold out the rolled up manuscript of my *Te Deum* and I know He shall be a compassionate judge.'

Also worth investigating

Symphony: No.6 in A (1881): agreeable, typical Bruckner but not frequently performed.

Symphony No.8 in C minor (1887, rev. 1890): eighty minutes long and a difficult listen on first hearing (the slow movement alone lasts half an hour, but in a great performance such as that recorded by Karajan, the Eighth can be an overwhelming experience).

Symphony No.9 in D minor (1896): magnificent, ethereal, and left unfinished.

Ferruccio BUSONI

'He could conceive wonderful things in music; unfortunately he could not consistently turn them into music' (Neville Cardus)

Born: 1 April 1866, Empoli, near Florence
Died: 27 July 1924, Berlin
Full name: Ferruccio Dante Michelangiolo Benvenuto Busoni
Influences: Bach, Brahms, Verdi, Wagner
Type of music: orchestral, concerto, opera, chamber, piano
Contemporaries: Edwin Lemare, DUKAS, GLAZUNOV, SIBELIUS, **BUSONI**, SATIE, Francesco Cilèa, GRANADOS, Hamish MacCunn, Scott Joplin

HIS LIFE AND MUSIC

With an Italian clarinettist for a father and Anna Weiss, an Italian-German concert pianist, for a mother, it was not surprising that their extravagantly-named offspring should become a musician. Busoni was playing the piano in public from the age of eight, made his debut in Vienna at ten and conducted his own choral work in Graz, to where the family had moved, at twelve. For the rest of his life he managed to combine the role of international virtuoso (and Busoni was one of *the* great pianists of history) with that of composer, developing his own complex theories of music and art. A man of formidable intellect, a philosopher of music, he sought to combine in his work the warmth of Italy and the formality of Germany. Among his avant-garde theories, he postulated the idea that the octave could be divided into thirty-six intervals; he also advocated the possibilities of electronic music and microtonal music – yet none of this appeared in his

own work. He was strictly a classicist at heart and could not bring himself to write music as daring as his theoretical ideas.

With its leanings towards stolidity and convoluted thought, little of Busoni's music has survived beyond his many masterly transcriptions of Bach's instrumental works, which have remained standard repertoire for pianists.

Busoni held various teaching posts during his career, in Helsinfors – where one of his students was Sibelius – Moscow, New England and Bologna, but was based mainly in Berlin with his wife and two sons. Among the musicians who passed through his hands were Egon Petri, Dmitri Mitropoulos, Percy Grainger, Kurt Weill and the extreme avant-garde composer Edgar Varèse but, in the end, when he died of kidney disease aged fifty-seven, it was clear that his importance was as an influence on the next generation of pianists and not as a trail-blazing composer.

Essential works

Turandot Suite, Op.41 (1904): Busoni's second opera is based on Carlo Gozzi's fairy tale, the source also of Puccini's opera; this suite gives a flavour of Busoni's sumptuously-orchestrated style; in *Das Frauengemach* (Intermezzo from Act 2) are heard the familiar strains of 'Greensleeves': Busoni apparently thought the tune was of Oriental origin.

Sonatina No.6 Chamber-Fantasy on Carmen (1920): a brilliant piano précis of themes from Bizet's opera in a post-Lisztian style.

Variations on a Chopin Prelude (1884 rev. 1922): Busoni bases nine variations on the sombre C minor Prelude Op.28 No.20, demonstrating his supreme mastery of pianistic textures.

Chaconne in D minor (1897?): a classic and monumental transcription for piano of the chaconne from Bach's Partita No.2 in D minor for solo violin (BWV10047).

Busoni made many piano transcriptions of Bach's organ works; among the most effective and frequently played are his versions of the Toccata, Adagio and Fugue in C (BVW564), and the choral preludes 'Sleepers awake!', 'In Thee is joy', 'I call to Thee', 'Come, Redeemer' and 'Christians, rejoice'.

Also worth investigating

Doktor Faust, opera (1916–24): an unfinished, mammoth work, it sums up Busoni's credo, and is a synthesis of all his styles. (He also provided his own libretto.) It is a great intellectual achievement but makes poor theatre because of its lack of emotional involvement and dramatic conflict. A difficult listen.

Piano Concerto, Op.39 (1904): not frequently performed due to its sheer length and the massive forces required – a male chorus in the last movement; but it is one of Busoni's most accessible and melodic works, especially memorable in the recording by John Ogdon.

Dietrich BUXTEHUDE

Born: c.1637, Oldesloe (Holstein, then part of Denmark)
Died: 9 May 1707, Lübeck
Type of music: organ music, church cantatas
Influences: His father Johannes Buxtehude, Jan Sweelinck, Sweelinck's pupil Samuel Scheidt
Contemporaries: Pietro Francesco Cavalli, LULLY, **BUXTEHUDE**, Alessandro Stradella, Marc-Antoine Charpentier, Pelham Humfrey, John Blow

HIS LIFE AND MUSIC

Better known for his influence on J.S. Bach than for any of the music itself, Buxtehude (pronounced: *books'*-ter-hoo-der) was one of the greatest organists of his day. In 1668 he succeeded Franz Tunder as organist of the Marienkirche in Lübeck, among the prime musical posts in Germany. One of the conditions attached to the post was that the newcomer marry the incumbent's daughter, which Buxtehude duly did. Thirty-five years later, the German composer Johann Mattheson applied to be his successor and took his friend Handel with him. 'We listened with much attention as good artists,' he wrote, 'but as a matrimonial alliance was proposed for which neither of us had the slightest inclination, we departed having had much enjoyment.' Apparently all five of Buxtehude's daughters were singularly lacking in appeal.

Lübeck became a Mecca for German musicians. Bach, aged twenty, is reported to have walked 200 miles from Arnstadt just to hear Buxtehude play, then overstayed his leave of absence and almost lost his job. Whether or not the story is true, the effect of Buxtehude's vocal and keyboard works on Bach was crucial.

Worth investigating

Buxtehude's works are usually identified by their BuxWV numbers, an abbreviation of *Buxtehude Werke-Verzeichnis* (Catalogue of Buxtehude's works). **Canzona in G, BuxWV170** and the **Gigue Fugue in C, BuxWV174** are two attractive examples of the composer's numerous organ works, many of which are more dry and pedantic, while three of his best cantatas – *Ich suchte des Nachts, Alles was ihr tut* and *Gott hilf mir* – make for interesting comparisons with the Italian choral writing of fifty years earlier.

William BYRD

'The English Palestrina'

Born: 1543, Lincolnshire
Died: 4 July 1623, Stondon Massey, Essex
Type of music: Polyphony; church music, madrigal, instrumental (keyboard in particular)
Influences: Tallis and the English choral tradition
Contemporaries: Roland de Lassus, Andrea Gabrieli, Alfonso Ferrabosco, **BYRD**, Tomás Luis de Victoria, Giovanni Gabrieli, Thomas Morley, Don Carlo Gesualdo

HIS LIFE AND MUSIC

If Thomas Tallis was the first important English composer, Byrd was the first English composer of genius, and unquestionably the greatest of the Elizabethan era. More than any other – even Purcell – he can claim to be the father of British music.

Byrd may have studied under Tallis as a young man, but what is certain is that at the age of twenty he was appointed organist of Lincoln Cathedral and in 1572 moved to London to become joint organist of the Chapel Royal with Tallis. The two composers obtained an exclusive licence to publish music in England – in effect, an early attempt to establish copyright. After Tallis' death, the licence passed into Byrd's hands. He was an astute businessman and well able to look after his affairs, which included protracted litigation over ownership of the property in Essex to which he had moved in 1593 with his second wife.

Like Tallis, Byrd was an ardent Catholic, as well as being a royal musician and wrote for both the Roman and English Churches, which gives some insight into the state of religious tolerance under Elizabeth I, though it must be said that much of his Latin music was written for private worship. Byrd's range was far wider than Tallis', and his liturgical music, motets, madrigals, chamber and keyboard works show him to be among the most complete musicians of the age.

What exactly did he add to the musical language? Like J.S. Bach, Byrd combined the passionate with the intellectual. He was adventurous in his harmony and experiments with structure, his music had rhythmic variety and complex syncopation to an unprecedented degree and he was more free in his melodic ideas than his contemporaries. Listening to Byrd's music one can hear many apparently 'wrong notes' or discords, where the independent intertwining melodic parts clash harmonically before being resolved. Such collisions seem logical – and not unusual to our modern ears – but Byrd was at the cutting edge of new music. 'What I have written are not misprints,' he once said; obviously he felt a need to make this clear!

Essential works

The three settings of the **Latin Mass** (for three, four and five voices, respectively) and his Anglican Great Service are considered to be Byrd's masterpieces.

Thirty-four **Cantiones sacrae** (1575): seventeen by Byrd, seventeen by Tallis; these make for a fascinating comparison of styles and, as the first music published in England, are historically important.

Psalmes, Sonets, and Songs of Sadnes and Pietie (1588): in which Byrd wrote 'The exer-

cises of singing is delightful to nature, and good to preserve the health of man. It doth strengthen all parts of the breast and doth open the pipes.'

Queenes Alman, **The Carman's Whistle**, **Quadran Paven** and **Wolsey's Wilde** are some of the exotic titles of his 140 pieces of keyboard music, much of which can be found in *My Ladye Nevell's Booke* (1591) and the *Fitzwilliam Virginal Book*, which contains lively dance and song variations for the virginals.

Joseph CANTELOUBE
(1879–1957)

Songs of the Auvergne

In some respects, Canteloube could be called the French Vaughan Williams: their careers were contemporaneous and strongly influenced by the folk music of their respective countries. Both went to extraordinary lengths to go out into the countryside and collect material with all the alacrity of butterfly-collectors. But there all similarity ends. Vaughan Williams was a far superior creative force.

Canteloube's full name was Marie-Joseph Canteloube de Malaret ('de Malaret' being the name of his ancestral estate). He had piano lessons from Amélie Doetzer, a former pupil of Chopin, but more importantly studied composition with the austere Vincent d'Indy. It is possible that d'Indy's *Symphony on a French Mountain Song* of 1887, based on folk songs from the Cévennes, inspired Canteloube. From 1900 to the end of his life he travelled all over France in search of folk songs, using elements of them to revivify contemporary French music.

Between 1923 and 1955 he published four sets of songs that he had discovered in the Auvergne, that dramatic and mountainous area dominated by its chain of extinct volcanic peaks or *puys*. Initially, he set them for piano and voice; later he orchestrated them in opulent fashion, and this is the form in which they are most often heard. By far the most popular, used in many a TV commercial, is Set 1 No.2 – 'Baïlèro' (pronounced Bye-ee-*lair'*-o), but any collection should also include 'Passo pel prat' ('Come through the meadow') from Set 3 No.2, 'Brezairola' ('Berceuse') from Set 3 No.4 and 'Chut, chut' ('Hush, hush') from Set 4 No.4 – charming, idiosyncratic and indispensable.

Emmanuel CHABRIER
(1841–94)

España, 1883

This exhilarating orchestral showpiece was written shortly after Chabrier had abandoned his career as a civil servant at the Ministry of the Interior in Paris to become a full-time composer. Up until then, an affluent background (his father was a successful barrister in the Auvergne) had allowed him to lead the life of a cultured dilettante. His many friends included not only leading musicians such as Fauré and d'Indy but also the writers Verlaine and Zola, and artists such as Renoir and Manet. In fact, not only did Manet die in his arms but Chabrier also owned, amongst his Renoirs and Sisleys, Manet's *Un bar aux Folies-Bergère*. After only fourteen years composing, Chabrier became a manic depressive and died on the verge of insanity. He was just fifty-three.

His music was influenced by two Spanish piano teachers from his childhood, and by Wagner whose scores he laboriously copied and studied. His first success was with the operetta *L'étoile*, written when he was still a civil servant; others, such as *Gwendoline* (1885) and *Le roi malgré lui* (1887) prospered less well, although their overtures are worth hearing, as are his heady and exuberant piano pieces, such as *Bourrée fantasque* and *Ten pièces pittoresques*. His *Marche joyeuse* (1888) is a worthy companion to *España*, whose tune a few of us might admit to first encountering in an unsyncopated version in the 1956 pop song 'Hot Diggity', a hit for Michael Holliday.

Gustave CHARPENTIER
(1860–1956)

Louise, opera, 1889–96

Most composers who suddenly have a hit on their hands are driven to capitalize on their success. Not so Charpentier who had been a pupil of Massenet and, like him, had won the coveted Prix de Rome. He was passionately devoted to the social problems of the poor and in 1900 formed a society devoted to the welfare of working-class girls, which went on to become an auxiliary Red Cross society during the First World War.

Louise, his extraordinary one-off success, has many autobiographical references: his mistress at the time was called Louise and she, like his heroine, was a dressmaker; the third act portrays a festive night in Montmartre organized for the poor, when a working-class woman is crowned Muse – Charpentier had been involved in such an event and incorporated the music he'd written for the occasion into his opera. Like Wagner, he provided his own libretto and adopted the older composer's *leitmotiv* device in the score in addition to such touches of realism as Paris street cries.

In 1913 Charpentier wrote a sequel, *Julien*, continuing Louise's story, but it was not a success. In spite of living to the age of ninety-five, he produced nothing else of significance, but perhaps it was enough to write the Act 3 aria 'Depuis le jour', in which Louise tells her lover how happy she is. Many composers couldn't write such music if they lived to be a hundred.

Ernest CHAUSSON

(1855–99)

Poème, Op.25, 1896

This richly lyrical masterpiece for violin and orchestra is one of the most beautiful of short works written for the instrument. A one-movement rhapsody full of soaring, melodic themes, it is tender, passionate and, at times, melancholic. Chausson's close friend Debussy said of it: 'Nothing touches us more with dreamy sweetness than the end of this *Poème*, where the music, leaving aside all description and anecdote, becomes the very feeling that inspired its emotion.' It is a piece that has always been close to violinists' hearts.

Poème is dedicated to the great Eugène Ysaÿe, who gave its first performance in London exactly a week after the premature death of Chausson in a bicycling accident. (While on a summer holiday near Limay, he lost control going down a steep hill and was smashed to death against a stone wall.) Chausson wrote few other works but well worth hearing are his Symphony in B flat, Op.20, the middle movement of which has a wonderful theme for the cor anglais and cellos, and the intense Concerto for violin, piano and string quartet. As a man of private means (his father was a building contractor who made a fortune from rebuilding the centre of Paris), Chausson never had to struggle to make a living. He already had a law degree and was married with a family by the time he decided to enrol at the Paris Conservatoire. Although he withdrew after a few months, he was able to study privately with César Franck for three years, and Franck and Wagner were the main influences on his music. A major creative talent had finally established itself by the end of his short life; its development and fruition were not to be.

Frédéric CHOPIN

'The poet of the piano'

Born: 1 March 1810, Żelazowa Wola, near Warsaw
Died: 17 October 1849, Paris
Full name: Fryderyk Franciszek (Frédéric François) Chopin
Type of music: piano solo, piano and orchestra, songs and chamber
Influences: Polish folk music, J.S. Bach, Mozart, Field, Bellini, Paganini, Hummel, Czerny
Contemporaries: Johann Hartmann, Michael Balfe, MENDELSSOHN, **CHOPIN**, Otto Nicolai, Félicien David, SCHUMANN, Samuel Sebastian Wesley, LISZT

Few composers command such universal love as Chopin; even less have such a high proportion of their output still remaining in the active repertoire. He is the only great composer whose every work involves the piano – no symphonies, operas or choral works and only a handful of compositions that involve other instruments. He wrote just under 200 works; 169 of these are for solo piano.

HIS LIFE

1810 The greatest of all Polish composers had a French father, Nicholas, who had gone to Poland as a young man and become a tutor to the family of Countess Skarbek at Żelazowa Wola. His mother was the Countess' lady-in-waiting, herself from Polish nobility. This dual nationality is reflected in Chopin's music – the epic struggle of the Poles and the refined elegance of the French. Shortly after Frédéric's birth, the family moved to Warsaw where Nicholas had a teaching post.

1816 Chopin had his first piano lessons from Adalbert Żwyny, an accomplished local musician, and made his public debut at nine.

1825 He became a piano student of Joseph Elsner, director of the Warsaw Conservatory. It is largely due to Elsner and Żwyny that Chopin became an original creative force: they let him develop in his own way.

1828 A friend of Chopin's father invited him to Berlin and the following year Frédéric gave two concerts in Vienna, which included his Variations on Mozart's 'Là ci darem la mano' after which Schumann made his famous judgment: 'Hats off, gentlemen! A genius.'

1830 The fading attractions of Warsaw and his unrequited love for a young singer persuaded him to leave Poland. Before he left in November, his old teacher Elsner presented him with a silver urn of Polish earth, saying, 'May you never forget your native land wherever you go, nor cease to love it with a warm and faithful heart.' The urn was buried with Chopin.

Despite a Polish revolt against Russian rule, Chopin headed for Vienna.

1831 After staying some time in Stuttgart, and intending to travel to London, he stopped off in Paris. It remained his home for the rest of his life.

1832 His Paris debut in January was not a success. The Parisians did not take to his playing or music immediately and Chopin considered leaving for America. His destiny was determined by Prince Radziwill who introduced him to the *salon* of Baron Jacques de Rothschild. Here, Chopin triumphed and from then on his career as a composer and highly paid teacher was one of unbroken success.

Chopin was a sensitive, fastidious man who never enjoyed robust health. The rich, privileged world of the aristocratic and wealthy *salons* not only appealed to his instincts (he liked to mingle with money and beautiful women) but also provided the perfect ambience for his music and particular style of playing. Where his friend Liszt was the thunderous, virtuoso showman, Chopin was the refined, undemonstrative poet, noted for his *rubato* style, where notes are not played in strict tempo but subtly lengthened and shortened 'like a tree's leaves in the breeze,' as Liszt said.

1837 His first great love in Paris was the flirtatious daughter of Count Wodzińska. The family terminated the affair. His next was perhaps the most unlikely woman of his circle: Aurore Dupin or Mme Dudevant, the radical, free-thinking novelist who wrote under the pseudonym of George Sand. By no means good-looking (photographs bear witness), she smoked cigars and wore men's clothing. 'What a repellent woman she is,' reacted Chopin initially. 'Is she really a woman? I'm ready to doubt it.' But she held a fascination for him, and a relationship developed that lasted for ten years; she was a mother figure who became the love of his life, although one of her personal letters implies that the physical side of their liaison was embraced less than enthusiastically by the composer.

1838 George Sand travelled to Majorca with her son and daughter and Chopin joined them there. Instead of the paradise they had hoped for, it was a disaster, with inhospitable and antagonistic locals, damp, wet weather and the breakdown of Chopin's health. He began haemorrhaging and having hallucinations, and it was only a prompt departure for the mainland that saved his life (he had another haemorrhage in Barcelona).

1839 For the next few years, Chopin was at the height of his creative powers; he was respected and internationally famous. Yet his health deteriorated, and he became more consumptive year by year.

1848 The increasingly tense relationship with George Sand came to an end. Sand seemed comparatively unaffected; 'Chopin,' said Liszt, 'felt and often repeated that in breaking this long affection, this powerful bond, he had broken his life.' A Scottish pupil of Chopin's, Jane Stirling, persuaded him to make a trip to England and Scotland with her but this and a few fund-raising concerts undermined his health further and when he returned to Paris he became a virtual recluse, too weak to compose or teach.

1849 He gave strict instructions that all his unpublished manuscripts be destroyed. Chopin had a good idea of his worth and was determined that only his best work should survive. He died from consumption on 17 October and was buried in the Père Lachaise cemetery in Paris, next to his friend, Bellini.

HIS MUSIC

More than any other, Chopin is responsible for the development of modern piano technique and style. His influence on succeeding generations of writers for the instrument was profound and inescapable. He produced a whole range of new colours, harmonies and means of expression in which he exploited every facet of the new developments in piano construction, which included a larger keyboard (seven octaves) and improved mechanism.

Few of Chopin's compositions translate successfully to other instruments. Interestingly, this most romantic of the Romantic composers disliked the association, borne out by the fact that, unlike his contemporaries Schumann and Liszt, his inspiration never came from literature or painting.

Unlike any other great composer, Chopin achieved his claim to immortality not by writing large-scale works but in miniatures (the nocturne, prelude, étude, mazurka and so forth), though these frequently encompass emotion of tremendous power. Even his two concertos and three sonatas are really shortish pieces sewn together into larger classical forms, which, he realized early on, were not his strength.

Chopin was hypercritical of everything he wrote and what we hear played with such inevitability and apparently effortless flowing melody cost him much. George Sand described Chopin frantically trying to capture on paper all that he had in his head; crossing out, destroying, beginning afresh, scratching out once more, and re-working a single bar countless times. There are few works by this composer that do not seem genuinely inspired. The inexhaustible variety of moods and ideas, the endless supply of beautiful melodies and discriminating taste combine to make his *oeuvre* one of the high points of musical creation.

Essential works

Piano Concerto No.1 in E minor, Op.11 (1830)
Piano Concerto No.2 in F minor, Op.21 (1829)

The Second Concerto, written when Chopin was nineteen, appeared in print after the First. The slow movements of these concertos are among Chopin's most beautiful.

Andante spianato and **Grande polonaise brillante in E flat, Op.22**: a sumptuous Nocturne followed by a lively Polonaise, played either as a solo or (more often) with orchestral accompaniment.

Four Ballades – No.1 in G minor, Op.23; No.2 in F, Op.38; No.3 in A flat, Op.47; No.4 in F minor, Op.52: four pianistic stories, among the most sublime creations of Romantic music. The first has been described as 'the odyssey of Chopin's soul'; the pianist John Ogdon thought No.4 to be the most powerful of all Chopin's compositions.

Twelve Etudes, Op.10 and **Twelve Etudes, Op.25**: Don't be put off by the title 'études' (studies), which in other composers' hands mean 'exercises'. Chopin's études are quite different. Each one concentrates on a different pianistic problem, such as arpeggios, octaves and chromatic scales, but they are all wrapped in incomparably beautiful music. They are *de rigeur* for every pianist. The best known études are:

Op.10 No.3 in E: this has come to be known as 'Tristesse' ('Sadness'); turned into a popular song called 'So deep is the night'.

Op.10 No.5 in G flat: 'The Black Keys' study, so called because the pianist's fingers touch only one white note.

Op.10 No.12 in C minor: the 'Revolutionary' étude inspired by the fall of Warsaw. More prosaically, it's the one Sparky played on his Magic Piano!

Op.25 No.1 in A flat: often called the 'Aeolian Harp' or 'Shepherd Boy' étude.

Op.25 No.11 in A minor: nicknamed the 'Winter Wind' and easy to see why.

Fantaisie in F minor, Op.59: at turns melancholic, heroic and tender, this inspiring work illustrates, perhaps more succinctly than any other, every facet of Chopin's genius.

Fantaisie-impromptu in C sharp minor, Op.66 (post.): one of the piano's most popular pieces, although Chopin himself did not permit its publication (he thought so little of it); it appeared after his death. The middle section (trio) provided two American songwriters with the 1919 hit, 'I'm always chasing rainbows'.

Mazurkas: Chopin composed fifty-six of these between 1830 and 1849; many of them are well known and of immense charm and subtlety, adapting, in an idealized way, his country's native dance.

Nineteen Nocturnes: The Irish-born John Field wrote the first nocturne in 1814 but Chopin developed the genre beyond Field's endeavours, transforming them into love poems in which the piano is the singer. Every collection should include: **Op.9 No.2 in E flat, Op.15 No.1 in F, Op.15 No.2 in F sharp minor, Op.27 No.2 in D flat, Op.32 No.2 in A flat**; the latter nocturne is famous through its appearance in *Les Sylphides*, the ballet score constructed from Chopin's music.

Polonaises Nos.1–6: Chopin wrote his first polonaise at the age of seven, and completed another eight before leaving Poland. But it is the six later pieces, written in Paris, that are the best, where he could idealize his native land from afar and transform a national dance into a national epic.

No.3 in A, Op.40: known as the 'Military', only exceeded in popularity by ...

No.6 in A flat, Op.53: the 'Heroic', with a cavalry charge in the middle, a succession of left-hand octaves.

Polonaise-fantaisie in A flat, Op.61: a late work in which Chopin is striving to develop the polonaise; many consider this to be one of his greatest works.

Twenty-four Preludes, Op.28: This extra-ordinary set of miniatures captures a world of emotion and mood, full of anguish and despair, serenity and melancholy. The critic James Huneker felt that the Preludes alone would make good Chopin's claim to immortality. 'If all Chopin's music were to be destroyed,' he wrote, 'I would plead for the Preludes.' They were composed at Valdemossa in Majorca where Chopin and George Sand spent a few unhappy months, the Preludes the only good thing to emerge from the visit. There is one for each major and minor key, each major key followed by its relative minor. Among them are:

No.4 in E minor: played on the organ, with Nos.6 & 20, at Chopin's funeral service at the Madeleine in Paris.

No.6 in B minor: the left hand plays a cello-like melody.

No.7 in A: as brief as it is famous. Used effectively in *Les Sylphides*.

No.15 in D flat: the 'Raindrop' prelude (the nickname is self-explanatory).

No.20 in C minor: twelve bars long, that's all. Rachmaninov and Busoni used it for a set of variations, and Barry Manilow based his hit song 'Could it be magic' on it.

Four Scherzi – No.1 in B minor, Op.20; No.2 in B flat minor, Op.31; No.3 in C sharp minor, Op.39; No.4 in E, Op.54: 'Scherzo' means 'a jest', but these characteristic works are far from light-hearted or playful. Mendelssohn made the scherzo synonymous with the 'caprice'; here Chopin extends the genre into 'breathings of stifled rage and of suppressed anger' (Liszt). The Four Scherzi, like most of Chopin's works, are extremely difficult to play but all are masterpieces, with passages of surpassing beauty.

Sonata No.2 in B flat minor, Op.35: this contains the famous Funeral March (third movement) and the spectral, impressionistic, whirlwind last movement described by Anton Rubinstein as 'night winds sweeping over churchyard graves.' Rachmaninov made a famous – if controversial – recording of the work that is unforgettable.

Sonata No.3 in B minor, Op.58: an imperfect masterpiece overweighed with its profusion of melodic ideas, but which has always been a favourite vehicle for pianists. The triumphant drama of the final presto is irresistible and has been rated the most technically demanding of all Chopin's works.

Waltzes: Chopin thought the Viennese waltzes composed by the Strauss family quite vulgar. These are high-spirited Parisian waltzes,

though 'never meant to be danced by ordinary mundane creatures of flesh and blood.' The most famous are:

Grande valse brillante in E flat, Op.18: beloved of all ballet schools.

Valse brillante in A minor, Op.34 No.2: said to be Chopin's favourite.

Waltz in A flat, Op.42: arguably the most perfect of Chopin's waltzes and certainly the most difficult to play.

Waltz in D flat, Op.64 No.1: the 'Minute' waltz; impossible to play within sixty seconds – the average is about ninety seconds.

Aaron COPLAND

'Composers tend to assume that everyone loves music. Surprisingly enough, everyone doesn't.' (Copland)

Born: 14 November 1900, New York
Died: 2 December 1990, New York
Type of music: symphony, orchestral, concerto, ballet, stage and incidental music, film, vocal, chamber, piano
Influences: Debussy, Ives, Boulanger, Stravinsky, Les Six, Schoenberg, Jazz
Contemporaries: Georges Auric, WEILL, George Antheil, **COPLAND**, Ernst Krenek, Gerald Finzi, Edmund Rubbra, WALTON, Maurice Duruflé

HIS LIFE AND MUSIC

Born in a humble street in Brooklyn to Lithuanian immigrants, Copland is generally regarded as the first indisputably great American composer. The piano came easily to him, and, after graduating from the local high school, he had lessons in harmony and counterpoint with the eminent (though conservative) teacher and composer Rubin Goldmark. His first published piece, *The Cat and the Mouse*, appeared in 1920.

Copland was able to scrape together enough money to go to Paris to study with Nadia Boulanger, the doyenne of European teachers. Here, during his four years at the New School for Americans at Fontainebleau (1921–25), Copland was introduced to an enormous range of musical influences, all of which he was encouraged to absorb. Jazz, the neo-classicism of Stravinsky and the whimsicality of Les Six made a particularly strong impression on him and they colour the first period of his mature compositions. With a thorough understanding of composition and orchestration under his belt, Copland returned to America, where he became involved in a wide range of musical activities – working as a pianist in a hotel, a lecturer and an organizer of various musical societies, in addition to composing.

The conductor, publisher and patron of music, Serge Koussevitsky, became an influential champion of Copland's music throughout his tenure as conductor of the Boston Symphony Orchestra; this gave an incalculable boost to Copland's growing reputation. Between 1930 and 1936, he entered a phase of experimental and dissonant writing – *Variations* and the Piano Sonata, for instance, are difficult works.

He then discovered the power of American folk idioms, and produced music as redolent of America as Mussorgsky's is of Russia – *El salón México*, the ballets *Billy the Kid*, *Rodeo* and *Appalachian Spring* are as American as apple pie. His *Lincoln Portrait* for speaker and orchestra, using texts from the president's speeches and letters, has been performed (for better or worse, but generally worse) by world leaders from Adlai Stevenson and Margaret Thatcher to Eleanor Roosevelt, John Wayne and General Norman Schwartzkopf. Copland's patriotic *Fanfare for the Common Man* (1942) has been used for the opening of every type of formal ceremony. His film scores, such as *The Red Pony*, *Our Town* and *Of Mice and Men*, are among the most distinguished ever written and he won an Oscar in 1950 for the score of *The Heiress*. He described film music as being like 'a small lamp that you place below the screen to warm it.'

Copland managed the feat of becoming a popular classical composer while retaining the respect of the 'serious musical establishment'. In his later works, he reverted to serial techniques, writing in a less approachable, more austere manner. Whatever one thinks of his virtually unknown middle- and late-period music, Copland has to be admired for his steadfast independence and unwillingness to court popularity for its own sake.

Essential works

El salón Mexico (1933–36): one of the first works of Copland's 'Americana' period, this catchy impression of a Mexican dance hall uses jazzy tunes and Latin-American rhythms.
Billy the Kid, ballet (1938): written in only five weeks, Copland's score (the suite usually heard is about two-thirds of the whole) tells the story of William Bonney, better known as Billy the Kid, who terrorized the American West in the 1880s; as well as an effective shoot-out, several cowboy songs are quoted as themes.
Rodeo, ballet (1942): the Four Dance Episodes from the complete score have become highly popular – *Buckaroo Holiday*, *Corral Nocturne*, *Saturday Night Waltz* and (especially) *Hoe-Down* – exuberant, robust and unmistakably Copland.
Appalachian Spring, ballet (1944): written for the choreographer Martha Graham, this is a tonal portrait of the landscape of the Pennsylvania farmlands; the penultimate section

includes a series of variations on a well-known Shaker hymn tune 'Simple Gifts'. Here are quintessential Copland orchestral textures, redolent of the American prairies and the great outdoors. For many, this is his finest work.
Symphony No.3 (1944–46): dedicated to the memory of Koussevitzky's wife, this impressive work reflects the 'general sentiments' during a time of war; in the last movement, arrestingly, Copland quotes his own popular **Fanfare for the Common Man**. This, his longest orchestral work, was described by Koussevitzky as 'the greatest American symphony'.

Also worth investigating

Ten Old American Songs (1950–52): in two sets: charming and whimsical.
Clarinet Concerto (1947–48): written for the jazz clarinettist Benny Goodman, this piece exploits all the characteristic qualities of 'the King of Swing'.

Arcangelo CORELLI

'Il divino'

Born: 17 February 1653, Fusignano
Died: 8 January 1713, Rome
Type of music: Baroque; concerto grossi, trio sonatas, solo sonatas
Influences: Giovanni Gabrieli, Ludovico Viadana, the Bologna school of violin-playing
Contemporaries: Pelham Humfrey, John Blow, PACHELBEL, **CORELLI**, Agostino Steffani, Michel-Richard Delalande, PURCELL, Alessandro Scarlatti

HIS LIFE AND MUSIC

Born into a wealthy family near Bologna, Corelli showed an early talent for the violin. After living in Rome, Paris and Germany, he returned to Rome, where he spent the rest of his life. His patron was the wealthy, music-loving Cardinal Ottoboni, nephew of Pope Alexander VIII, and Corelli provided the music for his household. The fame of the

Monday concerts that were held there spread throughout Europe, and Corelli's reputation as the leading violinist of his day, together with the widespread publication of his music, made him among the most influential musicians of the period. This is discernible not only in the music by Purcell, Vivaldi, Handel and J.S. Bach but also in the art of violin playing – such as requiring the performer to play more than one note with a single bow stroke (traditionally, it was always one note for each stroke) and playing two or three strings simultaneously (known as double and triple stopping). His pupils Francesco Geminiani and Pietro Antonio Locatelli in turn passed on what they had learnt.

Corelli insisted that the string players in his orchestra should all bow in the same way, a practice that led to unprecedented accuracy in performance and, according to a contemporary report, produced 'an amazing effect, even to the eye, as well as the ear.' In this, Corelli was the principal architect of modern orchestral playing and the composer who fashioned three new musical forms: the Baroque trio and solo sonatas, and the concerto grosso, a four- or five-movement work, the forerunner of the modern concerto, in which a solo passage interplays and contrasts with the whole orchestra.

Corelli was buried near Raphael in the Pantheon, Rome and left an estate of approximately £6,000 (an exceptional amount in those days) and a collection of over a hundred paintings, including works by Brueghel and Poussin.

His music itself is passionless, balanced, almost mechanical, but the slow movements demonstrate the lyrical powers of the violin as never before with great dignity and serenity, and the fast outer movements are crisp, concise and jolly – in other words, the classical form of Baroque music.

Worth investigating

Corelli's entire output is for orchestra or chamber groups and includes forty-eight trio sonatas and twelve concerti grossi. Unusually for the period, he wrote no vocal music. His best-known work is the **Concerto grosso Op.6 No.8**, the 'Christmas Concerto'. **No.2** in this set is the work on which Tippett based his *Fantasia Concertante on a Theme of Corelli*.

François COUPERIN

'I am more pleased with what moves me than with what astonishes me' (Couperin)

Born: 10 November 1668, Paris
Died: 11 September 1733, Paris
Known as: 'François Couperin le Grand'
Type of music: chamber, choral, instrumental (mainly keyboard)
Influences: Lully, Corelli
Contemporaries: Tommaso Vitali, Johann Christoph Pepusch, **COUPERIN**, Giovanni Bononcini, ALBINONI, Jeremiah Clarke, William Croft, VIVALDI

HIS LIFE AND MUSIC

The most prominent representative (hence le Grand) of a famous family of musicians whose dynasty began in the 1620s and expired when the last male Couperin died two centuries later: French rivals to the German Bachs. François spent most of his musical life in the service of the French court as a harpsichordist and organist, composing sacred music and chamber works for the royal pleasure of Louis XIV.

His lasting memorial is the series of extraordinary harpsichord works written towards the end of his life. Between 1713 and 1730 the four volumes of his *Pièces de clavecin* were published – 230 pieces in twenty-seven *ordres* (Couperin's name for suites), each *ordre* a series of dances. Their titles were all whimsical, witty or descriptive, like 'The Little Windmills' and 'The Knitters', and many defy translation because they referred to topical subjects: *Les culbutes jxcxbxnxs* [sic] and *Les tic-toc-choc*, for instance. The Romantics were keen on this kind of thing, as were Debussy and Satie in their piano pieces. They are musical postcards of the court, sketches of Couperin's life and personality.

His book *L'Art de toucher le clavecin* (1716) had an enormous influence on succeeding generations of keyboard players. Alfred Einstein wrote perceptively that 'in Couperin we see the beginnings of the French musical predilection for the exquisite, for studied brilliance, emotional discretion and roguish charm extending to sly wit.' It was not for nothing that Ravel wrote his tribute *Le tombeau de Couperin* two hundred years later.

Worth investigating

Livres de clavecin (1713–30): dip into these at random. Apart from those mentioned above, look out for **La fileuse** and **Les fastes de la grande et ancienne Mxnxstrxndxsx** [sic].

L'apothéose de Lully (1725), for strings and continuo.

Les nations (1726): trio sonatas and suites for violins and continuo.

Peter Maxwell DAVIES

Born: 8 September 1934, Manchester
Full title: Sir Peter Maxwell Davies
Type of music: symphony, concerto, opera, ballet, chamber, choral, keyboard
Influences: Medieval chants, Webern, Sessions, religious philosophy, the Orkneys
Contemporaries: GÓRECKI, Krzysztof Penderecki, BIRTWISTLE, **DAVIES**, PÄRT, Cornelius Cardew, BENNETT, Steve Reich, Philip Glass, John McCabe

HIS LIFE AND MUSIC

Some may have heard of the famous composer who lives on the Orkney island of Hoy; some may recognize the titles of a number of his pieces. Few could identify a note of his many compositions. In common with his peers, his critical reputation is not reflected by his success with the public. Sir Peter, hailed as a leading contemporary composer, can write as abstrusely as any. Yet he has produced some of the most accessible of new works.

At the Manchester (now Royal) College of Music he was part of the 'Manchester Group' of Birtwistle, Elgar Howarth and John Ogdon, who were promoting the avant-gardists of Europe. In 1957, he went to Rome on a scholarship, then served as director of music at Cirencester Grammar School for three years, which stimulated his lifelong interest in writing for young people. In 1968, after a period of study with Roger Sessions at Princeton University, a round-the-world lecture tour and a spell as composer-in-residence at Adelaide University, he returned to London. With Harrison Birtwistle, he founded the Pierrot Players (later reformed as the Fires of London), a chamber group at which he directed much of his output, including the haunting music-theatre piece *Eight*

Songs for a Mad King. Medieval and Renaissance music had always played an important part in his make-up, as did the sight and sound of the sea and the Scottish landscape after his move to Orkney in 1971; *An Orkney Wedding with Sunrise* and *Runes from a Holy Island* are two works with which to conduct initial explorations of Davies' complex world.

In 1977 Davies founded the St Magnus Festival in Orkney and it has seen the premiere of many of his works since then. He campaigns fervently for the causes closest to his heart, which include fighting for Britain's musical life and its orchestras as well as taking up the anti-nuclear-weapons banner and being a committed environmentalist.

Essential works

An Orkney Wedding with Sunrise (1985): for bagpipe and orchestra.

Runes from a Holy Island (1977): for flute, clarinet, violin, cello, piano and percussion.

Eight Songs for a Mad King (1969): a one-off where a solo male voice takes the part of the mad king, George III, and, going from one cage to another inhabited by musicians symbolizing birds, tries to convey by screams, whines and whimpers, the tunes inside his head.

St Thomas Wake (1969): foxtrot for orchestra based on a pavan by John Bull. Great fun.

Claude DEBUSSY

'Great painter of dreams' (Rolland)

Born: 22 August 1862, St Germain-en-Laye
Died: 25 March 1918, Paris
Full name: Achille-Claude Debussy
Type of music: Impressionist; orchestral, opera, chamber, piano, vocal
Influences: Medieval and Oriental music, Mallarmé (and French symbolist poets), Monet (and Impressionist painters), Satie
Contemporaries: ARENSKY, Enrico Bossi, Leon Boëllmann, **DEBUSSY**, DELIUS, Edward German, Horatio Parker, Gabriel Pierné, MASCAGNI

HIS LIFE

1862 The refined taste and exquisitely-coloured music of Debussy belonged to a man born above his parent's china shop on the outskirts of Paris. Neither his mother or father seem to have shown much interest in his development and it was his aunt Clémentine who noticed his musical gifts. She kept a dress shop and when she and her wealthy *amour* removed to Cannes in 1871, Debussy visited her there and had his first piano lessons.

1872 Back in Paris, he had further lessons from a pupil of Chopin. Just three years later, he was good enough to play Chopin's F minor Concerto, having entered the Paris Conservatoire aged ten. At about the same time, he started to compose.

He was a strange-looking young man with a bulging forehead (the French call it *un double front*), which he hated and tried unsuccessfully to cover with his hair. His teachers found him charming, while one fellow student described him as 'uncommunicative, surly and not attractive to his friends.' His piano teachers were the finest and he was thought to be headed for a career as a virtuoso. Early on, his few intimates noticed his impeccable taste and quiet obstinacy: rather than gorge himself on a bag of cheap sweets, Debussy would buy a small delicate pastry. Later he would surround himself with fine books and pictures, dressing in beautifully-cut clothes, usually sporting a broad-brimmed hat, and eating the best caviar, for he was something of a gourmet.

His friends and teachers were also made aware of his rebellious nature. At the Conservatoire, this would take the form of questioning everything that was presented to him. His composition teacher was Ernest Guiraud; one day, exasperated by his pupil's unwillingness to adopt the traditional method of harmony, he enquired what rules he followed. 'Mon plaisir,' came the curt reply.

1880–85 Debussy was recommended as household pianist to Mme Nadezhda von Meck, Tchaikowsky's patron. He was to teach her children and play four-hands with them. Not quite eighteen at the time, Debussy travelled to Switzerland, Italy and Russia with the family, staying in Moscow and the family estate in the summers of 1881 and 1882. Mme von Meck dispensed with his services when he fell in love with her eldest daughter. Between 1881 to 1884 Debussy prepared himself for the Prix de Rome and won the much-coveted prize at the second attempt with a cantata, *L'enfant prodigue*, that had all the necessary academic niceties in the writing to please the judges. Like passing the driving test, you must first know all the basics thoroughly before adopting your own idiosyncrasies and reaping the benefits of experience. Off he went to the Villa Medici in

Rome for three years; he hated it there but it gave him the chance to meet Liszt, who introduced him to the music of Lassus and Palestrina, the austere spirituality of which rubbed off on Debussy. Liszt's subtle pedalling when he played the piano also gave him ideas.

1886 Back in Paris and living with his parents, he fell under the influence of Wagner's music, like many other young composers of the time, although he was to reject it fairly swiftly, with the exception of *Parsifal* – a work in which he delighted for the rest of his life. Other influences were in play that resulted in music which was to be the very antithesis of Wagner's. First there was the eccentric Erik Satie, later to become the *éminence grise* of Les Six (see HONEGGER). He encouraged Debussy to write music that was not hidebound by academic tradition – 'Break the rules, defy convention' could have been his credo – and to find inspiration in the paintings of Monet, Cézanne, Renoir, Pissarro and others. Three influential exhibitions from 1874 to 1877 had led to the – initially derisive – term 'Impressionism' being used to describe their work, derived from a painting by Monet entitled *Sunrise – an Impression*. Debussy disliked his music being labelled 'Impressionist' but he could do nothing to alter the tag allotted him – his own tastes in painting were for Whistler and Turner, and the anti-Romantic Symbolist poets such as Mallarmé, Verlaine and Rimbaud were his preferred writers. Edgar Allan Poe, too, fascinated him and for a while Debussy worked on an orchestral work based on the story *The Fall of the House of Usher*.

1889 Yet another influence on his development was the Grande Exposition Universelle where he first heard a Javanese gamelan orchestra and fell in love with its exotic textures and counterpoint of which, he said, 'in comparison that of Palestrina is a child's game.' Debussy was a man of strong likes and dislikes and the deciding factor in his belief that music must go on a new path was his disinterest in Brahms and Tchaikowsky, the fact that Beethoven bored him and that he found the old structures stifling and lifeless. He gradually evolved a style that was indeed the musical equivalent of the Impressionist paintings. His musical colours, half-lit, delicate mezzotints are as different from the sound of the currently fashionable German, French and Russian schools as, say, the sound of King Oliver to Glenn Miller. Technically, Debussy achieved the sound by such means as using the Oriental pentatonic scale, the whole-tone scale, unresolved discords in succession, and consecutive perfect fifths and fourths; traditional construction and formal development of themes, principles on which classical music had securely rested, were thrown out of the window.

If Debussy's music was unconventional for the time, so was his private life. A chain-smoking sybarite, he was a sensualist and egoist who cared little for few other people than himself. Short, plump, pale and bearded, with that bulging forehead, he was not, on the surface, the most attractive of men – his resemblance to some medieval paintings of Christ earned him the nickname 'Le Christ hydrocéphalique' – but he had enormous magnetism. Colette referred to 'his unrelenting gaze [in which] the pupils of his eyes seemed momentarily to dart from one spot to another like those animals of prey hypnotized by their own searching intensity.' In the late 1880s he met up with Gabrielle Dupont – 'green-eyed Gaby'. They lived in a shabby apartment in Montmartre while Debussy struggled to make ends meet. He wrote the String Quartet in 1893 and *Prélude à l'après-midi d'un faune* the following year, the two works with which we may say that Impressionism in music was born. Slowly he began to make a name for himself.

1899   Gaby's reward for her support and care while her lover established himself was rejection when Debussy married Rosalie Texier. He had already separated from Gaby to live with 'Lily-Lilo', as Debussy called his new love, and threatened to kill himself if she did not marry him. Gaby Dupont shot herself, survived and disappeared into oblivion; years later, the pianist Alfred Cortot ran into her – she was dressed as a poor working woman.

1904–15   Only five years later, Debussy grew tired of Rosalie ('the sound of her voice makes my blood run cold,' he once said) and took up with Emma Bardac, the wife of a wealthy banker. Rosalie Texier, too, shot herself in despair; she, too, recovered. Debussy divorced her, and married Emma in October 1908. Older than Debussy, she already had grown children; their only child together was born in 1905, before Emma was divorced. This was Debussy's adored Claude-Emma (i.e. 'Chouchou,') to whom he dedicated his *Children's Corner* suite. She died in 1919 aged fourteen.

By the turn of the century, Debussy's music had begun to reach a wider public. His opera *Pelléas et Mélisande* was produced in 1902. Although controversial and opposed by Maeterlinck on whose play the opera was based, it won him many admirers and made his name internationally famous. He received the Légion d'honneur and was made an advisor on the board of the Paris Conservatoire. Financially secure from his second marriage and with increasing success as a composer, Debussy had at last 'arrived'.

He travelled throughout Europe and even as far afield as Moscow and St Petersburg (in 1913) but from 1909 his health started to deteriorate.

1915–18   He suffered from frequent haemorrhages and underwent an operation for bowel cancer, which left him with a colostomy bag. He had a second operation, radium and morphine were administered but it was no use. Towards the end of 1917 he wrote, 'Music has quite left me, and I have never forced anyone's love.' From the beginning of the following year he could not leave his room and died there at the end of March. Only a handful of his friends were present at his funeral.

HIS MUSIC

Christopher Headington considers Debussy to be 'perhaps the most subtly and profoundly influential of all the twentieth century's composers so far; and his influence, which has reached to a remarkable extent into popular music, appears to be increasing today as musicians once again seek for the essential bases of their art.'

Reading Oscar Thompson's summary of Debussy's art, one realizes just how revolutionary Debussy was. The sounds he invented are from another planet to that inhabited by Brahms, Wagner and Tchaikowsky, whose music ruled the roost while Debussy was struggling to become accepted. To Thompson, he was 'the poet of mists and fountains, clouds and rain; of dusk and glints of sunlight through the leaves; he was moonstruck and seastruck and a lost soul under a sky bespent with stars .... He was conscious of the perfumes of a summer's day and he could scent in fancy the odours of an Andalusian night. In transmuting Nature into harmony, he has made sonorous his own emotions; never with any beating of the breast or invoking the high heavens to look down upon his agony or his transport of joy. Always here is reticence; always sobriety.'

Essential works

Prélude à l'après-midi d'un faune (1892–94): inspired by Stéphane Mallarmé's poem of the same title, this famous orchestral work encapsulates the Impressionist and Symbolist influences in Debussy's work. The poem tells of a faun experiencing the delicious state between waking and dreaming; he imagines he has seen a nymph, he awakens, his feelings intense and turbulent, and then returns once more to sleep. Debussy describes the work as a prelude: in other words he sets the mood for the poem. An Impressionist painter would be interested not in the photographic realism of the scene but in interpreting its impression in light and shadows; the Symbolist poets would be as interested in the theme of the poem as they would be in the very sound of the words. Debussy's music is entirely analogous with these two schools.

Nocturnes for orchestra (1899): Debussy, unusually, provided a programme for each of the three movements and explained 'we are not concerned with the form of the Nocturne, but with everything that this word includes in the way of diversified impressions and special lights.' In *Nuages* (*Clouds*) marvellous woodwind writing evokes the movements of clouds, in *Fêtes* (*Festivals*) the composer is concerned with movement, rhythm and dancing, and in *Sirènes* (*Sirens*), heard less frequently, Debussy turns to a favourite subject, the sea.

La mer (1905): Debussy's most ambitious work for orchestra is a multi-faceted portrait of the sea. The work is in three movements, or 'sketches', as Debussy preferred to call them, but are subtly bonded together so that none successfully stands alone in performance unlike the Nocturnes – apart from anything else, the final movement repeats thematic material from the first. Debussy completed the score while staying at Eastbourne.

Ibéria (1910): this is the second and best known of the three works for orchestra collectively entitled *Images* (not to be confused with the two sets of works for piano also called *Images*). *Gigues* and *Rondes de Printemps* are the first and third sections of the suite. The three movements of *Ibéria* are not a portrait of Spain but an evocation of the feelings and impressions aroused by that country. In reality, Debussy's total experience of the real Spain was the result of a one-hour stop in San Sebastián where he went to a bullfight. Yet the music is as Spanish as any Spaniard could

write, the result of Debussy's *impressions* after reading books, listening to flamenco dancers and folk songs and looking at pictures.

String Quartet in G minor (1893): completed the year before *L'après-midi d'un faune*, this is a rare example of Debussy writing in a structural scheme not of his own devising. Yet, early as it was in his career, it has all the nebulous colours, timbres and harmonic language that he was to make his own.

Pelléas et Mélisande, opera (1893–1902): opera buffs rave about this seminal work: 'one of the most successful attempts to create a single artistic entity out of music and drama,' 'a watershed in the history of opera and classical music,' and so on. The word setting, in which the sung word becomes almost as natural as speech, the orchestral role, which does not link or accompany or comment on the action but provides a 'tonal backdrop', and the reticence of the score were new concepts in music theatre. This opera is not an easy listen and many people find it boring, especially those who like operas to have big tunes (there aren't any) and spectacular arias (look elsewhere). It is a misty, dreamy work of shadows and imagery, based on the play by Maurice Maeterlinck, a variation of the Tristan and Isolde story. 'I have tried,' wrote Debussy, 'to trace a path that others may follow, broadening it with individual discoveries which will, perhaps, free dramatic music from the heavy yoke under which it existed for so long a time.'

Piano music

Preludes (1910, 1913): many authorities believe the two sets of Preludes to be the most perfect distillation of Debussy's art and, in addition, that they constitute the first change of character and technique in piano writing since Chopin. Whereas Chopin's brief masterpieces express clearly defined moods and emotions, Debussy's miniatures resemble improvisatory sketches suggesting 'infinitely delicate auditory and visual sensations.' One other point of interest is that Debussy put the title of each prelude at the foot of the page, not at the head – he wanted them to be heard as objectively as possible, without preconceptions. *The* recording of these is by Walter Gieseking; in fact any Debussy played by Gieseking goes to the heart of the matter.

The best known of the twenty-four are (from Book 1) *Voiles*, *La fille aux cheveux de lin* ('The Girl with the Flaxen Hair'), among the most celebrated and exquisite pieces Debussy wrote – *La Cathédrale Engloutie* – a portrait of the Cathedral of Ys rising out of the waves, as legend has it, and *Minstrels* – music-hall and black-faced minstrels. From Book 2, less inspired, seek out the American cakewalk number *General Lavine-Eccentric* – a famous wooden puppet at the Folies Bergère, *Hommage à S. Pickwick, Esq., P.P.M.P.C.* – a celebration of Dickens' character with quotations from 'God Save the Queen', and, especially, *Feux d'artifice*, a brilliant firework – and keyboard – display.

Suite bergamasque (1890, rev. 1905): in four movements, although only one of them is generally played these days and *that* is played more than any other composition by Debussy, for the third movement is the lovely *Clair de lune*. His aim in this suite was to return to the grace and charm of the seventeenth-century French clavecinists without compromising his own harmonic ideas.

Estampes (1903): three 'prints' or 'etchings' capture a Chinese atmosphere in *Pagodes*, moonlit waters by the Alhambra in *Soirée dans Grenade* and falling rain in *Jardins sous la pluie*.

Images (1905, 1907): when Debussy sent the first of the two sets to his publishers he wrote,

'I think I may say without undue pride that I believe these three pieces will live and will take their places in piano literature ... either to the left of Schumann ... or to the right of Chopin.' No.1 of the first set, *Reflets dans l'eau* (*Reflections in the water*), is among the finest musical evocations of water.

Children's Corner, suite (1908): six short movements depict the magical world of a child. It was written for his daughter 'Chouchou' when she was only four and includes the *Serenade for the Doll* (No.3), the popular *Gollywog's Cakewalk* (No.6) – listen out for the sly quote from *Tristan und Isolde* in the middle – as well as a send up of a Clementi piano study in *Doctor Gradus ad Parnassum*.

L'île joyeuse (1904): one of Debussy's most sensuous works and a masterly piece of piano writing; it is an interpretation of Watteau's picture *Embarquement pour Cythère*.

Also worth investigating
Deux Arabesques, for piano (1891)
Pour le piano, suite (1894–1901): comprising *Prélude*, *Sarabande* and *Toccata*
Trois chansons de Bilitis (1897)
La plus que lente, for piano (1910)
Jeux, ballet (1912)
Sonata for violin and piano (1917)

Léo DELIBES

'Father of the modern ballet'

Born: 21 February 1836, St-Germain-du-Val, Sarthe
Died: 16 January, 1891, Paris
Full name: Clément Philibert Léo Delibes
Type of music: opera, operetta, ballet, incidental music for plays
Influences: Adam, Meyerbeer, Offenbach, Gounod
Contemporaries: Henryk Wieniawski, César Cui, SAINT-SAËNS, **DELIBES**, BALAKIREV, Emile Waldteufel, BIZET, BRUCH, MUSSORGSKY, Josef Rheinberger

HIS LIFE AND MUSIC
After early lessons with his mother, Delibes entered the Paris Conservatoire at the age of twelve but this precocious start led only to jobs as an organist and accompanist (Adolphe Adam, the composer of *Giselle*, had recommended him for the post at the Théâtre Lyrique in 1853) and as chorus master assisting Gounod, Berlioz and Bizet. He had a hit with his first work for the stage, the light-hearted one-act operetta *Deux sous de charbon*. This work established the direction of Delibes' career. He became a complete man of the theatre, and the Paris Opéra's presentation in 1866 of *La source* (subsequently revived as *Naïla*) was his first successful ballet; it was followed four years later by a second ballet commission, *Coppélia, ou La fille aux yeux d'émail*, to give the work its full title. With *Sylvia* (1876), Delibes achieved lasting fame as one of music's finest melodists. His deft and imaginative orchestration won him many admirers, among whom were

Tchaikowsky (whose own ballet music is noticeably influenced by Delibes) and, later, Stravinsky.

Delibes was not as successful with his operas, until, almost out of the blue, came his exotic masterpiece *Lakmé* in 1883.

None of Delibes' work has pretensions to depth or high aesthetic ideals like that of some of his contemporaries; he wrote expertly-crafted, delicately-drawn scores of tuneful, characterful music.

Essential works

Lakmé, opera (1883): the only score of Delibes' twenty-nine stage-works that is still heard today, excluding *Coppélia* and *Sylvia*. Set in nineteenth-century India, the unlikely plot (so what's new?) is saved by the music. 'The Bell Song' from Act 2 is among the most exacting of coloratura arias and has always been popular but, thanks to TV commercials for the 'world's favourite airline', this has been overtaken by the sensuous Act 1 duet 'Dôme épais le jasmin', better known as the Flower Duet.

Coppélia, ballet (1870): the plot is based on *The Sandman*, a short story written by E.T.A. Hoffmann and the same source as that used by Offenbach the following year for his opera *The Tales of Hoffmann*; the Act 1 Mazurka is well known.

Also worth investigating

From **Sylvia** comes the famous 'pizzicato' dance; from **Naïla** comes the *Pas de Fleurs*, turned into a virtuoso piano *soufflé* by Dohnányi; and finally, of interest is the incidental music Delibes wrote for a revival of Victor Hugo's play *Le roi s'amuse*. Beecham made a fine recording of this suite of dances – the *Pavane* comes from Arbeau's *Orchésographie* of 1589 and was used by Peter Warlock in his *Capriol* Suite.

Frederick DELIUS

'The poet of dawn and sunsets, of hills, the countryside, and the sea'

Born: 29 January 1862, Bradford
Died: 10 June 1934, Grez-sur-Loing, near Fontainbleu
Original name: Fritz Theodor Albert Delius
Type of music: orchestral, concerto, chamber, opera, choral
Influences: Thomas Ward, Grieg, Wagner, Debussy
Contemporaries: ARENSKY, Enrico Bossi, Leon Boëllmann, DEBUSSY, **DELIUS**, Edward German, Horatio Parker, Gabriel Pierné, MASCAGNI, Eugen d'Albert

HIS LIFE AND MUSIC

The sound world of Delius is immediately recognizable – warm, luminous orchestral colours, hazy, impressionistic tone-pictures tinged with a romantic glow. Hard to hum a Delius tune (yet they are there) or to see where the music is going (he was at his best fantasizing, dreaming and drifting) but the ravishing beauty of his music is equally hard to resist. No one followed in his footsteps, unless you include popular music arrangers. He belonged to no tradition; he led nowhere.

His father, Julius Delius, was a successful Prussian industrialist who had settled in the thriving North-country industrial town of Bradford, and become the owner of a wool company. Frederick was destined to follow in his footsteps and in 1882 was dispatched to run the orange groves his father had purchased in Solano, Florida. Here, he had a Damascus-like conversion: hearing the close harmony of Negro singers wafting across the St John River he realized that music must be his life. *Appalachia*, variations on an old slave song, reflects his time there. He had brought his violin with him, and he was skilled enough to impress people with the Mendelssohn Concerto. On a trip to

Jacksonville in search of a piano, he met up with an American organist, Thomas F. Ward, who gave him lessons in music theory. In six months, so Delius said, he learnt more from Ward than in the three years of formal training he undertook subsequently at the Leipzig Conservatory (father Delius had relented in the face of his son's determination and the oranges were left to ripen under someone else's care). '[Ward] showed wonderful insight in helping me to find out just how much in the way of traditional technique would be useful for me.'

However uncongenial he found Leipzig, one benefit was a meeting with Grieg and the two became close friends. Indeed, Scandinavia exercised a lifelong hold over Delius' imagination and music – he'd first travelled there as a young man – and when, after graduating in 1888, he moved to Paris, he mixed with painters and poets (more than musicians) who were predominantly Scandinavian.

Delius married the painter Jelka Rosen in 1897 and moved to the village of Grez-sur-Loing near Paris, which was to be his home for the rest of his life. Increasingly, he became more reclusive, visitors were rarely welcomed and when they were invited *chez* Delius, they would often be met with profound silence or dismissed abruptly when the host could stand their company no longer.

From the age of forty, his unique voice began to assert itself; the pleasant but derivative works of the previous two decades now gave way to the distinctive Delius sound, in *A Mass of Life*, *Sea Drift*, *Brigg Fair* and *In a Summer Garden*. Germany took to his music readily and England too, after a reluctant start, mainly due to Thomas Beecham, an ardent champion of Delius' work.

Delius and his wife spent the war years in England and Norway but by the early 1920s his creative powers had faltered. Paralysis and blindness set in, the result of contracting syphilis in Paris in the 1890s, 'a heavy defection of his favourite goddess Aphrodite Pandemos who had returned his devotions with an affliction that was to break out many years later,' as Beecham put it so quaintly. That might have been that, had it not been for the intervention of the young Yorkshire musician Eric Fenby who offered his services as amanuensis to the ailing Delius. (It is now difficult to imagine anyone but Max Adrian and Christopher Gable writing the music, so effective was Ken Russell's film of the partnership between Delius and Fenby.) In 1929 Beecham organized a festival of six concerts devoted entirely to Delius' music, and which the composer attended (Beecham mounted a second festival in 1949). 'He was carried in his invalid chair, propped up by cushions, down the gangway to a waiting ambulance,' wrote his sister. 'All that the pressmen could see  was a figure with silvered hair, wearing a grey felt hat, a heavy overcoat, with his sightless eyes shielded by tortoiseshell glasses and a pale, wrinkled, ascetic face.' This was the first and only time that Delius heard his music cheered to the echo by his compatriots. It was his last public appearance.

The final four years of his life were spent in excruciating pain alleviated by constant doses of morphine. When he died, he was buried at Grez but a year later friends arranged for the transferral of his body to England where he was buried in the quiet country churchyard of Limpsfield in Surrey.

Essential works

On Hearing the First Cuckoo in Spring (1912): quintessential Delius, a brief orchestral tone-poem that makes a perfect introduction to the sensuous, tranquil textures that dominate his best music. The picture of an Edwardian summer afternoon is exquisite – though its main theme derives from a Norwegian folk song. Its companion piece is the languorous *Summer Night on the River* (1911).

In a Summer Garden (1908): inspired by Delius' beautiful riverside garden at Grez and dedicated to Jelka; according to Eric Fenby, this was the last piece of music the dying composer heard.

A Song of Summer (1930): adapted from the unpublished *A Poem of Life and Love*, completed by the blind and paralysed composer, notated by Eric Fenby. 'Imagine we are sitting in the heather on the cliffs by the sea,' said Delius, as they began the task of dictation. Its richly-scored climax was used to powerful effect in Ken Russell's film biography of the same title.

Brigg Fair (1907): a set of variations on a Lincolnshire folk song (Percy Grainger introduced Delius to the tune) subtitled 'an English Rhapsody'; as with this work and all of

Delius' music, Beecham's recordings are still the benchmark.

The Walk to the Paradise Garden (1907): an orchestral interlude between the fifth and sixth scenes of Delius' opera *A Village Romeo and Juliet*, added to the score five years after its original composition and often played as a separate item in concerts.

Sea Drift (1904): some people think Delius' choral writing show him at his most idiosyncratic; this is a haunting setting of Walt Whitman's despairing poem, for baritone, chorus and orchestra.

Also worth investigating

A Mass of Life (1904–08): a grand celebratory choral and orchestral piece, though inspired by the discredited theories of Nietzsche, and lacking in rhythmic vitality.

La calinda (1904): from Delius' second opera, *Koanga*, this little piece has achieved worldwide popularity in Eric Fenby's arrangement for concert orchestra. Look out for the short Serenade from *Hassan*, of similar character.

Sleigh Ride (1890): No.3 of Three Small Tone-Poems; early and unrepresentative it may be, but what a jolly tune!

Ernst von DOHNÁNYI
(1877–1960)

Variations on a Nursery Song, Op.25, 1914

We are familiar with this tune from the nursery rhyme 'Twinkle, twinkle, little star'; the Americans call it the 'Alphabet song' while, to the French, who seem to have had it first in 1761, it is 'Ah, vous dirai-je, Maman'. Mozart wrote a set of keyboard variations on the tune (K.265), and Adolphe Adam, who composed *Giselle*, wrote some acrobatic vocal variations.

Dohnányi begins his variations for piano and orchestra with a portentous, puffed-up, Wagnerian tone-poem of an introduction. The listener anticipates a thunderous entry from the soloist with all guns blazing – octaves, arpeggios, the lot – but Dohnányi deftly whips the rug out from under our feet and humorously presents the tune played with two fingers. He then gives us eleven highly contrasted and deliciously witty variations, a compendium of virtually every nineteenth-century musical trend. He dedicated the piece 'to the enjoyment of lovers of humour, and the annoyance of others.'

Dohnányi began his career as a virtuoso pianist. He made many recordings — including two versions of the Variations – but abandoned full-time concerts and touring to concentrate on composing and teaching in Berlin and Budapest (his pupils included Sir Georg Solti). The Second World War brought personal tragedy: of his two sons, one was executed for his role in the abortive attempt on Hitler's life and the other was killed in combat. He himself was suspected of Nazi collaboration and acquiescence in some anti-Semitic measures, but was later exonerated. After the war he settled in America and came to be regarded as the Grand Old Man of Hungarian Music. His grandson is the distinguished conductor Christoph von Dohnányi.

There are many other fine works by this composer. His music is far more German in the late Romantic mould than the more nationalist works of his Hungarian contemporaries Bartók and Kodály. His orchestral Suite in F sharp minor and *Ruralia hungarica* (five pieces for orchestra) are well worth digging out, and pianists have always enjoyed at least two of his many piano solos, Rhapsody in C, Op.11 No.3 and Capriccio in F minor, Op.28 No.6.

Gaetano DONIZETTI

'He had a Midas gift of melody' (Donald Jay Grout)

Born: 29 November 1797, Bergamo
Died: 8 April 1848, Bergamo
Type of music: opera
Influence: Rossini
Contemporaries: Saverio Mercadante, Franz Berwald, SCHUBERT, **DONIZETTI**, Jacques Fromenthal Halévy, BELLINI, Josef Lanner, Albert Lortzing, ADAM

HIS LIFE

Imagine composing over twenty operas – some of them highly successful at the time – before finding your own way of doing things. That is what happened to the incredibly prolific Donizetti.

His father, a weaver and later a pawnbroker, would not countenance a musical career for his son at first but eventually he reluctantly allowed him to go to the Bergamo School of Music. Here Donizetti devoured the scores of his idol Rossini, who was only five years his senior, and determined that he would be an opera composer in the same mould. So his first opera, *Enrico di Borgogna* (1818), and the next twenty-two were written by the hand of Donizetti but with the voice of Rossini. Donizetti could not have known that Rossini would stop writing operas in 1829, but the strange fact is that as soon as Rossini *did* 'retire' (at the age of thirty-seven), Donizetti started writing music that bore his own distinctive style.

His finest operas were produced after 1830 – *Anna Bolena, L'elisir d'amore, Maria Stuarda, Lucia di Lammermoor, Don Pasquale* – some sentimental and tragic, others witty and subtle, and numbering seventy in all. As in the Rossini-influenced days, he could turn out as many as three or four a year, and was said to have sketched and written the last act of *La favorita* in only a few hours. Sir Charles Hallé, the German-born conductor, remembered visiting Donizetti and asking him if it was true that Rossini had really written *The Barber of Seville* in a fortnight. ' "Oh, I quite believe it," answered Donizetti. "He was always such a lazy fellow!" I confess that I looked with wonder and admiration at a man who considered that to spend a whole fortnight over the composition of an opera was a waste of time.' Not all have

stood the test of time; one wonders what such quixotic titles as *Alfredo il Grande*, *Alina Regina di Golconda* and *Elisabetta o Il castello di Kenilworth* contain.

Donizetti dashed all over Europe in the 1830s and '40s, producing, supervising and composing his operas, acclaimed in Vienna and Paris as much as in his native Italy.

With the appearance of *Don Pasquale* in 1843, Donizetti reached the height of his creative powers, but then Fate intervened. He had never got over the death in 1837 of his adored wife and began suffering bouts of fever and headaches, accompanied by intense depression and hallucinations. He continued to work through 1844, but in 1845 had a paralytic stroke and lapsed into insanity brought on by the final stages of syphilis.

HIS MUSIC

Rossini, Bellini and Donizetti: the great triumvirate of Italian opera composers in the first half of the nineteenth century. After Rossini's retirement and Bellini's premature death, it was Donizetti who paved the way for the young Verdi. He seems to have been an amiable man, well liked by all who met him, with a sense of his own place in musical history, aware that he was the heir of Rossini and aware too when his time was up: 'My heyday is over,' he wrote in a letter in 1844, 'and another must take my place.... Others have ceded their places to us and we must cede ours to still others.... I am more than happy to give mine to people of talent like Verdi.'

Donizetti was a practical man of the theatre and understood what appealed to audiences and how to make the most of the musical forces at his command. He appreciated the benefits of writing with a particular artist in mind to suit his or her ability, and the vocal opportunities he gave them helped keep the works so popular. Why else should singers of the calibre of Joan Sutherland, Maria Callas and Montserrat Caballé revive some of Donizetti's operas after years of neglect, such as *La favorita*, *Anna Bolena*, *La fille du régiment* and *Emilia di Liverpool*?

In some quarters, Donizetti is denounced for his indiscriminate fecundity, and there is some truth in Cecil Gray's remark that 'when he chose to take the trouble, he was capable of attaining remarkable heights.' Such criticism should be tempered by the fact that only a genius in complete control of his craft could have written the Sextet from *Lucia*.

Essential works

L'elisir d'amore, opera (1832): *The Elixir of Love* is one of Donizetti's best comic creations, and he wrote the music in just fourteen days. His forty-first opera, it contains one of the most popular arias: 'Una furtiva lagrima', from Act 2, one reason why all the foremost tenors have loved playing the role of Nemorino.
Lucia di Lammermoor, opera (1835): this is Donizetti's masterpiece. Based on Sir Walter Scott's novel *The Bride of Lammermoor*, it is one of the great soprano vehicles (the famous

Mad Scene from Act 3 is a veritable lexicon of coloratura technique) and contains the finest sextet in opera.
Don Pasquale, opera (1843): a wonderful comic work: Act 3 has the lovely Serenata, 'Com è gentil' ('How lovely it is').
Anna Bolena (1830), **Maria Stuarda** (1835), **La fille du régiment** (1840), **La favorita** (1840) and **Linda di Chamounix** (1842): these are the other Donizetti operas that are worth investigating.

Paul DUKAS
(1865–1935)

The Sorcerer's Apprentice, 1897

Anyone who has seen Walt Disney's *Fantasia* can never forget apprentice Mickey Mouse battling with the brooms and the tide of water sweeping into his master's den. Dukas' masterpiece, an orchestral scherzo, is a literal musical translation of Goethe's ballad 'Der

Zauberlehrling' (in French 'L'apprenti sorcier', which, in turn, should be more correctly translated as 'The Apprentice Sorcerer'). It is a 'pop' classic and was given its first performance in Paris in 1897. Ironically it is unlike anything else that Dukas wrote; the rest of his output, strongly influenced by his friend Debussy, tends to be dour, humourless and non-programmatic. Among his more extended works are the Symphony in C, the opera *Ariane et Barbe Bleu* and the dance-drama *La péri*, but for a further brief and attractive glimpse of Dukas try his *Villanelle* for French horn and piano.

Dukas puts in a strong claim for the 'most boring life of a composer' award. He devoted all of it to studying, teaching and composing music in Paris. He was said to be a mild-mannered, self-centred man. He was certainly self-critical: he completed very little music after 1910 and, just before his death, destroyed most of what he had written.

Antonin DVOŘÁK

'I should be glad if something occurred to me as a main idea that occurs to Dvořák only by the way' (Brahms)

Born: 8 September 1841, Mühlhausen, Bohemia (near Prague)
Died: 1 May 1904, Prague
Type of music: Romantic, nationalist; symphony, orchestral, concerto, opera, choral, chamber
Influences: Beethoven, Schubert, Smetana, Brahms, Wagner
Contemporaries: TCHAIKOWSKY, Johann Svendsen, CHABRIER, **DVOŘÁK**, SULLIVAN, MASSENET, Arrigo Boito, GRIEG, Pablo de Sarasate, RIMSKY-KORSAKOV

HIS LIFE

The greatest of all Czech composers, whose best works are among the finest of the nineteenth century, who was recognized internationally and a hero among his countrymen, died impoverished. The violinist Fritz Kreisler visited him at his home in 1903 and said the scene recalled something out of *La bohème*. Dvořák had sold his music for a pittance, and the money from his tours and his work in America had gone. 'I had been playing some of Dvořák's Slavonic Dances,' wrote Kreisler, 'and visited the old man to pay my respects. I asked him whether he had nothing further for me to play. "Look through that pile," said the sick composer, indicating a pile of unorganized papers. "Maybe you can find something." I did. It was the Humoresque (in G flat, Op.101 No.7).' (Now among Dvořák's – not to say classical music's – best-known pieces, the Humoresques were transcribed for violin and piano by Kreisler.)

If his father had had his way, Dvořák would have followed in his footsteps and become a butcher. Instead the young man's extraordinary musical gifts led him elsewhere, although recognition was a long time coming. He learnt the violin as a child, became a chorister in his native village and played in local orchestras. When Dvořák was twelve, he was sent away to study music and learn German, financed by an uncle. The headmaster of the school, Antonin Liehmann, was an excellent musician who taught Dvořák the piano, viola and organ and gave him a good grounding in music theory.

Throughout the 1860s Dvořák was an orchestral violinist and violist, playing in cafés and theatres, and composing prolifically. He performed in a concert of Wagner excerpts conducted by the composer himself and came under his spell, later playing in the Prague National Theatre Orchestra under the father of Czech music, Smetana. Life was a struggle both financially and creatively. Dvořák existed for music and nothing else except trains. Like Hindemith half a century later, the composer was one of music's great trainspotters; he knew off by heart all the time-tables from the Franz-Josef Station in Prague, and often said that he would have liked to have invented the steam locomotive, 'one of the highest achievements of the human spirit.'

In 1873, he abandoned the orchestra for the organ loft of St Adalbert's in Prague, a less demanding job that gave him more time to compose. The same year he married Anna Cermakova, his former pupil. Suddenly, a succession of masterly pieces appeared, including the Serenade for Strings. News of his music spread, and before five years had elapsed he found himself hailed throughout Europe as a major creative force. His achievement had been to recognize that his writing up to 1873 was derivative, a copy of Wagner, Brahms and other German late-Romantics. As soon as he turned to Czech nationalism and began using the musical character and folk rhythms of his native land, a personal, fresh, distinctive voice emerged. His Symphony No.3 won him the Austrian State Prize as well as the respect of Brahms, who was on the jury, and the relationship between the two men developed into one of lifelong friendship. Brahms was instrumental in finding a publisher for the younger man's work, and Dvořák won the same award three years in succession.

Dvořák's frequent visits to England during the 1880s spread his fame further – his choral works were eagerly received – and he was awarded many prestigious honours, culminating in 1891 when he was made a professor of composition at the Prague Conservatory, and was awarded an honorary doctorate by Cambridge University as well as being offered the directorship of the National Conservatory of New York at an annual salary of $15,000. Dvořák moved to the United States in 1893, after a string of farewell European tours. A combination of homesickness and the discovery of American indigenous folk music combined to inspire a series of masterpieces, including the 'New World' Symphony, the Cello Concerto and the 'American' String Quartet.

On returning to Prague, he resumed his professorship, was made director of the Conservatory in 1901 and was appointed a life member of the Austrian House of Lords, the first musician to be so honoured. During this final period, Dvořák turned to writing symphonic poems based on old Czech legends and operas, including the only one that remains in today's repertoire, *Rusalka*. Although his last months were clouded by the fiasco of his new opera *Armida* (he died of an apoplectic stroke six weeks after its premiere), his death was marked by a national day of mourning.

HIS MUSIC

If Smetana was the founding father of Czech music, Dvořák was the composer who popularized it. He was a country boy, a rustic, noted for his sunny, outgoing disposition. A love of the countryside and nature pervades his work. Wherever one turns there is an inexhaustible freshness and effortless invention.

His melodic gifts can be compared with Schubert – the tunes just kept on pouring out – and like Smetana he did not use actual folk tunes but rather absorbed their essence, painting their character in his own more vivid colours. Although by no means an intellectual (he was barely more than literate), Dvořák had an instinctive grasp of classical music structure, which enabled him to write within a strict discipline without academic pedantry. All these qualities are reflected in his music. There is no turmoil in his character or his music, no neuroticism, no dark, brooding side. It is true he was no instigator of musical form and in many ways his work is conservative, but its supreme attractions are its directness and innocence for, as one writer put it, 'life was a very wonderful, uncomplicated thing to him.'

Essential works

Dvořák wrote the Beethovian number of nine symphonies during his life but, because he disowned the first four, the numbering of these can be confusing, and five of the symphonies are known by two different numbers. They are:

No.1 in C minor, 'The Bells of Zlonice' (1865)

No.2 in B flat (1865)

No.3 in E flat (1873)

No.4 in D minor (1874)

No.5 in F (sometimes known as No.3) (1875, rev. 1887)

No.6 in D (sometimes known as No.1) (1880)

No.7 in D minor (sometimes known as No.2) (1884–85)

No.8 in G (sometimes known as No.4) (1889)

No.9 in E minor ('From the New World') (sometimes known as No.5) (1893)

The first four symphonies are rarely performed, although some people make big claims for the Symphony No.3 in E flat. As to the others:

Symphony No.6 in D, Op.60 (1880): Dvořák was determined that a Brahms should come out of Bohemia and in this symphony, his first mature attempt at the most demanding of musical structures, he pays tribute to Brahms and *his* Symphony No.2 in D, written just three years earlier.

Symphony No.7 in D minor, Op.70 (1885): this is Dvořák at his most terse, except for the gorgeous third movement, one of his finest; musicians love playing this – and indeed all Dvořák's orchestral scores – because everyone, not just the first players, has a rewarding part to play, something that Dvořák's decade of playing in an orchestra had taught him.

Symphony No.8 in G, Op.88 (1889): the most nationalist of the symphonies, the second movement being almost a miniature tone-poem of Czech village life, with its bird song and rustic country band.

Symphony No.9 in E minor ('From the New World'), Op.95 (1893): when 'the New World' first appeared, fierce debate raged about whether Dvořák had used Negro and American Indian tunes as the basis for this most loved of symphonies, or whether it was a Czech work that had captured the spirit of American national melodies. A century later it seems hugely unimportant when we are swept along with Dvořák's masterly orchestration and his unforgettable themes. The first movement hints at the spiritual 'Swing Low, Sweet Chariot', and the ravishing second movement

Largo was adapted into the song 'Goin' Home' – a tune that, in Britain, has become irrevocably associated with the North Country, brass bands and a certain brand of brown bread after a particularly powerful TV commercial claimed the music.

Carnival, Op.92 concert overture (1891): the third in a cycle of three concert overtures Dvořák originally intended to be played together, portraying the 'three great creative forces of the Universe – Nature, Life and Love.' The trilogy idea was abandoned: *In Nature* and *Othello* are played separately, but the boisterous *Carnival* is by far the most famous.

Scherzo capriccioso, Op.66 (1883): among Dvořák's most popular shorter works for orchestra, a fiery scherzo, followed by a spacious middle section.

Eight Slavonic Dances, Op.46 (1878)

Eight Slavonic Dances, Op.72 (1886)

Dvořák became known throughout Europe and America with these pieces, and there can hardly be a piano stool in Britain that didn't have a copy of **Op.46 No.8** in it at one time. **Op.46 No.1 in C** and **Op.72 No.1 in B** are the other two instantly recognizable works (much-played) but try also the tender **Dance in E minor, Op.72 No.2**. These irresistible miniatures make use of Czech dance rhythms such as the Dumka, Polka, Furiant, Sousedska and Skoena.

Serenade for Strings in E, Op.22 (1875): a five-movement suite, full of memorable tunes you can't get out of your head and one of Dvořák's most delectable scores.

Cello Concerto in B minor, Op.104 (1895): arguably the most popular cello concerto in the repertoire, it is certainly one of the greatest works for the instrument. It was inspired by the Cello Concerto No.2 by the operetta composer Victor Herbert. When Brahms initially saw Dvořák's score he is said to have exclaimed: 'Why on earth didn't I know that one could write a cello concerto like this? If I had only known, I would have written one long ago!' The balance between the soloist and the orchestra in this work is masterly, and the magisterial and poignant themes can leave few listeners untouched.

Piano Quintet in A, Op.81 (1887): if chamber music means 'forbidding', you should start with this most sunny of chamber works, full of bright harmonic colours, lively Czech dance rhythms and Dvořák's bountiful tunefulness.

String Quartet No.12 in F, 'American', Op.96 (1893): while Dvořák studied Negro songs during his American sojourn, he also became fascinated by American Indian music; here he uses the peculiarities of Indian rhythms and folk song. Unbelievably, especially in our politically correct age, until the 1950s this work was known as 'The Nigger' Quartet.

Piano Trio No.4 in E minor, 'Dumky', Op.90 (1891): 'Dumky' is the plural of the Russian word 'Dumka' ('passing thought'), and in this generally reflective Slavic folk song contrasted with exuberant interludes, Dvořák captures the spirit of the Dumka to perfection.

'O silver moon' (from Rusalka, Op.114) (1901): one of ten operas written by Dvořák, Rusalka is rarely performed outside Czechoslovakia, but this achingly beautiful soprano aria is, justly, a recital favourite.

Stabat mater, Op.58 (1877): once the staple diet of British choral societies, this lovely setting is a tuneful reminder of Dvořák, the composer of large-scale vocal works, now somewhat neglected compared with the popularity of his orchestral works.

… not forgetting **'Songs my Mother taught me'** (from seven Gypsy Melodies, Op.55, 1880) and the ubiquitous **'Humoresque'** (in G flat, No.7 of eight Humoresques, Op.101, 1894). Hackneyed, over-played pieces, but part of the fabric.

Also worth investigating
Nocturne in B for strings, Op.40 (1875)
Piano Concerto in G minor, Op.33 (1876)
Violin Concerto in A minor, Op.53 (1880, rev.1882)
Romance in F minor for violin and orchestra, Op.11 (1879)
Requiem Mass, Op.89 (1890)

Edward ELGAR

'The first composer to bring English orchestral music to the front rank' (Basil Maine)

Born: 2 June 1857, Broadheath, near Worcester
Died: 23 February 1934, Worcester
Full title: Sir Edward William Elgar
Type of music: symphony, orchestral, concerto, oratorio, cantata, chamber, instrumental
Influences: Brahms, Wagner, the English choral tradition
Contemporaries: JANÁČEK, SOUSA, CHAUSSON, Anatoli Liadov, SINDING, **ELGAR**, LEONCAVALLO, Cécile Chaminade, PUCCINI, Dame Ethel Smyth, Sergei Liapunov

HIS LIFE

'I am self-taught in the matter of harmony, counterpoint, form, and, in short, the whole of the "mystery" of music.…When I resolved to become a musician and found that the exigencies of life would prevent me from getting any tuition, the only thing to do was to teach myself. I read everything, played everything, and heard everything I possibly could.' Elgar was not only self-taught but self-made, in the best Edwardian tradition. His background, belying the bluff, stiff-upper-lipped character in the photographs, was one of genteel poverty in the English countryside. His father ran a piano-tuning business from his music shop in Worcester and was the organist of Worcester's Roman Catholic Church, a post he held for nearly forty years. His mother, the daughter of a farmer, was more inclined to literary interests, exerting a lasting influence on Elgar's development.

Elgar's father was at the centre of Worcester's musical life, on friendly terms with the local gentry and clergy connected with the Anglican cathedral. By the age of twelve his son was deputizing for him at the organ and, under his father's guidance, had taught himself the violin so that he could join in the music-making of local ensembles. He also won a reputation for his improvising abilities on the piano. Having left school at fifteen and spent an unsuccessful year in a lawyer's office, he determined on a career in music.

This took the form of giving piano and violin lessons locally and, in 1879, being made bandmaster at the County Lunatic Asylum. During his five years' involvement there, he wrote and arranged dozens of works for the ensemble to play at dances, entertainments and so forth – a formative experience, for he could experiment with every kind of instrumental combination at will. Simultaneously, he played in an orchestra in Birmingham and conducted another amateur group in Worcester.

By the time of his marriage in 1889, Elgar was thoroughly versed in the ways of composing – he was to become an orchestrator of unsurpassed brilliance – and his new wife, Caroline Alice Roberts (one of his piano pupils and the daughter of a retired Major-General), introduced him into moneyed society. His marriage also gave his creative impetus and his musical ambitions the boost they needed. All of Elgar's important music was written during the thirty years of his life with Alice. They had one child, their daughter Carice, who was born in 1890 and died as recently as 1970.

The couple first lived in London, but conditions were unfavourable and they returned to Worcestershire in 1891 to settle in Malvern. The following thirteen years saw the transformation of Elgar from a provincial small-time musician to a great composer of international standing, culminating in a knighthood in 1904. Orchestral and choral works were his main preoccupations. The demand for new choral works was insatiable, and Elgar's lifelong connection with choirs and his immersion in the Catholic faith stood him in good stead. The success of his religious and secular cantatas *The Black Knight*, *The Light of Life*, *King Olaf* and *Caractacus* paved the way for his 1900 masterpiece *The Dream of Gerontius*. By then, Elgar's name was widely known as a composer of individuality and depth, particularly after the appearance in 1899 of another masterpiece and perhaps his most loved work, the orchestral portraits of his friends featured in the *Enigma Variations*.

It is appropriate that by far his most played composition should be a piece involving chorus and orchestra. In March 1901 Elgar had premiered his Military Marches *Pomp and Circumstance* Nos.1 & 2 in Liverpool to huge popular success. When Henry Wood conducted them for the first time in London at a Promenade concert, he recalled: 'The people simply rose and yelled. I had to play it again – with the same result; in fact they refused to let me go on with the programme .... I played the march a third time. And that, may I say, was the one and only time in the history of the Promenade concerts that an orchestral item was accorded a double encore.' Queen Victoria had died in January 1901 and Elgar was asked if he would provide something for the forthcoming coronation. A set of verses was sent to him as a suggestion, written by Arthur Benson, a schoolmaster at Eton and son of the Archbishop of Canterbury. During a November performance of the *Pomp and Circumstance* Marches, Elgar was seated next to the indomitable contralto Clara Butt. She asked the composer to write her something that was similar to the tune of the Trio in March No.1, to which Elgar responded, 'You shall have that one my dear.' Benson supplied some new verses which fitted *the* tune and began with the words 'Land of Hope and Glory'. (Incidentally, there is no evidence to suggest, as sometimes stated, that it was Edward VII who came up with the idea of putting words to Elgar's tune.) They made their first triumphal appearance together in the conclusion of the *Coronation Ode* (1902), and 'Land of Hope and Glory' was published separately soon afterwards.

Now living in London and his religious faith receding, Elgar turned his attention to what he considered to be the pinnacle of the composer's art: the writing of a symphony. He achieved his ambition in no small measure, producing two masterworks, the First in 1908, the Second in 1911. A third large-scale work, the inspired Violin Concerto, was premiered the previous year by Fritz Kreisler. One of the saddest omissions in gramophone history is the lack of a recording of the work by Kreisler; he was booked to do it, but the event never took place.

Elgar was awarded the highest British honour for artists, the Order of Merit, in 1911. The following year saw the completion of his final large-scale choral work, *The Music Makers*, in which Elgar used thematic ideas from his past work, uniting them in one single vision. This was strangely prescient: how could he have known that, after his Symphonic study *Falstaff* (1913), he would write nothing more of importance until 1919 when, with a final magnificent autumnal flourish, he composed the Cello Concerto, String Quartet and Piano Quintet – and then, nothing. After his wife's death in 1920, he lost the urge to create, although he tried, unsuccessfully, to complete a third symphony.

He was made Master of the King's Musick in 1924 and given a baronetcy in 1931, but for the last fourteen years of his life, returned to his roots in Worcester, he was all but silent as a composer. The destruction of the world he knew by the First World War, the dissonance and fads of contemporary music – the new era meant little to him.

HIS MUSIC

Anthony Burgess, in *The Observer* in 1983, wrote: 'I know that Elgar is not manic enough to be Russian, and not witty and *pointilliste* enough to be French, not harmonically simple enough to be Italian and not stodgy enough to be German. We arrive at his Englishry by pure elimination.' It is strange that history has come to recognize Elgar as the first significant English composer since Purcell, the man who rescued the country from its 'land without music' label. His immediate predecessors, Hubert Parry and Charles Villiers Stanford, wrote a considerable amount of music as inspired and worth-while as some of Elgar's, and it was Vaughan Williams, with the folk song movement, who can truly be said to have established a specific 'English' musical renaissance.

Elgar wrote in the mid-European tradition – the world of Brahms is never far away. Yet Elgar's music is without question quintessentially English. You don't need a Ken Russell to overlay footage of the Malvern Hills with the Introduction and Allegro for strings or the *Enigma Variations* to tell you that. Elgar may give us what we now perceive as a picture of a long-vanished England, of a British Empire that is no more, but the emotions and pictures his music evokes reassure us of unfashionable concepts such as patriotism, love of one's country and pride in one's nation; his pastoral voice conjures up the tranquil beauty of the English countryside; his pomposity and ebullience remind us of the British bulldog – one with teeth.

Elgar's friend, the critic Ernest Newman, described 'the sunset quality' of Elgar's music. The yearning, self-questioning and reflection amid the bombast and heroics is vastly affecting. It cannot be said that he was an innovative composer, he worked firmly within the nineteenth-century harmonic and structural traditions, but his orchestral and compositional techniques are all the more remarkable for his having had no formal academic training, unlike the vast majority of great composers. Perhaps, above all, it is his melodic genius that singles him out. The small selection below is ample proof.

Essential works

Elgar himself, a highly proficient conductor, recorded a vast amount of his music, both by the acoustical process and the later electrical method; despite variable sound quality, his interpretations are fascinating historical documents to set beside the modern recordings by such models as Barbirolli, Boult and Handley. **Symphony No.1 in A flat, Op.55** (1908): to compose your first symphony at the age of fifty is exceptionally late; Elgar had been thinking about the work since 1898, and when the great conductor Hans Richter prepared for its premiere he said to the orchestra: 'Gentlemen, let us now rehearse the greatest symphony of modern times, written by the greatest modern composer, and not only in this country.' The symphony's opening theme, marked *nobilmente*, is typical and one of Elgar's finest.

Symphony No.2 in E flat, Op.63 (1911): dedicated to the memory of Edward VII, who had died in 1910, an event reflected in the funereal slow movement, this is a rumbustious, self-assured work, but it never attained the popularity of the First Symphony. A famous 'out-take' exists of Elgar rehearsing the orchestra just prior to recording.

Enigma Variations, Op.36 (1899): what's the 'Enigma'? Scholars have been arguing for nearly a century now, but Elgar wasn't telling. 'Auld lang Syne', 'Rule Brittania', a Mozart symphony? If there *is* a hidden theme (some say the 'enigma' is an unplayed theme that fits over the opening statement), it doesn't distract from the inspired variations Elgar wrote upon it, each one portraying his friends, his wife and, in the last movement, himself. Variation IX, *Nimrod*, was recently voted the fourth most popular piece of classical music by radio listeners. Why 'Nimrod'? Elgar's publisher was his friend August Jaeger. 'Jaeger' is the German for 'huntsman'; in Genesis we read of 'Nimrod the mighty hunter before the Lord'.

Pomp and Circumstance, Op.39, five military marches (1901–30): much imitated, but never equalled. The title comes from Shakespeare: 'Farewell the neighing steed and the shrill trump, / The spirit-stirring drum, the ear-piercing fife, / The royal banner, and all quality, / Pride, pomp, and circumstance of glorious war!' (*Othello*, Act 3). The Trio of March No.1 to which we sing 'Land of Hope and Glory' is now a second national anthem. Elgar knew it would be a winner ('I've got a tune that will knock 'em – knock 'em flat,' he said), but he disapproved of its jingoistic words and became as sick of hearing it as Rachmaninov did of his Prelude in C sharp minor. March No.4 is the next most popular; it accompanied the Prince and Princess of Wales down the aisle in 1980.

Cockaigne (In London Town), Op.40 (1901): a concert overture presenting a bustling, swaggering portrait of London.

Falstaff, Op.68, symphonic study (1913): Elgar's letters reveal a whimsical, sparkling sense of humour; in this musical depiction of Falstaff and his relationship with Prince Hal the same characteristic emerges, with the usual Elgarian mix of brio and sadness.

Introduction and Allegro, Op.47 (1905): here is Elgar, bright and breezy, walking on the Malvern Hills; this wonderfully accomplished work uses a string quartet set against a string orchestra, like a latterday concerto grosso. It undoubtedly influenced later compositions by Vaughan Williams and Tippett. Try also the Serenade for string orchestra in E minor, Op.20, a slighter but equally enjoyable essay for strings and one of Elgar's first successes.

The Dream of Gerontius, Op.38 (1900): using a text by Cardinal Newman on the soul of Gerontius as it passes from life into death (a text Dvořák was offered but turned down, incidentally), Elgar fashioned this most awesome of British choral works (he disapproved of the title 'oratorio' and it does not appear on the score) into a powerful meditation on the soul's immortality. Not everyone liked it: Delius thought it 'a nauseating work,' Stanford found it 'stinking of incense', and George Moore said it was 'Holy water in a German beer barrel'.

Concerto for violin and orchestra in B minor, Op.61 (1910): one of the longest and most taxing concertos in the repertoire. Elgar dedicated it to Fritz Kreisler. The score is inscribed 'Aquí está encerrada el alma de ... ('Herein is enshrined the soul of ...'). Whose soul? The violin, or the American Mrs Worthington at whose villa the Elgars were staying when sketches of the work were begun? Its most famous recording was made by the young Yehudi Menuhin with Elgar conducting; arguably its most faithful interpreter was Albert Sammons in the ancient recording he made with Sir Henry Wood.

Concerto for cello and orchestra in E minor, Op.85 (1919): this is Elgar wearing his heart on his sleeve for once; gone is the outgoing man who loved society, here is a poignant, elegiac, introspective masterpiece reflecting his wife's failing health and other personal concerns. Has anyone improved on the recording of it made by Jacqueline du Pré and Sir John Barbirolli?

Also worth investigating

Quintet for piano and strings in A minor, Op.84 (1919): if nothing else, listen to the slow movement.

La capricieuse, Op.17 (1891): an unlikely, but successful, virtuoso fiddle encore.

Organ Sonata No.1 in G, Op.28 (1895): the first movement is especially worth hearing.

Caractacus, Op.35 (1898): its jingoistic text is laughable, but the music is magnificent, and the finale should be played at full volume.

Sea Pictures, Op.37 (1899): five settings of 'sea-poems'; 'Where corals lie' is the most popular, and the Janet Baker/Sir John Barbirolli version is still the yardstick.

And three Victorian *salon* pieces par excellence: **Salut d'amour, Op.12, Chanson de nuit, Op.15 No.1** (1897) and **Chanson de matin, Op.15 No.2** (1897).

Manuel de FALLA

'An unceasing quest for the musical soul of Spain' (Gilbert Chase)

Born: 23 November 1876, Cadiz
Died: 14 November 1946, Alta Gracia, Argentina
Full name: Manuel de Falla y Matheu
Type of music: opera, ballet, concerto, chamber, vocal, instrumental
Influences: Grieg, Felipe Pedrell, Spanish (especially Andalusian) folk music, ecclesiastical chants and flamencan song, French Impressionism
Contemporaries: Albert Ketèlbey, KREISLER, William Hurlstone, **FALLA**, Ermanno Wolf-Ferrari, Havergal Brian, Sergei Bortkiewicz, Roger Quilter

HIS LIFE AND MUSIC

Felipe Pedrell, the *eminence grise* of Spanish nationalism in music, persuaded Falla (as he had Albéniz and Granados) to use his country's character and folklore to express himself in composition. But, like Grieg whose music he greatly admired, Falla preferred not to make direct use of folk melody but rather to capture the essence and spirit of his native land as reflected in his own personality.

He began by writing *zarzuelas*, then, as now, popular, light musical entertainments in Spain, and won a prize for his opera *La vida breve* (1905). After its success he decided to visit Paris for a few weeks. There he met and befriended Debussy, Ravel and Dukas, became swept up in French musical life and ended by staying seven years. Influenced and greatly encouraged by these men (listen to Debussy's *Ibéria* from *Images* and piano prelude *Soirée dans Grenade*!), Falla made his way back to Spain in 1914. This blend of Impressionism and his own ambitions for Spanish music resulted in his three best-known works: *Nights in the Gardens of Spain* and the ballet scores *El amor brujo* and *El sombrero de tres picas*.

In 1919, Falla settled in Granada, leaving only infrequently to conduct or attend performances of his work. A lifelong bachelor, he was a recluse by nature, hated publicity and went out of his way to avoid attention. Stravinsky once described Falla as 'the most unpityingly religious person I have ever known – and the least sensible to manifestations of humour.' Despite coming from a wealthy family, he had no desire for money, possessions or honours; all he wanted was to worship God, write music and lead a simple life. This austerity comes across in his music, which is far more aloof and spare than the spontaneity, warmth and ebullience of Albéniz and Granados. Towards the end of his life he became a hypochondriac: believing that a full moon was bad for his health, when such an occurrence was due in March or in September, he refused to see anyone.

At first he sided with Franco during the Spanish Civil War, but the anti-religious sentiment that became prevalent after the overthrow of the monarchy forced him into self-imposed exile, knowing that his frail health prevented him from setting foot in his native country again. After his death at his home near Cordoba, Argentina, his body was brought back to Spain and buried in the crypt of Cadiz Cathedral.

Essential works

El amor brujo (Love, the Magician) (1915): originally a one-act ballet but better known as an orchestral suite; *The Dance of Terror* and the *Ritual Fire Dance* in particular are immensely popular. They are also known in piano transcriptions, a speciality of the great pianist Arthur Rubinstein.

El sombrero de tre picos (The Three-cornered Hat) (1919): as much as anything the work that made Falla's name; commissioned by Diaghilev and designed by Picasso. *The Miller's Dance* comes from this ballet.

Noches en los jardines de España (Nights in the Gardens of Spain) (1907–16): fountains, cypresses, Moorish palaces, orange trees, palms, guitars, a gentle summer evening breeze – this is a lush, masterly (if melancholy) evocation for piano and orchestra.

Also worth investigating

Two irresistible, foot-tapping encores that were made famous by Fritz Kreisler in his own arrangements for violin and piano of *Jota*, a transcription of *Canciones populares Españolas No.4*, and *Dance Española No.1* from *La vida breve*.

Gabriel-Urbain FAURÉ

'Marvellous musical horizons overflowing with freshness and light' (Roussel)

Born: 12 May 1845, Pamiers, Ariège (French Pyrenees)
Died: 4 November 1924, Paris
Type of music: chamber, piano, choral, vocal
Influences: Schumann, Chopin, Gounod, Saint-Saëns, church music (especially of earlier times)
Contemporaries: RIMSKY-KORSAKOV, Stephen Adams, WIDOR, **FAURÉ**, PARRY, Xaver Scharwenka, Vincent d'Indy, STANFORD, HUMPERDINCK

HIS LIFE AND MUSIC

The essential character of Fauré's music has been compared to the painting of Chardin or Fragonard; the musicologist Paul Landormy observed that 'his language, always moderate, is like well-bred discourse. He never raises his voice too high. He works in quiet colours. He is most discreet. He leaves much to be inferred. And his reserve is something quite as eloquent as louder outbursts.'

For proof of this last quality, all you have to do is listen to Fauré's Requiem, perhaps the most widely loved setting of the text by any composer. It seems small-scale and untheatrical in contrast to the Requiems by Berlioz, Verdi and Brahms, and Fauré tellingly omits the full text of the *Dies irae* – the cue to unleash full orchestral and choral forces – preferring to include only the pleading *Libera me* section of the text, yet few would say that the grander scores are more eloquent or moving.

He led a quiet, undramatic life. The son of a village schoolmaster who was promoted to assistant inspector of primary schools, Gabriel was the sixth, and unwelcome, child to be born to the family. He was fostered until he was four years old and never seems to have enjoyed much warmth or family love. It is said that a blind woman heard the eight-year-old boy playing the harmonium one day and urged his father to take him to Paris to study music. Fauré was introduced to the newly opened École Niedermeyer, the 'École de musique religieuse et classique', and Louis Niedermeyer was so impressed with him that he offered him a place at the school free of charge. With the death of Niedermeyer in 1861, Saint-Saëns became Fauré's teacher and the two developed a close, lifelong friendship.

Fauré's career thereafter is notable for its lack of thrust. He spent four years in Rennes as the church organist, returning to Paris in 1870 on the eve of the Franco-Prussian War, and he joined the light infantry for a short spell. He found a succession of increasingly important organ posts, eventually landing the top job at the Madeleine in 1896. In addition to this he took conducting and composition classes at the École Niedermeyer, becoming a professor of composition at the Paris Conservatoire. Meanwhile, in 1883 he had married the daughter of a successful sculptor.

As a link to the Impressionists and as a teacher of the future generation of French composers, Fauré was of the utmost importance. One only has to read the names of those who came under his undemonstrative tutelage: Ravel, Enesco, Roger-Ducasse, Florent

Schmitt and, arguably the most influential teacher of the twentieth century, Nadia Boulanger. Unlike his contemporaries Chabrier, d'Indy and Lekeu, Fauré did not succumb to the fashionable habit of Wagner-worship, and throughout his songs and chamber work there is an unmistakable 'Frenchness' about the language. He was unsuccessful in larger forms – operas and symphonies were not his forte – but his songs and idiomatic piano and chamber music attracted a growing number of admirers from the mid-1870s.

Fauré was appointed director of the Conservatoire in 1905, a post he retained for fifteen years until increasing deafness made it impossible for him to continue. His final works, the Second Piano Quintet and the Trio in D minor, were written when he was stone deaf. Throughout his tenure he was determined, rather pathetically, to keep his handicap a secret. Close friends helped him in this and, when his predicament was revealed four years after his death, many people who knew him were shocked. 'I have been reserved all my life,' he wrote in a letter to his wife, 'and have only been able to let myself go in certain situations.' To his son, Philippe, he confided: 'For me ... music exists to elevate us as far as possible above everyday existence.' Quite so.

Essential works

Requiem (1888, rev.1893 and 1900): whichever orchestration you prefer, one magical setting follows another in this most ethereal of choral works; who could remain unmoved by the *Sanctus*, *Pie Jesu* and *In Paradisum*? Two things distinguish this Requiem from its predecessors: its humility and the fact that, as confirmed by Fauré's son, the composer was 'not a believer but a sceptic.' At the École Niedermeyer, Fauré had absorbed the art of the church musician from the age of nine. He was forty-one when he wrote this much-cherished work, prompted, perhaps, by the recent death of his father. It received its first performance in 1888, the year in which his mother died.

If you like the Requiem, you will almost certainly fall for the equally lovely **Cantique de Jean Racine, Op.11** (1865).

Pavane, Op.50 (1887): a gentle, pastoral, orchestral trifle, with which many will be familiar.

Ballade in F sharp, Op.19 (1881): scored for piano and orchestra, this beautiful, 13-minute-long, one-movement work was originally written for piano solo. It should be heard more often, as should the haunting **Fantaisie in G, Op.111**, written in 1919 in Fauré's old age.

Violin Sonata No.1 in A (1876): written a decade before Franck's better known and even more adventurous Violin Sonata in the same key, and sounding today pleasurably melodic and romantic, it is easy to forget that in its day Fauré's Sonata was thought daring in harmony and structure.

Piano Quartet No.1 in C minor, Op.15 (1879): this is Fauré's most popular chamber work, though he received no payment for it from the publisher. Written after a broken engagement to the beautiful daughter of the famous singer Pauline Viardot-Garcia, the Adagio in this quartet says it all.

Dolly Suite, Op.56 (1897): these six movements of great tenderness were composed for Fauré's young friend Hélène, or 'Dolly', Bardac. Originally for piano duet, they were orchestrated in 1912 by Henry Rabaud. Readers of a certain age will forever associate the opening Berceuse with BBC Radio's *Listen With Mother*.

Berceuse, Op.16 (1880): for violin and orchestra

Elegie for cello and orchestra, Op.24 (c.1883, orch. 1901)

Two unpretentious miniatures typical of Fauré's entrancing melodic and lyrical gifts.

Piano music

Dip into any selection of Fauré's **Nocturnes**, **Barcarolles** and **Impromptus** and you are bound to make friends with many unexpected delights – Nocturne in C sharp minor (1898), for example. The Chopinesque titles were deliberate – he modelled them on the earlier composer's – but you could never mistake Fauré for Chopin; his piano works have fragrant harmonies and melodic developments all their own. It is a short step from here to Debussy.

Songs

Fauré composed nearly a hundred songs during his life, reflecting his development as a composer. One of the earliest, **'Après un rêve', Op.7 No.1**, is well known both as an instrumental solo and in its original form. His later songs, especially the settings of Verlaine's poems, use increasingly advanced harmonies, with an accompaniment that is of equal importance to the vocal line.

His two 'cycles', or collections, **Cinq mélodies** (1890) and **La bonne chanson** (1894), are impressive, but the most important collection, confirming Fauré as one of France's greatest songwriters, is **L'horizon chimérique, Op.118**. Others to look out for are 'Nell, ici-bas!', 'Les berceaux', 'Les roses d'Isaphan', 'Au cimetière', 'Soir', 'Clair de lune', 'Chanson d'amour', 'Spleen' and 'Rencontre'.

John FIELD

Born: 26 July 1782, Dublin
Died: 23 January 1837, Moscow
Type of music: piano concerto, solo piano
Influences: Bach, Mozart, Clementi, Dussek, Bellini
Contemporaries: François-Adrien Boïeldieu, Bernhard Crusell, HUMMEL, **FIELD**, PAGANINI, AUBER, Louis Spohr, WEBER, Henry Bishop, HÉROLD, Carl Czerny

HIS LIFE AND MUSIC

The 'inventor of the nocturne' came from a family of musicians. At the age of twelve he was taken by his ambitious father to London where he studied with Muzio Clementi and was also employed as a kind of salesroom demonstrator for Clementi's pianos. His mentor took him on a trip to Paris, Vienna and St Petersburg, where Field decided to settle. Perhaps he might have become an important composer, but a succession of extra-marital affairs and too much drink meant that compositions appeared irregularly, though he was popular as a teacher – Glinka was among his pupils. From 1824 to 1831 he lived in Moscow, by which time he was already suffering from cancer. He returned to England in 1832 for a series of concerts and an operation. Reunited with his mother, it was said that she hardly recognized him because he had aged so much. At the end of his resources, Field toured Europe before returning finally to Moscow in 1835 an alcoholic and incurably ill.

Field wrote almost exclusively for the piano and today he is remembered only for his Nocturnes, where the right hand plays a song-like melody accompanied by a flowing left hand. It was Chopin who developed the form and, compared with his miniature master-pieces, Field's are merely charming trifles, but pleasant nonetheless.

Worth investigating

Eighteen Nocturnes: try a selection from these.

Piano Concerto No.2 in A flat (1811): the best of his seven piano concertos, with catchy themes; a contrast to some of the thundering virtuoso works of his contemporaries.

A John Field Suite (1939): orchestral arrangements by Sir Hamilton Harty of a selection of Field's piano works. The opening Polka and final Rondo are orchestral lollipops.

César FRANCK

'Pater Seraphicus'

Born: 10 December 1822, Liège, Belgium
Died: 8 November 1890, Paris
Type of music: orchestral, chamber, organ and piano works
Influences: Bach, Liszt, Wagner
Contemporaries: OFFENBACH, SUPPÉ, Henri Vieuxtemps, Joachim Raff, **FRANCK,** LALO, Carl Reinecke, SMETANA, BRUCKNER, JOHANN STRAUSS II, Stephen Foster

HIS LIFE

Name a famous Belgian! Well, here's one, even though César Franck spent most of his life in Paris and became a naturalized Frenchman in 1873. It is questionable whether there has ever existed a milder, more humble man who was also a great composer. His ambitions were simple: to serve music and God with equal reverence.

Franck's music was ignored for most of his life, his first taste of success coming only months before his death. He didn't seem to mind, despite the insults of the critics and the dreadful things said to his face. 'Does it please you?' asked the conductor Edouard Colonne halfway through a rehearsal of Franck's symphonic poem *Les Djinns*. Franck replied yes, he was delighted. 'Well,' said Colonne turning to the orchestra, 'it's all frightful music but we'll go on with it anyway.' After the premiere of Franck's Symphony in D minor, Charles Gounod described it as 'the affirmation of incompetence pushed to dogmatic lengths'. Saint-Saëns was the pianist in the first performance of Franck's Piano Quintet. He hated it so much he refused to return to the stage and acknowledge the applause, leaving the music on the piano: Franck had dedicated the work to him. Perhaps the most humiliating rebuff was the first (private) performance of his oratorio *Les béatitudes*, completed in 1879 after ten years' work. Franck invited all the notable French musicians of the day to hear it at his home; in the event just two people turned up.

He began his career as a piano prodigy and was twelve when his father sent him and his brother Joseph, a violinist, on tour. After studying at the Liège Conservatory, he entered the Paris Conservatoire where his ability to improvize and transpose on the organ and piano became legendary. Part of his first-year examination was to sight-read a concerto composed by Hummel. Some mischievous streak led him to transpose it, at sight, from A minor down to F sharp minor, an incredible feat.

He looked set for a successful and profitable career as a soloist – his tyrannical father wanted nothing else from his talented son – but the young man was not interested and settled into a routine that altered little thereafter: rising at half-past five to compose for two hours, then teaching pupils all over Paris and playing the organ at various churches. In 1858 he became organist at St Clothilde, a post he held for the rest of his life.

People remembered him rushing from one appointment to another through the streets of Paris, his coat too large, his trousers too short, the absent-minded music professor, untouched by the lack of worldly recognition. 'He possessed the soul of a child,' wrote Debussy. 'The discovery of a beautiful harmony was sufficient to make him as happy as the day was long.' His pupils at the Conservatoire, where he became organ professor in 1872, adored him. They included Lekeu, Duparc, d'Indy, Chausson and Pierné.

His marriage in 1848 to the daughter of a well-known actress – his family were horrified and broke off relations with him – was not a success. He discovered he had exchanged his overbearing father for an oppressive wife who disliked his music and lack of ambition even more. The love of his pupils was some recompense, in particular the Franco-Irish Augusta Holmès with whom it is said he had an affair – the Piano Quintet is a love letter to her and is full of erotic intensity. His one taste of public success came in April 1890 with the premiere of his String Quartet. Shortly after, he was on his way to a lesson when he was knocked down by a bus. Although he continued working – he even made it to the pupil's house –his health deteriorated and he died of pleurisy.

HIS MUSIC

For some, Franck's music is too sentimental, so imbued with religiosity that it is like listening to a stained-glass window. Much of it meanders along, loosely constructed, so that it seems one is hearing an example of his famous improvisations rather than a carefully worked, fully structured piece. Yet a handful of works are clearly masterpieces, individual and unmistakably 'Franck'. Evident in all his music is the influence of his organ playing: it is easy to visualize, even in purely orchestral scores, the hands transferring from one manual to another, subtly changing the registration by pulling out a different stop, modulating constantly, shifting harmonies. Evident also is the same serenity of spirit and feeling of peaceful acceptance in these works as in his own character.

His most adventurous innovation as a composer was in cyclic form, where themes are developed from short melodic phrases, then manipulated and expanded throughout the whole composition to bind the work together. Liszt had experimented with this thematic transformation in the 1840s and 1850s.

Most of Franck's greatest works were composed in the last four years of his life; exceptionally, his creative powers rose instead of declined as he grew older.

Essential works

Symphony in D minor (1886–88): his only symphony, apart from an unpublished youthful attempt, alternates passages of Wagnerian solemnity with joyous exuberance; its stately slow movement is equally memorable.
Symphonic Variations for piano and orchestra (1885): a continuous one-movement work, much recorded, much loved, a good introduction to Franck's music.
Sonata for violin and piano in A (1886): one of the finest in the repertoire, standing alongside those of Beethoven and Bach. Written as a wedding present for the great Belgian violinist, Eugène Ysaÿe.
String Quartet in D (1889): the late work that brought Franck success at last.
Three Chorales for organ (1890)
Pièce héroïque in B minor for organ (1878):

Franck's works for this instrument are part of the organist's standard repertoire in the same way that Bach's are. The Chorales exchange moments of grandeur and drama with contemplative fantasy; the thrilling finale of the *Pièce héroïque* makes the walls vibrate!
Prélude, aria et final for piano (1886–87)
Prélude, choral et fugue for piano (1884)
Underrated, unknown by the general public, these beautiful, richly harmonized works are masterpieces.

Other works
'Panis angelicus', sacred song (1872)
Piano Quintet in F minor (1878–79)
Le chasseur maudit (1882), **Les Éolides** (1875–76), **Les Djinns** (1884) and **Psyché** (1887–88): four symphonic poems.

George GERSHWIN

'He is the prince who has taken Cinderella by the hand and openly proclaimed her a princess to an astonished world' (Walter Damrosch)

Born: 26 September 1898, Brooklyn, New York
Died: 11 July 1937, Beverly Hills, California
Original name: Jacob Gershvin
Type of music: orchestral, concerto, opera, piano, popular song
Influences: Tin Pan Alley (especially Jerome Kern), jazz, ragtime, Yiddish music, Charles Hambitzer, Debussy, Stravinsky
Contemporaries: Roger Sessions, Virgil Thomson, KORNGOLD, **GERSHWIN**, Roy Harris, POULENC, Carlos Chávez, Georges Auric, WEILL, George Antheil

HIS LIFE

Is there anyone who doesn't get a kick out of Gershwin? Few composers have done more to weld the two opposing cultures of serious and popular music together – a road that is still in the process of being mapped out, let alone built. The tragedy is that George Gershwin didn't live long enough to develop all his ideas.

His father, Morris Gershovitz (he shortened the name to Gershwin when he emigrated to America in 1891), bought a piano in 1910 initially for Ira, the older son, but it was Jacob, later George, who took to it. Within four years he was good anough to get a job playing popular songs in music shops. He had lessons with the top New York teachers – piano with Ernest Hutcheson and Charles Hambitzer, harmony with Edward Kilenyi and Rubin Goldmark – but no one can teach a composer the gifts with which Gershwin was blessed. Before he was twenty he had written a Broadway hit, *La La Lucille*, which included the hit song 'Swanee'. It sold more than a million copies in sheet music and over 2.25 million records, setting him up for life. An early string quartet went by unnoticed, as did a serious one-act opera, while he turned out hit after hit musical containing songs such as 'Fascinating Rhythm', 'Lady Be Good' and 'The Man I Love', with the lyrics usually written by his brother Ira.

Gershwin was a man possessed of phenomenal energy and ambition and it was inevitable that he should want to prove himself with more demanding music. The bandleader Paul Whiteman provided the catalyst by asking Gershwin for a concert piece.

The result was *Rhapsody in Blue*. Its first performance, on 12 February 1924, was attended by the likes of Rachmaninov, Stravinsky and Toscanini. The work was a triumph, if controversial, and it made George Gershwin internationally famous overnight.

The only question mark was over his ability to orchestrate. Ferde Grofé, Paul Whiteman's arranger, had done the orchestration for *Rhapsody in Blue*, but in the following year Gershwin produced his Piano Concerto in F, which effectively had been orchestrated by himself. Successful as he was, and while continuing to write Broadway shows, Gershwin still felt that

he was under-educated musically and asked to study with Ravel and Nadia Boulanger. Ravel turned him down. 'Why do you want to be a second-rate Ravel,' he asked, 'when you're already a first-rate Gershwin?' It was said that he also approached Stravinsky for lessons. When the composer of *The Rite of Spring* enquired how much Gershwin earned, he was told, 'About 250,000 dollars a year.' Whereupon Stravinsky asked Gershwin for lessons instead!

Other concert works followed (*Second Rhapsody* and *Cuban* Overture), but it was the inspired *An American in Paris* that scored Gershwin his next major success.

During the last years of his life Gershwin spoke of plans he had for a symphony, a string quartet, a ballet and a cantata based on the Gettysburg address. None of these plans were realized. What he did complete was an ambitious folk opera based on the novel *Porgy* by Dubose and Dorothy Heyward. It was not immediately popular: some eminent black composers, including Duke Ellington, did not like it, the serious music critics sniffed at it, and Gershwin's usual audience was bamboozled by its very serious-ness. The eminent critic and composer, Virgil Thomson, wrote of *Porgy and Bess* that it was 'a libretto that should never have been accepted on a subject that should never have been chosen [by] a man who should never have attempted it.' Its acceptance as one of the indisputably great operas of American music came only after Gershwin's premature death at the age of thirty-eight from an inoperable brain tumour.

HIS MUSIC

Leonard Bernstein, writing about *Rhapsody in Blue* in 1955, said: 'It's not a composition at all. It's a string of separate paragraphs stuck together – with a thin paste of flour and water … I don't think there has been such an inspired melodist on this earth since Tchaikowsky… but if you want to speak of a *composer*, that's another matter.'

Gershwin mixed with the most skilled musicians of his day and was painfully aware of his technical shortcomings. The conservatory-trained academics and critics took delight in pointing out the defects in his major works – the occasional awkward modulations, the strained transitions – but, as Rhett Butler might have put it, 'Frankly, my dear, no one gives a damn,' for the so-called flaws fade into insignificance against the genius of his melodic gifts and his originality. *Rhapsody in Blue* was criticized for its lack of form and development, while the jazz purists complained that it wasn't the genuine article. Prejudice against a successful Tin Pan Alley artist crossing over into another field also played its part in the musical establishment's initial unwillingness to take Gershwin seriously as an American composer of importance. Gershwin was equally determined that he *should* be taken seriously.

His melodies are fresh, spontaneous, reassuring and able to stand the test of time. The works he fashioned are among the most treasured of all American music, and the Piano Concerto is the most frequently performed of any American concerto. Most importantly, he made the use of popular music respectable and a valid idiom for 'serious' composers to utilize: Kurt Weill, Constant Lambert, William Walton and Aaron Copland have all acknowledged their debt to him.

Essential works

Rhapsody in Blue, for piano and orchestra (1924): it is conceivable that no other work in musical history has been so successful so soon after its completion; it has been arranged and adapted for every possible combination (and, incidentally, became Paul Whiteman's signature tune), and the royalties from sheet music, records and performances were astronomical. As musicologist David Ewen put it, 'Few works written by Americans before 1924 have such an unmistakable national identity as this one. It is American to the core, just as rodeos and baseball are American.' In the same way that the waltzes of Strauss evoke the Vienna of the nineteenth century so Gershwin's *Rhapsody in Blue* is America in the 1920s.

Concerto in F for piano and orchestra (1925): Gershwin was a fine pianist in his own works and he played the piano part for the premiere of this piece. (He recorded *Rhapsody in Blue* several times, but no official recordings were made of him as soloist in the concerto, though off-air recordings exist.) Some critics thought the Concerto in F was the work of a genius, but others considered that it was too derivative, relying too much on Debussy. Its charm, vitality and popularity remain unabated; its themes, if not its construction, are the equal of Rachmaninov.

An American in Paris (1928): this tone-poem for orchestra was sketched and completed in Paris, orchestrated in Vienna and premiered by the New York Philharmonic under Walter Damrosch. It was memorably choreographed and danced by Gene Kelly. Although it contains no piano part, there is a recording with Gershwin playing the small celeste role in the score.

Porgy and Bess, opera (1935): the first (and still the foremost) American opera, a firm departure from the European tradition. The score of this opera draws on banjo and percussion and incorporates indigenous folk songs and speech patterns (Gershwin immersed himself in the culture of the South), popular music idioms, jazz and spirituals. He introduced another interesting device in the opera: the white people only speak, the black people only sing. It took him a year and a half to complete the 560 pages of score. The 'hits' include 'Summertime', 'I Got Plenty o' Nuttin', 'Bess, You Is My Woman' and 'It Ain't Necessarily So.'

Three Preludes for piano (1926): three miniature masterpieces in contrasting jazz moods, unmistakably Gershwin.

Also worth investigating

Cuban Overture, **Second Rhapsody**, **'I Got Rhythm' Variations** and **Song transcriptions for piano solo**.

Orlando GIBBONS

'It is proportion that beautifies everything' (Gibbons)

Born: 1583, Oxford
Died: 5 June 1625, Canterbury
Type of music: English church music, madrigals, instrumental and keyboard works
Influences: Polyphonic school, Byrd
Contemporaries: Thomas Tomkins, Thomas Weelkes, ALLEGRI, **GIBBONS**, Girolamo Frescobaldi, Heinrich Schütz, Pietro Francesco Cavalli, LULLY

HIS LIFE AND MUSIC

Gibbons served as a chorister with King's College, Cambridge and was just twenty-one when he was made organist of the Chapel Royal, a position he retained until his death. He enjoyed considerable royal patronage throughout his career; in 1619 he was appointed one of 'the musicians for the virginalls to attend on his hignes privie chamber'

at a salary of £46 and in 1623 became organist of Westminster Abbey (his seven children were all baptized 'next door' at St. Margaret's). In 1625 he conducted the music for James I's funeral. Two months later the new king, Charles I, summoned the Chapel Royal to Canterbury to greet the arrival of his queen, Henrietta Maria, from France. Before she arrived, however, Gibbons had an apoplectic fit and died. He was buried in the cathedral the following day.

English composers during the reign of Elizabeth I had become the envy of all Europe. Gibbons continued the tradition into the reign of James I, becoming the first composer of sacred music to write exclusively for the Anglican church. He introduced an important technique in this field – the 'verse anthem', a work for solo voices and choir in which the solo passages have an independent accompaniment (which is played by viols and/or organ) – but wrote much that was in the *a capella* style of Palestrina. Apart from his anthems, Gibbons is best remembered for his madrigals. *The Silver Swan* is still deservedly popular and comes from the 1612 collection of *Madrigals and Mottets.*

He was equally adept at composing for the viol and virginal, although many of these works are restrained and sombre in mood. His string pieces include a set of nine fantasias, which was the first music ever to be cut on copper plates, though this and all but a small number of his compositions were published only after his death.

Essential works
Anthems
'O Lord in Thy Wrath', 'Almighty and ever-lasting God', 'Hosanna to the Son of David', 'This is the record of John' (Gibbons' most popular verse anthem), 'O clap your Hands', 'O Lord increase my faith' and 'Lift up your heads'.

Instrumental
Pavan and Galliard 'Lord Salisbury', composed for virginal.
Madrigals
'The silver swan', 'Now each flow'ry bank', 'What is our life' and 'Dainty fine bird that art encaged'.

Alexander GLAZUNOV

'The Russian Mendelssohn'

Born: 10 August 1865, St Petersburg
Died: 21 March 1936, Neuilly-sur-Seine
Full name: Alexander Konstantinovich Glazunov
Type of music: symphony, orchestral, concerto, ballet, chamber, piano, vocal
Influences: Liszt, Brahms, Wagner, Russian Nationalists
Contemporaries: NIELSEN, Edwin Lemare, DUKAS, **GLAZUNOV**, SIBELIUS, BUSONI, SATIE, Francesco Cilèa, GRANADOS, Hamish MacCunn

HIS LIFE AND MUSIC

Glazunov is a composer ripe for re-evaluation but not among those otherwise-forgotten composers with one overwhelming success to their names, nor among the all-time giants. Few would be able to name, let alone sing something from, a Glazunov work, with the possible exception of the last part of his ballet *The Seasons*. Yet in his day, he was hailed as a genius, 'the Little Glinka', the heir to the Mighty Handful and Tchaikowsky. He may not have been an innovator, but most pieces of Glazunov's that are given an airing make one think, 'Why isn't this played more often?'

He was born into a wealthy family (his father was a successful book publisher) and at fifteen was studying orchestration, counterpoint and harmony with Rimsky-Korsakov. A year later he had completed his First Symphony, a work that astonished Balakirev, who conducted the premiere, and Cui, who commented that it was 'frightening in its precocious maturity'. Liszt also conducted it at Weimar. Glazunov was regarded as the flag bearer of new Russian music and, at twenty-one, was considered to be among her foremost composers. Having been appointed professor of composition at the St Petersburg Conservatory in 1899, he was made director in 1905, a post he retained through the Revolution until 1928. Though a self-confessed musical conservative, among the students who passed through his hands were Prokofiev, Stravinsky and Shostakovich.

Glazunov felt no great love for Lenin and his regime, but in truth his creative powers waned before 1917. Whether he was being facetious or not is a moot point when he told H.G. Wells in 1920 that he didn't have much manuscript paper left and as soon as it ran out he would stop composing altogether. He certainly did not write much after that.

In 1928 he left Russia for Paris and conducted tours in America, but he died an exile in the French capital. Many people were shocked when they heard of his death: they had assumed he had died years earlier.

Essential works

The Seasons, Op.67, ballet, (1899): the ballet is rarely mounted now, but the four seasonal movements fashioned from the full score remain popular, especially the opening Bacchanale of *Autumn*. Glazunov himself conducted an untidy recording of the work.
Violin Concerto in A minor, Op.82 (1904): romantic, sweeping and superbly well-crafted, this is Glazunov at his best. Old-fashioned for its time it may be, but its three-movements-in-one don't contain a dull moment.
Stenka Razin, Op.13, symphonic poem (1885): portrait of a ruthless Cossack murderer of the seventeenth century, executed in Moscow in 1671. Begins and ends with the 'Song of the Volga Boatman' (yes, the one that goes 'Yo-ho, heave-ho').

Also worth investigating

Méditation in D for violin, Op.32 (1891): brief, lusciously romantic sister of the Méditation from *Thaïs* (*see* MASSENET); the most-performed of Glazunov's compositions.
Saxophone Concerto (1934): a surprising and attractive use of an instrument with a small concerto repertoire.
Of his eight underrated, under-played **Symphonies, Nos.4, 5 & 6** are full of good things. **No.5** is probably the best to begin with; **No.8** has almost Elgarian breadth and power.

Mikhail GLINKA

'The father of Russian music'

Born: 1 June 1804, Novospasskoye (Smolensk), Russia
Died: 15 February, 1857, Berlin
Full name: Mikhail Ivanovich Glinka
Type of music: orchestral, opera, chamber, piano
Influences: Donizetti, Bellini, Berlioz, Spanish and Russian folk music/culture
Contemporaries: Josef Lanner, Albert Lortzing, ADAM, BERLIOZ, **GLINKA**, Julius Benedict, Johan Hartmann, Michael Balfe, MENDELSSOHN, CHOPIN

HIS LIFE

Coming from a monied family, Glinka was financially secure all his life. His only paid employment was with the Ministry of Communications in St Petersburg for a few years and later, in 1836, when he was made Master of the Imperial Chapel. At other times he relied on his mother's generosity and was able to indulge his passion for music without the need to worry where the next rouble was coming from. His health, though, was never strong and this gave him a valid reason to travel to warmer climes for recuperation.

Along the way he picked up a musical education: he was a natural pianist and had a few lessons with John Field in St Petersburg; he took singing lessons in Italy where he met Bellini, Donizetti and Mendelssohn; a famous German theorist, Siegfried Dehn, taught him composition in Berlin; and he befriended Russian literary giants Pushkin and Gogol. In 1834, on the death of his father, he returned home to take care of his family's affairs.

This haphazard, unfocused development culminated in the writing of an opera that changed the course of Russian music and which, in turn, had a significant effect internationally. Glinka's aim was to write a thoroughly Russian work, patriotic and nationalistic. 'As if by magic,' he wrote, 'the plan of the whole opera and the idea of the antithesis of Russian and Polish music, as well as many of the themes and even details of the working-out – all this flashed into my head in one stroke.' *A Life for the Tsar* (1836) was the first opera written by a Russian which quoted Russian folk songs, had a Russian subject and was concerned with peasants instead of nobility. Curiously, an obscure Italian composer, Catterino Cavos, had written an opera using the same story twenty years earlier and it had been performed in St Petersburg.

Glinka followed this with another opera, *Ruslan and Ludmilla*, but its music was too advanced for the Russians of the day and it was not a success. He was to compose nothing of equal importance again. Depressed by the reaction to *Ruslan*, he took himself off on a tour of France and Spain, collecting folk tunes and trying to learn Spanish. 'My feet were all right,' he said, 'but I couldn't manage the castanets.' A string of dark-eyed beauties added to the pleasure of his travels; if they were teenagers or empty-headed, so much the better. His marriage in 1835 had ended in separation four years later and he was divorced in 1846. After further adventures in Warsaw, St Petersburg and Paris, he eventually arrived in Berlin where he had come to study Bach and choral music. There he caught a cold and died.

HIS MUSIC

Before Glinka, all Russian concert music had been dominated by foreign influences. With two (imperfect) works, this amiable dilettante gave his countrymen a musical identity, a new Russian perspective on which succeeding generations capitalized. He had opened the door and cleared the path; others built a grand new road. What was it about Russian music that was different and made such an impact elsewhere? The national temperament, with its violent and rapid changes of mood and emotion, was highlighted and the exotic qualities of the indigenous folk music were exploited. The boundaries of the empire embraced Oriental as well as Slavic influences and Russian folk music often featured unusual rhythmical metres (time signatures of 5/4 and 7/4) that were rarely used in Western music up until then.

A Life for the Tsar had a lasting influence on Tchaikowsky and Rimsky-Korsakov (both far more gifted composers than Glinka). It also used the device of *leitmotiv* some years before Wagner applied it so successfully. In 1836, when the opera was first performed in the presence of the Imperial family, it was revolutionary and stood alone. Six years later, in *Ruslan and Ludmilla*, Glinka introduced new and distinctive harmonies, making use of authentic Oriental themes. *Ruslan* is a strange, uneven work, advanced enough to be the first to incorporate the use of a whole-tone scale in opera while falling back on slavish imitations of Bellini and Donizetti.

Essential works

Ruslan and Ludmilla (1842): the overture, which is all that is heard nowadays, is an invigorating orchestral curtain-raiser, invariably played too fast at the beginning of a concert.

Kamarinskaya, orchestral fantasy (1848): Tchaikowsky wrote, 'The present Russian school is all in *Kamarinskaya*, just as the whole oak tree is in the acorn ... From it, all Russian composers (including myself) draw contrapuntal and harmonic combinations whenever they have to deal with a Russian dance tune.'

Jota Aragonesa (also known as the **Spanish Overture No.1**): the result of Glinka's sojourn in Spain and among the first orchestral attempts by a European composer to capture the idiomatic Hispanic melodies and rhythms.

Grand Sextet for piano and strings in E flat major (1832): preceding *A Life for the Tsar*, thoroughly under Mendelssohn's influence and none the worse for that, bubbling with irrepressible *joie de vivre*. His **Trio pathétique** (1832) only just falls short of this.

Christoph Willibald GLUCK

'There is no musical rule that I have not willingly sacrificed to dramatic effect' (Gluck)

Born: 2 July 1714, Erasbach, near Weidenwang (Upper Palatinate)
Died: 15 November 1787, Vienna
Full name: Christoph Willibald Ritter von Gluck
Type of music: opera, ballet
Influences: Sammartini and Italian opera
Contemporaries: W.F. Bach, John Stanley, Niccolò Jomelli, **GLUCK**, C.P.E. BACH, Johann Stamitz, Antonio Soler, Gaetano Pugnani, HAYDN

HIS LIFE

Gluck's place as one of the seminal figures in music history is due to his pioneering operas. 'Anyone meeting Gluck ... would never have taken him for a prominent person and a creative genius,' observed Johann Christoph von Mannlich, a court painter in Paris. 'He was about 5 feet 6 inches tall, stocky, strong and muscular without being stout. His head was round, his face ruddy, broad and pockmarked. The eyes were small and deeply set. He called things by their name and therefore, twenty times a day, offended the sensitive ears of the Parisians used to flattery. He was a hearty eater, never denied being grasping and fond of money, and displayed a goodly portion of egotism, particularly at table, where he was wont at sight to claim first right to the best morsels.'

His father was a forester and, like Handel's, actively discouraged his son from playing any musical instrument although it was obvious that he had such a talent. Gluck left home at eighteen and for the following twenty-five years flitted through Europe in pursuit of a musical career: first to Prague where he supported himself by playing at dances and singing in churches, then to Vienna, and later, in 1737, to Milan. Here he studied with Giovanni Battista Sammartini, one of the first symphonic composers, and Gluck absorbed all there was to know about Italian opera. Four years later he had his first success with *Artaserse* and decided to move on to London, where he met Handel who liked him but couldn't stand his music. 'My cook understands more about counter-point than he does,' Handel remarked. (Actually, his cook and valet at the time was a professional musician, Gustavus Waltz.) Gluck kept a portrait of Handel in his bedroom for the rest of his life.

Leaving London, he travelled the length and breadth of Europe for the following fifteen years as a composer and conductor, writing operas in the Italian style and becoming more and more dissatisfied with what he was doing. Eventually, he married the daughter of a wealthy Viennese banker, which made him financially independent. Then in 1760, famous and successful as he was and collaborating with two others, he wrote a ballet, *Don Juan*, based on Molière's play, which broke with convention: it was more human, more truthful and aspired to far greater dramatic effect than anything currently on offer. In 1762, one of his collaborators, the extraordinary playwright, critic and lottery organiser Raniero de Calzabigi, who was entirely in tune with Gluck's ideas, came up with the libretto for *Orfeo ed Euridice*. This work did for opera what *Don Juan* had done for ballet. Audiences had heard nothing like it before; neither had musicians. Gluck was a perfectionist with an acute ear and simply would not tolerate sloppy playing. His abrupt manner and dictatorial demands made him the Toscanini of his day, insisting that players repeat passages twenty or thirty times until he was satisfied with the result.

In 1773, he visited Paris with his wife and adopted daughter, a fine singer. Here he composed *Iphigénie en Aulide* and also produced it, after long rehearsals in which he had to correct acting and vocal styles that had not altered since the days of Lully. It precipi-tated a furore among French musicians and commentators, rival composers and music lovers. Even Marie Antoinette played a small part in the battle by coming to the defence of Gluck – before her marriage, he had taught the Austrian princess singing and harpsi-chord. In the end, the powerful Italian clique, headed by the composer Niccolò Piccinni, was defeated and Gluck returned to Vienna triumphant, though greatly saddened by the premature death of his daughter.

Perhaps his own health persuaded him to remain in Vienna after 1779, for he had suffered several 'apoplectic seizures' – probably minor thromboses. Hailed throughout Europe as its leading musical master, he survived for a further eight years until a final stroke killed him after entertaining to lunch two friends from Paris.

HIS MUSIC

All Gluck's early operas are in the conven-tional Italian style and most have libretti by the Austrian poet Pietro Metastasio. But one, *L'innocenza giustificata*, with a text by Count Giacomo Durazzo, showed him the possibilities of getting away from the empty vocal gymnastics and cardboard cut-outs with which he was continually presented.

Then, in 1760, Gluck came across a book by a French ballet-master, Jean-Georges Noverre, which proposed that the

most important elements of a ballet or an opera are the story and the feelings of the characters within that story; the music and singing must contribute to the plot and the understanding of the personalities. Gluck put these ideas into practice with his ballet *Don Juan*, followed by his first opera on these lines, *Orfeo ed Euridice*. In this, he unleashed a string of hitherto untried orchestral effects to enhance the colour and heighten the dramatic effects of the action, such as the wrath of the Furies or the ethereal calm of the Elysian Fields.

Gluck was one of the first composers to use clarinets, cor anglais and trombones in opera scores (Mozart later used trombones in *Don Giovanni* and even then it was considered unusual). Gluck included cymbals, triangles and bass drums and – perhaps the most noticeable change of all – dispensed with the harpsichord as an accompaniment for the singers.

In the preface of his opera *Alceste*, Gluck wrote: 'I have tried to restrict music to its true role of backing up poetry by means of expression and by following the situations of the plot, without holding up the action or stifling it with a useless superfluity of ornaments.' Gluck established his supremacy as the most significant opera composer of his time in a succession of operas based on Greek legends: *Iphigénia en Aulide*, *Orfeo ed Euridice* and *Alceste* (in new French versions), *Armide* and *Iphigénie in Tauride* – the five 'reform operas', as they are known.

His influence was not immediate – Mozart's early operas, for example, are entirely based on the old Italian way of doing things – but Gluck had paved the way for the rapid evolution of opera that took place over the following century. For, after the later operas of Mozart came those of Weber, and after the minor revolution of Weber came the apocalyptic vision of Wagner.

Essential works

Orfeo ed Euridice, opera (1762): 'The Dance of the Blessed Spirits' is the popular flute solo depicting the Elysian fields. The two arias 'Che puro ciel!' and 'Che faro senza Euridice' are justly famous; the latter is better known in the UK as 'What is life to me without thee', a much-loved recording of which was made by the contralto Kathleen Ferrier.

Alceste, opera (1767): 'Divinités du Styx'

('Gods of the Styx') is a celebrated aria sung by Alcestis defying the powers of death.

Paride ed Elena, opera (1770, Vienna): a ravishingly lovely aria in this opera is 'O del mio dolce ordor' ('O thou belov'd'), which was originally written for a *castrato*. The aria is sung by Paris when he arrives in Greece, happy in the knowledge that he will soon be with his Helen.

Henryk GÓRECKI
(1933–)

'Symphony of Sorrowful Songs': Symphony No.3, Op.36, 1976

Górecki was born in Czernica, Poland, not far from Katowice where he received his musical education and near the town of Oswiecim on the Polish-Silesian border, which we know by its German name of Auschwitz.

There are three movements in Górecki's Third Symphony (all of them marked to be played *lento*). The settings of the three movements are: the lamentation of the Holy Cross Monastery, written during the second half of the fifteenth century; a prayer inscribed on the wall of a cell in the Gestapo's headquarters, Zakopane, by an eighteen-year-old girl who had been imprisoned there in 1944; and a folk song in the dialect of the Opole region in Poland: 'And you, God's little flowers / May you blossom all around / So that my son / May sleep happily.' Some people find that the symphony's continuous and naive minimalism is rather sleep-inducing; for others it provides a deep spiritual experience. The work has the same reassuring lullaby effect as Pachelbel's Canon at ten times the length.

Górecki's name was all but unknown in the West five years ago, although he had been composing industriously since his first published work, Toccata for two pianos, in 1955. Then a recording of his 'Symphony of Sorrowful Songs' featuring an unknown soprano, Dawn Upshaw, and the small-time London Sinfonietta conducted by David Zinman, was released in 1992. No one involved could have predicted anything but a specialist interest from the public. The work had been around since 1977 and, like Górecki's previous two symphonies, had aroused little attention amongst the wider music-loving public. The new record's inclusion in Classic fM's regular playlist and repeated requests from listeners to hear its haunting, mesmeric song of sorrow, prayer and exhortation put it at the top of the classical charts for months. It has sold well over a million copies to date, the equal and better of many major rock groups, whose record promoters know better than anybody that repetition pays dividends.

Louis Moreau GOTTSCHALK

'An American composer – bon Dieu!' (La France musicale)

Born: 8 May 1829, New Orleans
Died: 18 December 1869, Rio de Janeiro
Type of music: symphony, but mostly solo piano
Influences: Chopin, Liszt, Creole, Latin-American and Afro-American dance rhythms
Contemporaries: JOHANN STRAUSS II, Stephen Collins Foster, **GOTTSCHALK**, RUBINSTEIN, Karl Goldmark, Joseph Joachim, BORODIN, BRAHMS, Julius Reubke

HIS LIFE AND MUSIC

'I was dreadfully sorry to hear of poor Gottschalk's death,' wrote the American pianist Amy Fay. 'If anything more is in the papers about him you must send it to me, for the infatuation that I and 99,999 other American girls once felt for him still lingers in my breast.' Gottschalk was the first native American composer to achieve international success as a composer and virtuoso pianist. From an exotic background (a Jewish father born in London, and a mother who came from the French nobility) he was born a Creole. He gained his musical education in Paris, where he was sent when he was only twelve years old, and became the darling of the *salons*; Berlioz and even Chopin praised his unique gifts.

Returning to the United States in 1853, he was lionized – especially by the ladies in his audiences – throughout his incessant and interminable perambulations all over the American continent; during the Civil War it was said he travelled 95,000 miles giving 1,100 concerts in the process. He spent much of his time in South America where he eventually ended his days; some say he died during a recital in Rio de Janeiro while playing his composition *Morte!!*, others say it was in a brothel, from a ruptured abscess in the abdomen. He was forty years old.

During his lifetime, his piano music was phenomenally popular. He thrilled audiences with scintillating versions of national tunes and operatic themes, introduced for the first time the sensual dance rhythms of Latin America and, fifty years before Scott Joplin, was writing ragtime – all allied to disciplined European pianism. The last quarter of this century has seen a strong revival of interest in his music. He may not be a Great Composer but he is certainly great fun.

Worth investigating
Symphony No.1, 'A night in the tropics'
Symphony No.2, 'À Montevideo'
Solo piano
La savane, ballad créole, Op.2: variation on a Louisiana folk song.
Le bananier, chanson nègre, Op.5: The Banana Tree – a catchy early work.
Le banjo, fantaisie grotesque, Op.15: a ragtime cakewalk from c.1854.
Souvenir de Porto Rico, Op.31: march of the Gibaros (Puerto-Rican peasants).
'Columbia', caprice américain, Op.34: 'stride piano' treatment of Stephen Foster's 'My Old Kentucky Home'.

Manchega, concert study, Op.38: uses Spanish rhythms half a century before the modern Spanish school of Albéniz and Granados.
Ojos criollos, dance cubaine (1860): a marriage of polka and tango, one of Gottschalk's most popular pieces.
The Union, concert paraphrase on National Airs, Op.48 (1862): a synthesis of 'Yankee Doodle', 'The Star-Spangled Banner' and 'Hail Columbia'.
Grand triumphal fantasy on the Brazilian national hymn, Op.69: also in an arrangement for piano and orchestra.

Charles GOUNOD

'God sends me down some of his angels and they whisper sweet melodies in my ear' (Gounod)

Born: 17 June 1818, St-Cloud
Died: 18 October 1893, Paris
Full name: Charles François Gounod
Type of music: opera, symphony, orchestral, choral, vocal, chamber
Influences: Palestrina, Bach, Rossini, Mendelssohn, Schumann
Contemporaries: Sterndale Bennett, Niels Gade, LITOLFF, **GOUNOD**, Antonio Bazzini, OFFENBACH, SUPPÉ, Henri Vieuxtemps, Joachim Raff, FRANCK

HIS LIFE

Gounod is an intriguing man, an endearing mix of the profane and sacred, rather like his music. Perhaps someone like Ken Russell will one day make a film of at least one episode in his life. His father was a clever but unsuccessful painter who died when Gounod was four; his mother, also a talented artist, taught music and ran her late husband's lithograph business profitably. Gounod picked up both skills quickly but at the age of thirteen, after attending a performance of Rossini's *Otello*, he decided on music as his profession. 'I felt as if I were in some temple,' he recalled later, 'as if a heavenly vision might shortly rise upon my sight … Oh that night! What rapture! What Elysium!'

His mother insisted on the completion of a thorough academic education before allowing him to study music; Gounod duly complied then, aged eighteen, entered the Paris Conservatoire. After three attempts he won the coveted Prix de Rome in 1839 and hurried off to immerse himself in Italy and its music. Unlike Berlioz's experience, it proved formative and he became captivated by the music of Palestrina, making a serious study of sixteenth-century ecclesiastical music. His absorption led him to start writing church music of his own.

On leaving Rome to return to Paris, he travelled by way of Vienna and Leipzig where he spent several days with Mendelssohn and heard the choral music of J.S. Bach for the first time. His first position on arriving back in Paris was as organist for Les Missions Etrangères (the Chapel for Foreign Missions). The early composers he had come to love were introduced into the services amidst opposition – they were not the same as the fashionable sentimental music played in most Catholic churches at that time. Gounod's profound religious nature led him to begin theological studies in preparation for entering the priesthood, but the pull of music was too strong – and so, it proved, was that of the flesh – for him to progress beyond the novitiate stage. Nevertheless, he affected the wearing of a clerical garb and signed himself Abbé Gounod, rather like Liszt, who was challenged by similar temptations. Gounod was even known in some quarters as 'the philandering monk'. He was clearly an outgoing character who was irresistible to other people, a man of impish humour and enormous charm. The actor Edmund Got recorded in his diary that Gounod was 'as talented musically as he is exuberant and shamelessly pushy as a man'.

A chance meeting with the influential prima donna Pauline Viardot led her to ask Gounod to write an opera. Gounod had no difficulty in falling in love with one of her daughters, although the eventual engagement did not lead to marriage. The only way for any composer to make money from music in Paris was from writing opera and, although he had had no experience of writing for the stage, Gounod set to his task with a will. The result was *Sapho* (1850) – which was enough of a success to encourage him to write more.

In 1852 he was appointed conductor of the Orphéon, a union of choral societies; this was a position his new father-in-law had arranged, for Gounod had married Agnes Zimmerman, daughter of Pierre Zimmerman, the famous teacher of piano at the Paris Conservatoire. Four years later Gounod began work on the opera that was to make him world famous, *Faust*.

After its premiere in 1859, the composer was the most celebrated in France. For the remainder of his life he tried to repeat its extraordinary effect; his own favourites, *La Reine de Saba*, *Mireille* and *Roméo et Juliette*, were not failures but came nowhere near the popularity of *Faust*. To be strictly accurate, the first production of the opera was not an overwhelming triumph and Gounod had to wait another ten years for its revival before it really took off to become the most popular French opera of the nineteenth century. In less than fifty years it had notched up over 2,000 separate performances worldwide, and to date it has been performed in over fifty countries and translated into twenty-five different languages. Yet no publisher would touch it at first. Some did not like the treatment of Goethe's play on which it was based, and others objected to a love scene following a church scene. However, a newcomer in the publishing field, Choudens, took it up. It made the company's fortune. Years later, it is said, Gounod met Choudens who was wearing a fine fur coat and a shabby hat. Gounod touched the coat and asked: '*Faust?*' A moment later he pointed to Choudens' hat: '*Roméo et Juliette?*'

At the outbreak of the Franco-Prussian War, Gounod and his wife, along with Viardot and other artists, fled to London. Here he remained from 1870 until 1875, rather longer than the duration of the war. He lived in Tavistock House, once the home of Dickens, with a Mr and Mrs Weldon, and seduced the influential, eccentric and mentally unstable Georgina Weldon. Gounod's wife returned indignantly to Paris, while the composer remained in London in a turbulent *ménage à trois*, with Georgina managing his affairs. At length, Gounod's son Jean was sent over to sort things out. He promptly attempted to seduce Mrs Weldon too, and was thrown out. During this time, Gounod had met with great success in England, founding the Gounod Choir (later named the Albert Hall Choral Society and then the Royal Choral Society). Soon he tired of Mrs Weldon, whose mental health was rapidly deteriorating, and he left for Paris. Instead of forwarding the scores, effects and all the money he had loaned the Weldons, Georgina issued a counter-suit including a bill for three years' board. After protracted legal wranglings, judgment was given against Gounod for the sum of £11,640.

For the last decade of his life, Gounod turned to religious mysticism and the writing of liturgical music, but, after 1870, he produced little of significance. 'He might well have echoed Tennyson's despairing cry,' wrote Martin Cooper, 'that he was the greatest master of English living and had nothing to say.'

HIS MUSIC

Between 1852 and 1870 only five new French operas were added to the repertoire of the Paris Opéra, while the Opéra-Comique relied on works by Auber and Adam that had been written in the 1830s. The French operatic tradition was stagnant and the theatres were dominated by the epic spectacles of Meyerbeer and the operettas of Offenbach. Gounod was the first home-grown composer to break the mould. He brought to his music a sweetness of melody, spicy harmonies, graceful orchestration (more lightly scored than similar German work) and the Gallic poise and elegance that Massenet was to refine and to which Bizet was so indebted.

The other area in which Gounod made an impact, one that is virtually ignored today, was French song. It was a line that was to stretch from Fauré to Debussy and Ravel. The bulk of his religious music was seen by contemporaries (Saint-Saëns in particular) as the key to Gounod's un-doubted place among the immortals of music. England especially responded to his disguised eroticism in works such as *Mors e vita* and *La rédemption* but, though the St Cecilia Mass has impressive moments, the saccharine sentimentality of his settings soon began to cloy. The reason for Gounod's ultimate fate as a good second-rate composer rests on his essential superficiality ('face-powder music', according to Wagner) and lack of talent as a musical dramatist.

Essential works

Faust, opera (1859): Neville Cardus, writing in the Manchester *Guardian* in 1938, observed, 'How ironical that the world's profoundest expression of the denying spirit and of man's genius for creative life [Goethe's *Faust*] … should have served as the basis of an opera which glorifies insincerity of mind and senti-ment' [Gounod's *Faust*]. Assuredly, Gounod's *Faust* is not Goethe's *Faust*, the metaphysical considerations of the play are ousted in favour of the love story. The Germans (who rarely mount it) call this opera *Maragarethe* to disassociate it from the work of their great poet, but audiences don't care tuppence for such niceties and revel in the elements of this work that seem to constitute all popular operas: wonderful writing for the voice, memorable melodies, exotic and colourful set-tings, rousing choruses and contrasting moods and pace. Its five acts tell the story of the ageing philosopher Faust who makes a pact with Mephistopheles: his soul in exchange for the lovely Marguerite. The famous passages include Faust's aria 'Salut! demeure chaste et pure' ('Hail, saintly dwelling'), the 'Jewel Song' ('Ah! je ris de me voir' – 'I am laughing with joy'), a favourite soprano showpiece, the celebrated 'Soldiers' Chorus' (Act 4) beloved of Welsh male voice choirs (Gounod originally wrote this passage for his unfinished opera *Ivan the Terrible*) and Ballet Music between Acts 4 and 5.

Roméo et Juliette, opera (1867): an inconsis-tent work that nevertheless sticks pretty faithfully to Shakespeare's play and contains much fine music, including the lovers' duet in the tomb, Romeo's garden-scene cavatina and, especially, Juliet's ever-popular 'Waltz Song'.

Messe solonnelle de Sainte-Cécile (1855): composed in the country near Avranches, Gounod was concerned above all to render it worthy of the patron saint of music: 'The Mass! … In music!… by a paltry man!… My God, take pity on me,' he wrote. 'At first one was dazzled,' recalled Saint-Saëns after its first performance, 'then charmed, then conquered.'

Funeral March of a Marionette (1872): one of the movements for a planned *Suite burlesque* for piano, this short novelty item – Gounod's most popular concert work – describes the funeral procession of a marionette who is killed after a duel: one of those 'so-that's-what-it's-called!' tunes.

'Jésus de Nazareth'
'Quand tu chantes' ('Serenade')
'Où voulez-vous aller?'
Ave Maria (1853): Gounod's best-known piece, originally a 'meditation for violin based on Bach's Prelude No.1 in C'. The complete prelude is used as an accompaniment to a moving religious melody; words were added in 1859. Also worth investigating: **Petite symphonie for nine wind instruments** (1885)

Percy GRAINGER

Born: 8 July 1882, Melbourne
Died: 20 February 1961, White Plains, New York
Full name: George Percy Aldridge Grainger
Type of music: orchestral (mainly short works), choral-orchestral, brass band, chamber, piano
Influences: folk music, Grieg, Delius
Contemporaries: SZYMANOWSKY, Manuel Ponce, Joaquín Turina, **GRAINGER**, KODÁLY, STRAVINSKY, WEBERN, Alfredo Casella, Lord Berners, BAX

HIS LIFE AND MUSIC

Most people are familiar with *Country Gardens* (based on an English Morris dance) and probably with *Molly on the Shore*, *Shepherd's Hey*, *Mock Morris* and *Handel in the Strand*. Their popularity has tended to overshadow the rest of Grainger's considerable and varied output and, though he would never be put on a pedestal to join the pantheon of immortals, he is unorthodox, original and deserves better than to be dismissed by the more puritan arbiters of musical taste. There is a tendency to overlook real craftsmanship when it is put to – sometimes – frivolous use.

The amusing and bizarre aspects of Grainger's life are well documented in John Bird's biography: his habit of jogging from one concert venue to the next with a heavy rucksack on his back, his abnormally close relationship with his formidable mother Rose, her suicide, his predilection for physical self-flagellation, his 'blue-eyed' Nordic views and his substitution of Italian and German music terms for Anglo-Saxon ones (such as 'Room Music' for chamber music, 'louder' for crescendo, and 'middle-fiddle' for viola).

Grainger (born George Percy, adopting his mother's maiden name, Aldridge, later) first made his reputation as a concert pianist. His teacher in Melbourne, Louis Pabst, had been taught by Anton Rubinstein. Grainger made a strong impression on all who heard him, including Grieg and Delius with whom he developed close friendships. After living in Britain for a time he became an American citizen. In 1926, married his 'Nordic Princess' Ella Viola Ström in the Hollywood Bowl before a paying audience of 20,000.

As a composer he was virtually self-taught and his best music relies on conventional harmonies, with an emphasis on vigorous rhythms and traditional tunes. He was tirelessly curious in trying out new combinations; he wrote for the solovox, theremin, marimba, harmonium, banjo and other under-used instruments, as well as experimenting with electronic music as early as 1937.

Dying of cancer, he requested that, when the flesh had been removed from his skeleton, he should be placed for preservation and display in the Grainger Museum, Melbourne. His request was denied.

Essential works
The Warriors, music for an imaginary ballet (1912–16): Grainger's own favourite work.
Colonial Song (1911): this piece was once described by Beecham as 'the worst orchestral piece of modern times', but you should judge for yourself.
Lincolnshire Posy (1940): this suite is based on English folk songs. Grainger himself had

collected most of the folk songs for this work early in the century.

In a Nutshell, suite (1905–16): this piece includes *Arrival Platform Humlet* and the *Gum-sucker's March*.

Blithe Bells: 'a free ramble' on 'Sheep May Safely Graze' from J.S. Bach's Cantata *Was mir behagt*, BWV 208.

Folk-song arrangements: *Country Gardens, Molly on the Shore, Shepherd's Hey, Mock*

Morris, Handel in the Strand, all of which show Grainger at his outdoor, exuberant best. *Irish Tune from County Derry* (*The Londonderry Air* 'dished up' by Grainger) and *Harvest Hymn* are succinct but moving.

Special mention must be made of Martin Jones' recordings of the complete piano music of Percy Grainger on six Nimbus CDs. On Vol.1 is *Bridal Lullaby*, used to magical effect in the film *Howard's End*.

Enrique GRANADOS

Born: 27 July 1867, Lérida, Spain
Died: 24 March 1916, English Channel
Full name: Enrique Granados y Campiña
Type of music: Spanish nationalist; opera, zarzuela, piano
Influences: Liszt, Spanish music, Felipe Pedrell
Contemporaries: SIBELIUS, BUSONI, SATIE, Francesco Cilèa, **GRANADOS**, Hamish MacCunn, Scott Joplin, Sir Granville Bantock, Albert Roussel

HIS LIFE AND MUSIC

Falla, Albéniz and Granados: the triumvirate responsible for the establishment of a modern Spanish school of music. In fact, Granados' father was Cuban, an officer serving in the Spanish army; his mother was a Montañesan from Santander in the north, and the elaborate ornamentation of the indigenous music of Montañesa is a notable characteristic of her son's work.

His initial career was as a pianist, studying in Barcelona and, thanks to a wealthy patron, at the Paris Conservatoire. Returning to Spain he established himself as one of the leading Spanish musicians of the day – there are even some primitive recordings of his piano playing.

His early piano pieces *Danzas españolas* attracted the praise of Massenet, Saint-Saëns and Grieg, but it was his opera *Maria del Carmen* (1898) that brought him esteem as a composer. Five subsequent operas were failures, due to poor libretti. His masterpieces, however, are the two books of piano pieces *Goyescas*. These were converted into a short opera and first performed in 1916 at the Metropolitan Opera in New York (not at the Paris Opéra, as originally intended, because of the outbreak of the First World War). Granados and his wife crossed the Atlantic to attend the premiere. A newly composed Intermezzo greatly helped its modest success, which led to an invitation from President Wilson for Granados to play at the White House, delaying the couple's return to Europe. When Granados and his wife did so, their ship, the *Sussex*, was torpedoed by a German submarine on the journey from Liverpool to Dieppe. Although the ship was brought back safely to port, Granados drowned in an unsuccessful attempt to save his wife.

Little of Granados' music is played today, other than the works below, but it is well worth listening to some of his songs (the fifteen *Tonadillas al estilo antiguo*, for instance) and the *Allegro de concierto* for piano and orchestra.

Essential works

Twelve Danzas españolas, piano (1892–1900): atypical examples of the new Spanish nationalistic idiom encouraged by Granados' teacher, Felipe Pedrell. No.5 *Andaluza* (also

known as *Playera*) achieved (and still has) enormous popularity with guitarists as well as pianists.

Goyescas, suite for piano (1911): inspired by

his love of Domenico Scarlatti's music and the paintings of Goya, Granados wrote these seven ballades, which rank among the finest of Spanish keyboard works. 'Goyescas is a work for all time,' wrote Granados. 'I am convinced of this fact.' No.4 is perhaps the finest and certainly the best known piece – *Quejas, o la maja y el ruiseñor*, which we know as *The Maiden and the Nightingale*, equally lovely in its vocal version.

Edvard GRIEG

'The Chopin of the North' (Hans von Bülow)

Born: 15 June 1843, Bergen
Died: 4 September 1907, Bergen
Full name: Edvard Hagerup Grieg
Type of music: concerto, stage music, chamber, piano, song
Influences: Mendelssohn, Schumann, Chopin, Liszt, and the Norwegian landscape and people
Contemporaries: CHABRIER, DVOŘÁK, SULLIVAN, MASSENET, Arrigo Boito, **GRIEG**, Pablo de Sarasate, RIMSKY-KORSAKOV, Stephen Adams, WIDOR, FAURÉ, PARRY

HIS LIFE

Grieg's great-grandfather was a Scot who emigrated to Bergen, Norway after the Battle of Culloden, changed his name from Greig and became British Consul, a post subsequently held by his son and grandson. Edvard was introduced to music by his mother, a talented amateur pianist, but it was largely due to the persuasion of the Norwegian violinist Ole Bull, who had heard the young Grieg play the piano, that a musical career came about. His parents were reluctant and Grieg, who had considered becoming a priest, hated the Leipzig Conservatory to which he was sent. The young Arthur Sullivan was a fellow-student.

Nevertheless, during his time there Grieg had the opportunity of hearing Clara Schumann play her late husband's Concerto, and Richard Wagner conduct *Tannhäuser*. Here, too, he developed pleurisy, which left his left lung seriously impaired, bequeathing him precarious health and diminished energy for the rest of his life.

He returned not to Oslo but to Copenhagen in 1863, where the revered Niels Gade, founding father of the new Scandinavian school of composition and Denmark's leading composer, befriended Grieg, inspiring him to form the Euterpe Society dedicated to promoting Scandinavian music. This he did with the aid of another gifted young composer, Rikard Nordraak. 'From Nordraak,' wrote Grieg, 'I learned for the first time to know the nature of Norwegian folk tunes and my own nature.' Alas, Nordraak died in 1866 at the age of twenty-four, though not before he had written what is today's Norwegian national anthem.

In 1867 Grieg married his cousin, the talented singer Nina Hagerup, who would become the chief interpreter of his songs, but a period of despair ensued: he had found the key to his musical voice yet his missionary zeal in promoting Norwegian composers and music met with opposition; then his first and only child, a thirteen-month-old daughter, died in 1869. It was a letter from Franz Liszt not only praising his music but inviting him to Rome that did more to encourage him than anything. After meeting Liszt in 1869, he returned to Norway and opened a Norwegian Academy of Music.

In 1869 he gave the first performance of his familiar Piano Concerto in A minor. This, with the first set of *Lyric Pieces* for piano and two Violin Sonatas that had already been published, established him as one of the foremost composers of the time. Subsequently,

Ibsen approached him to write the incidental music for the stage version of his *Peer Gynt*, a job that occupied the composer for two years. Grieg had now become so famous that the government granted him an annuity to relieve him of financial burdens so that he could concentrate on composing. Ironically, apart from the *Holberg Suite*, all his most successful works were written by the time he was thirty-three.

He visited England frequently and was showered with honours and decorations wherever he went; a much-loved figure, he was admired, most unusually, by both Brahms *and* Tchaikowsky and he became an honorary Doctor of Music of Cambridge *and* Oxford Universities. But he was a shy, retiring, modest man, a Republican not much impressed by medals and orders bestowed by royalty, though he confessed they were useful for putting on the top layer of his trunks when travelling. 'The Customs officials are always so kind to me at the sight of them,' he said. As he grew older, Grieg became physically weaker and more reclusive, preferring the company of his wife and the tranquillity of his home at Troldhaugen overlooking the Hardanger fjord near Bergen. He died of a heart attack and, following a state funeral, his ashes were sealed in the side of a cliff by the fjord at Troldhaugen.

HIS MUSIC

Von Bülow's description of Grieg as 'the Chopin of the North' is precise – not that Grieg imitated Chopin's style, but both composers were more comfortable in miniatures than in large forms (Grieg's early symphony is not a success); both used the piano for most of their poetic, musical expression, and both fed off a proud nationalism without (at least, very rarely) relying on extant folk tunes. Somehow, Grieg's music is a tonal portrait of Norway in the same way that Elgar's and Vaughan Williams' are of England. It is full of the idioms of Norwegian folk music synthesized with the German Romantic tradition.

Only a year after Grieg's death, Arnold Schoenberg composed his first atonal piece; no music of two composers could be more dissimilar. Certainly Grieg is a conventional, undemanding composer – Debussy described experiencing his music as if 'one has in one's mouth the bizarre and charming taste of a pink sweet stuffed with snow' – but to Louis Elsen in his study of Grieg, and to many others, 'in these days when much music suggests nervous maladies and the mad house ... Grieg comes like a whiff of pure air.'

Essential works

Piano Concerto in A minor, Op.16 (1868): perhaps the most frequently played of all piano concertos, *de rigueur* for every pianist, and Grieg's only successful work in an extended form. He revised it substantially several times, the last in 1906, the version played today.

Peer Gynt Suites Nos.1 & 2 (1876): culled from the complete incidental music to Ibsen's play, the first suite includes *Morning, Ase's Song, Anitra's Dance* and *The Hall of the Mountain King*; from the second comes the magical *Solveig's Song*. Grieg took on the task of providing incidental music to the play with

reluctance. Now the music far exceeds Ibsen's play in performance and popularity.

Holberg Suite, Op.40 (1884): originally for piano but transcribed by Grieg for string orchestra, this was a tribute to Ludvig Holberg, founder of Danish literature, whose centenary was celebrated in 1884.

Ballade in G minor, Op.24 (1875): variations on a Norwegian folk song; the most technically difficult and certainly the most heartfelt of Grieg's piano works, it is rarely played now.

Lyric Pieces (1867–1901): sixty-six short piano pieces in ten volumes; some of the best

known are *Papillons*, *To Spring* and *Wedding Day at Troldhaugen* (all of which were recorded by Grieg in 1903 in very primitive sound) but the whole collection is a treasure house.
Songs: of the 140 songs Grieg composed, inspired mostly by his wife, 'Ich liebe dich' ('I love thee') has always been a favourite. The words are by Hans Christian Andersen and it was written in 1865 for Nina during the time that her parents opposed her marriage.

George Frideric HANDEL

'To him I bow the knee' (Beethoven)

Born: 23 February 1685, Halle
Died: 14 April 1759, London
Original name: Georg Friedrich Händel (Handel adopted the anglicized form)
Type of music: opera, oratorio, concerti grossi, instrumental
Influences: Purcell, madrigalists, the German School, Scarlatti, Corelli
Contemporaries: RAMEAU, J.S. BACH, DOMENICO SCARLATTI, **HANDEL**, Benedetto Marcello, Niccolò Porpora, Jean-Baptiste Senaillé, John Galliard

HIS LIFE

1685 Handel's father was a barber-surgeon and valet to the Prince of Saxe-Magdeburg. He was in his mid-sixties when his son was born, and he hated music. Somehow young Handel managed to learn the organ and spinet; one story has it that his sympathetic mother smuggled a spinet up to the attic where the strings were smothered with cloth to muffle the sound. From these unpromising beginnings flourished the greatest keyboard instrumentalist of the day – and it happened quickly.

1693 The Duke of Saxe-Weissenfels heard the boy play the organ at one of the Sunday services, filled his pockets with gold coins and insisted that he was allowed to study music. Handel was put in the care of Friedrich Zachow, the organist of the Lutheran church in Halle, who soon realized he had a genius on his hands. After three years, Zachow confessed there was nothing more he could teach the boy. Handel was just eleven. He doesn't appear to have had any further instruction from anyone.

1702 After studying law for a while in Halle, he was appointed organist at the cathedral

of Moritzburg – only eighteen years old and already people were talking of 'the famous Handel' – and then moved to Hamburg, the seat of German opera.

1706 Fed up with the petty jealousies and cabals there, Handel went to Italy, where he turned to writing opera in Florence and Venice and oratorio in Rome. All were triumphs and soon 'Il Sassone' ('The Saxon') was one of the most talked about musicians in Italy. Here he absorbed and studied all the music that was being written and came into contact with such figures as Corelli, Alessandro Scarlatti and his son Domenico with whom he had a celebrated keyboard 'duel' to determine whom was the finer player. Result? Scarlatti was adjudged to be the better harpsichordist but Handel the finer organist. Scarlatti admitted that until he heard Handel play the organ he had no conception of its powers. The two retained a lifelong mutual admiration.

1710 From Italy, Handel moved to Hanover as court musician to the Elector – a prescient decision as it turned out. After a year he was given leave to go to England where he wrote an opera (*Rinaldo*, 1711) which was an astonishing success. Back to Hanover, but London was too tempting and he returned to England and further triumphs. Two years passed and Handel was still absent from the Hanoverian court.

1714 When Queen Anne died, who should succeed her on the throne? None other than Handel's German employer, the Elector of Hanover. If George I was displeased at his musician's cavalier attitude it didn't last long, for soon Handel had a royal pension of £400 a year – with an additional £200 from the Princess of Wales – and he was able to embark on a series of operas underwritten by the nobility and cast with the finest European singers. The Royal Academy of Music in London (not the present-day college, which was founded in 1822) was set up to present Italian opera and the entrepreneurial Handel was made its artistic director. He was, unassailably, the most powerful musician in the land.

We know very little of his private life – he was almost obsessively secret – but he was said to be gruff and curt and certainly had a violent temper. 'Madame,' he told the temperamental soprano Francesca Cuzzoni, 'I know you are a veritable devil, but I would have you know that I am Beelzebub, the head devil.' To another singer who threatened to jump on his harpsichord, he responded: 'Let me know when you will do that and I will advertize it. For I am sure more people will come to see you jump than to hear you sing.' People were much amused by his comical accent, his huge bulk (he was known as 'the great bear'), his bow legs and his habit of muttering to himself as he waddled round the streets of London. He was a glutton, too, and his eating habits were said to be 'repulsive'.

Perhaps it was his very success or his foreignness or the fact that he was dictatorial in his demands that exposed him frequently to attacks and ridicule. Despite royal patronage and his popularity with the public, despite his capacity for making friends and support-ing the underprivileged, Handel found he had many enemies. One particular rival appeared in the form of Giovanni Bononcini and for a time there was intense competi-tion as to who was the better composer. Handel saw him off in the end, of course, but not before the poet John Byrom had written:

> Some say, compared to Bononcini
> That Mynheer Handel's but a ninny.
> Others aver that he to Handel
> Is scarcely fit to hold a candle.
> Strange all this difference should be
> 'Twixt tweedledum and tweedledee.

And that's how the phrase was coined.

1728 Not long after Handel became a British citizen, public taste for Italian opera waned; audiences had discovered John Gay's *The Beggar's Opera* to be more accessible, with tunes they already knew. Handel, now quite wealthy from shrewd investment, sunk £10,000 of his own money into another Italian opera company and lost the lot.

With bankruptcy and the debtors prison looming, Handel's health deteriorated, rheumatism set in and he suffered a paralytic stroke; he appears to have had some sort of breakdown and then … he changed course. He wrote himself back into financial success and public favour by resurrecting a genre that was relatively unknown in England – the oratorio. These were dramatized Bible stories set to music of the same verve as the operas but with massive choruses and grand orchestral writing. Nothing like them had been heard before. In the interludes he would appear at the organ to play a concerto, improvising the brilliant solo part.

1741 Inspired by an invitation to Dublin from the Duke of Devonshire and the Lord Lieutenant to present one of his works for charity, he wrote *Messiah*, completed in a feverish twenty-five days, one of man's grandest musical achievements and most remarkable bursts of creativity. A succession of oratorios followed – among them *Semele, Judas Maccabaeus, Joshua* and *Solomon* – showing Handel to be at the height of his powers. The 'great Handel' ruled the musical world again, only to be knocked sideways by another cruel blow. He became blind, a condition not helped by being operated on by the same quack surgeon who attempted to save Bach's eyesight.

Indomitably, he continued to play the organ and conduct, one of the wonders of London, for people flocked to hear him. As Harold Schonberg observed: 'His blindness aroused pity, and that too helped. When *Samson* was presented, and the tenor John Beard stood next to the blind composer to sing:

> Total eclipse – no sun; no moon.
> All dark, amid the blaze of noon

There must have been an audible gulp from the audience.'

Handel was buried in Westminster Abbey. Despite his request for a private service, 3,000 people attended, and the monument he requested to be erected in his memory shows him at his working table with the score of *Messiah* open at 'I know that my Redeemer liveth'.

HIS MUSIC

Handel and Johann Sebastian Bach (born only a hundred miles away four weeks later) summed up in their different ways all that had preceded them, represented all contemporary schools and styles of musical thought and provided the signposts for the future. The two composers never met, although on three occasions Bach made special journeys to Halle in order to meet his far more famous peer. Each time, they missed each other.

Handel was the cosmopolitan musician, widely travelled, the subject of royal patronage, working with Italian and English texts and not too concerned about the intellectual rigours of composition. His is happy, confident and melodic music imbued with the grace of Italian vocal writing, an easy fluency in German contrapuntal writing and the British choral tradition inherited from Purcell. Handel wrote an enormous amount of music in more forms and with far more variety than any of his contemporaries. True, he borrowed a great deal from himself and others. With the amount of music he had to write in tandem with all his other responsibilities he simply did not have the time to do everything. There are many examples of movements from one work which reappear in a different guise and tempo elsewhere. Everybody did it, but Handel was a plagiarist on a grand scale – and got away with it. When he was asked why he lifted material from Bononcini he replied: 'It's much too good for him; he did not know what to do with it.'

Yet, in spite of all this, little of Handel's music is now heard apart from a few much-(over?-) played works. Why? The forty-six operas that he wrote are difficult to revive. Their mythological subjects and the lack of true drama in the plots make them irrelevant to today's audiences and no amount of clever designs, effects and over-inventive direction can disguise that fact. The fashion for oratorios died with the Victorian age and revivals of any of his thirty-odd works, apart from *Messiah*, are few and far between; only individual items are included in concerts. Works such as his *Chandos Anthems*, written when he was in the service of the Duke of Chandos, and the Concerti Grossi, surely the finest of their kind, are hardly ever heard in the concert hall. The same applies to his numerous instrumental pieces.

Handel is rated as one of the most popular of all classical composers, yet a proportionately small amount of his music is ever played with any regularity. By contrast, most of Bach's work, more forbidding in the minds of some, is performed widely the world over. Handel was a great man in physical stature, spirit and vision. But perhaps the most striking thing of all was his calm ability to separate the adversities of life (the everyday turmoil as well as the personal tragedies and attacks that befell him) from his apparently inexhaustible creativity.

Essential works
Vocal
Below are the most famous passages from Handel's oratorios and operas. The more intrepid will want to hear the whole work but if two hours of *Jephtha*, for instance, doesn't appeal, this is the best way of getting to know Handel's wondrous vocal writing – in snippets.

Messiah, sacred cantata (1741): this includes 'Every valley shall be exalted', 'For unto us a Child is born', 'How beautiful are the feet', 'Hallelujah Chorus', 'I know that my Redeemer liveth' and 'The trumpet shall sound'.

Israel in Egypt, oratorio (1739): includes 'I will sing unto the Lord' and 'The people shall hear and be afraid'.

Jephtha, oratorio (1752): 'Waft her, angels'.

Joshua, oratorio (1748): 'Oh had I Jubal's lyre'.

Judas Maccabaeus, oratorio (1747): 'Sound an alarm'.

Samson, oratorio (1743): 'Let the bright seraphim', sung at the wedding of the Prince and Princess of Wales by Dame Kiri te Kanawa; and 'Total eclipse'.

Semele, secular oratorio (1744): 'O sleep why dost thou leave me' and 'Where'er you walk'.

Theodora, oratorio (1750): 'Angels ever bright and fair'.

Xerxes (or **Serse**), opera (1738): 'Ombra mai fu' is among the best known of all classical pieces and universally known as 'Handel's Largo' (even though the music says *larghetto*).

Atalanta, opera (1736): 'Care selve' ('Come beloved').

Tolomeo, opera (1728): 'Silent worship' is among the loveliest of all pining love songs.

Rodelinda, opera (1725): 'Dove sei' ('Art thou troubled?'): especially as sung by Kathleen Ferrier.

Ariodante, opera (1735): 'Doppo notte' ('After night')

Other vocal works
Acis and Galatea, masque (1718) 'Love in her eyes sits playing', 'Ruddier than the cherry' and 'As when the dove'; the work has one of Handel's sunniest overtures.

Zadok the Priest, anthem (1727): the first of four anthems written for the coronation of George II, this has been heard at almost every coronation since; the fourth is the equally inspired, 'My heart is inditing'.

Alexander's Feast, ode for St Cecilia's Day (1736): 'War is toil and trouble'

Salve Regina (1707): for soprano and strings
Ode for St Cecilia's Day (1739)
Ode for the Birthday of Queen Anne, 'Eternal source of light divine' (1713)
L'Allegro, Il Penseroso ed Il Moderato (1740): for tenor, soprano, bass, chorus and orchestra

Dettingen Te Deum (1743): written in thirteen days to celebrate the English victory over the French at Dettingen.

Chandos Anthems (1717-20): written when Handel was the composer in residence at the home of the first Duke of Chandos. **No.6**, 'As pants the hart' and **No.9** 'O praise the Lord with one consent' are two of the finest.

Instrumental
Water Music (1717): a suite of twenty short pieces composed to accompany a royal trip up the river Thames which can be heard either in its original form, in the three concerti grossi arrangements Handel made, or in the modern orchestral version of five movements made by Sir Hamilton Harty.

Music for the Royal Fireworks (1749): another uncomplicated, joyful suite of six movements, which Handel wrote for entertainment purposes.

Twelve Concerti Grossi Op.6 (1739): ranked as the summit of the concerto grosso form are Handel's equivalent of the 'Brandenburg' Concertos – though this set is scored only for strings. The most attractive of the twelve are **No.6 in G minor, No.7 in B flat and No.10 in D minor**.

Organ Concertos Op.4 and Op.7 (1738, 1760): Handel wrote these two sets of six concertos as interludes for his oratorios, ad libbing much of the solo parts. There are three others, one of which is nicknamed 'The Cuckoo and the Nightingale', written for the first performance of *Israel in Egypt* (Handel also turned it into a harp concerto). Don't let any idea you may have of an organ concerto being dull put you off; these marvellous works contain some of the most high-spirited, life-enhancing music ever written.

Harpsichord Suite No.5 in E (1720): the air and variations are called 'The Harmonious Blacksmith'.

Arrival of the Queen of Sheba (*Solomon*, oratorio) (1749): especially in the famous recording made by Sir Thomas Beecham.

On the subject of Beecham, those with a penchant for the unfashionable should get hold of his ballet suites, *The Gods go a'begging*, *Love in Bath*, *The Origin of Design* and *The Faithful Shepherd*, which are culled from a cross-section of Handel's works. Also his over-blown orchestration of *Messiah* will have the authentic brigade hopping up and down; others will be on the edges of their seats during the big choruses.

Joseph HAYDN

'Papa Haydn'

Born: 31 March 1732, Rohrau, Lower Austria
Died: 31 May 1809, Vienna
Full name: Franz Joseph Haydn
Type of music: symphony, concerto, stage, choral, oratorio, chamber, keyboard
Influences: Stamitz and the Mannheim School, Handel, C.P.E. Bach, Mozart
Contemporaries: Johann Stamitz, Antonio Soler, Gaetano Pugnani, **HAYDN**, François Gossec, J.C. Bach, Johann Albrechtsberger, BOCCHERINI

HIS LIFE

1732 Haydn's father was a wheelwright and the village sexton. Joseph was the second of his twelve children. His brother Michael, born five years later, also became a composer. Haydn's father had taught himself to play the harp by ear, and a paternal cousin, Johann Mathias Franck, was a local choral director, but otherwise there was nothing in his ancestry to indicate a musical career. His first lessons were from his cousin, and he was only eight when admitted to St Stephen's Cathedral in Vienna as a chorister.

1748 After leaving the choir when his voice broke, Haydn was thrown back on his own resources, borrowing money to rent an attic where he could practise the harpsichord. He made a thorough study of C.P.E. Bach's keyboard works, read as much musical theory as he could absorb and had a few lessons from the then famous Italian composer Nicolò Porpora, who was living in Vienna.

1759 His first compositions began to be noticed and he was engaged as music director and composer to the Austrian Count Maximilian von Morzin at his estate in Lukavec.

1760 Haydn married – one of the biggest mistakes of his life. He had been in love with one of his pupils in Vienna, and when she became a nun he married her sister Maria Anna Keller, who had no love of music, no appreciation of Haydn's greatness and even used his manuscripts as hair-curlers. They were separated for most of his life, but he still sent her money. It is said that, although they corresponded, he never opened her letters.

1761 The turning point in Haydn's career came when Prince Anton Esterházy, who had heard one of his symphonies at Lukavec, invited him to become second Kapellmeister at his estate in Eisenstadt. The prince died the following year, but he was succeeded by his brother Nicholas – the fanatical music-loving 'Nicholas the Magnificent' who entertained on a truly lavish scale and at Esterháza had one of the most splendid palaces in Europe, which included a 400-seat theatre.

Haydn remained in Eisenstadt until 1790 and it was here that he composed most of his eighty-three string quartets, eighty of his 104 symphonies, and nearly all his operas and keyboard works, as well as a huge amount of music written for the prince to play himself. In addition to the daily performance of chamber music, Haydn and his orchestra had to present two operas and two concerts every week. His salary was generous and Haydn was encouraged to compose as he wished. He recalled: 'As a conductor of an orchestra I could make experiments, observe what produced an effect and what weakened it, and was thus in a position to improve, alter, make omissions, and be as bold as I pleased. I was cut off from the world, there was no one to confuse or torment me, and I was forced to become original.' The members of the orchestra loved him, hence his nickname 'Papa Haydn', and the composer even got on well with the prince – it must have seemed like a dream.

1781 By this time Haydn was acknowledged throughout Europe as a genius, honoured by all. He made only brief annual visits to his beloved Vienna but on one of them he met Mozart for the first time. Mozart was twenty-five, nearly a quarter of a century younger than Haydn. The two became close friends; Mozart admired Haydn's music and dedicated his first six string quartets to him, while the ever-generous Haydn described Mozart as 'the greatest composer known to me either in person or by name' and set about promoting Mozart's works rather than his own. The two learned much from each other.

1790 Prince Nicholas died, succeeded by his son Paul Anton who was more interested in paintings than music. Nevertheless, an annuity of 1,000 florins kept Haydn as the nominal Kapellmeister at Eszterháza, allowing him to live permanently in Vienna. The same year, the enterprising impresario Johann Peter Salomon invited Haydn to London for a series of concerts. The composer was feted wherever he went and he returned to Vienna eighteen months later with a small fortune.

1794 Haydn visited London again, achieving further triumphs, and later in the year returned to Eszterháza. Paul Anton had died, succeeded by his son, another Prince Nicholas, who planned to revive the Haydn orchestra. As Kapellmeister, Haydn now turned his attention to choral works. From this period come the *Nelson Mass*, *The Creation*, *The Seasons* and the Austrian National Anthem, first performed on the Emperor's birthday, 12 February 1797. (Its original text, 'Gott erhalte Franz den Kaiser', was changed in the year of European revolution, 1848, to 'Deutschland, Deutschland über alles' with its later connotations of German imperialism.)

1800 In his mid-sixties Haydn's health began to fail and he resigned as Kapellmeister in 1802, though Prince Nicholas II increased his pension to 2,300 florins and paid all his medical bills so that Haydn should suffer no financial burden.

1808 Haydn made his last public appearance at a concert given in his honour and conducted by Salieri.

1809 Vienna capitulated to Napoleon who ordered a guard of honour to be placed round Haydn's house. When Haydn died, the music at his funeral service was a Requiem by his favourite composer, Mozart.

1820 Before his reinterment at Eisenstadt, Haydn's head somehow became separated from his body and it was exhibited in a glass case in the hall of the Gesellschaft der Musikfreunde in Vienna for some years.

1954 On 5 June, Haydn's skull was reunited with his body at Eisenstadt.

HIS MUSIC

'He alone has the secret of making me smile and touching me at the bottom of my soul,' wrote Mozart. 'There is no one who can do it all – to joke and terrify, to evoke laughter and profound sentiment – and all equally well: except Joseph Haydn.'

In the half century of Haydn's creative activity, Johann Sebastian Bach died, precipitating the end of the contrapuntal period of music, and Beethoven's Third Symphony was given its premiere, announcing the Romantic era. During those fifty years, the old forms of the mass, the oratorio and the concerto grosso were replaced by the symphony, the sonata and the string quartet. Instead of the church being the focal point for musical activity, the palaces of the nobility and, shortly afterwards, the concert platform assumed central importance. This in turn led to a change in musical values, including a further advance in poetic, subjective expressiveness.

In all this, Haydn was a pioneer. He is frequently, and inaccurately, described as 'the father of the symphony'. Some (Stamitz, for example, and those of the Mannheim School) had composed three-movement symphonies well before him, just as others had written keyboard sonatas and string quartets. But Haydn developed all these forms to a higher degree, and showed the way forward; he was at the forefront of modern musical thought. His early works are reflections of C.P.E. Bach; his last announce the very different world of Beethoven. Yet it wasn't until he was forty that he began producing compositions that marked any significant advance, and had he died as young as Schubert or Mozart he would be a mere footnote in musical history. It was his fertility, variety, unpredictability, wit, quality of invention and genius for musical construction that put Haydn head and shoulders above his contemporaries.

Essential works

Haydn's works are sometimes referred to by their H numbers, after the catalogue prepared by the Dutch bibliographer Anthony van Hoboken (1887–1983).

Symphonies

Many of Haydn's symphonies have acquired nicknames:

No.31 in D, 'Horn Signal' (1765): the first time a symphonic score called for four horns, it features many horn fanfares.

No.45 in F sharp minor, 'Farewell' (1772): in the closing pages of the finale of this symphony, the instruments leave the stage one by one until only the two first violins are left. Legend has it that this was Haydn's tactful way of telling his employer that the band needed a holiday.

Nos.82–87: known as the Paris Symphonies, these were composed for a concert organisation in Paris.

No.83 in G minor, 'La poule': a theme in the first movement suggests a clucking hen.

No.85 in B flat, 'La reine': much approved by Marie Antoinette.

No.92 in G, 'Oxford': this symphony was composed, though not played, for the occasion when Haydn was made a Doctor of Music at Oxford University.

Nos.93–104: known as the London (or Salomon) Symphonies, and composed for Haydn's two visits there under the auspices of the impresario J.P. Salomon. **No.94 in G, 'Surprise'**: known in German as 'Paukenschlag' (literally 'drumstroke'), because of the sudden and humorous break in the peaceful slow movement. **No.100 in G, 'Military'**: the use of Turkish percussion instruments in this symphony enthralled London audiences.

No.101 in D, 'The Clock': the second movement has a staccato accompaniment which sounds like a ticking clock. **No.103 in E flat, 'Drum Roll'**: this work opens with a kettledrum roll, hence its nickname. **No.104 in D, 'The London'**: confusingly, this work, which is part of the London series, is known as 'The London' Symphony.

Concertos

Piano Concerto in D (c.1784): some twelve keyboard concertos have been attributed to Haydn; this one is by far and away the most popular.

Cello Concerto in D (1761–65): a cornerstone of the cellist's repertoire.

Cello Concerto in C (1784): the manuscript for this work was discovered in the Prague National Museum as recently as 1961 and has become a firm favourite with audiences.

Trumpet Concerto in E flat (1796): written for the Viennese trumpeter Anton Weidlinger and still a marvellous display piece.

Piano sonatas

No.38 in F (H.xvi:23), **No.50 in D** (H.xvi:37), **No.58 in C** (H.xvi:48) and **No.62 in E flat** (H.xvi:52): these are some of the most frequently played of the fifty-two piano sonatas Haydn wrote.

String quartets

F minor Op.20 No.5 (1772): one of a set of six quartets known as *Die Grossen* or *Die Sonnen* (*The Sun Quartets*), which highlight the development of Haydn's style and technique and give each instrument greater individuality Op.20 No.5 has been described as 'the most nearly tragic work Haydn ever wrote'.

E flat Op.33 No.2: this piece comes from a set of six works entitled the Russian Quartets (they are dedicated to Grand Duke Paul of Russia). It is nicknamed *The Joke* because of the unexpected pauses Haydn inserted in the last movement to catch out the chattering ladies in the audience.

Six quartets Op.76 (composed between 1797 and 1798): in which Haydn's mastery of the form reaches its apex. **No.2 in D minor**: referred to as the *Quinten* (*Fifths*) because the opening theme of the first movement consists of descending fifths. Some call it *The Donkey* – a descending fifth sounds like one! The minuet is known as the *Hexen* (*Witch*) – the music is feverish and savage. **No.3 in C**: this is called the *Emperor* Quartet because it incorporates variations on Haydn's Austrian National Hymn. **No.5 in D**: this is known as the *Largo* Quartet because of its spiritually sublime slow movement.

Piano Trio in G, Op.73 No.2: the only one of his forty-four piano trios still regularly played; the well-known Hungarian or 'Gypsy' rondo is its last movement.

Choral works

The Creation (1796–98): Haydn's imagination is let loose in this magnificent, if sprawling, work. It has some of the most adventurous orchestral writing of the entire eighteenth century. The gentle 'In verdure clad' (for soprano) and 'The heavens are telling' (for chorus) are highlights.

The Seasons (1799–1801): this was one of Haydn's last works, though you wouldn't know it; full of impish humour and vivid musical pictures.

Mass No.11 in D minor, Nelson Mass: written to celebrate Nelson's defeat of Napoleon's army at the Battle of the Nile.

Ferdinand HÉROLD
(1791–1833)

Zampa Overture, 1831

'I am going too soon,' Hérold remarked to a friend a few days before his early death. 'I was just beginning to understand the stage.' He achieved much in his short life, for, with Adam and Auber, he was responsible for the establishment and huge popularity of *opéra comique*.

His musical genealogy is interesting: he began his career as a pianist and was taught by his father; his father had been taught by C.P.E. Bach who, in turn, had been taught by *his* father, Johann Sebastian – a long musical journey from the single Hérold work that remains in the orchestral repertoire. The opera itself is never performed now. It concerns Zampa, a sixteenth-century pirate who is dragged under the sea and drowned by a marble statue of his former bride.

One other piece 'by Hérold' is still popular. In 1960 John Lanchbery rearranged the music that Hérold had composed for the ballet *La fille mal gardée*, from which comes the oft-requested *Clog Dance*. Alas, the music for this particular number is not by Hérold at all, as is generally stated, but by the obscure German composer Peter Ludwig Hertel (1817–99).

Abbess HILDEGARD OF BINGEN

'A feather on the breath of God' (Hildegard)

Born: 1098, Bemersheim (Rheinhessen, Germany)
Died: 1179, Rupertsberg, near Bingen
Type of music: plainsong
Influences: monastic and church music
Contemporaries: Guido d'Arezzo, **HILDEGARD OF BINGEN**, Pérotin, Guillaume de Machaut, John Dunstable, Guillaume Dufay, Johannes Okeghem

HER LIFE AND MUSIC

St Hildegard was one of the most remarkable women of the Middle Ages: a visionary, writer, naturalist, poet and composer. She was the abbess of a Benedictine convent and, like other women of the time, became a prophet among her contemporaries. Her highly coloured 'revelations' were taken most seriously by four popes and various emperors, monarchs and eminent ecclesiastics, while her enemies condemned her as a fraud.

Women composers are a rare breed at any time and Hildegard can hardly be called seminal – but the plainsong melodies she wrote to her own texts are vivid and affecting examples of music in the Christian tradition of nine hundred years ago. Few were aware of her music before the appearance of a cult recording by Gothic Voices.

Worth investigating

Her collection of music and poetry called *The Symphony of the Harmony of Celestial Revelations* contains some of the Middle Ages' finest songs. Her *magnum opus*, written a hundred years before anything in the same genre appeared, is *Ordo virtutum*, a morality play. The actors represent the Devil and sixteen Virtues; only the latter have singing parts.

Paul HINDEMITH

'A twentieth-century Bach' (David Ewen)

Born: 16 November 1895, Hanau near Frankfurt
Died: 28 December 1963, Frankfurt
Type of music: orchestral, opera, ballet, chamber, choral, piano, vocal, functional music
Influences: Wagner, Richard Strauss, Stravinsky, Bartók
Contemporaries: E.J. Moeran, Walter Piston, Dimitri Tiomkin, **HINDEMITH**, Mario Castelnuovo-Tedesco, ORFF, Roberto Gerhard, Roger Sessions

HIS LIFE

When it came to a career in music, it seems Hindemith encountered parental opposition and, aged eleven, ran away from home to make his living playing the violin in theatres and cafés. With the money he made, he put himself through the local music conservatory in Frankfurt at the age of thirteen. His self-determination to live life on his own terms never left him: he was leader of the Frankfurt Opera Orchestra by 1919, had his first music published while still a student, co-founded and played the viola in the Amar Quartet, which became renowned for its performances of contemporary music, and, by the time he was thirty, was regarded as one of Germany's major creative figures.

Hindemith's status as a viola soloist – and he did as much as anybody to raise the profile of this Cinderella of the strings – led to him giving the first performance of Walton's Viola Concerto (1929), although, listening to recordings of Hindemith, the sound he makes is not the warm, luscious sound of present-day virtuosi. Indeed, two other famous violists of the time, William Primrose and Lionel Tertis, didn't have a good word to say about his playing.

Throughout the Twenties he produced savage, anti-Romantic scores, establishing himself as the leading musical *enfant terrible* of the day. Richard Strauss complained to him: 'Why do you write this way? You have talent,' to which Hindemith replied: 'Herr Professor, you make your music and I'll make mine.'

In 1927 he was offered the influential post of Professor of Composition at the Hochschule für Musik, Berlin. When he moved there, incidentally, three rooms of his new home were given over to his electric model railway; not only did he design its elaborate track layout, but he also made up detailed timetables. He was fanatical about trains and was said to know the complete European train timetable off by heart.

Eventually, his Jewish wife Gertrude Rottenberg, his many Jewish colleagues and his opera *Mathis der Maler* (*Matthias the Painter*) – which dealt with the sensitive subject of the defeat of German liberalism during the Peasant's War – led to him being denounced by the Nazis as 'musically degenerate'. His music was banned, and in 1935 Hindemith left for Turkey and then America. In 1940 he joined the staff at Yale University and became an American citizen. After the Second World War he flitted between Europe and the States, eventually settling in Switzerland. The flow of compositions and conducting engagements continued until his health declined in the 1960s. He died from a stroke.

HIS MUSIC

Few composers this century have been able to match Hindemith's musical accomplishments. He could play virtually every instrument in the orchestra and composed with incredible facility. He wrote for every combination of instruments and in every form, including works for player piano, mechanical organ (a film score for *Felix the Cat*, 1927), *Lehrstück* (an entertainment that has a singing part for the audience) and a trio for viola, piano and heckelphone: his list of *oeuvres* is as long as it is varied in interest and quality.

His music is termed 'neo-classic' because he applied new harmonic ideas to old musical forms, such as the sonata and fugue (just as his German predecessors Bach and Beethoven had done in their day) and it was his use of these forms, and his craftsmanship, that was so admired by fellow musicians. Indeed, it is they who most readily respond to Hindemith's muse; generally, his music appeals to the eye and mind first, and the ears and heart second.

That the general public has never taken to him is ironic because he thought his work was 'easily comprehensible for people with ears' and he passionately wanted to make modern music accessible to everyone. His credo was 'music should be useful first and beautiful second', and the word *Gebrauchsmusik* (literally 'music for use') was coined to describe the compositions he wrote for educational or social purposes (Hindemith later disowned the term). Music, he felt, need not be just a means of self-expression but purely functional.

Frequently, the result of this philosophy was, as Stravinsky put it, 'as arid and indigestible as cardboard'. Large amounts of Hindemith are grim and unsmiling in the best German tradition, but there are exceptions. Works of enormous grace and vigour are among his diverse and prolific output. You really have to stand on the side of the Hindemith swimming pool and jump in; there's no use dipping your toes in to see what the water's like.

Essential works

Symphonic Metamorphoses on themes by Carl Maria von Weber, suite, 1943: don't let the ponderous title put you off; this suite is not difficult, it is full of tunes (by Weber and Hindemith) and is a loud, lively, four-movement piece.

Mathis der Maler, symphony, 1934: uses themes from Hindemith's opera of the same name. The narrative concerns the life of the sixteenth-century painter Matthias Grünewald, but its allegorical significance and religious symbolism lightly disguises the composer's main argument – the artist's role in times of political turmoil.

Der Schwanendreher (The swan-turner), viola concerto 1935: written in Hindemith's least acidic vein, using old German folksongs for its themes.

Kammermusik, Nos.1–7, chamber music (1922): the works by which Hindemith first made his name, eschewing post-Romanticism and Impressionism. The advanced contrapuntal writing led critics to dub them the 'Brandenburg Concertos – upside down'.

Piano Sonata No.3 in B flat (1936): the last and weightiest of the three piano sonatas, concluding with a double fugue.

Ludus tonalis, studies in counterpoint, tonal organization and piano playing (1943): for the even more adventurous, this set of twelve fugues is seen as a modern *Well-tempered Clavier* (*see* J.S. BACH).

Gustav HOLST

*'Never compose anything unless the not composing of it becomes
a positive nuisance to you'* (Holst)

Born: 21 September 1874, Cheltenham
Died: 25 May 1934, London
Original name: Gustavus Theodore von Holst
Type of music: orchestral, opera, choral, chamber
Influences: literature, Wagner, Eastern philosophy, English folk music
Contemporaries: Max Reger, RACHMANINOV, Joseph Jongen, **HOLST**,
Reynaldo Hahn, SCHOENBERG, IVES, Samuel Coleridge-Taylor, RAVEL

HIS LIFE AND MUSIC

Think of Holst and one thinks of *The Planets*. Little else springs to mind and, indeed, his output is comparatively slender – he was a late starter and a slow worker – and few of his compositions were performed in his lifetime. He wrote other works of interest, yet *The Planets* is such an overwhelming, original piece that everything else pales into insignificance in scale and concept.

Holst's paternal great-grandfather left Sweden and settled in England in 1807. His father was an organist, and his mother a piano teacher but when he went to study at the Royal College of Music in 1893 (he was a pupil of Stanford for composition) it was the trombone that became his main instrument. Vaughan Williams was a fellow student and became a lifelong friend. At first Holst earned his living as a trombonist in various theatres and opera companies before changing course to become a teacher at St Paul's Girls' School in 1905 and, two years later, at Morley College, both in London. They were positions he held for the rest of his life.

His early work is dominated by the influence of Wagner, then tempered by his interest in religious philosophy and the mysticism, poetry and spiritualism of the East. In addition, Vaughan Williams introduced him to English folk music. By 1915 he had absorbed these influences and found at a voice of his own.

During the First World War, plagued by suspicions of German sympathies because of his name, he dropped the 'von' and went out to Salonika and Constantinople to organize concerts for the British troops. *The Planets*, written between 1914 and 1916, had to wait until 1920 for its first complete public performance, when it established his name as a leading composer. In February 1923 he suffered concussion as the result of a fall, causing a rapid deterioration in his health (never strong) which thereafter severely limited all his musical activities except composition. He became more reclusive, declining many honours and taking little interest in public affairs. His daughter Imogen, also a musician, described how 'he sank into a cold region of utter despair ... a grey isolation'. Summing it all up, Holst pinpointed 'Four chief reasons for gratitude ... Music, the Cotswolds, RVW [Vaughan Williams] and having known the impersonality of orchestral playing.'

Essential works

St Paul's Suite (1913): written for St Paul's Girls' School orchestra, a delightful suite in the character of English folksongs, although few are actually quoted; the last movement uses 'Greensleeves' as a counterpoint.

The Planets (1916): this seven-movement orchestral suite depicting the characters of each planet was the work in which all of Holst's previous influences gelled with dramatic, emotional, lyrical and ethereal orchestral effects, not least in the hidden choir of women's voices at the end of *Neptune*. *Jupiter*, its best-known section, is also the hymn tune *Thaxted* (an Essex town where Holst played the organ), to which the words 'I vow to thee my country' are sung. An awful arrangement of it served as television's Rugby World Cup Theme in 1991, sung by Dame Kiri Te Kanawa. Holst was not a confident conductor and his 1926 recording of *The Planets* is merely a curiosity.

Also worth investigating

The Hymn of Jesus (1917): a distinct, un-solemn, choral-orchestral cantata highlighting Holst's great skill as a choral writer.

A Somerset Rhapsody (1906–07): orchestral work based on two English folksongs.

A Fugal Overture, Op.40 No.1 (1922): originally the overture to his opera *The Perfect Fool*.

Fugal Concerto for flute, oboe and strings, Op.40 No.2 (1923): a jolly and instantly-likeable concerto, despite what one may think from its title.

Egdon Heath (1927): a tone-poem inspired by Thomas Hardy's novel *The Return of the Native*, this is another side of Holst, dark and brooding. The Parisians hissed it; Holst thought it his best work.

Arthur HONEGGER

Born: 10 March 1892, Le Havre
Died: 27 November 1955, Paris
Full name: Arthur Oscar Honegger
Type of music: opera, ballet, concerto, orchestral, chamber, vocal, instrumental, radio, theatre, film
Influences: Ravel, Debussy, Stravinsky, Prokofiev
Contemporaries: Frank Martin, PROKOFIEV, Sir Arthur Bliss, **HONEGGER**, Ferde Grofé, Herbert Howells, MILHAUD, Kaikhosru Sorabji, Arthur Benjamin

HIS LIFE AND MUSIC

Born in France of Swiss parents, Honegger spent most of his life in France and retained dual citizenship throughout his life. Much of his music reflects this Franco-Teutonic background. Prolific as he was adventurous, Honegger composed his first music for the cinema as early as 1923 for *La roue*, and went on to write the scores for Abel Gance's silent masterpiece *Napoléon* (1927) and the Leslie Howard / Wendy Hiller version of Shaw's *Pygmalion* (1938), among many others.

During the Nazi occupation of Paris, Honegger lived as a virtual recluse in the capital but was allowed by the Germans to continue to compose and, through an oversight, act for the French Resistance. After the war, he was invited to America by Serge Koussevitzky to teach at the Berkshire Music Center at Tanglewood but while there he developed angina, the disease from which he eventually died.

Honegger is a difficult composer to define because his large corpus of compositions, few of which have found their way into the concert hall let alone the public consciousness, contains a wide variety of styles that leave the listener wondering what his musical voice sounds like. He vacillated between modern conservatism and advanced polytonal dissonance.

His best known piece is, ironically, not typical of most of his output. 'Pacific 231', his musical portrait of a huge steam locomotive, was once considered the last word in adventurous dissonance and jarring rhythms but can now be admired for its clever realism. The Concertino for piano and orchestra, which appeared the following year, could have been written by a different composer – it is light (not to say slight), witty and jazzy. It was Honegger's one concession to Les Six, the celebrated group of composers dreamt up by the critic Henri Collet who seemed, erroneously, to think that Honegger, Poulenc, Milhaud, Auric, Tailleferre and Durey had a common musical creed. However, the label stuck and was at least useful in promoting their music.

Honegger was more serious in his approach than Poulenc and Milhaud, the only other composers of Les Six who amounted to anything. (Durey became famous for his membership of the French Communist Party rather than for his music, while Tailleferre and Auric produced amiable music for films and concerts.) Indeed, Honegger's muse is altogether more sombre than satirical and this became clear when his style crystallized between the two World Wars.

Essential works
Pastorale d'été (1920): a gentle, languorous picture of country scenes for small orchestra, occasionally programmed by conductors like Toscanini who would follow it, by contrast, with: **Mouvement symphonique No.1 'Pacific 231'** (1923): 'I have always had a passionate love of locomotives,' wrote Honegger in his preface to this piece. 'What I have sought to accomplish ... is not to imitate the noises of a railway engine, but rather to translate into music a visual impression and a physical sensation.' It is ingeniously scored, the train slowly moving off and getting up steam as Honegger piles dissonance on dissonance until it comes to a metallic, grating stop. The title describes an American locomotive – the British equivalent is a 4-6-2: where we count the wheels, the Americans count the axles.

Mouvement symphonique, No.2 'Rugby', (1928): a musical impression of a game of rugby (Honegger had already composed a sport ballet in 1921 entitled *Skating Rink*). The piece was premiered in a football stadium.
Le roi David, oratorio (1921): this work, which established Honegger's name, calls for a narrator, as well as soloists, chorus and orchestra. The form and approach remind one of Handel; the music does not.

Also worth investigating
Concertino for piano and orchestra (1925)
Jeanne d'Arc au bûcher (Joan of Arc at the Stake), dramatic oratorio (1938)
Symphony No.2 for string orchestra (1941): a deeply felt work, embodying much of the mood of occupied Paris.

Johann Nepomuk HUMMEL

'Mozart, Beethoven and Hummel, great masters of all of us' (Chopin)

Born: 14 November 1778, Pressburg
Died: 17 October 1837, Weimar
Type of music: opera, ballet, church music, concerto, chamber, keyboard
Influences: Mozart, Clementi, Albrechtsberger, Haydn, Salieri, Beethoven
Contemporaries: François-Adrien Boïeldieu, Bernhard Crusell, **HUMMEL,** FIELD, PAGANINI, AUBER, Louis Spohr, WEBER, Henry Bishop, HÉROLD

HIS LIFE AND MUSIC
Physically, Hummel was not an attractive man, with 'an unpleasant, common-looking face that constantly twitched' and which was pitted by smallpox scars. He puffed and panted and perspired when he played the piano, grew to be monstrously stout and 'wore utterly tasteless clothing and diamond rings on almost all his fingers'. Yet his music is elegant, superbly crafted, full of memorable themes and, at its best, the sort of music Mozart could have written had he lived longer. It is certainly underrated.

Hummel seemed assured of immortality: one of the brilliant piano virtuosos of the day, he lived with Mozart in 1785 for two years and studied with the older composer, then with Salieri, Clementi and Haydn. He toured throughout the continent, including

Russia until, by 1820, he was considered one of the supreme musicians of the age. Friend of Beethoven and Goethe, Chevalier of the Legion of Honour, Hummel eventually settled in Weimar as court Kapellmeister in 1819, a post he held until his death. He was said to be the equal of Beethoven as a keyboard improviser and a significant number of musicians held him as quite the equal of Beethoven as a composer, too. His compositions had a tremendous influence on the young Romantics; Mendelssohn, Schumann and Liszt all revered him and Chopin was captivated by his work – Hummel's influence can be heard by comparing his Piano Concerto in A minor of 1821 with the E minor Concerto composed by Chopin in 1830. The Polish composer must also have been familiar with Hummel's now-forgotten set of twenty-four preludes in all the major and minor keys. Hummel's music is expertly crafted, rich in melodic invention and contrapuntal skill. Yet, immediately after his death, his music fell out of fashion. Edward Dannreuther, in the first edition of Grove (1889), dismissed Hummel as 'quite incapable of humour or passion, but fully equipped with every musical virtue that can be acquired by steady plodding, he appears expressly cut out for the hero of respectable mediocrity.' Listening to the works listed below reveals just how wrong that judgment is.

Incidentally, Hummel's wife lived until as late as 1883 and today his great-great-grandson is a successful industrialist in Los Angeles.

Essential works

Piano Concerto in A minor, Op.85
Piano Concerto in B minor, Op.89
These lively works, successors to Weber's two concertos and anticipating the Mendelssohn and Chopin concertos, were rescued from oblivion by Stephen Hough's recordings.
Piano Quintet in E flat, Op.87: 'Incapable of humour'? Try the sparkling finale.
Piano Septet in D minor, Op.74: scored for flute, oboe, horn, viola, cello, double bass and piano, arguably his finest work.

Piano Septet in C, 'Military Septet', Op.114 : scored for flute, clarinet, trumpet, violin, cello, double bass and piano.
Piano Sonata No.5 in F sharp minor, Op.81: for the more adventurous listener; this sonata had an overwhelming effect on the young Schumann.
Trumpet Concerto in E flat: son of Haydn's masterpiece in the same key, the final *rondo alla polacca* is a show-stopping virtuoso display.

Engelbert HUMPERDINCK
(1854–1921)

Hansel and Gretel, opera (1890–93)

Not the Indian-born crooner (real name Arnold George Dorsey) who plucked the name of our man out of a dictionary. The German composer, who first studied architecture, won a music prize in 1881 which enabled him to visit France and Italy. In Italy he met Wagner who invited him to his house in Bayreuth and the two of them got on famously, Humperdinck helping the great man to prepare the score of *Parsifal* for publication. After professorial spells in Barcelona and Frankfurt, Humperdinck hit the jackpot in 1893 with his fairy tale opera, which had a libretto by his sister, Adelheid. The German public had had enough of Wagnerian bombast and to return to a familiar story (based on the tale by the brothers Grimm) with music inspired by folk tunes was exactly what they wanted. Yet that was it; Humperdinck could never repeat the success. Neither, it must be said, could the host of imitators who sprang up.

In 1929, the Manchester Schoolchildren's Choir and the Hallé Orchestra under Sir Hamilton Harty recorded, on one side of a 78-r.p.m. disc, Purcell's 'Nymphs and Shepherds' and on the other the Dance Duet ('Brother come and dance with me') from Act 1 of *Hansel and Gretel*. It was an instant, if unlikely, hit and has never been out of the catalogue since.

Charles IVES

'All the wrong notes are right. Just copy as I have – I want it that way'
(Ives to his copyist on the score of The Fourth of July)

Born: 20 October 1874, Danbury, Connecticut
Died: 19 May 1954, New York
Full name: Charles Edward Ives
Type of music: symphony, chamber, instrumental, vocal
Influences: his father, natural dissonance, hymn tunes, patriotic songs, military bands and the European tradition of Bach, Beethoven and Brahms (from his teacher Horatio Parker)
Contemporaries: Max Reger, HOLST, Reynaldo Hahn, SCHOENBERG, **IVES**, Samuel Coleridge-Taylor, RAVEL, Reinhold Glière, Albert Ketèlbey, KREISLER

HIS LIFE AND MUSIC

Ives' music takes you by the scruff of the neck, sticks two fingers in your face and challenges any pre-conceived ideas you may have on the subject – it comes hard to anyone brought up on a diet of Rachmaninov, Holst or Ravel, Ives' contemporaries. He was an extraordinary man who wrote extraordinary music. One can only sit back and wonder at his stubbornness, the way he expressed his personal vision and his refusal to be tied to any received wisdom. The devices that he introduced into his music – atonality, polytonality, dissonance, multiple rhythms, jazz and collage – were in advance of Stravinsky, Schoenberg and Debussy. They arrived at their own answers later and their work was widely performed; not so Ives – most of *his* was not performed until the 1950s. Only then did it become clear how much he had been ahead of his time. His stream-of-consciousness technique has been compared with the James Joyce of *Ulysses* and *Finnegan's Wake* (though Ives anticipated Joyce in this, too).

Where did it come from? Perhaps his father, a remarkable bandleader who encouraged his son to 'open his ears' and listen to the noise made by two military bands playing different marches simultaneously and to note the out-of-tune singing of hymns in church: in other words, to accept natural dissonance, not dismiss it. He even encouraged Ives to sing 'Swanee' in a different key to that in which it was being played on the piano. The young Ives began to experiment writing in a combination of several keys, first as a spoof, then as a serious proposition. No wonder his teacher at Yale was baffled by someone to whom Chopin was 'soft ... with a skirt on', Mozart was merely 'effeminate' and who felt Debussy 'should have sold newspapers for a living'. He had higher opinions only of J.S. Bach, Beethoven, Schumann and Brahms.

After graduating, Ives, with assured unpredictability, went into insurance. In 1907 he established the firm of Ives and Myrick (afterwards Mutual of New York) and proved an able businessman, ending up a millionaire. When, in 1918, he suffered a massive heart attack and was no longer able to work (diabetes added to the complications) he was able to publish at his own expense some of the vast amount of music he had written 'out of office hours' and distribute it gratis to interested parties. Few were aware of his double life and Ives made no effort to procure performances of his work – he felt he had no hope of commercial success. When it *was* performed, he seemed indifferent. By 1930 he had all but stopped composing. He retired to his farm in Connecticut and became increasingly reclusive; he never went to concerts and did not have a record player or radio. Slowly, his music began to be played and his Third Symphony, written in 1903, won a Pulitzer Prize in 1947, but it was only after his death that his real achievements were recognized. He has become something of a cult figure, an example to any composer who feels faint-hearted in following his instincts and developing independent musical thought. 'Ivesian' has entered the language to describe a certain kind of music.

Essential works

Variations on 'America': written for the organ when Ives was just seventeen, this is his most frequently played piece, a humorous set of variations on our national anthem (the Americans purloined the same tune for their own ends in the 1830s).

Piano Sonata No.2, 'Concord': 'this is not a nice sonata for a nice piano player,' wrote Ives, 'but something the writer had been long thinking about.' It was begun in 1910, completed in 1915 and not performed in its entirety until 1939 by John Kirkpatrick in New York. Forty-five minutes long, unlike conventional sonatas which build from simplicity to complexity, the 'Concord' does the reverse. A difficult listen but it's worth persevering; perhaps start with the second movement, *Hawthorne* – Nathaniel Hawthorne, one of the Transcendentalist movement (c.1836-1860) of

writers in Concord, Massachusetts who inspired the work.

Symphony No.3, 'The Camp Meeting' (1904): also inspired by New England, it uses hymn tunes to portray the camp meetings held in Danbury when Ives was a boy. Listen to 'What a friend we have in Jesus', 'O for a Thousand Tongues' and 'Just Am I'. Not difficult; indubitably, authentically American.

Three Places in New England (1904): the second movement, *Putnam Park*, has the technically extraordinary feat of two bands approaching playing different marches in different tempos.

114 Songs: written between 1888 and 1921 in styles ranging from beguilingly Romantic to starkly dissonant. A selection to sample are 'Charlie Rutlage', 'Slow March', 'In the Alley', 'The Side Show' and 'The Circus Band'.

Leoš JANÁČEK

'I do not play about with empty melodies. I dip them in life and nature' (Janáček)

Born: 3 July 1854, Hukvaldy, Moravia
Died: 12 August 1928, Ostrava, Austria
Type of music: orchestral, opera, choral, chamber, piano
Influences: Russian literature and Moravian folk music and culture
Contemporaries: STANFORD, HUMPERDINCK, MOSZKOWSKI, **JANÁČEK**, SOUSA, CHAUSSON, Anatoli Liadov, SINDING, ELGAR, LEONCAVALLO

HIS LIFE

The ninth of fourteen children, Janáček (pronounced *Yan'*-er-check) was brought up in the magnificent mountains and forests of north-east Moravia on the Polish border. When he was eleven, his father, the village schoolmaster, decided to send him to the Augustine monastery in Brno, the Moravian capital, where the choirmaster was a family friend. From there Janáček graduated to the Brno Teachers' Training College (1872–74), the Organ School (College of Music) in Prague (1874–75) and thence to the Leipzig and Vienna Conservatories. He returned to Brno, married and settled into teaching and conducting locally.

Like Bartók and Kodály in Hungary and Vaughan Williams and Holst in England, Janáček became fascinated by his country's folk music and set off with a friend, Frantisek Bartos, to collect folk material. Certain elements of this found their way into his early compositions and he evolved a theory that music should follow the rhythms of human speech, of animal and bird noises. For the following twenty years, Janáček continued to live and work in Brno in total obscurity, writing music of little significance.

It wasn't until his late forties that he found his own distinctive voice in his opera *Jenufa* which was first performed in Brno just before Janáček's fiftieth birthday. The work took another twelve years to reach Prague, making Janáček sixty-two when the world of music discovered this unorthodox and original composer. He had twelve more years to live. An

intense period of creative activity ensued, including the production of the *Glagolitic Mass*, the Sinfonietta and two extraordinary string quartets.

The foundation of the Czech Republic in 1918 inspired him; freedom from German domination and his love of Russia and the Russian language provided further spurs to his efforts. An additional catalyst was Janáček's love life: in 1917 he had an affair with a singer in the Prague production of *Jenufa* and the following year met Kamila Stösslová, the pretty wife of an antique-dealer. Her husband had been able to provide food for the Janáčeks during the war and the composer was later in a position to save the Stösslovás from being expelled from the country as aliens. Separated from his wife, Janáček became infatuated with Kamila and began a voluminous correspondence in the last sixteen months of his life, amounting to nearly 700 letters. Kamila did not reciprocate his feelings but Janáček transformed her into the heroine of three of his final works – *Kát'a Kabanová*, *The Cunning Little Vixen* and *The Makropoulos Affair*. She was also the inspiration for his song cycle *Diary of One Who Disappeared*. His creative urges were undiminished when he caught a cold after a walk in the woods near his home village. This became bronchial pneumonia from which he died aged seventy-four.

HIS MUSIC

The final twenty-four years of Janáček's life won him a place among the greatest of Czech composers, with Dvořák and Smetana. Most of Dvořák's best known works had been written by the time he was thirty-five; Janáček had to wait three-quarters of his life before receiving any recognition. There were only fourteen years between their ages; their mature music is separated by half a century.

The sound world Janáček created is as individual in its way as that of Debussy or Stravinsky. The key influences were nature and folk music but equally important in his vocal works was his adaptation of his abrupt native Lachian dialect into musical phrases. No wonder he has been called 'The Moravian Mussorgsky': both composers evolved their melodies from speech patterns ('melodies of the language' as Janáček called them). Like Mussorgsky, Janáček was not a skilled technician and what his music loses in sophistication and polish it gains in force and passion.

Essential works

Jenufa, opera (1894–1904): most of Janáček's nine operas are on Russian subjects, but his first triumph is based on a tale of Moravian peasant life. It is the disturbing tale of Jenufa, a peasant girl, and her baby who is drowned by Jenufa's stepmother. Janáček's own daughter, Olga, died while he was completing the opera (the second of his children to die). There is much 'singable' music which does not always comply with Janáček's speech-pattern theory – *Jenufa*'s opening 'Ave Maria', for example, and the final duet which is one of the most affecting moments in opera. The strength of the work comes from the dramatic power of Janáček's melodies.

The Cunning Little Vixen, opera (1921–23): though by no means instantly accessible, this is probably the best Janáček opera to try first. You'll need a libretto to follow the action – even a Czech would need a translation as it is written in dialect. The story, a parable, switches between humans and animals and concerns a young vixen, Bystrouska, who is caught and raised by a gamekeeper. The vixen is eventually shot by a poacher but when the gamekeeper returns to the forest he is surrounded by a group of animals which includes the vixen's daughter, demonstrating nature's infinite capacity for renewal.

Taras Bulba (1915–18): a rhapsody for orchestra in four movements sparked off by Gogol's epic novel about the fifteenth-century Cossack Taras Bulba. Murder, revenge, capture and execution are all here in highly dramatic, vivid colours. The piece ends in a radiant section when Taras Bulba prophecies that a Tsar will arise and bring victory to the Russian Orthodox faith.

Sinfonietta (1926): an orchestral *tour de force* in five movements: the melodic and rhythmic ideas are all derived from Moravian folk songs and dance but its spirit is of ebullient pride in the newly formed Czechoslovakia.

Glagolitic Mass (1926): this is Janáček's choral masterpiece, full of triumphal brassy fanfares and bursting with energy. The composer wanted to celebrate Czechoslovak independence by writing something in the language of the missionaries, Cyril and Methodius, the brothers who first rendered a Slav translation of the Scriptures in the ninth century. He chose to set the Old Church Slavonic Mass text (slightly different to the Latin Mass) to 'portray the nation's faith not on

a religious basis', wrote Janáček, 'but on a strong moral one which calls God to witness'. *The* recording, as of much else of Janáček's music, is by Sir Charles Mackerras.

String Quartet No.1 'The Kreutzer Sonata' (1923)

String Quartet No.2 'Intimate Letters' (1928) The first of these remarkable string quartets was written in a week and is another of Janáček's works inspired by Russian literature, in this case Tolstoy's novella of the same name. Janáček's passionate involvement with the subject was acute; he wrote of 'a woman, wretched, careworn, beaten, even to death as Tolstoy depicted in his story.' The second quartet was 'written in fire', the passion he felt for Kamila inspiring a white-hot three weeks of creative activity; its subtitle was to have been 'Love Letters'.

Also worth investigating
The Excursions of Mr Brouček, opera (1917)
Kát'a Kabanová, opera (1921)
The Makropoulos Affair, opera (1923–25)
The Diary of One Who Disappeared, song cycle (1919)
Mládí ('Youth'), wind sextet (1924)
Along an Overgrown Path (1901–08), fifteen pieces for piano
In the mists (1912), for piano

JOSQUIN DES PRÉS

'Josquin is master of the notes; others are mastered by them' (Martin Luther)

Born: c.1440, probably in Picardy
Died: 27 August 1521, Condé-sur-l'Escaut, Hainault
Full name: Josquin des Prés, also written as Després, Despréz or des Préz; known also simply as Josquin
Type of music: masses, motets and secular songs
Influences: Dufay, Ockeghem and the Italian polyphonic school
Contemporaries: Guillaume Dufay, Johannes Okeghem, **JOSQUIN DES PRÉS**, Martin Luther, John Taverner, Hans Sachs, TALLIS, Jacobus Clemens non Papa

HIS LIFE
Every other composer of the late fifteenth century is eclipsed by Josquin. No one is sure when or where he was born, although it is known that during his lifetime he was always referred to by his first name, which itself is a pet name for Josse or Joseph; hence most reference books list him under 'J'.

What little is certain about Josquin's early life suggests that he may have sung in the French royal chapel. In 1459 he moved to Italy and joined the private choir of the Duke Galeazzo Maria Sforza in Milan before service in the papal chapel, where he remained from 1487 to 1494. Why this devotion to church music? In common with many others at this time, Josquin believed that artistic gifts were a divine loan to be repaid to God in the form of loyal service.

Yet he was also fond of the good things in life such as hunting, fine food and wine and, most unusually, he had a sense of fun and humour. This sometimes appears in his music and is a combination of the formal Italian and the boisterous Flemish; he was a musician who, in painting terms, could produce a Raphael Madonna with the same ease as a Brueghel peasant.

After 1502, Josquin was connected with the chapels and courts of Duke Hercules I at Ferrara, Louis XII of France, the Archduchess Margaret of Austria and the Emperor Maximilian I, ending his life as Provost (religious overseer) of Notre-Dame church in Condé-sur-l'Escaut in Hainault. The epitaph on his tomb is preserved in a manuscript at Lille, though both the tomb and church were destroyed during the French Revolution.

HIS MUSIC

Josquin's stature among his contemporaries is confirmed by the fact that Ottaviano dei Petrucci, the inventor of music printing, published no less than three volumes of his masses. No other composer was granted more than one. Rabelais and Luther were among those who praised him highly. Few composers are hailed as geniuses in their own lifetime, so what were the special qualities that made Josquin so outstanding? He had a tremendous creative vitality which impelled him to develop accepted forms and structures, making his music a synthesis of everything that had gone before, more expressive and far richer than anything previously written, highly accomplished technically (Josquin could write in canon as easily as Bach later wrote in fugue) and the harmony and polyphony in his scores are more sophisticated. Just listen to music by his peers and the generation immediately preceding him (Dufay or Ockeghem, for example) and you'll hear the difference.

Josquin's work also encompasses a wider range of emotions: compare the gaiety of the *frottola* (a type of early madrigal) *El grillo* (*The Cricket*), in which Josquin wittily imitates the clicking of the insect, with the sombre grandeur of the *Missa 'Pange lingua'* and the tender-hearted *Ave verum*. An additional device for which Josquin became famous, although he wasn't the first to do it, was to borrow snatches of his own and other people's work – bits of popular songs, well-known settings of masses and motets – and incorporate them into his next piece. It helped the important and satisfying process of thematically unifying a piece of music.

Essential works

Josquin wrote nineteen masses, about fifty secular pieces and more than 150 motets with sacred texts. The most beautiful masses are **'Pange lingua'**, **La sol fa re mi** and **De Beata Virgine**.

Also worth investigating are the four-part motets **Absalon fili mi** and **Planxit autem David (the lament for Saul and Jonathan)**, the five-part motet **Miserere mei, Deus** and the six-part motet **Ave Maria … virgo serena**.

Dmitri KABALEVSKY

Born: 30 December 1904, St Petersburg
Died: 16 February 1987, Moscow
Full name: Dmitri Borisovich Kabalevsky
Type of music: concerto, symphony, opera, chamber, instrumental
Influences: Mussorgsky, Borodin, Tchaikowsky, Scriabin, Miaskowsky
Contemporaries: Luigi Dallapiccola, Richard Addinsell, **KABALEVSKY**, Constant Lambert, Marc Blitzstein, Alan Rawsthorne, Dag Wirén, TIPPETT

HIS LIFE AND MUSIC

No one would claim that Kabalevsky was one of the twentieth century's greatest composers but there is a handful of works which are irresistible despite their often derivative nature. Like Khachaturian, a close contemporary and fellow student of Nikolai Miaskowsky at the Moscow Conservatory, his work is largely inspired by folk music. He towed the party line more dutifully than most, rising to become a great musical power in the land as director of music for Soviet Radio and the Institute of Arts History, and was the regime's leading musical ambassador.

One element informs all of his compositions – optimism, a rare quality in recent music and one not to be despised when it is served up with such panache and wit, and in expertly crafted scores. His music for children is particularly notable.

Essential works

Colas Breugnon, overture (1936–38): surely one of the most exuberant opera overtures. It is a miniature portrait of the principal character, a crafty Burgundian craftsman of the sixteenth century who loved the good things in life. This overture featured frequently in Toscanini's concerts.
Symphony No.2 in C minor Op.19 (1934): a tuneful, high-spirited, immediately appealing work, the type that won official Soviet approval. Like most of Kabalevsky's music it is direct and not particularly deep.
The Comedians, Op.26 suite for orchestra,

(1940): incidental music for a children's play, *The Inventor and the Comedians*; No.2, the Galop, is almost as popular – and frenetic – as Khachaturian's Sabre Dance.
Piano Concerto No.3 in D, 'Youth', Op.50 (1952): the final work of a trilogy dedicated to the young; the others are the **Violin Concerto, Op.48** and **Cello Concerto, Op.49**. A bubbling, infectiously charming romp.
Piano Sonata No.3, Op.46: said to be Kabalevsky's answer to Prokofiev's three so-called 'War Sonatas' Nos.6, 7 & 8; stunningly recorded by Vladimir Horowitz.

Aram KHACHATURIAN

Born: 6 June 1903, Kodzhori, Tiflis (now Tbilisi)
Died: 1 May 1978, Moscow
Full name: Aram Il'yich Khachaturian
Type of music: symphony, concerto, ballet, chamber, vocal, piano
Influences: Russian Orientalism, Armenian folk music and Nicolai Miaskovsky
Contemporaries: Maurice Duruflé, RODRIGO, Boris Blacher, **KHACHATURIAN**, Luigi Dallapiccola, Richard Addinsell, KABALEVSKY, Constant Lambert

HIS LIFE AND MUSIC

To his critics, Khachaturian is 'watered-down Prokofiev'. His music is, for the most part, certainly less grim and more accessible than that of many of his contemporaries. He can be accused of conservatism and of crude populism at times but he could both write wonderful melodies *and* not be afraid to use them – two qualities in short supply in twentieth-century music. He was also a brilliant and imaginative orchestrator. Listen to his *Masquerade Suite*, in particular its well-known Waltz, and one could almost be listening to Tchaikowsky. Not that Khachaturian avoided dissonance and contemporary compositional techniques but his musical heart always led him back to his roots. Whereas many nationalist composers had adopted the musical idioms of the Russian Orient, Khachaturian was actually born in one of the Caucasian countries.

Khachaturian (the correct, if rare, pronunciation is Hach-a-tur-*yan*, the 'H' sounding like a German 'CH') was the son of an Armenian bookbinder and was slow to reveal his talent for composition. His first instrument was the tuba but it was as a biology student that he went to Moscow University. Within a year he had switched to the Gnesin School of Music to study cello, an instrument he had never played before. (Mikhail Gnesin himself had been a pupil of Rimsky-Korsakov.) In 1929 Khachaturian went on to the Moscow Conservatory where his composition teacher, Miaskowsky – another Rimsky-Korsakov pupil – was perhaps the strongest influence on him. His arresting First Symphony was written for his graduation 'in honour of the fifteenth anniversary of Soviet Armenia'.

After the international success of his Piano Concerto, official recognition was quick to follow and he was awarded the coveted Stalin Prize three times and the Order of Lenin in 1939. In 1948, however, he was hauled up before the Central Committee of the Communist Party, with Prokofiev and Shostakovich, for writing the wrong sort of music, and accused of 'decadent formalism'. An interesting charge, because Khachaturian had already been writing the kind of music that was now being requested. Over the following three decades he made many visits abroad conducting his own works, and was one of the Soviet Union's most eminent musical representatives.

Essential works

Piano Concerto (1936): Prokofiev meets Liszt and Borodin. Oriental-inspired themes, exotic melodies and exuberant rhythmic drive with a liberal use of the percussion department – typical of so much of Khachaturian's music. The slow movement features the flexatone (musical saw) to haunting effect.

Violin Concerto (1940): engaging folk material with a virtuoso solo part, as in the Piano Concerto. The virile, passionate outer movements with a central lament make it one of Khachaturian's most poignant works.

Masquerade, suite for orchestra (1944): the incidental music composed for Lermontov's play *Masquerade* about the upper classes of Russia in 1830. Light music, but highly infectious; the Waltz and Galop are popular hits.

Gayaneh, ballet (1931–57): also known as *Gayne*, this ballet contains the brash, fiery

Sabre Dance, Khachaturian's most famous piece.

Spartacus, ballet (1955–67, rev.1969): based on the 73 BC slave revolt led by the Thracian warrior Spartacus against the Romans. Banish all thoughts of Kirk Douglas, and revel in the un-Roman romanticism of the lush score that includes the *Adagio of Spartacus and Phrygia*, the theme used in BBC television's 1970s family shipping saga *The Onedin Line*.

Symphony No.1 (1934): makes use of trans-Caucasian folk music for its themes and development; the first time these had been incorporated into that most European of musical forms, the symphony.

Also worth investigating
Symphony No.2 (1943)
The Valencian Widow, ballet suite (1953)

Zoltán KODÁLY

'Some day the ringing tower of Hungarian music is going to stand' (Kodály)

Born: 16 December 1882, Kecskemét
Died: 6 March 1967, Budapest
Type of music: orchestral, concerto, opera, choral, song, chamber, piano, incidental music
Influences: Gregorian chant, Bach, Bartók, Debussy, Brahms
Contemporaries: Manuel Ponce, Joaquín Turina, GRAINGER, **KODÁLY**, STRAVINSKY, WEBERN, Alfredo Casella, Lord Berners, BAX, Sir George Dyson

HIS LIFE AND MUSIC

The two men who changed the direction of Hungarian music first met in 1900 at the Budapest Conservatory. Bartók and Kodály became lifelong friends, their relationship cemented by a common cause: the vision of an educated Hungary. Together they undertook several expeditions collecting Hungarian folk songs. In view of the primitive equipment – bulky machines with fragile cylinders – their determination must be wondered at. They collected between three and four thousand tunes. The results were published jointly and their findings systematically catalogued. Hitherto no one had thought to reap this rich natural harvest and re-invest it in their country's living heritage, although Vaughan Williams and Holst were doing the same thing simultaneously in England. Previously influenced by Brahms and then Debussy, Kodály now found his own voice using Hungarian folk songs and rhythms. His first mature work, the symphonic poem *Summer Evening* (1906) dates from this period as does his first teaching post at the Academy in Budapest. This profession was not merely a means of earning money while he composed: he saw teaching as an essential part of his mission.

He composed diligently without much recognition for the following fifteen years and certainly achieved nothing as momentous as Bartók's contemporary pieces. However, in 1922 Kodály, Bartók and Dohnányi were each asked to supply a new work for the fiftieth anniversary of the unification of Buda and Pest. The work chosen was Kodály's *Psalmus hungaricus*, which brought him international recognition. His folk opera *Háry János* followed in 1926 and by the mid-thirties he was a national hero. What makes his music attractive is its directness, its lyrical and melodic appeal and swinging sense of rhythm; Bartók chose another path, preferring to distort the folk-based material, moulding it into something more subjective and obscure.

During the Second World War, Kodály remained in Budapest, surviving under the German puppet government; Bartók, already withdrawing from Hungarian musical life, had left for the United States. The Nazis ordered Kodály to divorce his Jewish wife – he refused, and, though threatened by the Gestapo with torture, he was active in the underground movement. It was probably his reputation that saved his life, for the Nazis finally decided to leave him alone. After the war, with Bartók dead, Kodály was acclaimed as the country's greatest living composer. He was certainly the most powerful: his music-teaching system was used throughout the country and, although he composed less and less, his influence and decisions dominated Hungary's musical life until his death.

Essential works

Psalmus hungaricus, Op.13 (1923): an outstanding choral work using an old Hungarian adaptation of Psalm 55 and set to the music of native folk songs and styles.

Háry Janós, suite (1925–277): the music fashioned from Kodály's comic opera about Háry Janós, a familiar figure in Hungarian folklore, who is a liar of fabulous conceit and bravado. It is in six movements, the first one prefaced by an orchestral sneeze, for legend has it that if someone sneezes while a tale is being told, the story must be true.

Dances of Galánta (1933): a five-movement dance suite for orchestra played without pause. 'Galánta is a small Hungarian market town,' wrote Kodály, 'known to travellers between Vienna and Budapest. The composer passed there seven years of his childhood.'

Erich Wolfgang KORNGOLD

'Ein Genie! Ein Genie!' (Mahler)

Born: 29 May 1897, Brno, Austria
Died: 29 November 1957, Hollywood
Type of music: opera, ballet, symphony, concerto, chamber, instrumental, film
Influences: Puccini, Mahler, Richard Strauss
Contemporaries: Roger Sessions, Virgil Thomson, **KORNGOLD**, GERSHWIN, Roy Harris, POULENC, Carlos Chávez, Georges Auric, WEILL

Many reference books on classical music ignore Korngold. He wrote film scores in Hollywood, so he can't really be a serious classical composer, can he? Film buffs revel in his sumptuous scores for *Captain Blood*, *The Adventures of Robin Hood*, *The Sea Hawk*, *The Private Lives of Elizabeth and Essex*, all of which starred Errol Flynn, and *Kings Row*, with Ronald Reagan. Few are familiar with his concert music.

Korngold began life as one of the most precociously gifted children in musical history, the son of a highly respected music critic. Puccini admired him, Mahler called him a genius and Richard Strauss was 'filled with awe' – all three composers had an influence on his early work. Korngold's pantomime, *Der Schneemann*, created a sensation when presented at the Vienna Court Opera, his Piano Trio was played by Bruno Walter and his Piano Sonata by Artur Schnabel – all before he reached his teens. Arthur Nikisch, the music director of the Gewandhaus Concerts in Leipzig and the greatest conductor of the day, commissioned the thirteen-year-old Korngold for his first orchestral work ('Schauspiel' Overture, Op.4), an unprecedented honour for an adolscent. The critic Ernest Newman wrote: '[His music] is the spontaneous product of a most subtly organised brain that at the first span embraces practically all we know and feel today in the way of harmonic relation.' After more orchestral works, chamber music lieder, Korngold turned in his mid-teens to dramatic music for the theatre. Mature operatic successes followed – *Der Ring des Polykrates* and *Violanta* – culminating in 1920 with *Die tote Stadt* (an international hit, given productions in 83 opera houses) and his own favourite *Das Wunder der Heliane* in 1927.

In 1934 Korngold accepted an invitation from the director Max Reinhardt to go to Hollywood and adapt Mendelssohn's music for the film of *A Midsummer Night's Dream* (in which Mickey Rooney starred as Puck). The Nazis made it impossible for him to return to Austria, and Korngold eventually settled in Hollywood, becoming an American citizen in 1943. After the Second World War, he returned to composing orchestral music while also producing film scores, a genre of composition which, with Max Steiner and Alfred Newman, he pioneered.

Essential works

Sinfonietta (1912): the hand of Richard Strauss hovers over the music, but this is Korngold's own voice, an extraordinary work by a fifteen-year-old.

Die tote Stadt, opera (1920): lush, late-Romantic score; Act 1 contains the achingly lovely duet 'Glück das mir verblieb', featured in the film *Diva*. A 1924 recording by Richard Tauber and Lotte Lehmann still sends a tingle up the spine.

Violin Concerto (1946): written for Bronislav Hubermann, who died before playing it, and recorded incomparably by the great Jascha Heifetz; the themes for each movement in this concerto are taken from the film scores of *Another Dawn*, *Anthony Adverse* and *The Prince and the Pauper*. 'More Korn than Gold'

one critic said. Really? Just try the second movement.

Symphony in F sharp, Op.40 (1951–52): a huge four-movement symphony which includes parts for marimba and bass tuba as well as enlarged percussion. The sombre Adagio is masterly.

Piano Trio in D, Op.1 (1910): composed when Korngold was not yet twelve, this is a remarkably mature four-movement work of expansive lyricism with Korngold's melodic gift already much in evidence.

Violin Sonata in G, Op.6 (1912): for any composer, let alone a fifteen-year-old, this violin sonata is an adventurous and assured piece with a nod towards Bartók and his own later Violin Concerto.

Fritz KREISLER

'A most valuable symbol of a whole epoch' (Josef Gingold)

Born: 2 February 1875, Vienna
Died: 29 January 1962, New York
Type of music: operetta, violin
Influences: Strauss, Lehár, Viennese dance, Baroque music
Contemporaries: RAVEL, Reinhold Glière, Albert Ketèlbey, **KREISLER,**
William Hurlstone, FALLA, Ermanno Wolf-Ferrari, Havergal Brian

HIS LIFE AND MUSIC

One of the most acclaimed violinists in history, Kreisler was the composer of many delectable short pieces for the instrument which have held their own on the concert platforms and record labels of the world; his *Tambourin chinois* is among the most requested tracks on Classic fM.

He was only twelve when he won the Grand Prix (gold medal) of the Paris Conservatoire against forty competitors, making his American debut the following year in 1888. He then abandoned music to study medicine in Vienna and art in Rome, after which he was called up into the Austrian army. He resumed his music career in 1899 and became one of the highest paid artists in the world before being recalled into the army for the First World War. He was wounded in 1915 and discharged. From then on, until deafness took its toll, he remained at the top of his profession, and was one of the most beloved of all musicians, noted for his humanity and kindness wherever he went.

In 1935 he caused a furore in the classical world by admitting that some violin pieces he had 'discovered' in 1910, and had performed since, were really forgeries, his own clever pastiches of earlier composers. Some critics were outraged at this unethical behaviour, but more probably because they had been hoodwinked. Few, if any, have equalled Kreisler in his own inimitable recordings of these 'forgeries' and his other compositions, and singers, as well as all string instrumentalists, use them to learn about musical phrasing. They should be listened to and absorbed by anyone who wants to know about the arts of *rubato* and making music. Light and insubstantial Kreisler's compositions may be, but few have written for the violin with more skill and charm.

Essential works
Pieces for violin and piano
Liebeslied: Rachmaninov made piano transcriptions of this and *Liebesfreud*.
Liebesfreud
Schön Rosmarin
Tambourin chinois
Caprice viennois
Marche miniature viennois

Prelude and Allegro: (attributed to Pugnani)
Sicilienne and Rigaudon: (attributed to Francoeur)
Also innumerable arrangements of other composers' works, including a re-working of the first movement of Paganini's Violin Concerto No.1 – an over-the-top arrangement and enormous fun.

Édouard LALO

(1823–92)

Symphonie espagnole, 1874

Lalo was over fifty before he had any success as a composer. Indeed, the lack of recognition had caused him such depression that he abandoned composition and, in the words of a contemporary, 'turned for precarious solace to matrimony with a contralto'. His

Violin Concerto in F, Op.20 was played by the great Spanish violinist Pablo de Sarasate in Paris in 1874. The same year, Lalo composed the *Symphonie espagnole*, Op.21, and dedicated it to Sarasate. This one work, a violin concerto in all but name, secured him international fame. Tchaikowsky praised it in a letter to his patron, Madame von Meck: 'It is so fresh and light, and contains piquant rhythms and melodies which are beautifully harmonized .... Like Delibes and Bizet, Lalo is careful to avoid all that is *routinier*, seeks new forms without trying to be profound, and is more concerned with musical beauty than with tradition, as are the Germans.'

The work is in five movements though invariably given without the Intermezzo which is generally considered not to be of the same quality as the others. His opera *Le roi d'Ys* was enormously successful in its day but the two other works of Lalo's that are worth investigating are his Cello Concerto (1877) and Schumannesque Symphony in G minor (1886), both highly rewarding.

Lalo, who came from a military family in Lille and whose father had been decorated on the battlefied of Lützen by Napoleon, became one of the most distinguished figures in French music. He had the appearance of an Austrian diplomat, even after an attack of paralysis in the early 1880s left him walking with a limp. In the later years of his life, the paralysis returned, further aggravating his poor health and deepening his depression.

Franz LEHÁR

Born: 30 April 1870, Komarón, Hungary
Died: 24 October 1948, Bad Ischl
Type of music: opera
Influences: Johann Strauss II, Slav and military music
Contemporaries: Guillaume Lekeu, Louis Vierne, Leopold Godowsky, **LEHÁR**, SCRIABIN, VAUGHAN WILLIAMS, Hugo Alfvén, Max Reger, RACHMANINOV

HIS LIFE AND MUSIC

Lehár was the last of the great Viennese operetta composers, and a dollar millionaire by the age of thirty-five. Only a year after the premiere of his first international hit, *The Merry Widow*, it had been performed more than 5,000 times in the United States and five productions were playing simultaneously in five different languages in Buenos Aires. The musical heir to Johann Strauss II, Lehár brought a blend of nostalgia and sophisticated humour to the frivolous operetta which suited perfectly the spirit of privileged gaiety in Vienna at the turn of the century.

Lehár was the son of a military bandmaster. He entered the Prague Conservatory to study the violin when he was twelve, and on showing Dvořák a couple of sonatas he had written, the great Czech is supposed to have said, 'Hang up your fiddle, my boy. Concentrate on composing.' At twenty he was the youngest bandmaster ever appointed in the army, but after writing an opera, *Kukuschka*, the interest of a publisher finally persuaded him to act on Dvořák's advice. He soon made a name for himself as a composer of operettas with a string of works for Vienna's Theater an der Wien but it wasn't until the performance of *Die lustige Witwe* in 1905 that he hit the jackpot.

After a few failures, Lehár tapped into a winning streak again and within the space of three months, October 1909 to January 1910, Vienna saw the first nights of *Das Fürstenkind* (*The Prince's Child*), *Zigeunerliebe* (*Gypsy Love*) and *Der Graf von Luxemburg* (*The Count of Luxembourg*). Rich and famous, he and his wife Sophie moved to the Salzkammergut, a ski resort where the Emperor Franz Josef had his hunting lodge. With the death of the emperor and the outbreak of the First World War, Lehár's success subsided. It wasn't until he met the renowned opera and *Lieder* singer Richard Tauber that his career was revitalized. Lehár wrote a succession of operettas tailored to Tauber's magnetic personality and voice and a second string of triumphs followed, including *Friederike* in 1928, *Das Land des Lächelns* (*The Land of Smiles*) in 1929 – the biggest hit since *The Merry Widow* – and *Giuditta* in 1934.

Again, war intervened, forcing Tauber to leave for England when the Nazi menace spread. Lehár retired to his villa at Bad Ischl and remained there for the duration of the war. He was a favourite composer of Hitler and, incredibly, re-wrote the overture to *The Merry Widow* and dedicated it to the Führer. Whether it was an act of homage or done to save his Jewish wife from the Gestapo is a moot point. It didn't help the Jewish librettist of his *The Land of Smiles* and *Giuditta*, who was executed in a concentration camp while his work was still playing in Vienna.

The Lehárs moved to Switzerland after the war. Sophie Lehár died late in 1947, Tauber a few months later and Lehár not long after that.

Essential works

Die lustige Witwe (The Merry Widow) 1905: Lehár was second choice as composer for this work. Richard Heuberger, another Viennese composer, had already turned down the libretto. The directors pronounced Lehár's score 'tuneless and unmusical' (what *were* they listening to?) and would allow only a low-budget production. It was an immediate hit and in New York and Paris, Merry Widow hats and dresses became instantly fashionable. The opera has been filmed on a number of occasions, most bizarrely in a 1925 *silent* film directed by Erich von Stroheim. Among the most popular soprano requests is Hanna's (the Merry Widow's) 'Vilia, oh Vilia, the witch of the wood' from Act 1 and the Waltz Song 'Lippen schweigen' ('Silent love') from Act 3, in which Danilo declares his love for Hanna.

Das Land des Lächelns (The Land of Smiles): with English lyrics by Harry Graham, this operetta includes 'Patiently smiling', 'Love, what has given you this magic power?' and, above all, 'You are my heart's delight', forever associated with Richard Tauber, who was said to have sung it over 3,000 times.

The high spots in the Lehár–Tauber operettas were the *Tauberlied*, the songs specially written for Tauber, many of which have proved far more enduring than the operas from which they came: the Serenade from *Frasquita* (1922), entitled 'Farewell, my love farewell', 'Girls were made to love and kiss' (*Paganini*, 1925) and 'O maiden, my maiden' (from *Friederike*, 1928) are idiomatic. They were recorded incomparably by Tauber with Lehár conducting.

Ruggiero LEONCAVALLO
(1857–1919)

Pagliacci, opera, 1892

Cavalleria rusticana by Mascagni and *Pagliacci* – 'Cav and Pag' as they are referred to in the trade, for these works are invariably presented together – are one-act operas that provided their composers with their only triumph. Why neither man could produce a further work of comparable distinction is one of music's curiosities. It certainly was not for lack of trying.

Leoncavallo's first opera, *Tommaso Chatterton* (based on the story of the young English poet who committed suicide by drinking strychnine), was about to be produced in 1878 when the manager absconded with the funds. Thereafter, Leoncavallo made a living by playing the piano in cafés all over Europe, Egypt and Turkey before settling in Paris. Here he made a thorough study of Wagner's scores and resolved to emulate the great German by writing a trilogy on the Italian Renaissance. The research alone took him six years. Having completed the first part and sketched the rest, he couldn't find a publisher.

Enraged at the lack of interest, Leoncavallo turned to Sonzogno, the publisher of Mascagni's *Cavalleria rusticana*, which had just become a huge hit. In five months, Leoncavallo had written the libretto, music and orchestration for *Pagliacci* in a deliberate attempt to emulate the success of Mascagni. Ironically, it is the antithesis of a Wagner opera: both works represent the ultimate in Italian *verismo,* that is lowlife as opposed to epic drama. He based the work on a true incident with which he had some connection: during his childhood in Calabria, a jealous actor had killed his wife after a performance; the magistrate who had tried the case was Leoncavallo's father. *Pagliacci* (*Clowns*) – not *I Pagliacci* (*The Clowns*) as it is often incorrectly called – was an instant and international success, with Toscanini conducting the first performance in Milan in May 1892. Sonzogno now had under his control the most popular one-act operas ever written.

Could Leoncavallo hit the jackpot again? He could not. The premieres of the first part of his Italian Renaissance trilogy and *Tommaso Chatterton* were greeted with indifference and then he had the misfortune to write *La bohème* only a year after Puccini had tackled the same subject. A light opera *Zazà* (1900) fared slightly better, but for all intents and purposes that was it. He kept on turning them out without making any impression at all. Just one hour of music for immortality!

'Vesti la giubba' from Act 1 of *Pagliacci* is among the greatest of tenor arias and was recorded in 1902 by Enrico Caruso. It made him the earliest recorded artist to sell more than a million copies of one disc. In 1904 he recorded Leoncavallo's song 'Mattinata' with the composer at the piano and three years later, *Pagliacci* became the first complete recording of an opera to be issued in the UK.

Franz LISZT

'The most important germinative force in modern music' (Cecil Gray)

Born: 22 October 1811, Raiding, near Ödenberg, Hungary
Died: 31 July 1886, Bayreuth
Original name: Ferenc Liszt
Type of music: orchestral, concerto, oratorio, chamber, piano, organ, vocal
Influences: Beethoven, Paganini, Berlioz, Chopin
Contemporaries: Félicien David, SCHUMANN, Samuel Sebastian Wesley, **LISZT**, Ambroise Thomas, Vincent Wallace, Sigismund Thalberg, Friedrich von Flotow

HIS LIFE

Composer, teacher, Abbé, Casanova, writer, sage, pioneer and champion of new music, philanthropist, philosopher and one of the greatest pianists in history, Liszt was the very embodiment of the Romantic spirit, yet he remains the most contradictory personality of all the great composers. He was as arrogant and egocentric as he was humble and generous; he was profoundly spiritual yet delighted in the pleasures of the flesh – and had at least twenty-six major love affairs and several illegitimate children (Ernest Newman said, 'He collected princesses and countesses as other men collect rare butterflies, or Japanese prints, or first editions'); attracted to the life of a recluse, he loved luxury and the adulation of the public; he practised at the highest level of his art yet could demean himself with meretricious theatrics: all in all, a fascinating man.

1811 His father, Adam, was an excellent musician, an official on the Esterházy estate and a cello player in the court orchestra. As a young man he had been a Franciscan novice for two years.

1820 Young Liszt was introduced to the piano at an early age. By nine he could not only play Hummel's difficult B minor Concerto in public but was also able to extemporize on themes submitted by the audience.

1821 Prince Nicholas Esterházy was impressed enough to arrange for a group of Hungarian aristocrats to fund the musical education of the prodigy to the tune of 600 florins a year and Liszt, with his mother and ambitious father, moved to Vienna. His piano mentor here was Carl Czerny, who refused to accept payment for the pleasure of teaching the Hungarian *Wunderkind*. Liszt's composition teacher was Antonio Salieri – the same Salieri who had been so much a part of Mozart's life. Soon Liszt was giving concerts. Beethoven attended one, in which Liszt played an arrangement of a Beethoven Piano Trio from memory; the great master is said to have kissed his brow and exclaimed, 'Devil of a fellow! –such a young rascal!' Liszt also made his debut as a composer at this time, when he was asked to contribute a variation on a theme by Diabelli.

1823 Still only twelve and a masterly pianist, Liszt left Vienna for Paris to try for admission to the Conservatoire. However, the director, Luigi Cherubini, had an aversion to child prodigies and the establishment did not admit foreigners, so it was left to private teachers to administer a little French polish to Liszt's talent.

1824 A concert at the Paris Opéra in March established Liszt as one of the finest pianists ever heard; allegedly, the orchestra in the concerto item stopped playing to listen to him, enraptured. The fashionable *salons* in both Paris and London welcomed him.

1827 By the age of sixteen Liszt was famous throughout Europe and financially self-sufficient. Adam Liszt died suddenly of typhoid fever the same year, enjoining his son to hand over his fortune to his mother in recognition of the person who had made it possible. Liszt, exhausted by constant touring, bowed out of the limelight for a few years, teaching, reading everything he could get his hands on and embarking on the first of his many passionate love affairs, with Caroline de Saint-Cricq, a sixteen-year-old whose father, the French Minister of Commerce, nipped the romance in the bud. Religion and philosophy for a time replaced music as the dominant force in Liszt's life.

1830 He then encountered three musicians who were to change everything: Chopin, Berlioz (then virtually unknown) and Paganini. From Berlioz he learnt about the potential sonorities of the orchestra – Liszt's later orchestral works testify to that; from Chopin he absorbed the poetry and refined, sensitive taste of the Pole's piano style. But it was the electrifying effect of Paganini's stage presence and the spectacular demands of his music that immediately fired Liszt's imagination. Paganini had dramatically extended the possibilities of the violin with his astounding technical prowess and Liszt consciously set out to emulate on the piano what Paganini had accomplished on his instrument. To achieve this involved creating a new technique.

1831–33 For the following two years Liszt shut himself away to master his objectives, practising to the point of exhaustion. He described his routine: 'Here is a whole fortnight that my mind and fingers have been working like two lost spirits – Homer, the Bible, Plato, Locke, Byron, Hugo, Lamartine, Chateaubriand, Beethoven, Bach, Hummel, Mozart, Weber are all around me ... I study them, meditate on them, devour them with fury. Besides this, I practise four to five hours of exercises (thirds, sixths, eighths, tremolos, repetitions of the notes, cadenzas, etc.). Ah! provided I don't go mad you will find an artist in me. Yes an artist such as you desire, such as is required nowadays.'

Liszt's re-emergence on the concert platform was a major artistic event and the pianistic artillery he had acquired swept all rivals aside. He played Beethoven's sonatas inimitably and Chopin's intimately, but what the public really adored were the stupendous opera fantasies and dare-devil concoctions of his own. The conductor and pianist Charles Hallé heard him at about this time and recorded that he sat speechless in 'a stupor of amazement' after the experience and then went home with a feeling of thorough dejection. 'Such marvels of executive skill and power I could never have imagined .... Liszt was all sunshine and dazzling splendour, subjugating his hearers with a power that none could withstand. For him there were no difficulties of execution, the most incredible seeming child's play under his fingers.'

1834 Liszt met and fell in love with the beautiful Comtesse Marie d'Agoult in 1834. The fact that she had a husband and three children was of no importance when it came to such a grand passion. Within a year, she had left them and joined Liszt in Geneva where Blandine, their first child, was born; she died in 1867. Cosima, their second child, destined to become the wife of Richard Wagner, was born in 1837 and lived until 1930. In 1839, their third child, Daniel, was born in Rome; he died at the age of only twenty.

1839–47 For the following eight years, Liszt toured all over the continent, from Turkey and Russia to Portugal and Ireland, amassing a fortune, heaped with honours, the intimate of royalty and statesmen wherever he appeared. Indeed, he was not averse to giving royalty a dressing-down if their behaviour interfered with his music-making.

1847 At the height of his powers, he changed direction. The relationship with Marie d'Agoult had gradually disintegrated and, when they finally parted, Liszt took the children to live with his mother in Paris. Here his mistresses included Marie Duplessis (immortalized by Dumas *fils* as the Lady of the Camellias and by Verdi in his opera *La traviata*) and the dancer Lola Montez. While on a concert trip to Kiev in 1847 he met the Polish-born Princess Carolyne Sayn-Wittgenstein, a cigar-smoking, unhappily-married intellectual who suffered from a morbid fear of fresh air. This was Liszt's last

great love. The two discovered a mutual interest in religion and mysticism and within a short time the princess had abandoned her husband and thirty thousand serfs to join Liszt in Weimar where he had been made Kapellmeister to the Grand Duke.

1848–61 They lived at the court as an unmarried couple for the following ten years. Liszt's duties were to direct performances of orchestral and operatic works, and, by the end of the decade, he had transformed Weimar into one of Europe's most notable musical centres, the headquarters of the Music of the Future. Musicians flocked to Weimar like pilgrims to Mecca. The works Liszt presented and conducted were of the widest variety, from premieres of new and experimental works to quality revivals of the classic repertoire.

Liszt never allowed his personal preferences to dictate what he produced. Even composers he personally disliked or whose music he did not care for had a hearing. He was also courageous enough to present a revival of Wagner's *Tannhäuser*, a work by a political revolutionary sought by the authorities. He then followed it up with the world premiere of *Lohengrin*. He fought for funds to present other works by the composer, and the duke's refusal to fund the enterprise was one of the reasons for Liszt's eventual departure. Other avant-garde works of the day, such as Peter Cornelius' *The Barber of Baghdad*, were hissed by the resentful inhabitants of Weimar and the reaction to the premiere of Cornelius' opera was the final straw.

Two other activities occupied Liszt during his reign at Weimar. Piano students came to him from all over the world, among them the brilliant Carl Tausig – considered to be the equal of Liszt as a pianist but who, alas, died young – and Hans von Bülow, the future ardent Wagnerian who was to marry Liszt's daughter Cosima before being cuckolded by Wagner. Perhaps most astonishing of all was the time Liszt devoted to composition. Most of his music was written in this period. The amount he produced is simply staggering; what we hear today is only the tip of the iceberg. These years include twelve symphonic poems, the *Faust* and *Dante* Symphonies, two Piano Concertos and the *Totentanz* for piano and orchestra, the great B minor Piano Sonata, and literally hundreds of other pieces for the piano as well as revisions of all the piano music he had written in the 1830s and 1840s.

1861–71 Although he resigned from his musical duties in 1859, Liszt remained in Weimar until 1861. In the hope that he could marry Princess Carolyne, he travelled to Rome but the Pope revoked the sanction for her divorce at the last moment. However, he decided to remain in Rome. The religious life again attracted him and in 1865 Pope Pius IX conferred on him the dignity of Abbé. In 1879 he received the tonsure and the four minor orders (ostuary, lector, exorcist and acolyte) but was never ordained a priest; yet he was allowed to discard the cassock and even marry if he so wished.

1871–86 From now on Liszt divided his time between his religious interests in Rome and teaching piano in Pesth (now Budapest) and Weimar, where he was invited back in 1869. The number of famous musicians who came into contact with him runs into hundreds; the letters he wrote, in French and German, run into thousands, and they are all in longhand for he never employed a secretary. Musicians from all over Europe sent him music to promote, to play, to comment upon. He reviewed, he gave concerts and he continued to compose.

Liszt's influence on the following generation of music-makers is hard to exaggerate; Borodin, Balakirev, Rimsky-Korsakov, MacDowell, Smetana, Debussy, Saint-Saëns, Fauré, Grieg and Brahms all benefited from his advice and encouragement. He nurtured a whole school of pianists, giving his time with a generosity that has rarely been matched, and he never asked for any fees. Towards the end of his life, one Liszt pupil, the great pianist Moriz Rosenthal (whose recordings attest to his prodigious gifts) summed up Liszt thus: 'He was more wonderful than anybody I have ever known.'

1886 His final triumph was a visit to England. Although aged and suffering from dropsy, he gave some public concerts, including a private recital at Windsor Castle for Queen Victoria. He also attended a performance of his oratorio *St Elizabeth*. The reception given to him wherever he went moved him deeply and he stayed on an extra week before travelling to Bayreuth for the Festival. During a performance of *Tristan und Isolde* he had to be taken from the auditorium: pneumonia had set in, swiftly followed by congestion of the lungs. The last word he uttered was 'Tristan'.

HIS MUSIC

Liszt worked in every field of music except ballet and opera, and to each he contributed a significant development. (To be accurate, he did write *one* opera in 1825, entitled *Don Sanche*, which was given a couple of performances, then shelved; fifty years later it was thought that the score had been lost in a fire at the Paris Opéra but it resurfaced again in 1903. Liszt never tackled the medium after the effort of his fourteenth year.)

So much of his music has still to be heard this century that, of necessity, judgement must be made on the relatively small proportion that is available. The project that the Hyperion record label initiated a few years ago with the pianist Leslie Howard gives some idea of the amount he wrote. Howard will be the first person ever to have played and recorded all the piano works of Liszt when he completes the cycle in about 1998. There will be over 1,200 separate titles in fifty volumes – on almost 200 CDs. And that's just the piano music!

Quantity by no means equals quality in Liszt's case, however. Among his works are many examples where effect becomes a substitute for substance; again, some of the more apparently profound pieces can seem phoney and manufactured after a while. The artist mirrors the composer: he can be wildly exciting, dramatic and overwhelming one moment and then genuinely poetic and moving the next; music of charged physicality, even eroticism, can alternate with a subdued, reflective spirituality. Two further qualities rarely commented on are his brilliance as an orchestrator and his melodic gift – the amount of memorable and famous themes he produced really should not be allotted to just one composer.

All this, important as it is, is of secondary consideration beside his main genius as a musical liberator. A common inspiration for his work was an external influence – a painting, a book, some religious experience or a walk in the mountains – and he set as an ideal 'the return, change, modification and modulation of the musical motives, conditioned by their poetic idea.' The outcome of this was the symphonic poem or 'tone-poem', a one-movement orchestral work – of Liszt's invention. He made use of the idea of 'transformation of themes' in which all the themes in a work are derived from a single basic idea – the *idée fixe* as Berlioz called it. *Leitmotiv*, evolved by Wagner in his operas, was also a feature of Liszt's mature work. Both these developments exercised an enormous influence on orchestral writing during the second half of the nineteenth century. In parallel with Wagner, Liszt experimented with harmony, particularly in enhancing chromatic harmony, which results in unprepared modulations into unrelated keys. Young composers everywhere copied his bold strokes of imagination and his frequent dissonances. The famous chord with which Wagner's opera *Tristan und Isolde* begins (the so-called '*Tristan* chord', cited as the first indication that music could dispense with tonality) was used, with one small difference, by Liszt in a song written in 1845, years before *Tristan* was conceived. Wagner, writing in 1859, admitted, 'since my acquaintance with Liszt's compositions, my treatment of harmony has become very different to what it was.' As early as 1837 he incorporated the whole tone scale into the *Dante* Sonata and his late piano pieces contain experiments with atonality. In these and his little-known oratorios he uses the whole tone scale and other unconventional devices that anticipate the methods of Debussy, Bartók and Schoenberg.

Finally, one must consider Liszt's contribution to the piano. There is no doubt that he was one of the greatest pianists in history, and, incidentally, an extraordinary sight-reader. None of his contemporaries could compete with his brilliance, personal magnetism or the sheer volume of sound he produced. Since his death, it has been the fashion to talk of Liszt the flamboyant showman to the exclusion of almost everything else. Now he can be seen as the pianist who combined showmanship with technique and poetry to a higher degree than any of his peers. He invented the piano recital – programmes had previously been shared between artists; he was the first to play the piano sideways-on to the audience – he knew how to make the most of his striking good looks and let the ladies see him in profile instead of from behind, as was the custom. (In fact, he sometimes employed two pianos on the stage so that he could change sides and let the audience see his other profile and, not incidentally, his hands.) He made the piano sexy and, after him, the many lions of the keyboard who modelled themselves on him, more or less successfully, were accorded the same sort of celebrity as today's top opera singers. The music he wrote for the instrument was equally liberating, adventurous and experimental. He devized the concept of the Rhapsody and his compositions revolution-ized keyboard technique; the innovations to express both his profound thoughts and his more vulgar showpieces were a significant advance on what had gone before. Every composer for the piano thereafter was indebted to Liszt.

Liszt was an important composer and yet most of his works are woefully underrated; there was a long period when he fell out of fashion. Whether or not he is a great composer of the first division is still fiercely debated, but to a growing number of people he is one of the seminal figures of the nineteenth century and the least acclaimed genius in the history of music.

Essential works

Piano and orchestra

Concerto No.1 in E flat (1849 rev. 1853, 1856): sometimes called the 'Triangle' Concerto because of the instrument's brief but prominent appearance in the third section, this, the most played of Liszt's works for piano and orchestra, is in four unified movements performed without interruption. A *tour de force* for every virtuoso, thrilling and effective with one of the most notoriously difficult openings to play of any concerto. Berlioz conducted the first performance with the composer as soloist.

Concerto No.2 in A (1839 rev. 1849–61): another one-movement concerto, which Liszt called a Concerto Symphonique to emphasize the symphonic nature of the work. The themes are transformed and varied, at times graceful and lyrical, at others strident and martial.

Fantasia on Hungarian Folk Themes (1860): an adaptation of the *Hungarian Rhapsody* No.14 for piano solo (see below) composed eight years earlier; it is a spectacular crowd-pleaser of contrasting moods, fiery rhythms and Hungarian melodies.

Totentanz (1849 rev. 1853 & 1859): subtitled 'Dance Macabre', the fantasy was inspired by a fresco, *The Triumph of Death*, in the Campo Santo in Pisa. The *Dies irae* is the leading theme with spectacular flights of virtuosity from the soloist in a work that exudes diabolism – especially in the hands of a pianist such as Georges Cziffra or Raymond Lewenthal.

Polonaise brillante (Weber–Liszt)

Wanderer Fantasy (Schubert–Liszt)

These two examples of Liszt's 're-workings' for piano and orchestra of other composers' solo works – there are a few other examples – are rarely heard. If you like glittering piano playing in a grand Romantic setting, these are for you.

Piano solo (original)

Almost all Liszt's masterpieces were published after 1848 when he had abandoned the life of a touring virtuoso, though many of the compositions that appeared were revisions of works conceived in this earlier period.

Années de pèlerinage: Book 1: Suisse, Switzerland (1848–54); **Book 2: Italie, Italy** (1837–49); **Book 3:** (1867–77): these three books of tone-poems, the results of Liszt's travels all over Europe, can be compared to an artist such as Turner sketching his impressions of the sights and sounds he encounters and then producing a finished canvas as a masterly souvenir. Switzerland was the inspiration for

Book 1 of *Years of Pilgrimage* (seven pieces) and contains one of the finest musical evocations of water in *Au bord d'une source* (No.4 of the set). Also worth listening to is the hair-raising recording by Vladimir Horowitz of No.6, *Vallée d'Obermann*.

Book 2 (seven pieces) was inspired by the paintings of Michelangelo and Raphael, the Sonnets of Petrarch (Nos.4, 5 & 6 are devoted to these) and a poem by Victor Hugo, the *Fantasia quasi sonata 'Après une lecture de Dante'*; the latter is a tremendously effective piece lasting nearly seventeen minutes.

Book 3 (seven pieces) is less impressive but has another remarkable water painting that anticipates the Impressionism of Debussy – No.4 *Les jeux d'eau à la villa d'Este*.

Études

Six Études d'exécution transcendante d'après Paganini (1838, rev. 1851 as *Grandes Études de Paganini*)

Three Concert studies (1848): *Il lamento, La leggierezza, Un sospiro*

Twelve Études d'exécution transcendante (1851)

Two Concert studies (c.1863): namely, *Waldesrauschen* and *Gnomenreigen*. Taking advantage of recent improvements to the instrument, Liszt's *Paganani études* are all derived from Paganini's Twenty-four Caprices for solo violin, apart from No.3 which is based on the rondo from the earlier composer's Violin Concerto No.2 in B minor, now known as *La campanella*. No.6 of this set is a Theme and Variations on the famous Caprice No.24 in A minor on which Rachmaninov, Brahms, Lutosławski *et al* based their variations.

With the even more extravagant *Transcendental Études*, Liszt threw down a challenge to his peers: 'This is what is now possible on the piano – if you have the technique and daring.' As the title suggests, any pianist attempting them must have a transcendental technique. Written in six relative major and minor keys, the set is a veritable compendium of pianistic devices. The best are No.4 *Mazeppa*, No.5 *Feux Follets*, No.6 *Vision*, No.8 *Wilde Jagd*, No.10 *Allegro agitato molto* and No.12 *Chasse-neige*.

Two sets of shorter, more lyrical studies have always been popular with top pianists, *La leggierezza* and *Un sospiro* (*A Sigh*). Rachmaninov's recording of *Gnomenreigen* is one of the great piano discs.

LISZT

Rhapsodies

Nineteen Hungarian Rhapsodies (1846–85): **Nos.1–15** all date from the early 1850s; **Nos.16–19** are less good, and were written almost three decades later. Musical snobs consider them to be shallow display pieces; the rest of us can sit back and succumb to their gypsy high spirits. As a Hungarian, Liszt had an obvious attraction to his national folk music – even if the finished results are more well-bred than their original – and in most he keeps the form of the *Csárdás* dance with its slow *lassan* introduction leading to the lively *friska*.

By far the best known of these is the now, unfortunately, hackneyed and over-played Second Rhapsody in C sharp minor. The best of the rest are **Nos.6, 9** (*Carnival of Pesth*), **No.10** (which imitates a cembalon rather successfully), **Nos.11 & 12** (No.12 was Liszt's favourite) and **Nos.13 & 14** (No.14 revamped later as the basis of the *Hungarian Fantasy – see* above). The complete rhapsodies as recorded by Cziffra are jaw-dropping.

Rapsodie espagnole (c.1863): about sixteen minutes in duration; this is a thrilling show-stopper that uses two traditional melodies, *Jota Aragonesa* and *Folies d'Espagna*. It has also been effectively arranged for piano and orchestra by Busoni.

Piano Sonata in B minor (1852–53): in any discussion of piano music, the Liszt Sonata, as it is known, looms large: the crowning glory of his achievements as a writer for the piano and one of the nineteenth century's musical monuments. It lasts about half an hour and is full of ground-breaking ideas: it expands the usual form of the sonata (three or four contrasted movements with appropriate development sections) into a tightly knit structure using five themes or *motifs* to unify one huge single movement which nevertheless retains the outward vestiges of the traditional sonata. The American critic James Gibbons Huneker thought that 'Nothing more exciting is there in the literature of the piano.' When played by Martha Argerich or, in a more wilful but iridescent recording made in 1932 by Vladimir Horowitz, one is inclined to agree.

Mephisto Waltz No.1 (1860): also for orchestra, this miniature tone-poem, inspired by Nikolaus Lenau's poem 'Faust', is subtitled 'The Dance at the Village Inn'. The daring opening, with Mephistopheles tuning up his violin, could be by Bartók; its seductive middle section was an influence on Scriabin. The final pages will put you on the edge of your seat.

Harmonies poétiques et réligieuses (1845–52): an uneven set of ten pieces containing two masterpieces: **No.3 Bénédiction de Dieu dans la solitude**, mystical and ecstatic by turns, and No.7 *Funérailles*,

dedicated to the memory of Chopin, with its middle section of tumultuous octaves, fringed with black despair.

Also worth investigating

Consolation No.3 in D flat (c.1850)
Liebesträume No.3 in A flat (c.1850)
Scherzo and March (1851)
Venezia e Napoli (1840, rev. 1859)
Deux Légendes (1863): *St Francis of Assisi preaching to the birds*; *St Francis de Paule walking on the water*

Late piano works

In order to see how far Liszt had journeyed in musical terms during his long life and how he was still experimenting and keeping abreast of all the latest developments when he was in his seventies, it is essential to hear these pieces and then compare them with his early work. Technically, these other-wordly miniatures use whole-tone scales, chords in fourths and have an ambiguous tonality: some of the essential ingredients for Impressionism and Expressionism. Liszt's contemporaries thought that he had lost his way; Debussy, Stravinsky and Bartók were amazed by them. In Leslie Howard's words, 'they work out all the possibilities that composers would need for about fifty years after his death – with the caveat that Liszt did them better.'

Elegy No.2 (1877)
Nuages gris (1881)
Csárdás macabre (1881–82)
La lugubre gondola Nos.1 & 2 (1882)
En rêve (1885)

Piano solo (arrangements of music by other composers)

The amount of time Liszt spent in promoting the music of others – producing, conducting, advising and guiding – must surely have been equalled by the time he spent adapting for the piano music both old and new. To reduce the then-unknown Berlioz's *Symphonie fantastique* to a piano solo was indicative of his altruism, but to transcribe every one of Beethoven's nine symphonies is a breathtaking achievement.

Audiences liked nothing better than to hear a pot-pourri of themes from the latest opera and literally hundreds of composers obliged, but Liszt's operatic paraphrases are of a different order. Sometimes he reproduces the subject that takes his fancy in a straightforward way, at others he adds his own pianistic elaborations and harmonies; frequently he takes different themes and works them up into a completely independent creation of his own.

A third area of transcription was songs. Liszt's piano versions of Schubert and Schumann *Lieder* contain some of his finest works. But the range of composers whose works he adapted is remarkable, a tribute to an extraordinary

catholic knowledge and taste. Who else would have had the capacity to tackle Bach's organ preludes and fugues, a Handel Sarabande and Chaconne as well as works by Rossini, Saint-Saëns, Tchaikowsky and dozens of others? Here are the best of those that are generally known and still played:

Six chants polonais: No.1 *Mädchens Wunsch*, No.5 *Meine Freuden* (Chopin)

Polonaise from Eugene Onegin (Tchaikowsky)

Réminiscences de Don Juan (Mozart)

Réminiscences de Lucia di Lammermoor (Donizetti)

Réminiscences de Norma (Bellini)

Réminiscences de Robert le Diable – Valse infernale (Meyerbeer)

Rigoletto: paraphrase de concert (Verdi)

Schubert–Schumann song transcriptions

Tannhäuser Overture (Wagner)

Liebestod from Tristan und Isolde (Wagner)

Wedding March and Dance of the Elves (Mendelssohn)

Widmung and **Frühlingsnacht** (Schumann)

Faust Waltz (Gounod)

Organ

Fantasia and Fugue on **Ad nos, ad salutarem undam**, from Meyerbeer's *Le prophète* (1850): The *Ad nos* is considered to be one of the monuments of the instrument's repertoire, lasting nearly half an hour, and a work which set the stage for the organ symphonies of Guilmant, Widor and Vierne.

Prelude and Fugue on the Name B-A-C-H (1850, rev.1870): these last are two wall-shaking examples from Liszt's small list of organ works.

Orchestral

A Faust Symphony (1854–57): for tenor, chorus and orchestra, a version of Goethe's *Faust*. Instead of interpreting the whole poem, Liszt devotes each of his three movements to a portrait of the protagonists, Faust, Marguerite and Mephistopheles. In effect, the 'symphony' is a suite of three symphonic poems.

Symphonic Poems – Les préludes (1848, rev. 1854), **Mazeppa** (1851), **Tasso** (1849 rev.1851): of Liszt's twelve works under this generic title of his invention only *Les préludes* has achieved any popularity. Its programme is taken from Lamartine's *Méditations poétiques*: 'What is our life but a series of preludes to that unknown song of which death strikes the first solemn note.' *Tasso*, inspired by the life of the sixteenth-century Italian poet, and *Mazeppa*, a musical description of Victor Hugo's poem, receive occasional performances.

Vocal

Liszt wrote about sixty songs for voice and piano, some of them strikingly beautiful, most of them little known. Among them are:

'Du bist wie eine Blume'; 'Ich finde keinen Frieden'; 'Die Lorelei'; 'Es muss ein wunderbares sein'; 'Die Macht der Musik'; 'Jeanne d'Arc au bûcher'; 'Wenn ich schlafe'; 'Wie, fragten die Burschen'

Henry LITOLFF
(1818–91)

Scherzo, from Concerto symphonique No.4 in D minor, Op.102, c.1852

Litolff composed five *Concerto symphoniques* – another term for piano concertos. The second movement of No.4 is a scintillating *presto* Scherzo, a rollicking dialogue between piano and orchestra with a mock-solemn chorale in the middle. It has long been a classical lollipop but the whole four-movement work is enormous fun and worthy of revival, although there is no current recording. Nothing else of Litolff's work has survived in performance, though his overture *Robespierre*, incorporating the *Marseillaise* and a vivid depiction of the execution, was once a concert favourite.

Litolff was highly regarded in his day as a composer and pianist; Liszt dedicated his First Piano Concerto to him, a work which shares with Litolff's concerto the distinction of being the first to include piccolo and triangle in the score. Son of an Alsatian father and English mother, Litolff eloped at seventeen with his first wife, toured Europe as a pianist and divorced. Imprisoned for debt, he escaped with the help of a prison guard's daughter, fled to Holland and married the widow of a distinguished music publisher to become one of the pioneers of cheap editions of classical music. His third wife was the Comtesse de Larochefoucauld; when *she* died in 1870 he married a fifteen-year-old girl.

George LLOYD

Born: 28 June 1913, St Ives
Type of music: symphony, opera, concerto, choral, instrumental
Influences: Elgar, English early twentieth-century school
Contemporaries: BRITTEN, LUTOSŁAWSKI, Tikhon Khrennikov, **LLOYD**, Andrzej Panufnik, Humphrey Searle, Alberto Ginastera, BERNSTEIN

HIS LIFE AND MUSIC

Lloyd's works have been scandalously neglected until the past decade or so. He began studying music seriously at fourteen, playing the violin (he studied with the great English violinist Albert Sammons for five years) and writing opera, encouraged by his father who supplied the libretti. His first work, *Iernin*, was produced at the Lyceum Theatre, London when he was twenty-one. It won the praise of Beecham and Vaughan Williams and for some years it seemed as though a long and distinguished career lay ahead. His second opera, *The Serf*, was produced at the Royal Opera House, Covent Garden. The Second World War brought everything to an abrupt end: Lloyd served in the Royal Marines and nearly lost his life when his ship, in one of the Arctic convoys to Russia, was sunk. For some years he suffered from the effects of shellshock. A measure of the man is that his next work was a symphony not of bitterness or a commentary on war but of celebration and good humour. However, no performance was forthcoming and his Symphony No.4 lay unperformed for thirty-five years. After spending some years at his wife's home in Switzerland, he returned to England, his health only partially regained. The strain of writing and the production of his third opera, *John Socman*, for the 1951 Festival of Britain led to a further deterioration in his health.

Lloyd, disillusioned with the lack of interest in his work, retreated to Dorset in the early 1950s, to farm carnations and then, most successfully, mushrooms. For nearly twenty-five years he had almost no contact with musicians, with the exception of the pianist John Ogdon. The use of the muscles and nerves of his left hand, which had become partly uncontrollable after the war, returned; he took up the violin again and once more began composing. It was not until 1977 when the BBC finally broadcast a Lloyd work (his Symphony No.8) that recognition began to come. An overwhelming public response to this contemporary composer who wrote in a language that was at once accessible and rewarding led to the recording of all his twelve symphonies. Now he is enjoying an Indian summer, an able, not to say inspiring, conductor of his own work.

Lloyd has never forgotten the audience and, as he himself has said, 'So many people have no religion, no spiritual outlet. So they go for music. You can see it in their eyes when they listen: they are searching desperately for something to feed their souls. Twelve-note music gave them nothing. Whereas I often get letters from people who tell me they have had trouble, even tragedy, in their lives – and that when they play my music they feel better.'

Essential works

Symphony No.4 in B (1946): composed after his convalescence from shellshock, its Scherzo and exuberant finale in particular are immediately appealing.
Symphony No.12 (1989): the last of Lloyd's symphonies, written on a 'theme-and-variation' format and, though relatively light-weight, concludes with a serene movement of great intensity.
A Symphonic Mass (1993): Classic fM was the first radio station to broadcast this work, commissioned for the 1993 Brighton Festival. It is already well on the way to becoming one of the most popular choral works of the past fifty years. Linked by the same single glorious melody, the work climaxes shatteringly in the middle with Lloyd's magnificent setting of the *Sanctus*; it ends with a touching *Dona nobis pacem*. The composer's own performance must receive special mention, in a recording by Albany Records who have done so much to promote Lloyd's work.

Jean-Baptiste LULLY

'Prince of French Musicians' (Titon du Tillet)

Born: 28 November 1632, Florence
Died: 22 March 1687, Paris
Original name: Giovanni Battista Lulli
Type of music: opera, ballet, choral, instrumental
Influences: Pietro Cavalli, Italian *bel canto* school
Contemporaries: Heinrich Schütz, Pietro Francesco Cavalli, **LULLY**, BUXTEHUDE, Alessandro Stradella, Marc-Antoine Charpentier, Pelham Humfrey

HIS LIFE

An unusual start, colourful middle years and bizarre end mark out this Italian-born musician who was to become the founder of French opera. The son of a poor miller, he was taught the elements of music by a Franciscan monk. He could play the guitar and violin and he could sing; the latter attracted the attention of the Chevalier de Guise, who took the fourteen-year-old boy to Paris to be *valet de chambre* to Mademoiselle d'Orléans. Lully was in the habit of entertaining the domestic servants in the kitchen with improvisations on the violin; this was observed by the Count de Nogent and Lully was found a place in Mademoiselle's private band. In 1652, after losing her favour, he entered the service of her young cousin, who happened to be the Dauphin, later Louis XIV. Lully was also an excellent dancer, a talent shared with his royal master, and the two appeared together in a ballet in 1653, the first of many such occasions. Louis danced the part of 'le roi soleil' and carried it off so well that the title stuck with him for the rest of his life. He appointed Lully to the royal band (the famous *Vingt-quatre violons du Roi*) and in 1656 allowed him to train sixteen specially-selected violin-players. Lully's smaller band, *Les petits violons*, was soon acknowledged as being far superior to the king's; this led to Lully's appointment as conductor of the 'King's Violins', which was probably the finest musical ensemble in existence at that time.

From then on, Lully's story is one of increasing power and influence, first in royal music circles and later as one of the King's *secrétaires*, among his most trusted and important personal advisors. He was a shrewd courtier, ambitious, arrogant, ruthless and determined, a man who knew when to be obsequious and when to flatter. In 1661 he was appointed official composer to the king and in the following year was made music master to the royal family; at this time he was earning the enormous sum of £30,000 a year, a factor which, coupled with his avariciousness, did not endear him to his contemporaries. With the acquisition of the licence to operate the Académie Royale de Musique and various patents from the king, Lully was able to establish a virtual monopoly in the Parisian theatre, depriving any of his rivals from making a reputation. The stage works that he produced over the following fifteen years marked the beginnings of a new school of opera.

During the performance of a *Te Deum* he had written in celebration of the king's recovery from serious illness, Lully accidentally stabbed his foot with the sharp-pointed cane he used for conducting. An abscess developed, he contracted gangrene and died shortly after from blood poisoning.

HIS MUSIC

Lully's art would never have flourished without the approval of the king, but having won that support he could never be criticized for not making the most of it. The ballets composed for the court led to the series of *comédie-ballets* that he wrote in collaboration with the dramatist Molière using comical and satirical subjects; these ballets, including *Le bourgeois gentilhomme*, were the seeds of *opéra comique*. From here, too, evolved the classic 'French' overture – its characteristics being a slow opening with dotted-note rhythms, a quick and sometimes fugal middle and a slow end. *Alcidiane* from 1658 is the earliest example.

The work he produced at the Académie Royale de Musique eventually led to the founding of the Paris Opéra; the Académie was really the first French national opera house. And it was in the realm of theatre that Lully found his true calling. He set French texts to music with a far greater sensitivity and flexibility than anyone before him, abandoning what had become the Italian convention for doing things with endless vocal decoration and repetitive variations of arias; he gave dramatic interest to choral ensembles and increased the prominence of the orchestra in opera. The subject material tended to be drawn from Greek mythology with five acts and continuous music, a genre of entertainment known as *tragédie en musique* ('tragedies set to music') which developed into French *opera seria*.

Violinist, dancer, singer, courtier, director, stage manager, conductor and a man of business, Lully had extraordinary energy and a disregard for obstacles. A perfect combination for the man who also wrote the first notable minuets and was among the first to use the newly invented oboe.

Essential works

Les amants magnifiques, ballet (1670) and **Le bourgeois gentilhomme**, ballet (1670): both written with Molière.
Overtures to: **Cadmus et Hermione** (1673);

Thésée (1675); **Psyché** (1678); **Armide et Renaud** (1686): the latter was Lully's penultimate opera; produced posthumously, it is considered his finest achievement.

Witold LUTOSŁAWSKI

Born: 25 January 1913, Warsaw
Died: 7 February 1994, Warsaw
Type of music: symphony, orchestral, concerto, chamber, instrumental, choral, film, radio
Influences: Stravinsky, Bartók, Debussy, Ravel, Schoenberg, Webern, Berg
Contemporaries: John Cage, Jean Françaix, BRITTEN, **LUTOSŁAWSKI**, Tikhon Khrennikov, LLOYD, Andrzej Panufnik, Humphrey Searle

HIS LIFE AND MUSIC

Few of the many Polish composers who have followed in the footsteps of Karol Szymanowski have made an impact in the West. The works of such composers as Aleksander Tansman, Karol Rathaus, Stanislaw Wiechowicz, Michal Kondracki and Roman Palester have yet to be assessed. Andrzej Panufnik and Krzysztof Penderecki have their followers but, until the development of the cult interest in Henryk Górecki, the most widely known was Lutosławski.

Born into a wealthy family, he studied at the Warsaw Conservatory before becoming a full-time composer. His career was interrupted by the Second World War: he joined the Polish army but was made a German prisoner-of-war, returning to Warsaw to earn his living by playing the piano in cafés and cabarets. His writing having been temporarily halted by the Nazis, Lutosławski then found his First Symphony banned by the Communists as being 'formalist' and until the mid-1950s he spent much of his time creating scores for radio and film, teaching and writing a series of compositions based on Polish folklore. The Overture for Strings (1949), Concerto for Orchestra (1954) and the First Symphony (1947) all employ quotations from folk music, worked in a modern context. In other pieces, such as *Funeral Music* for string orchestra (1958), dedicated to the memory of Bartók, Lutosławski made use of atonalism in a personal manner. He also made forays into aleatory methods (scoring the precise notes but leaving it up to the players to determine the length and placing of the notes).

Showered with honours during the sixties and seventies, with the fall of Communism he became a touring musical ambassador of his country, conducting his own music of which he was a fine exponent.

Essential works

Concerto for Orchestra (1954): obviously inspired by Bartók's virtuosic masterpiece of the same title, this spirited work was criticized as lacking in personality when it first appeared, but it is a good piece with which to make an acquaintance with Lutosławski. More accessible than Bartók's, its brilliant spiky scoring is laced with folk music *motifs* and tunes.

Cello Concerto (1970): commissioned and recorded by Rostropovich, this striking and taxing virtuoso work is a demanding listen, but full of interesting effects – shrieking trumpets and horns – and it incorporates some aleatory practices in the score.

Variations on a theme of Paganini (1941): this piano duet based on the same Paganini violin Caprice (No.24 in A minor) that attracted Rachmaninov, Brahms *et al*, is a barnstormer, written during Lutosławski's time in Warsaw under the Nazi occupation.

Edward MACDOWELL

Born: 18 December 1860, New York
Died: 23 January 1908, New York
Type of music: orchestral, concerto, choral and piano
Influences: Schumann, Raff, Liszt, Grieg, Anton Rubinstein
Contemporaries: Mikhail Ippolitov-Ivanov, WOLF, **MACDOWELL**, ALBÉNIZ, MAHLER, Ignacy Paderewski, Emil von Rezniček, CHARPENTIER

HIS LIFE AND MUSIC

If Gottschalk was the first American-born composer to make use of indigenous American and Latin-American material, MacDowell was the first to be hailed as the equal of his contemporaries in Europe. His training on the continent included study with some of the finest teachers of the day: Ehlert – himself a pupil of Mendelssohn – Joachim Raff, Carl Heymann and, eventually, Liszt. When MacDowell returned to the United States in 1888 he was feted as a famous composer and pianist. In 1896 'the greatest musical genius America has produced' was offered the position of head of the newly established music department at Columbia University.

Tragedy followed. Relations with the university authorities deteriorated and he resigned his post in 1904. It is debatable whether his periods of deep depression and irritability contributed to the unhappy situation or whether the situation exacerbated his condition. At any rate, MacDowell lapsed into total insanity and his last years were spent in an asylum reduced to a childlike state, unaware of his surroundings. His devoted wife outlived him by nearly half a century. She died in 1956 at the age of 99.

MacDowell was unable to develop any nationalistic trait in his many works despite some of the fanciful titles, such as *From an Indian Lodge* and *Of Br'er Rabbit*. They are written in the traditional European Romantic manner – pretty, well-crafted and tuneful, like the average German composer of his day which essentially he was.

Worth investigating

Piano Concerto No.2 in D minor, Op.23 (1884–86): despite the obvious influence of Liszt in this concerto, it is a sparky, showy virtuoso vehicle, which has, rightly, held its place on the fringes of the repertoire. Big tunes, passionate outbursts, and the second movement (Scherzo) is a real winner.

To a Wild Rose, from **Woodland Sketches, Op.51** (1896)
Witches' Dance, from **Two Fantastic Pieces, Op.17** (1884)
Two piano encores still played occasionally, the former of simple and enduring charm, the latter a devilish finger-twister.

Gustav MAHLER

'Only when I experience intensely do I compose; only when I compose do I experience intensely' (Mahler)

Born: 7 July 1860, Kaliste (on the borders of Bohemia and Moravia)
Died: 18 May 1911, Vienna
Type of music: symphony, vocal
Influences: Wagner, Bruckner
Contemporaries: WOLF, MACDOWELL, ALBÉNIZ, **MAHLER**, Ignacy Paderewski, Emil von Reznicek, CHARPENTIER, ARENSKY, Enrico Bossi

HIS LIFE

'Thin, fidgety, short, with a high, steep forehead, long dark hair and deeply penetrating bespectacled eyes' was how the conductor Bruno Walter, Mahler's one-time assistant, described him. Mahler was also a manic-depressive, an egomaniac, one of music's great despots, a neurotic who had a mother fixation (according to Freud, who analysed him) and undoubtedly a genius. As with his music, people either loved or hated him. 'The dedicated Mahlerians,' wrote Harold Schonberg, ' regard [those who dislike his music] the way St Paul regarded the Heathen. It is hard to think of a composer who arouses equal loyalty. The worship of Mahler amounts almost to a religion … Mahler's [music] stirs something imbedded in the subconscious and his admirers approach him mystically.'

His tragic childhood stalked him throughout his life. His grandmother had been a ribbon seller, going from house to house selling her wares. His father had transcended these humble origins. He was the owner of a small brandy distillery and had married the daughter of a wealthy soap manufacturer. It was an ill-tempered, badly matched marriage and the young Gustav Mahler frequently witnessed the brutality and abuse meted out on his long-suffering mother by his ambitious father. Of their twelve children, five of them died in infancy of diphtheria, Mahler's beloved younger brother Ernst died from hydrocardia aged twelve and his oldest sister died of a brain tumour after a brief and unhappy marriage. Another sister was subject to fantasies that she was dying, one brother was a simpleton in his youth and became a forger in his adult life, while yet another brother, Otto, a humble musician, committed suicide rather than accept the mediocrity that fate had assigned him.

When he was six, Mahler discovered a piano in the attic of his grandmother's house. Four years later he gave his first solo piano recital and aged fifteen he enrolled at the Vienna Conservatory. Here he not only developed as a pianist but also won prizes for his compositions and discovered a talent for conducting. His professors noticed the diligence and single-minded application that would mark his professional career. Within a short space of time, conducting and composition took over his life with a totality that left little time for anything else. Realizing he could not make a living as a composer writing the sort of music he dreamed of, he took up conducting, first in Bad Hall, Austria

then in a permanent position at Laibach (now Ljubljana). In 1882 he moved to Olmütz and the following year to Vienna and Kassel – the traditional path of the aspiring conductor, going from opera house to opera house, slowly building a reputation. In 1885 he was in Prague, and then got a break in Leipzig working in harness with another brilliant young conductor, Artur Nikisch. In one season Mahler conducted over 200 performances, edited a Weber opera, fell in love with the wife of Weber's grandson and finished his First Symphony. One quality that Mahler had in abundance was energy, something he inherited from his mother. From his father came his drive and tenacity. His next step was to take over the Royal Opera House in Budapest from 1886 to 1888. Here he built up a fine company that won the praise of Brahms. When he moved on to Hamburg, Tchaikowsky allowed Mahler to conduct *Eugene Onegin* in his stead. 'The conductor here is not of the usual kind, but a man of genius who would give his life to conduct the first performance,' he wrote.

Then, in 1897, Mahler quietly converted to Catholicism. Shortly after this he was appointed to the position he had yearned for. With the enthusiastic backing of Brahms, he became artistic director of the Vienna Opera and, soon afterwards, of the Vienna Philharmonic. He remained at the Opera for ten years and during that decade he raised its fortunes to a height which some say has never been equalled since. Here he reigned as king, choosing the repertory and singers, staging many of the productions himself and overseeing every aspect of life in the opera house; he engaged the great stage designer Alfred Roller and experimented with lighting and stage effects: this was Mahler's Wagnerian idealism put into practice – combining all the arts of the music theatre in a single man's vision. Above all, he moulded the orchestra into one of the finest in the world. The players respected him as a musician but they hated him as a man; Mahler's quest for perfection was implemented by the uncompromising martinet that he was. He had a tendency to pick on individual players and reduce them to tears; he would even discipline the audience, forbidding latecomers to enter the auditorium during the first act, an unheard of demand in those days. Every work that he laid his hands on came up 'Herrlich wie am ersten Tag' as they say in Vienna – 'Glorious as on the first day' – and he did it all at a profit.

Inevitably, Mahler made enemies. Not just because of his despotic methods and lack of social niceties – he had no small talk and was nervous among people – but because he was a Jew and a genius. He was merciless with his tongue, with his contempt for those who opposed him and with his anger at those who failed to match his standards.

In 1901 he married Alma Schindler, the step-daughter of the avant-garde Viennese artist Carl Moll. She was beautiful, well-read and a composer in her own right, having studied under Alexander Zemlinsky, Schoenberg's teacher. It was a remarkable marriage but one in which Mahler demanded complete freedom. His wife was to be mother, wife and amanuensis, she was to give up her composing and be totally subservient to his whims. The first five years of their marriage saw Mahler at the height of his powers and at his happiest. He continued to compose as he had during the previous decade in the one form to which he aspired and – to his austere way of thinking – in the purest, highest form of musical expression, the orchestral symphony. By 1906 he had completed the Fifth, Sixth and Seventh Symphonies. Each one was vaster in scale than its predecessor; each one was met with hostility, misunderstanding and vituperation. Mahler was impervious to all around him, convinced that 'my time will come'.

Then personal tragedy hit. One of his little daughters died from scarlet fever. Mahler was distraught with grief and forever after carried around with him the guilt that he had been responsible in part for his child's death, guilt for tempting fate: in 1903 he had composed a set of songs using poems by Rückert entitled *Kindertotenlieder – Songs of the Death of Children*.

In 1907 he decided to leave Vienna and, the same year, was told he had a serious heart condition. The remaining three years of his life were focused on America. He first went to the Metropolitan Opera for two full seasons. Indifferent performances and the presence of Arturo Toscanini led to friction and more unhappiness. Worse came when he took over the conductorship of the New York Philharmonic in 1909. The audience disliked him, the orchestra loathed him, the critics reached for their poisoned pens. The feeling was entirely mutual. The Philharmonic was, in Mahler's words, 'the true American orchestra – without talent and phlegmatic'. The orchestra board was dominated by ten wealthy American women. 'You cannot imagine what Mr. Mahler has suffered,' Alma Mahler told the press. 'In Vienna my husband was all-powerful. Even the Emperor did not dictate to him, but in New York he had ten ladies ordering him around like a puppet.' In September 1910 he was in Munich to conduct the premiere of his mammoth Eighth Symphony which met with overwhelming acclaim, one of the few triumphs he ever witnessed as a composer. He returned to New York in late 1910 but early the following year collapsed under the strain of sixty-five rigorous concerts. An infection set in which serum treatments in Paris did nothing to alleviate. In a nursing home in Vienna he died of pneumonia, aged fifty.

HIS MUSIC

Mahler is the last great Romantic symphonist, his music is conceived on the grandest scale, employing elaborate forces and conveying 'lofty concepts of universal art.' He was not an innovator in his harmonic writing but there is much harmonic daring, especially in the Ninth Symphony. Scholars make much of Mahler being the stepping stone between Wagner and Schoenberg. Schoenberg's Five Orchestral Pieces of 1908 are far in advance of anything Mahler conceived, yet Scriabin, who was forging his own path, was more adventurous than Mahler as early as 1905. Richard Strauss and Debussy were more 'modern' than Mahler. To some, Mahler is Alpha and Omega (even his wife remarked that he was always telephoning God); to others he is a sentimental and self-absorbed Austrian neurotic.

Although Mahler's music was never entirely ignored after his death – conductors such as Bruno Walter and Willem Mengelberg saw to that – it wasn't until after the Second World War that it began to be played regularly and in the past forty years Mahler has become central to the repertoire of every orchestra.

His output is comparatively small, concentrated almost exclusively on the symphony. There is no mature chamber music, nothing for solo instruments, no opera, no smaller choral works – only songs and symphonies. He could compose only when not tied up with his duties as conductor and then only when able to devote himself entirely to the work in hand. In Austria, he would take himself off for the summer to his property at Maiernigg on the Wörthersee. Here he worked in total silence – dogs and cats were banished and even the cows were ordered to have their bells removed.

What are his themes, his impulses? 'Whoever listens to my music intelligently,' he said, ' will see my life transparently revealed'. Death is there, of course, and suffering. This is balanced by Mahler's response to nature, to the beauty of the world around him: his music is full of simple, almost naïve folk songs evoking the Austrian countryside and recalling the pastoral moods of Beethoven. Pain and joy intermingle, sensual gratification and human suffering become inseparable from each other – these were the images he worked with. He never forgot witnessing a brutal rape in Prague at the age of eleven.

The Mahlers lived near a military barracks – marching, military associations with death and conflict permeate his music. But above and beyond all this, Mahler wanted to express his view of the human condition, to set down his lofty ideals about Life, Death and the Universe in 'great works', as he put it, 'if I am to achieve an immortal role for posterity. My symphonies represent the contents of my entire life; I have written into them all my experience and all my suffering,' he wrote. 'There too will be found my *Angst* – my anxiety, my fear.' Mahler revelled in his *Angst*, in his own neuroses, and wanted the world to see how much he was suffering – perhaps that is why it strikes a chord with so many ardent admirers in our own anxiety-ridden age.

Essential works

Mahler's biographer, Paul Stefan, has divided the nine symphonies into three groups: the first four are subjective, representing a personal struggle against cosmic forces; the next four are the probings of the musician-philosopher seeking an answer to the riddle of the universe; in the last, his struggle with himself and the eternal verities is over – Mahler steps back and seeks inner peace.

Symphony No.1 in D 'The Titan' (1884–88, rev.1893 & 1898): the composer described this symphony as 'the sound of nature' and it is full of the countryside, ingratiating dance melodies and rhythms. Despite his lifelong aversion to attaching titles and programmatic interpretations of his work, he endowed this symphony with precise labels, breaking it into two parts, the first *Days of Youth, Flowers and Thorns*, the second *A Chapter of Flowers*, and each of the four movements was also given a descriptive title. Later he gave the whole work the title of 'The Titan'. Later still he disowned all the titles.

Symphony No.2 in C minor 'Resurrection' (1888–94 rev.1896): Mahler considered this symphony to be the sequel of 'The Titan'. It calls for gargantuan forces – a pipe organ, church bells, off-stage horns, trumpets and percussion, a soprano, contralto and chorus. If the work were subjected to a programmatic interpretation one could say that the first movement is about death, the second about youthful optimism, the third about life's vulgarities and the fourth about spiritual life; the last movement is Judgement Day. In other words, the symphony is an allegory on the life of man.

The finale is certainly loud enough to wake the dead, one of the most thrilling and shattering climaxes of any symphony.

Symphony No.4 in G (1900): the most joyous of all the symphonies and one of the shortest, culminating in a fourth movement in which a soprano sings the text of an old Bavarian folk song. This is perhaps the best of the nine symphonies for Mahler beginners; it was, he said, a child's conception of heaven and the colour of blue sky.

Symphony No.5 in C sharp minor (1902): the Adagietto, the heartachingly beautiful fourth movement, has become Mahler's best known piece of music, thanks largely to its memorable and effective use in Visconti's overrated film of Thomas Mann's novel *Death in Venice*. The work has five movements and its unusual structure begins with a funeral march.

Symphony No.8 in E flat, 'Symphony of a Thousand' (1906): in two gigantic sections, this vast score calls for a huge orchestra with quintuple woodwind, seven soloists, a boys' chorus and a mixed double chorus. The electrifying first half of the symphony is a setting of the Latin hymn 'Veni Creator Spiritus', while the second takes the final scene from Goethe's *Faust* in which Faust's redeemed body is drawn heavenwards.

Das Lied von der Erde, song cycle (1909): *The Song of the Earth* is considered by many to be the most beautiful and personal of Mahler's works. He began writing a Tenth Symphony but never completed it (leaving others to provide its conjectural end) but Mahler referred to this work as 'a symphony', which it is in all but name. The completion of nine symphonies frequently had a terminal effect on composers' lives (viz. Beethoven, Bruckner and Dvořák) and the superstitious Mahler was determined to outwit Fate. In *The Song of the Earth* he uses poems by Chinese writers, which examine human life as a

transient stage in a constant process of earthly renewal.

Also worth investigating
Symphony No.3 in D minor (1896 rev.1906)
Des Knaben Wunderhorn, song cycle (1892–98)

Pietro MASCAGNI
(1863–1945)

Cavalleria rusticana, opera, 1888

Like the composer of 'Pag' (*see* LEONCAVALLO), the composer of 'Cav' was unable to repeat the success – or come anywhere near the inspiration – of this most engaging of all one-act operas. Its story of betrayal and passion based on a tale by Giovanni Verga (who had already turned it into a play as a vehicle for the great actress Eleonora Duse), its richly Romantic score and its gratifying roles have ensured its place in opera houses throughout the world from the time of its first performance in 1890 to the present day. Its glorious *Easter Hymn* (the whole action takes place on Easter Sunday) and the *Intermezzo* (a favourite with makers of TV commercials) are the musical high points but Mascagni tops these dramatically with the *brindisi* (drinking song) 'Viva, il vino' and the final lament 'Mama, quel vino e generoso'. *Cavalleria rusticana (Rustic chivalry)* is the epitome of Italian *verismo* opera, then a new style of opera in which the dramatic development is highly condensed and the action is based on stark realism rather than, say, legends and fairy tales.

Its first performance came about as a result of being one of three winners of a competition for one-act operas, an idea dreamt up by the publisher Sonzogno who would later also publish Leoncavallo's *Pagliacci*. So great was the opera's success that medals were struck in Mascagni's honour and the King of Italy bestowed upon him the Order of the Crown of Italy, an honour that even Verdi had to wait for until middle age. His sixteen other operas were, apart from *L'amico Fritz* (1891), not merely unsuccessful but in the case of *Le maschere* (1901) booed off the stage before the final curtain in Genoa. 'It was a pity I wrote *Cavalleria* first,' Mascagni admitted, 'I was crowned before I was King.'

In later life, Mascagni became an ardent supporter of Mussolini and Fascism, and most of his friends deserted him. Stripped of all his honours, his last days were spent in comparative poverty in a small hotel in Rome.

Jules MASSENET

'Érotisme discret et quasi-religieux' (Vincent d'Indy)

Born: 12 May 1842, Montaud, near St-Étienne, Loire
Died: 13 August 1912, Paris
Original name: Jules Emile Frédéric Massenet
Type of music: opera, ballet, incidental music
Influences: Adam, Thomas, Wagner, Gounod
Contemporaries: Johann Svendsen, CHABRIER, Dvořák, SULLIVAN, **MASSENET**, Arrigo Boito, GRIEG, Pablo de Sarasate, RIMSKY-KORSAKOV, Stephen Adams

HIS LIFE AND MUSIC

'To know *Manon* is to know Massenet' it has been said. The opera has wonderful melodies, a story of strong emotions and a frisson of eroticism, and music that combines the sentimental lyricism of the French tradition, exemplified by Gounod, with the dramatic and orchestral advances of Wagner – but not too much. There had to be nothing too demanding to spoil a pleasant night out for the bourgeoisie. Massenet was called disparagingly both 'la fille de Gounod' and 'Mademoiselle Wagner' by his critics.

He was as shrewd a composer as he was an investor, handling the vast amounts of money he made with business-like acumen. He was interested primarily in giving the public what they wanted. In this he succeeded more than any French opera composer of the late nineteenth century. He had studied at the Paris Conservatoire with Ambroise Thomas, who was about to achieve fame with his opera *Mignon*. An able pianist, he won the Prix de Rome in 1863 which took him to Italy for three years. Here he met Liszt who introduced him to the girl he would marry. His first success as a composer came in 1872 but his methods did not endear him to colleagues who saw him as a cynical opportunist, ready to sacrifice personal and musical ideals for commercial advantage. Rimsky-Korsakov called him 'a crafty fox'; Massenet himself admitted to d'Indy that, in spite of the pseudo-religious oratorios and operas he was writing, 'I don't believe in all that creeping Jesus stuff, but the public likes it, and we must always agree with the public'.

Manon (1884), based on the same short story by Abbé Provost that Puccini would use nine years later for his *Manon Lescaut*, was an enormous hit. He had to wait until 1892 for a comparable success with his masterpiece *Werther*. These two, of the twenty-seven operas that Massenet composed, are the only survivors in the modern repertory.

Essential works

Manon, opera (1884): Massenet uses *leitmotiv* (like Wagner) throughout the score and adroitly spins some wonderful melodies; he departs from the original story more than Puccini but achieves greater dramatic unity. Beecham said he would give 'the whole of Bach's 'Branden-burg' Concertos for *Manon* and would think I had vastly profited by the exchange'. The famous arias are 'Adieu, notre petite table' (sung by the heroine), 'En fermant les yeux' from Act 2 (the *Dream Aria*) and 'Ah fuyez, douce image!' from Act 3 both sung by Manon's devoted lover Des Grieux.
Werther, opera (1892): based on Goethe's story 'The Sorrows of Young Werther', this has

been described as 'a sugary cake but baked by a high-class confectioner'. 'Pourquoi me réveiller' (Ossian's Song) in Act 3 is a powerful aria for Werther (with a tune that is a minor key version of 'Ta-ra-ra-Boom-de-ay'!).

Other works

Méditation from Thaïs (1894): the beautiful violin solo is an Intermezzo from this quasi-mystical piece of morality set in fourth-century Egypt.
Élégie: a 'pop' classic; originally a piano piece, *Mélodie*, No.5 from *Dix pièces de genre*, Op.10 (1866), and then used as part of the orchestral music for de Lisle's play *Les erinnyes* (1873).

Felix MENDELSSOHN

'The Mozart of the nineteenth century' (Schumann)

Born: 3 February 1809, Hamburg
Died: 4 November 1847, Leipzig
Full name: Jakob Ludwig Felix Mendelssohn-Bartholdy
Type of music: symphony, orchestral, stage and incidental, oratorio, sacred, cantata, concerto, chamber, piano, organ, song
Influences: Handel, Bach, Mozart, Beethoven
Contemporaries: Johan Hartmann, Michael Balfe, **MENDELSSOHN**, CHOPIN, Otto Nicolai, Félicien David, SCHUMANN, Samuel Wesley, LISZT

HIS LIFE

Mendelssohn is one of the Sunshine Composers who, like Rossini and Saint-Saëns, wrote optimistic music effortlessly. *Felix* is Latin for 'happy man' and there are few important composers who have led such happy, untroubled lives and whose music so exactly reflects their own character.

His background was wealthy and cultured. Moses Mendelssohn, his grandfather, was a hunchbacked pedlar who became one of Germany's major intellectual figures of the eighteenth century, a philosopher who was known as 'the modern Plato'. The talents of Felix's father lay elsewhere. He built up a powerful Hamburg bank and was a man of considerable wealth, while his wife – a linguist, musician and gifted painter – provided the intellectual life of the family.

1809–21 Both Felix and his sister Fanny proved to be exceptionally talented, studying piano, violin, languages and drawing from an early age. When it was clear that music was to be the boy's future, Mendelssohn's father decided to convert from the Jewish faith to Protestantism. He saw how many paths were closed to Jews in the musical world and, after one of Felix's fellow choristers in the Singakademie had sneered 'The Jew-boy raises his voice to Christ' after a performance of Bach's *St Matthew Passion*, he took both his children to be converted to Christianity. Later, he and his wife followed suit, adding 'Bartholdy' to their name to distinguish them from other Mendelssohns who were still Jewish. By the time he was nine, Felix was a good enough pianist to appear in public; at ten he joined the Singakademie in Berlin, then under the direction of his teacher Karl Friedrich Zelter, and by 1821 had composed several symphonies, two operas, fugues for string quartet and other works. In all this, he was encouraged by his parents though not spoilt – Mendelssohn was made to rise at 5 a.m. each day for a full period of study.

The Mendelssohn house was often filled with the distinguished and influential. Notable musicians, including Weber, would gravitate there for informal concerts and when, in 1821, Zelter took Felix to Weimar and introduced him to Goethe, the seventy-year-old writer and the twelve-year-old prodigy became firm friends. All who met the young Mendelssohn and heard him play left amazed; Spohr, Cherubini, Moscheles – all were incredulous. Here, without a doubt, was a second Mozart.

1825 This assertion was not fanciful, for by the time he was sixteen Mendelssohn was composing music of far greater maturity than that written by Mozart at a similar age: the overture to *A Midsummer Night's Dream* and his Octet are extraordinarily assured and original. The remaining incidental music for Shakespeare's play, written fifteen years later, is no different in its mastery.

1829 Mendelssohn was only twenty years old when he conducted a performance of Bach's *St Matthew Passion* at the Berlin Singakademie, an event which, more than any other, encouraged a general revival of interest in Bach's music. Not long afterwards, he made the first of ten visits to England, feted as a celebrity and conducting the premiere of his C minor Symphony before travelling to Scotland. This visit inspired his overture *Fingal's Cave* and the 'Scottish' Symphony, just as his subsequent tour of Italy provided the spark for his Symphony No.4 'Italian'.

1830–35 Established as one of the leading composers, conductors and pianists of the day, Mendelssohn accepted the appointment of musical director of the Lower Rhine Music Festival, Düsseldorf. This proved one of his few unsuccessful periods; his demands were too high, causing some hostility and resentment, and he left after six months. Within a year, though, and still only twenty-six years old, he was made musical director of the famous Leipzig Gewandhaus Orchestra. Over the following five years, Mendelssohn made the orchestra into the finest in the world. His care and concern over preparation and interpretation proved to be an evolutionary point in the history of conducting.

1836–45 During a stay in Frankfurt he met and fell in love with the seventeen-year-old daughter of a French Protestant clergyman, Cécile Jeanrenaud. They were married in

March 1837 and enjoyed an idyllically happy life together with their five children. In 1840, the King of Prussia appointed him head of the music department of a projected academy of arts in Berlin. The idea came to nothing and he was made Kapellmeister to the king, a post which, to his immense relief, did not require residence in the capital, but which gave him the chance to realize a long-held ambition – to found a conservatory in Leipzig. The King of Saxony gave his permission and the Leipzig Conservatory opened in April 1843 with Mendelssohn and Schumann teaching piano and composition and Ferdinand David in charge of the violin department: not a bad line-up.

1846–47 Mendelssohn was now working at a furious pace – conducting, teaching, composing, giving concerts – and his health began to suffer; pains in the head and abnormal fatigue were recurrent. He visited Birmingham for the triumphant premiere of his oratorio *Elijah* in August 1846 before returning to Leipzig, followed by a further visit to England in the spring of 1847. Here he played yet again for Queen Victoria, his long-time, fervent admirer.

In May, news reached him that his beloved sister Fanny had died suddenly. Her loss had a devastating effect on him. Hearing of her death, he became unconscious, rupturing a blood vessel in the brain. He only partially recovered and began suffering terrible depressions and agonizing pain. Less that six months later, he too was dead. He was thirty-eight. Memorial services were held in most of the principal cities in Germany as well as in London, Manchester, Birmingham and Paris. For which composer today would such events take place?

HIS MUSIC

The titles of the works below attest to Mendelssohn's undiminished popularity – an extraordinary number of his works are appreciated by lovers of both classical and light music. In such works as the E minor Violin Concerto or *Fingal's Cave* the two main ingredients of Mendelssohn's music can clearly be heard – a mixture of Classical form and structure with the Romantic's gift of self-expression. The sonata and concerto, the symphony and the fugue are from a previous era and Mendelssohn, one feels, is totally at home with them – this gives his music its wonderful poise, balance and clarity. The combination of this with his astonishing melodic gift and powerful ability to express youthful exuberance, triumph, poetic fantasy, tenderness, serenity and celebration of life's joys put Mendelssohn into a class of his own.

Essential works

Symphony No.3 in A minor 'Scottish', Op.56 (1842): inspired by his visit to Scotland in 1829, this was composed, performed and published in the space of one year; it uses Scottish melodies and rhythms and paints a marvellous sound portrait of the country. The lilting second movement is one of his finest achievements.

Symphony No.4 in A 'Italian', Op.90 (1833): the most popular of his five mature symphonies and, in fact, one of the most popular of all Romantic symphonies; an entrancing and spontaneous flow of melody from first to last, ending with a spirited *Saltarello* and *Tarantella* (two Italian peasant dances).

Symphony No.5 in D 'Reformation', Op.107 (1830): written to commemorate the tercentenary of the Augsburg Protestant Confession (the creed of the Lutheran Church, hence the title), the symphony abounds with religious *motifs*, notably Luther's 'Ein feste Burg' in the third and fourth movements.

A Midsummer Night's Dream, Opp.21 and 61, incidental music to Shakespeare's play, (1826–42): the famous Overture, written when Mendelssohn was only seventeen, is a miracle for the work of a boy; here, already, is his mature style with its 'light, aerial, fairy' reaches. Few could spot the join between this and the remaining parts of the incidental music written at the request of the King of Prussia thirteen years later. The most frequently heard sections are the Scherzo and the Wedding March; the latter has accompanied goodness knows how many happy couples down the aisle, a tradition that was established after the fashionable royal wedding of Queen Victoria's daughter, the Princess Royal, in 1858.

The Scherzo is also well known from the prodigiously difficult transcription for solo piano by Rachmaninov, the most remarkable recording of which is by Benno Moiseiwitsch, made in a single take in 1939.

Fingal's Cave or The Hebrides Overture, Op.26 (1830): inspired by a visit to this cave off the Isle of Mull in 1829; listening to the opening, one can almost see the waves rolling in.

Octet for strings in E flat, Op.20 (1825): composed when he was only sixteen and one of the miracles of music; Mozart had nothing similar to show at the same age.

Violin Concerto in E minor, Op.64 (1844): among the most eloquent, and certainly one of the most frequently recorded, concertos of all time, a splendid display vehicle for the soloist; it's been called 'an Eve to Beethoven's Adam'.

Piano Concerto in G minor, Op.25 (1831): a brilliant, compelling work, with dazzling writing for the piano and piquant orchestration; the three movements are played without a break. His other piano concertos well worth getting to know are **No.2 in D minor, Op.40** and **Capriccio brillant in B minor, Op.22** (also for piano and orchestra). The writing in all three had a profound influence on many composers.

Piano Trio in D minor, Op.49 (1839): inspired melodies, rich, idiomatic writing for each instrument, heart-warming in character, this is one of the masterworks of the genre.

Andante and Rondo capriccioso, Op.14 (1830 and 1824): quintessential Mendelssohn, with its combination of Classical and Romantic techniques; it ends, as David Dubal put it, ' in a paroxysm of blind octaves'. Less well known is **Variations sérieuses in D minor, Op.54** (1841), an intensely emotional piano masterpiece, the finest set of variations of the period.

Forty-eight Lieder ohne Worte (Songs without Words), Opp.19, 30, 38, 53, 62, 67, 85, 102 (1830–45): these gems include some of the world's best-loved piano pieces. Who does not know *Spring Song*, once *de rigueur* for Victorian parlour pianists and now hackneyed beyond salvation. Many were given titles by publishers.The best include: *Sweet Remembrance* (the first of the set); *Hunting Song*, the three *Venetian Gondola Songs*, *Spinning Song* (or *The Bees' Wedding*), the *Duetto* and *Volkslied*.

Elijah, oratorio (1846): Mendelssohn at his most profound; the music has an overwhelming humanity ('O Rest in the Lord', 'If with all your Hearts' and 'It is Enough' are among the fine arias) as well as dramatic force and thrust (try the great double chorus 'Baal we cry to thee').

Hear my prayer (1844): 'hymn for soprano, chorus and organ', in most choirs' repertoires before 1927 when it appeared on an inspired recording (still in the catalogue) featuring boy soprano Ernest Lough and the Temple Church Choir of London. 'O for the wings of a Dove' is the concluding section.

Also worth investigating
Symphony No.2 in B flat 'Hymn of Praise', Op.52; Overture Ruy Blas, Op.95; War March of the Priests (from the incidental music to *Athalie*); **Concerto in E for two pianos; Rondo brillant in E flat, Op.29; Piano Trio in C minor, Op.66; Six Lieder, Op.34** (No.2 is 'On Wings of Song')... not forgetting 'Hark the Herald Angels Sing'.

Olivier MESSIAEN

'Fantastic music of the stars' (Stockhausen)

Born: 10 December 1908, Avignon
Died: 28 April 1992, Paris
Type of music: orchestra, opera, choral, chamber, organ, piano
Influences: Gregorian chant, birdsong, Hindu ragas, Indian and Greek verse, gamelan orchestras, Catholic church, religious and spiritual literature
Contemporaries: SHOSTAKOVICH, Elisabeth Lutyens, Paul Creston, **MESSIAEN**, Elliot Carter, BARBER, William Schuman, Bernard Herrmann, Gian Carlo Menotti

HIS LIFE AND MUSIC
Probably the only composer to have a mountain named after him (Mount Messiaen, Utah), Messiaen is among the most strikingly individual of twentieth-century composers. He entered the Paris Conservatoire aged eleven, specialising in organ, improvisation and composition and studying with Dukas of *The Sorcerer's Apprentice* fame and with the great French organist Marcel Dupré. When he graduated in 1930, he not only became organist at the Trinity Church in Paris, playing there regularly until the end of his life, but also began a distinguished teaching career and co-founded 'La Jeune

France', a group that had the express intention of promoting modern French music. He joined the French army at the outbreak of the Second World War but was taken prisoner and spent two years in a German prison camp in Görlitz, Silesia. Here he composed *Quatuor pour la fin du temps*. Repatriated in 1942, he resumed his post at the Trinity Church and was appointed to the faculty of the Paris Conservatoire. His career as France's leading living composer developed apace, and by the early fifties he had an international standing and a generation of young composers eager to study with him, including Pierre Boulez, Karlheinz Stockhausen and Iannis Xenakis.

Messiaen came from a family of literary intellectuals and his breadth of knowledge and interests coloured his music: he was an expert ornithologist, and his *Oiseaux exotiques* (1955–56), *Catalogue des oiseaux* (1956–58) and *Réveil des oiseaux* (1953) are just some of the complex works inspired by birdsong; he studied Greek and Indian verse and, above all, he was a religious philosopher who had a knowledge of the world's religions and was a devout Roman Catholic. The mystic and the celebratory are at the root of all his music.

Essential works

L'ascension for organ, (1933–34): Messiaen provides each of the four movements with a title and an explanatory caption drawn from the Catholic liturgy and scripture (for example, 'Majesty of Christ Beseeching His Glory of His Father. "Father, the hour is come; glorify Thy Son, that Thy Son may glorify Thee"', the latter describing the programme for the music). Orchestrated by the composer, the original organ suite remains the most effective (try the incandescent *Transports de joie* at full bore – when the neighbours are out!).

Quatuor pour la fin du temps (1940): considered by some to be the greatest quartet of the century, it employs a violin, cello, clarinet and piano. Messiaen wrote this remarkable, ardently inspired work in a Nazi camp where he was imprisoned; it was first performed there in 1941 by Messiaen and three prisoners.

Turangalîla symphonie (1948): rhythm was a particular preoccupation of Messiaen's and nowhere is this demonstrated more vividly than in his massive ten-movement 'apotheosis of rhythm', commissioned by the Koussevitzky Foundation and conducted by Leonard Bernstein at its premiere in 1949. 'Turangalîla' is derived from Sanskrit, 'turanga' meaning 'time' and 'lîla' meaning 'love'. Although a complicated work that requires many hearings to absorb, it can be an overwhelming experience for first-time listeners, who usually remark on the use of a vast array of percussion instruments and the other-worldly sound of the *onde martenot*, an electronic keyboard invented in 1928 by Maurice Martenot – after an initial wave of enthusiasm for its possibilities in the 1930s, the instrument has since been used rarely by composers. The acid-tongued Stravinsky was not a fan of Turangalîla: 'Little more can be required to write such things than a plentiful supply of ink!'.

Also worth investigating
Vingt regards sur l'enfant Jésus (1944): twenty pieces for piano.
La Nativité du Seigneur (1935): a nine-movement suite for organ.
Les visions de l'amen (1943): eight movements 'full of the music of bells' for two pianos.
Chronocromie (1960): an orchestral *tour de force*, with birdsong and percussive rhythm as its springboard.

Giacomo MEYERBEER

'The luck to be talented and the talent to be lucky' (Berlioz)

Born: 5 September 1791, Vogelsdorf, near Berlin
Died: 2 May 1864, Paris
Original name: Jakob Liebmann Beer
Type of music: opera, choral, orchestral
Influences: Rossini, Auber, Spontini, Salieri
Contemporaries: WEBER, Henry Bishop, HÉROLD, Carl Czerny, **MEYERBEER**, ROSSINI, Ignaz Moscheles, Saverio Mercadante, Franz Berwald, SCHUBERT

HIS LIFE AND MUSIC

A century ago, Meyerbeer would have merited a detailed entry in any book on music. Today, he is viewed differently: his epic grand operas, which so delighted the public, are now seen as vapid, melodramatic spectacles compared with those by Verdi or Wagner, both of whom owed him much. A shame, for though his melodic invention is limited and his construction flawed, there are many passages of great originality.

A child piano prodigy born into a prosperous Jewish banking family, he was only seven when he performed Mozart's Concerto in D minor in public and two years later was considered one of Berlin's finest pianists. (He changed his name in recognition of a legacy from a relative called Meyer; the fashion for things Italian in music prompted the 'Giacomo'). He had lessons from Muzio Clementi and went on to study at Darmstadt; one of his fellow students was Weber. An interest in composition took over and Salieri encouraged him to enliven his heavy German contrapuntal style with the Italian wit of Rossini. He began a long association with the librettist Eugène Scribe in 1827 and, after moving to Paris in 1834, rapidly became the leading active composer of opera in France.

Success followed success and he became a wealthy man. Star-studded casts, vast crowd scenes and magnificent stage spectacles with elaborate scenery and effects dazzled the audience, and he used his money to publicize his work to maximum effect – he was the Sir Andrew Lloyd Webber of his day. Yet few composers have been so insecure about their work. He was forever altering his scores, sometimes orchestrating them in two ways, in different coloured inks, so that he could try the alternate effects, resulting in endless rehearsals. He told Gounod that sometimes he was ill for a month after a first night.

Meyerbeer had his enemies, and none more despicable than Wagner, whose early career he had helped promote and who called him 'a miserable music-maker'and 'a Jew banker to whom it occurred to compose operas'.

Worth investigating

L'africaine, opera (1865): a free rendering of the story of Vasco da Gama. Meyerbeer began work on this project in 1838. It was finally staged the year after his death and was a phenomenal success despite lasting about six hours. 'O Paradis' is still a favourite tenor aria.

Dinorah, opera (1859): contains the famous 'Shadow' Aria ('Ombre légère') from Act 2.

Les Huguenots, opera (1836): in five acts, this archetypal Meyerbeer work, arguably his finest, is based on the massacre of the Huguenots, which took place in Paris in 1572 on St Bartholomew's night.

Le prophète, opera (1849): still popular at the turn of the century, this opera is based on the historical episode of the coronation in 1535 of Jan Beuckelszoon, the Anabaptist 'prophet' who was crowned in Münster, Westphalia. The *Coronation March* is still heard sometimes.

Robert le Diable, opera (1831): Meyerbeer's first major triumph. Look out for the dramatic arias 'Nonnes qui reposez' (Act 3) and 'Oh, toi que j'aime' (Act 4).

Les patineurs, ballet suite (1837): a beguiling arrangement by Constant Lambert of excerpts from *Le prophète* and *L'étoile du nord*.

Darius MILHAUD

'Milhaud is the most gifted of us all' (Honegger)

Born: 4 September 1892, Aix-en-Provence
Died: 22 June 1974, Geneva
Type of music: every genre
Influences: Provençal and South American folk music, Debussy, Stravinsky, Jewish music, jazz
Contemporaries: HONEGGER, Ferde Grofé, Herbert Howells, **MILHAUD**, Kaikhosru Sorabji, Arthur Benjamin, Peter Warlock, E.J. Moeran, Walter Piston

HIS LIFE AND MUSIC

Milhaud is an entertainer, albeit a rather demanding one at times. His music is written in a wide variety of styles, as his influences might suggest, but his shorter pieces tend to be more successful than his many operas, concertos and symphonies. He was one of the first composers to make conscious use of polytonality and jazz in a symphonic score (his jazz ballet *La création du monde* pre-dates Gershwin's *Rhapsody in Blue*); experiments with electronic music, with counterpoint – his String Quartets Nos.14 & 15 are designed to be played separately or as an octet – and exploitation of West Indian and South American rhythms are, despite their diversity, all part of a recognizable Milhaud style.

His father was a wealthy almond merchant from an old Jewish Provençal family. He was picking out tunes on the piano from the age of three, and entered the Paris Conservatoire in 1909 where d'Indy, Widor and Dukas were among his teachers. Early on he became associated with Erik Satie and Jean Cocteau. Also in this circle was his friend the poet Paul Claudel who was made French Ambassador to Brazil in 1917, engaging Milhaud as his secretary there. In 1920 Milhaud was one of six young French composers labelled Les Six (Poulenc, Honegger, Auric, Tailleferre and Durey were the others) but although he flirted briefly with their high-spirited fun, he was always far too independent to belong to any stylistic group.

The onset of crippling rheumatoid arthritis in the late 1920s did nothing to diminish his prolific output in all forms and styles, or his concert appearances as pianist or conductor of his own work. The Second World War forced him to move to America, where he became professor of composition at Mills College, California, a position he retained until 1971 when he retired with his wife to Switzerland.

Essential works

Le boeuf sur le toit (The ox on the roof), pantomimne or farce (1919): 'a merry, unpretentious divertissement', in Milhaud's own words. Reflecting his recent trip to South America, the colourful score is awash with exuberant Latin-America rhythms. Jean Cocteau turned it into a stage work, *The Nothing-Doing Bar*, set in prohibition America. It was a sell-out and made Milhaud's name.

La création du monde, ballet (1923): after visiting Harlem in 1922, Milhaud was inspired to write this 'Negro ballet', the first to make a success of symphonic jazz.

Scaramouche, suite for two pianos (1937): adapted from his music for a seventeenth-century play *Le médecin volant*, the first movement is French farce, the second languid and amorous, the third a rollicking samba.

Claudio MONTEVERDI

'The prophet of music'

Born: 15 May 1567, Cremona
Died: 29 November 1643, Venice
Full name: Claudio Giovanni Antonio Monteverdi
Type of music: opera, secular and sacred choral, madrigal
Influences: Early Italian School, Giaches de Wert
Contemporaries: Jan Sweelinck, John Bull, John Dowland, **MONTEVERDI**, Thomas Tomkins, Thomas Weelkes, ALLEGRI, GIBBONS, Girolamo Frescobaldi

HIS LIFE

Monteverdi's life and musical career fall into three distinct sections. The first took place in Cremona, where his father was a chemist who practised as a barber-surgeon and where the young Monteverdi studied with the *maestro di cappella* at the cathedral. He had his first compositions published when he was only fifteen – motets, madrigals and similar pieces written in the conventional manner of his teacher. A stroke of good luck in 1592 led him to a position in the court of Vincenzo I, Duke of Mantua, as a viol player and singer. His patron was in the habit of taking a musical retinue with him wherever he went, whether it was to Hungary to fight a war or to Flanders to take a water-cure for gout. Monteverdi was thus free to hear the musical trends current elsewhere on the continent. He was made head of the musical household, married one of the court singers and was free to write what music he wanted, with the duke paying for its publication. Perfect. Then it all went wrong.

His wife of eight years died in 1607 and he suffered a nervous breakdown from which he took some time to recover; Vincenzo I died, to be succeeded by Francesco Gonzaga who summarily dismissed the composer, despite Monteverdi's enormous fame, and he went to live with his elderly parents. Next, a fire destroyed the manuscripts of twelve operas he had written and, when he was appointed head of music at St Mark's in Venice in 1613, which was by far the most prestigious church appointment outside Rome, he was set upon by highwaymen on his way there and robbed of everything he owned.

He remained in Venice for the rest of his life. Even after taking holy orders in 1632, Monteverdi continued to produce both secular and sacred music, though at a slower pace, seemingly more content in the service of God than the Venetian court, but the opening of the first opera house in Venice in 1637 inspired him, in old age, to write a remarkable five more operas.

HIS MUSIC

Although Monteverdi didn't write the first opera (that honour fell to Jacopo Peri), his *Orfeo* is credited as the first with any truly dramatic character, and the first in which the orchestra is used to comment on and add to the drama; the score is an amalgam of madrigals, recitatifs and diverse instrumental styles. He was the first to be able to blend the old polyphonic style with the new monodic, declamatory style; the first to use the string *tremolando* and *pizzicato* effects; he introduced certain chords in his harmony that no one had thought of using previously, and he was the first to point the way to the modern orchestra. In each of the books of madrigals he published, Monteverdi became more and more adventurous in his harmony and performance concepts; for instance, some have a continuo part, which was most unusual for the time, and later there are solos, duets and trios with accompaniment. The whole is greater than the parts and Monteverdi must be considered as one of the great original minds of music.

One distinguished critic wrote: 'He is first and foremost a musician who enjoys the splendour of richly flowing coloraturas and the colours of the orchestra, but who never forgot the main purpose of a composer: to build up a well-organized structure.' Monteverdi's work reveals the culmination of the Renaissance and the beginnings of the new Baroque period and beyond – some of Monteverdi's works could be mistaken for music written two centuries later.

Essential works

La favola d'Orfeo, opera (1607): after hearing Peri's opera *Euridice* performed in Milan for the wedding of Maria de'Medici to Henri IV of France in 1600, the Duke of Mantua, not to be outdone, urged Monteverdi to try this hand at this new form of dramatic and musical expression. The result was *La favola d'Orfeo*, or *L'Orfeo* as it's more commonly called, using a mixture of monody, madrigals and new instrumental form. It was lavishly produced and, nearly 400 years later, it is the earliest opera still in the active repertory.

Vespro della Beata Vergine (Vespers of the Blessed Virgin) (1610): Monteverdi's outstanding work in terms of religious music is this richly-scored setting for the service of Vespers; the variation of the instrumental groups and the compositional techniques employed set the Vespers apart; they were written by the 44-year-old Monteverdi after the loss of his wife and only daughter.

L'incoronazione di Poppea (The Coronation of Poppea) (1642): having moved to St Mark's in Venice, Monteverdi continued to compose both sacred and secular music for the state and other courts, including at least a dozen more operas. These have all been lost, except *Il ritorno d'Ulisse in patria* and his last great work, the first opera to make use of a historical event rather than a myth, *L'incoronazione di Poppea*. Most operas written in the interim had been aimed at the court audience; this was for the general public. Not until Mozart began composing, over a century later, would an opera appear with the same subtlety of characterization and dramatic force. Monteverdi wrote this when he was 75 years old, during a creative Indian summer that his compatriot Verdi would later emulate. Particularly moving

is the final duet from the opera 'Pur ti miro', in which Poppea and Nerone proclaim their love.

Worth investigating
Nine books of madrigals: 250 pieces covering a wide range of subject and expression. Such beauties as *Ecco mormorar l'onde* (1590), *Cruda Amarilli* (1605), *Hor ch'el ciel e la terra* (1638) and *Madrigali guerrieri et amorosi* (*Warlike and Amorous Madrigals*) (1638) represent his development of the form.
Il ballo delle ingrate, ballet (1608)
Arianna, opera (1608): of which only the lovely 'Ariadne's Lament' survives.
Il ritorno d'Ulisse in patria, opera (1640)

Moritz MOSZKOWSKI

'Glittering... yet innocent as a baby's birthday' (J.B. Priestley)

Born: 23 August 1854, Breslau (now Wrocław, western Poland)
Died: 4 March 1925, Paris
Type of music: concerto, orchestral, ballet, instrumental (especially piano)
Influences: Mendelssohn, Schumann, Chopin, Liszt
Contemporaries: Vincent d'Indy, STANFORD, HUMPERDINCK, **MOSZKOWSKI**, JANÁČEK, SOUSA, CHAUSSON, Anatoli Liadov, SINDING, ELGAR, LEONCAVALLO

HIS LIFE AND MUSIC

Moszkowski (pronounced Mosh-*kov*'-skee) wrote music that does not seem to have a care in the world. But even if, as has been said, it fails to stimulate our intellects, it does set our pulses tingling – and that is not a craft to dismiss lightly.

A century ago, his *Spanish Dances* Op.12 for piano duet and Serenade in D, Op.15 (piano solo) were among the bestselling pieces of music of all time. Moszkowski, the son of a wealthy Jewish businessman, was rich and famous by the time he was thirty; a concert pianist who toured all over Europe, he was well respected as a composer and teacher. He settled in Paris, where he married the sister of Cécile Chaminade. A generous host, Moszkowski was renowned for his wit. 'The difference between a Polish liar and any other nationality,' he was fond of saying, 'is that the Pole believes what he says.' And in response to Hans von Bülow's pompous pronouncement 'Bach, Beethoven, Brahms: tous les autres sont crétins' ('all the others are cretins'), Moszkowski replied: 'Mendelssohn, Meyerbeer and your humble servant: tous les autres sont des chrétiens' ('all the others are Christians').

Like many other composers of his day, Moszkowski was overshadowed by the greater talents of Brahms, Wagner and Debussy. But because a composer is not an innovator does not mean that his music is not worth listening to, and the pieces listed below serve as a reminder that the best '*salon* music' has an honourable place in the history of music along with the Olympian peaks. Ignacy Paderewski considered that 'after Chopin, Moszkowski best understands how to write for the piano, and his writing embraces the whole gamut of piano technique.' Most of Moszkowski's best pieces are, like those written by Grieg and Chopin, short piano works but he was not unsuccessful with now long-forgotten orchestral compositions such as his symphonic poem *Joan of Arc*, which influenced Richard Strauss.

The last part of Moszkowski's life was in stark contrast to his early years. In 1908, at the age of fifty-four, he was a recluse, constantly ill with stomach trouble. He had lost his wife and daughter, and his son was summoned to serve in the French army; he gave up taking pupils in composition because 'they all want to write like artistic madmen such as Scriabin, Schoenberg, Debussy and Satie.' He sold all the copyrights of his music and invested the capital in German, Polish and Russian bonds. With the advent of the First World War, he lost everything, lingering on for another ten years as a pauper. In 1923, fourteen of the world's greatest pianists gave a charity concert in Carnegie Hall to raise money for Moszkowski; $10,000 was collected. The funds from a second concert the following year arrived too late: he died of cancer at the age of seventy-one.

Essential works

Spanish Dances, Op.12: five short postcards from Spain, originally for piano duet but now more often heard in their orchestral version; jolly and entertaining.

From Foreign Lands, Op.23: almost as popular in their day as the above, these are musical impressions of Russia, Germany, Spain, Poland, Italy and Hungary.

Violin Concerto in C, Op.30: recorded just once, the neglect of this gorgeously romantic work is inexplicable; it demands resurrecting.

Piano Concerto in E, Op.59: arguably the best unknown Romantic piano concerto in the literature; enthusiasts of the Grieg and Chopin Concertos will love this, too.

Caprice espagnol, Op.37: a once favourite, end-of-recital barnstormer, much played by Shura Cherkassky and his teacher Joseph Hofmann.

Étincelles (Sparks), Op.36 No.6: an explosive piano firecracker made famous in a breath-taking recording by Vladimir Horowitz.

Wolfgang Amadeus MOZART

'Music more beautiful than it can ever be played' (Artur Schnabel)

Born: 27 January 1756, Salzburg
Died: 5 December 1791, Vienna
Original name: Johannes Chrysostomus Wolfgangus Theophilus Mozart
Type of music: opera, symphony, concerto, chamber, choral, vocal, piano
Influences: Leopold Mozart, Bach, Handel, Haydn
Contemporaries: Antonio Salieri, Muzio Clementi, **MOZART**, Ignaz Pleyel, Jan Dussek, Samuel Wesley, BEETHOVEN, Gaspare Spontini

HIS LIFE

Mozart was arguably the most naturally gifted musician in history. His inspiration is often described as 'divine' but he worked assiduously to become the greatest composer of his day, the finest conductor, pianist and organist in Europe and a good violinist. He was supreme not just in one area of music but in all. It is reassuring to know that he was mere flesh and blood like the rest of us; tactless, arrogant, impulsive and far from physically glamorous – his head was too big for his body, he had protruding eyes, a yellowish complexion and a face pitted with smallpox scars.

1756 There has never been a child prodigy in musical history to rival Mozart. Mendelssohn was writing better music at sixteen years old and Saint-Saëns was giving performances as a pianist of Beethoven's Violin Sonatas when he was only four, but Mozart could do everything – compose and play the piano and violin by the time he was six. His father Leopold was a composer and violinist in the service of the Prince Archbishop of Salzburg, hoping to become Kapellmeister. Wolfgang and his sister Anna Maria (who was nicknamed Nannerl) were the only two of Leopold's seven children to survive infancy.

1760 Both children were musically talented and when, at the age of four, Wolfgang could not only memorize a piece in an hour and a minuet in half that time, but also play it faultlessly, Leopold realized he had a prodigy on his hands. There is no doubt that part of Leopold's motive was to make a great musician of his son and let the world know about his God-given talents, but he exploited these gifts to the full.

1762 The children set off on their first tour with their father, intending to play at various European courts, visiting Munich and the Elector of Bavaria, and then Vienna where Nannerl and Wolfgang played in front of the Empress Maria Theresa and the seven-year-old Marie Antoinette.

1763 Mozart's first compositions were published in Paris and his first symphonies were written in the following year. The family tour continued to London where audiences flocked to hear the two prodigies, amazed at Wolfgang's powers of improvisation. Johann Christian Bach befriended them; one of the brothers Grimm (of fairy tale fame) heard Mozart improvize and wrote: 'I cannot be sure that this child will not turn my head if I go on hearing him often; he makes me realize that it is difficult to guard against madness on seeing prodigies. I am no longer surprised that St Paul should have lost his head after a strange vision.'

1766 The Mozarts arrived back in Salzburg where Wolfgang applied himself to the serious study of counterpoint under his father's tutelage.

1767 The following year, the family were in Vienna where his first opera *La finta semplice* was begun; his next stage work, a *Singspiel* entitled *Bastien und Bastienne,* was produced at the home of Dr Mesmer, discoverer of the therapy known as Mesmerism.

1769–71 Wolfgang and his father spent nearly two years in Italy during which, legend has it, he wrote out the entire score of Allegri's *Miserere* from memory. Here, he benefited from his meetings with the distinguished Italian composer Padre Martini. This was followed by a period in Salzburg in which he composed his first important works, including the Violin Concertos and the popular 'Haffner' Serenade.

1777 Accompanied by his mother, Mozart journeyed to Paris. This, unlike previous tours, which were financed by expensive gifts from the various courts, had to make money *en route*. Around this time he fell in love with Aloysia, one of the daughters of the music copyist Fridolin Weber. His mother's death in Paris and Aloysia's rebuttal of his affections persuaded him to return to Salzburg where he spent the following two years composing in the service of the archbishop. *Idomeneo* (1780), his first major opera, was among the commissions he received. Frustrated by the stultifying demands of his employer, he resigned from the archbishop's service.

1781 Mozart decided to make Vienna his home and it remained his base for the rest of his life; the move marks the beginning of his golden years as a mature composer. His first lodgings were with the Weber family and it wasn't long before he had fallen in love with Constanze, the flighty younger sister of his old love, who was now married.

1782–86 After his wedding in August, a string of fine works appeared: the 'Haffner' and 'Linz' Symphonies, a set of five string quartets dedicated to Haydn – the two had become close friends – as well as *Le nozze di Figaro (The Marriage of Figaro)* in 1786. Throughout this period, the Mozarts' finances were perilously poised, despite many commissions and concert appearances. No court appointment had materialized and, although stories of his poverty at this time are exaggerated, he felt poor enough to write begging letters to his friends and they make pathetic reading. Many were to his fellow Mason, the Viennese banker Michael Puchberg. The loans were never repaid and Mozart seems to have had no scruples in not paying his debts. It is a curious fact that whenever any of these carefully preserved begging letters appear on the market today, they fetch hundreds of times the amount of money Mozart originally requested. And yet, in spite of this, between 1784 and 1786 one masterpiece followed another. How could a human being compose nine of the greatest piano concertos under such circumstances? In 1786, three of these concertos were written concurrently with *The Marriage of Figaro.*

1787 October 1787 saw the appearance of *Don Giovanni*, Mozart's second operatic masterpiece; the following month he secured an appointment as Kammermusicus in Vienna in succession to Gluck, but whereas Gluck's stipend had been 2,000 gulden, Mozart's was a paltry 800. However, this change in his fortunes may have softened the blow of his father's death earlier in the year.

1788 This is the *annus mirabilis* in which Mozart composed his final three symphonies – No.39 in E flat, No.40 in G minor and No.41 in C, the 'Jupiter' – as well as *Eine kleine Nachtmusik*, the String Quintet in G minor and the exquisite Clarinet Quintet in A.

1789 In the spring, Mozart travelled to Berlin where he played for Friedrich Wilhelm II and was offered the post of Kapellmeister at a good salary, but Vienna drew him back. He returned to complete *Così fan tutte*, his third opera masterpiece and his third collaboration with the librettist Lorenzo da Ponte. Da Ponte had already established himself in London and the opportunity arose for Mozart to go there, but he declined.

1791 The Clarinet Concerto and Piano Concerto No.27 in B flat, *Die Zauberflöte (The Magic Flute)*, the old-fashioned, Italian-style opera *La clemenza di Tito* and the Requiem – any one of these would have been sufficient to make their composer immortal. But all by the same man? In one year? The achievement is breathtaking.

The circumstances of Mozart's death are well known – the mysterious visitor commissioning a Requiem Mass, Mozart thinking the stranger had come from another world and that the Requiem was for his own soul. The caller was in fact an employee of an

eccentric nobleman, Count Franz von Walsegg, who intended the work for his late wife and to pass it off as his own. Mozart did not live long enough to complete it; his terrible death occurred a few weeks before his thirty-sixth birthday, his body assaulted by streptococcal infection, Schönlien-Henoch Syndrome and renal failure which led to fever, polyarthritis, swelling of the limbs, vomiting, cerebral haemorrhage and terminal bronchopneumonia.

His funeral was the cheapest that Constanze could afford and after the service, with Mozart's body probably already putrefying, none in the party elected to accompany the coffin to St Marx Cemetery, which is about an hour's walk from the city centre. The location of his burial place has never been confirmed.

HIS MUSIC

'There is no feeling – human or cosmic, no depth, no height the human spirit can reach that is not contained in Mozart's music,' wrote the pianist Lili Kraus. It is perhaps true to say that of all the great composers none are revered and loved as much as Mozart. Writers and musicians for the past two centuries have often wanted to express in words what his music means to them. The critic Sir Neville Cardus reflected after hearing the opening of the Piano Concerto in A (No.23) that, 'If any of us were to die and then wake hearing it, we should know at once that (after all) we had got to the right place.' Another, Karl Barth, wrote, 'When the angels sing for God, they sing Bach; but I am sure that when they sing for each other they sing Mozart – and God eavesdrops.'

Mozart was able to cope with musical organization in a way that is given to few: he could hear lengthy works and write them down note for note afterwards and he could score a complicated piece while planning another in his head, gifts that are beyond the comprehension of ordinary mortals. He was not a great innovator of form but, rather like Bach, he welded together all the musical ideas of his time and raised them to a new plateau. Again, not all his compositions are masterpieces: much of his early work is humdrum, without much individuality and distinctly superficial; likewise there are many dance movements that have been tossed off the production line and some of the piano sonatas he wrote for his pupils are of less interest than the works of genius he was writing simultaneously.

What makes him stand apart? His melodies sing, his harmonies are full of emotion and personal expression; his handling of the technical aspects such as counterpoint and orchestration are effortless, full of rich imagination and colour. Instruments such as the clarinet and horn are allowed to flower in their own right, while the brass section is given weighty dramatic roles. Mozart's main instrument was the piano and the pieces he wrote were both display vehicles for himself (entertainment pieces) and, as in some of the piano concertos, the means by which he expressed himself most personally. He exploited all the potential of the new pianos of the day (these had smaller keyboards and a limited range of tone compared with today's concert grands) and, years before Chopin, used the expressive device of *rubato* when playing, where the left hand keeps strict time while the right hand takes subtle rhythmic licence. Lastly, his writing for the voice has rarely been matched. He composed with specific singers in mind and so was able to exploit the particular ability of each artist, writing not just to show off the voice, as had been the practice until then, but to use it as a means of expression. We meet real people with recognizable emotions in his operas, with music that evokes pathos and comments upon the drama. Perhaps that is why his four operatic masterpieces have held the stage for longer and are performed more frequently than those of any other composer.

Essential works

Mozart's works are identified by their K (or KV) numbers, an abbreviation of Köchel (or *Köchelverzeichnis*), meaning 'Köchel list' (pronounced 'ker'-kle). Ludwig von Köchel (1800–77), an Austrian nobleman, botanist, mineralogist and musical amateur, published his chronological catalogue of Mozart's work in 1862.

Orchestral

Serenade No.7 in D 'Haffner', K250
Serenade No.10 in B flat for thirteen wind instruments, K361
Serenade No.13 in G, Eine kleine Nachtmusik, K525

Mozart wrote an enormous number of compositions to accompany dances or merely as background music. Dip into the piles of Divertimenti, Minuets and Contredanses and you will probably come across Mozart the hack. The 'Haffner' and *Eine kleine* serenades are quality examples of his eighteenthth-century muzak, the first written for a family wedding of the Haffners, his patrons in Salzburg. Mozart would have been surprised to find that such a slight work (in his terms) as *Eine kleine* had become so popular today.

Occasionally, he went deeper and produced a masterpiece of the genre, such as the Serenade for thirteen wind instruments. The slow movement, when the long oboe note creeps in, was used to poignant effect in Peter Schaffer's play *Amadeus*, when Salieri, on

hearing it through a window, says, in wonder: 'It seemed to me I had heard a voice of God.'
Symphony No.29 in A, K201
Symphony No.31 in D 'Paris', K297
Symphony No.35 in D 'Haffner', K385
Symphony No.36 in C 'Linz', K425
Symphony No.38 in D 'Prague', K504
Symphony No.39 in E flat, K543
Symphony No.40 in G minor, K550
Symphony No.41 in C 'Jupiter', K551

Mozart wrote his first symphony when he was eight, his last when he was thirty-two. Haydn, when he wrote his 104 symphonies, knew that he had a guaranteed performance for them; under the circumstances, Mozart, without such a guarantee, was astonishingly prolific. Most are from his apprentice years or are entertainment fare, rather like the serenades and divertimentos, and as a body of work are not as important as the piano concertos. But with the later symphonies, things change. All those listed above should be in any record collection. (You'll look in vain for Symphony No.37; the one numbered 37 is by someone else – Mozart had copied the score out for a friend.)

The essence of Mozart the symphonist is in the final three, which were written close together but are highly contrasted: after the introduction, No.39 is all sunshine and smiles; No.40 is gloom and despair – the opening theme of the first movement is one of his most famous, helped to some extent, alas, by a hideous pop version from Waldo de los Rios in 1971; No.41 is the crowning glory of symphonic writing in the eighteenth century – no one is certain how it acquired its nickname the 'Jupiter', probably from England in the early 1820s. It opens with a stately procession and ends with a breathtaking display of musical invention where six themes are juggled simultaneously, inverted, played in canon and built to a glorious conclusion.

Concertos

Concertos for horn and orchestra: No.3 in E flat, K447; No.4 in E flat, K495: Mozart wrote four horn concertos between 1782 and 1786 for the Viennese horn player Igna Leitgeb, a former member of the Salzburg orchestra who had retired to Vienna to become a cheesemonger. Mozart scatters insults to Leitgeb throughout these light-hearted scores, yet, particularly in No.3, also manages to touch the heart. The final movement of No.4 is a classical lollipop, given lyrics by Flanders and Swann in their witty song 'Ill Wind'. The classic recording of all four concertos remains that made in the 1950s by Dennis Brain.

Concerto for bassoon and orchestra in B flat, K191: the only surviving bassoon concerto of at least four composed by Mozart. Among his earliest concertos in any form, it was composed in 1774, using the whole range of its compass. It's underrated, particularly in view of the slow movement.

Concerto for clarinet and orchestra in A, K622: one of music's masterpieces, written only two months before Mozart's death for his friend, the virtuoso Anton Stadler. Jack Brymer's recording with Beecham deserves special mention.

Concerto for piano and orchestra No.9 in E flat, 'Jeunehomme', and for orchestra No.10, K271

Concerto for piano and orchestra No.12 in A, K414

Concerto for piano and orchestra No.14 in E flat, K449

Concerto for piano and orchestra No.15 in B flat, K450

Concerto for piano and orchestra No.17 in G, K453

Concerto for piano and orchestra No.20 in D minor, K466

Concerto for piano and orchestra No.21 in C, K467

Concerto for piano and orchestra No.22 in E flat, K482

Concerto for piano and orchestra No.23 in A, K488

Concerto for piano and orchestra No.24 in C minor, K491

Concerto for piano and orchestra No.27 in B flat, K595
Concerto for 2 pianos in E flat, K365

The list of concertos may seem overlong – but it is deliberately so, for the piano concertos are Mozart's autobiography and among the high points of Western culture. His personality is revealed in these works more than anywhere else. His first original keyboard concerto was written when he was seventeen (the first four are concerto arrangements of other peoples' work) and the last in the year of his death. Of the thirteen masterpiece concertos written after K415 (i.e.1784) only Nos.16 & 18 are not included in the repertoire of the major pianists.

Each has different delights to offer: though No.12 was said to be Mozart's favourite, Nos.20–25 are considered to be the 'heart of the matter' and they are amongst the most venerated works in the concerto literature. No.20 was the first to be written in a minor key, and alternates between despair and defiance; No.21 has the ravishing, serene middle movement made famous by the 1967 film *Elvira Madigan*; the popular No.23 has, arguably, the most heart-breaking slow movement that Mozart wrote, and was the only occasion on which he used the key of F sharp minor; No.24, the other minor-key piano concerto, is sublime, far from the diverting entertainments of Haydn, but looking forward to Beethoven, full of emotional turmoil and pathos. No.27, written when Mozart was already ill, contrasts brilliant, childlike spontaneity with autumnal resignation. The two-piano Concerto provides tricky moments for the players and an exhilarating romp for the audience.

Concerto for violin No.4 in D, K218
Concerto for violin No.5 in A 'Turkish', K219
Mozart composed five violin concertos in quick succession in 1775. Of these, the last two are the best, No.5 being considered one of the greatest of all violin concertos. Its nickname comes from the last movement, a theme retrieved from an earlier ballet by Mozart, *The Jealous Women of the Harem*.

Chamber

Oboe Quartet in F, K370
Clarinet Quintet in A, K581
String Quintet No.3 in G minor, K516
String Quartet No.14 in G, K387
String Quartet No.15 in D minor, K421
String Quartet No.16 in E flat, K428
String Quartet No.17 in B flat 'Hunt', K458
String Quartet No.18 in A, K464
String Quartet No.19 in C 'Dissonance', K465

Choosing which of the twenty-seven piano concertos to investigate is a different matter to choosing from more than 200 chamber works.

Certainly the delectable oboe and clarinet works are indispensable and if you feel that Mozart's intimate side is more rewarding than any other, then you would not be alone in placing the G minor String Quintet among the most sublime of all his works, though many make claims for No.5 in D major, K593.

There are twenty-three string quartets. Mozart wrote a dozen before 1773 and then stopped using this medium for nine years. Between 1782 and 1785, he produced six quartets that dwarf his earlier efforts, written for, and inspired by, his friend Haydn, who played first violin to Mozart's viola in quartet performances; Nos.14–19 are known as the 'Haydn Quartets'. The first movement of No.15, in D minor, is said to have been inspired by Constanze's labour cries; the 'Hunt' was so named because of the galloping opening; the 'Dissonance' Quartet is an astonishingly advanced work for the time, its opening bars giving the impression of an ambiguous tonality. Until Beethoven, there were no further significant developments in quartet writing.

Instrumental
Piano Sonata No.8 in A minor, K310
Piano Sonata No.10 in C, K330
Piano Sonata No.11 in A, K331
Piano Sonata No.14 in C minor, K457
Mozart's eighteen piano sonatas are a less consistently exalted group of works, as many were written for pupils and teaching purposes. But they include some treasures: K310 with its declamatory opening theme is often played but nothing like as frequently as K330 (*Sonata facile*), with which every budding pianist begins. K331 has the famous *Rondo all turca* (*Turkish Rondo*) as its last movement, and this is often played separately; K457 is frequently coupled with the Fantasia in C minor, K475, composed a year after the C minor Sonata and perhaps Mozart's greatest solo work.

Religious music
Ave verum corpus, K618, motet: written in the last year of Mozart's life, one of the simplest and most poignant choral works ever written.
Exsultate, jubilate, K165, motet: a joyful, extrovert three-movement work for soprano and orchestra, the last one being an uplifting setting of the one word 'Allelujah'.
Laudate dominum: a setting of Psalm 116 for soprano and choir from the *Solemn vespers* of 1780 (K339); a famous old recording by Ursula van Diemen was once registered in a poll as the most popular classical request of all time.
Mass No.18 in C minor 'Great', K427
Mass No.19 in D minor 'Requiem', K626
Excluding these two, Mozart wrote at least sixteen settings of the mass, most of them triumphal, bustling and distinctly unsolemn. The 'Great' C minor Mass, the first not written

to a commission, is a far more personal affair; it was produced at the peak of his creative genius and yet, curiously, was left unfinished. The Requiem, composed in the certain knowledge that it was to be his own requiem, is another unfinished masterpiece.

Operas
Così fan tutte, K588 (1790): the full title, *Così fan tutte, ossia la scuola degli amanti*, translates literally as 'Thus do all women, or the School for Lovers' – which indicates what it is about: a cynical comedy on love and relationships. It did not achieve the popularity of his three other great operas until this century. The vocal highlights are the famous trio from Act 1, 'Soave sia il vento' ('May the gentle breeze') and 'Come scoglio' ('Like a rock'), a prodigiously difficult coloratura test piece.
Don Giovanni, K527 (1787): at least thirty other operas have been written on the story of the irresistible seducer and blasphemer, but this one, commissioned by the Prague opera house as a direct result of its success with *The Marriage of Figaro*, is the only one that is of any consequence, alternating between high comedy and tragedy. The *Catalogue aria*, 'Là ci darem la mano' ('Give me your hand') and the *Champagne aria* are all in Act 1, while in Act 2 is the touchstone of tenor arias, 'Il mio tesoro' ('My Treasure').
Die Zauberflöte (The Magic Flute), K620 (1791): Beethoven considered this to be Mozart's best work. Whether seen as a fairy tale, an allegorical pantomime or an evening glorifying Freemasonry, it is a work of universal appeal. Among the many celebrated extracts are 'Dies Bildnis ist bezaubernd schön' ('O loveliness beyond compare'), sung by Tamino, and one of Mozart's finest arias for the tenor voice; 'O zittre nicht' ('O tremble not') and 'Der Hölle Rache kocht in meinem Herzen' ('The pangs of hell are raging') – the two thrilling arias for the Queen of the Night that send the soprano up to an inhuman top F (written for Mozart's sister-in-law).
Le nozze di Figaro (The Marriage of Figaro), K492 (1786): the first of Mozart's three collaborations with the librettist Lorenzo da Ponte and written in Italian rather than German to cater for the taste of the Viennese public. *Figaro* is still frequently performed. It is one of the masterpieces of comedy in music, the ostensibly superficial plot and characters given depth and subtlety by Mozart's marvellous music. Apart from the sparkling overture, the many highlights include the arias 'Non so più' (sung by Cherubino), 'Non più andrai' (Figaro), 'Porgi amor' (Countess), 'Voi che sapete' (Cherubino), 'Dove sono' (Countess) and the 'Letter Duet' from Act 3, 'Che soave zefiretto' (Countess and Susannah).

Modest MUSSORGSKY

*'He trampled on the rules and crushed the life out
of them'* (Pierre d'Alheim)

Born: 21 March 1839, Karevo
Died: 28 March 1881, St Petersburg
Type of music: opera, orchestral, piano, song
Influences: Beethoven, Schumann, the Russian nationalism of Balakirev and
Borodin, Rimsky-Korsakov, Dargomijsky
Contemporaries: BALAKIREV, Emile Waldteufel, BIZET, BRUCH, **MUSSORGSKY**,
Josef Rheinberger, Sir John Stainer, TCHAIKOWSKY, Johann Svendsen, CHABRIER

HIS LIFE

A striking photograph exists of the young Mussorgsky, taken in about 1856, resplendent
in army uniform. Born into the landowning aristocracy, he was described by a friend as
'an impeccably dressed, heel-clicking society man, scented, dainty, fastidious'. It comes
as a shock to look at the famous painting of Mussorgsky by his friend Ilya Repin,
completed just weeks before his death: here is a tousle-headed, straggle-bearded,
dissolute face with a toper's nose. What happened?

Mussorgsky's musical talent was nurtured by his mother; at nine he was good enough
to play a John Field concerto and at thirteen, when a cadet at the military academy, he
began writing an opera, without any formal musical training. In 1856 he took a commission in the élite Preobrajensky Regiment. Borodin, then a medical army officer,
remembered him as something of a fop with signs of pretentiousness: 'He spoke through
his teeth and his carefully chosen words were interspersed with French phrases ... he
showed quite unmistakably perfect breeding and education.' In 1857 he met Balakirev
and Cui and became friendly with the critic Vladimir Stasov, a champion of Russian
national music. Already a heavy drinker, he abandoned his military career.

In 1861, when the serfs were emancipated, his family went bankrupt, forcing him into
paid work as a clerk in the Ministry of Communications. During the following four years
he composed continuously, although his lack of a musical education led him to abandon
most of the works he began. He resigned from his job in 1865 and when, two years later,
Stasov made his famous declaration about the 'mighty handful of Russian musicians'
(*see* BALAKIREV) Mussorgsky was ready to take up the challenge with his comrades-in-
arms Balakirev, Borodin, Cui and Rimsky-Korsakov: the Mighty Handful.

Mussorgsky was now living in abject poverty and well on the way to becoming an
alcoholic, struggling to get his thoughts down on paper. In 1869 he entered government
service again, this time in the forestry department. Simultaneously he worked on what
was to become his masterpiece, the opera *Boris Godunov*, which, after many revisions,
saw the light of day in St Petersburg in 1874. Its success was tempered by strong criticism
from Mussorgsky's fellow musicians and this upset him considerably. Cui attacked the
work for its immaturity and 'lack of technique'.

Mussorgsky began a second opera, *Khovanshchina* (left incomplete), still managing to
write some fine music but both his lifestyle and concentration had disintegrated. The
artist Repin recalled how often Stasov 'on his return from abroad was hardly able to get
him out of some basement dive, nearly in rags, swollen with alcohol.' Intermittently,
Mussorgsky appeared as a pianist and accompanist but he was now suffering from
delirium tremens and epileptic fits. He died from a fit just after his forty-second birthday.

HIS MUSIC

Of the group known as the Mighty Handful, Mussorgsky was the most original and
uncompromising, as well as being the most widely cultured and the most perceptive

thinker. He wrote a pitifully small amount of music and, unlike the others, lived only for that, taking his credo from Dagomijsky who, in 1857, had written: ' I do not intend to debase music to the level of mere amusement ... I want the notes to express exactly what the words express. I want truth.'

Mussorgsky wanted to depict the Russian people in music. 'When I sleep I see them, when I eat I think of them, when I drink – I can visualize them, integral, big, unpainted and without any tinsel.' Pushkin's play *Boris Godunov* provided the basis for his own libretto of the work in which he brought all his ideas to fruition. After fifteen months, the opera was ready but it was rejected for performance. It lacked a female role and the committee of the Imperial Theatre in St Petersburg recorded their shock at its novelty and bleakness – in other words, its truthfulness. Persuaded by Stasov to revise it, Mussorgsky made it more conventional, introducing a soprano role and an entirely new act. It was this 'sanitized' version that Cui criticized; it was 'de-Mussorgskyfied' further by his friend and admirer Rimsky-Korsakov and this is the version that is generally performed today. As Rimsky-Korsakov put it, he ironed out 'the countless absurdities in its harmonies and at times in its melodies.' But experts today feel that it is Mussorgsky's original work that is the strongest. The music is raw and innovative, while the later version emasculates the original.

Some see Mussorgsky's music as that of an inspired dilettante with ingenuous mistakes and awkward passages that would offend academically trained musicians; others see him as a rule breaker, writing awkward passages *on purpose* to convey his aims and his truth. He forged his own path regardless, as Debussy recognized: 'He is unique and will remain so because his art is spontaneous and free from arid formula.'

Essential works

Boris Godunov, opera (1868–73): this long, complex work (it is essential to follow it with an English translation and it lasts over three hours) is regarded as one of the most significant epic operas; it is difficult on first hearing but ultimately rewarding. It is also the first truly Russian opera, with a Russian subject. The music springs from the inflections of speech, translated into natural melody. The highlights of the opera are *The Coronation Scene*, Varlaam's song 'In the town of Kasan' and the famous *Death of Boris* in Act 4. The recording of the latter by the great bass, Feodor Chaliapin, is unforgettable.

Pictures at an Exhibition (1874): arguably the most important piano work by the Russian nationalists was inspired by a memorial exhibition of paintings and drawings by Mussorgsky's friend Victor Hartmann; it reflects a visitor to the exhibition promenading from one work to the next. It is even more popular in its orchestral version by Ravel.

Night on the Bare Mountain (1867): available both in the original and the better-known version by (once again) Rimsky-Korsakov; the work is a portrait of a midsummer night when the witches' Sabbath is held on the Bare Mountain near Kiev.

Carl NIELSEN

'Music is life, and, like it, inextinguishable'
(Nielsen's motto for his Symphony No.4)

Born: 9 June 1865, Nørre-Lyndelse, near Odense, Denmark
Died: 3 October 1931, Copenhagen
Full name: Carl August Nielsen
Type of music: symphony, concerto, stage work, chamber, instrumental
Influences: Gade, Grieg, Brahms, Liszt, later chromatic and dissonant music
Contemporaries: RICHARD STRAUSS, Alexander Grechaninov, **NIELSEN**, Edwin Lemare, DUKAS, GLAZUNOV, SIBELIUS, BUSONI, SATIE, Francesco Cilèa

HIS LIFE AND MUSIC

Anyone seeking a gentle introduction to twentieth-century music could do worse than listen to the symphonies of this remarkable composer, neglected by all but Scandinavia during his lifetime and only internationally recognized in the 1950s for what he was: Denmark's most important composer. In his charming autobiography, *My Childhood*, Nielsen tells of his life on the Island of Fyn, or Funen, where his father was a labourer. The Danish soil and character, rather than its folk music, pervade his work; there is an attractive, unsentimental directness about it and, although it has its bleak moments, a life-affirming spirit abounds in music of clear-cut colours and structures.

Nielsen received rudimentary music lessons from his father, a keen fiddle player, and then took up the trumpet in the local band, although his first job was as a shepherd. His elementary musical education at school was all the tuition he had before composing a string quartet, which qualified him for admission to the Royal Conservatory in Copenhagen. Among his teachers was the esteemed Niels Gade, friend of Mendelssohn and Schumann and the founding father of the Scandinavian school of composition. Neilsen's career was devoted to playing the violin in the Royal Chapel Orchestra, conducting all over Denmark and Europe, and composing. He died of a heart attack shortly after being made director of the Copenhagen Conservatory, a national hero.

Essential works
Six Symphonies

Dvořák and Brahms were Nielsen's models for the symphony but in each successive work he tried out something new. He was interested in changing tonalities – the First Symphony begins in one key and ends in another; the Second, inspired by a group of paintings depicting the four temperaments, has a memorable third movement (*Andante malincolico*) and a rollicking, swaggering finale; the Third, so-called (all the subtitles were Nielsen's) because of its expansive nature, has contributions from soprano and baritone soloists;

the Fourth begins with his reaction to war and ends with unquenchable optimism; in the Fifth the side-drum tries to drown out the orchestra – a magnificent work; the Sixth is a caustic look at his own work and others. The list is:

No.1 in G minor, Op.7 (1890–92)
No.2 'The Four Temperaments', Op.16 (1901–02)
No.3 'Sinfonia espansiva', Op.27 (1910–11)
No.4 'The Inextinguishable', Op.29 (1914–16)
No.5, Op.50 (1921–22)
No.6 'Sinfonia semplice' (1924–25)

Jacques OFFENBACH

'The Mozart of the Champs-Élysées' (Rossini)

Born: 20 June 1819, Cologne
Died: 5 October 1880, Paris
Original name: Jakob Eberst
Type of music: French comic opera
Influences: Halévy, Rossini, the operas of Gluck, Donizetti, Wagner and Meyerbeer
Contemporaries: LITOLFF, GOUNOD, Antonio Bazzini, **OFFENBACH**, SUPPÉ, Henri Vieuxtemps, Joachim Raff, FRANCK, LALO, Carl Reinecke

HIS LIFE AND MUSIC

Ironically, the composer who came to epitomize the frivolity of the Second Empire, 'the King of the Paris Boulevards', was a German – born Jakob Eberst, the son of a Jewish cantor and bookbinder. 'Jakob' became 'Jacques' and his father, known as Isaac der Offenbacher after Offenbach-am-Main where he lived, decided to change the family name to 'Offenbach'. By the age of fourteen, Jacques was at the Paris Conservatoire

studying the cello, and the city remained his base for the rest of his life. He then became a cellist in the orchestra of the Opéra Comique and started to compose both operettas and pieces for his instrument. In 1850 he was appointed conductor at the Théâtre Français. By the mid-1850s he was well versed in every aspect of operetta production.

An eccentric, wiry-looking man with a head like a mangy parrot with glasses, he had little success as a composer until his forties when he opened his own theatre to mount the work that had been consistently rejected. In 1855 the Théâtre Comte was re-named Bouffes-Parisiens and for the following ten years, under Offenbach's direction, it was *the* place to be seen. 'The Bouffes-Parisiens,' reported the *New York Tribune* of 1863, 'is so little as to be almost a joke ... It is the David of opera houses and, in an indirect way, scatters worse wounds among the Goliaths, its big rivals, than they would care to acknowledge ... They go to listen to the brightest and newest music, to witness the best acting, of its order, that the French stage affords. And they are never disappointed. Absolutely never.'

During this time, Offenbach elevated burlesque opera into an art form of his making. His melodic invention and skill as a composer and orchestrator won him immense respect but it was the subjects of his operettas that made him popular; he satirized composers such as Wagner and Meyerbeer, the army, the social order, the government, Greek mythology and many other victims. Wagner wrote that his music was 'a dung heap on which all the swine of Europe wallowed' – proof of the light-hearted, inconsequential nature of the entertainments to which the grateful Parisians flocked.

For twenty years, Offenbach reigned supreme as the master of his particular art. By the mid-1870s, the public had begun to tire of him, a series of spectacular productions failed, leaving him bankrupt, and Johann Strauss, whom he had encouraged to write operettas, conquered Paris with *Die Fledermaus*. Offenbach took off to America where he was offered $1,000 a night for a minimum of thirty performances. When he returned home in 1876 to write what would prove to be his masterpiece, *The Tales of Hoffmann*, it was to show a more serious side. He did not live to orchestrate the work. It was his one-hundred-and-second piece for the stage.

Frivolous and undemanding as his music is, it is also original and easily identifiable. The rollicking melodies, bright and breezy orchestration and irreverent humour suited the time to perfection: what Strauss was to the waltz of Vienna, Offenbach was to the polka and can-can of Paris and he paved the way for the operettas of Léhar and Sullivan. Commentators have identified a recurrent theme of cynicism and fatalism hidden beneath the merriment of the Second Empire. At least one contemporary found this mirrored in Offenbach's frothy operettas: 'The laughter I hear in Offenbach's music,' he wrote, 'is that of the Empress Charlotte gone mad.'

Essential works

Orfée aux enfers (Orpheus in the Underworld) (1858): the first true operetta: an opera that didn't take itself seriously. It pokes fun at Gluck's *Orpheus and Euridice*, the government and other targets. The popular Overture was composed not by Offenbach but by one Carl Binder, for the 1860 Vienna production; the most famous section is the Can-can in Act 4.

La belle Hélène (1864): a huge success all over the world; it is a skit on the story of Helen of Troy, and mocks the Second Empire and its preoccupation with sex and lax morals.

Les contes d'Hoffmann (The Tales of Hoffmann) (1881): lengthy (three Acts plus prologue and epilogue), based on stories by the extraordinary German writer, music critic, caricaturist and composer E.T.A. Hoffmann. Look out for *The Legend of Kleinzack* (Prologue) and the celebrated *Doll Song* (Act 1) in which the coloratura soprano is 'wound up'. Its best-loved number is the *Barcarolle* (Act 3): 'Lovely night, oh night of love'. The tune was originally a ghost song from Offenbach's 1864 opera-ballet *Die Rheinnixen*.

Worth investigating

La vie parisienne (1866)

La Grande-Duchesse de Gérolstein (1867)

La périchole (1868): includes the *Letter Song*, one of Offenbach's finest. Richard D'Oyly Carte, needing a curtain-raiser for its 1875 London production, asked Gilbert and Sullivan to provide one; the result was the *Trial by Jury* and the beginning of the writers' partnership.

Les brigands (1869)

Concerto Rondo in G for cello and orchestra

Gaieté Parisienne: a ballet concocted in 1938 from Offenbach scores by Manuel Rosenthal.

Carl ORFF
(1895–1982)

Carmina burana, 1937

Coming from a musical family in Munich with strong army associations, the young Orff had his first works published when he was sixteen and in just six months in 1911 wrote over fifty songs; he flirted with the ideas of Schoenberg and the works of Richard Strauss but by the early twenties he still hadn't found his own voice. It was, of all things, a school for gymnastic dancing that opened the door. He met Dorothee Günther in 1924 and they founded the Günther Schule with the aim of 'reviving the natural unity of music and movement' in children. The Orff methods were widely adopted in schools all over Germany, England, Russia and America. His interest in primitive rhythms and simple, monodic melodies led him to stage presentations of Monteverdi and Bach and from there to his masterpiece.

Carmina burana was first performed in June 1937. Orff described it as a 'scenic cantata', intending the orchestra, chorus and soloists to be accompanied by dance and mime. The words, in Latin and German, are from thirteenth-century student poems found in the monastery of Benediktbeuren in Bavaria, which are bawdy celebrations of drinking, lovemaking and other earthy delights. Its wide appeal – a message to many contemporary composers – comes from its rhythmic vivacity, its raw, direct energy and its fusion of traditional, jazz and modern compositional techniques.

Not surprisingly, Orff was sniffed at by the critics ('a rich man's banjo player,' said one). It would not have been because he was wearing the well-known make of aftershave with which the opening chorus 'O Fortuna' has, alas, become irrevocably associated as a result of its lengthy use in a British TV commercial.

Johann PACHELBEL
(1653–1706)

Canon in D

The first part of the Canon and Gigue in D for three violins and basso continuo has become a 'pop' classic, used in many TV commercials. It takes the form of a series of variations over the repeated short bass phrase of the introduction. Born in Germany,

Pachelbel's main claim to fame during his lifetime was as an organist and composer – he wrote dozens of (generally uninspired) chorales for organ and ninety-five fugues as interludes to the Magnificat, as well as non-liturgical toccatas, preludes, keyboard suites and similar pieces; the list of his motets is a long one indeed. As a friend of the Bach family, he taught Johann Christoph Bach, who in turn taught Johann Sebastian. More importantly, he pioneered musical symbolism by using such devices in his sacred music as repeated notes to illustrate steadfastness, minor keys for sorrowful moods, major keys for joy and, to portray evil, a broken diminished seventh chord.

Niccolò PAGANINI

'Paganini begins where our reason stops' (Meyerbeer)

Born: 27 October 1782, Genoa
Died: 27 May 1840, Nice
Type of music: concertos and other works for the violin, pieces for the guitar
Influences: Viotti, Kreutzer and the French school, Duranowski, Locatelli, Rossini, Bellini, Donizetti
Contemporaries: Bernhard Crusell, HUMMEL, FIELD, **PAGANINI**, AUBER, Louis Spohr, WEBER, Henry Bishop, HÉROLD, Carl Czerny

HIS LIFE

The extraordinary fact about Paganini is that, in a concert career of forty-three years, he was forty-five before he played outside Italy and he made his last public appearance only nine years after that. The impact of this brief period was truly astounding.

His father taught him the mandolin and the violin – he would also become a virtuoso on the guitar and viola – and Paganini made his first public appearance when he was eleven. He was only sixteen when he wrote his famous Twenty-four Caprices, which remain to this day a compendium of fiddle technique. So in advance of anything previously written, they seem to have arrived out of the ether. In fact, Paganini was greatly influenced by a now-forgotten violinist, August Duranowski, from whom he later admitted 'many of my most brilliant and popular effects were derived to a considerable extent.' Another influence was the French violinist Rodolphe Kreutzer and also, from a century earlier, the Twenty-four Caprices by Pietro Locatelli; Paganini quotes Locatelli's Caprice No.7 in his own Caprice No.1 as a tribute.

At nineteen, Paganini left home and spent the following eight years in Lucca. Most of the money he earned was lost at gambling. At one concert in Livorno he turned up without an instrument and was loaned a Guarnerius to play by a wealthy amateur. After the gentleman heard Paganini perform, he refused to take it back.

From 1805 he became violinist and, by rumour, lover to Napoleon's sister, Princess Elise, in Lucca and here he developed some of the violinistic 'tricks' that so captivated the audiences and led to his unwarranted reputation in some quarters as a charlatan, and *grande pagliaccio* of the violin. He would enter the stage with just two strings on his violin – the E-string representing a woman and the G-string representing a man – and play 'an amorous scene' between the two. At other times he would cut three strings of the violin 'by accident' and continue to play on just the G-string, a musical feat that demands incredible athleticism and accuracy. One contemporary reviewer wrote: 'In a sense, Paganini is without question the foremost and greatest violinist in the world. His playing is truly *inexplicable*. He performs certain passages, leaps and double stops that have never been heard from any violinist.'

The most enduring relationship in Paganini's life was the four-year liaison with the singer Antonia Bianchi whom he met on tour in northern Italy in 1824. Their son Achille was born in 1825 and although the relationship foundered, Paganini was a devoted father. Achille accompanied him on his travels wherever he went. He died in 1895.

Paganini began his conquest of Vienna, Berlin, Paris and London in 1828. In three years he became the most famous musician alive. People flocked to hear and see him despite the doubling of ticket prices; among them was the young Liszt who vowed to become the 'Paganini of the piano'. On the way he amassed a fortune – enough to give Berlioz 20,000 francs after hearing him conduct a concert of his work and to leave Achille 'nearly half a million dollars'.

By 1834 his health was broken and there was a gradual decline in his powers. He had had all his teeth removed in 1828 and two operations on his jawbone. In 1837 he suffered from laryngeal phthisis (paralysed larynx), which robbed him of his speech. Eventually he could barely swallow. Condemned as a heretic (it was frequently said that he was in league with the devil – how else could those sounds come out of that box?) the church denied him a burial and his body was stored in a cellar for several years. In 1845 the Grand Duchess of Parma authorized the removal of his remains to the Villa Gaione; they were re-interred in Parma cemetery in 1876 and yet again in 1896 in a new cemetery.

Paganini's Guarneri del Gesù violin is preserved in the Museo Municipale in Genoa. His life formed the basis for Lehár's operetta *Paganini* (which starred Richard Tauber and contained the hit 'Girls were made to love and kiss') and for the film *The Magic Bow*, in which Stewart Grainger artfully faked away with the help of clever camera angles.

HIS MUSIC

No other composer or performer of the first two decades of the nineteenth century so mesmerized the public as Paganini; his impact was enormous on the succeeding genera-tion of musicians now loosely called 'the Romantics'. Paganini was the archetypal Romantic: tall, emaciated, with wavy black hair to his shoulders, dressed in black, immobile; a showman, a dare-devil and the greatest violinist who had ever lived. His charisma and technical wizardry introduced virtuosity as an important element of music-making, while his compositions rocketed the instrument to another level.

The fact that so many of Paganini's best-known works are display pieces sometimes disguises his true worth as composer. Although he rarely played the music of other composers, he had a fine musical mind, encouraged Berlioz, the leading avant-garde composer of the day, and played all of Beethoven's string quartets. The Twenty-four Caprices not only revolutionized violin playing but had a similar effect on the piano, too: they led directly to the Op.10 and Op.25 studies of Chopin and Liszt's *Études transcendentales*, as well as inspiring a number of composers to write variations on them; Liszt and Schumann also transcribed some for keyboard.

The remainder of Paganini's music was not published during his lifetime. He jealously guarded his scores, gathering up the handwritten orchestral parts after each performance lest anyone should think of copying his secrets. The six concertos he wrote for the instru-ment can be seen as the synthesis of all the violin's idiosyncratic qualities – dazzling pyrotechnics and expressive *cantabile* – with performance skills calculated to thrill and physically excite an audience. They are also expertly and imaginatively orchestrated, with trombones, timpani, cymbals and bells included in the scores. This and the purely technical innovations he devised, such as left-hand *pizzicato*, ricochet bowing and double-stop harmonics, are masterfully scored in music of drama, energy and passion.

Essential works

Twenty-four Caprices, Op.1 (published 1820): short, unaccompanied studies, each of which tackles a different violinistic problem. Although all are musically attractive, it is best to dip into them. No.24 inspired Brahms' Varia-tions (for piano), Rachmaninov's Rhapsody on a theme of Paganini (for piano and orchestra) and Lutosławski's Variations for two pianos, as well as the less substantial work for cello by Lloyd Webber (*The South Bank Show* theme).

Violin Concerto No.1 in D, Op.6 (1817–18): the bouncing bow and double-stop harmonics feature in the popular last movement; *the* recording to hear is by the tragically short-lived Michael Rabin with the Philharmonic Orchestra and Lovro von Matačić. (*See also* KREISLER.)

Violin Concerto No.2 in B minor, Op.7 (1826): the last movement is nicknamed *La clochette* or *La campanella* in which the soloist imitates a little bell. Liszt wrote a difficult piano version of this piece.

Le streghe (Witches' Dance), Op.8 (1813):

among the most requested of Paganini's recital pieces.

Moto perpetuo Op.11 (after 1830): a non-stop, perpetual motion, whirlwind of notes – 2,248 to be exact – played at the rate of about thirteen a second.

Fantasia on the G string (on a theme from Rossini's *Mosè in Egitto*): literally played on just one string.

I palpiti, Op.13 (Variations on 'Di tanti palpiti' from Rossini's Tancredi) (1819): triplets with double notes, double harmonics and left-hand *pizzicati*, they are all here in this testing piece.

Giovanni da PALESTRINA

'He is the real king of sacred music, and the Eternal Father of Italian Music' (Verdi)

Born: c.1525, Palestrina, near Rome
Died: 2 February 1594, Rome
Original name: Giovanni Pierluigi
Type of music: Latin church music for unaccompanied choir
Influences: music of the Catholic Church, Josquin, the Franco-Flemish school
Contemporaries: Jacobus non Papa, Antonio de Cabezón, **PALESTRINA**, Roland de Lassus, Andrea Gabrieli, Alfonso Ferrabosco, BYRD, Tomás de Victoria

HIS LIFE AND MUSIC

As a boy chorister in Santa Maria Maggiore in Rome, Palestrina's first job was as organist at the cathedral in Palestrina. In 1551 he was back in Rome as *maestro di cappella* of the Julian Chapel, having married and produced two sons in the meantime. After dedicating a book of masses (the first of over one hundred) to Pope Julian III, Palestrina was

rewarded with a place in the papal choir without having to take the usual audition. This caused some annoyance among his fellow choristers, as he was said not to have a good voice. Shortly afterwards the new Pope, Paul V, dismissed Palestrina on the grounds that he was a married man. After a string of appointments and an offer from Emperor Maximilian to be maestro of the court in Vienna – an offer that came to nothing after Palestrina asked for an exorbitant fee – he found himself back in the Julian Chapel as maestro under Pope Gregory XIII, where he remained until his death. In 1580 his wife and sons died from the plague and, in despair, he took the first steps towards entering the priesthood. He was persuaded to do otherwise by the wealthy widow of a furrier and, combining music with his new wife's business and a talent for real estate, he again prospered.

Palestrina was no innovator, nor was he particularly versatile. Berlioz wrote of his madrigals that 'the most frivolous and gallant words are set to exactly the same music as those of the Bible ... the truth is he could not write any other kind of music.' There is little forceful or imaginative expression in his music, which includes over 250 motets, sixty sacred and one hundred secular madrigals, as well as lamentations, psalms, litanies and masses. What he was aiming for – and achieved – was a pure beauty of sound. He is acknowledged as the greatest composer of the Catholic Church and one of the finest masters of classical polyphonic writing: Palestrina is still held up as a model for students.

He was working for the Vatican during the Counter-Reformation when the Roman Church was doing all it could to strike back at the Protestant movement. This called for music that avoided elaborate contrapuntal settings, which tended to obscure the words. Palestrina knew exactly what was wanted – an ethereal cloud of sound to fill St Peter's. It was here, indeed, that he was buried, his coffin bearing the epitaph *Musicae Princeps*.

Essential works

Missa Papae Marcelli (1567): a prime example of the new, pure religious style; Palestrina dedicated this work to Pope Marcellus II, who reigned just 55 days and never heard it.

Missa brevis (1570): for four voices; Palestrina at his most spare and direct.
Missa Assumpta est Maria: considered to be Palestrina's finest setting.
Stabat mater: motet for eight voices.

Hubert PARRY
(1848–1918)

'Jerusalem', choral song (1916)

Parry is hardly a 'One-Hit Wonder'. But that is how he tends to be viewed today. It is ironic that 'Jerusalem' – not only Parry's shortest work, but also one that he allegedly threw into the fire in dissatisfaction (it was rescued by a friend) – should be the only piece by which he is generally remembered. Perhaps Parry felt – as some do now – that its musical triumphalism did not correspond with the inferred subject of Blake's poem: the world of infant factory labour, child chimneysweeps, underpaid farm labourers and men transported for poaching hares. No matter, the setting, suggested to Parry by the then Poet Laureate Robert Bridges, quickly caught on after its first performance at the Queen's Hall, London in 1916. It became the song for the 'Votes For Women' campaign in 1918 and was later taken up by the National Federation of Women's Institutes, besides being an indispensable finale to the BBC Promenade Concert season.

Why has his music all but disappeared? Parry wrote plenty of good music before Elgar made his substantial mark, but was the victim of fashion – his Victorian style and sentiment quickly dated. Recent recordings of his symphonies and orchestral works have revealed what an inspired music-maker he could be – the Symphony No.1 shows how wrong history's judgment has been in at least one instance.

Parry's setting of Milton's 'Blest Pair of Sirens' was the staple fare of choral societies for decades, and no one should miss the elegiac *Six Songs of Farewell* (including 'My soul there is a country' and 'Lord, let me know thine end'). But his choral masterpiece is undoubtedly the anthem *I Was Glad*, the exultant setting of Psalm 122 composed for the coronation of Edward VII (the interpolated cries of 'Vivat Regina Elizabetha' were added, to spine-tingling effect, at the 1953 coronation). Two other notable Parry works are the hymn tunes for 'Praise ye the Lord' and 'Dear Lord and Father of mankind' – but who associates the forgotten composer with them?

The son of an English country gentleman and Eton-educated, Parry became director of the Royal College of Music in 1894, Professor of Music at Oxford in 1897, was knighted the following year and created a baronet five years later. It comes as a surprise, therefore, to learn from his friend, the musicologist Percy Scholes, that 'he was prominent in almost every branch of athletics and constantly ran into every kind of danger that land and water could afford, suffering almost every possible injury short of the immediately fatal.' More importantly, the writer goes on: 'His geniality, generosity, moral character, and artistic ideals had an influence that those who received it hope they may be enabled in some measure to pass on to future generations; indeed, he was everything that is implied by the description "English gentleman".'

The English choral tradition, if nothing else, was safe in Parry's hands, passed from Tallis to Byrd, from Byrd to Gibbons, Gibbons to Purcell, Purcell to Battishall and Greene, on through the Wesleys to Parry, from Parry to Vaughan Williams and Holst; Parry deserves greater recognition for his role in the renaissance of English music.

Arvo PÄRT

Born: 11 September 1935, Paide, Estonia
Type of music: at first serialist, now minimalist; symphony, orchestral (including film scores), cantata, oratorio, chamber, piano
Influences: Schoenberg, Gregorian chant, Renaissance composers, Russian Orthodox Church music
Contemporaries: GÓRECKI, Krzysztof Penderecki, BIRTWISTLE, DAVIES, **PÄRT**, Cornelius Cardew, BENNETT, Steve Reich, Philip Glass, John McCabe

HIS LIFE AND MUSIC

Until 1980, Pärt's music was unknown in the West. Now he is something of a cult with followers as devoted as those of John Tavener and Henryk Górecki, whose music reflects many elements of Pärt's. By the time he emigrated to Vienna and thence to Berlin in 1980, Pärt had already had two distinct careers as a composer: writing in the twelve-note system and experimenting with collage techniques and, while working as a technician for Estonian Radio (1958–67), composing more than fifty film scores.

He finally abandoned these methods and underwent a voluntary period of compositional silence, during which he meditated and studied religion. When he began writing again, his music emerged quite differently: 'I have discovered it is enough when a single note is beautifully played,' he has said. 'This one note, or a moment of silence, comforts me. I work with very few elements – with one voice, with two voices. I build with primitive materials – with the triad, with one specific tonality. The three notes of a triad are like bells. And that is why I call it tintinnabulation.' The result is music of undramatic, uneventful, monk-like simplicity. There is an undoubted spiritual purity behind this hypnotically simple language – Górecki's popular Third Symphony will have prepared you for Pärt if you have not heard his music. Some find it restful and 'the most beautiful sound next to silence'; others fall asleep waiting for something to happen.

Worth investigating

Tabula rasa (1977): the movements *Ludus* and *Silentium* are scored for two solo violins, strings and prepared piano – screws are inserted between the strings; at over fifteen minutes, it is one of Pärt's longer works.

Cantus in memory of Benjamin Britten (1977): Pärt's empathy with the 'unusual purity of [Britten's] music' inspired this tribute for string orchestra and a single bell.
Summa (1978): his most recorded choral work.

Amilcare PONCHIELLI
(1834–86)

Dance of the Hours (from *La Gioconda*),1876

Poor Ponchielli. His career coincided with Verdi's, and, shortly after his death, one of his pupils made quite a name for himself: it was Giacomo Puccini. The son of a shopkeeper, and brought up in poverty near Cremona, he had a tough life, not achieving any real recognition until the last ten years of his career. One of his works remains in the repertoire: his opera *La gioconda* (*The Joyful Girl*). It is an important work because Ponchielli, inspired by Wagner, aimed to make the music more continuous, more suited to the action and with a richer orchestral texture than had been heard previously in Italian opera. Singers are attracted to its dramatic and lyrical *bel canto* roles; it contains the celebrated tenor aria 'Cielo e mar!' (Act 2) and the impassioned 'Suicidio!' from Act 4, for the soprano heroine. Yet the part that everyone knows is the ballet from Act 3. It is a classical hit, featuring in Walt Disney's *Fantasia*, and is the tune to which – can we admit it? – Alan Sherman sang the words 'Hello muddah, hello faddah / Here I am at Camp Granada!' Poor Ponchielli.

Francis POULENC

'Above all do not analyse my music – love it!' (Poulenc)

Born: 7 January 1899, Paris
Died: 30 January 1963, Paris
Full name: Francis Jean Marcel Poulenc
Type of music: opera, ballet, concerto, chamber, choral, vocal, piano
Influences: Schumann, Chabrier, Fauré, Viñes, Satie, Neo-classicism, Stravinsky
Contemporaries: KORNGOLD, GERSHWIN, Roy Harris, **POULENC**, Carlos Chávez, Georges Auric, WEILL, George Antheil, COPLAND, Ernst Krenek

HIS LIFE

One of Poulenc's friends described him as 'moitié moine, moitié voyou' ('half monk, half guttersnipe'), which suits his physical appearance perfectly and goes halfway to describing his music. His face resembled that of the French clown Fernandel and, especially in his early work, Poulenc does seem to have revelled in the role of the clown of French music. This was balanced by the Catholic faith that he was born into, that he lost and finally rediscovered in 1935.

Poulenc's father was a wealthy pharmaceutist; his mother, who came from a family of cabinet-makers, was the music lover, and gave Francis his first piano lessons. In 1916, when he was seventeen, he continued his studies with one of the most respected pianists of the day, the Spaniard Ricardo Viñes, who gave the premieres of many of the works by Ravel and Debussy. Years later, Poulenc admitted, 'I owe him everything … it is really to Viñes that I owe my first flights in music and everything I know about the piano.' It was also in 1916 that he was introduced to the father figure of a young, irreverent group of French composers – Erik Satie. Shortly afterwards, Poulenc's first composition, *Rapsodie nègre,* was published. He rapidly became the centre of the avant-garde circle in Paris and befriended the group of composers who came to be known as Les Six – Auric, Durey, Honegger, Milhaud and Tailleferre (*see* HONEGGER) – aware of his own lack of formal musical training.

After serving in the French army from 1918 to 1921, and composing his popular *Trois mouvements perpétuels* while he was on the Vosges front, he decided to take his musical education a little more seriously, though not too seriously: one of the charms of the music composed by Poulenc is that it is untainted by preconceived ideas and an academic conservatory outlook; you don't come across fugues and counterpoint in his work and, indeed, Poulenc liked nothing better than to cock a snook at the musical establishment.

He embraced the gay social life of 1920s Paris, producing a string of expertly crafted, witty, tuneful scores 'sometimes verging on triviality but never falling into vulgarity', as the critic Roland-Manuel neatly put it. Ballet commissions from Diaghilev, piano pieces of charm and elegance and, especially, songs flowed from his pen. In this latter field, he found his ideal interpreter in the gifted baritone Pierre Bernac. The two men became lifelong companions and, rather like Benjamin Britten and Peter Pears, provided inspiration for each other.

In 1935, Poulenc's religious faith, which had diminished after his father's death in 1917, was revived following a visit to the shrine of Notre-Dame de Rocamadour. While he never abandoned his role as the worldly, *chic* jester, a religious vein recurs throughout the remainder of his music. Among these are the Litanies à la Vierge noire de Rocamadour (Litanies to the Black Virgin of Rocamadour, 1936), the Mass in G (1937), Quatre Motets pour un temps de pénitence (Four Motets for a Time of Penitence, 1939), Exultate Deo and Salve Regina (1941) and the Stabat Mater (1951).

Chamber music of the highest quality was also an important part of Poulenc's output, characterized by the typically-French wit and polish in the handling of woodwind writing. His final works were the Oboe Sonata, which was written in memory of Prokofiev, and the Clarinet Sonata, written in memory of Honegger. Poulenc himself died suddenly in Paris, in the same year that claimed several others from the music world – the pianist Benno Moiseiwitsch, the conductor Fritz Reiner, the soprano Amelita Galli-Curci, Poulenc's sometime collaborator Jean Cocteau and his fellow-composer Paul Hindemith.

HIS MUSIC

Poulenc may have begun as the clown of French music but he has certainly ended up having the last laugh as far as many of his contemporaries are concerned. His works are more widely played than those of Milhaud and Honegger, his two important peers in Les Six. Poulenc has worn well, for all his derivative, lightweight reputation.

The successor to Chabrier's unique brand of Gallic insouience, Poulenc progressed from being an *enfant terrible*, digging fun at older composers and using fashionable neo-classicism, to taking an interest in the way music was developing, without embracing any new -isms or ideologies.

He had a wonderful eye for a good text and an equally fine ear for setting it to music, and many believe his songs are the finest in the language since Fauré. What informs his music above all is his Schubertian gift for melody. Almost every Poulenc piece has something to send you away humming a tune that just will not leave your head – the opening of the *Gloria* or the last part of the Organ Concerto, for instance. The variety of styles adopted within a short framework dazzles the ear – one moment it seems one is listening to a music hall number, the next sweeps the listener up on to some heavenly plateau, basking in the serenity of a touching, fragrant little passage before being thrown to earth with a loud raspberry.

In fact, though Poulenc's music can be fun, underneath all the surface merriment there is undoubtedly an underlying melancholy; Poulenc at heart was a sad and somewhat lonely man. In his music he never stays in the same mood for long, afraid to expose his true feelings and too knowing to overplay the comedy. One of his great strengths was that he knew his limitations; he also knew he was no innovator. He once commented, 'I think there's room for new music which doesn't mind using other peoples' chords.

POULENC

Wasn't that the case with Mozart and Schubert?' The result, despite its narrow range, means that he has as individual a voice as any composer who has written in the twentieth century.

The 1920s and 1930s refused to take Poulenc seriously: at that time, if you were not writing dissonant or atonal or serial music, you were nothing. Some people still have the idea that Teutonic profundity, form and structure is the only worthwhile music. 'When Poulenc has nothing to say, he says it,' opined musicologist David Brew. If you listen to Poulenc, you will discover whether or not you are in this camp.

Essential works

Aubade for piano and eighteen instruments
(1929): a 'choreographic concerto' in which ten brief sections, played without interruption, give the impression of childlike repartee between the soloist and the chamber group, its sharply contrasted moods rapidly shifting from Gallic wit to melancholy.

Concerto in D minor for two pianos (1932):
this has proved to be one of his most frequently played works, quintessential with its charm, wit, engaging tunes (typically two-bar phrases without any development), tongue-in-cheek dissonances and quirky rhythmic effects.

Concerto for organ, strings and percussion in G minor (1938): conceived in the style of a Buxtehude Fantasia, the work was commissioned by the Princess Edmund de Polignac and it is dedicated to her. It is in one continuous movement; it begins with a thunderous opening chord, after which you're never sure whether you're in a church or a variety theatre!

Piano Concerto (1949): spontaneity and individuality are the key to this brilliant and admittedly slight piece, written for a visit to America. The last movement of the concerto quotes the French song 'À la claire fontaine' – or is it 'Way down upon the Swannee River'?

Sextet for Piano and Wind Quintet (1930–32, rev.1939): Poulenc's sophisticated Gallic wit is much in evidence in the three movements, whose moods constantly catch one off-guard.

Clarinet Sonata (1962): in the repertoire of every clarinettist and no wonder: it is not only a workout for the two players but the central movement is one of Poulenc's loveliest ... before the fire-eating finale.

Trois mouvements perpétuels (1918): the first of these is instantly recognizable, especially to those of a certain age who grew up to *Listen With Mother*.

Les soirées de Nazelles (1930–36): little known and, for some reason, detested by Poulenc himself, these eight variations (small pastel sketches) contain some of his finest keyboard writing. They were improvized at a country house in Nazelles and written down as a souvenir of pleasant evenings in the country with friends round the piano.

L'histoire de Babar (Babar the Elephant) (1940–45): with a story by Jean de Brunhoff, this children's tale has continued to charm generations of youngsters; the music is catchy and tuneful but makes no concessions. It is usually performed by a TV personality and is thus rarely heard at its best; there is also an orchestral version, by Jean Françaix, but this is not as piquant as the original piano version.

Vocal

La Voix humaine (The Human Voice), lyric tragedy in one act (1958): an opera with a single character — a 'phone call, forty-five minutes long, by a woman bidding farewell to her ex-lover.

Gloria (1959): for soprano, chorus and orchestra; this uplifting and deeply felt work, a mixture of celebration and prayer, will haunt you for days.

Of Poulenc's nearly 200 songs, containing some of his finest music, the collections to experience first could be:

Le bestiaire (The Bestiary) (1919): six settings of poems by Poulenc's favourite writer, Guillaume Apollinaire.

Chanson gaillardes (1926): eight songs with texts written by anonymous seventeenth-century writers.

Fiançailles pour rire (1939): six songs with words by Vilmorin.

Banalités (1940): a further five settings of works by Apollinaire.

Chansons villageoises (1942): texts by Fombeure.

Deux poèmes (1943): words by Louis Aragon; the first is called simply 'C' and is one of Poulenc's best.

Also worth investigating

Stabat mater (1950)

Les biches, ballet (1923): notable especially for its 'hits' – the Adagietto and Rondeau; Poulenc's first big success, a commission from Diaghilev for his Ballets Russes.

Concert champêtre for harpsichord and orchestra (1928): written for the great harpsichordist Wanda Landowska.

Trio for oboe, bassoon and piano (1926)

Pastourelle: piano arrangement from the ballet *L'éventail de Jeanne*, by various composers.

L'embarquement pour Cythère (1951): 'valse-musette', a short encore piece for two pianos.

Sergei PROKOFIEV

'I abhor imitation and I abhor the familiar' (Prokofiev)

Born: 27 April 1891, Sontzovka, near Ekaterinoslav (Ukraine)
Died: 5 March 1953, Moscow
Type of music: symphony, orchestral, incidental, concerto, opera, ballet, choral, film, chamber, piano, vocal
Influences: Russian School, Stravinsky, Les Six
Contemporaries: Bohuslav Martinů, Jacques Ibert, Frank Martin, **PROKOFIEV**, Sir Arthur Bliss, HONEGGER, Ferde Grofé, Herbert Howells, MILHAUD

HIS LIFE

Prokofiev died on the same day as Stalin. Apart from the final years of his life, he managed – not totally but more successfully than the other great Russian composers living under the dictatorship – to maintain his musical ideals.

He was a brilliant student. By the age of thirteen, when he entered the St Petersburg Conservatory, he was already a good pianist and had produced an opera (aged nine), an overture and other works. He had the best teachers, including Glière, Liadov and Rimsky-Korsakov (who was still on the staff as professor of composition). Anna Essipova, who had been married to one of the most acclaimed piano teachers of the nineteenth century, Theodor Leschetizky, taught Prokofiev piano. Such a precocious, blazing talent

inevitably rebelled against the stifling conservatism that confronted him. Like Shostakovich and Britten, his style seemed to be pre-formed and completely original; it remained constant for his entire creative life. Even before graduation, he caused a stir in musical circles with some of his compositions – the First Piano Concerto was controversial with its violent keyboard gymnastics, unexpected harmonic and melodic twists and angular rhythms. Before he was twenty, he was famous. But Prokofiev was no *Wunderkind* who burns out after initial brilliance.

In 1918 he left Russia and travelled through Siberia to Japan and America, giving concerts of his own music, and in 1920 he arrived in Paris. Here, he met another ex-patriot, Sergei Diaghilev, who commissioned three ballets from him – *Chout*, *Le pas d'acier* and *L'enfant prodigue*. Further commissions came from his publisher, Sergei Koussevitzky, and in 1921 he visited America again for the premiere of his opera *The Love for Three Oranges*.

After returning to Russia in 1927, where he was greeted as a celebrity, Prokofiev flitted between his mother country, Paris and other European cities before deciding in 1932 to settle in Russia for good. Quite why he did this is open to question. Surely he knew to what political pressures artists were subjected. Stravinsky stated that it was because Prokofiev was politically naïve and also because he had not met with much success in America: Prokofiev's return to Russia, he said, was 'a sacrifice to the bitch goddess'. Why did he not live and work abroad in peace, like Stravinsky and Rachmaninov? Perhaps he thought he was famous enough to be treated differently by the authorities. In this he was sadly mistaken and, after an initial period of co-habitation, the authorities and Prokofiev were at loggerheads. Nevertheless, some of his finest music was written in the 1930s and during the war years, despite increasing ill-health and the break-up in 1941 of his marriage after an affair with a 25-year old student, Mira Mendelson.

When the Central Committee of the Communist Party denounced Prokofiev, Shostakovich and others for 'formalism' – music that had no immediate function and did not extol the virtues of the Stalinist regime – a humiliating public apology appeared: 'We are tremendously grateful to the Central Committee of the All-Union Communist Party and personally to you, dear Comrade Stalin, for the severe but profoundly just criticism of the present state of Soviet music…. We shall bend every effort to apply our knowledge and our artistic mastery to produce vivid, realistic music reflecting the life and struggles of the Soviet people.'

Thereafter, in the few years left to him, Prokofiev churned out inconsequential scores, the equivalent of the paintings of tractors and chemical works that Soviet artists were executing.

HIS MUSIC

Writing of Prokofiev's music, the critic Stephen Walsh summarized: 'Twentieth-century music has been so full of attitudes, so self-conscious, so often a vehicle for ideas, feelings and manifestos which themselves have nothing to do with music, that it is peculiarly refreshing and reassuring to come back to a composer who wrote music simply out of an instinctive and irrepressible feeling for that medium.'

Prokofiev is one of the most performed of all twentieth-century composers; some pieces such as *The Montagues and Capulets* from *Romeo and Juliet* have achieved the status of classical 'pops', while others, such as the Third Piano Concerto, the *Lieutenant Kijé* suite and the 'Classical' Symphony, are central repertoire works.

Prokofiev was the dominant force among domiciled Russian composers during the thirties and forties. Shostakovich, Khachaturian and the awful Tikhon Khrennikov, a Stalin apologist, all borrowed from Prokofiev and all kowtowed to officialdom. The 1948 denunciation excepted – life itself would not have been possible had he not conformed – Prokofiev was admirably obstinate in his determination to write the music *he* wanted.

His voice is unmistakable after a few bars. His novel harmonic and melodic ideas are quite idiosyncratic: perhaps he'll begin with a banal little tune and then suddenly have it leap up an unexpected interval; he uses orthodox chords in unorthodox relations and, equally markedly, he is witty – not in the elegant French way, but ironic and sardonic (though many of his early works are self-consciously cocking a snook at traditions in much the same way that Les Six were to do). Some of the music is intentionally dissonant and aggressive – at times it is physically violent to perform – but it never abandons tonality completely, for, despite the effects and shock tactics, he remains a pupil of Rimsky-Korsakov, in a chain that links him to Mussorgsky, Tchaikowsky and Balakirev, singing the songs of old Russia in his own modern dress. Underneath he's an old softy.

Essential works

'Classical' Symphony, Op.25 (1917): one of Prokofiev's most popular works; a delightful pastiche of the classical symphonies of Mozart and Haydn but with Prokofiev's own piquant harmonies, quirky, hummable themes and masterly economy of writing. An easy and enjoyable introduction to twentieth-century music. How strange that such an infectious, bright piece should have been composed during the Russian Revolution.

The Love for Three Oranges, Op.33, opera (1919): not an easy listen and the nonsensical libretto would take pages to elucidate – it is one to catch in the theatre for it to make its full

impact – but the March and the Scherzo have become concert favourites.

Lieutenant Kijé, Op.60, symphonic suite (1934): this was the first music Prokofiev wrote after returning to Russia. Composed for a film of the same name, it is a comedy revolving round the deeds of the mythical Kijé; the music matches the story's satirical vein. Especially well known (and played to distraction every Christmas) is the Troika ('Sleighride').

Romeo and Juliet, Op.65 (1935): the music for the ballet (based on Shakespeare's play) became popular only after the appearance of three orchestral suites based on the score; the second is the most successful, opening with the strutting *Montagues and Capulets*, sometimes called *The March of the Nobles*.

Piano Concerto No.3, Op.26 (1921): the most frequently played of the Prokofiev concertos and among the most popular of the twentieth century. The solo part is particularly brilliant, with the strongly percussive element so characteristic of Prokofiev's piano music much in evidence, but not without a stream of lyrical themes. The composer made a revealing recording of the work, although the sound is less than ideal. There are four other Piano Concertos, and No.1 (which caused such a stir when he was a student) is well worth trying next; the fourth was written for the one-armed pianist Paul Wittgenstein (who never played it – too difficult!), for the left hand alone.

Violin Concerto No.2 in G minor, Op.63 (1935): the slow movement is one of Prokofiev's loveliest creations, the concerto itself among the finest written this century; it is full of unforgettable melodies – very Russian in atmosphere – with an exciting finale of incisive and impulsive rhythms typical of Prokofiev.

Peter and the Wolf, Op.67 (1936): 'symphonic fairy tale for narrator and orchestra' is the subtitle for this evergreen entertainment, written to teach children the different sounds of the instruments of the orchestra: the cat is the clarinet, the duck portrayed by the oboe, the wolf by three French horns and Peter by a string quartet. Everyone from Sir Ralph Richardson to Richard Baker and from Sting to Angela Rippon have had a crack at the narration – with varying degrees of success.

Piano Sonatas Nos.6, 7 & 8, Opp. 82–84 (1939–44): of Prokofiev's nine piano sonatas, these three, sometimes known as the 'War' Sonatas, are the best and most often played. No.6 in A is the longest and most demanding of all nine, tonal but with a bitter, dissonant flavour; No.7 in B flat is wiry and athletic – Sviatoslav Richter's performance of this and, indeed, the other two sonatas, captures the full impact; No.8 in B flat has a surprisingly lyrical opening, contrasted with a motor-driven finale.

Symphony No.5, Op.100 (1944): like the sonatas, the symphonies should not be heard one after the other: they are not all immediately accessible and together they could prove, let us say, 'emotionally draining'. The Fifth Symphony is probably the best of the seven – composed within a single month in the summer of 1944 – and its Adagio is one of compelling emotional intensity.

Giacomo PUCCINI

'I shall feel it as an Italian, with desperate passion'
(Puccini talking of Manon Lescaut)

Born: 22 December 1858, Lucca
Died: 29 November 1924, Brussels
Full name: Giacomo Antonio Domenico Michele Secondo Maria Puccini
Type of music: opera
Influences: Verdi, Wagner, Debussy, Richard Strauss and Stravinsky
Contemporaries: ELGAR, LEONCAVALLO, Cécile Chaminade, **PUCCINI**, Dame Ethel Smyth, Sergei Liapunov, Mikhail Ippolitov-Ivanov, WOLF

HIS LIFE

As a child Puccini showed little enthusiasm for music, a reversal of the usual scenario of someone born into a musical family. The fifth of seven children, he was the fifth and, as it turned out, the last generation of a dynasty of Italian musicians: his great-great grandfather Giacomo, his great-grandfather Antonio, his grandfather Domenico and his father Michele all had positions as organists and church composers in Lucca.

Puccini's mother was determined that her son should continue the family tradition and sent him to the Instituto Musicale in Lucca, where his teacher, Carlo Angeloni, fired up the boy's passion for music. Before long, he was playing the piano and organ like a good Puccini was expected to. But it was a visit to Pisa in 1876 to see a production of *Aida* that had a revelatory effect on him: from that time forward he was determined to follow in Verdi's footsteps.

First, though, he rounded off his studies in Lucca by composing a mass. Then he went to the Conservatory in Milan, assisted by funds from a great-uncle and a stipend from Queen Margherita, for serious study with Antonio Bazzini (now remembered for his dazzling violin piece *La ronde des lutins*) and Amilcare Ponchielli, famed as the composer of the opera *La gioconda*. In 1883, the publisher Edoardo Sonzogno announced the first of a series of competitions for a one-act opera (Mascagni's *Cavalleria rusticana* was to win the 1889 competition). Puccini, encouraged by Ponchielli, wrote a work with a young journalist, Ferdinando Fontana. This was *Le villi*, a story that used the fashionable operatic theme of deserted lovers changing themselves into spectres and dancing the loved one to death. It was written within a few weeks and was not even mentioned when the prizes were announced in 1884. However, at a party soon afterwards in company with Arrigo Boito, the librettist and composer, and other influential people in the musical world, Puccini was asked to sing extracts from *Le villi*. The direct result was a production of the work at the Teatro dal Verme in May 1884. It was an immediate triumph, the great Italian publishing house of Ricordi snapped up the rights and commissioned Puccini to write another. He remained with the firm for the rest of his career.

Five years passed before he completed this next opera, *Edgar*. It was a failure, one of only two that he experienced. Puccini admitted it was 'a blunder' but during this time he began his affair with Elvira Gemignani. Being married in Catholic Italy meant that divorce from Elvira's merchant husband was impossible. Nevertheless, she bore Puccini an only son in 1886, and it was not until 1904, after Elvira's husband died, that the couple could marry. Meanwhile, Puccini had been searching for a good librettist. His choice was a disaster. The subject he had selected was a cheeky and daring one in the circumstances for he decided to write an opera based on the same story, *Manon Lescaut*, as that with which Massenet had had a huge success only nine years earlier (*Manon*, 1884). The original libretto by Domenico Oliva was entirely rewritten by Puccini and Giulio Ricordi, with contributions from Leoncavallo, Marco Praga, Luigi Illica and Giuseppe Giacosa. In the final score of *Manon Lescaut*, no librettist is credited, a unique curiosity in the annals of opera. Paradoxically, the work provided Puccini with unprecedented success. It is the opera in which he discovered his own musical voice and which made his name internationally famous. George Bernard Shaw, then a music critic, remarked pertinently that 'Puccini looks to me more like the heir of Verdi than any of his rivals.'

With his next opera, *La bohème*, Puccini confirmed that prediction, although initial reaction was far cooler than the enthusiastic welcome accorded to *Manon Lescaut*; in fact, no first night of a Puccini opera ever approached that of his first great composition. *La bohème* was more conversational in style, more grittily real, and the orchestral score was more impressionistic. The conductor for the premiere was the young Arturo Toscanini, just beginning to make a name for himself (his broadcast performance of the work was captured in 1946). Within a short time the opera had been produced all over the world; it is still regarded by many as Puccini's supreme masterpiece.

With fame came wealth, and in 1900 he built a fabulous villa in the village of Torre del Lago by the lake of Massaciuccoli near Florence – he'd been living in the area since 1892 – and began work on his next project. It was based on Victorien Sardou's 1887 play

La Tosca. Using the same team from *La bohème* – librettists Luigi Illica and Giuseppe Giacosa – Puccini completed the work in 1893. Now one of the best loved of all operas with some of the most celebrated arias, *Tosca* divided the critics. It was Puccini's first excursion into the world of operatic *verismo*, a movement that had been initiated by Bizet's *Carmen* and was epitomized in Leoncavallo's *Pagliacci* and Mascagni's *Cavalleria rusticana*. Shaw referred to Sardou's melodramas as 'Sardoodledom', describing the original play as 'a cheap shocker'. The remark was copied fifty years later by the American critic Joseph Kerman, when he described Puccini's opera as 'that shabby little shocker' – which just goes to prove that one must never trust the judgment of critics.

Four years after the premiere of *Tosca* came the last in this remarkable trilogy written by the same three men, *Madama Butterfly*. It took its plot from a play by David Belasco, itself based on a magazine article by John Luther Long, which in turn was based on a real incident. Puccini once more went to great pains not to repeat himself musically, and created an exotic atmosphere for his setting, using authentic Japanese folk tunes in the score. The first performance, in March 1904, was a fiasco orchestrated by Puccini's rivals, but after many cuts and revisions it was re-presented two months later at Brescia, where it triumphed.

Puccini described himself as 'a mighty hunter of wild fowl, opera libretto and attractive women' – one of the reasons for living in Torre del Lago was so that he could indulge in his addiction to shooting wild ducks and other game birds. He could also have said that he liked fast cars, fast boats and fast women. The older he became, the more attractive he grew to women: tall, a dandy when it came to clothes, aristocratic in looks and bearing, with a carefully trimmed moustache and dark, heavily lidded eyes. He had numerous affairs and, as Puccini's biographer Mosco Carner points out, it is interesting to note that seven of his twelve stage works are named after the opera's heroine and that 'he treats them with a most subtly calculated mixture of true affection and refined sadism, possibly traced to primitive drives and fantasies in his unconscious.' After Puccini and Elvira Gemignani were married in 1904, what had been a passionate relationship soured into one of frequent and violent quarrels. They employed a servant, Doria Manfredi, at the villa. Elvira became convinced that Puccini was having an affair with Doria and went mad with jealousy. Her public accusations and harassment of the girl eventually drove Doria to kill herself by taking poison; the autopsy revealed that she was still a virgin. Puccini fled to a hotel in Rome and remained there for days, weeping, it is said. Elvira was sentenced to five months in prison.

Another Belasco play, *La fanciulla del West (The Golden Girl of the West)*, furnished Puccini with the material for his next venture in the unlikely operatic setting of the 1849 Californian gold rush. It had an American premiere in 1910, with Toscanini conducting and Caruso starring as the hero Dick Johnson, but although it has many fine moments and is liked by the public, it has never caught on in the same way as the previous three operas. His next work, *La rondine*, was Puccini's second professional failure, which perhaps can be attributed to its uneasy mix of opera and operetta. Challenging himself once more, Puccini then conceived the idea of an evening of three one-act operas; *Il trittico (The Triptych)* is made up of *Il tabarro (The Cloak)*, *Suor Angelica (Sister Angelica)* and the comedy *Gianni Schicchi*; the latter is by far the best of the three.

Puccini's final opera presented even greater self-imposed challenges. He was a shrewd operator and kept abreast of all the latest musical developments, so that *Turandot*, with its setting of Peking in ancient times, incorporates contemporary music techniques not normally associated with Puccini. It was an adventurous work, and the last opera written in the twentieth century to have entered the standard repertoire *and* remain beloved by the public at large.

The composer never finished the score – the last two scenes were completed from sketches by Franco Alfano. Puccini died aged sixty-five from a heart attack while undergoing treatment for cancer of the larynx.

HIS MUSIC

Of the four most frequently played pieces of music on Classic fM, two are by Puccini –
'O mio babbino caro' from *Gianni Schicchi* and 'Vissi d'arte' from *Tosca*; among listeners'
requests, the fourth most popular number is 'Che gelida manina' from *La bohème*. If one
item of classical music is more responsible than any other for the current wave of enthusiasm for opera, then it is 'Nessun dorma' from *Turandot*. Few classical composers can
claim to have had their music played on jukeboxes, and few opera houses have a season
that does not include at least one of Puccini's operas. In other words, Puccini straddles
popular and classical tastes in music, guaranteeing ticket sales the world over. It is a
strange coincidence that many of his best known arias fit so neatly on to one side of a 78-
r.p.m. disc – the first great composer to benefit from the four-minute musical sound-bite.

Arnold Schoenberg (who else?) remarked that 'there are higher and lower means,
artistic and inartistic .... Realistic, violent incidents – as for example the torture scene in
Tosca – which are unfailingly effective, should not be used by an artist, because they are
too cheap, too accessible to everybody.' Benjamin Britten was once asked by Shostakovich
what he thought of Puccini's operas. 'I think his operas are dreadful,' replied Britten.
'No, Ben, you are wrong,' riposted Shostakovich. 'He wrote marvellous operas, but
dreadful music.' Yet ironically, the public would willingly exchange all the operas of
Britten and Shostakovich for one *La bohème*. It is true that Puccini's music is highly
charged, and as a manipulator of audience emotion, he was second to none – but that is
a large part of what theatre is about. Many putative opera composers die without
realizing it.

As a composer, Puccini belonged to no school and led to no others. Verdi is his most
obvious role model, but he absorbed elements of Wagner, Debussy and even, later on,
Stravinsky. Whatever atmosphere he wanted to create, be it ancient China or contemporary Japan, the sound is instantly and uniquely Puccini's, with its opulent yet clear-cut
orchestration and miraculous fund of melodies with their bittersweet, tender lyricism.
Regardless of the harmonic or orchestral novelties he introduced – and his incomparable abilities as an orchestrator are often overlooked – he was adroit enough to take his
public with him: the jump from *Manon Lescaut* to *Turandot* is quite a big one. He was
an inspired craftsman who was also adventurous and skilful enough to seek fresh
challenges in each new work. In 1922 he wrote of the then current state of opera as he
saw it: 'By now the public for new music has lost its palate. It loves or puts up with
illogical music devoid of all sense. Melody is no longer practised – or, if it is, it is vulgar.
People believe the symphonic element must rule, and I, instead, believe this is the end
of opera.' It is a view that may fall on sympathetic ears today.

It was not only as a musician that Puccini's contribution to opera was significant – his
instinct for the theatre was almost infallible. He drove his librettists frantic as he strove
to achieve the dramatic effects he knew were needed. He spent large amounts of time
seeking out the right subject, researching and checking every aspect of its authenticity,
its psychological and historical accuracy. Poignancy and believable human characters are
a constant in all his operas. The canvases may be smaller than those of Wagner and Verdi
but the emotions are no less intense and involving. And intricately linked to this is the
masterly writing for the voice, the string of roles that have attracted the world's greatest
singers, guaranteeing that Puccini's operas will be around for many more years for us to
wallow in.

Essential works

Manon Lescaut (1893): based on the novel
*L'Histoire du Chevalier des Grieux et de Manon
Lescaut* by Abbé Provost, Puccini's first mature
opera was the third to use the story, preceded
by Auber's in 1856 and Massenet's in 1884.
Puccini follows the novel more closely than
Massenet, in four relatively disjointed scenes
set in eighteenth-century Amiens, Paris, Le
Havre and Louisiana. Listen out especially for
Manon's beautiful aria from Act 2 'In quelle
trine morbide' ('In this gilded cage') – one of
Puccini's finest arias – and her 'L'ora o Tirsi, è

vaga e bella' ('These are hours of joy's creating'), ending on a *pianissimo* top C.

La bohème (1896): many have become hooked on opera by being taken to see *La bohème* – it is a marvellous introduction to the whole experience, with some of music's best-known arias and a touching tale of doomed love. There is high passion, drama and heart-rending lyricism: you have to be pretty hard of heart not to respond to Puccini's sumptuous score. Rodolfo's Act 1 'Che gelida manina' ('Your tiny hand is frozen' – known in the trade as 'You're tiny – and it's frozen') must be one of the most popular of all tenor arias, while Mimi's answering 'Si, mi chiamano Mimi' ('Yes, they call me Mimi') is hardly less well loved. Then there's 'Quando me 'n vo' ('When I am out walking') known as *Musetta's Waltz Song* and the melting quartet from Act 3 'Addio, dolce svegliare'. Buy the recording with Jussi Björling and Victoria de los Angeles, conducted by Beecham.

Tosca (1900): the counterpart of *La bohème*, for while the music is no less ardent and lyrical, the love interest is sombre and tragic. The painter, Cavaradossi, is one of *the* tenor roles, Tosca has a rewarding soprano role, and Scarpia, the chief of police and an unusually believable villain, provides great acting opportunities for the baritone. Three arias stand out in this opera: 'Recondita armonia' ('Strange harmony') from Act 1, where Cavaradossi sings to the miniature he holds of Tosca; 'Vissi d'arte' ('I have lived for art'), Tosca's outpouring in Act 2 when she is confronted with the possibility of having to surrender herself to Scarpia; and 'E lucevan le stelle' ('Stars were shining'), Cavaradossi's farewell in which he recalls his meetings with Tosca on starlit nights. Of the many fine record-ings made of the work, essential listening is that by Callas, di Stefano and Gobbi, conducted by De Sabata.

Madama Butterfly (1904): Puccini came to London in 1900 and saw a production of Belasco's play of the same title. Although he didn't understand a word of it, apparently, he was so deeply moved by what he saw that, according to the colourful but unreliable memoirs of Belasco, Puccini embraced the author and, with tears in his eyes, begged him for the rights to it. Belasco agreed at once and Puccini started to work on it in the autumn of 1901. He himself felt that the opera was 'the most felt and most expressive opera that I have conceived' and it was his personal favourite. The story is about the young geisha Cio-Cio San and her love for Lieutenant Pinkerton of the US Navy. It is a heartbreaker and contains such wonderful music as 'Dolce notte' ('Sweet Night'), the exquisite love duet

that comes at the end of Act 1; 'Un bel dí vedremo' ('Some day he'll come', or 'One Fine Day' as it is usually called), one of the most popular soprano solos in all opera; 'Tutti I fior', known as the *Flower Duet*; and the Intermezzo between Acts 2 and 3, known as the *Humming Chorus*.

Turandot (completed 1926): there had been at least ten other operas on this subject written in the previous century, none of which had made any impression; even Busoni's 1917 *Turandot* did not dissuade Puccini from using the fairy tale in which Turandot, the bewitching daughter of the Chinese emperor, promises to marry any man of royal blood who can answer three riddles; he who fails to answer correctly is put to death. Those expecting the sound of *La bohème* and *Tosca* are in for a surprise, for here Puccini employs features from contempo-rary music, with dissonance and polytonal vocal and orchestral passages, and the result is, arguably, Puccini's most powerful dramatic work.

The opera combines the heroic, the comic and the lyrical in equal measure. Its two most celebrated passages are Turandot's spine-tingling account of how one of her forebears had been abducted – 'In questa reggia' ('In this same palace') – special mention should be made here of Dame Eva Turner's historic recording of the aria made in 1929; and the ubiquitous 'Nessun dorma' ('None shall sleep') from Act 3, in which Calaf, who has answered the riddles correctly, relishes the moment when he will win Turandot's hand. 'Nessun dorma' has now become Pavarotti's theme song, but his versions should be compared with those of Beniamino Gigli or Jussi Björling. All of them hold on to the penultimate note (a high B natural – 'vin-cer'-o!') to thrilling effect, although Puccini wrote it as a short (semiqua-ver) note. Who can blame them?

Also worth investigating

La fanciulla del West (The Golden Girl of the West) (1910): another Puccini opera based on a play written by Belasco. This one is set during the time of the California gold rush and tells of the love of Minnie, the owner of a saloon, for Dick Johnson who, in reality, is the notorious bandit Ramerrez.

Gianni Schicchi (1918): part three of *Il trittico*, a one-act opera set in Florence in 1299, showing that Puccini could be a dab hand at comedy when he chose; the hit aria is 'O mio babbino caro' ('O my beloved father'), which was given a new lease of life by its use in the Merchant-Ivory film *A Room with a View*.

Messa di Gloria (1880): this was a student work and is an uneven one, but the central section, the *Gloria,* is tremendous.

Henry PURCELL

'The Orpheus Britannicus'

Born: 1659, London
Died: 21 November 1695, Westminster, London
Type of music: opera, stage and incidental, vocal, keyboard
Influences: Cooke, Humphrey, Blow, French and Italian schools
Contemporaries: Agostino Steffani, Michel-Richard Delalande, **PURCELL**,
Alessandro Scarlatti, Tommaso Vitali, Johann Pepusch, COUPERIN

HIS LIFE

Many regard Purcell as the greatest English composer of all time. That is arguable, but considering his importance in the history of British music, it is ironic that so little is known about his short life. There is even some dispute as to who his father was: Henry or his brother Thomas Purcell. Both were singers in the Chapel Royal and thus in the musical service of Charles II.

Young Purcell's rise to fame was precocious: at fifteen he was a mere 'organ tuner'– in other words, he pumped the bellows; at eighteen he was composer to the king's private band, at twenty he was organist of Westminster Abbey. Thereafter he was one of the busiest men in England, and one of the best known, for he composed music of such variety and for so many different occasions that wherever there was music, from lewd drinking songs to ceremonial odes, from opera and incidental theatre music to chamber works, dances and anthems, there was also the name Purcell.

Five days after his death, he was buried in Westminster Abbey. The music he had composed the previous year for Queen Mary's funeral was played at his own service. His epitaph reads: 'Here lies Henry Purcell Esquire, who left life and is gone to that blessed place where only his harmony can be exceeded.'

HIS MUSIC

In 1690, John Dryden dedicated his play *Amphitryon* to Purcell 'in whose person we have at length found an Englishman equal with the best abroad'; Purcell's friend Roger North said that 'a greater musical genius England never had.' 'Genius' is an over-used term, especially of those who die young, so what exactly is it that makes it an appropriate description? His diversity and tremendous technical accomplishment in every area of the art of music would alone merit the label, but it is confirmed in his individual handling of the material and the certainty of an original voice that combines the best Italian and French traditions of harmony and drama with his own heritage of English church music and folk song.

Purcell's 'royal music', written for Charles II, James II and Queen Mary, includes Welcome Songs and odes for birthdays and St Cecilia's Day, as well as the powerful and noble anthems that strongly influenced Handel. There are trio sonatas written in the contemporary style and other chamber works in which he uses the polyphonic style of the old masters – his *Fantasy Upon One Note* is a famous example of this: four strings weave their melodies round a fifth viol, which plays nothing but the note middle C. Purcell's *Lessons* or suites are collections of marches, airs and minuets, in which his favourite ploy is to write variations of a tune played over a repeated or ground bass line. One of his most loved arias, the heart-breaking 'Dido's Lament' from *Dido and Aeneas*, uses the same device.

Purcell had a unique ability to set English words with more sensitivity and facility than any previous composer. His melodies can be flowery and embellished or direct and simple, but he knew instinctively how to capture the cadences peculiar to English verse in an imaginative and dramatic way. An example is in the famous Frost Scene from his semi-opera *King Arthur*, where he indicates the bass should sing with a shiver on every note; such a device might sound obvious now, over three hundred years later, but it was daringly original then.

Purcell was at his best in his music for the theatre. *Dido and Aeneas* was his first and only opera, a masterpiece written in 1689 for the 'young gentlewomen' of a fashionable girls' school in Chelsea, and the earliest English opera still regularly staged. His other work for the theatre comprises instrumental music and songs for plays, masques and semi-operas such as *The Fairy Queen*, *The Indian Queen*, *King Arthur* and *The Tempest*, seldom heard nowadays; the music is glorious but the plays are unrevivable and the texts usually poor. The best way to get to know Purcell's theatre music is through recordings.

Essential works

Dido and Aeneas, opera (1689): especially the Overture and 'When I am laid in earth', known as 'Dido's Lament'

The Fairy Queen, semi-opera (1692): particularly 'Hark! the echoing air'

King Arthur, semi-opera (1691): especially the Frost Scene from Act 3 and 'Fairest Isle'

Laudate Ceciliam (Ode for St Cecilia's Day) (1683)

Funeral music for Queen Mary (1695)

Come ye sons of art, away (Ode for the birthday of Queen Mary II (1694)

'I was glad when they said unto me', anthem (1685): compare this with Parry's setting for the coronation of Edward VII.

Te Deum and Jubilate in D (1694)

Tell me, some pitying angel (or The Blessed Virgin's expostulation) (1693)

Chaconne in G minor for strings

Fantasia in F (Upon One Note) for five viols (c.1680)

Sonata for Trumpet and Strings No.1 in D (c.1694)

Trumpet Tune and Air in D: not the Trumpet Voluntary entitled *The Prince of Denmark's March*, often attributed to Purcell but in fact composed by Jeremiah Clarke.

Music from **Abdelazar** (1695): includes the famous Rondeau on which Britten based his *Young Person's Guide To The Orchestra*.

Music from **The Libertine** (c.1692): includes 'Nymphs and Shepherds', made famous in a million-selling but stylistically anachronistic recording by the Manchester Schoolchildren's Choir in 1929 with the Hallé Orchestra and Sir Hamilton Harty.

Sergei RACHMANINOV

'How can I compose without Melody?'
(Rachmaninov, when asked in 1924 why he was not composing)

Born: 1 April 1873, Oneg, district of Novgorod
Died: 28 March 1943, Beverly Hills, California
Type of music: symphony, orchestral, opera, choral, concerto, chamber, piano, vocal
Influences: Schumann, Chopin, Henselt, Liszt, Tchaikowsky, Borodin, Godowsky
Contemporaries: Hugo Alfvén, Max Reger, **RACHMANINOV**, Joseph Jongen, HOLST, Reynaldo Hahn, SCHOENBERG, IVES

HIS LIFE

'I try to make my music speak simply and directly that which is in my heart at the time I am composing. If there is love there, or bitterness, or sadness, or religion, these moods become part of my music, and it becomes either beautiful, or bitter, or sad, or religious. For composing music is as much a part of my living as breathing and eating. I compose music because I must give expression to my feelings, just as I talk because I must give utterance to my thoughts,' wrote Rachmaninov.

Few musicians have successfully followed two musical disciplines with equal success, but Rachmaninov managed three: composer, conductor and pianist. The music came from his father, its nurture from his mother. His grandfather had been a good amateur pianist and a pupil of John Field; Rachmaninov's aristocratic and expensively amorous father Vassili was also a pianist. For many landowning families, times were hard in the 1870s and, when Rachmaninov was nine, the estate was sold, his parents separated, and he went with his mother and five siblings to live in St Petersburg. With such a background, music would have been closed to him as a profession. Now, without property or income, he was free to embark seriously on the study of music, for he had clearly inherited the family talent for the piano.

After a couple of years at the St Petersburg Conservatory, Rachmaninov entered the Moscow Conservatory in 1885 on the advice of his cousin, the pianist Alexander Siloti. Under the strict regime of Zverev, he quickly developed into a formidable player. He studied composition with Taneiev and Arensky, Tchaikowsky took an interest in the young man's work and, by the age of nineteen, he had written his First Piano Concerto and the group of *Five Pieces*, Op.3 (dedicated to Arensky); these include the celebrated Prelude in C sharp minor, one of the most popular of all piano compositions. He found a publisher, his one-act opera *Aleko* made a considerable impression at its premiere in 1893 and he won the Great Gold Medal for the piano when he graduated; altogether an impressive start to a career.

Then came a profound setback. For two years he worked on the composition of his First Symphony. The premiere was a disaster: the piece was derided by the critics and the performance was a fiasco, poorly conducted by Glazunov, rumoured to be drunk. The 23-year-old composer destroyed the score denouncing it as 'weak, childish, strained and bombastic'. (Although the orchestral parts were preserved, the work was not heard again until 1945.) This humiliation prompted a period of severe self doubt and depression. His confidence was boosted by an invitation to appear in London as conductor, composer and soloist; his tone-poem *The Rock* was given and the by now inevitable C sharp minor Prelude; but when he returned to Moscow and tried to complete a second piano Concerto, his depression returned.

Rachmaninov consulted a psychologist, Dr Dahl, and after a course of 'positive suggestion therapy' (hypnosis), during which Dahl insisted that Rachmaninov would 'start writing, and the work will be excellent', the composer indeed was able to complete the Second Piano Concerto. It bears the dedication 'To Monsieur N. Dahl', the only time a piece of music has been dedicated to a hypnotist. The concerto has become the most popular of the genre written this century. It formed the model for countless lesser works for piano and orchestra, and the affection in which it is held remains undiminished.

The premiere under Siloti was in 1901; another relation was now to play an important part in Rachmaninov's life – he married his cousin Natalie Satina in 1902. During the following few years, he managed to conduct at the Bolshoi (1904–06), compose, if not prolifically, and appear as a soloist. He and his family moved to Dresden for two years, enabling him to concentrate on composition, returning to Moscow in 1909, then travelling to America for his first tour of the country. For this he wrote his Third Piano Concerto, playing it twice in New York, the second time under the baton of Mahler. The success of this visit led to him being offered the conductorship of the Boston Symphony Orchestra, which he turned down – the offer was repeated in 1918 and again declined.

From 1910 to 1917 he remained in Moscow, conducting the Philharmonic concerts and composing, as well as making many acclaimed foreign tours. When the Revolution came, it changed his life forever. In November 1917, he and his family left Russia for a Scandinavian tour, providing the catalyst that decided him against living under the new regime. Rachmaninov never returned to Russia.

When he eventually settled on America as his base, he arrived with very little money. Changing career, he became a professional concert pianist. This involved an extraordinary amount of work, as he had a small repertoire compared with most pianists, but by specializing in the music the public wanted to hear – Chopin, Schumann, Liszt and, of course, his own compositions – he made a sensational success. His career as a conductor evaporated, despite the many engagements he carried out, and he wrote comparatively little music after he left Russia. Instead, Rachmaninov became one of the most famous pianists in history.

He bought a house on Lake Lucerne in Switzerland – his grandmother's house on the banks of the River Volchov had inspired a lifelong love of rivers and boats – and made annual tours of Europe. In 1935 he decided to make New York his home, later settling in Los Angeles. His home there was an exact replica, down to the food and drink, of the home he had left in Moscow. Composition gradually became more and more difficult for him but he continued to play in public until a month before his death from cancer, a few weeks after becoming an American citizen. He was buried in the Kensico Cemetery in New York.

HIS MUSIC

To the thousands who love Rachmaninov's work (and most know him mainly through his piano music) it comes as a surprise to learn that it has attracted so much criticism. But here is a case where public opinion has, for once, triumphed. Some pianists, including Brendel and Barenboim, refuse to play his piano music because they consider it vulgar. Certainly, Rachmaninov is less popular in Italy, France and Germany than in Britain and America, and it is true that he was no innovator. He relied on the traditions and techniques he learnt from others, the language he had inherited from Tchaikowsky and the cosmopolitan Russian school; he had little sympathy with the Mighty Handful, much as he loved Mother Russia. He was temperamentally opposed to any kind of dogma or creed attached to music. Scriabin's work, which had made such an impression on Russian music during his early years, held little appeal for Rachmaninov and, although intellectually stimulated by the younger generation of Russians such as Stravinsky and Prokofiev, he made no acknowledgement of their developments. Although he was a fan of an artist such as Art Tatum, the influence of jazz appears nowhere in his music; neither does atonalism or serialism. Rachmaninov's work is strictly tonal, classically structured and imbued with harmonic beauty and melodies of overpowering expressiveness. He was, in other words, a Romantic, writing after the Romantic era had passed. These are the faults cited by his critics. 'I feel like a ghost wandering in a world grown alien,' Rachmaninov is reported to have said. 'I cannot cast out the old way of writing and I cannot acquire the new. I have made intense efforts to feel the musical manner of today, but it will not come to me.'

The characteristics of his music are that it has an unmistakable Russian melancholy – brooding, wistful, yearning – epitomized in one memorable theme after another.

Rachmaninov was described by Stravinsky as 'a six-and-a-half-foot scowl'; he rarely smiled in public and this gave rise to the legend that he was a miserable man with no sense of humour. It is true that he did not suffer fools gladly, but his music is peppered with sardonic humour and moments of tongue-in-cheek fun. (There's the famous story of the occasion when he and his friend, the violinist Fritz Kreisler, were giving a recital. Kreisler had a memory lapse, sidled up to Rachmaninov and whispered urgently; 'Where *are* we?' Back came the reply, quick as a flash: 'Carnegie Hall.') There are other, more hidden, features to listen out for: his tunes tend to move in a stepwise fashion of tone and semitones; there are frequent references to death and the *Dies irae* theme, and the sound of bells often appears; these held a lifelong fascination for him, having heard the pealing of the St Petersburg and Moscow churches when he was young man.

As for his piano music, Rachmaninov is listed in the *Guinness Book of Records* as having the largest hands of any musician and, of course, he wrote for those hands. The scores are loaded with complicated textures and note-spinning. Frequently, the sheer physical difficulty puts it beyond the reach of many players, probably because the configurations and stretches often have to be made at lightning speed to achieve their effect. His left hand could play C-E flat-G-C-G; his right could accommodate an amazing C (second finger)-E-G-C-E (the thumb held under on the E). Try it!

Few pianists have come close to the perfection Rachmaninov achieved when playing his own music, if the recordings we have are anything to go by. His discography, which includes the four piano Concertos, the *Paganini Rhapsody* and many keyboard pieces by himself and others, is arguably the most consistently glorious of any pianist.

Essential works

Symphony No.2 in E minor, Op.2 (1907): the most rewarding of the three symphonies, it shows a clear debt to Tchaikowsky. Its four movements are dominated by the lush Adagio, one of the most heartfelt and moving in all Russian music, followed by its antithesis, a boisterous, joyful finale.

Symphony No.3 in A minor, Op.33 (1936, rev.1938): written thirty years after the Second Symphony and completed in Switzerland, the work, which Rachmaninov himself recorded, has been characterized as 'a profusion of those sweeping cantabile phrases, darkened by moods of melancholy and brooding and impassioned stress.... Sombre, lyrical, defiant, it is a work wholly representative of the Slavic genius and Rachmaninov in particular.'

Symphonic dances, Op.45 (1940): written in Long Island and his last major work, this is 'Rachmaninov's apotheosis of the dance'. It consists of three movements for orchestra inspired by the dance and is intoxicating in its rhythmic ingenuity and brilliant scoring.

Piano Concerto No.1 in F sharp minor, Op.1 (1891, rev.1917): written while still a student at the Moscow Conservatory but later revised (the version we hear today), this is a dazzling display piece drawing on Chopin for its poetry, Tchaikowsky for its brilliance and Liszt for its technical demands. Those who need to be convinced of its worth should listen to the recording by Byron Janis with Kyril Kondrashin.

Piano Concerto No.2 in C minor, Op.18 (1901): with Tchaikowsky's No.1, this is the world's most beloved of piano concertos, and the work with which Rachmaninov's name is most readily identified. It is easy to see why with its wonderful themes, tender and passionate at turns, its drama of emotional climaxes and exciting solo part. In David Lean's film *Brief Encounter* it is used to unforgettable effect. From its famous introductory nine unaccompanied chords to the exultant coda, this work fails to touch only a very few.

Piano Concerto No.3 in D minor, Op.30 (1909): arguably the most technically difficult concerto in the standard repertoire for the soloist, who rarely gets a break in this 'magnificent knucklebreaker'. This is the finest of Rachmaninov's works for piano and orchestra, tightly constructed, with 'big tunes' in every movement, Russian melancholy and luxuriant orchestration. Its dedicatee, Josef Hofmann, never played it; for a display of transcendental pianism, listen to the recording Vladimir Horowitz made in 1951 with Fritz Reiner.

Piano Concerto No.4 in G minor, Op.40 (1927, rev.1941): the least successful of the four, perhaps because it doesn't have the memorable themes, and the second movement threatens to break into 'Three Blind Mice', yet in the hands of a great pianist such as Arturo Benedetti Michelangeli, one can still be convinced that this is a masterwork.

Rhapsody on a theme of Paganini, Op.43 (1934): second to the C minor Concerto in popularity, and Rachmaninov's last work for piano and orchestra; it consists of twenty-four variations on the Paganini violin Caprice No.24. Divided into three groups, this work takes the form of a three-movement concerto, although it is played without a break. The famous theme, used by a string of composers, from Brahms and Lutosławski to Sir Andrew Lloyd Webber, is artfully transformed, played in counterpoint with the *Dies irae* and inverted for the lovely Eighteenth Variation, which was used as the score for the film *The Story of Three Loves*.

Five pieces, Op.3 (1892): the second of this set of early pieces is the notorious C sharp minor Prelude, nicknamed by the composer as 'It', because at every recital he was forced to play 'It'. Detractors have said that this short piece represents everything that Rachmaninov had to say. Untrue, but it does contain all the hallmarks of his mature work – nostalgia, Slavic melancholy, a minor key, chanting, bells, keyboard virtuosity and a precisely judged emotional climax. But don't dismiss the rest of this set, which includes the poignant *Élégie* and lively *Polichinelle*.

Ten Preludes for piano, Op.23 (1901–03)
Thirteen Preludes for piano, Op.32 (1910)
Like the C sharp minor prelude and Chopin's work in this genre, these twenty-four miniatures cover every major and minor key and are a distillation of Rachmaninov's unique keyboard style. Pianistic texture and rhythmic *motifs* rather than melodies concern the composer here. It's best to dip in and get to know the preludes one by one; the gems are Op.23 No.5 in G minor, the most popular, Op.32 No.5 in G, especially when played by Rachmaninov, and Op.32 No.10 in B minor, his own favourite.

Piano Sonata No.2 in B flat minor, Op.36 (1913, rev. 1931): an over-ambitious work both in its original and its shortened version, but there are many things about this brutal piece, full of wild despair, that command attention – not least the electrifying finale.

Polka de V.R.: a deliciously knowing encore using a theme that was improvized by Rachmaninov's father, Vassili. Frequently played to perfection by Shura Cherkassky in his recitals, this piece was dedicated to the Polish-American pianist-composer Leopold Godowsky, whose keyboard writing had a great influence on Rachmaninov .

Vocalise, Op.34 No.14: Rachmaninov published seven sets of songs consisting of seventy-one separate numbers; among the most inspired are 'Spring Waters', 'Lilacs', 'To the Children' and 'Daisies' but the loveliest of all is this wordless song, the ultimate of the Op.34 set. An orchestral arrangement was recorded by the composer but the version by the soprano Anna Moffo with Leopold Stokowski has been described by Bryce Morrison as 'the most perfect vocal recording ever made'.

Piano transcriptions
Rachmaninov was a master in this field and most virtuosos have at least one in their repertoire. They include:

Scherzo from A Midsummer Night's Dream (Mendelssohn): Rachmaninov's friend, the pianist Benno Moiseiwitsch, made *the* recording of this inimitable arrangement.

Prelude (from Violin Partita No.3) (J.S. Bach)

The Flight of the Bumble Bee (Rimsky-Korsakov)

Liebesfreud and Liebeslied (Kreisler)

'Daisies' and 'Lilacs' (two Rachmaninov songs)

Also worth investigating
Isle of the Dead, Op.29, tone-poem for orchestra (1909)
Variations on a theme by Corelli, Op.42, for piano (1931)
Cello Sonata in G minor, Op.19 (1901)
The Bells, Op.35, choral symphony (1913)
Vespers, Op.37 (1915)

Jean-Philippe RAMEAU

'The expression of thought, of sentiment, of the passions, must be the true aim of music' (Rameau)

Baptized: 25 September 1683, Dijon
Died: 12 September 1764, Paris
Type of music: opera, ballet, theatre, choral, instrumental
Influences: Italian opera, Lully, André Campra
Contemporaries: VIVALDI, TELEMANN, Jean-François Dandrieu, **RAMEAU**, J.S. BACH, DOMENICO SCARLATTI, HANDEL, Benedetto Marcello

HIS LIFE AND MUSIC

Although Rameau was revered as among the most influential and important French composers of the eighteenth century, little of his music is heard today. He had a strangely disjointed career. At seven he could sight-read anything that was put before him on the harpsichord, and for the first forty years of his career he was, like his father, a provincial organist, moving from Avignon to Clermont-Ferrand to Paris, Dijon, Lyon and back to Clermont again. In 1722 he returned to Paris and published a controversial and revolutionary textbook on harmony, *Traité de l'harmonie*, which, with the reputation he had won as one of the country's leading organists, helped make his name. Then he changed course and in 1733, backed by the wealthy tax gatherer and arts patron Le Riche de la Poupelinière, devoted himself to writing opera. For the following thirty years, Rameau produced some thirty pieces for the theatre in one form or another. Although he was no judge of libretti, he raised the musical aspects of opera to a new level and in his ballets introduced many novel descriptive effects such as the earthquake in *Les Indes galantes*. Audiences found them deafening; musicians felt them to be complex and demanding. Wagner came in for much the same criticism a century later.

Worth investigating

Les Indes galantes, 'ballet heroïque', (1735): dance scenes on an Indian Ocean island, a Peruvian mountaintop, at a Persian court and in an American Indian forest are features of this piece, plus an earthquake, storm at sea and volcanic eruption.

Pièces de clavecin, vols.2 & 3 (1741): includes No.16 *Le rappel des oiseaux*, No.20 *Tambourin*, and his most famous piece, No.43 *La poule*, which cleverly imitates the clucking of a hen. Saint-Saëns parodied it in 'The Carnival of the Animals'. There are many other charming and descriptive pieces among over fifty titles in this collection.

Maurice RAVEL

'Music must be emotional first and intellectual second' (Ravel)

Born: 7 March 1875, Ciboure, Basses-Pyrénées
Died: 28 December 1937, Paris
Full name: Joseph Maurice Ravel
Type of music: orchestral, opera, ballet, chamber, piano, vocal
Influences: Weber, Chopin, Debussy, Fauré, Chabrier, Satie, gypsy music, jazz, Spanish and Far Eastern music.
Contemporaries: SCHOËNBERG, IVES, Samuel Coleridge-Taylor, **RAVEL**, Reinhold Glière, Albert Ketèlbey, KREISLER, William Hurlstone, FALLA

HIS LIFE

There seems to be no constant factor in determining whether a child will be musical or not, regardless of the parents' talent, or lack of it. Take Ravel's mother and father, for example. Pierre-Joseph Ravel (pronounced with the emphasis on the second syllable), of Swiss descent, was an engineer involved in the construction of the Spanish railways when he met his wife, whose family had been Basque fishermen or sailors for generations. Both their sons, Edouard and Maurice, were musical. Nothing in the family history had suggested that their son would become one of France's greatest composers.

The family moved to Paris when Maurice was three months old, and his talent was encouraged. Music lessons began in 1882 when he was seven, and he entered the Paris Conservatoire in 1889, where Fauré was among his teachers; he remained a student for a further sixteen years – an unusually long time. One reason for this was his strenuous attempts to win the coveted Prix de Rome, which Berlioz, Bizet and Debussy had been awarded. He was placed second in 1901, tried and failed in 1902 and 1903 and then was eliminated, humiliatingly, in 1905 before the final stage of the competition. However, by this time he was already established as a respected composer; the lovely *Pavane pour une infante défunte*, his piano piece *Jeux d'eau*, his String Quartet and the three songs with orchestra, *Schéhérazade*, had been well received. The jury, whose decision became a *cause célèbre*, was charged with favouritism, which led to the resignation of the Director of the Conservatoire, Théodore Dubois, with Fauré taking his place. When the scandal had died down, Ravel was famous. Over the following decade or so, he wrote some of his finest work – *Rapsodie espagnole*, *Gaspard de la nuit* and *Daphnis et Chloé*.

The First World War had a decisive and ultimately fatal effect on Ravel: he volunteered his services for the army and the air force, but neither could use him because of his very light weight (about seven stones) and his frail physique. Instead, he became an ambulance driver at the Front in Verdun. Although short, at a little over five feet, and sensitive by nature, his health up to that time had been good, but the war broke him physically and emotionally; dysentery led to him being released from his driving duties, and he was compelled to recuperate in hospital. His mother's death followed shortly afterwards; this deeply affected him, and he began to suffer from insomnia and what he called 'nervous debility'. Thereafter, despite producing a number of masterpieces, inspiration came less frequently. Nevertheless, his career continued smoothly.

Ravel never married. Soon after the war he moved to a small villa called Belvédère about thirty miles to the south-west of Paris in Montfort-l'Amaury and lived in semi-seclusion. All his affection was lavished on his beautiful home, which, according to his

biographer Madeleine Goss, 'became his mother, wife and children … the only real expression of his entire life.' There he lived with his housekeeper, a collection of mechanical and clockwork toys and a family of Siamese cats, a passion he shared with Debussy. He accepted few pupils but gave friendly advice to many, including Vaughan Williams. In fact, Ravel comes across as an isolated, reserved and aloof individual, 'more courteous than cordial… and more ingenuous than anything else', as his lifelong friend Roland-Manuel described him. After Debussy's death in 1918 he was hailed as France's greatest living composer and honours were heaped

upon him, although, perhaps in retaliation for the Prix de Rome debacle, he vehemently turned down the Légion d'honneur in 1920. He accepted invitations for him to conduct his music all over Europe (in this and as a piano soloist he was only adequate).

In the autumn of 1932, Ravel had a road accident in a Paris taxi from which he never fully recovered. The following year he began to notice problems in muscle co-ordination and, although his mind remained clear, he described his physical state as 'living in a fog'. Despite trying to divert him with travel, friends would see him gazing out from his villa for hours on end, motionless. When asked what he was doing, he would reply, 'Waiting.' Gradually, he lost his memory. Stravinsky, who described Ravel and his music as 'the perfect Swiss clockmaker', said: 'Gogol died screaming, Diaghilev died laughing but Ravel died gradually – and that is the worst of all.'

Eventually, suspecting a brain tumour, an operation was decided upon. No tumour was found. Nine days later, having briefly regained consciousness and calling for his brother, Ravel passed away. Shortly before, he had heard a performance of his own

Daphnis et Chloé and is reported to have said, in tears, 'I still have so much music in my head. I have said nothing. I have so much more to say.'

HIS MUSIC

Ravel was one of the greatest orchestrators in musical history and he put it to use in music ranging from delicate impressionistic pictures to fantasies concerning children and animals, from the world of the Viennese waltz to the seductive charms of Spanish dance and life. Hardly anything is known of Ravel's inner emotional life. Uniquely among important composers, intimate relationships beyond his family appear to be almost non-existent. He seems to have poured all his emotion and thought into music and, ironically, the amount that he wrote was relatively small. What he did produce is pure gold, all of it clearly stamped 'made by Ravel' with its instantly recognizable sound. He worked slowly and carefully at each composition, polishing every face of the jewel. 'One must spend time in eliminating all that could be regarded as superfluous in order to realize as completely as possible the definitive clarity so much desired,' he wrote. Later, he regretted, 'I am not one of the great composers. All the great have produced enormously. There is everything in their work, the best and the worst, but there is always quantity. But I have written relatively very little ... and at that, I did it with a great deal of difficulty. I did my work slowly drop by drop. I have torn all of it out of me in pieces.'

Ravel's significance lay in establishing, with Debussy, a distinct French school of music. The tradition of Germany, and Wagner in particular, had dominated the musical thinking of Gounod, Massenet and the previous generation of French composers. Both Ravel and Debussy are classified as Impressionists and there are many similarities between the two: both used colourful titles for their music and the same musical techniques such as medieval church scales, the pentatonic scale and rich chords with vibrant dissonances; both were master orchestrators. But there the similarity ends; Debussy's music is more sensuous and emotional, the harmonies and forms he employed are more adventurous and vague. Ravel's music is precise and piquant, objective and classical – crystalline, clear-cut and elegant as opposed to amorphous, nebulous and opaque. Debussy was Ravel's senior by thirteen years and the two were inevitably compared, many critics deciding that Ravel was an imitator, even a plagiarizer, of his rival. Some titles are similar: Ravel wrote a *Rapsodie espagnole*, Debussy his *Ibéria*; Ravel wrote the piano piece *Miroirs*, Debussy his *Images*; Ravel wrote *Jeux d'eau*, Debussy *Reflets dans l'eau*. It seems, in retrospect, that the one influenced the other – there is nothing unusual about two men arriving at the same conclusion about the same subject simultaneously. The different characters of the two men represent the nature of their individual musical styles.

Essential works

Alborada del gracioso (1904–05): 'Alborada' suggests 'morning serenade' and 'gracioso' is a jester. Orchestrated in 1912, this is one of Ravel's Spanish pieces, the fourth of a set of five entitled *Miroirs* and originally written for piano. In either form it is highly effective but it can be judged at a hearing just how brilliant an orchestrator Ravel was by playing the two versions one after the other.

Boléro (1928): lovemaking set to music, Torvill and Dean's celebrated ice-dance, 'a piece for orchestra without music' (as Ravel described it) – however you see this seventeen-minute orchestral crescendo, and whether you respond to it or not, it is unforgettable. It came about as a result of a commission from the dancer Ida Rubinstein, although the idea of building a composition from a single theme without development or variation had interested Ravel for some time. 'Once the idea of using only one theme was discovered,' he said, 'any Conservatory student could have done as well.' The same ceaseless, maddening beat proceeds for no less than 326 bars until the final release of tension comes with its one key modulation (from C to E). It is difficult to conceive how popular *Boléro* became after its premiere. It was given its final accolade of immortality when Paramount Pictures, thinking that *Boléro* was an opera, paid Ravel a fabulous sum for the film rights, then, discovering that it was only a piece of music, used it as background for a box-office hit starring Carole Lombard and George Raft. Its title? *Bolero*!

Daphnis et Chloé, ballet (1909–12): having discovered the genius for ballet of Stravinsky, de Falla and Prokofiev, Diaghilev turned to Ravel. Diaghilev had been presented with a scenario for a ballet based on the story of Daphnis and Chloé by the choreographer Michel Fokine. Curiously, Diaghilev did not like the finished work, which took Ravel two years to complete, and the first performance by the Ballet Russe, with Nijinsky leading the cast, was not a success. It is an extraordinary score, Ravel's masterpiece, more of a vast symphony than a conventional ballet and today it is regarded as the finest in the modern French repertory. Even more famous are the two suites Ravel prepared from the full score; the second, and most popular, opens with one of music's most impressive 'sunrises'. The skill and subtlety with which he paints his impressionistic colour and atmosphere makes this one of the twentieth century's landmark scores.

Pavane pour une infante défunte (1899, orch. 1905): whether in its original piano form or orchestral version, this stately and wistful dance is one of Ravel's best-loved pieces, a tender elegy for a dead Infanta – that is to say, a Spanish princess. Ravel chose the title for the alluring sounds of the words.

Rapsodie espagnole (1907): this four-movement orchestral rhapsody, another of Ravel's Spanish pieces, was his first successful work for orchestra; the third movement Habanera is an orchestrated version of his earlier Habanera for two pianos.

La valse, piano (1919–20; piano version 1921): a commission from Diaghilev gave Ravel the chance to fulfil his ambition of writing a Viennese waltz of his own for use in a ballet – he had always loved the waltzes of Schubert and Johann Strauss. What emerged was a piece that begins in 1855 and ends in 1919, for the initial gaiety of the music, in the best traditions of Strauss, is dispelled by increasingly violent and disruptive episodes, the music becoming more desperate in its merriment until it becomes clear that the dancers are dancing themselves to annihilation. Diaghilev disliked the result and never used it. Ravel was hurt and when the two men met in 1925, he refused to shake the impresario's hand; Diaghilev was insulted and challenged Ravel to a duel – the Russian was eventually persuaded to back down, but the two never met again.

Piano Concerto for the left hand (1929–30): the magical opening to this marvellous work sets the scene for the most inventive and original of all the concertos written for the left hand alone. It was commissioned by the one-armed pianist Paul Wittgenstein, brother of the famous philosopher, who had lost an arm in the First World War, although if the recording he made is anything to go by, he was not equal to the task. You'd never know that just one hand was playing the solo part, the writing is so skilful. This and the concerto below were Ravel's last important works.

Piano Concerto in G (1929–31): Ravel explained he 'conceived the concerto in the strict sense, written in the spirit of Mozart and Saint-Saëns'. It took him two years to compose but this brilliant piece flashes by; its first movement is gay and witty, the second is as tender as a Mozart or Bach slow movement, the last has its emphasis on syncopated rhythm. Ravel obviously knew Gershwin's concerto and the whole work is heavily influenced by jazz. The composer conducted a recording of the work in 1932 with its original soloist Marguerite Long but the unsurpassed version is by Arturo Benedetti Michelangelo.

Gaspard de la nuit (1908): Ravel's masterpiece for the piano is among the twentieth century's most important keyboard works. His conscious aim was to write a transcendentally difficult piano piece, the equivalent of Balakirev's *Islamey*. In this he certainly succeeded – the soloist needs wrists and fingers of steel to get through it – but the three movements (*Ondine*, *Le Gibet* and *Scarbo*) inspired by a poem by Aloysius Bertrand contain some of the most arresting piano music ever heard.

Jeux d'eau (1901): 'Fountains', inspired by Liszt's *Jeux d'eau à la Villa d'Este* and *Au bord d'une source*, is a vivid water portrait, 'liquid poetry' as the pianist Alfred Cortot described it. It also paved the way for a new world of sounds on the piano.

Introduction and Allegro for flute, clarinet, harp and string quartet (1905): making use of the newly invented pedal harp, Ravel evokes a world of cool, Gallic *chic* and poise with this unusual combination, emphasizing again what Debussy said of him, that he possessed 'the finest ear that ever existed.'

Tzigane (1924): a rhapsody for violin and orchestra (or piano) in which Ravel set out to write a stylization of Hungarian gypsy music after hearing the violinist Jelly d'Aranyi improvize such pieces at the home of a friend. The long solo cadenza with which it begins is terrifyingly difficult; played on the G-string only (shades of Paganini), the work ends in a whirlwind of fiddle fireworks. D'Aranyi gave the first performance when the accompaniment was played on a short-lived invention, the lutheal – an organ-like attachment to the piano.

L'enfant et les sortilèges, opera (1925): *The Child and the Sorcerers*, based on a fairy tale play by Colette, is a curious work in two parts. In some places the music is tongue-in-cheek, 'in the spirit of American operetta', as Ravel described it, with a duet in cat language and a burlesque on the fox-trot; elsewhere the score contains some delicate music that conjures up a child's world of enchantment.

Worth investigating
Ma mère l'oye, ballet (1908–11): originally a suite for piano duet (1908–10)
String Quartet in F (1902–03)
Piano Trio in A minor (1914)

Valses nobles et sentimentales for piano (1911)
Le tombeau de Couperin (suite for piano 1913, orch. 1917)
And not forgetting Ravel's orchestration of Mussorgsky's famous piano suite *Pictures at an Exhibition*, the version that is most often heard.

Ottorino RESPIGHI

'A middle-class scenic artist' (Percy Young)

Born: 9 July 1879, Bologna
Died: 18 April 1936, Rome
Type of music: Romantic-Impressionist; symphonic poems, ballet, opera, chamber
Influences: Rimsky-Korsakov, Richard Strauss, Debussy, Puccini
Contemporaries: Joseph Holbrooke, Rutland Boughton, **RESPIGHI**, Frank Bridge, CANTELOUBE, John Ireland, Cyril Scott, Nicolai Medtner

HIS LIFE AND MUSIC

Beginning his career as a violinist and viola player, Respighi went to Russia in 1900, where he played first viola in the Imperial Opera Orchestra in St Petersburg. Here he took lessons from Rimsky-Korsakov, who proved to be a decisive influence on his compositional style, leading Respighi to become one of the century's most masterly orchestrators, fond of splashy, flamboyant effects. His scores are notable for their imaginative, luscious harmonies and 'sound colour.'

In 1902 he spent some time in Berlin, studying with Max Bruch, and continued his career as a violin soloist and as viola player with the Mugellini Quartet of Bologna. He was made a professor of composition at the Santa Cecilia Academy in Rome in 1913 and became its director in 1923. He remained in the post for only two years, leaving to concentrate on composition full time. Respighi's works may lack individuality but it was he and Busoni who revived the Italian instrumental tradition after the domination of the country's great opera composers.

Essential works
The Fountains of Rome (1914–16)
The Pines of Rome (1924)
Roman Festivals (1928)
This triptych of symphonic poems, each with four movements, is Respighi's evocative tone-portrait of Italy. *Fontane di Roma* is generally considered to be the best, while *The Pines of Rome* has, written into the score, a gramo-phone recording of a nightingale.
Violin Sonata in B minor (1916–17): Respighi wrote this grand but underrated work as a vehicle for himself; it was rescued from oblivion by Jascha Heifetz, who made a classic recording of it.

The Birds (1927): suite for small orchestra based on the 'bird music' (such as the night-ingale and the cuckoo) of Pasquini, Rameau and other eighteenth-century masters; the Prelude was used as the signature tune for BBC TV's *Going For A Song*.
Ancient airs and dances for the lute: three suites of orchestral arrangements of Italian music of the seventeenth and eighteenth centuries.
La boutique fantasque (1919): *The Fantastic Toy Shop*, a ballet commissioned by Diaghilev and fashioned from short piano works by Rossini.

Nikolai RIMSKY-KORSAKOV

'A cultured aromatist' (Neville Cardus)

Born: 18 March 1844, Tikhvin, near Novgorod
Died: 21 June 1908, Liubensk, near St Petersburg
Full name: Nikolai Andreievich Rimsky-Korsakov
Type of music: symphony, orchestral, opera, choral, chamber
Influences: Glinka, Balakirev, Berlioz, Wagner, Liszt
Contemporaries: Arrigo Boito, GRIEG, Pablo de Sarasate, **RIMSKY-KORSAKOV**,
Stephen Adams, WIDOR, FAURÉ, PARRY, Xaver Scharwenka, Vincent d'Indy

---

HIS LIFE

How many of us know Rimsky-Korsakov's music beyond *Scheherazade* and *The Flight of the Bumble Bee?* Compared with the music of Tchaikowsky and Rachmaninov, a meagre amount is ever played. And his operas, the works that Rimsky-Korsakov believed to be his finest achievements, are all but unknown. Yet, perhaps because it sounds like a music-hall joke, his name must be one of the most familiar of all classical composers. His place in the development of Russian music cannot be overstated for, apart from his own work, he was an important teacher, numbering among his pupils Glazunov, Liadov, Ippolitov-Ivanov, Arensky, Gretchaninov, Miaskovsky, Prokofiev and Stravinsky.

From a wealthy, aristocratic, landed family where music was part of everyday life, Rimsky-Korsakov was discovered to have a natural talent for the piano at an early age but his ambitions were focused on joining the navy like his elder brother. He entered the Naval School in St Petersburg in 1856 but also took piano lessons and began to form ideas for composition, enthused by performances of various operas – especially Glinka's *A Life for the Tsar* and *Ruslan and Ludmilla.* He was introduced to Balakirev and, like many, fell under his charismatic influence, which led to him attempting a symphony. In time, he would become the fifth (and youngest) member of the Mighty Handful (*see* BALAKIREV).

In the meantime, the call of the sea was more powerful and on graduating in 1862 he joined the clipper *Almaz* for a voyage that kept him from St Petersburg for two and a half years. On his return, Balakirev conducted a performance of Rimsky-Korsakov's First Symphony in December 1865, which, as much as anything, finally determined its composer to make music his life. He was still considered a gifted musical amateur by the circle in which he moved – and he was certainly musically under-educated – when Cui asked him to help orchestrate an unfinished opera by Dargomyzhsky, *The Stone Guest.* This proved to be a formative experience, providing a vivid and intense lesson in the arts of dramatic construction and orchestration.

His astonishment can be imagined then, when, at the age of twenty-seven, he was offered the post of Professor of Composition at the St Petersburg Conservatory. He remained on the faculty from 1870 until his death. As he himself said, 'I did not know at that time how to harmonize a chorale properly,' confessing that he had 'never written a single contrapuntal exercise in my life, and had only the haziest understanding of strict fugue; I didn't even know the names of the augmented and diminished intervals or chords' – irrelevant terms for the layman, perhaps, but basic considerations for a teacher of composition. Instinct alone had got him thus far, a deficiency he set about correcting with an iron regime of contrapuntal study.

Although still officially in the navy, Rimsky-Korsakov was made Inspector of Russian Military Bands in 1873, but this again inspired him to an intense study of orchestration.

From this point, Rimsky-Korsakov's history is one of increasing influence as a teacher and administrator, which runs parallel to his development as one of Russia's most celebrated composers. By the mid-1870s, the basic characteristics of his music had flowered: a love of fantasies and fairy tales and a dedication to nationalistic music coloured, like the work of the other four of the Mighty Handful, by Orientalism. Overwork brought him to the verge of a nervous breakdown in 1889, to be followed, after a relapse of two years, by a creative outburst that established him as the most famous of the Five, whose power in the musical world of St Petersburg was absolute.

Rimsky-Korsakov, though, was no dictator. Indeed, when the conservatory students rebelled against the authorities in 1905, Rimsky-Korsakov took the side not of the establishment but of the students and was dismissed from his post for his pains. It made him something of a hero. Glazunov resigned in protest. When he was recalled and made Director, Glazunov immediately reinstated Rimsky-Korsakov. 1907 saw his last appearance abroad, in Paris, where he conducted two concerts of Russian music staged by Diaghilev. His last work, the opera *Le coq d'or*, was banned by the censor – it dealt with the bungling administrators of Russia and a stupid Tsar – and he died of angina pectoris before the situation was resolved.

HIS MUSIC

Nationalism and Orientalism aside, it is Rimsky-Korsakov's use of the orchestra that immediately attracts attention; his unexpected but highly effective combinations of instruments, imaginative idiomatic writing for solo or ensemble passages and a range of tone and colour to summon up location, character or atmosphere have rarely been surpassed. These brilliant effects, in which clarity is never sacrificed, have become something of a lexicon for composers and his famous book on orchestration, in which many examples from his own works are quoted as illustration, is a constant source of reference for anyone interested in scoring for an orchestra. His position as the most important and industrious of the Mighty Handful is due to his greater technical proficiency and classical, structural assurance, the discipline and dedication he brought to his music – he was the only one of the five to shake off thoroughly the shackles of amateurism – and the significant work he did both in producing the next generation of Russian composers and promoting the music of his predecessors.

Perhaps soon his operas will become more popular, so different are they from the social realism of Mussorgsky, yet still unmistakably Russian, described by Gerald Abrahams as 'half-real, half-supernatural, a world as limited, as distinctive and as delightful as the world of Grimm's fairy tales and as Alice's Wonderland'. Throughout his operas and, indeed, his entire *oeuvre* there runs the same bounteous melodic fountain, tender Russian lyricism and violently contrasted moods couched in rich orchestral textures. It may be true that the manner in which it is said is more important than what is said but, as a whole, Rimsky-Korsakov's music is the most sophisticated Russian music produced to that date.

Essential works

Scheherazade, symphonic suite (1888): Rimsky-Korsakov's most celebrated composition, this is a four-movement setting of several episodes from *The Arabian Nights*: The Sultan, convinced of the faithlessness of women, determines to kill each of his wives after the first night he spends together with them, but one of his wives, the Sultana Scheherazade, saves her life by diverting him with stories that she relates over a period of a thousand and one nights. There are two significant themes that recur throughout the work – the powerful opening, which represents the Sultan, and a romantic melody for the solo violin portraying Scheherazade.

Capriccio espagnol (1887): Rimsky-Korsakov explained that this work belonged to 'that period of my creative life at the end of which my orchestration had reached a considerable degree of virtuosity and bright sonority without Wagner's influence, within the limits of the usual make-up of Glinka's orchestra.' Its five movements, using Spanish themes of different dance characters, are played without pause and form a popular and effective orchestral showpiece.

Russian Easter Overture (1888): this overture is based on themes of the Russian Orthodox Church; the slow, lengthy introduction gives way to an exciting second half that was described by Rimsky-Korsakov as 'expressing the transition from the solemnities of Passiontide to the vociferous communal rejoicings of Easter.'

Sadko, opera (1894–96): Rimsky-Korsakov's sixth opera and one of his finest, using the eleventh-century legend of Sadko, the wandering minstrel. Among his adventures is a scene in the harbour of Novgorod where he wagers his life against the combined wealth of local merchants that he can catch a net full of golden fish – he wins the bet, of course. In this act, we hear Rimsky-Korsakov's most famous aria 'Song of India' or 'Chanson Hindu' as well as the popular 'Song of the Viking Guest'; a notable recording of this is by the great bass Feodor Chaliapin.

Also worth investigating

Tsar Sultan, opera (1900): an uneven work but it contains many glorious pages apart from its big hit: for reasons that are far too complex to go into here, Prince Guidon is advised by a swan to transform himself into an insect. This is the launching pad for one of music's most over-played tunes, *The Flight of the Bumble Bee*. In its operatic setting (Act 3) it has very different clothing to the arrangements for solo instruments in which it is most often heard – and it has been arranged for *every* instrument from the accordion to the xylophone. Piano buffs will be aware of the incredible version that was recorded by the legendary Georges Cziffra.

Overture to May Night (1878–79): the composition of Rimsky-Korsakov's second opera was bound up with the courtship of his wife; its conventionally shaped overture is a distillation of recurring 'Rimskian' elements – romantic melody, fantasy, folk songs and a vivacious, brilliant finale.

The Snow Maiden, opera (1881): one of Rimsky-Korsakov's most successful operas of the thirteen he wrote; the score, and orchestral suite from it, include the well-known *Dance of the Buffoons*.

And not forgetting the orchestration of Borodin's *Prince Igor* and Mussorgsky's *Night on the Bare Mountain*, *Khovanshchina* and *Boris Godunov*.

Joaquín RODRIGO
(b.1901)

Concierto de Aranjuez, 1939

Rodrigo and his wife, the Turkish pianist Victoria Kamhi, moved to the little town of Aranjuez just outside Madrid in 1939, having spent much of the previous decade in Paris. Here he put the finishing touches to a guitar concerto that has firmly planted itself in the affection of music lovers. Has there ever been a more vivid musical picture of Spain than this, the work of a man who has been blind since the age of three? (All his works are notated and played through by his wife.) The sunshine and sangria is there but also nostalgia in its wistful and beautiful Adagio.

It comes as something of a surprise to learn that not only is Rodrigo not a guitarist but he was also a pupil of Paul Dukas, the composer of *The Sorcerer's Apprentice*. Not surprisingly, the success of the *Concierto de Aranjuez* inspired Rodrigo to write other works for guitar and orchestra, a notoriously difficult combination when scoring the weak-toned instrument against a full orchestra. These include his *Fantasia para un gentilhomme* (1954) the *Concierto madrigal* (for two guitars and orchestra, 1969) and the *Concierto Andaluz* (for four guitars, 1967).

Gioachino ROSSINI
'The Swan of Pesaro'

Born: 29 February 1792, Pesaro
Died: 13 November 1868, Paris
Full name: Gioachino Antonio Rossini
Type of music: opera, other vocal works
Influences: Haydn, Mozart, the Italian opera tradition
Contemporaries: Henry Bishop, HÉROLD, Carl Czerny, MEYERBEER, **ROSSINI**, Ignaz Moscheles, Saverio Mercadante, Franz Berwald, SCHUBERT, DONIZETTI

HIS LIFE

Rossini's father was the town trumpeter for Pesaro and played brass instruments in various theatres as well as doubling as a municipal inspector of slaughterhouses; his mother was a small-time opera singer. Rossini's gifts were noted at an early age and by the time he reached his teens he could not only play the piano, the viola and the horn but also was much in demand as a boy soprano.

On leaving the Liceo Musicale in Bologna he had composed a large amount of music, including five accomplished string quartets. He wrote his first opera *Demetrio e Polibio* in 1808 and this led to his first commission – *La cambiale di matrimonio*, a one-act opera which in turn prompted further commissions. Rossini's career snowballed rapidly. His first full-length opera, *Tancredi*, was an enormous success and the aria 'Di tanti palpiti' was the equivalent of one of today's pop hits; less than three months later he had an even greater triumph with his comic opera *L'Italiana in Algeri* (*The Italian Girl in Algiers*). At the age of twenty-one he was famous throughout Italy.

Venice had been the stage for his early work. Rossini then moved on to Naples and had a brief stay in Rome, having been asked to write an opera for the Teatro Argentina. Desperate for a story to use, he decided to use Beaumarchais' play *Le barbier de Séville*. There were at least four other musical versions of the play doing the rounds when Rossini wrote his, the most popular of these by Giovanni Paisiello. It was an audacious choice

for any composer, but, according to Rossini, he composed the 600 pages of *The Barber of Seville* in only thirteen days (his biographer says it was nineteen). Despite borrowing from some of his previous work, the composition of this opera remains one of the most astonishing feats of sustained, instant musical creation.

The premiere was a fiasco – one of the singers tripped and had to sing with a bloody nose, a cat wandered on stage and distracted the audience's attention, and the partisan first-nighters booed some of the music they recognized from previous Rossini works and hissed their disapproval of his choice of the same subject used by Paisiello. The second performance of the opera, however, was a triumph. Paisiello's work was consigned to oblivion and Rossini's *Il barbiere di Siviglia* has continued to delight audiences throughout the world ever since.

Based in Naples, Rossini began an affair with the prima donna Isabella Colbran and continued his triumphant progress with *La Cenerentola* (1817), *Mosè in Egitto* (1818), *La gazza ladra* (*The Thieving Magpie*) (1817) and *Zelmira* (1822). Between 1808 and 1829 he produced no less than forty operas. Now married to Colbran, Rossini moved to Vienna where he met Beethoven and composed *Semiramide* (1823), his next big hit. Then on to London where he was fêted by public and royalty alike – George IV sang duets with him – and treated as the greatest living composer. In 1824 he headed for Paris where he adapted his style to French tastes with *Le Comte Ory* (1828), following it with his grand opera masterpiece, *Guillaume Tell* (1829). Rossini was now immensely wealthy and at the height of his creative powers. Then his life took a completely unexpected course. He simply stopped composing. Apart from his *Stabat mater* and *Petite messe solennelle* of 1863, he wrote nothing else of importance. No one has yet come up with a completely convincing explanation for this decision – lack of inspiration? worn out? neurasthenia? inability to find good singers? afraid of competition? It could be none or any of these reasons.

In 1832 Rossini met Olympe Pélissier, a celebrated Parisian beauty who became his mistress. They left Paris for Bologna in 1836 and, when Isabella Colbran died in 1845, the two were married. From 1848 to 1855 they lived in Florence, after which they returned to Paris. Here Rossini's home became a focal point for many of the great artists of the day. He was renowned for his generosity, his hospitality and, of course, for his food. *Tournedos Rossini* was just one of the dishes that he invented. Although Rossini suffered from depression for some twenty years, his wit and *bon mots* were famous. 'Wagner,' he said, 'has lovely moments but awful quarters of an hour.' After hearing Berlioz's *Symphonie fantastique* Rossini commented, 'What a good thing it isn't music.' He had been born in a leap year and took great pleasure in celebrating his nineteenth birthday in 1868. Like many Italians, Rossini was extremely superstitious and was terrified of Friday 13th. He died on 13 November 1868 – a Friday. There were 6,000 mourners in his funeral procession, four military bands and a chorus of 399 that sang the Prayer from his *Mosè in Egitto*.

HIS MUSIC

Rossini's contribution to the development of opera was immense – indeed he dominated the opera world for the first half of the nineteenth century. Where he led, Donizetti and Bellini followed, each making their decisive contributions but working in the shadow of Rossini's astonishing success.

He once said: 'Show me a laundry list and I will set it to music,' and there is certainly a significant amount of superficial, production-line music among the composer's vast output. He was indecently prolific and not always as self-critical as perhaps he should have been. Yet he delighted his audiences and his work continues to captivate us today. 'Delight must be the basis and aim of this art,' he once wrote. 'Simple melody – clear rhythm!' As Thomas Pynchon commented in his book *Gravity's Rainbow*, published in 1973, 'The point is … a person feels good listening to Rossini. All you feel like after listening to Beethoven is going out and invading Poland. … There is more of the sublime in the snare-drum part of *La gazza ladra* than in the whole Ninth Symphony.' Technically, Rossini extended the range of both instrumental textures and lyric ornamentation; he was the first to eliminate unaccompanied recitative, giving the whole work the same musical fabric; and he wrote out all vocal ornaments and cadenzas instead of leaving it to the dubious taste of singers. And there was the 'Rossini rocket', an orchestral crescendo where the same passage is repeated again and again, each time with more instruments joining in. The effect created is of mounting excitement such as in 'La calunnia' from Act 1 of *The Barber*. But it was the degree of sophisticated wit in the music (*The Barber* again) as well as the dignified and dramatic (*William Tell*) that Rossini managed incomparably well – and the ability to drench his life-enhancing scores in an endless flow of melody.

Essential works

Il barbiere di Siviglia (The Barber of Seville) (1816): this is the perfect comic opera for both audience and singers; the latter relish the splendid opportunities it offers, especially the mezzo or soprano appearing as Rosina. The Overture and many of the individual pieces in the opera are loved even by those who have never heard a complete opera. Act 1 alone includes 'Ecco ridente' (Count Almaviva's serenade), 'Largo al factotum' (Figaro's introductory tongue-twisting show-stopper) and 'Una voce poco fa' (among the most popular of all coloratura arias).

La Cenerentola (Cinderella) (1816–17): pronounced La Chay-nay-*ren'*-toe-lah, this is Rossini's setting of the same story we know from pantomime. Like *The Barber*, it is full of quick-fire invention, patter songs, brilliant ensembles and thrilling coloratura solos. Act 2 contains the famous Rondo aria 'Non più mesta', with which Cinderella forgives her stepsisters, recorded with breathtaking agility by Cecilia Bartoli.

Le Comte Ory (1828): one of his first French operas; it is relatively neglected, undeservedly.

Semiramide (1822–23): pronounced Sem-eer-*am'*-ee-day (Semiramis was the Queen of Babylon). Based on a Voltaire story, the Overture is one of his finest; 'Bel raggio lusinghier' is a favourite coloratura workout for sopranos.

Mosè in Egitto (1818): *Moses in Egypt* has the stirring 'Dal tuo stellato soglio' ('From your Starry Throne'), sung at Rossini's funeral and the subject of some extraordinary variations by both Paganini (violin) and Sigismund Thalberg (piano).

The Barber and **La Cenerentola** are the best Rossini operas to begin with, but no collection should be without the Overtures to **La scala di seta, Il Signor Bruschino, L'Italiana in Algeri, La gazza ladra** and, of course, **William Tell**, which is still one of the most popular of all classical concert pieces, and rightly so. Each opera, too, has many rewards to offer – some more consistently than others.

'Di tanti palpiti', from **Tancredi** (1812–13): possibly the most famous aria of its day. Rossini is said to have composed it in four minutes while waiting for rice to cook, which is why it is sometimes known as the *aria del risi* (*The Rice Aria*).

Stabat mater (1831–42, in various versions): from this comes the glorious tenor solo 'Cujus Animam'.

Petite messe solennelle (1863): the earlier chamber score is preferable to the later orchestration of 1867.

Many composers, particularly Respighi and Britten, have used Rossini's works as the inspiration for their own compositions.

Anton RUBINSTEIN

Born: 28 November 1829, Vikhvatinetz, Podolia, South-west Russia

Died: 20 November 1894, Peterhof, near St Petersburg

Full name: Anton Grigor'ievich Rubinstein

Type of music: concerto, symphony, chamber, instrumental (especially solo piano), song, opera

Influences: Beethoven, Schumann, Mendelssohn and the German tradition, Liszt

Contemporaries: Stephen Collins Foster, GOTTSCHALK, **RUBINSTEIN**, Kárl Goldmark, Joseph Joachim, BORODIN, BRAHMS, Julius Reubke

HIS LIFE AND MUSIC

In the last half of the nineteenth century, Anton Rubenstein – the first great *international* Russian pianist, a teacher, conductor, man of vision and a prolific composer – was a giant in the musical firmament. Hans von Bülow called him 'the Michelangelo of Music'. Today his reputation has dwindled to nothing.

He looked so like Beethoven had as a young man that Rubinstein was rumoured to be the composer's illegitimate child; Liszt referred to him as 'Van II'. His family were prosperous Jewish merchants who were baptized in 1831. They moved to Moscow when Anton was five years old, and he began piano studies at the age of eight with Alexander Villoing. 'By my thirteenth year,' wrote Rubinstein in his autobiography, 'I had no other teacher.'

He made concert tours all over Europe before going to Berlin with his talented brother Nicholas to study composition. He returned to St Petersburg in 1848, where, in 1862, he founded the Imperial Conservatory. He attracted much opposition from the Mighty Handful (Balakirev, Borodin, Cui, Rimsky-Korsakov and Mussorgsky), the group striving to promote Russian nationalism in music. Cui condemned him: 'It would be a serious error to consider Rubinstein a Russian composer. He is merely a Russian who composes.' All Rubinstein's musical and cultural roots were German–European based, and his tastes were conservative. 'He is behind our time,' observed George Bernard Shaw, 'and indeed hardly up to his own in musical development.'

In spite of opposition from Balakirev's Free School, it was Rubinstein's court-subsidized venture that succeeded. Nicholas Rubinstein founded the Moscow Conservatory in 1866. In this way, the brothers won official recognition for the

professional musician for the first time in Russia and, while Glinka laid the roots for the nationalist composer, the Rubinsteins laid the roots for the country's instrumentalists and teachers of today. In the first twenty years of the existence of the Imperial and Moscow Conservatories, Tchaikowsky, Rachmaninov, Siloti, Essipov, Gabrilowitsch and a host of other important artists and composers had passed though their doors.

In 1867, Rubinstein left the running of the Imperial Conservatory to others for two decades, while he toured, conducted and composed. He made a triumphant tour of America during 1872–73, giving 215 recitals and amassing a small fortune on the way. He created a sensation by playing without music, a virtually unheard-of practice, and presented a famous cycle of concerts surveying keyboard literature from Byrd to contemporary works – 140 different pieces in total. Not many could or would attempt that today.

Much of his music has a depressing anonymity about it, for, like many fluent composers, Rubinstein suffered from being insufficiently self-critical. Chopin, Schumann and Mendelssohn look over his shoulder, but 'moderns' such as Liszt and Berlioz are rarely in his company. The music poured out in every form: six symphonies, five piano concertos, songs, chamber music, choral works, operas, ballets, cantatas and thirteen operas. Very little is performed now, yet scattered among the garnets are a few real gems. In spite of all he achieved, Rubinstein had few illusions about himself: 'For the Jews, I am a Christian, for the Christians, a Jew,' he wrote. 'For the Russians, I am a German, for the Germans, a Russian; for the classicists, I am futuristic, for the futurists, a reactionary. Conclusion: I am neither fish nor flesh, a deplorable individual.'

Essential works

Piano Concerto No.4 in D minor, Op.70: Rubinstein's only piano concerto still played; a thunderous, dramatic, virtuoso work with some pretty tunes. A musical Chinese meal.

Melody in F, Op.3 No.1: a perennial favourite of pianists, a Chopinesque *salon* piece. Its companion Op.3 No.2 is never played.

Kammenoi Ostrow, Op.10 No.22 (also known as *Rêve angélique*) and **Romance in E flat, Op.44 No.1**: two further pieces to make the young ladies swoon.

Valse-Caprice in E flat and **Grande étude in C, 'Staccato', Op.23 No.2**: two taxing pieces with which the composer sometimes ended his

recitals. One listener reported, 'The impression was so overwhelming, my nerves were so wrought up that I felt stifled. I glanced at my neighbour – she had left the room weeping. We all had a feeling of involuntary terror as if in the presence of some elementary power of nature.' Such was his effect on audiences.
Symphony No.2 in C, 'Ocean': once widely performed, this seven-movement monster lasts over seventy minutes.

Camille SAINT-SAËNS

'The only great composer who wasn't a genius'

Born: 9 October 1835, Paris
Died: 16 December 1921, Algiers
Full name: Charles-Camille Saint-Saëns
Type of music: symphony, orchestral, opera, ballet, concerto, chamber, vocal, piano, film
Influences: Bach, Mozart, Beethoven, Mendelssohn, Liszt
Contemporaries: PONCHIELLI, Henryk Wieniawski, César Cui, **SAINT-SAËNS**, DELIBES, BALAKIREV, Emile Waldteufel, BIZET, BRUCH, MUSSORGSKY

HIS LIFE

Saint-Saëns was one of the most remarkable child prodigies in the history of music – indeed, he had an altogether remarkable mind: organist, pianist, conductor, caricaturist, dabbler in science, mathematics and astronomy, critic, traveller, archaeologist, writer of plays, poetry, philosophy, essayist on botany and ancient music, editor of music and the composer of more than 300 works touching every area of composition.

His father, a minor official in the Department of the Interior, died from consumption a year after his marriage. Taught by his great-aunt, Saint-Saëns began playing the piano at two and a half, gave a performance in a Paris *salon* at five, started composing at six and made his official debut aged ten. As an encore he offered to play any one of Beethoven's thirty-two sonatas from memory. After studying at the Paris Conservatoire he competed unsuccessfully for the Prix de Rome in 1852; he did so again in 1864 when he was an

established composer. His First Symphony appeared in 1853, presented anonymously as the work of a German composer (it's Mozart in structure, Mendelssohn in mood). Gounod was present and sent an admiring note of encouragement. As a pianist and organist of exceptional ability he was much in demand, and at the age of twenty-two he was appointed to the most prestigious organ post in France at the Madeleine. It was here that he developed his legendary gift for improvisation – Liszt called him the greatest organist in the world – and soon, famous musicians visiting Paris would make a point of stopping off at the Madeleine to hear him play, among them Clara Schumann, Anton Rubinstein and Sarasate. Hans von Bülow rated Saint-Saëns as a score reader and all-round musician higher than Liszt. 'Wagner and I were in conversation with Saint-Saëns in the same room. Saint-Saëns who could not follow German, became bored and picked up the full-score manuscript of *Siegfried*, not yet completed, put it on the piano and began to play. Wagner and I stopped talking. Never had I heard such score-reading and it was all *prima vista*. Scarcely an effect was lost. Wagner was speechless. I too can play from score, but neither I nor any living man could have performed that feat after Saint-Saëns. He is the greatest musical mind of our time.'

Saint-Saëns toured extensively as a pianist, both in solo concerts and in performances of his own piano concertos; his technique was apparently effortless and it is possible to hear what a phenomenally agile player he was through the hiss and crackle of some ancient recordings. He became a professor of piano at the École Niedermeyer in 1861 and ten years later helped found the Société Nationale dedicated to the performance of music by French composers.

He composed at great speed: the *Oratorio de Noël* was completed in twelve days; a commission he had forgotten about produced twenty-one pages of full score in two hours; the Second Piano Concerto took three weeks from concept to concert. 'Not having had time to practise it sufficiently for performance, I played very badly,' wrote Saint-Saëns. 'Except for the Scherzo, which was an immediate success, it did not go well.'

By the late 1860s, Saint-Saëns was numbered amongst the top living composers, awarded the Légion d'honneur at only thirty-three, befriended by the leading musicians of the day and an habitué of the *salon* of Princesse Mathilde, a member of the Imperial family and mistress of the Ministre des Beaux-Arts. His own private life was not so successful. He was forty when he married the nineteen-year-old Marie Truffot, sister of one of his pupils. The couple had two children but Saint-Saëns had little time for family life and in the first three years of his marriage he completed his opera *Samson et Dalila*, his Piano Concerto No.4, the oratorio *Le déluge*, a suite for orchestra and a symphonic poem, he visited Russia (where he became close friends with Tchaikowsky), composed numerous other short works, gave concerts and, in the spring of 1878, returned from Switzerland after writing a Requiem Mass. His arrival coincided with a terrible tragedy: his two-and-a-half-year-old son André had fallen from a fourth floor window and died; barely six weeks later his second son died suddenly of an infant malady. Three years after that, Saint-Saëns and his wife were on holiday when the composer, without warning, disappeared. Marie Saint-Saëns never saw her husband again, although they did not divorce, and she died, aged nearly ninety-five, in January 1950.

In December 1888, Saint-Saëns' mother died at the age of eighty; she was the only adult to whom he was ever really close. After 1890, he wrote little of consequence and began to indulge his passion for foreign travel, frequently visiting the Canary Islands and Algeria, and venturing as far afield as Colombo and Saigon where, allegedly, he developed a close interest in the natives – usually young boys. As his music became less and less appreciated by each generation, he became proportionately more irritable and outspoken in his condemnation of new music. He abhorred the operas of Richard Strauss, was left speechless by *The Rite of Spring* and loathed Debussy and his music. He made enemies and, like many before him who chose not to move with the times, was left like a dried fossil on the beach, an arch-reactionary but still the Grand Old Man of French music (pictured opposite, seated, with Charles Harford Lloyd, Herbert Brewer and Elgar in 1913 after the premiere in Gloucester of his oratorio *The Promised Land*).

He was still giving recitals three months before his death, completing a concert tour of Algiers and Greece at the age of eighty-five. When he announced his retirement in August 1921, he had been before the public for seventy-five years.

HIS MUSIC

Saint-Saëns has been called 'the French Mendelssohn' and the two have much in common, with their effortless, fluent techniques, their love of neatness in form, structure and harmony, and the undemanding, untroubled pleasure that their music brings. Mendelssohn, arguably, dug deeper; Saint-Saëns certainly allowed much second-rate work to escape. 'I produce music as an apple tree produces apples,' wrote Saint-Saëns and on another occasion: 'I live in music as a fish in water.'

But amongst the less successful works is music as inspired as any of the first-division composers. His importance in the history of French music is unassailable and the contempt in which he is held in some circles is partly a reflection of his long life – in his eighty-six years he saw the births and deaths of Bizet, Rimsky-Korsakov, Debussy and Tchaikowsky and the premieres of works by Bellini, Donizetti and Schumann as well as Schoenberg, Prokofiev and Bartók. Saint-Saëns may have been no innovator, but his mastery of contrapuntal writing, the sonority and resourcefulness of his orchestration and other qualities were at first resisted by those who were used to a lighter French music. He was also the main exponent in his country of the Lisztian symphonic poem and among his works are an unusually wide acknowledgement of the music of other nations: the Egyptian Fifth Piano Concerto, Africa Fantasy, Russian and Arabian Caprices, a Breton rhapsody, an Algerian suite and Persian songs. His craftsmanship and taste were impeccable, second to none: 'The artist who does not feel completely satisfied by elegant lines, by harmonious colours, and by a beautiful succession of chords does not understand the art of music,' wrote Saint-Saëns – and that was his *credo*. Everything sounds so well and, though he may not move the listener, he delights with the elegance, purity and tunefulness of his music.

Essential works

Symphony No.3 in C minor (with organ), Op.78 (1886): dedicated to his friend Liszt, this is the best and most popular of Saint-Saëns' three mature symphonies, in four distinct but unbroken sections. The organ makes its appearance in the lovely slow movement, but it is the *fortissimo* entry in the finale that is particularly well known, its theme used to triumphal effect in the 1995 film *Babe*.

Danse macabre, Op.40 (1874): based on a poem by Henri Cazalis that tells of Death playing his violin for the dance of the skeletons on a dark wintry night, the music is a firm concert favourite.

Le carnaval des animaux (The Carnival of the Animals) (1886): it's ironic that the most popular work by Saint-Saëns should be one that he never intended for publication; indeed the only section he allowed to appear in print during his lifetime was *The Swan*, that most famous of all cello solos. Fearing that his reputation as a serious composer might be harmed, he kept his little *jeu d'esprit* under lock and key until his death; its first public performance was not until April 1922. Each creature in his *Grande fantaisie zoologique* (the work's subtitle) gave him with the pretext for an exhibition of pure musical craftsmanship and caricaturing the music of Rossini, Mendelssohn, Berlioz, Offenbach and himself (*Danse macabre*) to enchanting effect. Ogden Nash wrote some tediously unfunny verses that are sometimes interpolated between sections.

Piano Concerto No.2 in G minor, Op.22 (1868): Bach, in the first movement, meets Offenbach, in the last movement. Of his five piano concertos, this is the most frequently heard, composed in three weeks at the instigation of Anton Rubinstein who conducted the first performance. Pure, ear-tickling delight from start to finish, with its rumpty-tumpty Scherzo and thrilling *presto* finale.

Piano Concerto No.4 in C minor, Op.44 (1875): the lesser known Fourth Concerto is the best constructed of his five piano concertos, written at the same time as the 'Organ' Symphony, which also begins in C minor and ends in C major, uses chorale melodies and has a similar structure.

Violin Concerto No.3 in B minor, Op.61 (1880): although less demanding technically than his two earlier violin concertos, this work is far more musically rewarding. It is dedicated to the renowned violinist Sarasate, and the final movement has a memorable soaring secondary theme.

Violin Sonata No.1 in D minor, Op.75 (1885): a typically Gallic and light-textured work of immense charm (the fiery *moto perpetuo* finale is one of Saint-Saëns' finest); the main theme of the first movement is the famous 'little phrase' in the head of the imaginary composer Vinteuil in Proust's *A la recherche du temps perdu*, a character who was based partly on Saint-Saëns.

Introduction and Rondo capriccioso in A minor, Op.28 (1863): among the most recorded of all miniatures for violin and orchestra and part of every fiddle player's repertoire, again dedicated to Sarasate.

Havanaise, Op.83 (1887): a popular violin piece, its theme a smokily sensuous Habanera.
Septet in E flat, Op.65 (1881): written for the unusual combination of trumpet, piano and strings, this is one of the composer's happiest inspirations, its four movements sparkling with wit but not without a tinge of nostalgia.
Variations on a theme of Beethoven for two pianos, Op.35 (1874): the theme is the Trio in the Minuet of Beethoven's Sonata in E flat, Op.31; Saint-Saëns builds ten ingenious and contrasted variations on it.
Samson et Dalila, opera (1877): Saint-Saëns' only opera (out of twelve) still in the repertoire. The first performance was under Liszt's auspices in 1877 in Weimar, as Saint-Saëns could not get it produced in France; it was not heard in Paris for another fifteen years. The

highlights include Dalila's two celebrated arias 'Printemps qui commence' (Act 1) and 'Mon coeur s'ouvre à ta voix' (Act 2), and the Act 3 *Bacchanale* – a terrific orchestral showpiece preceding Samson's arrival in the temple.

Also worth investigating
Tone-poems: **La jeunesse d'Hercule, Phaéton** and **Le rouet d'Omphale**.
Cello Concerto No.1 in A minor, Op.33
Piano Concerto No.5 in F 'Egyptian', Op.103
Suite algérienne in C, Op.60: from this comes the exuberant Marche militaire française.
Étude en forme de valse, Op.52 No.6: also in the arrangement by Ysaÿe for violin and piano.
Cyprès et Lauriers, Op.156: for organ and orchestra.
Fantaisie in E flat (1857): for organ.

Erik SATIE
(1866–1925)

Trois Gymnopédies, 1888

Originally written for the piano, Nos.1 & 3 were arranged for orchestra by Debussy, and it is in this form that these lullabies of hypnotic simplicity are most often heard today. Inspiration for them probably came from a Greek vase, whose decoration showed naked youths performing a stately dance before the statues of their gods at the Gymnopedia (a yearly festival held in honour of those who fell at Troy). Satie enjoyed composing in groups of three, presenting three different views of the same object, like looking at a sculpture from opposite angles.

The apparent artlessness of many of Satie's pieces, their thin textures and strange, unprepared harmonies, coupled with his idiosyncratic sense of humour, have led many people to view him as the madman of French music. Certainly, some of his jokes are as banal as some of his compositions – Satie holds the dubious distinction of being the world record-holder for the longest duration of any piece of music ever composed: his *Vexations*, which was played in New York in 1963, is a 180-note piano piece carrying the instructions for it to be played 840 times. It took five pianists working in relays overnight to complete the task. Satie's colleagues were puzzled by him; he was a man who worked as a cabaret pianist in Montmartre, wrote popular songs and gave his (mainly piano) compositions titles such as *Flabby Preludes for a Dog, Bureaucratic Sonata, Desiccated Embryos* and *Three Pieces in the Shape of a Pear*; the last composition was written in response to a critic who had commented that Satie's music had no form. Some of his works are witty, concise, satirical, effervescent – such as his *La belle excentrique* for two pianos; others are more lyrical and reflect his spiritual interests – he was involved with the Rosicrucians.

Harmonies are revealed in his *Sarabandes* (1887) that anticipate those that later brought fame to Debussy. Satie rebelled against the excessive emotionalism of the Romantics and the dominating influence of Wagner, and was instrumental in returning music to simpler, sparser textures. Musically under-educated and realizing his technical shortcomings, Satie was forty when he decided to become a pupil of d'Indy and Roussel. This period of study made him more ambitious; it resulted in his most accomplished work, the Cubist ballet *Parade* (a collaboration with Pablo Picasso and Jean Cocteau, commissioned by Diaghilev) which calls for a siren, a typewriter and a revolver. Satie kept his place at the head of the avant-garde as he grew older; revered by the younger French composers, he became the father figure of Les Six, mocking Debussy towards the end of his life, along with the excesses of Impressionism just as, earlier, he had mocked those of the Romantics. He died in poverty, from cirrhosis of the liver, aged fifty-nine.

Domenico SCARLATTI

'He seems to spring full-armed into the view of history'
(Hubert Parry)

Born: 26 October 1685, Naples
Died: 23 July 1757, Madrid
Full name: Domenico Giuseppe Scarlatti
Type of music: operas, cantatas and sacred music, and, especially, keyboard sonatas
Influences: his father Alessandro, Italian and Spanish dance music
Contemporaries: RAMEAU, J.S. BACH, **DOMENICO SCARLATTI**, HANDEL, Benedetto Marcello, Niccolò Porpora, Jean-Baptiste Senaillé

HIS LIFE AND MUSIC

A century before Liszt brought an unprecedented dazzling virtuosity to the piano, Domenico Scarlatti did the same for the harpsichord. He was initially overshadowed by his illustrious father Alessandro, who was then the most celebrated opera composer in Europe. Today, the works of Scarlatti *père* are never heard, while pianists and harpsichordists continue to delight in the ebullient, sparkling, keyboard sonatas written by Scarlatti *fils*.

Scarlatti began by composing operas in Rome, where he became *maestro di cappella* in the Vatican. He then took up a similar position to the royal family in Lisbon. As music master to the talented Infanta Maria Barbara, Scarlatti followed her to Madrid when she married the heir to the Spanish throne in 1729, and remained in the comparative isolation of the Iberian peninsula for the rest of his life. Spain and the music-loving royal couple provided the environment in which his genius could flourish. Only thirty of the nearly 600 sonatas that he composed were published during his lifetime; they are extraordinarily rich and varied, ranging from imitations of Spanish guitars and folk music, to whirlwind prestos, keyboard acrobatics, sensuous, elegiac song-movements and witty musical jokes. More than two-and-a-half centuries later, Scarlatti's sonatas remain as fresh and vivid as they were when they were written. The most astonishing thing is, there's hardly a dud among them.

Essential works

With the **keyboard sonatas**, two numbering systems are used to identify each sonata. These are, confusingly, totally different: L numbers, after Alessandro Longo, and Kk, after the American harpsichordist Ralph Kirkpatrick. All of Scarlatti's sonatas have been recorded on the harpsichord; some feel that they lose their character when played on the piano – but this is a matter of personal preference. The most frequently heard are:
Sonata in E, L23 'Cortege'
Sonata in D minor, L413 'Pastorale' (also in

a once-popular arrangement by Tausig: *Pastorale and Capriccio*).
Sonata in D, L465 'La chasse'
Sonata in G, L487 'Presto'
Sonata in G minor, L499 'Cat's fugue'
Sonata in A, L345
Sonata in A major, L483.

Also worth investigating

The Good-Humoured Ladies, orchestral ballet suite (1917): an arrangement of Scarlatti sonatas by Vincenzo Tommasini (1878–1950).

Arnold SCHOENBERG

'I believe art is born, not of "I can" but of "I must"' (Schoenberg)

Born: 13 September 1874, Vienna
Died: 13 July 1951, Los Angeles
Original name: Arnold Franz Walter Schönberg
Type of music: orchestral, concerto, opera, choral, chamber, piano, vocal
Influences: Brahms, Wagner and Richard Strauss
Contemporaries: Joseph Jongen, HOLST, Reynaldo Hahn, **SCHOENBERG**, IVES, Samuel Coleridge-Taylor, RAVEL, Reinhold Glière, Albert Ketèlbey, KREISLER

HIS LIFE

The events in the life of this brave musical giant can be briefly sketched; his work and ideas need a book to themselves. His father Samuel, who ran a shoe shop and sang in local choral societies, died when Schoenberg was sixteen, forcing him to take a job in a bank to support his mother and sister. For the man who was to become the most revered musical theoretician of the age and a great teacher, Schoenberg had remarkably little formal training, beyond counterpoint lessons with Alexander Zemlinsky, who became his brother-in-law in 1901.

To those who think of Schoenberg as a purveyor of squeaky-gate music, it comes as a surprise to hear his first two undoubted masterpieces, *Verklärte Nacht (Transfigured Night)* (1899) and the mammoth *Gurrelieder* (1911), which are lusciously scored, richly romantic works in the traditions of Brahms and Wagner. From the early 1900s he became increasingly adventurous, and his compositions provoked a furore whenever they were played. Schoenberg was frustrated by what he saw as the limitations of musical language. What Wagner and others had been hinting at, he now openly embraced: music that, for the first time, had no key – atonal music. The sounds that emerged were greeted with incomprehension; it seemed to those listening as though they were being subjected to an assault of cacophonous, random, improvized notes. This wasn't music as they understood it – and, indeed, Schoenberg was writing in a new language, so how could they understand? To many it was meaningless gibberish.

After a spell in Berlin, where he conducted a kind of intellectual cabaret called *Überbrettl*, he moved back to Vienna; there he devoted himself to composition and teaching, gradually gaining a reputation as a formidable musical thinker and attracting devoted disciples who shared his experimental aims. Among them were Alban Berg and Anton von Webern, with whom he formed a group that musical history now refers to as the Second Viennese School (the first had been the school of Haydn and Mozart). Critical hostility to his music in Vienna extended to anti-Semitic smears and violent abuse, but Schoenberg pugnaciously held his ground.

During the First World War he served sporadically in the Austrian army. Once the war had ceased, discouraged by the lack of performances of his work, he founded the Society for Private Performances. Here his music, and that of his followers, could be heard in ideal conditions – critics were not invited, and expressions of approval or disapproval were discouraged. In 1922, at about the time the Society was disbanded, he began work on the Suite for piano, Op.25, the first formal twelve-note piece to be composed.

Three years later, he was made a Professor at the Prussian Academy of Arts in Berlin. The rise of the Nazis ensured that he was dismissed from his post. Although born a Jew, he had converted to the Christian faith in 1898; moving to Paris in 1933, confronted with the German persecution of Jews, he reconverted to Judaism and left Europe for America, at the same time changing the spelling of his name from Schönberg to Schoenberg.

He spent the first year in Boston, but in 1935 he was made a Professor at the University of Southern California; in 1936 he moved on to U.C.L.A., where he taught for eight years until he reached the mandatory retirement age of seventy. On 11 April 1941 he became an American citizen. In 1946 he had a near-fatal illness during which his heart momentarily stopped beating; after this, Schoenberg's health declined rapidly.

HIS MUSIC

Mention Schoenberg's name to the average man in the street and he won't have heard of him; play a work such as the Five Orchestral Pieces to the same man, and he will listen in bewilderment. A Schoenberg concert can still empty a concert hall faster than a bomb scare. Some of the works that have caused him to be hailed as one of the greatest and most influential composers of the twentieth century, first appeared in the early years of this same century and yet are still not tolerated by the public. Beethoven and Wagner, two other seminal forces in the course of music, never experienced such battles to gain acceptance for their music. In fact, no musical revolutionary in history has had so much time and promotion devoted to him as Schoenberg – and with so little effect on the musical tastes of the public.

His development as a composer can be marked in three stages, excluding the juvenilia. The first is the Brahms- and Wagner-dominated period, which produced *Verklärte Nacht* and *Gurrelieder*; these were written in the late-Romantic, highly-chromatic style not dissimilar to that of Richard Strauss, with its sensuous, surging phrases and richly expressive harmony. Others, such as Bartók, Busoni and Scriabin, were at this time also writing music that hinted at atonality. Schoenberg took the plunge into the pool that none had quite dared enter: on 19 February 1909, he completed his Piano Piece Op.11 No.1 – the first musical composition to dispense with any reference to tonality. The piece was not merely doing away with the traditional ideas of consonance and dissonance: it was atonal. Schoenberg himself disliked the term, preferring to describe it as 'pan-tonality'. To most who heard his *Kammersymphonie* No.1 and the Three Piano Pieces Op.11, all they could make out was a chaotic nightmare. It was, in fact, highly organized and structured, but written in a language for which the audience did not have a dictionary.

Thus, from Romanticism Schoenberg progressed to becoming an Expressionist – his second 'period'. Rather than portray the world about him in the fleeting images of the Impressionists, Schoenberg and other artists, especially painters such as Kandinsky (with whom Schoenberg studied), wanted to project their own inner feelings into their work. But the chords, intervals and rhythms – the building blocks of all music that had gone before – were not those with which Schoenberg could express *his* feelings as *he* wanted. His new language required signposts: in Five Orchestral Pieces the instruments sound as if they are playing against each other, rather than blending together, and in the last section, the score becomes so complicated that he introduces the device of marking the principal part of a particular moment with an H (*Hauptstimme* = 'principal voice'). In his song cycle for female singer / reciter, *Pierrot lunaire*, the singer glides from pitch to pitch in strange rhythmic patterns, a technique Schoenberg called *Sprechstimme* ('speaking voice').

The third part of his development came after the First World War, when he took stock, feeling the need to systematize the new language. There were no longer any major or minor chords and scales, no key or tonic to hang on to. He needed a codified framework, and in 1921 gave a lecture entitled 'Method of Composing with Twelve Tones'.

Simply put, there are twelve notes, or tones, in a chromatic scale: C, C sharp, D, E flat, E, F, F sharp, G, G sharp, A, B flat, B. In writing a piece in twelve-note technique, the composer makes a tone-row, a series (hence 'Serialism', an alternative name for the technique), and arranges them in a certain order. Any suggestion of tonality is avoided by arranging the tones in a series where they would not be played together in a triad (*see* GLOSSARY). The tone-row has four forms: the original, the original backward, the original upside-down and the original upside-down-backwards. Each form of the tone-rows can then be transposed onto any other of the eleven tones of the chromatic scale.

This gives a total of forty-eight possible series of tones built on the original row. These series make up the composer's thematic material. He can then develop it with all the traditional devices of composition. There is only one restriction: once a tone has been sounded, it may not be repeated until all eleven other tones of the row have been used.

Just as Beethoven could employ the notes of a major scale to make a lively dance, a wistful melody or a series of dramatic chords, so Schoenberg too could let his imagination run free and do the same, given the imposed restrictions. Of course, his lively dances, wistful melodies or dramatic chords sound very different to Beethoven's who was, nevertheless, also working under a set of restrictions. Twelve-note technique has been used in every field of music, from cartoons and film scores to symphonies and operas. Schoenberg's innovations have influenced every generation of composers since the 1920s. In his writings and teaching, and through his many pupils, he may be said to have been one of the most influential musicians in history.

Yet many music lovers have struggled to come to terms with Schoenberg's ideas. Some see it as academicism or music by mathematical patterns, appealing to the intellect and not the soul. Should music be so forbidding in its calculations, they ask, or so ugly in the sound it makes? To those who admire what has come from the Second Viennese School it is as richly romantic as works in the traditional manner, even more expressive and profound, written from the heart. The musicologist Percy Scholes, in 1927, summed up his feelings on Serialism thus: 'Nothing is really wasted in Art. Even the puzzle-canons of the Flemish helped in their way the progress of music, and in these new methods of musical construction there is much of the puzzle-canon.' Audiences are still puzzling over Schoenberg. Almost fifty years after his death, he remains a composer's composer, admired by musicians but unloved by the public at large: the bogey-man or hero of music, depending on your point of view.

Essential works

Verklärte Nacht (Transfigured Night), Op.4 (1899): now usually heard in the version made for string orchestra in 1917, this is pre-atonal Schoenberg, deeply emotional, passionate and romantic. It was inspired by the poem 'Weib und di Welt' by Richard Dehmel and tells the story of a couple's walk through a moonlit grove; the woman confesses she has been unfaithful, the man forgives and forgets, and thus, through forgiveness, the world becomes transfigured. In 1907, Schoenberg's wife Mathilde had an affair with a young painter, Richard Gerstl, who was living in their house. Friends persuaded her to return to her husband and two small children; Gerstl could not accept the situation and committed suicide, aged twenty-five.

Gurrelieder (1911): lasting ninety minutes, this gargantuan work is based on a poem telling the story of the love between King Waldemar and the heroine Tove, who lived in Castle Gurre in Denmark. The style is dramatically reminiscent of Wagner and Richard Strauss, the scale is enormous – the work requires five solo voices, a speaker, three male choruses, an eight-part mixed chorus and a huge orchestra. Schoenberg had to score it on specially-made paper containing forty-eight staves. The first part was completed in 1901; the piece was then delayed for ten years – and was finally performed in 1913. This came after

the public had been introduced to Atonal Man and there was some expression of relief that the composer had regained his senses, as they supposed the case to be. Yet, despite the obvious ardent Romanticism of the *Gurrelieder*, fights broke out at the first performance, a woman fainted and there was a lawsuit brought for assault. Strange: Ravel, Debussy and Stravinsky were writing much more advanced music at the time.

Three Piano Pieces, Op.11 (1909): although Schoenberg was not a pianist, the six sets of piano pieces written between 1894 and 1931 provide the clearest, most concise survey of the composer's development; the early Piano Pieces of 1894 are a world apart from these three ground-breaking miniatures, in which tonality was dispensed with for the first time. It is 'open-ended' music, in which no single note or passage is more important than the other, and the ear cannot anticipate structure or musical argument.

Five Orchestral Pieces, Op.16 (1909): the quaint titles of the five sections – *Premonitions, Yesteryears, Summer Morning by a Lake, Peripetia* and *The Obbligato Recitative* – remind one of Schumann; the most interesting of these is the third movement, where Schoenberg experiments with what he called *Klangfarbenmelodie* ('sound-colour melody'). Here a melodic effect is transformed by changing the way in which a single note or chord is played. The first performance was given not in Germany or Austria but in London in 1912, under the baton of Sir Henry Wood.

Pierrot lunaire, Op.21 (1912): here, in this cycle of twenty-one short poems or melodramas, Schoenberg arrives at the threshold of Expressionism – not twelve-note but atonal and dissonant. The solo voice becomes a musical instrument, part of the chamber ensemble texture. So complex is the music in this piece that it required forty rehearsals before the premiere in Berlin in 1912 where it provoked a scandal.

Five Piano Pieces, Op.23 (1923): the first published formal example of serial music and so of great musical interest. Glenn Gould felt that 'I can think of no composition for solo piano from the first quarter of this century which can stand as its equal.'

Franz SCHUBERT

'The first lyric poet of music' (Harold Schonberg)

Born: 31 January 1797, Vienna
Died: 19 November 1828, Vienna
Full name: Franz Peter Schubert
Type of music: symphony, chamber, piano, mass, song, opera, stage, ballet
Influences: Haydn, Mozart, Beethoven, Rossini
Contemporaries: Saverio Mercadante, Franz Berwald, **SCHUBERT**, DONIZETTI, Jacques Fromenthal Halévy, BELLINI, Josef Lanner, Albert Lortzing

HIS LIFE

1797 Schubert was the son of a modest schoolmaster; his mother was a cook. When his musical talent began to emerge, it was encouraged, but with no higher ambition than that he should grow up to be a respectful, hard-working teacher like his father, whose diligence and thrift had allowed him to buy the schoolhouse where the family lived. His early lessons were with his father and brother, but Schubert was soon far beyond their modest accomplishments. Even the parish choirmaster, who taught him singing, had to admit, 'He seems to know each lesson perfectly before I can begin explaining it to him.' By the age of ten, Schubert could play the piano, organ, violin and viola.

1808 He became a member of the imperial court chapel choir in Vienna, which meant that his education, board and lodging at the chapel school were paid for. Among his teachers was Antonio Salieri. 'You can do everything,' he announced to this timid, diffident little boy, 'for you are a genius.'

1811 Schubert began composing while at school and the first of his more than 600 songs, 'Hagars Klage', is dated 30 March 1811.

1813–16 When Schubert's voice broke, rather than stay on a scholarship and continue his education, he decided to leave the school and return to his father's house to follow in his footsteps and become a teacher (an added bonus of the profession was that it meant avoiding military service). Schubert was singularly unsuited to teaching; he could not keep discipline and simply wasn't interested in the subjects he had to teach. All he wanted to do was to write music. And write it he did. In this period he completed five symphonies, four masses, several string quartets, stage music, an opera and some of his most famous *Lieder* – 'Gretchen am Spinnrade', for example, written when he was just seventeen and 'Erlkönig' when he was eighteen – songs of astonishing maturity and originality. In 1815 alone he composed no less than 140 songs (on 15 October alone, he composed eight in one day!).

1816 Schubert finally abandoned the teaching career he loathed so much, and took his chances as a full-time composer. He befriended the poets Johann Mayrhofer and Franz von Schober and while lodging with the latter and his widowed mother, he met the renowned baritone Johann Vogel who was to champion so many of Schubert's songs (he gave the first performance of 'Erlkönig'). Other friends in his loyal circle, which included clerks, customs officers and postmen as well as singers, actors and poets, described Schubert as 'a lump of fat… short, somewhat corpulent, with a full round face, but with eyes so sparkling that they revealed at once the inner fire.' He was 5 feet 1½ inches tall, nearsighted and almost always wore glasses – some said he even kept them on in bed so that he could start composing the minute he woke in the morning. 'If you pay him a visit [at that time],' said Schober, 'he says "Hello, how are you? – Good!" and goes on working, whereupon you go away.'

His self-discipline enabled him to produce an enormous amount of music, and he wrote as much in twenty years as Brahms wrote in fifty. Every morning was devoted to composing. After two o'clock, the afternoon would be taken up with friends, walking in the countryside or chatting in one of Vienna's coffee houses. The evenings were given over to music at the homes of his friends, where Schubert presided as the life and soul of the party, gatherings which came to be known as 'Schubertiads'. Unlike Beethoven, he felt uncomfortable in aristocratic circles, preferring the Bohemian, intellectual, art-loving circle of Vienna.

1818   The meagre income Schubert earned was supplemented by teaching music to the daughters of Count Esterházy at his summer estate in Zelésk, Hungary. Unlike Haydn before him, there was no permanent post for Schubert there, and unlike Beethoven, he never found a rich and permanent patron.

1820   By now, he had composed over 500 works embracing every branch of composition, yet only two of them had been heard in public – the Mass in F in 1814 and a solitary song in 1819. The music commissioned for a play and an opera were both critical flops, and it wasn't until 1821 that his first works, a volume of songs, were published – and then only because his friends clubbed together to pay the costs.

1823   Failure and lack of recognition now began to bite hard. His incidental music to *Rosamunde* was accused of being 'bizarre' and of his opera *Alfonso und Estrella*, Weber remarked dismissively, 'First puppies and first operas should be drowned.' Poverty and having to live on the charity of friends made him increasingly despondent and, added to this, he had to cope with the effects of venereal disease. 'Each night when I go to sleep,' wrote Schubert, ' I hope never again to waken, and every morning reopens the wounds of yesterday.' Yet in the midst of this, he wrote the 'Unfinished' Symphony No.8.

1827   The death of his idol Beethoven came as a terrible blow and Schubert's ambition from then on was to be buried next to him. And still, amidst his many troubles, the most divine music continued to flow – the String Quintet, the last three great Piano Sonatas, the Mass in E flat and the songs that after his death would be gathered into the cycle *Schwanengesang*.

1828   On 26 March in the Musikverein of Vienna, for the first time there was given a programme entirely devoted to Schubert's music. It was put on by his friends, of course, but, though successful, was never even reviewed – Paganini was in Vienna and his concerts took up all the newspaper space. Less than eight months later, Schubert died in a delirious state, babbling of his idol Beethoven. Ostensibly, his symptoms were those of typhoid poisoning, although it now seems likely that tertiary syphilis was wreaking its final damage. He was 31, and was buried as near to Beethoven as was practicable, with the epitaph 'Here lie rich treasure and still fairer hopes.' Schubert left no estate at all – except his manuscripts.

1838 It seems incredible at this remove that so little of Schubert's music should have been heard or published during his lifetime. After his death, piles of manuscripts were left, forgotten, bundled up and stuck into cupboards. It was only by chance and the diligence of a few musicians that some came to light; in 1838 Schumann visited Schubert's brother and came across the 'Great' Symphony in C (the Ninth) and urged its publication; the 'Unfinished' Symphony was not heard until 1865, after the score was found in a chest; and George Grove (of *Grove's Dictionary*) and the young Arthur Sullivan (of Gilbert and Sullivan) unearthed Schubert's Symphonies Nos.1, 2, 3, 4 & 6, sixty songs and the music for *Rosamunde* in a publisher's house in Vienna in 1867.

1978 Over a century later, the sketches for a tenth symphony were discovered in another Viennese archive.

HIS MUSIC

Schubert was not the first of the Romantics but he was, in the words of Harold Schonberg, 'the first lyric poet of music'. The ideas came tumbling out like water from a spring. Not for him the titanic inner struggles of Beethoven. He rarely revised his work – his natural instinct and feel for musical shape was enough. Surprisingly for such a fecund composer, there are comparatively few second-rate works. But that is not to say his music was without faults; his knowledge of counterpoint was weak, and in longer forms, such as the symphonies and some of the sonatas, the themes are not developed or enlarged in the traditional manner. The same material is presented in a different guise, with a change of key or instruments, or, more usually, new ideas emerge. While it is not accurate to say that Schubert was a miniaturist, it was in smaller forms that his genius flowered, none more notably than in his songs. Altogether, he set poems by ninety-one different authors, generally in strophic form – where the same tune is used for all the verses – but not dogmatically so, for there are songs of every shape and style. And what music! It comments on the words, illustrates the moods or scenes depicted and somehow heightens both, elevating the art of song to an entirely new level.

Schubert's gift of melody has, quite probably, never been equalled. It is not merely the beauty of the ideas but their variety of character that is truly astonishing, encompassing every emotion and mood. It's the way in which he harmonizes this fount of melody that makes him so original, offering surprises ('the element of the unexpected that is yet so inevitable') as well as taking the listener exactly where he or she hopes the music will go, without ever being mundane or banal.

Essential works

Schubert's works are identified both by their Op. Nos. and their D numbers – after Otto Erich Deutsch (1883–1967), the Austrian musicologist who published a complete thematic catalogue of Schubert's work in 1951.

Orchestral

Of the nine symphonies, the first three are early works, although in **No.2** Schubert has already found his feet; **Nos.5 & 6** are elegant and beautiful but not among his best. **No.4 in C minor** (Schubert himself called it The 'Tragic' Symphony) is undoubtedly the finest of the symphonies before the two final master-pieces. **No.7** was sketched out but never completed.

Symphony No.8 in B minor 'Unfinished', D759 (1822): one of the most popular of all symphonies, though why it was left unfinished, with two complete movements instead of the usual four, is a mystery – there are sketches for a third movement and some say that he did indeed finish four movements but that his friend Hüttenbrenner, to whom Schubert gave the score, lost the last two .... Or did Schubert not feel able to better the two movements we know today? He rarely began a composition before completing the previous one.

Symphony No.9 in C 'Great', D944 (1825–28): when Schumann discovered the manuscript of this symphony at Ferdinand Schubert's house, he wrote to Clara Wieck: 'It is not possible to describe it to you. All the instruments are human voices. It is gifted beyond measure, and this instrumentation,

Beethoven notwithstanding – and this length, this heavenly length, like a novel in four volumes ....' One of Schubert's last works, packed with ideas, heading off in new directions and developing the symphonic form from where Beethoven had left it.

Rosamunde, D797, incidental music for a play, (1823): the overture and enchanting second dance from the ballet music (in G major) are universally loved, but unmissable is the Entr'acte No.3 (in B flat), one of Schubert's most heavenly tunes. He used it again in the slow movement of his A minor String Quartet and in the Impromptu in B flat for piano.

Chamber music

Octet in F, D803, (1824): a marvellous work, the result of a commission to provide a companion piece to Beethoven's Septet, built on the scale of a symphony, it is airy, light-hearted and tuneful.

String Quintet in C, D956, (1828): the serene melancholy of the first movement and the uniquely lovely second movement make this a very special work, among the last that Schubert wrote. One of the cornerstones of any classical collection.

Piano Quintet in A 'Trout', D667, (1819): written when Schubert and his friend Vogl were on a holiday, this magical work has none of the resignation or elegiac grief of the String Quintet. It has five movements, the fourth being a jolly set of variations on his song 'Die Florelle' ('The Trout').

Adagio and Rondo concertante in F, D487, (1816): little-known but captivating short two-movements-for-piano quartet, like a miniature piano concerto with an unforgettable Rondo theme.

Not all of Schubert's fifteen String quartets are of equal merit. Worth investigating are:

String Quartet No.13 in A minor, D804 (1824): the themes of this quartet's first three movements are reminiscent of his *Lieder*, while the fourth begins with a lively Hungarian dance.

String Quartet No.14 in D minor 'Death and the Maiden', D810 (1824): so-called because Schubert used part of his famous song 'Der Tod und das Mädchen' in the second movement; death and funerals hang heavy over the whole work.

Piano Trio No.1 in B flat, D898 (c.1828)
Piano Trio No.2 in E flat, D929 (c.1828)
Both trios are quintessential Schubert; the slow movement of No.1 is a good example of how he can take the listener by surprise: the music is in the key of A flat when suddenly it switches to the remote key of E – 'The effect is of the heavens opening up.' A historic recording of this work was made in 1927 by the legendary partnership of Pablo Casals, Alfred Cortot and Jacques Thibaud. The slow movement of the

less well-known **E flat Trio** is another beauty, based on a Swedish folk tune; it was used in the film *Barry Lyndon*.

Sonata in A minor 'Arpeggione' D821: the arpeggione (a cross between a cello and a guitar) was invented in 1823, and Schubert wrote its for its one exponent, Vincent Schuster; the instrument never caught on, but the music did, played nowadays on the cello.

Piano music

Six Moments musicaux, D780 (1823–28): a form that Schubert invented and which describes fleeting musical thoughts; No.3 in F minor is especially popular.

Eight Impromptus, D899 and D946 (1828): a form not originated by Schubert but made popular by him, these are like short improvisations. There are two sets: D899 Nos.1–4 and D935 Nos.1–4; all are, without exception, miniature masterpieces.

Fantasia in F minor, D940 (1828): a piano duet and a late work whose opening theme – another example of Schubert's 'serene melancholy' – takes the breath away.

Fantasy in C 'Wanderer Fantasy', D760 (1822): an extended solo piano work, enormously testing to play, which begins and ends in heroic style. Liszt made a highly effective version for piano and orchestra.

Sonatas

Schubert wrote about twenty sonatas for the piano. Like the string quartets, they are uneven – some don't hang together successfully and themes are underdeveloped, giving them an unsatisfying feel; yet all are brimming with wonderful musical ideas. The best are:

Sonata in C minor, D958 (1828)
Sonata in A, D959 (1828)
Sonata in B flat, D960 (1828)
These piano sonatas were written in quick succession in the last weeks of Schubert's life. Composed in less than four weeks, they are among the greatest of his works, stretching the sonata form and, like the String Quintet and Ninth Symphony, showing an inventiveness that puts them on a level of inspiration way above that of the tunesmith and miniaturist. They are known as the three 'posthumous sonatas' because they were not published until 1838. Today, the B flat Sonata is required playing for all pianists, and some feel that its *Andante sostenuto* ranks with the greatest slow movements ever written.

Of the other sonatas, the earlier **Sonata in A, D664** (1819) has a youthful freshness that brings a smile to the face, and the lengthy (nearly forty minutes) **Sonata in D, D850** (1825) has an enchanting slow movement, ending with a perky finale like a Swiss clock (also popular as a violin encore).

Marche militaire in D, D733 (1818): one of Schubert's best-known works; the first of a set of three, attempted by every beginner on the piano and a favourite orchestral 'classical pop'.

Vocal

Schubert's incomparable songs typify the school of German Romantic *Lieder* that was soon to be developed by Schumann, then Hugo Wolf and Richard Strauss. Of his over 600 essays in the genre, seventy-two are of poems by Goethe, forty-seven by Mayrhofer and forty-six by Schiller. They cover everything from dramatic narrative to philosophic meditation, from exuberant joy to deep melancholy. Liszt made persuasive piano arrangements of a selection. Dip in anywhere and you'll find something to admire.

Among the best-loved ones are:

'**Gretchen am Spinnrade**', '**Erlkönig**', '**Horch, horch die Lerch**', '**Die Forelle**', '**Ave Maria**', '**Auf dem wasser zu singen**', '**An Sylvia**', '**An die Musik**', '**Wiegenlied**' (D498),

'**Der Hirt auf dem Felsen**', '**Litanei**', '**Frühlingsglaube**', '**Der Musensohn**' and '**Der Tod und das Mädchen**'.

Schubert also wrote several song cycles (a group of songs united by a single theme):

Die schöne Müllerin has twenty songs with words by Müller, in which the miller of the title passes through the stages of joy, disillusionment and thoughts of suicide. It includes 'Das Wandern', 'Wohin?' and 'Ungeduld'.

Die Winterreise: with twenty-four songs, and lyrics by Müller, this cycle was composed in 1827 when Schubert was at his lowest ebb. Highlights are 'Gute nacht', 'Der Lindenbaum', 'Die Krähe' and 'Frühlingstraum'.

Schwanengesang: includes fourteen songs with words by Rellstab, Heine and Seidl, of which 'Liebesbotschaft', 'Am Meer' and (one of the greatest of all love songs) 'Ständchen' are the best known.

Robert SCHUMANN

'Everything beautiful is difficult, the short the most difficult'
(Schumann)

Born: 8 June 1810, Zwickau
Died: 29 July 1856 Endenich, near Bonn
Full name: Robert Alexander Schumann
Type of music: symphony, concerto, chamber, instrumental, choral, song
Influences: Bach, Beethoven, Mendelssohn
Contemporaries: CHOPIN, Otto Nicolai, Félicien David, **SCHUMANN**, Samuel Wesley, LISZT, Ambroise Thomas, Vincent Wallace, Sigismund Thalberg

HIS LIFE

Mendelssohn, Chopin, Schumann, Liszt, Verdi and Wagner were born within four years of one another; Schumann is a key figure in the Romantic movement epitomized by these composers and, arguably, none investigated the Romantic's obsession with feeling and passion quite so thoroughly as he did. For most of his life, Schumann suffered from inner torment – he died insane – but then some psychologists argue that madness is a necessary attribute of genius.

1810 Schumann's father was a Saxon bookseller and publisher, well-to-do and cultured. Robert was his fifth child and although he and his wife were not musical, they encouraged their son's musical talents, commencing with piano lessons at the age of ten. For a career, however, he was persuaded to study law in nearby Leipzig, where, at the same time, he studied piano with his future father-in-law, Friedrich Wieck.

1829 A series of events, *deus ex machina*, then took place – events that twisted and turned the paths Schumann might have expected to travel trouble-free. His elder sister, Emilie, committed suicide in 1826, and shortly afterwards his father died at the age of fifty-three from a nervous disease that no one has been able to diagnose. (Of Schumann's three brothers, only one reached late middle age.) Schumann became absorbed in the fashionable Romantic malaise of *Weltschmerz*, or world-weariness, exemplified by the writings of Novalis, Byron and Lenau, among others, all of whom died young in romantically tragic circumstances.

1830 Schumann persuaded his mother and his guardian to allow him to study music and the same Friedrich Wieck was recommended. He returned to his tutor's house, where he lodged and boarded, determined to become a world famous virtuoso like his teacher's talented young daughter, Clara. Schumann's mature career as a composer dates from about this time.

1832 A second tragic event intervened when he developed an ailment in the index and middle fingers of his right hand. He tried all the fashionable remedies available, including a mechanical device that purported to help strengthen and lift the middle finger. It permanently crippled his right hand, so much so that he was exempted from military service – a certificate exists showing that Schumann was unable to pull the trigger on a rifle. That was the end of his ambitions as a concert pianist.

1833 Worse was to come. Some theories have it that the original problem with his two fingers was caused by the side-effects of mercury treatment for syphilis. He was a handsome man and enjoyed the company of young ladies, but from this date onwards he noted unaccountable periods of angst and momentary losses of consciousness, bouts of breathing difficulty and aural hallucinations; he also suffered from insomnia and acrophobia, and confided in his diary that he was afraid of going mad. He thought of killing himself.

Nevertheless, throughout this decade Schumann's career as a composer slowly grew, while he also developed his literary activities. In 1834 he co-founded a progressive journal, the *Neue Zeitschrift für Musik*, which fulminated against the vapid *salon* music of the day. His sharp and perceptive writing made him one of the foremost critics of the time, the first German critic to recognize Chopin, writing as early as 1831, under the name of Eusebius, 'Hats off, gentlemen, a genius!', and was among the first to champion Berlioz and predict Brahms' greatness. Sometimes his judgments have proved to be askew, but in general Schumann's musical criticism was as fine as the style of his prose.

He also translated his journalistic and musical convictions into real life. He formed an association of intimate friends, which he named *Davidsbündler* ('David against the Philistines'), a group that would oppose philistinism in the arts and give passionate support to all that was new and imaginative. Schumann immortalized these friends in his piano work *Davidsbündlertänze*.

Concurrent with all this, a fourth event took place – one that had the benign effect of inspiring his music to heights which (who knows?) he may not have reached had he not fallen in love with Clara Wieck and been prevented from marrying her. Perhaps surmising that Schumann was an unstable character, Friedrich Wieck violently opposed the relationship, and his actions over the following seven years won him a place in music history, not as the obscure teacher of a great composer or as the father of a great pianist (which Clara would become) but as the disagreeable father-in-law who thwarted young love. He forced the couple to separate, opened their love letters and initiated a campaign of personal vilification against Schumann, so set was he against his daughter's marriage.

1840 The affair ended in court, judgment went against Wieck and the happy couple were married on 12 September, the day before Clara's twenty-first birthday. Was it a happy marriage? Schumann's career as a composer clearly entered a new stage: in 1840 alone he wrote over a hundred songs and in 1841, over four days, he sketched out his Symphony No.1 in B flat, the 'Spring' Symphony. Many other masterful works followed rapidly but although Clara was intensely ambitious for her husband, they found it hard to balance the need for a pianist to practice and a composer to work in silence.

1844 On tour, he found it galling to be introduced as the husband of Clara Schumann and returned home before her from Russia. His mental health began to fail, he resigned from the teaching post Mendelssohn had created for him at his new Conservatory in Leipzig, and the Schumanns moved to Dresden. The great Piano Concerto was completed here, along with the Second Symphony and more songs, but from the late 1840s it was clear that Schumann was becoming increasingly unbalanced.

1850 He accepted the post of Director of Music in Düsseldorf. It proved to be a disaster. Schumann was no conductor, a talent that the position demanded, and with his natural reserve (Liszt and Wagner found him boring) now exaggerated by his inability to communicate and, at times unaware of his surroundings, he was forced to resign.

1854 Aural hallucinations were now accompanied by visions of demons and angels, and on 27 February he tried to kill himself by drowning in the Rhine. He was rescued and placed at his own request in an asylum at Endenich near Bonn. Here, Brahms was one of the few welcome visitors; some sources say Schumann refused to see Clara or any of their seven children, others that Clara would not visit for fear of upsetting him.

1856 Schumann lived on in this unhappy state for a further two years. Shortly before he died, Clara did visit him. He had aged so much that she did not recognise him initially. 'He smiled at me and put his arms around me with great difficulty, for he had almost lost control of his limbs,' wrote Clara. 'Never shall I forget that moment. I would not give up that embrace for all the treasures on earth.' He died in Clara's arms and was buried the following day in Bonn. Opinions vary as to whether the cause of his final illness was tertiary syphilis, sclerosis of the brain (his own doctor's verdict), *dementia praecox* or starvation induced by psychotic depression. Whatever, it was the cruellest and most un-Romantic of ends.

HIS MUSIC

Schumann's finest music is for the piano, closely followed by his songs. Up until 1840 he wrote little else but for the piano, works that are at the heart of every pianist's repertoire, an enormous proportion of which are played and recorded regularly by every major soloist; like Shakespeare's plays, they provide an unending source of pleasure and challenge in their interpretation. The moods and forms they encompass are myriad, filled with poetic flights of fancy and the wildest imagination. Although he wrote successfully in some of the traditional forms such as the sonata, he added to the Romantic practice of loosely-knit structures the idea of painting many small cameos and combining them onto one huge canvas.

After 1840, he wrote more for the voice. Schumann's sensitivity to literature, both prose and verse, allied with his extraordinary melodic facility make his songs among the most important gifts to the art of *Lieder*, and make him a worthy successor and companion to Schubert. He brings the same tenderness, passion and humanity to his settings as the older composer, but with touches of irony and self-deprecating wit that is missing from the works of other Romantics.

Like Schubert, Schumann was not as happy with the large forms as he was with the small. Musicologists tut-tut at his orchestration and his inability to find a cohesive structure for the Symphonies and they wince at the awkward writing of his chamber music. Yet the music returns again and again, entrancing the listener with its invention and spring-like inspiration. The lyrical beauty he could summon up at will, the warmth and sheer well-being that his works engender, silences criticism after all.

Essential works
Piano music

Carnaval, Op.9 (1835): Schumann loved word play, acrostics and double meanings; this captivating collection is subtitled 'little scenes on four notes'. He wrote the work for Ernestine von Frick when he was in love with her (a brief departure from Clara); Ernestine lived in the Bohemian town of Asch and in German notation, our notes A, E flat, C and B natural become A, Es (S), C and H. The four notes permeate the work; they are also the only musical letters in Schumann's name, a fact that intrigued him. But beyond the private jokes, the succession of fleeting character sketches that follow in quick succession combine to make one of the piano's masterpieces. Notable are the recordings by Arthur Rubinstein or (earlier) by Sergei Rachmaninov.

ASCH also appears in **Papillons Op.2**, while A,B,E,G and G form the notes of the theme for the **Abegg Variations Op.1**, named after the Countess Meta von Abegg, to whom Schumann was also romantically attached.

Fantasiestücke, Op.12 (1837): Schumann used two pen-names for his contributions to the *Zeitschrift für Musik*: Eusebius and Florestan. These eight short, contrasted pieces reveal the two opposing sides of their natures, as well as the two faces of Schumann's personality – one forceful and dominant, the other a gentle dreamer; *Des Abends*, *Warum?* and *Traumes Wirren* are three favourites.

Études symphoniques, Op.13 (1834–52): a theme and twelve variations are a bland way of describing this work, but Schumann invented a new form of writing variations – he felt it unnecessary to hear the theme during each variation but rather used snippets of the melody or a harmony or rhythm as the impulse for the next variation. It was a process that would influence Brahms profoundly. The theme came from the adoptive father of his former love, Fraulein von Frick.

Kinderszenen, Op.15 (1838): an album of childhood scenes through an adult's eyes, the thirteen brief musical pictures include the ever popular *Träumerei* (*Daydreams*), which every student of the piano will have encountered.

Fantasie in C, Op.17 (1838): dedicated to Liszt, this is another revered piano work. Schumann wrote to Clara: 'I do not think I ever wrote anything more impassioned than the first movement. It is a profound lament about you.' After this comes a heroic march, followed by a final movement, a meditation that has been described as 'a pure stream of beatific melody.'

Orchestral

Symphony No.1 in B flat, 'Spring', Op.38 (1841)

Symphony No.3 in E flat, 'Rhenish', Op.97 (1850)

For those coming fresh to Schumann's four symphonies, these are the best to sample first. The 'Spring' is immediately attractive – bursting with energy, graceful dance melodies and Mendelssohnian high spirits. The 'Rhenish', in five instead of the usual four movements, was originally subtitled 'Episode in a life on the banks of the Rhine river'. The fourth movement is called the *Cathedral Scene*, an evocation of the enthronement of a cardinal in Cologne Cathedral, which Schumann had once witnessed.

Piano Concerto in A minor, Op.54 (1841–45): Schumann's most popular composition and one of the most loved of all piano concertos. Like Grieg, he wrote just one in the key of A minor, and although he began three earlier piano concertos he abandoned them all. Famously, the work begins with a single dramatic blow from the orchestra, followed by the piano's downward cascade of chords before the beautiful first theme, which is recognizable to every German as the 'Leben Sie wohl' ('Fare you well') phrase from Schubert's *Wanderer's Nightsong* (Mendelssohn quotes it in his overture *A Calm Sea and a Prosperous Voyage* (requoted in Elgar's *Enigma Variations*) and Beethoven used it in the *Les Adieux* sonata). Dinu Lipatti's recording of the work has achieved classic status.

Two other lesser-known works for piano and orchestra are worth getting to know:

Konzertstück (Introduction and allegro appassionato) in G, Op.92, (1849)

Introduction and Allegro in D minor, Op.134, (1853)

Chamber

Piano Quintet in E flat, Op.44 (1842): the one chamber work of Schumann's that can be thoroughly recommended on all counts, a pioneering work for the combination of piano and string quartet, and the inspiration for later works by Brahms, Dvořák and Franck. There is a tangible, white-hot, creative force behind it – Schumann sketched it in five days and scored it within a fortnight. It is dedicated to Clara. Mendelssohn was the pianist for the first performance after Clara fell ill at the last moment: he sight-read the part.

If you fall for this, try also the **Piano Quartet in E flat, Op. 47** (also 1842) and the **Piano Trio in D minor, Op.63** (1847).

Songs

Dichterliebe, Op.48 (1840): the most noted singers of the world have always counted this song-cycle (*A Poet's Love*) among their most treasured possessions. The sixteen settings of Heine's poems show what an unusual sensitivity Schumann had for verse. The piano plays as important a role as the singer, commenting on and defining the character and emotional content and sometimes given proportionately long introductory and concluding passages, raising the art of *Lied* to new heights. Look out especially for No.1 ('Im wunderschönen Monat Mai'), No.6 ('Im Rhein, im heiligen Strome') and No.15 ('Aus alten Märchen winkt es').

Among Schumann's 250 other songs, essential listening are:

'Frauenliebe und leben, Op.42' (Woman's Life and Love): a cycle of eight songs, following the protagonist from her first love, marriage and childbirth to betrayal, as well as

'**Mondnacht**', '**Der Nussbaum**', '**Aufträge**' and '**Die beiden Grenadiere**' and '**Widmung**'.

Also worth investigating
Konzertstück for four horns and orchestra, Op.86 (1849)
Cello Concerto in A minor, Op.129 (1850)
Papillons, Op.2 (1829–31), piano
Toccata in C, Op.7 (1829–32), piano
Kreisleriana, Op.16 (1838), piano
Piano Sonata No.2 in G minor, Op.22 (1833–38)

Alexander SCRIABIN

'I wish I could possess the world as I possess a woman' (Scriabin)

Born: 6 January 1872, Moscow
Died: 27 April 1915, Moscow
Full name: Alexander Nikolaievich Scriabin
Type of music: symphony, orchestral, concerto, piano
Influences: Chopin, Liszt, Wagner, Nietzsche
Contemporaries: Louis Vierne, Leopold Godowsky, LEHÁR, **SCRIABIN**, VAUGHAN WILLIAMS, Hugo Alfvén, Max Reger, RACHMANINOV, Joseph Jongen

HIS LIFE AND MUSIC

Scriabin's career divides into two halves: until about 1900 he was a latter-day Russian Chopin, executing the sort of piano pieces that the Polish composer might have written had he lived longer; then Scriabin increasingly came to believe that he was God. This makes him and his music not uninteresting. He wasn't mad, but he was certainly a hypochondriac, an obsessive and a megalomaniac on a scale not matched even by Wagner. His music broke with all previous forms and traditions. It has enormous originality, the ideas and theories were truly messianic but he did not have Wagner's

determined pragmatism or a long enough life to see his grandiose schemes come to fruition. Little of his work has been accepted into the mainstream repertoire. Ultimately Scriabin has been seen to lead nowhere, despite the 1960s revival of interest in his mystic and psychedelic fusions – a brief, intense meteor.

Scriabin's father was a young law student, his mother a talented concert pianist who died of tuberculosis shortly after Alexander's birth. He was brought up by a doting aunt and grandmother, who pampered him; over-concerned to protect him from danger and illness, they would not allow him to play with other children. He was fourteen before he went out into the street unaccompanied and this early seclusion led to his later hypochondria – Scriabin could not tolerate being on his own, he was a compulsive hand-washer, he wore gloves in case he should come into contact with germs and he never wore a hat (unheard of at the time) fearing it would make him go bald. With his super-ego and sense of self-adoration, it was not surprising that it should be his own music that affected Scriabin most. One contemporary watching him, said 'I have seldom seen a composer's face and figure so mobile while listening to his own music. It was as if he could not constrain himself to conceal the profound experiences he derived from it.'

The teachers who developed his prodigious gifts were the best in Moscow – men such as Conus, Zverev, Taneiev and Safonov. Scriabin was a fellow student of Rachmaninov's at the Moscow Conservatory and was destined to be a great pianist like him, until he damaged his right hand trying to outdo the pianistic feats of another Safonov pupil, Josef Lhevinne. Thereafter, Scriabin never quite regained the keyboard fluency he had enjoyed and played only his own works in public. He stayed on at the Conservatory to study fugue with Arensky but never completed the course. By this time he was writing his first pieces in the manner of Chopin and was taken up by the publisher Belaieff who offered him a contract. A successful European tour ensued and by the late 1890s Scriabin was giving concerts devoted entirely to his own music.

In 1897 he married a fellow pianist, Vera Isakovich with whom he had three children. From 1898 to 1903 he taught piano at the Moscow Conservatory. So far, so conventional.

In 1898 a shift in style emerged, the classical outlines became blurred, the harmonies cryptic and unusual; he completed two huge symphonies incorporating the germs of his new creative thoughts, and started reading Nietzsche and the mystic musings of Helena Blavatsky. Scriabin began to form the theory that music was something greater, more all-encompassing than the mere sounds that emerged. 'I can't understand how to write only "music" now,' he wrote to friends. 'How uninteresting it would be. Music, surely, takes on idea and significance when it is linked to one single plan within the whole of a world viewpoint .... Music is the path of revelation.'

He devised the so-called 'mystic chord' (C, F sharp, B flat, E, A, D) and worked out entire pieces based on this. He abandoned key signatures and the music became more dissonant. Curiously, although the theories of Arnold Schoenberg were being developed at around the same time and have nothing to do with Scriabin's theories, the sound of their two languages in certain pieces is extraordinarily similar.

After Belaieff's death, Scriabin was financed by a wealthy Moscow merchant. Shortly afterwards, in 1905, he seduced his former pupil, the eighteen-year-old Tatiana Schloezer, and left his wife for her with the explanation, 'I have to make a sacrifice for the sake of my art.' Vera accepted her fate, even to the extent of spreading the gospel of Scriabin throughout Europe in her recitals. Tatiana joined Scriabin in the United States in 1906 for a concert tour but the couple were advised to leave because of their 'immoral' relationship – Vera refused to grant Scriabin a divorce and the puritan Americans did not take kindly to common-law wives.

In 1908, Scriabin acquired another wealthy patron in the person of the conductor Serge Koussevitzky. His publishing house was devoted to Russian composers and Russian music. Scriabin, controversial and provocative, was exactly what Koussevitzky required and Scriabin, in turn, needed money and a publisher. They toured together as soloist and conductor and, although the relationship did not last long – each was too convinced of his own importance – Koussevitzky continued to support the Scriabin cause, including giving the first performance of his last major work for orchestra, *Prometheus*. This was a preliminary study for the apocalyptic masterpiece he planned entitled *Mystrerium*; Koussevitzky's money (5,000 roubles a year for five years) helped finance the composition.

By now Scriabin had formed his personal Superman theory, convinced he was the musical messiah destined to unite the world by his mystic art. His verse writing includes such lines as 'I am God! I am nothing, I am play, I am freedom, I am life. I am the boundary. I am the peak. I am God!' For *Prometheus*, he had produced a system whereby different sounds corresponded to different colours; C = red, E = 'pearly white and shimmer of moonlight', F sharp = bright blue, G sharp = purple, and so on, and a colour organ was invented to play with the score (such a contraption was actually made but it proved impractical and was dropped). *Mystrerium* was to be a cataclysmic synthesis of all the arts, a multi-media extravaganza, a 'sacred action' involving dance, orchestra, piano, colour, incense and sculpture, to be performed in a temple in India with 'a reflecting pool of water… and bells suspended from the clouds'. 'I shall not die,' said Scriabin. 'I shall suffocate in ecstasy after the *Mysterium*.' To prepare himself for the event, Scriabin bought a Sanskrit grammar and a sun helmet.

However, it was not to be; the First World War intervened. In March 1914 he was in London for a concert conducted by the adventurous Sir Henry Wood, which included Scriabin's Piano Concerto and *Prometheus*; he gave his last recital in Petrograd just over a year later on 15 April 1915. In London a boil had developed on his upper lip but healed without medical attention. Back in Moscow after the Petrograd recital, a carbuncle grew in the same place. This time it did not heal. Scriabin developed a fever and before long gangrene covered his entire face. Within a few days he was dead.

Essential works

Symphony No.3 in C, 'The Divine Poem', Op.43 (1902–04): of his five symphonies, this is the first in which Scriabin merged his theories of music and philosophy; all three of the latter works are more tone-poems than symphonies. The movements of 'The Divine Poem' (*Struggles*, *Delights* and *Divine Play*) represent Tatiana Schloezer's programmatic theosophic text invoking 'the evolution of the human spirit … which attains its unity with the universe (the divine 'Ego')' – make of it what you will.

Symphony No.4 in C, 'Poem of Ecstasy', Op.54 (1905–08): when Scriabin played part of this work to a group of eminent Russian musicians, one of them, Rimsky-Korsakov, denounced it, saying, 'He's half out of his mind.' But this is probably the most successful of the three later symphonies. It describes the 'ecstasy of untrammelled action, the joy in creativity' with different instruments representing five leading theosophic motives: the flute for Yearning, trombones for Protest, horns for Apprehension, the trumpet for both Will and for Self-Assertion – the work's central idea.

Symphony No.5 in F sharp, 'Prometheus: The Poem of Fire', Op.60 (1910): Scriabin was planning his *Mysterium* at the same time as composing this work. Here, Man is represented by the piano as he struggles against the Cosmos (the orchestra); eventually the two merge, and the ecstatic ending has a mixed chorus joining the orchestra with a wordless chant.

Piano Concerto in F sharp minor, Op.20 (1896): an uneven work written in Scriabin's Chopinesque style, but which bears repeated hearings; the last movement has a searingly romantic second subject.

Piano sonatas

Scriabin wrote ten sonatas, and they chart the course of his development as a composer. The first three are indebted to Chopin and Liszt (**No.2 in G sharp minor, Op.19 'Sonata-Fantasy'** is well worth a listen). With **Sonata No.4 in F sharp minor, Op.30** – written in 1903 when his musical thinking had altered – Scriabin switches to a one-movement form, which he continued to use in the subsequent sonatas and, gradually, the music becomes more difficult to play and comprehend.

Sonata No.5 in D sharp minor (1907): written in a key rarely used, this is the first to exploit Scriabin's new mystical musings, involving extreme violence and dissonance and exploring every corner of the piano's sonority. **Sonata No.6** (1911): dispenses with a key signature. **Sonata No.7, Op.64** (1911): the composer's personal favourite; he called it 'The White Mass'. **Sonata No.8, Op.66** (1912–13): the longest of the one-movement sonatas. **Sonata No.9 in F, Op.68** (1912–13): 'The Black Mass', only eight minutes long. **Sonata No.10** (1913): exceeds them all in complexity and obscurity. In the hands of a great pianist such as Vladimir Horowitz, these works, at first daunting, can sound thrilling, dangerous and, yes, visionary.

Eighty-five Preludes and **Twenty-four Études**: dip into these at will. They are variable, rising from the banal to the ravishing; the later the opus number, the more demanding the music becomes. Not to be overlooked are:

Étude in C sharp minor Op.2 No.1 (1887): composed when Scriabin was fourteen and one of his best known works.

Twelve Études, Op.8 (1894)

'One of the finest late-nineteenth-century sets

of concert études,' according to David Dubal. The most famous of these – **Étude in D sharp minor, Op.8 No.12** – is also Scriabin's most frequently played work. Louis Biancolli wrote: 'Whoever plays it feels momentarily like a god. To have composed that étude is to have married the piano.' The recordings by Horowitz and Simon Barere reveal what he means.

Prelude in C sharp minor for the left hand alone, Op.9 No.1 (1894)

Nocturne in D flat for the left hand alone, Op.9 No.2 (1894)

Scriabin wrote these last two when he injured his right hand trying to outdo the pianistic feats of his classmate, Josef Lhevinne.

Vers la flamme, Op.72 (1914): of all the late Scriabin works, this encapsulates his essence. *Towards the Flame* summons up an apocalyptic vision – Hiroshima on the piano – in which Scriabin 'was setting his soul on fire'.

Dmitri SHOSTAKOVICH

'The conscience of Soviet music' (Khachaturian)

Born: 25 September 1906, St Petersburg

Died: 9 August 1975, Moscow

Type of music: symphony, orchestral, opera, film, stage, ballet, choral, chamber, piano

Influences: Mahler, Tchaikowsky, Glazunov, Stravinsky

Contemporaries: Alan Rawsthorne, Dag Wirén, TIPPETT, **SHOSTAKOVICH**, Elisabeth Lutyens, Paul Creston, MESSIAEN, Elliott Carter, BARBER

HIS LIFE

After his death, the government of the USSR issued the following summary of Shostakovich's work, drawing attention to a 'remarkable example of fidelity to the traditions of musical classicism, and above all, to the Russian traditions, finding his inspiration in the reality of Soviet life, reasserting and developing in his creative innovations the art of socialist realism and, in so doing, contributing to universal progressive musical culture.'

It wasn't always like that, despite his three Orders of Lenin and other Soviet honours. Shostakovich's life happened to run in tandem with the Communist regime and he frequently fell foul of the authorities, accused of not writing the correct type of music. Nevertheless, while Prokofiev and Stravinsky had grown up under the Tsars, Shostakovich was the first and arguably the greatest composer to emerge from Communism.

His first music lessons on the piano came from his mother, a professional pianist (his father was an engineer employed in the weights and measures office) but it was Glazunov who took him under his wing when Shostakovich entered the St Petersburg Conservatory at the age of thirteen. His graduation composition was his First Symphony, which made him internationally known at the age of twenty and has subsequently proved to be one of his most popular works. His Second Symphony 'To October', was less successful despite its rousing choral finale and revolutionary sentiments.

Shostakovich, child of the Revolution, believed it was the duty of an artist to serve the state. Yet his next venture, the satirical opera *The Nose*, was attacked by the arbiters of Soviet musical taste as 'bourgeois decadence'. The same year, his Third Symphony, subtitled 'The First of May', its finale saluting the 'International Workers Day' was criticized as being no more than 'a formal gesture of proletarian solidarity'. This was nothing compared to the reaction to his opera *Lady Macbeth of the Mtzensk District* (1934). Soviet musicians generally welcomed it as a significant work, as good as anything being produced in the West. But its scenes of adultery, murder and suicide shocked puritan officialdom and, after the opera's Moscow production, the official Communist party newspaper *Pravda* published an article headed 'Chaos instead of Music' accusing Shostakovich of creating 'a bedlam of noise', 'a confused stream of sounds' and 'petty bourgeois sensationalism'. Stalin may have recognized his own resemblance to its corrupt chief of police.

Shostakovich showed little confidence when he apologized for his errors. He said that he would try to do better and would henceforth write music that fell in line with 'socialist realism' (whatever that meant), even though he thought that that was what he had been doing. After his next stage work, the tepid ballet *The Limpid Brook*, was also condemned by *Pravda* as being insufficiently dignified on the subject of Soviet life, Shostakovich decided to abandon the theatre and between 1938 and 1955 he wrote chiefly symphonies and string quartets.

His Fourth Symphony fared no better as far as musical officialdom went – even the orchestral musicians criticized it in rehearsal – and it was withdrawn before its first performance. With the Fifth Symphony (1937) Shostakovich was allowed in from the cold. It is certainly a magnificent work; the miracle is that the Soviet regime agreed, hailing it as a 'model of true Soviet art'.

During the war, Shostakovich volunteered for active service but was turned down because of his poor eyesight; however, in the 1941 siege of Leningrad by the Nazis, he served in the fire brigade before being flown to the temporary Soviet capital Kuibishev to complete his Seventh Symphony 'The Siege of Leningrad'; the ever-mindful authorities feared for the safety of their valuable People's Artist. Its theme, the rampant German army overcome by the victorious Russians, led to performances in every Allied country and its composer became a kind of artistic war hero.

Even this esteem was not enough to save him from being denounced in the famous edict of 1948 when he, with Prokofiev and other prominent Russian composers, was accused of 'formalism' and 'anti-people art'. He defended himself with some dignity, while accepting the political dogma behind the criticism, but was nevertheless dismissed from his professorship at the Moscow Conservatory and wrote only film scores and patriotic music until after Stalin's death in 1953. Symphonies Nos.9, 10 & 11 created small interest, Symphony No.12 (which he dedicated to the memory of Lenin) created a little more, but with his Symphony No.13, Shostakovich again came up against official criticism. This time the criticism came from the Communist Party chairman Nikita Khruschev who complained that the text of the choral part in the symphony, referring to the massacre of the Jews in Kiev during the Second World War, did not pay sufficient attention to the others who were slaughtered. The text was amended to meet the chairman's objections. Shostakovich's final two symphonies passed the political quality test without controversy.

His first wife died in 1954 and he was remarried two years later to a young teacher. Meanwhile, his son Maxim, born in 1938, was progressing with his musical studies and has since become one of his father's most distinguished interpreters. In the sixties, Soviet restrictions on the arts were slackened. Shostakovich was left in peace to compose as he wished and many of the works previously condemned by the regime were given a clean bill of health. At the time of his death, *The Times* wrote in its obituary that he was beyond doubt 'the last great symphonist'.

HIS MUSIC

Throughout his 147 opus numbers, Shostakovich maintained a remarkable uniformity of style. Once he had found his musical voice, he made little change to it. The result is that his music is recognizable after only a few bars. What are its characteristics? Melody, folk song and rapid exchange of emotional extremes (very Russian) from the sublime to the banal and from mordant, sarcastic wit to brooding melancholy. He uses dissonant harmonies and other modern compositional techniques, but never abandons tonality. It is a style that has won him many admirers who like contemporary music that is challenging and arresting without being experimental or inaccessible.

However, the truth must be admitted: Shostakovich is horribly uneven. At his best he is among the most vital and original of twentieth-century composers but suddenly, after an overpowering passage, he will become 'as naive as a schoolboy, almost as if he cannot discriminate between the good and the bad,' as one writer put it. And his worst music is full of clichés and apparent vulgarity. How much of this conceals the hidden codes and parodies of a secret dissident is a matter for conjecture.

Essential works

Symphony No.1 in F minor, Op.10 (1924): Shostakovich was not quite twenty years old when this early masterpiece was performed by the Leningrad Philharmonic under Nicolai Malko. Glazunov was amazed at his young pupil's technical assurance. Here, ready formed, is Shostakovich's voice from which he never deviated. Some think it is the freshest symphony he ever wrote.

Symphony No.5 in D minor, Op.47 (1936): with the subtitle 'A Soviet Artist's Practical Creative Reply To Just Criticism', the Fifth Symphony was written after the rebukes Shostakovish had received for his opera *Lady Macbeth*. The work was a triumphant success with both the audience and the critics. It was cheered to the echo and, indeed, it remains the most popular and frequently heard of all this composer's symphonies, a majestic and powerful conception that ends in a blaze of brass and timpani.

Symphony No.7 in C, Op.60 (1941): the historical importance of this symphony is, frankly, greater than its musical content, which frequently teeters into cheap effects. 'Neither savage raids, German planes, nor the grim atmosphere of the beleaguered city could hinder the flow of ideas,' wrote Shostakovich. 'I worked with an inhuman intensity I have never before reached.'

Symphony No.10 in E minor, Op.93 (1953): for many people this is Shostakovich's finest achievement; its odd-number movements are dark and melancholy, while the two even-number movements are ebullient. He manages to work in his personal monogram as a theme once more, too – the notes D, E flat, C and B natural (D, Es, C, H in German notation = D.S.C.H.). The symphony was completed immediately after the death of Stalin, perhaps reflecting the dark ages that had passed and optimism for a better future.

Piano Concerto in C minor, Op.35 (1933): scored, unusually, for piano, trumpet and string orchestra, this is bursting with youthful zest and sarcasm. As with the Piano Concerto No.2 there is a splendid recording of the composer in the solo part.

Piano Concerto No.2, Op.102 (1957): this was written for Shostakovich's son, Maxim, and apparently contains many private family jokes in the piano solo (one is a reference to some infamous student finger exercises). It is a thoroughly enchanting work with its 'What shall we do with a drunken sailor' first movement subject and the melting slow movement.

Twenty-four Preludes and Fugues, Op.87 (1951): written for the late Tatiana Nikolayeva (who made two wonderful recordings of them) and inspired by the bicentennial of Bach's death, these are Shostakovich's major contributions to piano literature.

Worth investigating

Fifteen String Quartets (1938–74)

Violin Concerto No.1 in A minor, Op.99 (1948, rev.1955): written for the renowned violinist David Oistrakh.

Lady Macbeth of the Mtzensk District, Op.29, opera (1934)

On a lighter note, try the **Polka** from the ballet *The Age of Gold* (genuine musical humour, for once!) and the **Romance** that Shostakovich wrote as part of the music for the 1955 film *The Gadfly* (Op.97 No.8), which in the UK we also know as the theme music for the TV series *Reilly, Ace of Spies*.

Jean SIBELIUS

*'Golden gifts I do not ask for, and I wish not for thy silver, only bring
me back to my country'* ('Kalevala', Finnish epic poem)

Born: 8 December 1865, Hämeenlinna, Finland
Died: 20 September 1957, Järvenpää, Finland
Full name: Johan Julius Christian Sibelius
Type of music: symphony, orchestral, theatre, concerto, chamber, vocal
Influences: Grieg, Tchaikowsky, Brahms, Bruckner
Contemporaries: NIELSEN, Edwin Lemare, DUKAS, GLAZUNOV, **SIBELIUS**,
BUSONI, SATIE, Francesco Cilèa, GRANADOS, Hamish MacCunn, Scott Joplin

HIS LIFE

To most people Sibelius is the composer of *Finlandia* and the *Karelia* Suite, to others he
is one of the great symphony composers, to the people of Finland he is all these things
and a national hero. While he was still alive the Finnish government issued stamps with
his portrait and would have erected a statue to him had Sibelius not discouraged the
project. Perhaps no composer in history has meant so much to his native country as did
Sibelius. He still does. 'He is Finland in music; and he is Finnish music,' is a description that sums him up exactly.

Sibelius came along at the right time. Not only did his formative years coincide with
the burgeoning musical nationalism of other countries, but Finland was under the
despotic rule of Tsarist Russia – patriots were imprisoned, newspapers suppressed and
Finnish culture and history were subsumed into the Russian empire. He was born in a
small town in central-south Finland, the son of a regimental doctor who died during the
cholera epidemic of 1867–68 and was brought up by his mother and grandmother. He
adopted the name Jean after coming across a set of visiting cards used by his seafaring
uncle, who had gallicized his name from Johan to Jean.

The usual early music lessons on piano and violin led to his first composition aged
ten, followed by a series of juvenilia influenced by the likes of Mozart and Grieg. The
law drew him briefly to Helsinki University but music quickly took over. Busoni was on
the staff of the city's Music Academy and a lifelong friendship developed between the
two. In 1889 Sibelius travelled to Berlin for further study, then to Vienna as a pupil of
Karl Goldmark. On his return to Finland in 1891 he produced his first major composition, the *Kullervo Symphony*, based on an episode from the great Finnish epic poem
Kalevala. Overnight, this ambitious score established him as the country's most
important composer.

Finnish mythology had a profound effect on Sibelius and he became ambitious to
create music that resonated with these ancient legends and so reflected the spirit and
unique culture of his people and country. Works like *En Saga*, *The Swan of Tuonela* and
his First Symphony had a tremendous impact. Above all, *Finlandia*, an overtly patriotic
orchestral work, identified him with the growing nationalist movement.

A grant from the enlightened Finnish Senate enabled Sibelius to give up all other work
and concentrate entirely on composing. This was not enough to keep him out of debt,
however, and he and his wife, Aino Järnefelt, whom he had married in 1892, were beset
with financial worries from the 1890s to the end of the First World War. Ironically, he
sold one of his most popular compositions, the little *salon Valse triste*, to his publishers
for 300 marks – it made them a fortune. Sibelius was also a heavy drinker with a fondness
for beer and cognac as well as fine cigars, none of which helped improve his situation.
In 1901, a disease of the ear threatened to make him totally deaf; it was successfully
treated but seven years later he had to undergo thirteen operations on his throat to

remove a malignant growth that had initially been diagnosed as cancer. His music during this period, which included the *Valse triste* and the melancholy Fourth Symphony, reflect his morbid frame of mind.

By 1914, honours were being heaped upon him as he travelled through Europe and even to America to conduct his music. The war not only curtailed his foreign visits and royalties, it also heralded the complete cessation of all creative activity. Apart from some trivial piano music, only the Fifth Symphony was composed during the conflict, completed in time for his fiftieth-birthday celebrations. Finland proclaimed its independence after the October Revolution and was plunged into a civil war after a *coup d'état* by the Red Guards. Sibelius' brother was murdered, and the composer, whose sympathies were with the Whites, was forced to flee the Villa Ainola, which since 1904 had been his home in Järvenpää, to the north of Helsinki.

After the war, he composed his Sixth and Seventh Symphonies, the symphonic poem *Tapiola* and the incidental music to a production of *The Tempest*. He travelled, he toured, he conducted, but his last-known work was completed in 1929. After that, silence. He would potter down to the village occasionally for a drink and a smoke, walk in the forests or work in his garden, but he discouraged visitors and disliked discussing his music. After the Second World War he was a virtual recluse. Rossini amused himself in his old age by writing little *jeux d'esprits*; for the last thirty-one years of his life Sibelius seems not to have put pen to paper. He was ninety-one when he died of a cerebral haemorrhage.

One other surprising fact about Sibelius: that huge, bald, craggy head – he must have one of the most recognizable faces of any of the great composers – was not the result of alopecia but vanity. At the age of forty or thereabouts, his hair began to turn grey. Rather than be thought an old man, he shaved it all off and kept it shaved.

HIS MUSIC

Sibelius' early work up to the first two symphonies is clearly derivative of Brahms and Tchaikowsky, and is none the worse for that, but as early as *En Saga*, a completely different sound to that of the German and Russian Romantics begins to emerge. For a decade from 1903, there is a gradual turn to a more personal, deeper style in his work, particularly in the Violin Concerto (1903), *Pohjola's Daughter* (1906) and the spare, concise Fourth Symphony (1911), the textures of which are far removed from the complexity and richness of Mahler, Scriabin or Richard Strauss. He liked to compose in enormous arching phrases, and as his themes are so generously broad, the orchestration becomes sparer, bleaker and more economical with long, singing solo passages. Later still, he developed a new technique that involved the use of short, terse *motifs* woven together into an immense mosaic of monumental power.

There is very little merriment in Sibelius' music – the light touch was not part of his make-up. A kind of austere grandeur, an icy, brooding quality impels admiration and inspires awe, for here in sound is the bleak Finnish landscape at the mercy of the unforgiving elements. So completely does Sibelius conjure up the character of his country that, listening to music, one feels convinced that the theme must be a Finnish folk melody. In fact, Sibelius' melodies are all his own.

There is a defiant, elemental mood in much of the music, with frequent outbursts of passion and colour. He took nothing from the opulence of Strauss and Scriabin and remained aloof to later developments, listening to performances of music by such men as Schoenberg, Prokofiev and Bartók on the radio with interest but without involvement. He was 'the last representative of nineteenth-century nationalistic Romanticism,' as one writer put it. Inevitably for a composer who had found his style and saw no need to move with new musical thought, he was thought of as an anachronism by many professionals long before he died.

Essential works

The essential Sibelius is to be found in his symphonies, which are all very different in character. He has been acclaimed as 'the greatest master of the symphony since Beethoven'. All seven symphonies were composed between 1899 and 1926; there were some rumours of a long-anticipated Eighth Symphony, which he almost certainly completed, as parts were sent for copying in the early 1930s, but Sibelius withdrew the score and destroyed it. Although recorded in the mid-1950s, the Sibelius cycle with the London Symphony Orchestra and conductor Anthony Collins remain benchmark readings.

Symphony No.1 in E minor, Op.39 (1899): both this symphony and No.2 are often criticized for being influenced by Russian music – and that is true – but there is no mistaking their individuality. The texture and the themes of these works sound nothing like Tchaikowsky, despite the over-dramatic, Slavic, heart-on-sleeve treatment.

Symphony No.2 in D minor, Op.43 (1901): the Finns regard No.2 as a sort of national testament – making this and No.5 the most popular of the symphonies – but it is by no means representative of Sibelius. It is emotional, theatrical, and easy on the ear, with powerful climactic surges. The big tune in the overwhelming finale was said to represent 'hope entering the breasts of the Finns and comfort in the anticipated coming of a deliverer'.

Symphony No.4 in A minor, Op.63 (1911): compared with the opulence of the preceding symphonies, No.4 is austere indeed, a meditative and melancholy affair indicative of the bleak state of the composer's mind at the time.

Symphony No.5 in E flat, Op.82 (1915, rev.1919): although the listener would not be aware of it, Sibelius had great difficulties in its construction. He felt he had to suffer for 'obstinately composing symphonies at a time when all other composers have sought other means of expression,' but this was the form in which he felt he could best convey his ideas. The first version of the symphony (1915) was withdrawn and, after heavy revision and rewriting, the work was given four years later. The heroic theme of the last movement has

been described as 'Thor swinging his hammer' and ends with a famous succession of crunching, separated chords. Not without reason, Sibelius' Fifth has been called his 'Eroica'.

Symphony No.7 in C, Op.105 (1926): here Sibelius' four traditional movements are compressed into a single one, marking the culmination of his evolving symphonic technique. The symphony lasts for nineteen minutes, the same duration as a Richard Strauss tone-poem, and was named by the composer as a *Fantasia sinfonica*. There are reminders of earlier symphonies, particularly in the build-up of repeated themes and great melodic curves that conjure up vast vistas and almost Olympian serenity.

Violin Concerto in D minor, Op.47 (1903, rev.1905): the violin was Sibelius' first study instrument and in his youth he nourished ambitions to become a virtuoso (he could manage the first two movements of Mendelssohn's concerto) and as late as 1891 auditioned for the strings of the Vienna Philharmonic. This is a difficult work to play but not to hear, and is now core repertoire for every great soloist, a superb romantic showpiece with passionate, memorable melodies and invigorating rhythms.

En Saga, Op.9 (1892, rev.1902): there is no particular saga attached to this tone-poem, the music tells its own dark and threatening story. This is Sibelius' first undoubted masterpiece and, with it, Finnish national music achieved artistic significance for the first time.

The Swan of Tuonela, Op.22 No.2 (1893): the second of a suite of four orchestral *Lemminkäinen Legends* is based on the epic poem *Kalevala*; Tuonela is the Finnish equivalent of Hades and, on the black river encircling it, glides a swan. This bird is portrayed by the cor anglais and is among the most beautiful solos ever written for the instrument.

Karelia Suite, Op.11 (1893): the inhabitants of Karelia, in the eastern part of Finland, are noted for being far jollier than their counterparts in the western part – which accounts for Sibelius' gayest music. The three short movements (*Intermezzo*, *Ballade* and *Alla marcia*) in this suite are simple, clear-cut classical 'pops' and were conceived for a student theatre production.

Finlandia, Op.26 (1899, rev.1900): this tone-poem is Sibelius' most famous work and in a recent poll was voted the sixth most requested piece of classical music. It made the composer's name known internationally and, with lyrics added to its central section, gave the Finns their equivalent of *Land of Hope and Glory*. The Russians even banned the work for political reasons, so powerfully did the music evoke national sentiments.

Tapiola, Op.112 (1926): Sibelius' last work, his final tone-poem. Like his first, *En Saga*, it has no specific programme but depicts the dark, brooding forests of the Northland and Tapio,

the 'forest's mighty God' while 'wood-sprites in the gloom weave magic secrets'.

Pelleas and Melisande, Op.46, (1905): the first section of this music, written by Sibelius for Maeterlinck's play, is *At the Castle Gate*, which is famous as the signature tune for the long-running television programme *The Sky at Night*.

Worth investigating
Valse triste, Op.44 No.1, (1903, rev.1904)
Pohjola's Daughter, Op.49, symphonic fantasia (1906)
Nightride and Sunrise, Op.55, (1909)
Romance for Strings, Op.14, (1911)
The Oceanides, Op.73, tone-poem (1914)

Christian SINDING
(1856–1941)

Rustle of Spring, 1896

When he was living in Berlin, Sinding ordered a large amount of manuscript paper from his publishers. No bill was ever received. He ordered more; still no demand for payment. Eventually he wrote requesting an account as he was sure the sum owed must be thousands of marks. Yes, his publishers replied, you do owe us thousands of marks, but in view of the large profits of *Rustle of Spring*, the debt is cancelled. Both composer and publisher had made a small fortune out of the work. There can hardly be an aspiring pianist anywhere in the world who has not tackled the piece, yet it is now rarely included in recitals as it's considered to be too hackneyed. A pity, for a pianist like Shura Cherkassky can still make its tarnished surface glitter.

In fact, Sinding, whose total number of works runs to 132 opus numbers, was considered by the Norwegians to be Grieg's successor and he was honoured as such. He was too indebted to Schumann, Liszt, Brahms, Wagner and Grieg himself to be precisely that, but some of his music is far from negligible. The works that are worth investigating are his Piano Concerto in D flat (1889), Piano Quintet, Op.5 (1884) and, above all, his Suite in A minor for violin and orchestra, which have been recorded by both Perlman and Heifetz.

Bedřich SMETANA
'The father of Czech music'

Born: 2 March 1824, Leitomischl
Died: 12 May 1884, Prague
Full name: Bedřich Friedrich Smetana
Type of music: symphonic poem, opera, chamber, piano
Influences: Mozart, Liszt, Wagner, Bohemian folk music
Contemporaries: Joachim Raff, FRANCK, LALO, Carl Reinecke, **SMETANA**, BRUCKNER, JOHANN STRAUSS II, Stephen Collins Foster, GOTTSCHALK

HIS LIFE

Czechoslovakia did not exist in Smetana's day; the lands of Bohemia merely constituted part of the Austrian Empire. During the nineteenth century, nationalist movements developed all over Europe, culminating in the 'Year of Revolution' – 1848. It was the Prague uprising, during which the previously apolitical Smetana helped man the barricades, that was crucial to his development as the first composer to give a voice to Czech music. But it took him some time to realize his ambition.

'With God's help and grace, I will be a Mozart in composition and a Liszt in technique,' Smetana wrote ambitiously in his diary in 1843. Prodigiously gifted as a child, he was proficient enough to play first violin in a Haydn quartet at the age of five, and made his public debut as a pianist a year later, but because of parental opposition, his talent was not allowed to flourish immediately. At nineteen he had had little formal training and his ambitions seemed unlikely to be realized. Then luck started to play a part: his girlfriend, Kateřina Kolářová, persuaded her own music professor to give him lessons and simultaneously he became the piano teacher to the family of Count Leopold Thun, which enabled him to write his first compositions. Yet eight years after the Prague uprising, Smetana had made little progress. He had married Kateřina but tragedy coloured their relationship – of their four daughters only one, Zofie, survived, and Kateřina showed signs of tuberculosis from 1855.

In 1856, encouraged by Liszt, he made the bold step of moving to Göteberg in Sweden and his life started to take shape: he attracted an enthusiastic band of pupils, he at last established himself as a pianist and he composed three symphonic poems, *Richard III*, *Wallenstein's Camp* and *Haakon Jarl*, which attracted much attention.

Kateřina died in 1859 and Smetana returned to Prague in 1861, having married the sister-in-law of his brother Karl the previous year. The political situation had improved, and Smetana was now a mature composer with a considerable reputation. He knew Glinka's nationalistic operas, with their Russian melodies and librettos, and determined to do the same for Bohemia. He was given the important job of music director of the Prague Provisional Theatre, and his first opera, *The Brandenburgers in Bohemia* (1863) made use of his new credo. Three years later he wrote his masterpiece *The Bartered Bride*. His six other operas show a remarkable versatility in their different styles and content (Richard Strauss was strongly influenced by Smetana's *The Two Widows* of 1874) but *The Bartered Bride* remains the only one in the general repertoire outside Prague today. By 1952 the opera had notched up 2,000 performances at the Prague National Theatre alone. The 1870s saw Smetana at the height of his creative powers with such original and remarkable works as his cycle of symphonic poems *Má vlast* (*My Homeland*) and his wonderful E minor String Quartet inspired by reflections of his youth.

Like Donizetti, Smetana ended his days suffering from the effects of syphilis. He had become totally deaf, experienced headaches and hallucinations and frequently lost the power of speech. Having ceased to appear in public, he lived with his daughter Zofie and her husband in the country, before being confined to an asylum in 1884.

HIS MUSIC

As a composer, Smetana was of the utmost importance in the development of a new musical heritage for his country and was a major influence on Dvořák, Janáček and Martinů. It took time for him to find his voice; he did not attempt to write a letter in Czech until 1856, having been brought up to speak German exclusively, and the Prague authorities had to be persuaded of his musical aims. The Austrian regime had encouraged an operatic tradition that favoured the works of Meyerbeer and the Italian repertoire sung in Bohemian. 'Les Huguenots,' bewailed Smetana when he first saw the production at the Provisional Theatre in Prague, 'has armies of barely eight on each side ... the singers are so pressed together in the foreground that everyone must be careful not to hurt his neighbour when he turns.'

It was clearly time for national pride to assert itself, and there was much to initiate. Smetana was the first composer to demonstrate how Bohemian folk music and dance could be used in the service of serious art, albeit within the traditional mid-European musical language and much influenced by the orchestral devices of Liszt and Wagner. Welded to modern harmony and thematic construction, these influences produced fresh, vivid music that was unmistakably the voice and heart of the future Czechoslovakia.

Essential works

The Bartered Bride, opera (1866): (known as *The Battered Bride* in the trade!), Smetana made five versions of his comic masterpiece that delightfully conjures up Czech rural life. The score is filled with dance rhythms and folk songs and, as well as its ebullient Overture, often played separately, includes the popular orchestral Polka (Act 1) and *Furiant* and *Dance of the Comedians* (Act 2).

Má vlast (My Homeland), symphonic poems (1872–79): these six tone-poems include Smetana's most celebrated work *Vltava*, a bustling epic portrait of the river that flows through Prague. It is the second of the cycle and, ironically, has a theme derived from Swedish, not Czech, folklore.

String Quartet No.1 in E minor 'From my life' (1876): this is a superb and moving autobiographical work that encompasses the composer's youthful romance and his love of art, a joyful polka and the discovery of his national music and, finally, the terrible reflections at the onset of his deafness. In the coda of the final movement, Smetana explains that the long-drawn-out note [a high 'E'] 'is the fatal whistling in my ear in the highest registers that in 1874 announced my deafness. I permitted myself this little joke, such as it is, because it was so disastrous to me.'

Piano Trio in G minor (1855, rev.1857): a profound and tender elegy on the death of the composer's first daughter.

John Philip SOUSA

'The March King'

Born: 6 November 1854, Washington, D.C.
Died: 6 March 1932, Reading, Pennsylvania
Type of music: band marches, operetta, songs
Influences: German and American military music, Johann Strauss II
Contemporaries: STANFORD, HUMPERDINCK, MOSZKOWSKI, JANÁČEK, **SOUSA**, CHAUSSON, Anatoli Liadov, SINDING, ELGAR, LEONCAVALLO, Cécile Chaminade

HIS LIFE AND MUSIC

It was Sousa's view that 'a march should make a man with a wooden leg step out' and no one has offered more spirited, optimistic music in two-four with which to do it. Sousa's marches could only be American: simple, catchy tunes with little or no countermelody, brash, breezy and thoroughly patriotic. They are also extremely effectively scored and their vitality and rhythmic appeal seem to be undiminished a century after many of the more famous of them were written.

There is no truth in the delightful legend that his ancestors came from China with the name So and that the precocious John Philip added USA to his name. In fact, his mother was Bavarian and his father Portuguese, a trombonist in the US Marines Band. John Philip's instrument was the violin, and he first appeared as a soloist at the age of eleven. He joined the Marines Band at thirteen and supplemented this by playing in variety theatres in and around Washington. In 1877, he was a member of the special band assembled to play under Offenbach when the composer of the *Can-Can* visited the Philadelphia Centennial Exhibition in 1876. He was only twenty-six when he was made leader of the US Marine Corps Band, which he led for twelve years before being given the chance to start his own band. From then until the day he died, Sousa conducted, composed and toured all over the world with increasing acclaim. He lived to record some of his music, though he distrusted the process, and gave his name to the Sousaphone, a variation on the tuba with a detachable bell, first made for his band.

His marches are the only pieces of Sousa's music heard today, and of the 139 he wrote, only a handful are heard regularly. Few know that, apart from writing at least ten operettas (*El capitán* was his greatest success), he also composed a symphonic poem *The Chariot Race* (inspired by *Ben Hur*), orchestral suites and five novels.

Worth investigating

The best Sousa marches are also his most well known:

The Stars and Stripes Forever (1897): Sousa's monument, an American national treasure that earned him $300,000 in his lifetime. Piano buffs will know the astonishing piano transcription of this by Vladimir Horowitz. Also: **Semper Fidelis** (c.1888), **The Washington Post** (1889), **The High School Cadets** (c.1890), **The Liberty Bell** (1893), **Manhattan Beach** (1893), **King Cotton** (1895), **El capitán** (1896).

Charles STANFORD

Born: 30 September 1852, Dublin
Died: 29 March 1924, London
Full title: Sir Charles Villiers Stanford
Type of music: symphony, orchestral, concerto, opera, choral, organ, vocal
Influences: Brahms, folk music and culture of Ireland
Contemporaries: FAURÉ, PARRY, Xaver Scharwenka, Vincent d'Indy, **STANFORD**, HUMPERDINCK, MOSZKOWSKI, JANÁČEK, SOUSA, CHAUSSON, Anatoli Liadov

HIS LIFE AND MUSIC

Tennyson and Stanford had great respect for each other and one is just about as unfashionable as the other these days. That doesn't mean that their work is without merit. Stanford earns his place here because his music *is* unfashionable. Much of it deserves to be better known and his influence on the course of British music was incalculable. A list of just some of the musicians who passed through his hands during the forty years in which he taught composition at the Royal College of Music proves the point: Bliss, Boughton, Bridge, Goossens, Holst, Howells, Hurlstone, Ireland, Jacob, Moeran, Coleridge-Taylor and Vaughan Williams.

His instrument was the organ and his lasting contribution is to church music – every choirboy knows 'Stanford in B flat', the service he wrote aged twenty-seven, and there are numerous hymns and other settings of the canticles. He was an influential choral conductor of the Bach Choir, the Leeds Festival and others. His ten operas achieved little success and await re-assessment, though *Much Ado About Nothing* and *The Travelling Companion* have been revived recently. Another, based on Sheridan's play *A Tragedy Rehearsed*, has a nice musical joke: as one of the characters, dying after a duel, utters the immortal line 'O cursèd parry! – that last thrust in tierce was fatal,' the orchestra quotes the opening theme of 'Blest Pair of Sirens' by his contemporary Sir Hubert Parry.

His seven symphonies and six Irish Rhapsodies are variable and written in the German style, but who can blame him when he received more encouragement from Germany than his own country. The music is heavily influenced by his friend Brahms and there is a mite too much of the Professor at times and not enough of the Celt – but when the latter shines through, as it does often, Stanford shows up well alongside Parry and Elgar.

Essential works

Symphony No.3 in F minor 'Irish,' Op.28 (1887): a work that earned Stanford his international reputation; it was chosen for the opening concert of the new Concertgebouw in Amsterdam and was the most successful British symphony prior to Elgar's First.

Irish Rhapsody No.4 in minor, Op.141 (1914): this is the composer's own favourite of the six Irish rhapsodies; it is subtitled 'The Fisherman of Loch Neagh and what they saw'. A string of Irish tunes are quoted before the rowdy conclusion.

Clarinet Concerto in A minor, Op.80 (1902): you'd have to be pretty hard of heart not to be affected by this beautiful work, cast in a single-movement but with the traditional three movements clearly recognizable; the slow movement is meltingly lovely.

Piano Concerto No.2 in C minor, Op.126 (1915): begins like Rachmaninov's concerto in the same key – Stanford's has one of the most arresting openings of any piano concerto – but then their paths diverge. If you like romantic music with sweeping tunes and lush orchestration, you'll fall in love with this: the first movement contains music that has made grown men weep, especially in the recording made by soloist Malcolm Binns.

The Bluebird, Op.119 No.3 (1910): an unaccompanied part song, a setting of Mary Coleridge's poem, this is an exquisite little tone-poem and a lesson for any composer in vocal writing; it was once popular in a recording by the Glasgow Orpheus Choir.

Songs of the Sea, Op.91 (1904): five settings of poems by the lawyer–poet Sir Henry Newbolt, the most famous of which is 'Drake's Drum,' an ever popular party piece with baritones.

Ye choirs of New Jerusalem, Op.123 (1910): an anthem in the repertoire of every cathedral choir, a setting of an eleventh-century hymn by St Fulbert of Chartres.

Services in B flat, Op.10 (1879): otherwise 'Stanford in B flat,' the composer's first major contribution to the liturgy, which opens with the 'Te Deum,' performed at the coronation of King Edward VII in 1902.

Johann STRAUSS II

'The Waltz King'

Born: 25 October 1825, Vienna
Died: 3 June 1899, Vienna
Type of music: operetta, waltzes and other dance music
Influences: Ländler and Viennese café music, Johann Strauss I, Lanner
Contemporaries: Carl Reinecke, SMETANA, BRUCKNER, **JOHANN STRAUSS II**, Stephen Collins Foster, GOTTSCHALK, RUBINSTEIN, Karl Goldmark

HIS LIFE

Johann Strauss the Younger has a good claim to the title 'The World's Most Popular Composer' and his *Blue Danube* Waltz, which he penned in 1867, has a claim to be the best known piece of music ever written. (Whether it is the best loved is another matter – especially in the city of 'The Waltz King,' where it is played unceasingly day and night in every hotel, restaurant and café.)

The Strauss Family Story – filmed, televized, turned into an operetta – is that of the Viennese Waltz but it was Johann II who was the inspired composer, able conductor and sharp businessman, and whose work stands head and shoulders above the accomplishments of his father and brothers.

Johann II's grandfather was a humble innkeeper on the outskirts of Vienna who committed suicide after his second marriage; Johann I (1804–49) developed a love of music from the itinerant musicians who performed at his father's inn. His ambition was to play the kind of entertainment music he had grown up with and he set about learning the violin with a will. Within a year he was playing the viola in an orchestra. Here he befriended the charming violinist Josef Lanner (1801–43) and joined him when Lanner started up his own orchestra. So successful was the venture that they decided to run two bands – Lanner conducting one, Strauss the other, and although they soon went their separate ways, this had done much to establish Strauss the composer and conductor with the Viennese. Before long the Strauss orchestras were touring all over Europe, they were the official dance orchestra for Austrian court balls, and they played at Queen Victoria's coronation ball. This was the beginning of the dynasty; it died out in 1939 with the death of Johann Strauss III, son of Eduard, one of Johann II's brothers.

Johann I had six children by his wife Anna: Johann, Josef, Nelli, Therese, Eduard and Ferdinand (who died after a few months). He also had five illegitimate children by his mistress Emilie Trampusch and eventually left his family in order to live with her. With him went the opposition that had been put in the way of Johann II's musical ambitions. Although Anna had openly encouraged her son, Johann *père* had whipped him on one occasion when he found him playing the violin. Johann II assembled his first orchestra

at the age of nineteen, making his debut in October 1844. His success was instantaneous. The headline in a Viennese paper read, 'Good night, Lanner. Good evening, Father Strauss. Good morning, Son Strauss'. The two Strauss family orchestras ran in open rivalry with each other until 1849. The elder Strauss contracted scarlet fever from one of his illegitimate children and was found in his apartment dead, naked and abandoned by his mistress. She had taken her children and all her possessions and vanished off the face of the earth.

Johann Strauss II now combined both orchestras and, for the rest of his life, enjoyed a career of fabulous success, composing and conducting all over Europe. Eventually, he ran six orchestras simultaneously. With assistant conductors, copyists, librarian, publicists and booking agents, the Strauss music business was a highly lucrative concern. In 1872 he was invited to America to conduct his *Blue Danube* for the colossal fee of $100,000 for fourteen performances; at another concert he conducted a choir of 20,000 in front of an audience of a hundred thousand. He then went on a short tour, doubled his money and returned to Europe a millionaire.

Johann's brother Eduard took over as conductor of the court balls after 1871, enabling Johann to concentrate on composition. And that might have been that, turning out waltz after polka after march after galop from an inexhaustible gold-mine of melody. But in 1863 he met Offenbach, then at the height of his fame as the composer of French operettas, who had come to Vienna for a production of *Orpheus in the Underworld*. Both entered a competition to write the best waltz for a ball – and Offenbach won. This, as much as Offenbach's suggestion that Strauss should try his hand at operetta, was the spur to writing something for the stage. After a few flops, Strauss came up with one of the most perfect examples of the genre, *Die Fledermaus* (1874), and followed it in 1885 by another, *Der Zigeunerbaron*.

His flair, energy and creativity never left him until the last few years of his life. His third wife, Adele, had introduced him to Brahms and the two became close friends. The older composer was deeply depressed when Brahms died in 1897. Strauss died two years later from pneumonia.

HIS MUSIC

The only piece of Johann I's work that is at all well known is his *Radetzky* March, composed the year before his death. His music, though an advance on the simple *Ländler* (the precursor of the waltz), is not as melodically memorable as that of his famous son. Eduard and Josef Strauss were also composers – Eduard notched up 318 works, Josef 283, some of which are heard today. Their brother, Johann II, wrote 400 waltzes alone, 300 polkas, galops, marches and other dances. What is extraordinary about his music is that it aroused the admiration of sophisticated, serious musicians just as much as ordinary music-loving members of the public. His namesake, though no relation, Richard Strauss wrote of his appreciation thus:

'Of all the God-given dispensers of joy, Johann Strauss is to me the most endearing.... In particular I respect [his] originality, his innate gift. At a time when the whole world around him was tending towards increased complexity, increased reflectiveness, his natural genius enabled him to create from the *whole*. He seemed to me the last of those who worked from spontaneous inspiration. Yes, the primary, the original, the proto-melody – that's it .... As for the *Rosenkavalier* waltzes ... how could I have composed those without thinking of the laughing genius of Vienna?'

The construction of the famous works is artful, with a tender prelude, a chain of five or so contrasting themes and a rousing conclusion; their orchestration quite masterful, with more complex textures than hitherto. The swaying waltz melodies of Johann Strauss complement the elegant, easy-going lifestyle of the Viennese of the late-nineteenth century, living in the confident capital of the Hapsburg empire – at least, that is the rose-coloured picture of the fairy tale world that Strauss painted for us. The world today does not seem ready to tire of the past era that his music so effortlessly evokes.

Essential works

Die Fledermaus (The Bat) (1874): still the most popular of all operettas, the only one by Strauss actually set in Vienna. Even an average production can hardly fail to whisk you off your feet with its enchanting waltz tunes, its plot of comic intrigue, its romance and elegant sets and frocks. The Overture is often heard independently as well as Adele's famous Laughing Song 'Mein Herr Marquis' and the Csárdás (*Klänge der Heimat*), both from Act 2.

Der Zigeunerbaron (The Gypsy Baron) (1885): Strauss wrote sixteen operettas. This and *Die Fledermaus* are the only two revived regularly today; the others suffer from poor librettos. For *Eine Nacht in Venedig* (*A Night in Venice*), which is still occasionally played, Strauss composed the music without bothering to read the plot or dialogue beforehand.

An der schönen blauen Donau, Op.314 (1867): Originally called *On the beautiful, blue Danube*, the first version had lyrics with political overtones, causing hostility at its premiere. Today it is a second Austrian national anthem, arranged for every possible combination of instrument; the most famous is a dazzling piano elaboration by the otherwise obscure Andrei Schulz-Evler – the classic recording is by the legendary Josef Lhevinne. When Brahms signed Frau Strauss' fan, he wrote out the opening bars and then put 'Leider nicht von Brahms' ('Unfortunately, not by Brahms').

Other great waltzes

Geschichten aus dem Wienerwald (Tales from the Vienna Woods) (1868)

Wein, Weib und Gesang (Wine, Woman and Song) (1869): (not 'women,' as it is often incorrectly called).

Wiener Blut (Vienna Blood) (1870)

Rosen aus dem Süden (Roses from the South) (1878)

Frühlingsstimmen (Voices of Spring) (1883)

Kaiser (Emperor) (1889)

Tausend und eine Nacht (A Thousand and One Nights) (1871)

Künstlerleben (Artist's Life) (1867)

Morgenblätter (Morning Papers) (1864)

And don't forget: **Perpetuum Mobile** (1862), **Unter Donner und Blitzen (Thunder and Lightning)** polka (1868), **Tritsch-Tratsch** polka (1858) and many more....

Richard STRAUSS

*'Melody ... is the greatest of divine gifts, not to be compared
with any other'* (Richard Strauss)

Born: 11 June 1864, Munich
Died: 8 September 1949, Garmisch-Partenkirchen
Full name: Richard Georg Strauss
Type of music: symphony, orchestral, opera, choral, chamber, vocal
Influences: Berlioz, Brahms, Liszt, Wagner
Contemporaries: Eugen d'Albert, Johann Halvorsen, **RICHARD STRAUSS**,
Alexander Greghaninov, NIELSEN, Edwin Lemare, DUKAS, GLAZUNOV, SIBELIUS

HIS LIFE

Richard Strauss was a *Wunderkind*. He began piano lessons when he was four years old
and completed his first composition, a Polka in C, at the age of six. His Op.1, a *Festmarsch*
for Orchestra, written when he was twelve, was published in 1880. His father, Franz, was
the leading horn player in Munich. Although Wagner entrusted to him the important
horn solos in the premieres of *Tristan und Isolde*, *Die Meistersinger* and *Parsifal*, Franz
Strauss was openly scathing about Wagner's music. When the composer's death was
announced during an orchestral rehearsal in 1883, every man rose in silent homage –
except Franz Strauss. He lived until 1905, long enough to see, paradoxically, his son
Richard become the most passionate advocate of Wagner's music and among its most
brilliant interpreters.

Richard's formal academic schooling ran parallel to his musical studies. He very
quickly made a name for himself, his technical assurance, if not his style, seemingly pre-
formed. Few composers have their first symphony, a violin concerto and a second
symphony (played by the New York Philharmonic) completed and premiered by the age
of twenty. The influential pianist, composer and conductor Hans von Bülow, who had
been married to Liszt's daughter Cosima, before losing her to Wagner, took a shine to
the young Strauss. When he left his orchestra at Meiningen in 1885, Strauss replaced
him for a year. Von Bülow was an ardent Wagnerite, despite having been cuckolded by
the great man, and he introduced Strauss to the poet and musician Alexander Ritter, who
was married to Wagner's niece. Between them they convinced Strauss of the musical
aesthetics of Liszt and Wagner, the concept of 'music as expression', encouraging him to
abandon the classical, restricting forms of the German Romantic style. Wagner's music
dramas and Liszt's symphonic tone-poems were to be his models. From that point on,
Strauss' music would have a literary or philosophic outline.

The first venture in which he parted company from his traditional past was the
symphonic fantasy *Aus Italien*. It caused a furore. The audience hissed, considering it
ugly and confusing, bewildered by its occasional dissonance, notwithstanding the
quotation of 'Funiculi funicula' in one section, included under the mistaken apprehension that it was an Italian folk song. Strauss was undeterred, now convinced of his destiny
and never averse to a little controversy. In the decade after 1887, during which he wrote
a succession of tone-poems, he made his name throughout the musical world. Such
masterpieces as *Don Juan*, *Till Eulenspiegel* and *Ein Heldenleben* are now as much a part
of basic orchestral repertoire as Beethoven's symphonies, but when they were first heard
the critics could not find enough adjectives with which to condemn them. *The Times* of
8 March 1897 wrote of the tone-poem *Also sprach Zarathustra*: 'While every kind of
instrumental elaboration is exhibited, including an amorphous and remarkably hideous
fugue, the actual material of the themes is of the poorest and least convincing order; and
for many pages at a time, the possibilities of cacophony seem to be exhausted.' 'If *Don*

Quixote is no music,' opined the New York *Musical Courier* of December 1898, 'it may possibly be something else – a big, huge, monumental, colossal joke, a joke of such magnitude as only a master and a genius like Strauss is able to perpetrate. I can see him chuckling over his morning coffee as he reads the learned essays upon anaesthetic noises made by the herd of bleating muttons.'

By the turn of the century, Strauss was recognized as being not only among the most important and provocative composers of the time but also in the front rank of conductors. In 1898 he was appointed to one of the most prestigious musical posts in the world – the conductorship of the Berlin Philharmonic. He was to retain this post for twelve years. Using his immense influence he introduced a system whereby, for the first time, German composers would be entitled to receive a royalty from every performance of their work given by a major orchestra or opera house.

Composed concurrently with the tone-poems were his operas. *Guntram* (1894) and *Feuersnot* (1901) were failures. The soprano lead in *Guntram* was Pauline de Ahna; she married Strauss in September 1894, remaining with him, despite a stormy relationship, until the end of his life, dying only months after him. In 1900 Strauss met the poet Hugo von Hofmannsthal, a librettist who was to have a profound effect on his career in the theatre. Their collaboration began with *Salome*, premiered in 1905, followed by *Elektra* in 1909. These works managed to provoke the same hearty opprobrium as the tone-poems had done: 'There is a vast deal of ugly music in *Salome* – music that offends the ear and rasps the nerves like fiddlestrings played on by a coarse file ...' (*New York Tribune*); the distinguished critic W. J. Henderson of the *New York Sun* was sure that 'Strauss has a mania for writing ugly music: a modern harpy, he cannot touch anything without besmearing it with dissonance.' And so on. As if by way of concession, von Hoffmansthal and Strauss' next venture could not have been more different, evoking the graceful world of eighteenth-century Vienna in their charming comedy *Der Rosenkavalier*, which remains among the most cherished of all operas.

Strauss became something of a legend in his own lifetime. Music lovers would make pilgrimages to his beautiful villa in Garmisch in the Bavarian Alps to pay their respects. He continued composing for the rest of his life – and writing good music, too – but the truth is that he wrote little after the First World War to compare with his early tone-poems and operas. Although an immensely cultured man and congenial company, there was a darker side to him: conceited, jealous of rivals and notoriously, even psychopathically, mean, Strauss was anything but the munificent Great Composer; even his photographs seem to portray a petty-minded businessman. He demeaned himself by rearranging his compositions for smaller forces, specifically so that his music would attract more performances and thus more money. His wife, who ruled him with a rod of iron, held the purse strings and gave him a small allowance to live on. This he supplemented by insisting that members of the orchestra join him in the card game Skat (who were they to refuse?), at which he was uniquely skilled. Even though the musicians could not afford the amount of money they invariably lost to him, he would insist on being paid. Their discomfort seemed to be a source of delight to him. In Bayreuth one year, some of them lost so much money that they refused to continue playing in the orchestra until Winifred Wagner reimbursed them.

It is not easy to excuse Strauss' behaviour in Germany during the thirties. He accepted the position of President of the Third Reich Music Chamber and supported the boycott of Jewish music in Germany; and when Bruno Walter was removed from his post as head of the Leipzig Gewandhaus Orchestra, Strauss promptly substituted for him. Toscanini refused to conduct at Bayreuth; Strauss accepted. True, he resigned from his official post in 1935 and spoke out against the Nazi regime when he insisted on working with the Jewish librettist Stefan Zweig on his opera *Die schweigsame Frau* (*The Silent Woman*). But when he was asked why he did not leave the country, Strauss reportedly replied: 'Germany had fifty-six opera houses; the United States had two. It would have reduced my income.'

He and his wife lived in Switzerland for most of the Second World War but returned to their villa in the Bavarian Alps after the war had ended. He was allowed to remain there by the American Army, cleared of Nazi affiliations in 1948 after facing a special court in Munich.

Despite all this, so revered was he by the musical world that he was feted during his visit to London in 1947 and his eighty-fifth birthday was celebrated worldwide, just a few months before he died.

HIS MUSIC

Strauss' tone-poems, operas and songs composed between 1885 and 1910 are startling in their originality of concept and sound. Naked passion and sensuality were on display, virtuosic treatment of the orchestra, sounds that had never been heard before, with bold excursions from tonality, while never completely abandoning it, and wild passages of dissonance that shocked audiences and fellow composers.

Of *Till Eulenspiegel*, Debussy said 'This piece might be called "An hour of original music in a lunatic asylum"'; Stravinsky thought *Der Rosenkavalier* 'cheap and poor'; Tchaikowsky thought that 'such an astounding lack of talent was never before united to such pretentiousness.' Famously, after the band of the Grenadier Guards had played a potpourri from *Elektra*, George V sent a message: 'His Majesty does not know what the Band has just played, but it is *never* to be played again.' In the words of the musicologist Milton Cross, though, 'these early works were filled with pages of majestic, poetic, inspired music, which burst on the closing of the nineteenth century like a blinding flash of sunlight.' The dramatic power in his operas and tone-poems, their soaring intensity and grandeur had certainly never been equalled.

With the completion of *Der Rosenkavalier*, this burning originality disappeared and for his remaining forty years, Richard Strauss, while certainly not resting on his laurels, fell back on his extreme technical accomplishment, his professional adroitness and sophistication. Mannerisms recur and, instead of white-hot inspiration, insipid copies appear, not without occasional flashes of his youthful genius but unsustained and often laboured. It is interesting to note that in his final works – the concertos for horn and oboe and the opera *Die Liebe der Danae* – he returned to the styles of his first two heroes, Brahms and Wagner.

Essential works
Tone-poems
Don Juan, Op.20 (1888): listening to this ardent, passionate music more than a century after its composition it is hard to see what it was that made it such controversial music when it was first performed. This tone-poem is a thrilling portrait, lasting about eighteen minutes and based on a poem by Nikolaus Lenau, of the famous lover and his search for the perfect woman. The opening is notoriously difficult to conduct and is often given as a test to aspiring baton wavers.

Tod und Verklärung, Op.24 (1889): *Death and Transfiguration* is in four sections played without a pause: the first section is *Sleep, illness, revery*; this is followed by *Fever and struggle with Death*, then *Dreams, childhood memories, and Death*; the final section is *Transfiguration*. The work is an unusual case of a piece of music inspiring a poem (by Strauss' friend Alexander Ritter) and not the other way about.

Till Eulenspiegels lustige Streiche (Till Eulenspiegel's Merry Pranks), Op.28 (1895): five years passed before Strauss attempted another tone-poem; this is one of sheer delight, telling the story of the incorrigible rogue of German legend who escapes punishment – Strauss sends him to the gallows!

Also sprach Zarathustra, Op.30 (1896): as long as a three-movement symphony, *Thus Spake Zarathustra* has one of the most famous openings of any piece of music, thanks entirely to Stanley Kubrick, who used it to powerful effect in his film *2001: A Space Odyssey*. Now inescapably linked to lunar exploration, the tone-poem, which was based on Nietzsche's philosophy, was intended, according to the composer, 'to convey an idea of the development of the human race from its origin, through the various phases of evolution, religious as well as scientific, up to Nietzsche's ideas of the Superman.'

Don Quixote, Op.35 (1897): subtitled 'fantastic variations on a theme of a knightly character', the work is in three parts: an introduction, theme and variations, then a finale. Don Quixote is represented by a solo cello, Sancho Panza by a tuba, bass clarinet and, later, solo viola.

Ein Heldenleben, Op.40 (1898): the last of these famous tone-poems is over half an hour in duration and contains six sections, which are are played without pause. It portrays a hero who is beset by adversaries and atempts to overcome his foes in order to build a new and better world. The hero in this case is R. Strauss who, in the final section of this marvellous work, quotes from a number of his own compositions.

Operas

Salome, Op.54, one-act opera (1905): biblical in its origins, this unpleasant little episode was dramatized by Oscar Wilde and has Herod's daughter, Salome, asking for the head of her beloved John the Baptist as payment for gyrating her way through the 'Dance of the Seven Veils' and is then erotically excited by the prophet's decapitated head. Strauss based his opera on Wilde's play and succeeded in shocking turn-of-the-century audiences to the core. The tortuous melodies and rhythms are openly lascivious. The opera is not an easy listen, but it is a challenging and immensely powerful work.

Der Rosenkavalier, Op.59, opera (1911): 'The Cavalier of the Rose' is the literal translation of the title; 'a comedy for music' was how the composer described this glorious work, which combines the elements of intrigue, farce and satire, as well as truly touching pathos. Where the scores for *Salome* and *Elektra* were dissonant, here Strauss piles on lush late-Romanticism; the string of waltz themes are worthy successors to the work of Johann Strauss. Set in eighteenth-century Vienna, the opera tells the story of the love between the Princess von Werdenberg (always referred to as the Marschallin), her young suitor Octavian and his beloved Sophie. To many people, this is the last great Romantic opera; it is certainly the most popular German opera to have been written this century. The *Waltz Suites* from the opera are often played separately, but essential listening is the famous Trio (Act 3) sung by the three lovers, among the most ravishing passages in all opera – especially in the recording featuring Gueden, Reining and Jurinac conducted by Eric Kleiber.

Songs

Four Last Songs, (Op.post. 1948): Strauss wrote almost 150 songs during his career but none are lovelier than these autumnal final utterances; the songs are conceived for the orchestra as much as the voice – symphonic songs, if you like – and they provide a gentle compliment to *Lied von der Erde,* composed by Mahler. Each of the first three songs ends with a solo passage for horn, an instrument as close to Strauss' heart as the soprano voice for which these were written.

Other Strauss songs to look out for include the beautiful '**Morgen, Op.27 No.4**', '**Wiegenlied, Op.41 No.1**', '**Ständchen, Op.17 No.2**', '**Cäcilie, Op.27 No.2**' and (Strauss's own favourite) '**Traum durch die Dämmerung, Op.29 No.1**'.

Worth investigating

Burlesque for piano and orchestra (1885)
Serenade for thirteen wind instruments, Op.7 (1881)
Horn Concerto No.1 in E flat, Op.11 (1882–83)
Eine Alpensinfonie ('Alpine' Symphony), Op.64 (1915): the score asks for organ, glockenspiel, herd bells, thunder machine, wind machine and off-stage horns and trumpets.
Le bourgeois gentilhomme, Op.60 (1918): suite of music to Molière's play.
Metamorphosen for twenty-three solo strings (1945)
Elektra, Op.58 (1909): one-act opera
Ariadne auf Naxos, Op.60 (1916): opera
Capriccio, Op.85 (1942): one-act opera

Igor STRAVINSKY

*'He is a liberator. More than anyone else he has freed
the musical thought of today'* (Satie)

Born: 17 June 1882, Oranienbaum, near St Petersburg
Died: 6 April 1971, New York
Full name: Igor Fyodorovich Stravinsky
Type of music: ballet, opera, symphony, orchestra, chamber, choral, piano
Influences: Impressionists, Rimsky-Korsakov and Russian nationalists, Handel,
Mozart, Webern, jazz
Contemporaries: Joaquín Turina, GRAINGER, KODÁLY, **STRAVINSKY**,
WEBERN, Alfredo Casella, Lord Berners, BAX, Sir George Dyson, Edgard Varèse

HIS LIFE

Stravinsky's father Feodor was a famous bass singer with the Russian Imperial Opera,
where he created the role of Varlaam in Mussorgsky's *Boris Godunov*; as a result, Igor,
one of four brothers, had his first musical experiences in a renowned opera house. His
father's scores, which he became adept at reading, provided further food for thought, but
it was a performance of Tchaikowsky's 'Pathétique' Symphony, played in memory of the
composer, who had just died, that was 'the beginning of my conscious life as an artist
and musician.'

   His father discouraged him from such a course and in 1901 sent him to study criminal
law and legal philosophy at St Petersburg University. His acquaintance with Vladimir
and Andrei Rimsky-Korsakov, sons of the great composer, led to Stravinsky becoming a
family friend and frequent visitor to Rimsky-Korsakov's house. With Feodor Stravinsky's
death in 1902, Igor began taking lessons in orchestration free of charge from Rimsky-
Korsakov, who was something of a father-figure to the young man. These lessons and
his own study of counterpoint were the only formal musical studies Stravinsky undertook
– he never went to a music conservatory or completed a degree in music. His early
progress as a composer was unusually slow, although he had shown some promise as a
pianist, and Rimsky-Korsakov was hesitant to encourage his young friend to become a
full-time composer. His Symphony in E flat, given its first complete performance in St
Petersburg in 1908, was a weak affair, presaging none of the remarkable writing
Stravinsky was soon to produce. To celebrate the wedding of Rimsky-Korsakov's
daughter, Stravinsky wrote an orchestral fantasy *Feu d'artifice* (*Fireworks*). His adored
teacher died a few days after the wedding.

   If Stravinsky believed in fate then he was well rewarded, for in 1909, *Feu d'artifice*
together with his *Scherzo fantastique*, were given in a concert in St Petersburg. In the
audience happened to be Serge Diaghilev, ballet impresario, founder of the Paris-based
Ballets Russes and one of the great talent-spotters of musical history. He commissioned
Stravinsky to write a ballet score; the result was *The Firebird*. It was presented at the Paris
Opéra in 1910 and made Stravinsky instantly famous. Almost immediately, Diaghilev
persuaded him to write a second ballet score, another work for the musical theatre – the
world in which Stravinsky had been brought up. *Petrushka* provided him with a second
triumph. It also marked a turning point in twentieth-century music with its electric
rhythms, novel instrumental textures and daring polytonality, including passages written
for two different keys (C and F sharp) simultaneously. These innovations emphasized
the extraordinary development in a composer who only four years earlier had produced
such inexperienced and technically deficient works as the Symphony in E flat. Now he
was hailed as among the most significant of living composers, a fashionable icon to the
avant-garde of Paris.

This success, this revolution, was as nothing compared to the third masterpiece commissioned by Diaghilev. The premiere of *The Rite of Spring* at the Théâtre des Champs-Élysées in Paris on 29 May 1913 created possibly the biggest scandal in musical history. Exotically choreographed by Nijinsky with bizarre settings and costumes by Roerich, the first night ended in a riot, so violent was the reaction to the music. Catcalls and stamping feet from detractors threatened to drown out the music, while musicians such as Ravel and Debussy were on their feet yelling their support. Blows were struck, faces were spat in and the critics summoned up their most vituperative adjectives. *The Rite of Spring* was such a sudden, violent wrench from every musical tradition that had gone before that, to most people, it seemed like the work of a madman. A musician will explain that Stravinsky employed techniques such as dissonances of scales played at the intervals of major sevenths and superimpositions of major upon minor triads with the common tonic, rapid changes of metre and unorthodox instrumental combinations. Put more simply, the music has a tremendous tension, a primordial, elemental impact that dazzled its first audiences and announced in a single, shattering blow the birth of a new musical era.

The reception of *The Rite of Spring* at its London first night in July 1913 was better mannered but savaged by the critics again: 'It has no relation to music at all as most of us understand the word,' wrote one. The American premiere of the orchestral suite from the ballet, given as late as 1924, inspired the following verse in the Boston Herald:

> Who wrote this fiendish *Rite of Spring*?
> What right had he to write this thing?
> Against our helpless ears to fling
> Its crash, clash, cling, clang, bing, bang, bing!

Acceptance of the sound world of *The Rite* came slowly but inevitably. By 1940 it was so much part of the standard repertoire that it was included in Walt Disney's *Fantasia*, along with Beethoven's 'Pastoral' Symphony and Tchaikowsky's *The Nutcracker*.

Nothing Stravinsky wrote subsequently had the same impact on the musical world – certainly none of his later works are as well known to the general public – but it would

be misleading to think that he composed nothing else of importance or that he stood still. Far from it. Throughout his life, Stravinsky experimented, pushed himself and developed.

Two more ballets followed, *Le rossignol* and *Les noces*, in which he used smaller orchestral forces. Then came the Russian Revolution of 1917, and his life changed irrevocably. He and his wife (he had married his cousin Catherine Nossenko in 1906) had moved to Switzerland for health reasons, but always intended to return to his estate in Volhynia; when it was clear that his property in Russia would be confiscated and that his royalties would dry up, he opted for voluntary exile in Paris (he became a French citizen in 1934).

After the war, Diaghilev once again prevailed upon Stravinsky to produce another ballet. *Pulcinella* (1920) marked the beginning of a second stage in his musical development. The themes on which the music was based were from the eighteenth-century composer Pergolesi and other Italian contemporaries. Not only was the material 'classical' but the form in which this and future works were conceived relied on structures that had fallen out of fashion, as in the Piano Concerto and the Octet for wind instruments. These are far removed from the luxuriantly orchestrated, ferocious pre-war scores that he now abandoned in favour of what we now call 'neo-classicism'.

Running parallel with his career as a composer, Stravinsky, obsessed with earning enough money, produced a number of keyboard works in which he could be a capable soloist, and travelled all over Europe, North and South America in the two decades after the First World War. This was the period of the opera/oratorio *Oedipus Rex* (1927), *The Symphony of Psalms* (1930) and the ballet *Perséphone* (1933–34). In 1934 he became a French citizen but by the end of the thirties, he was tiring of Europe. His elder daughter Ludmilla died of consumption in 1938, his wife of the same illness the following year, his mother a few months later. With another war seeming inevitable, Stravinsky accepted an invitation from Harvard University to hold the chair of Professor of Poetry and in 1939 he moved to America, joined shortly afterwards by his long-time mistress Vera de Bosset – he'd been in love with her since 1922. They were married in 1940 and became American citizens shortly after the end of the Second World War.

In 1948 he agreed to return to the theatre by writing full-scale opera. With a libretto by W. H. Auden and Chester Kallman based on *The Rake's Progress*, a series of paintings by William Hogarth, the composition took Stravinsky three years. It was premiered in Venice in 1951, with the composer conducting, his first visit to Europe since the war. This proved to be almost his last work in the neo-classical style he had made his own, for, while working on *The Rake's Progress*, he was introduced to Robert Craft, a young American musician in his early twenties. Craft became his musical factotum and also introduced Stravinsky to recordings of the works of Schoenberg and the Second Viennese School. Stravinsky had always opposed Serialism – in fact, although he and Schoenberg were near neighbours in Hollywood, they never met – but now he began cautiously to experiment with it. Thus began the third period of his development, producing his first composition in the new form at the age of seventy-five (*Agon*, 1957). It must be said that none of the music from this period has found favour with the public.

With Craft's help, Stravinsky was able to resume the worldwide touring that characterized the thirties, and in 1962, just before his eightieth birthday, he made a triumphant return to Russia. Soon afterwards, his music, long denounced by the authorities, began to be played there. His last major work was the *Requiem canticales* (1966) after which ill-health slowed him down, but throughout the decade he was feted as few other composers in history, universally acknowledged as the greatest living composer. In 1966 he moved from Hollywood to New York where he died. A few weeks later his body was flown to Venice where he was buried on the island of San Michele, near the resting place of Serge Diaghilev.

Stravinsky bequeathed one ninth of his estate to Robert Craft. It was a valuable legacy. When the manuscript of *The Rite of Spring* came up for auction in 1982 it fetched $548,000, the highest price ever paid for any manuscript by any composer. The buyer was the Swiss philanthropist Paul Sacher whose fortune came from the pharmaceutical company that manufactures the drugs Valium and Librium. His Sacher Foundation building in Basel now houses 166 boxes of letters and 225 drawers of manuscripts – the entire Stravinsky archive – for which he paid $5,250,000.

HIS MUSIC

From 1910 to 1945, Stravinsky was the single strongest influence on contemporary music. The early ballets alone were enough to secure his place among the greats and they eventually succeeded in seducing the public; his second, neo-classical period has failed to achieve the same appeal, and the intellectual rigour with which Stravinsky worked during this time has led to the music being more respected than loved – by musicians, that is, for the average music lover knows little of this phase, let alone the third, serial, period. Few works from the fifties and sixties appear with any regularity either in the concert hall or on record.

In other words, in practical terms, Stravinsky's fame and the popularity of his music are founded on his three early ballets for Diaghilev; but these and the neo-classical works also had a decisive influence on the course of music. Harold Schonberg in his book *The Great Composers* doubts if any composer in the history of music, Bach and Webern included, displayed such logic in his music. Much of the pleasure in listening to Stravinsky is intellectual: the listener is aware of being in the presence of a great mind – fascinating, witty 'but above all organized,' writes Schonberg. 'Stravinsky's music can communicate strongly, but only to a certain type of mind, a kind of mind equivalent to Stravinsky's own – which means one that responds to form, technique, rhythm, stylization. Where a Beethoven, Schubert, or even Bach appeals to listeners on all levels, Stravinsky does not have that universal quality'. It seems as if he will remain, to the general public, more famous for those few works that changed the course of music than for the vast bulk of his later work.

Essential works

Stravinsky recorded a substantial proportion of his music, issued by Sony; these are revealing readings but the composer was not always his own best interpreter, despite his assertions to the contrary. His fee in 1965 for conducting half a concert and part of a rehearsal was $10,000. In a letter to a friend, his wife wrote: 'I have noticed that few people listen with attention to the music in these concerts and that, in fact, few seem to have come for that purpose. What they want is to be in his numinous presence. And although $10,000 may be a lot of money, so is Igor a lot of numen.' Gerard Hoffnung once drew a cartoon of Stravinsky conducting *Petrushka*, with one arm on his hip and the other holding a metronome.

The Firebird, ballet (1910): it was a bold gamble of Diaghilev's to entrust this commission to so inexperienced a young composer. The choreographer Michel Fokine guided and advised Stravinsky throughout its composition and the premiere in Paris, conducted by Gabriel Pierné – incidentally, the composer of *The March of the Little Lead Soldiers* – was a resounding success. Based on a Russian legend, the story is told with music of stunning originality and imagination, as though Rimsky-Korsakov had been suddenly propelled forward half a century, with a brilliant orchestral palette, distinctive melodic line and Stravinsky's own angular rhythmic force. He prepared three orchestral suites from the score, the second is the most frequently heard in concerts and includes *Dance of the Firebird*, *Dance of the Princess*, *Berceuse* and *Dance of the Kastchei*.

Petrushka, ballet (1911): the scene is set in the Shrovetide Fair held in the Admiralty Square in St Petersburg. Petrushka is a kind of Polichinelle, a poor hero always suffering from the cruelty of the police and unjust persecution. He is killed but returns as a ghost to frighten his enemy, his old employer, an allusion to the despotic rule of the Tsars. The score is even more brilliant than *The Firebird*, achieved with greater technical assurance, more harmonic daring and subtler evocation of moods and images. There is an orchestral suite, as well as a coruscating transcription of three movements for solo piano by the composer.

The Rite of Spring, ballet (1913): subtitled 'Scenes of Pagan Russia', this is Stravinsky's masterpiece, inspired by 'a vision' as he himself described it – a young girl dancing herself to death in a sacrificial pagan rite. He began writing it then laid the work aside until *Petrushka* was completed. He took the finished score to Debussy in a version for four-hands-one-piano (recorded occasionally and highly revealing) and the two played it through – Debussy was a fabulous score reader. This is interesting because there is more of Debussy in the score than any other composer, save Stravinsky himself. Even the famous opening bassoon solo is not that far removed from the opening of *Prélude à l'après-midi d'un faune*. In a letter to a friend in 1916, Debussy wrote of Stravinsky: '... he is a spoiled child who sometimes cocks a snook at music ... but for the moment he is unbelievable. He professes a friendship for me because I have helped him to mount a rung of the ladder from which he launches his squibs, not all of which explode. But once again, he is unbelievable.'

Pulcinella, ballet (1919–20): Diaghilev commissioned and produced, Picasso designed, Massine choreographed, Massine and Karsavina were among the principal dancers, Ernest Ansermet conducted – an impressive line-up over eighty years ago. Pulcinella is a traditional character from the Neopolitan theatre. Stravinsky goes further than merely adapting Pergolesi's music, which forms the basis of the work, and provides a musical portrait of Pergolesi and his times – as well as an enchanting ballet. He made an orchestral suite from the ballet score as well as two suites for violin and piano, the second of which is the attractive *Suite italienne*.

Les noces, cantata (1923): *Svadebka* in Russian, literally 'Little Wedding', these four 'Russian choreographic scenes' were designated a cantata. The unusual instrumental combination of chorus, soloists, four pianos and seventeen percussion instruments, the placement of the singers in the orchestra pit rather than on the stage, as well as some astringent, piercing sonorities did not lead to instant success. The London premiere in 1926 was notable, for the four pianos were played by four composers (Poulenc, Auric, Dukelsky and Rieti) and the work was defended, amidst much vicious criticism, by none other than H.G. Wells who 'did not know of any other ballet so interesting, so amusing, so fresh, or nearly as exciting as *The Wedding* ... a rendering in sound and vision of the peasant soul.'

Also worth investigating
Oedipus Rex, opera oratorio (1927)
Symphony of Psalms, for chorus and orchestra (1930)
Symphony in Three Movements (1945)
The Rake's Progress, opera (1951)

Arthur SULLIVAN

'They trained him to make Europe yawn; and he took advantage of their training to make London and New York laugh and whistle' (G.B. Shaw)

Born: 13 May 1842, London
Died: 22 November 1900, London
Full name: Sir Arthur Seymour Sullivan
Type of music: symphony, orchestral, concerto, ballet, choral and vocal, particularly opera and operetta
Influences: Mozart, Mendelssohn, Schumann, Bellini, Offenbach
Contemporaries: Johann Svendsen, CHABRIER, DVOŘÁK, **SULLIVAN**, MASSENET, Arrigo Boito, GRIEG, Pablo de Sarasate, RIMSKY-KORSAKOV

HIS LIFE

If ever a composer was born with a musical silver spoon in his mouth it was Sullivan, the son of an Irish bandmaster. By eight he could play every instrument in the band and became a chorister in the Chapel Royal when he was twelve. His first composition was published the following year and aged fourteen he won the newly established Mendelssohn Scholarship against stiff competition. This gave him three years of study in Leipzig, where his piano teacher was Moscheles, and where he met Liszt and Grieg. When he returned to London, his incidental music for *The Tempest* made him famous overnight. By the time his cantata *Kenilworth* had been performed at the 1864 Birmingham Festival, Sullivan had been marked out as a composer of the first rank. He looked set to become the most important English composer since Purcell.

It didn't happen for, as the world knows, he was introduced to a writer and librettist called William Schwenk Gilbert and their names are linked as surely as Rolls with Royce and Fortnum with Mason. Sullivan's first operetta, *Box and Cox*, was written not with Gilbert but with F.C. Burnand; the famous team's first collaboration in 1871, *Thespis*, was not a success (the score, incidentally, has vanished without trace). The impresario Richard D'Oyly Carte brought them together again four years later and the result was *Trial By Jury*, a one-act skit on the legal system (and the only one of their operettas with no spoken dialogue). From there, the run of success was extraordinary, with comic operettas that retain their freshness and popularity to this day. The operettas made Gilbert and Sullivan famous and rich, each of them earning an income of over £10,000 a year, twice as much as the Prime Minister, Mr Gladstone. Only *Princess Ida* (1884), *Utopia Limited* (1893) and *The Grand Duke* (1896) were less than box-office hits.

Gradually, however, the two men lost their will to work together – or rather, to continue to put up with each other. Although they had much respect for each other's gifts, they were as different as chalk and cheese – Sullivan was a good-looking, charming and elegant society man, befriended by royalty, while Gilbert was an acerbic, gruff, egoistical man of the theatre who was never happier than when there was a visit to the law courts in the offing.

Sullivan's health was never good. In 1892, reported to be dying while holidaying in Cannes, he was brought back to convalesce at Sandringham with his friends the Prince and Princess of Wales. He died of pneumonia in the last weeks of 1900 aged only fifty-eight. He was buried in St Paul's Cathedral.

HIS MUSIC

When Sullivan appeared on the music scene, he had no rivals. It was only natural that such precocious gifts should make him the great white hope for 'the land without music'. He never intended to be a composer of operettas and came to despise the genre, which had taken him away from his ambition to be a nineteenth-century Handel, a symphonist on a par with Schumann, whose works he revered and promoted. In truth, Sullivan was simply not that talented. His choral and orchestral music is supremely well-crafted but its invention is limited. There were going to be no major advances, developing the course of British music. His Symphony in E is a product of the German tradition with a touch of Bellini and Mozart thrown in for good measure. Yet, when his talents were matched with lyrics of immense verve and ingenuity, when music was called for that had to characterize or describe a ludicrous, satirical plot, Sullivan flowered with an amazing fount of melody, wicked send-ups of Verdi choruses and Rossini patter songs, writing with a facility that can only be compared to the latter. Sullivan may not have liked what he was doing but no one has done it better.

Essential works

The whole G&S canon has become known as the 'Savoy Operas', even though not quite all their works were produced at the theatre of that name, which did not open until 1881.

Trial By Jury (1875), **The Sorcerer** (1877), **HMS Pinafore** (1878), **The Pirates of Penzance** (1879), **Patience** (1881), **Iolanthe** (1882), **The Mikado** (1885), **Ruddigore** (1887), **The Yeomen of the Guard** (1888), **The Gondoliers** (1889).

The Tempest, incidental music (1861): the work with which Sullivan first made his name.

Symphony in E 'Irish' (1866): with a haunting 'Irish' tune in the Allegretto, this symphony is Schumannesque and confident.

Overture di Ballo (1870, rev.1889): a bright and infectious, Italian-style concert work.

'The Lost Chord' (1877): Sullivan wrote this work in memory of his brother, and it became the most popular ballad of the nineteenth century.

And the unforgettable hymn **'Onward! Christian soldiers'** (1871).

Pineapple Poll, ballet suite (1951): compiled and arranged by Sir Charles Mackerras from the operas.

Franz von SUPPÉ

'The German Offenbach'

Born: 18 April 1819, Spalato, Dalmatia (then Austria, now Split, in former Yugoslavia)
Died: 21 May 1895, Vienna
Original name: Francesco Ezechiele Ermenegildo Cavaliere Suppé Demelli
Type of music: comic opera
Influence: Offenbach
Contemporaries: LITOLFF, GOUNOD, Antonio Bazzini, OFFENBACH, **SUPPÉ**, Henri Vieuxtemps, Joachim Raff, FRANCK, LALO, Carl Reinecke, SMETANA

HIS LIFE AND MUSIC

Is there a military band in the country – or in the world – that doesn't include the *Light Cavalry* and *Poet and Peasant* overtures in its programmes? Suppé was a purveyor of light music to the gentry *par excellence* and the Viennese lapped it up. They still do.

Considering he was of Belgian descent, born in Austria of parents who lived in Italy for many years, his nickname seems inaccurate, but the comparison to Offenbach is apt. He could play the flute at eleven and, at fifteen, composed a mass. He studied music and philosophy in Padua, and after his father's death went to Vienna for further study at the Conservatory. His first musical post was as third conductor at the Josephstadt Theatre. He began composing incidental music for the plays presented there, both *Possen* (farces) and *Volksstücke* (folk plays) such as *Morning, Noon and Night*. Many of his overtures were used for more than one stage work. For instance, *Poet and Peasant* had been used for at least three others before he introduced it to the Theatre an der Wien, to which he had moved in 1846. Much-loved in Viennese musical circles, it was said that the start to a Suppé performance was heralded by a huge sneeze after he'd taken his pinch of snuff.

Over the following forty years he produced a prodigious amount of music – thirty comic operas of his own and 180 other stage pieces – which came to rival the work of Johann Strauss II in popularity. None of the operettas has survived in the repertoire but the tuneful, boisterous swagger of his overtures will always retain their appeal.

Essential works

Of the overtures, **Light Cavalry**, **Morning, Noon and Night in Vienna**, **Poet and Peasant** are the perennial favourites; those from **Fatinitza** (his extremely successful operetta), **The Queen of Spades**, **The Beautiful Galatea** (based on the Pygmalion-Galatea story), his one-act **Jolly Robbers** (which Sullivan must have known) and **Boccaccio** are also fun.

Karol SZYMANOWSKY

'The Polish Bartók'

Born: 6 October 1882, Timoshovka, Ukraine
Died: 29 March 1937, Lausanne
Full name: Karol Maciej Szymanowski
Type of music: symphony, orchestral, opera, vocal, chamber, piano
Influences: Beethoven, Wagner, Chopin, Richard Strauss, Scriabin, Stravinsky
Contemporaries: Nicolai Miaskovsky, Georges Enescu, **SZYMANOWSKY**, Manuel Ponce, Joaquín Turina, GRAINGER, KODÁLY, STRAVINSKY, WEBERN

HIS LIFE AND MUSIC

Szymanowski (pronounced She-mun-*ov'*-ski), the most important Polish composer of the twentieth century, is the link from Chopin to Lutosławski, Penderecki and Górecki, though very little of his music features in concert programmes. To the majority of people, his name is unknown.

Like his great compatriot, the piano was Szymanowski's first instrument (he composed at the piano). Both his parents played – they were wealthy and cultured landowners – and Szymanowksi took to the instrument and began writing at a very early age. The family were much given to home entertainments – plays, music, dances and fancy-dress balls – and Karol and his elder brother Felix composed the music for these occasions. Szymanowski's youthful music is rich with the influence of Chopin, a quality that must have appealed to the pianist Arthur Rubinstein whom he met after his entry to the Warsaw Conservatory in 1901. Rubinstein remained a lifelong friend and champion of his music.

Szymanowski's fame spread rapidly after the publication of his first pieces by the Association of Young Polish Composers (later known as Young Poland in Music), which he was instrumental in forming. Following his father's death in 1906, he travelled extensively, living in Berlin until 1908 and then moving on to Paris, Rome, Sicily, Greece, Algiers and Morocco.

From boyhood he had suffered from a slight limp, a condition that, with his homosexuality, contributed to his reserved, fastidious, highly sensitive personality, which he explored in a novel, *Efebos*, so that when his First Symphony (1907), much influenced by Richard Strauss, was criticized for being too elaborate, he agreed and withdrew the work. His Second Symphony, which shows a stylistic change influenced by Scriabin and Stravinsky, was better received. In the Third Symphony (1916) and the important opera *King Roger* (1925), his interest in ancient cultures, fostered by his foreign tours, was given full vent – the celebration of Dionysus is a central theme of both works.

In 1917, the family estate was plundered by the revolutionaries and Szymanowski lost everything. A third stage in his musical development emerged: he determined, like Mussorgsky in Russia, to define Polish music. Throughout the 1920s he spent much time in the resort of Zakopane, at the centre of the folk culture of the Tatra mountains, going on long walks to 'listen to the mountains' and gather folk material. The result was his ballet *Harnasie* (1926), which makes much use of the idiosyncratic music of the region. Here Szymanowski's musical style crystallized.

Although his writing is tonal, much of it is not readily accessible at a first hearing. His is a strange, individual voice often touched with the Oriental sensuality of Slavonic folk music and a vein of mysticism – highly expressive and lyrical but with dense, sumptuous harmonies and abrupt changes of rhythms and texture.

In 1926, with his music gradually gaining international recognition, he accepted the post of director of the Warsaw Conservatory, but his health was already in decline. His throat and lungs were affected by tuberculosis and, probably, cancer, not helped by his heavy smoking and fondness of vodka. He continued travelling and composing until a year before his death in a Lausanne clinic.

Essential works

Stabat mater (1925–26): an austerely beautiful setting for soloists, chorus and orchestra, one of Szymanowsky's finest works, mingling religious and national feeling. His first liturgical piece, it blends Polish rhythm and melody with sixteenth-century polyphony.

Harnasie, ballet (1923–31): a rhapsodic, vigorous and colourful score calling for a large orchestra, tenor and chorus, it was inspired by the life, music and dance of the inhabitants of the Tatra mountains, and Szymanowski shows himself to be a masterly manipulator of nationalist melody and intricate Slavonic rhythms. Listen for the *March of the Harnasie*, the *Drinking Song* and the *Peasant Dance* (also famous as a violin solo).

Symphony No.3 ('Song in the Night') (1916): a lavish, visionary choral symphony inspired by the pantheistic writings of the thirteenth-century Persian poet Jalal al-Din Rumi, the founder of the Mevelevi (Whirling Dervishes).

Symphony No.4, Symphonie concertante for piano and orchestra (1932): perhaps the most widely performed of Szymanowski's music, a concertante rather than concerto, emphasizing the equally important roles of piano and orchestra; Rubinstein was a fine exponent of the work.

King Roger, opera (1924): perfumed exoticism and awesome drama characterize this unusual

and rarely performed story about a shepherd – a mixture of Christ, Dionysus and Eros – who creates havoc in the lives of the king and his queen. One of the vocal highlights, *Roxana's Song*, is also an effective violin piece.

Also worth investigating
Concerto for violin No.1 (1916)
Concerto for violin No.2 (1933)
Three Myths for violin and piano (1915): No.1 from this set, **La fontaine d'Aréthuse**, is Szymanowksi's best-known piece.

Thomas TALLIS

'Father of English cathedral music'

Born: c.1505, London
Died: 23 November 1585, Greenwich
Alternative name: Thomas Tallys
Type of music: church music, motet, keyboard
Influences: English polyphonic tradition
Contemporaries: Martin Luther, John Taverner, Hans Sachs, **TALLIS**,
Jacobus Clemens non Papa, Antonio de Cabezón, PALESTRINA, Roland de Lassus

HIS LIFE AND MUSIC

Tallis is the first important English composer, yet little is known about his life. He held a succession of posts as an organist, most notably at Waltham Abbey in Essex until the dissolution of the monasteries in 1540, before joining the Gentlemen of the Chapel Royal in about 1543. He remained at the Chapel Royal for the rest of his life, serving under Henry VIII, Edward VI, Mary and Elizabeth I.

In 1572, William Byrd, forty years his junior, joined Tallis in the Chapel Royal, forming one of music's earliest significant partnerships. Tallis and Byrd became joint organists of the chapel and, in 1575, they were granted the sole right to print music in England. Their first publication was a joint venture – a volume of *Cantiones sacrae*, to which they both contributed seventeen motets. Tallis spent the last years of his life in Greenwich. He was described in 1577 as 'verie aged'. His epitaph reads: 'As he did live, so also did he die, in mild and happy sort, (O! happy man).'

Most of Tallis' music is, not surprisingly, for the church and his historic importance is in being one of the first composers to write for the Anglican service, bridging the transition from the Roman rite and establishing a church music tradition that is among the richest in music history. Although most of the texts Tallis chose to set are in Latin, as a Catholic one may guess that, after Queen Mary's reign, pragmatism took precedence over belief as

he adapted to Thomas Cranmer's English and his requirement of a 'playn and distincte note for every sillable'.

Tallis composed in the whole range of styles and forms then available. We can marvel at his handling of choral sonority, his technical assurance of grand polyphonic textures as well as in the simplicity of four-part hymn tunes. 'Tallis in D' is still in use today – No.78 in *Hymns Ancient and Modern Revised*. It first appeared in Archbishop Parker's *Psalter* of 1567, in which can also be found the tune on which Vaughan Williams based his *Fantasy on a Theme of Thomas Tallis*.

Essential works

'**Spem in alium**' (c.1570–1): literally 'sing and glorify', Tallis' masterpiece; an unaccompanied choral work for eight choirs of five voices; forty separate but harmonized vocal lines are interwoven in a glorious, uplifting act of creation.
'**Lamentations of Jeremiah**': a sombre and grave setting for five voices, again illustrating Tallis' mastery of counterpoint.

'**Salvator mundi**', '**O nata lux**', '**O sacrum convivium**', '**Audivi media nocte**', '**Gaude Gloriosa**' and '**In ieiuntio et fletu**': these are all striking and beautiful examples of Tallis' Latin motets, and worth tracking down. Among his English anthems are '**Hear the voice and prayer**', '**O Lord give Thy Holy Spirit**' and '**If ye love me**'.

Giuseppe TARTINI

Born: 8 April 1692, Pirano
Died: 26 February 1770, Padua
Type of music: violin concertos and sonatas
Influences: Veracini, Corelli, C.P.E. Bach
Contemporaries: Francesco Geminiani, Francesco Veracini, **TARTINI**, Louis-Claude Daquin, Giuseppe Sammartini, Pietro Locatelli, Johann Joachim

HIS LIFE AND MUSIC

'A complete romantic long before Romanticism had become the mainstream of musical expression' was the verdict of a later century on Tartini, the outstanding violinist and composer of his day. There are some pretty romantic legends attached to his life, too: he eloped with the niece of the powerful Cardinal Cornaro and, when the Cardinal ordered his arrest, he fled from Padua disguised as a monk. He sought refuge in the monastery of Assisi where a relative was custodian and hid there for two years. During this time he wrote his famous 'Devil's Trill' Sonata, inspired by a dream in which the devil showed him what could be done on the violin. He gave concerts from behind a curtain at the monastery until, on one occasion, a strong wind (or a deacon, depending on the source) blew the curtain aside and he was recognized. Tartini returned to Padua, reunited with his wife and forgiven by the Cardinal. There he founded a violin school which, apart from an absence of two years spent in Prague, he never left for the rest of his life. His final years were spent in some pain due to a malignant growth of the foot.

Tartini advanced the potential of the instrument more than anyone before him – the modern bowing technique owes its origins to Tartini. In his work, often inscribed with quotations in cipher, we hear music inspired by works of poetry, imbued with a sense of personal expression.

Worth investigating

The musicologist Minos Dounias (1900–62) catalogued Tartini's Violin Concertos in 1935; they are identified by D numbers.
Violin Concerto in E minor, D 56

Violin Concerto in A, D 96
Violin Concerto in A minor, D 113
Violin Sonata in G minor, 'Trillo del Diavolo' ('The Devil's Trill')

Peter Ilyich TCHAIKOWSKY

'A thrilling case of nerves' (Neville Cardus)

Born: 7 May 1840, Votkinsk, Viatka district
Died: 6 November 1893, St Petersburg
Name in native form: Pyotr Il'yich Tchaikovsky
Type of music: ballet, opera, symphony, concerto, song, chamber
Influences: Mozart, Mendelssohn, Schumann, Balakirev, Bizet, Russian folk song
Contemporaries: Josef Rheinberger, Sir John Stainer, **TCHAIKOWSKY**, Johann Svendsen, CHABRIER, DVOŘÁK, SULLIVAN, MASSENET, Arrigo Boito

---

HIS LIFE

Tchaikowsky was a comparatively late starter among the great composers: he learned the piano as a boy, and when the family moved to St Petersburg in 1850 it was decided that he should read law. It was not until he was in his twenties that he began to make something of his musical gifts. His father was a successful mining engineer while his mother was the artistic one, French by birth, and a good linguist. Peter was the second of her six children. He had a good education, a French governess and a stable beginning to his life. As early as eight years old, though, signs of neurosis began to manifest themselves, often brought on by listening to music.

1848 Tchaikowsky's father resigned his government post, hoping for a better position in Moscow. This did not materialize, and Peter and his elder brother, Modest, were packed off to boarding school. This second period of relative security ended in 1854 when his mother died of cholera. His relationship with her had been profoundly close, to the point of obsession, and it can be argued that he never recovered from this blow.

1859 His period at the St Petersburg School of Jurisprudence led to employment as a clerk in the Ministry of Justice, a job to which he was singularly unsuited. The decisive factor in his development was the founding in 1862 by Anton Rubinstein of what would become the St Petersburg Conservatory.

1863 Tchaikowsky followed his teacher Nicholas Zaremba to the Conservatory and the following year, in a gesture that none of the Mighty Handful could emulate, resigned his post to become a full-time musician. Only two years later, Rubinstein's brother Nicholas invited Tchaikowsky to teach harmony at the Moscow Conservatory.

For a time, he lived in Nicholas Rubinstein's house in Moscow while his first large-scale compositions began to emerge, Symphony No.1, 'Winter Daydreams' among them. His nervous disorder surfaced again in the forms of colitis, hypochondria, hallucinations and numbness in his hands and feet. One of his neuroses was his conviction that his head would fall off if he conducted an orchestra. Even later in life, when he was in constant demand to conduct his works, the experience terrified him and he conducted with the right hand holding the baton, the left hand holding his chin.

1868 The Belgian soprano, Désirée Artôt, part of an opera company visiting St Petersburg, became attached to Tchaikowsky, and for a while he contemplated marriage. She, however, was as celebrated for her sexual peccadilloes as her singing and soon after married a Spanish singer. Tchaikowsky appeared to accept it all philosophically. The music that followed the affair was the first version of his famous *Romeo and Juliet* Fantasy Overture, containing the most radiant love music he ever wrote.

Tchaikowsky's career progressed, untroubled, for the next few years. He contributed music criticism to Moscow newspapers, made many trips abroad, taught, and continued composing. Then came a series of crises.

1874 Late that year, Tchaikowsky finished his Piano Concerto No.1 and played it through to Nicholas Rubinstein to whom he had dedicated the work. Rubinstein denounced it as ugly and unplayable. Tchaikowsky was stunned (paradoxically, it is now his most frequently performed work; it was premiered in Boston, somewhat incongruously, in 1875 by the new dedicatee Hans von Bülow). Rubinstein eventually relented and became a fervent champion of the Concerto, but Tchaikowsky was flung into a morbid depression by Rubinstein's initial reaction to it, as well as by the initial failure of his ballet *Swan Lake*. He tired of his work at the Conservatory, had financial problems and, above all, nagging away at the back of his mind, was the guilt attached to his homosexuality.

1876 At exactly the right time a guardian angel appeared in his life. Through the violinist Josef Kotek, an affluent and cultured widow, Nadezhda von Meck, heard about Tchaikowsky and engaged him to write some music, offering him large fees for the work. She was a remarkable woman, forty-five years old, the mother of eleven children and passionately fond of music. But shortly after his introduction to Mme von Meck another crisis hit Tchaikowsky. A pretty 28-year-old music student named Antonina Milyukova became obsessed with him. She was a charming neurotic who threatened suicide if Tchaikowsky did not marry her. To read her love letters is to read the writings of an unbalanced woman (she would bite her fingernails to the quick until they bled). 'Some mysterious power drew me to the girl,' wrote Tchaikowsky later. To his brother Modeste, who was also homosexual, he confided, 'I am convinced that my inclinations are the greatest and insuperable barrier to my well-being, and I must by all means struggle against my nature.'

Without disclosing to Antonina his true sexual preference, without loving her, and thinking that marriage would scotch the current rumours about his 'deviancy', Tchaikowsky married her on 18 July 1877. It was a disaster. He was 'ready to scream' (he admitted) the first time they were alone together. Five days later, he was going out of his mind and wrote to Modeste, 'Physically, she is totally repulsive to me.' On 7 August he fled to his sister Alexandra's estate at Kamenka. Later he attempted to kill himself by standing in the freezing Moscow River. He next went to St Petersburg where another brother Anatol, a lawyer, made suitable arrangements for a separation. The couple were never divorced and never met again. Antonina continued to pester Tchaikowsky for years to come, badgering him for money and issuing veiled threats of blackmail. In 1896 she was confined to an insane asylum, where she died in 1917.

Nadezhda von Meck was kept informed of this relationship by Tchaikowsky, though never of the real cause of its failure, and in the same year (1877) she settled an annual allowance of 6,000 roubles on him. The fact that some of his finest masterpieces were produced subsequently has earned Mme von Meck an honoured place in the annals of music; for his Fourth Symphony, dedicated to his patron, the opera *Eugene Onegin* and the great Violin Concerto were but three of the works written shortly after she had given Tchaikowsky some financial security.

For the following thirteen years, this extraordinary relationship continued, one of the most curious and moving in musical history. They corresponded voluminously and frankly, often daily, Tchaikowsky pouring out his innermost thoughts, his aspirations and ideals, and Nadezhda von Meck responding with understanding, sympathy and encouragement. It was the perfect relationship for the composer, a replacement for his lost mother, a woman who had no personal or sexual interest in him, yet supported him financially and emotionally. Despite their touching friendship they never met. One of the conditions for her generous subsidy was that they should not become involved on a personal level. Sometimes they would be attending the same concert or would pass each other in the street; in Florence, where they were both staying only a short distance apart, Mme von Meck gave way and invited Tchaikowsky to visit her. Tchaikowsky declined, saying that one should never meet one's guardian angel face to face. Once they *did* accidentally come face to face; both turned crimson with embarrassment and fled without speaking.

1878–88 The initial burst of unqualified masterpieces was followed by an uneven period comprising his opera *Joan of Arc*, the Second Piano Concerto, *Capriccio Italien* and the Serenade for strings, the Piano Sonata and Piano Trio. By 1880 he was famous and respected. Then, between 1881 and 1888 he dried up.

He travelled extensively, each day enjoying a set routine wherever he was and, to the casual observer, living the life of a fastidious, disciplined bourgeois gentleman with only occasional bouts of heavy drinking giving a clue to the unhappy turmoil beneath. Tchaikowsky went to great lengths to conceal his sexual activities, using subterfuge and duplicity for fear of being discovered, entering cryptic annotations in his diary referring to 'Sensation Z'. It must not be forgotten that anyone convicted of a homosexual act in Russia was sentenced to death.

1888 Inspiration returned with the Fifth Symphony, the government settled an annual pension on him, and he made an extensive tour of Europe conducting his works to enormous acclaim. Then in 1890 came a letter from Nadezhda von Meck saying that, due to financial reversals, she was no longer able to subsidize Tchaikowsky. The composer replied expressing sympathy for her changed fortunes, pointed out that he was now financially self-sufficient and hoped their friendship would continue. The letter

went unanswered. So did many more. Then he learned that, in fact, Mme von Meck was not financially embarrassed and had used it merely as an excuse to discontinue the friendship. After thirteen years, his trusted confidante and mother-figure had abruptly terminated their relationship. Perhaps she had discovered the truth about his homosexuality; perhaps she had become bored with Tchaikowsky's letters; more likely, her family had put pressure on her to terminate the friendship and put an end to the society gossip about its nature. It was a shattering blow to Tchaikowsky's confidence and initiated a period of morbid depression.

1891 Tchaikowsky suffered considerably from homesickness during his first tour of the United States, despite being greeted with a rapturous reception wherever he appeared. He liked America and all its many attractions but wrote in his diary: 'I enjoy all this like a person sitting at a table set with marvels of gastronomy, devoid of appetite. Only the prospect of returning to Russia can awaken an appetite in me.'

1893 After Tchaikowsky returned home, his gloom became more profound. He was convinced that he would go insane. He completed his great Sixth Symphony, the 'Pathétique', and in June travelled to Cambridge to receive an Honorary Doctorate of Music. In October, he conducted the premiere of the 'Pathétique', but the work was coolly received. On 2 November, after an agreeable evening meal, he drank a glass of tap water. His friends were appalled. Didn't he know it was the cholera season in St Petersburg, that no water should be drunk without first boiling it? Tchaikowsky, it seems, was unconcerned.

There are many stories surrounding the death of this great composer. The question of 'Was it suicide or not?' has fascinated scholars for over a century and has provided the material for many plays, novels, doctorates and romantic biographers. The most likely theory is the simplest one – that Tchaikowsky was a fatalist: someone who, in the face of impending disaster, makes little effort to deal with it, belieiving that all events are subject to fate. It is unlikely that he would have deliberately tried to catch the same dread disease that had killed his mother. It is even more unlikely – though admittedly the better story – that he committed suicide by drinking arsenic. Tchaikowsky, it was rumoured, had had a homosexual relationship with the nephew of a high-ranking Russian nobleman or, in other versions, a member of the Russian Imperial family. As a result, it is said, he was 'tried' by a jury of his former classmates at the St Petersburg School of Jurisprudence and given the choice of suicide or Siberia. There is no doubt that Tchaikowsky did not want posterity to know he was homosexual and that he described his sexuality as 'unnatural' and a 'vice'.

The fact is that Tchaikowsky died four days after drinking the water. One troubling piece of evidence confusing the cholera theory is that the composer's body lay in state in his brother's bedroom. It was then taken to Kazan Cathedral, where mourners filed past in their hundreds to pay their respects and touch the body. Not one of them contracted the highly contagious disease.

In his last hours, the unconscious Tchaikowsky kept calling out the name of Mme von Meck, according to Modeste, and muttering 'Proklyataya', meaning 'Accursed one'. The word is in the feminine gender and was taken to refer to Nadezhda von Meck. By another of life's fearful symmetries, the lady herself died just two months later in Wiesbaden, Germany.

HIS MUSIC

Tchaikowsky is the most popular of all Russian composers. Many would say he is also the greatest. His music manages to combine nationalist elements of the Mighty Handful with the European tradition, but it is music that, from first note to last, could only have been written by a Russian.

In late-nineteenth-century Russia, music divided not just into two schools but also into two cities: Moscow was the cosmopolitan seat of composers like Tchaikowsky who preferred to go their own way; St Petersburg was the home of the nationalists, who accused Tchaikowsky of being too eclectic in style and too prone to be influenced by Western musical culture. Stravinsky thought that 'Tchaikowsky's music, which does not appear specifically Russian to everybody, is often more profoundly Russian than music that has long since been awarded the facile label of Muscovite picturesqueness. This music is quite as Russian as Pushkin's verse or Glinka's song, while not specifically cultivating in his art "the soul of the Russian peasant".'

Although he was personally on friendly, if distant, terms with all the Five (except for Cui, whom he despised), Tchaikowsky was writing from a different premise. Harold Schonberg expressed it well when he wrote, 'where Rimsky-Korsakov spread out his arms to embrace Russian antiquity and folklore, where Mussorgsky spread out his arms to embrace the entire Russian people, Tchaikowsky spread out his arms to embrace – himself.' Much of his music reflects his own state of mind – gloomy, passionate, troubled, despondent at turns – expressed with a heart-on-sleeve frankness that some find embarrassing. It isn't 'manly' to reveal your inner self like this, is the line; there's too much hysteria and self-preoccupation. Tchaikowsky himself was unerringly accurate about the worth of each composition – except *Swan Lake*, strangely, which he thought 'trash in comparison with *Sylvia*' by Delibes. He described his symphonic fantasy *The Tempest* as 'a motley pot-pourri' and *Francesca da Rimini* as too 'full of false pathos'. He was also equally sure of the merits of the Fourth Symphony and *Eugene Onegin*. As for the Sixth Symphony, he wrote to his nephew, 'I can tell you in all sincerity that I consider this symphony the best thing I have ever done.'

One thing distinguishes Tchaikowsky above all else from his Russian contemporaries – the gift of melody. It is the main reason why people love his music and want to return to it again and again: to hear those glorious tunes.

Essential works
Orchestral

Capriccio Italien, Op.45 (1880): inspired by a visit to Italy, this brilliant showpiece makes use of the country's folk tunes (the prominent figure for the trumpet at the beginning was based on bugle calls Tchaikowsky heard from a military barracks in Rome); the piece concludes with an exciting Tarantella. Shallow but effective.

Marche Slave, Op.31 (1876): more interesting than the better-known and overblown *1812* (both quote the Russian national anthem), leading to an impressive, if flashy, climax.

1812 Overture, Op.49 (1880): melodramatic, noisy and 'cheaply programmatic', the ever-popular *Ouverture solennelle* was commissioned to be played during the consecration of the Temple of Christ the Redeemer in Moscow, built as a memorial to Napoleon's defeat in Russia in 1812. The introductory theme is the Russian hymn 'God, preserve Thy people', followed by a realistic depiction of the battle of Borodino, with 'La Marseillaise' and 'God Save the Tsar' battling it out for musical supremacy. The Russian hymn is triumphant at last, the whole rounded off with the bells of Moscow ringing out. Vulgar? Yes, but breathlessly thrilling with or without canons.

Romeo and Juliet, Fantasy Overture (1869, rev.1870 and 1880): this wonderful work was written when Tchaikowsky was still an apprentice, though subsequently twice revised; the subject was suggested by Balakirev, who advised the young composer throughout its writing. It is not an overture in the usual sense of an introduction to an opera, but a descriptive concert piece (another use of the word), with 'fantasy' emphasizing the freedom of form in which the work is written. Based on Shakespeare's play, without following the plot scene by scene, it is easy to recognize the various elements of the tragic love story. Tchaikowsky wrote it after being jilted by the singer Désirée Artôt.

Serenade in C, Op.48 (1880): for string orchestra; written on impulse, Tchaikowsky confided, 'I felt it deeply from start to finish.' The four movements were orchestrated at the same time as the *1812* Overture and are a textbook of how to write for strings, from its sonorous hymn-like opening to the poignant Elegie to the Russian *furiant* finale.

Symphony No.4 in F minor, Op.36 (1877): the Fourth, Fifth and Sixth Symphonies offer a kind of cycle, revealing differing aspects of Tchaikowsky's dark and melancholy personality. The Fourth is concerned with destiny and, in the composer's own programme, 'the fatal power which prevents an impetus toward happiness from reaching its goal.' But throughout its four movements, an unkind fate is swept aside with vigour and contempt and the whole work is distinguished by its magnificent power and brilliance – and even flashes of humour – in a virtuoso piece of orchestral scoring.

Symphony No.5 in E minor, Op.64 (1888): few composers have been able to match Tchaikowsky in the musical expression of melancholy. Rather than weighing the listener down with sheer gloom, he somehow presents a healing balm. The Fifth is less exuberant than its predecessor and, in several departures from convention, replaces the usual third movement Scherzo with a Waltz. Its most famous movement is the second, the Andante Cantabile, with a haunting tune introduced by the solo French horn (turned into a pop song, inevitably, called 'Moon Love').

Symphony No.6 in B minor, 'Pathétique', Op.74 (1893): one of the greatest of this genre, the Sixth is a programme-symphony. Exactly what programme, Tchaikowsky teasingly chose not to divulge. 'Let them puzzle their heads over it,' he wrote. 'The programme is subjective through and through, and during my journey I often wept bitterly while composing it in my head.' Havelock Ellis, famous for his *Studies in the Psychology of Sex*, called the work 'a homosexual tragedy'. It is a lament for terrible woes, its final movement surely the most pessimistic utterance in all music. Among many points of interest along the way are the quote from the Russian requiem service 'And rest him with the Saints' in the first movement, the waltz-which-isn't-a-waltz of the second movement, written in a deceptive 5/4 measure, and the too-confident march of the third movement before the total resignation of the last. The whole work is proof that Tchaikowsky was happiest when he was sad, viewing his sorrows with detachment and encapsulating them in music of the utmost beauty.

Piano Concerto No.1 in B flat minor, Op.23 (1875, rev.1879 and 1889): the world's most frequently recorded piano concerto with just about the most famous opening pages has also spawned at least two million-selling discs. The recording in 1958 by Van Cliburn, conducted by Kiril Kondrashin, became the first classical album to go gold. It had sold two million by 1965. The other million-seller was the ghastly song 'Tonight We Love' based on the opening theme, a hit for Freddy Martin (who?) in 1941.

Whichever other recording you buy, you must hear the incandescent live performance of 1943 (not the earlier studio version) with Horowitz and Toscanini.

Piano Concerto No.2 in G, Op.44 (1880): if you've never tried Tchaikowsky's No.2, then you're in for a treat: it is better, though more conventionally, structured than No.1, full of glorious melodies again, and provides the soloist with plenty to do. In the hands of Shura Cherkassky, say, or Gary Graffman. it can knock you for six in either of the two versions in which it is performed – one by Siloti, with cuts and amendments, the other as conceived originally by Tchaikowsky. Balanchine used the score for his *Ballet Imperial*.

Violin Concerto in D, Op.35 (1878): *de rigeur* for all violinists and one of the four big concertos for the instrument (the others are by Mendelssohn, Beethoven and Brahms). The work was dedicated to the celebrated teacher Leopold Auer, then a professor at the St Petersburg Conservatory. Like Nicholas Rubinstein's reaction to the First Piano Concerto, Auer declared the work unplayable but later modified his opinion when the concerto caught on. Among Auer's pupils was Jascha Heifetz whose recording of the Concerto with Fritz Reiner and the Chicago Symphony Orchestra is still the touchstone by which others are judged.

Variations on a Rococco Theme for cello and orchestra in A, Op.33 (1876): a poised and eloquent set of variations on a theme of Tchaikowsky's own devising, the nearest he came to writing a cello concerto. It is an inspired and upbeat work, exploiting the instrument to the full, as in the Violin Concerto, stretching it to the limits.

Chamber

Piano Trio in A minor, Op.50 (1882): despite the row over the First Piano Concerto, which, in fact, had been forgotten by the time the Second Concerto was under way, Tchaikowsky was filled with sorrow at the death of Nicholas Rubinstein to whom he had owed so much at the outset of his career. Dedicated 'To the memory of a great artist', the Trio is cast in two lengthy movements: the first is called *Pezzo elegiaco* (*Elegiac piece*), and the second is a theme with variations, recalling Rubinstein's prowess as a pianist, judging from the difficulty of the piano part.

String Quartet No.1 in D, Op.11 (1871): composed while Tchaikowsky was a professor at the Moscow Conservatory, the quartet, sometimes known as the 'Accordion' because of the rise and fall of the opening chords, contains one of music's best loved movements, the Andante Cantabile. It has been arranged for every conceivable instrument, based on the folk song 'Sidel Vanya' ('Uncle Vanya sat on a divan and smoked a pipe of tobacco'), a song Tchaikowsky heard while visiting his sister at Kamenka in the Ukraine during the summer of 1869.

Piano

Tchaikowsky's solo piano music is generally less well known than his other works. A pity, for buried among the various *opus* numbers are some real gems. The tone is more intimate and less hysterical – there's certainly more humour and cheer – although Russian melancholy has its part to play as well. The pick of the bunch are:

Song without words, Op.2 No.3
Humoresque in G, Op.10 No.2 (1871)
Six Pieces, Op.19 (1873): the Nocturne (No.4) is famous but **No.6** contains a wonderful set of variations.
Six Pieces on One Theme, Op.21 (1873): a masterpiece that should be better known, the Impromptu (No.3) in particular.
Sonata in G, Op.37 (1878): long, sprawling and uneven, this is a dramatic composition when played by a great artist (Sviatoslav Richter, for example); not to be confused with the earlier, weaker, **Sonata in C sharp minor**.
The Seasons, Op.37b (1876): one piece for every month; **No.6** (June: Barcarolle) and **No.11** (November: Troika) will be instantly recognizable.
Chanson triste, Op.40 No.2 (1878)
Valse in A flat, Op.40 No.8 (1878)
Valse in F sharp minor, Op.40 No.9 (1878)
Dumka, Op.59 (1886): subtitled 'A Scene from Russian Life', this is a virtuoso work, 'a Lisztian Hungarian Rhapsody with a Volga accent' as David Dubal described it.

Vocal

Of nearly a hundred songs that Tchaikowsky composed, few are regularly included in recital, save one, 'None but the lonely heart', which is the last of his early **Six Songs, Op.6** (1869).
Six Songs, Op.16 (1872): No.1, 'Cradle Song' is particularly charming.
Six Songs, Op.38 (1878): the first of the set is 'Don Juan's Serenade', with words by Tolstoy.

Stage

Swan Lake, Op.20, ballet (1877): the earliest of Tchaikowsky's three ballets, *Swan Lake* was not a success at first, and this prompted Tchaikowsky to disparage it initially. But in this much-loved score he discovered a *métier* that ideally suited his talents, and the work has never been out of the repertoire. It, too, has its famous Waltz.

The Sleeping Beauty, Op.66, ballet (1890): music such as this and *The Nutcracker* inspired those involved in Russian ballet to carry the craft to an unprecedented height of perfection. The score is awash with glorious tunes and the Suite ends similarly – with one of those waltzes which Tchaikowsky enjoyed so much.

Eugene Onegin, Op.24, opera (1879): pronounced Yoo'-jeen On-*yay*'-ghin and known in the business as 'Eugene One Gin', this is Tchaikowsky's one indisputable operatic masterpiece. It was among the first fruits of his platonic relationship with Nadezhda von Meck and followed the disaster of his marriage to Antonina Miyukova. The libretto is based on a poem by Pushkin and tells the story of Tatyana's love for the elegant Onegin. Its most famous scene, known as the *Letter Scene,* is from Act 1 and ranks with the finest and most moving in all opera; in this scene the gauche Tatyana releases her pent-up feelings and writes to her beloved Onegin. It was the first part of the opera to be composed. The Waltz (Act 2) and Polonaise (Act 3) are often played separately.

The Nutcracker, Op.71, ballet (1892): a little girl dreams on Christmas night that the gift of a household nutcracker doll comes to life. Based on the fairy-tale by E.T.A. Hoffman, it provided Tchaikowsky with an opportunity to show his brilliance as an orchestrator and melodist in this enchanting score, which does not reveal a trace of his melancholy spirit. The Suite fashioned from the full score is better known, containing the famous *Miniature Overture,* March, *Dance of the Sugar Plum Fairy, Russian Dance, Arab Dance, Chinese Dance, Dance of the Flutes* and *Waltz of the Flowers.* At Christmas, every ballet company can be sure of a full-house of stage-struck, would-be ballerinas eager to enter into Tchaikowsky's magical world.

Also worth investigating
Symphony No.1 in G minor, 'Winter Daydreams', Op.13 (1866, rev.1874)
Symphony No.2 in C minor, 'Little Russian', Op.17 (1872, rev.1879)
Piano Concerto No.3 in E flat, Op.73 (1893)
Concert Fantasia in G, Op.56 for piano and orchestra (1884)
The Maid of Orleans, opera (1881)
The Queen of Spades, opera (1890)

Transcriptions
Tchaikowsky's works have attracted many composer-pianists to dress up the original music in effective transcriptions. Look out for:
Concert suite from The Nutcracker (Pletnyev)
Paraphrase on Waltz of the Flowers (*The Nutcracker*) (Grainger)
Paraphrase on the Polonaise from Eugene Onegin (Liszt)
Paraphrase on Eugene Onegin (Pabst)

Georg Philipp TELEMANN

'He had his hand almost upon the door' (Lawrence Gilman)

Born: 14 March 1681, Magdeburg
Died: 25 June 1767, Hamburg
Type of music: opera, church music, concerto, orchestral, chamber, instrumental
Influences: Lully, Vivaldi, Corelli
Contemporaries: Jeremiah Clarke, William Croft, VIVALDI, **TELEMANN**, Jean-François Dandrieu, RAMEAU, J.S. BACH, DOMENICO SCARLATTI, HANDEL

HIS LIFE AND MUSIC
Telemann was a close friend of both Bach and Handel though far more highly regarded than both of them during his lifetime. The son of a clergyman, he was a self-taught musician with an uncanny ability to soak up knowledge from a variety of disciplines. Science, languages and jurisprudence seem to have been Telemann's subjects at the University of Leipzig. By then he had picked up the violin, the zither and the oboe as well as having a reputation as a brilliant organist. Most of his music theory was gained by studying the scores of older masters like Lully.

He wrote operas and cantatas for the *Collegium Musicum* he founded while still a student in Leipzig and thereafter held a succession of posts – as organist and Kapellmeister in Sorau, Poland, and as music director in Eisenach and Frankfurt. In 1721 he was offered the prestigious job of music director of St Thomas' Church in Leipzig, which he turned down to become city musical director in Hamburg where he stayed for the rest of his life. The *third* choice for the post in Leipzig was Johann Sebastian Bach. (Telemann, incidentally, was godfather to Bach's son, Carl Philipp Emanuel.)

Telemann was a popular figure; his lively mind and genial high spirits are caught in his music, but his private life was not as happy: his first wife died in childbirth, he had eight sons and two daughters by his second wife, few of whom survived infancy, and she later abandoned him for a Swedish army officer. In addition, Telemann, like Bach and Handel suffered from failing eyesight as he grew older.

Handel said, famously, 'Telemann could write a motet for eight voices as easily as one could write a letter.' Whether or not the motet would be any good is another question. Music, Telemann thought, 'ought not to be an effort' and disarmingly asserted that 'a good composer should be able to set public notices to music.' Perhaps, but why?

Telemann was probably the most prolific composer in musical history – they started cataloguing his work in Germany in 1950 and they still haven't finished. He wrote almost as much as Bach and Handel put together, and each of *them* wrote a perplexing amount, his corpus includes 600 French overtures or orchestral suites, 200 concertos, forty operas and more than 1,000 pieces of church music. All of his music is extremely well-fashioned and elegant; his technique is sophisticated, combining the operatic elements of Italian baroque, the German contrapuntal style and the French school of dance-based suites. There are some quite wonderful works to delight the ears, but one has to pick and choose and listening to too much for too long jades the palate. One wants to move on to the broader canvases of Handel and Bach. Yet some of his music looks forward to Haydn and Mozart and there is, in Stephen Jackson's words, 'an earthy sharpness and pungent eclecticism to Telemann's finest music that eludes his famous contemporaries and which has led to his being called the Stravinsky of his day.'

Worth investigating

Concerto in G for viola and strings: the opening Largo is particularly poignant.
Suite in A minor for recorder and strings: this delightful seven-movement work encompasses French dances, an Italian air and a polonaise.
Concerto in G 'Polonois' for strings: Polish and Moravian influences in Telemann's work can be traced back to his time in Sorau, where the folk musicians inspired him greatly.

Concerto for trumpet and strings in D
Double Horn Concerto in E flat: from the third set of *Tafelmusik* (*Table Music*) of 1733. Each set contains a concerto, trio-sonata and one or two solo sonatas.
Overture in C ('Hamburger Ebb and Flow'): also known as *Wassermusik* and composed for a Hamburg celebration.
Magnificat in C

Michael TIPPETT

'A philosopher musician' (Percy M. Young)

Born: 2 January 1905, London
Full name: Sir Michael Kemp Tippett
Type of music: symphony, concerto, opera, choral, chamber, piano, vocal
Influences: Early English, Beethoven, Sibelius, English folk song, jazz
Contemporaries: Marc Blitzstein, Alan Rawsthorne, Dag Wirén, **TIPPETT**, SHOSTAKOVICH, Elisabeth Lutyens, Paul Creston, MESSIAEN, Elliott Carter

HIS LIFE AND MUSIC

Tippett was a comparatively slow starter. After a period at the Royal College of Music, he left to teach and compose, then returned to the college for further study, frustrated with what he was writing. It wasn't until 1934 that he allowed his first pieces to be performed publicly. His First String Quartet and the (now well-known) Concerto for Double String Orchestra attracted little attention.

His oratorio *A Child of Our Time* finally made his name, inspired by the case of a Jewish boy who assassinated a member of the German embassy in Paris in 1938. During the Second World War, he spent two months in Wormwood Scrubs for his pacifist beliefs. But it wasn't until the end of the war, when he was forty, that his music became readily available. As director of music at Morley College, London (1940–51) and director of the Bath Festival (1969–74), together with other appointments, he established himself at the centre of British musical life. He was awarded a CBE in 1959 and a knighthood in 1966.

Tippett's music is hard to categorize, unmistakably English but dissimilar in aim and content to that of his contemporaries Walton and Britten. He does not espouse atonalism or minimalism yet writes resolutely complex music that takes time to appreciate; his lyrical neo-Romantic impulses are obscured by his individual expression of harmony and rhythm. For all that and the critical acclaim and controversy his work has attracted, few of his works are known to the general public. Tippett admirers (and there are many) will demur, but the libretti of his operas (provided by himself) are pretentious and weak and it is unlikely that many of his stage works will stay the course. History has yet to decide.

Essential works

Fantasia concertante on a theme of Corelli (1953): commissioned by the Edinburgh Festival to celebrate the tercentenary of Corelli's birth, the Fantasia is scored for string orchestra and uses a theme from Corelli's Concerto grosso Op.6 No.2 in F. Its gracious lyricism and pastoral, sometimes impassioned, style have made the work deservedly popular.

Concerto for Double String Orchestra (1939): one of Tippett's most widely performed pieces, incorporating a divergence of musical styles from Beethoven, Orlando Gibbons and jazz to direct quotations of Scottish folk song (second movement) and Northumbrian bagpipe music (final movement). A rhythmically complex, rich and lucidly-scored work.

Piano Concerto (1956): 'It is easy to see now that it is the sound of [my opera] *The Midsummer Marriage* which is the true originator [of this work],' wrote Tippett, 'but it had its precise moment of conception years before when I was listening to a rehearsal of Beethoven's Fourth Piano Concerto with Giese-

king who had just returned to England after the war. I felt moved to create a concerto in which once again the piano might sing.'

The Midsummer Marriage (1955): Tippett was convinced that he had become 'the instrument of some collective imagination experience'. Inspired by this notion he set about writing this, his finest operatic work; it took him seven years to complete. Although the main theme is a mundane one (two people who believe they cannot marry until they have found themselves), the main characters are set against a series of magical, mystical events. Far more accessible than *King Priam* (1961), *The Knot Garden* (1969) and *The Ice Break* (1976).

A Child of Our Time (1939–41): despite its complex style, this powerful oratorio became a popular success after its first performance in 1944, the inclusion of negro spirituals heightening its emotional impact.

Also worth investigating are the **String Quartet No.1 in A** (1935) and the **Piano Sonata No.1** (1938).

Ralph VAUGHAN WILLIAMS

'What we want in England is real music [that] possesses real feeling and real life' (Vaughan Williams)

Born: 12 October 1872, Down Ampney, Gloucestershire
Died: 26 August 1958, London
Type of music: symphony, orchestral, opera, ballet, incidental and stage music, film, chamber, choral, song
Influences: Early English music, Purcell, English folk song, Bruch, Ravel, Sibelius
Contemporaries: Leopold Godowsky, LEHÁR, SCRIABIN, **VAUGHAN WILLIAMS**, Hugo Alfvén, Max Reger, RACHMANINOV, Joseph Jongen, HOLST, Reynaldo Hahn

HIS LIFE AND MUSIC

Down Ampney, the picturesque Cotswold village of Vaughan Williams' birth, is also the name of the hymn tune to which we sing 'Come down, O Love Divine'. With or without the words, it provides a perfect evocation of a village church in the tranquil English countryside. That, and *Sine nomine* (the tune of 'For all the saints'), *Monks Gate*, the folk tune he named after the place near Horsham, Sussex, where he first heard it, to which he set the words 'Who would true valour see' and his arrangement of the *Old 100th Psalm Tune* ('All people that on earth do dwell') may be his most performed music. They define the Englishness of the Church of England.

The family's original surname was Williams. Ralph (pronounced *Rayf*) Vaughan Williams was related to a distinguished family of lawyers on his father's side and to both Charles Darwin and Josiah Wedgwood on his mother's. He was brought up in the home of his maternal grandfather in Surrey, after his clergyman father died young. Music studies began at an early age with piano and violin and continued through his schooling at Charterhouse. Indeed, his studies were nothing if not protracted – he was fortunate in having a private income – and after the Royal College of Music, he took a Music degree at Trinity College, Cambridge, returned to the Royal College for lessons with Stanford, took off for Berlin for further study with Max Bruch and in 1908 at the age of thirty-six, still dissatisfied with what he was doing, went to Ravel in Paris for (as he put it) 'a little French polish'.

Despite this conservative English and German instruction, and modern French orchestral technique, Vaughan Williams emerged as an adventurous, unmistakably English composer with a distinct voice of his own. His discovery in the early 1900s of English folk song, through the recently formed English Folk Music Society, focused his style. 'VW' and Gustav Holst, lifelong friends who had met at the Royal College, went out seeking the source of their country's indigenous music (it was said that Vaughan Williams was dressed 'as though stalking the folk song to its lair'). Much of this material had never been written down before and the cataloguing and research that 'VW' and Holst undertook in this area was of considerable cultural significance. Before this, his early works sound like any one of a dozen accomplished composers writing at the turn of the century; afterwards, his music took on a different character. Apart from war service, for which he volunteered although he was over forty, Vaughan Williams devoted the rest of his long life to composition, teaching and conducting.

'The art of music above all other arts,' he wrote, 'is the expression of the soul of the nation.' It wasn't just the rhythm or melodies of English folk music that affected him, it was also their atmosphere. In this, he can be compared to nationalist composers like Mussorgsky and Bartók who wished to enshrine in their scores the essence of their countries and people. Musicologists analyze how Vaughan Williams achieved this through his use of modern harmony, parallel triadic progressions, modal counterpoint polytonality. His music has its demands, but never strains beyond clarity of texture and expression. None but an Englishman could have written the *Fantasia on a theme of Thomas Tallis*, the *Fantasia on 'Greensleeves'*, *The Lark Ascending* or the *Serenade to Music*. Vaughan Williams' best work transcends the folk music idiom, as all great nationalist music does, and is infused with the mysticism and poetry that were so important to him.

Vaughan Williams worked on into old age with undiminished creative powers – his Eighth Symphony appeared in 1955 (the score includes parts for vibraphone and xylophone) while his Ninth, composed at the age of 85, uses a trio of saxophones. After his wife's death in 1951, he married the poet and librettist Ursula Wood and moved from his home of many years – The White Gates, near Dorking in Surrey – to a house in London's Regent's Park. He was a familiar sight at the capital's concert halls and opera houses, his bulky figure, snowy-white hair and old-fashioned hearing aid doing nothing to detract from his role as the Grand Old Man of English music, the link between Elgar and Benjamin Britten.

Essential works

Vaughan Williams' operas and concertos are generally not as rewarding as his orchestral and vocal music.

Fantasia on a theme of Thomas Tallis (1910, rev.1919): scored for string quartet and double string orchestra, the theme for this serene and well-loved masterpiece is the third of the eight tunes Tallis composed in 1567 for the Metrical Psalter of Mathew Parker, Archbishop of Canterbury.

Fantasia on 'Greensleeves' (1934): this quintessential piece of English music is compounded of two folk songs: 'Greensleeves', an Elizabethan melody of unknown authorship, and 'Lovely Joan', a tune Vaughan Williams found in Norfolk in 1908. Originally he incorporated 'Greensleeves' into his composition for a 1912 production of *The Merry Wives of Windsor* and later into his opera *Sir John in Love* (1929). Falstaff commands: 'Let the sky rain potatoes, let it thunder to the tune of "Greensleeves",' further evidence that it was originally a vigorous dance tune.

Symphony No.2, (A London Symphony) (1913, rev.1920 & 1933): 'a better title,' wrote 'VW', 'would perhaps be "Symphony by a Londoner"... London (including its various sights and sounds) has suggested to the composer an attempt at musical expression.'

Symphony No.4 in F minor (1931–34): the strident, dissonant opening has often been used as music for dramas or documentaries depicting the horrors of war. Vaughan Williams employs jarring melodies and harmonies and complicated rhythms, light years away from the pastoral idiom. A striking and powerful work, there is a masterly recording of 'VW' conducting it; he liked to begin rehearsals for a concert by quipping, 'You start – I'll follow,' but he was far more than a mere time beater.

Symphony No.5 in D (1943, rev.1951): the four movements of this tranquil, introspective masterpiece have a unanimity of mood; 'it seems to fill the whole world with its song of goodwill,' wrote one reviewer after Vaughan Williams introduced it at a Promenade concert. The symphony is dedicated to Jean Sibelius.

Symphony No.6 in E minor (1944–47, rev.1950): one of the finest symphonies of the century; war and the post-war period reverberate throughout the work. The four movements, played without a break, contrast tragedy and turmoil with sober reflection – the last magical movement ebbing away into uncertain optimism, 'stillness made audible'.

The Lark Ascending (1914, rev.1920): an ethereal romance for violin and orchestra; it takes its title from a poem by George Meredith: 'He rises and begins to round / He drops the silver chain of sound ....'

Vocal

Serenade to Music (1938): composed for Sir Henry Wood's Golden Jubilee concert at the Royal Albert Hall on 5 October 1938 and dedicated to him 'in grateful memory of his services to music'. It contained parts for no less than sixteen famous singers who had been associated with him, and is a setting of the scene in the last act of *The Merchant of Venice*: 'How sweet the moonlight sleeps upon the bank! / Here will we sit, and let the sounds of music creep in our ears ....' There have been many fine recordings, but that made by Sir Henry soon after the premiere is a treasure.

'Silent Noon', song (1903): from *The House of Life* song cycle (words by Rossetti).

'Linden Lea', song (1903): 'Within the woodlands, flow'ry gladed, / By the oak trees' mossy moot ....'

'The Vagabond', song (1904): from the *Songs of Travel* song cycle (words by R.L. Stevenson) ...not forgetting many contributions to the English hymnal.

Worth investigating

The Wasps Overture (1909): written for a production of Aristophanes' play.

Symphony No.1, A Sea Symphony (1903–09, rev.1923): a choral symphony with text by Walt Whitman.

English Folk Song Suite (1923): originally for military band, but try the orchestral arrangement by Gordon Jacob.

On Wenlock Edge (1908): settings of A.E. Housman's poems, for tenor, string quartet and piano.

Job, masque for dancing (1931): a biblical ballet with parts for organ and saxophones.

Giuseppe VERDI

'He wept and loved for all of us' (d'Annunzio)

Born: 9 October 1813, Le Roncole, near Busseto, Duchy of Parma
Died: 27 January 1901, Milan
Full name: Giuseppe Fortunino Francesco Verdi
Type of music: opera, choral
Influences: Rossini, Donizetti, Bellini and Meyerbeer.
Contemporaries: Alexander Dargomizhsky, WAGNER, ALKAN, **VERDI**,
Stephen Heller, Adolf von Henselt, Sir William Sterndale Bennett, Niels Gade

---

HIS LIFE

The greatest of Italian opera composers was the son of a village innkeeper and began his long musical career as an organist, taking over the duties at the local church when still a small child. His father sent him to Busseto for formal music studies, thence, in 1821, to the home of Antonio Barezzi, a local merchant and patron of music. Barezzi supplied the funds for Verdi to progress to the Milan Conservatory but his protégé failed the entrance examination due to 'lack of piano technique and technical knowledge' according to some sources, 'over-age and insufficiently gifted' according to others.

1834 Verdi, a pale, short, pockmarked young man, taciturn, moody and intense, persevered in his ambitions by taking private lessons. After his studies with one Vincenzo Lavigna, from whom he acquired a thorough mastery of counterpoint, fugue and canon, Verdi applied for the post of *maestro di musica* in Busseto. He was turned down but instead was appointed Director of the Philharmonic Society.

1836 He married Margherita Barezzi the daughter of his patron, but tragedy intervened: their two infant children died and, in 1840, his beloved young wife died of encephalitis. During these four years he completed his first opera *Oberto, Conte di San Bonifacio* and moved to Milan; La Scala mounted the work with some success and he was given a contract to write more for the opera house. He was twenty-seven. His last opera, *Falstaff*, would be mounted at the same theatre in 1893 when he was eighty.

1840 *Un giorno di regno*, a comic opera, completed in the face of personal tragedy, was produced but was a fiasco. Its failure convinced Verdi he should abandon his operatic ambitions but the impresario Merelli persuaded him to undertake a third work, this time using the biblical subject of *Nabucodonosor*, or Nebuchadnezzar, later shortened to *Nabucco*. This was a turning point in Verdi's career and also for Italian opera. For the first time he found his own voice in a score that, although still much influenced by Rossini and Donizetti, confirmed his credentials as their successor. Verdi's fame spread rapidly throughout Italy.

1843 His next success, again a historical subject, came with *I lombardi alla prima crociata*, followed by another, based on Victor Hugo's drama, *Ernani*. This time the subject was more overtly political, the life of a revolutionary outlaw, and the work was acclaimed.

1851 For the following eight years, one opera followed another with varied success. During a stay in Paris where a French production of *I lombardi* (renamed *Jérusalem*) was being given, Verdi renewed his acquaintance with the soprano Giuseppina Strepponi who had created the role of Abigaille in the original production of *Nabucco*. After living together for several years, the couple were married in Savoy in 1859. By then, Verdi had written the three masterpieces that were to make him internationally famous. None of the operas written in the intervening years had come close to the successes of *Nabucco* and *Ernani*. Then, using another drama by Victor Hugo, *Le roi s'amuse*, he composed *Rigoletto* (1851). Soon every barrel organ in Europe was playing 'La donna è mobile', the teasing aria of the lecherous duke. Neither this number (which Verdi kept under wraps until the dress rehearsal for fear that someone would steal what he knew to be a hit tune) nor the opera show any sign of diminishing in popularity over 140 years later.

1853 *Rigoletto* alone would have been enough to establish his name as a fine composer of operas and Verdi would be remembered as another Mascagni or Leoncavallo. But to follow that with two more masterpieces within the space of a couple of years, and still have some of his greatest works ahead guaranteed him a place among the immortals of music. *Il trovatore* received its first performance in Rome in January 1853; *La traviata* followed less than two months later in Venice. By the age of forty he had eclipsed Meyerbeer as the most acclaimed living composer of opera.

1855 Two years elapsed before he completed his next work, his first in French, *Les vèpres Siciliennes*. It was given a rousing reception at its premiere in Paris, despite the fact that it dealt with the slaughter in medieval times of the French army of occupation in Sicily.

1857 Another two years brought another triumph: *Simon Boccanegra*. The winning pattern was repeated by the first performance in 1859 of *Un ballo in maschera*. Verdi was a fervent supporter of the Risorgimento, the reorganization of the numerous small Italian states into one country. The theme of resurgent nationalism in his early operas, the frequent clashes with the censor who suspected him of revolutionary tendencies, his political career in the 1860s when he sat reluctantly for five years as a deputy in that part of Italy already unified – all these things endeared him to the general public. The symbol of the nationalist movement was Vittorio Emmanuel, the future King of Italy. By coincidence, the initials V.E.R.D.I. stood for 'Vittorio Emmanuel, Re D'Italia' and all over Italy, the composer's name / political slogan was to be seen. Cries of 'Viva Verdi' could be heard as vociferously in the opera house as on the street. Verdi, however, disliked direct involvement with politics and withdrew from the first Italian parliament. He was made a senator in 1874, an honorary office which made no demands on him.

1862 During the summers, he and Giuseppina lived on a huge farm in Sant' Agata, enjoying a simple peasant existence. The winters were spent in their palatial home in Genoa. His frequent foreign travels included a special trip to St Petersburg to see the first performance of his latest creation, *La forza del destino* which the Imperial Opera had commissioned.

1867 The next milestone was his flawed masterpiece *Don Carlos*, a huge, sprawling affair subject to revisions and cuts – it was not given in its original version until a century after the premiere – which many opera lovers cite as the zenith of grand opera. In most people's minds, however, his next creation embodies all that grand opera should be.

1870 Verdi was commissioned by the Khedive (Viceroy) of Egypt to write a piece for the new opera house in Cairo. He requested a fee of $20,000, an enormous amount in those days, and received it without a murmur. Although the score of *Aida* was completed by 1870, the premiere was postponed until Christmas Eve 1871: Paris, from where all the scenery and costumes came, was besieged by the Prussian army in the Franco-Prussian war. The first performance was an international event but Verdi, who hated such glitzy occasions and loathed travelling by sea, refused to attend. Instead, he stayed in Milan to rehearse the singers for the forthcoming Italian premiere of *Aida*. The Khedive's assistant wired him from Cairo that the reaction had been one of 'total fanaticism … we have had success beyond belief.'

1873 The death of the Italian poet and patriot Manzoni prompted Verdi to write his great Requiem. Then, for thirteen years, he retired to the country and wrote nothing.

1887 It would have been reasonable to expect no more but, using a fine adaptation by Arrigo Boito of Shakespeare's *Othello* to compose an opera on the subject, he enjoyed a notable Indian summer.

1893 Verdi was seventy-nine when he completed his final opera, *Falstaff*, using material from *The Merry Wives of Windsor* and *Henry IV*, another collaboration with Boito. These two works – *Otello* and *Falstaff* – constituted new high points in Italian opera, showing that Verdi's creative powers, far from waning, had increased. After the premiere of *Falstaff*, the King of Italy offered to ennoble him and make him Marchese di Busseto but Verdi declined. 'Io son un paesano,' he told Victor Emmanuel, 'I am a peasant.'

1897 Giuseppina died from pneumonia in November. Verdi was desolate and he gradually lost the will to live. His sight and hearing deteriorated and he suffered paralysis but, setting aside 2,500,000 lire, he founded the Casa di Riposo per Musicisti in Milan, a home for aged musicians. The home is still in operation, supported by his royalties. In 1898 he composed his last work, *Quatro pezzi sacri* (*Four Sacred Pieces*). Verdi spent the Christmas of 1900 visiting his adopted daughter in Milan. It was here, at the

Grand Hotel, that he died from a sudden stroke. He was eighty-seven. A quarter of a million people followed his funeral cortège on the way to his final resting place in the grounds of the Casa di Riposa.

HIS MUSIC

What makes Verdi, with Puccini, the most popular of all opera composers? The ability to write glorious melodies with an innate understanding of the stage and how to write for the human voice, to express himself directly, unhampered by academicism and to score with technical brilliance, colour and originality. 'The theatre yesterday evening was filled to bursting; that's the only gauge to success,' wrote Verdi. He was as unlike Wagner, the other great figure of nineteenth-century opera born just five months earlier, as it was possible to be, although both were motivated by the same desire to create a musical art form that had dramatic truth and artistic validity. Harold Schonberg explained, 'The essential difference between Wagner and Verdi is the difference between German and Italian temperament, language and expression. Verdi invariably makes the vocal part the essence of his music…. On the whole the orchestral basis in Wagner and the vocal preponderance in Verdi remain the true sources of invention and style.'

Verdi was never a theoretician or academic, although he was quite able to write a perfectly poised fugue if he felt inclined, such as appears at the end of *Falstaff*. 'There is hardly any music in my house,' he wrote in a letter of 1869. 'I have never gone to a music library, never to a publisher to examine a piece. I keep abreast of some of the better contemporary work not by studying them but by hearing them occasionally at the theatre … I repeat, I am the least erudite among past and present composers.'

In his early work, the influence of Rossini and Bellini is clear in the emphasis on *bel canto* and stage effects but already by the time of *Nabucco* the dramatist in Verdi is struggling for an equal place with the musician. In his middle period – the operas from *Rigoletto* to *Aida* – he composed some of the most beautiful and memorable arias in all opera as well as achieving more penetrating characterization, highly developed dramatic conflict and keenly projected atmosphere and mood than Italian opera had ever produced before. For his last two masterpieces, one a comedy, one a tragedy, Verdi had clearly assimilated some aspects of Wagnerian music-drama but they are nothing but pure Italian, pure Verdi, a testament to a great man's ability to develop and learn. Here, more than in his previous work, words and music become one.

Essential works

Nabucco (1842): set in Jerusalem and Babylon in the sixth century BC. No one is certain whether Verdi was conscious of the parallels between the enslaved Hebrews of his opera and the plight of his fellow countrymen under Austrian oppression, but 'Va pensiero', the *Chorus of the Hebrew Slaves*, was taken up as the Italian anthem for independence and Verdi himself became a symbol of the resistance.

Rigoletto (1851): the story of the hunchback jester Rigoletto whose daughter Gilda is seduced by the libidinous Duke of Mantua, has been praised as 'even today among the finest manifestations of Verdi's genius. In unity of dramatic conception, in delineation of character, this music excels not only all the operas that preceded it, but most of the operas that succeeded it. If ever there was a case of sheer inspiration, *Rigoletto* constitutes such a one.' Its five best known numbers are often performed separately, enforcing the mistaken view that they are 'set pieces' and not integrated into the drama, but 'La donna è mobile', 'Quest' o quella', 'Caro nome', 'Pari siamo' and the great Quartet, the finest in all opera, are all germane to the action and characterization, and they are incomparable examples of musical and dramatic veracity.

Il trovatore (1853): *The Troubadours* was the most popular opera of the nineteenth century and has, ironically, one of the most implausible and imponderable plots of any work in this genre. Still, a ludicrous storyline never prevented an opera from being a success. It says something for Verdi's skill that its narrative has never affected its enduring hold on audiences for he provides a wonderfully varied musical feast and the roles of the four principal characters are a veritable encyclopaedia of the vocal arts. Verdi completed the score in the amazingly short time of thirty days, between 1 and 29 November 1852. Amongst its many highlights are the 'Anvil Chorus' (Act 2), the thrilling tenor aria 'Di quella pira' ('From that dread pyre') ending with a long top C (Act 3) and, from Act 4, Leonara's aria 'D'amor sull' ali rosee' ('On the rosy wings of love'), *Miserere* (at one time the most popular number from any opera) and the final duet 'Ai nostri monti' ('Home to our mountains').

La traviata (1853): the literal translation of the title, 'The Fallen Woman' or 'The Wayward Woman', is never used. The opera is based on the play (derived from the novel) *La dame aux camélias* by Alexandre Dumas *fils* about the legendary Parisian courtesan Marie Duplessis who died from tuberculosis in 1847 aged twenty-three. In the novel she becomes Marguerite Gautier; in the play – and film starring Greta Garbo – she is called Camille; in the opera she is Violetta Valéry, the fallen woman who sacrifices everything for love and is thereby redeemed. Today, the opera is so much a part of the international repertoire that it is easy to forget what a revolutionary piece it was when it first appeared: the realism of the text and music anticipates the later *verismo* movement; the sympathetic treatment of a courtesan was unique; the intimacy of the scenes with the principals approaches that of chamber music; indeed, the emphasis as a whole is not on the big scenes and choruses, although perhaps its best known passage is the *Brindisi chorus* (Drinking Song) from Act 1. Other highlights include Violetta's dazzling coloratura aria 'Sempre libera' ('Ever free') from Act 1 and the orchestral Prelude to Act 3.

Un ballo in maschera (1859): the attempted assassination of Napoleon III in Paris made the Naples authorities nervous of an opera which depicted regicide, for the original title of this work was *Gustavus III*, based on the real murder of the Swedish monarch at a masked ball in Stockholm in 1792. Verdi eventually agreed to change the location to Boston, Massachusetts, altered the title to *A Masked Ball* and made the central character Riccardo, Count of Warwick. Despite these somewhat bizarre anomalies, the opera was, and has remained, an enormous success. Look out particularly for the Act 1 Scene 2 ensemble 'È scherzo' ('It's a joke') and the baritone solo 'Eri tu che macchiavi quell'anima' ('It was you who stained my soul') in Act 3.

La forza del destino (1862): like *Il trovatore* and *La traviata*, *The Force of Destiny* is a tragic love story. Here the music and libretto are more uneven though critics acknowledge that the harmonies, orchestration and richer, more expansive melodies are an advance on Verdi's previous work, while it also contains throwbacks to his earlier style. The Overture is a particular favourite and its most famous aria is 'La vergine degli angeli' ('May angels guard thee') from Act 2. To those working in theatre, the mention of or quotation from *Macbeth* traditionally brings bad luck; *La forza del destino* is opera's equivalent for some reason.

Don Carlos (1867): despite its fanatical devotees, this is a flawed masterpiece; Verdi himself was dissatisfied with the original work and made two further versions. It is a long, sprawling five- or four-act work (depending on the version) written for the Paris Opéra and reflecting the Parisian love of spectacle and melodrama in the Meyerbeer manner. It has a fairly impenetrable plot exploring political, moral and personal themes and the conflict between Church and State. The astute characterization and lyrical beauty are there, however, and many see this as Verdi limbering up for *Aida*.

Aida (1871): the final magnificent work of Verdi's second period, using every element of his art: sublime large-scale choruses and poignant arias, pageantry, dance, spectacle and exoticism are all here, confirming his status as one of the greatest musical dramatists. The theme is doomed love – Radames, a Captain of the Egyptian guard, falls for Aida, an Ethiopian slave; he sings her one of the great tenor arias 'Celeste Aida' ('Heavenly Aida'); other memorable moments are Aida's 'Ritorna vincitor' ('Return victorious') and 'O patria mia' ('O my native land') and their duet before being entombed alive 'O terra, addio' ('O Earth, farewell'). And who can resist the *Grand March* (Act 2), with or without elephants?

Otello (1887): arguably Verdi's finest opera and his outstanding achievement. Nearly fifteen years separate *Aida* from *Otello* and Verdi felt increasingly as he grew older that he could not surpass the accomplishment of *Aida*. Wagner's operas were dominating the musical world and, though he admired Wagner, Verdi knew such methods were not for him. Having been presented with Boito's treatment of Shakespeare's *Othello*, however, the old man set to work. Even more than *Aida*, the musical and dramatic elements were welded indivisibly together, marking this out from the Verdi of *La traviata* or *Rigoletto*: there are few set arias or ensembles, for example, and the action fuses scene to scene without a pause. Those to look out for, however, are 'Credo in un Dio crudel' ('I believe in a cruel God') known as Iago's Creed (Act 2), Desdemona's moving 'Salce, salce, salce' ('Oh Willow, willow, willow') and 'Ave Maria' (Act 4). The opening of the opera, 'Esultate!' ('Rejoice!') was thrilling recorded by Francesco Tamagno, Verdi's original Otello, a remarkable document.

Falstaff (1893): Verdi had yearned to write a successful comic opera ever since the failure of *Un giorno di regni* half a century earlier. Egged on by Boito, he reluctantly set about working on this musical counterpart to *Otello*, 'just to pass the time' as he explained to his publisher. He spent two hours a day, every day for two years working on it. It is an astonishing creation for a man of nearly eighty; it brims over with youthful zest, freshness and high spirits. 'He has combined a schoolboy's sense of fun with the grace and science of Mozart,' wrote R.A. Streatfeild.

Requiem (1874): Verdi's only masterpiece not intended for the stage was aptly described by Hans von Bülow as 'Verdi's latest opera, in church vestments'. Its elegiac, spiritual moments (the tenor's 'Ingemisco', for instance, sometimes sung as a concert item) are combined with a heartfelt intensity and stirring theatricality setting it a long way from the masses of Bach or Mozart – try the awesome *Dies irae* and *Tuba mirum* sections!

Also worth investigating
I Lombardi (1843); **Ernani** (1844); **Macbeth** (1847); **Luisa Miller** (1849); and **Four Sacred Pieces** (1898).

Heitor VILLA-LOBOS
(1887–1959)

Aria (Cantilena) from *Bachianas Brasileiras No.5,* 1938

A serene, wordless melody sung by a soprano, which floats over the accompaniment of eight plucked cellos, this is one of those pieces that everyone knows but can't name. Villa-Lobos, by far the most significant Brazilian composer to date, composed nine suites with the same apt title, for the music's distinctive Brazilian rhythmic and melodic characteristics are fused with the style of J.S. Bach – an original and entirely successful conception. The Aria is the first part of the fifth suite and was composed in 1938; the lesser known second part (Danza) followed seven years later.

From the second suite comes 'The Little Train of the Caipeira', a clever and colourful sound picture of a busy little train chugging through the Brazilian countryside; the Prelude from *Bachianas Brasileiras No.4* is also lovely. There are some highly attractive Villa-Lobos works for guitar including twelve études (1929), five preludes (1940) and, in particular, Chôros No.1; and *Polichinelle (Punch)* from Book 1 of *Prole do bebe* is a hair-raising piano encore. These are mere glimpses of the profuse and bewilderingly diverse music of Villa-Lobos.

Antonio VIVALDI

'The Red Priest'

Born: 4 March 1678, Venice
Buried: 28 July 1741, Vienna
Full name: Antonio Lucio Vivaldi
Type of music: concerto, chamber, opera, liturgical settings
Influences: Corelli, Torelli and the Italian violin school
Contemporaries: ALBINONI, Jeremiah Clarke, William Croft, **VIVALDI**,
TELEMANN, Jean-François Dandrieu, RAMEAU, J.S. BACH, DOMENICO SCARLATTI

HIS LIFE

Fifty years ago, Vivaldi's reputation as a composer was so small that not even the exact date of his birth or the place and date of his death had been established; his music was very rarely played in the nineteenth century. Now he is considered to be one of the most important figures of the Baroque era. He's certainly the most popular.

He was born in Venice when the city, though long past the height of its mercantile power, was the musical capital of Europe. His father was a violinist at St Mark's and his son inherited his gift for the instrument, as well as his red hair, hence his nickname 'il preto rosso'. When he was fifteen he began training for the priesthood but, no sooner had he been ordained in 1703, than he was given a dispensation from saying Mass –

Vivaldi was a lifelong asthmatic and complained of chest pains during services. Strangely, these chest pains never seemed to occur while he was conducting or during his many foreign trips. The Church remained a useful backcloth for the rest of his life but it seems that his priestly duties were never taken very seriously.

What he took slightly more seriously was his position as *maestro di violino* (and later superintendent) of the Conservatorio dell'Ospedale della Pietà, one of Venice's most famous musical centres. Founded for the care and education of orphan girls, the standard of music-making there was so high that many leading figures would perform in concert with the foundlings.

Vivaldi took up the post in 1704 and a year later saw the first publication of his music. In the following two decades of the century he was incredibly productive. He established himself as one of the foremost violinists and composers in Europe, producing operas (at least one a year from 1713 to 1738, sometimes three or four) and instrumental works, including his two most famous sets of concertos *L'estro armonico*, Op.3 and *Il cimento dell'armonia e dell'inventione*, Op.8 from which come *Le quattro stagioni* (*The Four Seasons*). In 1718 Vivaldi left Venice to work for three years in the service of Prince Philip of Hesse-Darmstadt, governor of Mantua, and here he met Anna Giraud, known as La Giró. She took the leading soprano role in many of Vivaldi's operas and, with her sister Paolina, became his travelling companion; both were said to be his mistresses, a rumour that Vivaldi strongly denied.

During 1728 he had several audiences with the music-loving Emperor Charles VI. It was said that Charles spoke more with Vivaldi during the two weeks of their meetings than he had with ministers during the previous two years. Vivaldi dedicated his twelve concertos *La cetra*, Op.9 to the emperor.

The 1730s saw his powers wane. Philip of Hesse-Darmstadt died, the Church authorities took action against Vivaldi because of his lapsed priesthood and his association with La Giró, and after that his contract with La Pietà was not renewed. His music began to fall out of favour and he left for Vienna in 1740, possibly with the intention of seeking a post with the Imperial Court there. It was not to be. Charles VI died in October 1740 and the once-wealthy Vivaldi, now ill and poverty-stricken, died some months later. He was buried in a pauper's grave near St Stephen's – like another great composer of half a century later, Mozart.

Twenty-five years after Vivaldi's death, Count Giacomo Durazzo acquired Vivaldi's scores from La Pietà. His heirs kept them secret, even stipulating that none of the works in their possession should be published or performed. It was not until the late 1920s, when the terms of the will were overthrown, that the treasures came to light.

HIS MUSIC

No one knows to this day exactly how much music Vivaldi composed. The present tally stands at about 770 works, made up of forty-six operas (only twenty-one of which are extant), 344 solo concertos, eighty-one concertos for two or more instruments, sixty-one sinfonias and numerous secular and liturgical works, both instrumental and vocal. Stravinsky said that Vivaldi did not write 400 concertos but only one and then copied it out 399 times! This is unfair, but it cannot be denied that, if one had to exist solely on a diet of Vivaldi, then everything would soon begin to taste the same.

Having said that, he was one of the most original and innovative composers at a time when concertos were being churned out left, right and centre by everybody, most of little individuality or quality. Vivaldi's writing for the violin, to take just one area of his output, expanded the possibilities of the instrument. He also developed orchestral writing, introduced the concept of programme music and laid the seeds of the eighteenth-century symphony. For the first time, a soloist is pitted against an orchestra, the conflict and drama between the two consciously highlighted; for the first time, too, slow movements, fashioned from the soulful arias of his operas, are given instrumental treatment: the concerto form is developing.

Vivaldi wrote music of immense charm and optimism without the intellectual rigour of the German school. Nevertheless, in much of his work Vivaldi's virtuosity strained the credibility of the time. Haydn was influenced by *The Four Seasons* and Bach based the construction of his own keyboard concertos on Vivaldi's compositions. The sunny, prosperous, cultivated world of contemporary Venice shines through all his works, composed with innate and intuitive craftsmanship, mirroring his own extrovert, roguish character. With Vivaldi, Italian Baroque music reaches its zenith.

Essential works

Vivaldi's works are usually identified by their RV numbers. They were catalogued by the Danish scholar Peter Ryom; RV stands for Ryom *Verzeichnis*, meaning 'Ryom's Catalogue'. Collections of concertos are assigned a chronological Opus number; each concerto within that set has its own RV number.

Twelve Concerti (L'estro armonico) (Harmonic Imagination) Op.3 (1711)

Twelve Concerti (Il cimento dell'armonia e dell'inventione) (The Contest between Harmony and Invention) Op.8) (1725): The

Four Seasons are the first four concertos of this set: No.1 *Spring*, in E (RV269); No.2 *Summer*, in G minor (RV315); No.3 *Autumn*, in F (RV293); and No.4 *Winter*, in F minor (RV297). No.5 is *La tempesta di mare*, in E flat (RV253).

Twelve Concerti for violin and strings (La cetra) , Op.9 (1727)

Twelve Concerti for violin and strings (La stravaganza), Op.4

Concerto for violin, strings and continuo in D, RV234 (L'inquietudine)

Concerto for violin, strings and continuo in E, RV271 (L'amoroso): the 'other' theme used in the film *Elvira Madigan*.
Concerto for strings and continuo in G, RV151 (Alla rustica)
Concerto for two violins, strings and continuo in A minor, RV523

Six Concerti for flute and strings, Op.10: includes another entitled *La tempesta di mare*, in F (RV433) and *La notte*, G minor (RV439)
Concerto for mandolin and strings in C, RV425
Concerto for two trumpets in C, RV537
Gloria in D, RV589

Richard WAGNER

'Had he been a little more human, he would have been great for all time' (Debussy)

Born: 22 May 1813, Leipzig
Died: 13 February 1883, Venice
Full name: Wilhelm Richard Wagner
Type of music: opera, orchestral, choral, piano, song
Influences: Palestrina, Mozart, Beethoven, Weber, Meyerbeer
Contemporaries: Friedrich von Flotow, Alexander Dargomizhsky, **WAGNER**, ALKAN, VERDI, Stephen Heller, Adolf von Henselt, Sir William Sterndale Bennett

HIS LIFE

'I am not like other people. I must have brilliance and beauty and light. The world owes me what I need. I can't live on a miserable organist's pittance like your master, Bach.' The words of Richard Wagner give some indication of the most massive ego in musical history. 'I am being used as the instrument for something higher than my own being warrants…I am in the hands of the immortal genius that I serve for the span of my life and that intends me to complete only what I can achieve.' It is not overstating the case to say that Wagner thought he was divine. More than one writer has observed the parallels of his life with that of a deity: the mystery of his birth, the gospel of Wagner in words and music, the fanatical disciples, the temple he built in Bayreuth in which his works could be celebrated and he himself worshipped, the rejection of all who did not believe in him.

No composer has had so much written about him; no one man has had so deep an influence on the course of his art, either before or since. That he was a genius, a philosopher, a man of letters and a first-rate conductor, apart from being one of the key composers in history and one of the most remarkable figures of the nineteenth century, begins to make one wonder whether he was not right in his self-assessment. But with genius at this level, there is always an underside and Wagner had a very unpleasant underside indeed. In getting what he wanted for himself and his art he would lie, deceive, cheat, borrow money without any intention of repaying it, use people unscrupulously, and regard with contempt anyone who did not adore him. He was as indifferent to the pain that he caused others as he was neurotically obsessed with the pain that anyone caused him.

His megalomania approached madness, his egocentricity was Napoleonic – like Napoleon he was a short man, about five feet five inches in height. He was also a racist, a virulent anti-Semite and a believer in the Nietzschean theories of superman and the German super-race. No wonder the Nazis loved him.

1813 At one time there was a suspicion that Wagner might be 'tainted' with Jewish blood, and the Nazi archivists were dispatched to ensure that their hero was ethnically sound. To their immense relief, the researchers found that his likely natural father, an actor named Ludwig Geyer, was pure Aryan. In fact, there is indirect evidence that Geyer was indeed a Jew, which, if ever confirmed, would make an amusing paradox. The controversy arose because of doubts as to Wagner's paternity. His mother, Johanna, was the daughter of a baker in Weissenfels, although some papers show that she may have been the illegitimate daughter of Prince Friedrich Ferdinand Constantin of Weimar. At the time of Wagner's birth, she was married to a police registrar, Karl Friedrich Wagner, who died when Richard was only six months old. Johanna had already been having an affair with Geyer and had a daughter Cäcilie six months after they were married in 1814. Ludwig Geyer proved to be a profound influence on the young Wagner, surrounding him with books and paintings and introducing him to the theatre and music.

1821 Geyer died when Wagner was eight, but the seeds had been sown. It was litera-ture that proved to be the initial attraction, though, not music. Wagner was only eleven when he wrote a drama, drawn from Shakespeare and the Greeks, in which forty-two characters died in the first four acts, some of which reappeared as ghosts in the fifth. His latent passion for music was aroused by a performance of Weber's *Der Freischütz*; when he heard Beethoven's *Fidelio* for the first time at the Gewandhaus, Leipzig, music became an obsession. He made arrangements of Beethoven's symphonies, began to absorb scores and produced his first compositions: two orchestral overtures.

1829 These overtures were premiered in Leipzig. All this before he had had any formal training! His future character traits were also beginning to emerge – a rebel, he was expelled from the Thomasschule in Leipzig, where Bach had reigned a century earlier, and was more concerned with duelling, drinking, gambling and women than his law studies at the University of Leipzig. During his brief sojourn there (he never took his degree) he became well known as a compulsive talker and for his dogmatic views.

1831 Wagner left to undertake six fruitful months of studying counterpoint with the cantor of the Thomaskirche. His teacher, Theodor Weinlig, admitted that after that period there was nothing more he could teach him. As far as we know, this was the only professional instruction he ever received. Then Wagner struck out on his own, writing a symphony and three operas – *Die Hochzeit* (1832) and *Die Feen* to his own bloodcurdling libretti and *Das Liebsverbot*, based on Shakespeare's *Measure for Measure*.

1835 At twenty-two, Wagner was the conductor of a small opera house in Magdeburg. One reason for taking the job – the theatre was on the verge of bankruptcy – was his pursuit of a pretty young actress named Minna Planer. He, in turn, was pursued by creditors claiming their gambling debts. In March 1836, the opera house produced *Das Liebesverbot*. It was such a fiasco that the theatre was empty at the second performance. It bankrupted the opera house. Wagner, overwhelmed with financial demands, left with Minna for a similar conducting post in Königsberg. They married in November 1836. The two of them then went on to Riga in Russian Poland (now Latvia) to another opera post where they stayed unhappily for two years. Eventually, Wagner was dismissed, hounded by creditors, his passport confiscated and forced to flee Russia via a smuggler's route. At length, the couple arrived in Paris.

1839–42 Wagner and Minna lived in poverty and on two occasions he was imprisoned for debt. But then came his first success. His opera *Rienzi*, which he had begun in 1837, was accepted for production at the Dresden Opera. Written in the approved Meyerbeer style, it was a resounding triumph and made his name known throughout Germany. Dresden next offered a production of *Der fliegende Holländer* (*The Flying Dutchman*), Wagner's first tentative steps towards a new style of opera. It was a complete failure.

1843 In February, Wagner was made director of the Dresden Opera. During the following six years he raised the standard of performance there to unprecedented heights with a series of painstakingly produced performances, including, in October 1845, the premiere of his own *Tannhäuser*. By 1848 he had almost completed a third operatic masterpiece, *Lohengrin*.

1848 This was the year of revolution in Europe and by 1849 its spirit had spread to Saxony. Wagner sided with the revolutionaries, producing radical pamphlets, making political speeches and sympathizing with the rioters. When the revolution came to nothing he was forced to flee Germany and for the following thirteen years lived in exile in Zurich. Here, he formulated his radical ideas about opera and the 'music of the future': the concept of 'music drama' involving a synthesis of all the arts. The plan that began to occupy his mind was a giant project of four dramas in which all his theories would be realized, an opera cycle called *Der Ring des Nibelungen* (*The Ring of the Nibelungs*). It took him a quarter of a century to complete it.

1850 Meanwhile, Franz Liszt had mounted the world premiere of *Lohengrin* at Weimar. Its astounding success made Wagner the most famous living composer of German opera, though he was unable to attend any performances of his work there. At one time he lamented that he was just about the only German who had never seen a performance of *Lohengrin*. While working on *The Ring*, Wagner interrupted his labours with two other music dramas, *Tristan und Isolde* (1859) and *Die Meistersinger von Nürnberg* (1867). The friendship and generosity of a wealthy silk merchant, Otto Wesendonck, allowed him to live in a luxurious villa in Zurich while he was working on *The Ring* and *Tristan*. These kindnesses were repaid by Wagner having a passionate affair with Otto's wife, Mathilde. As early as 1850, Wagner had had an extramarital affair but the lady in question, Jenny Laussot, the twenty-one-year-old English wife of a wine merchant, saw the light and returned to her husband. Mathilde Wesendonck was a different case. Much of *Tristan* was written under her influence; she may even have been the inspiration for the work, though it is just as likely that Wagner fell in love with her *because* he was working on the opera. Whatever, *Tristan und Isolde* is one of the most important works of the nineteenth century and its harmonic innovations exercised an enormous influence on the future of music, paving the way for Mahler and Schoenberg.

1859 At length, the domestic situation in Zurich became impossible. Otto Wesendonck was fully aware of the situation and, eventually, he provided funds for Wagner and Minna to travel to Paris. Wagner's marriage had broken down irretrievably, and soon, a third married woman had entered his life.

1862 Wagner fell in love with Cosima, the daughter of Franz Liszt and the wife of his friend and champion, the pianist and conductor Hans von Bülow. The mesmeric power Wagner exercised over his admirers is no better illustrated than by Bülow. Wagner and Cosima had an illegitimate daughter named Isolde; Cosima then became pregnant with a second illegitimate daughter, Eva. Only at this point, and after Minna had conveniently died in 1866, did Cosima desert her husband and set up house with Wagner. Throughout, Bülow remained devoted to Wagner and wrote to Cosima, 'You have preferred to devote your life and the treasures of your mind to one who is my superior. Far from blaming you I approve your action from every point of view and admit you are perfectly right.' Cosima was the woman for whom Wagner had been searching all his life, someone of great intelligence and independence of mind who would provide stability, adulation and understanding whenever it was needed. He remained with her for the rest of his life – well, nearly. After Wagner's death, the imperious Cosima, born in 1837, became the guardian of the Wagner shrine and survived until 1930.

1860–70 In the meantime, a political amnesty allowed Wagner to return to Germany. Four years later, his fortunes changed dramatically when the young, homosexual Ludwig II ascended the throne of Bavaria. He invited Wagner to Munich and promised unlimited support for all his projects. It is very likely he was in love with Wagner but, at any rate, a mutual admiration flourished on a grand scale and, between 1865 and 1870, Munich was host to the world premieres of *Tristan und Isolde*, *Die Meistersinger*, *Das Rheingold* and *Die Walküre*, the latter two forming the first completed sections of *The Ring*. Ludwig's lavish support of Wagner soon brought him into conflict with the Bavarian Cabinet, who advised that the whole economy would collapse if the king continued his patronage on such a reckless scale. They were also disturbed by Wagner's political dabbling and his hold over the king, and they were scandalized by his morals (everyone knew of his relationship with Cosima). They observed this arrogant musician with more than a little concern. Wagner retreated to a palatial estate on Lake Lucerne, paid for by Ludwig, where he was joined by Cosima. Here, Eva was born (1867) and their first son Siegfried (1869). Cosima and von Bülow were divorced in July 1870; Wagner and Cosima married the following month.

1871 Wagner announced plans for another gargantuan scheme. Not a music-drama but a building, a special festival theatre where his works could be mounted under ideal conditions, produced to Wagner's own specifications. The council of the little Bavarian town of Bayreuth offered him a site, and in May 1872 the cornerstone was laid. It was a huge undertaking, and Wagner, characteristically, took to realizing his dream with extraordinary vigour and determination. No setback troubled him – he persuaded wealthy patrons to provide part of the subsidy, he conducted concerts to help raise money, King Ludwig coughed up 100,000 talers – and the Bayreuth Festival Theatre was unveiled on 13 August 1876.

1876–78 The opening performance was the first complete presentation of *The Ring* cycle, *Siegfried* and *Götterdämmerung* (*The Twilight of the Gods*) receiving their premieres. The event attracted world attention. Four thousand visitors were crammed into Bayreuth including the Emperor and Empress of Germany, the Emperor and Empress of Brazil and Grand Duke Vladimir of Russia, along with other crowned heads and many of the greatest living composers, including Tchaikowsky, Gounod, Saint-Saëns, Grieg and Liszt. Such novelties as gas-lighting linked to electric projectors and a magic lantern illuminating the 'Ride of the Valkyries' matched those of the operas themselves. The festival made a huge deficit but at the closing party Wagner had the good grace to pay tribute to Liszt. He owed him, he said, everything. Today, the Bayreuth theatre remains a living shrine to Wagner's music and vision.

Everyone was talking and writing about Wagner, and composers worked overtime to emulate him, the way he composed, the subjects he chose, the way he dressed – everything. He was the most famous composer in the world, like his music or not. He had achieved his dream – and that is not given to every man.

Basking in his fame, relative wealth and security (although money worries continued to nag), living in the comfort of the Villa Wahnfried (meaning 'Free from Delusion') a few miles from the festival theatre in Bayreuth, Wagner settled down to other things. He had a final fling with a married woman. This time it was the beautiful daughter of the poet Théophile Gautier, and wife of the poet Catulle Mendès. Judith Mendès, who was forty years younger than Wagner, actually moved into the Villa Wahnfried – Cosima turned a blind eye – before returning to her husband in 1878. Wagner finished his last opera or 'consecrational play', *Parsifal*, while producing a series of pamphlets and publications. In his all-embracing wisdom, he promulgated his lofty views on any number of topics. He believed the world could be saved if everyone ate vegetables instead of meat; he ranted on about racial purity – the Jews were former cannibals, Christ was not a Jew but an Aryan, the Aryans had sprung from the gods, and so forth – all the things that led Hitler to say 'Whoever wants to understand National Socialist Germany must know Wagner.'

1882 In August, Wagner conducted a performance of *Parsifal*. It was his last public appearance as a conductor. He was exhausted and began to have premonitions of death. Later that year he travelled with Cosima and their children to Venice for a lengthy holiday. As a birthday gift to his wife, he conducted a private performance of his youthful symphony on 24 December 1882. Six weeks later, he died of a massive heart attack. His body was brought back to Bayreuth, where it was buried in a vault in the garden of his villa to the accompanying strains of the Funeral March from *Götterdämmerung*.

King Ludwig was faithful to the end to his 'divine friend', the man to whom he wrote, 'I can only adore you…an earthly being cannot requite a divine spirit.' His 'mental state deteriorated' (i.e. the authorities wanted to conceal their monarch's sexual preferences) and he was committed to an asylum. On 13 June 1883, three months to the day after Wagner's death, Ludwig overpowered a psychiatrist who was escorting him on a walk and dragged him to the bottom of the Starnberg Lake, drowning himself in the process.

HIS MUSIC

Wagner not only changed opera single-handedly, he also altered the course of music. Throughout this book you will come across references to 'Wagnerism', 'the influence of Wagner on so-and-so', 'the rejection of Wagner's theories by another', and so on. In almost every work of musical reference, the entries devoted to Wagner will be longer than those devoted to anyone else.

From the 1870s onwards, his music had a profound effect on each new generation of composers. Richard Strauss, Bruckner and Mahler all extended his grandiose vision to symphonic works; Dvořák and even Debussy were affected by him; Rimsky-Korsakov followed the spirit of *Parsifal* in his opera *The Legend of the City of Kitezh*; the harmonies of *Tristan* led directly to Schoenberg's first major composition *Verklärte Nacht*; the works of poets and painters reflected the themes and characters in the operas; French literature of the late-nineteenth century is full of allusions to Wagner. No single figure in music has ever achieved such a pervasive global influence and no succeeding composer could ignore his innovations.

These innovations are on two levels, the purely musical and the aesthetic. German opera since Gluck had been heading towards Wagner's ideal, the synthesis of all the arts into one new, grandiose form. Thus, Wagner's operas combine poetry, music, drama, lighting, design and acting into an indivisible entity. Gluck had dreamed about it, Weber had approached it, but Wagner achieved it – and in spectacular style. The concept of music-drama, which he had formulated in the 1840s and 1850s, used myths, gods and goddesses and ancient legends. These, he felt, should be the proper concerns of the human spirit and, dressed in poetic garb, they became expressions of eternal verities, symbols of our souls, our innermost thoughts and feelings. To express this, Wagner became his own librettist, adapting the epic poems on which the operas are based into monumental poetic utterances.

The music, Wagner believed, must grow from the libretto, there must be no showpiece arias just to please the public and gratify the soloists, everything must evolve organically; the music, like the narrative must never cease, for the music *is* the story and the story *is* the music – it comments on the characters and action just as much as the words of the libretto. As a device to underpin the whole score, Wagner introduced short, descriptive tunes associated with different characters and different moods. This is the famous technique of *Leitmotiv*, another component in Wagner's total concept. In *Das Rheingold*, for instance, familiar material is echoed in *Götterdämmerung* to stunning effect. (When Sir Thomas Beecham was rehearsing the opera, he was quoted as saying: 'We've been rehearsing for two hours and we're still playing the same bloody tune!').

All previous music in the Austro-German tradition had relied on tonality; the ear knew in which key the music was and thus could follow it to its conclusion. It gave music a satisfying logic and inevitability. Wagner wanted to experiment with this concept. His need for endlessly flowing melody to express his ideals helped in achieving this goal. The perceived tonality of the piece became more uncertain, more fluid; the listener becomes increasingly unsure of where the music is going or in which key it will be resolved. The Prelude to *Tristan und Isolde* is the most celebrated example of this technique. Such developments formed the basis of the new methods of composition, adopting a free flow of modulating progression. From there we arrive at Mahler and, shortly afterwards, Schoenberg. It remains, almost a century and a half later, a brick wall to some people, for whom music without a clear tonality is unattractive to listen to.

Wagner made the orchestra an equal partner in the drama. No longer did it merely accompany the story; now it actually characterized the action of the story. Singers underwent special training in the new style of interpretation in order to perform the works – and to make themselves heard over the loudest sounds yet summoned from an orchestra. Hence the advent of the 'Wagnerian soprano' and the *Heldentenor* – the heroic or 'Wagnerian tenor'. Wagner even devised a new form of tuba to achieve exactly the right sound in the brass section. The musical army at his disposal produced an enriched vocabulary and harmony far beyond what had been written previously. It might have been dreamt of, but not realized.

The flaw in Wagner's ideal is that if every part of the music-drama is to have equal importance, then the various ingredients must be of equal quality. Yet music dominates, simply because he was a far better musician than anything else, no matter what Wagner himself might have thought. It is always dangerous to write your own script and then star in it – you need an objective eye to make objective judgments. Wagner, of course, would not have countenanced such a thought. His libretti, as a result, are astonishingly poor for the most part – repetitious, grandiloquent, verbose, barely adequate as far as poetry goes, notably lengthy and dramatically static and dull. A second flaw in Wagner's dream was to think that he was the ultimate, that there was nowhere to go after his truth. But every ideology becomes fashionable and then *un*fashionable; there was bound to be a reaction and, within two decades, Debussy had denounced, if not completely rid his work of Wagner, and Stravinsky was producing stridently anti-Wagnerian music, to be followed by the French School of Les Six. Composers found the orchestral textures of Wagner too stifling, over-written and stodgy. Audiences tired of complex analogies, and stage symbols to which they could not relate –they now longed for the lavish escapism of Verdi and a few simple tunes. Today, at least, in the words of Harold Schonberg, we can be sure that 'Verdi will never be underrated again and Wagner never overrated, never again to be taken as seriously as he was taken at the turn of the century, when he all but dominated the intellectual life of the Western world.'

Essential works

A good way of getting to know the composer and his idiom is to first sample some operatic highlights, the Overture to *Tannhäuser*, for example, or the Prelude to Act 3 of *Lohengrin*.
The Flying Dutchman (1843): the best complete opera with which to commence a Wagnerian odyssey may be this, *Der fliegende Holländer*. Musically, it falls between his earlier Meyerbeer-influenced operas and the later, more advanced style of *Tristan*, although, in fact, Wagner's 1860 revision incorporates some *Tristan*-style writing. During a particularly rough voyage in 1839, when his ship was nearly wrecked three times and forced into the safety of a Norwegian harbour, Wagner heard the story of the Wandering Jew of the ocean who was condemned to sail the seas for eternity after boasting that he could sail round the Cape of Good Hope in any conditions. The curse allowed him to put into port once every seven years, and would only be lifted if he could find a woman who would be faithful to him until death. Love through Redemption is one of Wagner's favourite themes, and the opera follows Senta's love for the ghostly Flying Dutchman. The Overture includes one of the mightiest musical storms but the most famous passage is the *Spinning Chorus* (Act 2).

Tannhäuser (1841–45): the opera's full title is *Tannhäuser and the Singing Contest on the Wartburg*. This is considered the most important, and popular, of Wagner's early operas. Its subject is taken from history; it is set in Thuringia in the thirteenth century and tells of the love of the knight Tannhäuser for Elisabeth. His passionate song in praise of Venus makes him an outcast and he has to seek atonement by travelling to Rome. The narrative is not exactly gripping stuff, but the score contains some of Wagner's most celebrated pages – the Overture is among the finest in all opera; Act 1 contains the *Venusberg Music* and *Bacchanale* as well as *The Pilgrims' Chorus*. 'Dich teure Halle' ('This blessed room') is Elisabeth's expressive aria when she sees her beloved Tannhäuser, followed by the *Procession of the Guests* and *Festal March*. 'O du mein holder Abendstern' ('O star of eve') is sung to the Evening Star by Wolfram, who also loves Elisabeth.

Lohengrin (1845–48): opera connoisseurs rate this as Wagner's first true masterpiece, based on several poems and legends and set in Antwerp in the first half of the tenth century. Here Wagner makes some bold developments, replacing the traditional overture with a Prelude that concentrates on the story's inner significance; it is a better dramatic prospect and it makes significant use of *leitmotivs*, associating different musical themes with certain characters; set-piece arias are less in evidence, with a seamless recitative expressing the emotional truth of the narrative. Liszt, who conducted the first performance, showed a good deal of courage in producing the opera while Wagner was in exile after his revolutionary activities.

The story revolves round Elsa of Brabant, accused of murdering her brother, who dreams of a knight defending her from the charge. A knight does appear and will stay as long as she never asks his name or from whence he came. It emerges that he is Lohengrin, son of Parsifal, keeper of the Holy Grail. The Prelude brilliantly suggests a vision of the Holy Grail 'shedding', in Wagner's words, 'glorious light on the beholder like a benediction' – this is perhaps the opera's crowning glory, music of the greatest genius. The Act 3 Prelude is a bustling impression of the wedding festivities of Elsa and Lohengrin, followed by the ubiquitous *Bridal Chorus* (…*Here comes the bride*).

Tristan und Isolde (1856–59): a psychological music-drama of great importance in the history and evolution of music, as revolutionary in its day as Gluck's *Orfeo* was in his. To musicologists, Wagner's use of chromaticism to express the themes of love and death heralded the break-up of tonality, and pointed the way forward to composers like Arnold Schoenberg. It is the starting point of modern music and its very opening, the famous Prelude, breaks with tradition and is not written in any definable key.

Tristan can be heavy going, and there is little in the way of dramatic action. But if it's not approached casually and you've had a chance to study some of the background, *Tristan* becomes a remarkable, even overwhelming experience. The opera is based on the Arthurian legend of Tristan and Isolde (another pair of Wagner's doomed lovers) and it provides an opportunity for sensual, passionate love music: the rapturous duet 'O sink' hernieder, Nacht der Liebe' (from Act 2) and, especially, 'Liebestod' ('Love-Death'), the name given to Isolde's final and ecstatic declaration of love.

Die Meistersinger von Nürnberg (1845 and 1861–67): *The Mastersingers of Nuremberg* is Wagner's only 'comedy' and it is frequently described as such – 'comic masterpiece', 'greatest comic opera ever written', and so on. Beware. Here, comedy does not mean Offenbach or Gilbert and Sullivan; it means the human comedy. For a man who took himself as seriously as Wagner did, there is no such thing as laughter or even gaiety – two of music's most precious rewards – in any of his music. Set in sixteenth-century Nuremberg, the allegorical story is based on fact. Having written in *Tannhäuser* of the aristocratic medieval *Minnesingers* (groups of noblemen who sang of love), Wagner took the subject of the later middle-class trade guilds who modelled themselves on the *Minnesingers* and were known as *Meistersingers*. The most famous of these was Hans Sachs, who lived in Nuremberg from 1494 to 1576. The winner of the next Mastersinger song contest is promised the hand of Sach's daughter Eva. It all works out for knightly Walther von Stolzing, despite the machinations of the pedantic critic Beckmesser.

Whatever the longueurs of the opera, the magnificent Overture, often heard independently, is a masterly piece of writing using many of the themes from the opera (the Mastersingers' motif, Walther and Eva's, and the motif of the March of the tradesmen) are all combined at the climax with tremendous skill. *The Prize Song*, with which Walther wins the fair Eva, has become, justifiably, a great tenor favourite.

Der Ring des Nibelungen (1848–74): *The Ring of the Nibelung* (or just *The Ring*, as it is popularly known) is one of man's greatest creative achievements. Its length alone, regardless of its dramatic and musical content, makes it unique. The libretti of the four operas were actually written in reverse order. Having become interested in the North-European sagas, Wagner's first literary text was *Siegfried's Death*, written in 1848, later becoming *Götterdammerung*. Realizing that the story needed an introduction, he then wrote *Young Siegfried* (1851). This in turn was prefaced by *Die Walküre* explaining Siegfried's parentage. Finally, as a prologue, he wrote *Das Rheingold*.

The whole poem was completed in 1852 and published privately in 1853. Wagner thus began the project in 1848 and completed the music in 1874. The cycle lasts fifteen hours and is played over four evenings. The summary below cannot hope to convey the breadth and depth of the drama, but might give a flavour of its narrative.

Das Rheingold (1851–54): literally *The Rhine Gold*. Three Rhinemaidens, swimming in the river, guarding the gold, tell Alberich (Lord of the Nibelungs) of their treasure and that anyone who fashions a ring from it shall be master of the world. This conceit is the spring-board for the cycle. Alberich steals the gold, so Wotan (king of the gods) and Loge (god of fire), who want itd for their own pruposes, capture Alberich and take him to Valhalla. Alberich utters a curse on the Ring and its possessors.

Die Walküre (1851–56): this is the one with *The Ride of the Valkyries*. The Valkyries are the nine daughters of Wotan and the earth goddess Erda, wild horsewomen of the air whose task it is to bear the bodies of dead warriors to Valhalla. Wotan has given the Ring to the giants Fasolt and Fafner, to pay for the building of Valhalla, and Fafner, in the form of a dragon, guards the gold. Wotan has fathered human sons to regain the gold. One of these sons is Siegmund, who falls in love with his married sister Sieglinde. Fricka, Wotan's wife, demands that Siegmund be slain for taking another's wife and Wotan orders Brünnhilde, a Valkyrie, to do the deed. Brünnhilde disobeys, Wotan kills Siegmund and Brünnhilde is punished by being put into a sleeping trance on a rock surrounded by fire. The *Magic Fire Music*, with which the opera closes, is sometimes played independently.

Siegfried (1851–52, 1857, 1864–65 and 1869): Siegfried, Wotan's grandson (offspring of Siegmund and Sieglinde) slays the dragon Fafner and awakens Brünnhilde in her circle of fire to claim her as his bride. Wotan loses his authority to Siegfried and realizes that the old gods are facing their twilight and that Siegfried and Brünnhilde are the rulers of the future.

Götterdammerung (1848–52 and 1869–74): in *The Twilight of the Gods*, Brünnhilde is tricked into thinking that Siegfried has deceived her and Hagen (son of Alberich) stabs him, demanding the Ring as spoil, Brünnhilde learns of Siegfried's true steadfastness and, understanding that an act of self-sacrificing love will cleanse the curse of the Ring, she mounts her horse and rides into Siegfried's funeral pyre. The waters of the Rhine engulf the pyre, Hagen is drowned in a last attempt to gain the Ring, and Valhalla goes up in flames.

Parsifal (1857, 1865 and 1877–82): Wagner didn't call this an opera or a music-drama, but a 'stage-consecrating festival play'. Whereas *Tristan und Isolde* was concerned with physical love, *Parsifal* centres on spiritual love. Wagner had no religious belief, but the legend of the Holy Grail, the cup from which Christ drank at the Last Supper, greatly attracted him, fulfilling his long-held ambition to write a religious music-drama.

To some, *Parsifal* is the apotheosis of Wagner's art, his greatest work, his last will and testament; others think it terminally boring with its lack of action, artificial characters and endless monologues. Both sides have a case, for what is lost in the weak text is gained by some of the most sublime music Wagner ever wrote.

Siegfried Idyll (1870): this eloquent lullaby for chamber orchestra was conceived in secrecy as a birthday present for his new bride, Cosima. At half-past seven on the morning of Christmas Day, fifteen musicians assembled quietly on the stairs leading to Cosima's bedroom and played this tender piece. All the themes (apart from one) are taken from *Siegfried*.

William WALTON

'I seriously advise all sensitive composers to die at the age of thirty-seven' (Walton, 1939)

Born: 29 March 1902, Oldham
Died: 8 March 1983, Ischia
Full title: Sir William Turner Walton
Type of music: symphony, orchestral, opera, cantata, concerto, chamber, film
Influences: Elgar, Stravinsky, Prokofiev, Hindemith, Lambert, jazz
Contemporaries: Ernst Krenek, Gerald Finzi, Edmund Rubbra, **WALTON**, Maurice Duruflé, RODRIGO, Boris Blacher, KHACHATURIAN, Luigi Dallapiccola

HIS LIFE AND MUSIC

Elgar's heir, before handing the crown to Britten, Walton was the most important English composer of the inter-war years. The Neo-Romantic vein in which Walton wrote, characterized by pungent orchestration, a driving sexual energy and virile rhythms, all still imbued with an unmistakable Englishness, makes his music easily accessible. For modern music, there is more than the usual amount of lyricism and tenderness, tinged with a melancholic streak at times.

Both Walton's parents were singers – his father was an organist, choirmaster and singing teacher – and at the age of ten, he won a place as a chorister at Christ Church, Oxford. He was encouraged in his youthful attempts at composition: when Sir Hubert Parry was shown some of Walton's work he remarked, 'There's a lot in this chap, you must keep your eye on him.' Dr (later Sir) Hugh Allen, then the organist at New College, sponsored Walton's admission to Christ College, enabling him to matriculate at the early age of sixteen.

While at Oxford, he met the Sitwell family – Edith, Osbert and Sacheverell – who took him under their wing. For the next decade and more, Walton lived with them in their houses in Chelsea and Italy as a sort of adopted brother. He was only nineteen when he composed *Façade*, the work that was to first bring his name to public attention. The combination of Walton's witty, exuberant music and Edith Sitwell's nonsense verses were a *cause célèbre* after their first outing, the poetess 'declaiming' her own words through a megaphone, hidden behind a curtain.

Such hedonistic high spirits were not enough foundation for a serious career, however, and Walton soon proved that he was capable of great things with his Viola Concerto, the concert overture *Portsmouth Point* and, above all, the magnificent dramatic cantata *Belshazzar's Feast* and his fizzing Symphony No.1. He composed his first film score in 1934 for *Escape Me Never*, discovering a medium to which his lyrical-dramatic gifts were ideally suited. During his work on the film of Shakespeare's *As You Like It* (1936), he met Laurence Olivier, and the three Shakespeare films in which he collaborated with the actor put him in a class of his own as a composer for the medium. Much of the music for *Henry V* was written (before Walton had even seen a rough cut) by working in response to Shakespeare's text, yet afterwards, Olivier generously said that 'the music actually made the film.' *Hamlet* followed in 1947 and *Richard III* in 1955.

As early as 1939, Walton, 'the white hope of British music,' pronounced prophetically, 'today's white hope is tomorrow's black sheep... I've just gone through the first halcyon periods and am just about ripe for my critical damnation.' Indeed, he wrote little during the decade after the Second World War. He married the Argentinian Susana Gil in 1948 in Buenos Aires, and shortly afterwards, they settled on the island of Ischia off the coast of Naples. His opera *Troilus and Cressida* (1954), Cello Concerto (1956) and Second Symphony (1960) were all coolly received by the critics, a reaction to his unfashionable late-Romanticism. By the time he died – and after his knighthood in 1947 he had been awarded, like Elgar, the Order of Merit (1967) – the comparatively small amount of music he wrote was once again coming back into fashion.

Essential works

Façade (1921–22): for reciter(s) and chamber ensemble, this much-performed, inimitable, entertainment is equally effective in the purely orchestral suites made from some of the music; amongst the quotes from *William Tell* and 'I do like to be beside the seaside' are the catchy Polka, Tarantella and 'Popular Song' (signature tune of BBC TV's *Face the Music*).

Belshazzar's Feast (1929–31): officially entitled 'Cantata', this is the most significant British oratorio since Elgar's *The Dream of Gerontius*. It is a powerful and thrilling experience: apart from the solo baritone, chorus and orchestra, the score has an expanded brass section, supposedly in response to Sir Thomas Beecham's remark before its Leeds premiere, 'As you'll never hear the thing again why not throw in a couple of brass bands?' Walton's choral writing, in the great Anglican tradition, is masterly.

Symphony No.1 in B flat minor (1931–35): with Vaughan Williams' Fourth (1934) this is the most important symphony of the inter-war years; much of it was written in Switzerland while he was living with the young widow Baroness Imma von Doernberg. 'With this,' confided Walton, 'I may be able to knock Bax off the map.'

Portsmouth Point, overture (1925)
Scapino, overture (1940)
Johannesburg Festival Overture (1956)
Capriccio burlesco (1968)
Although they were composed at different periods in his life, one thing these brief orchestral showpieces have in common is wit – an unusual commodity in modern music. Whether it is the high jinks of the lusty *Portsmouth Point* or the flashing and angular rhythms of the *Capriccio*, of two things you are never in doubt: that whoever wrote this music had a twinkle in his eye and was a master orchestrator.

Partita for orchestra (1957): a sadly neglected score of vintage champagne, its three short movements were written, said Walton, 'in the hope that it may be enjoyed straight off.'

Viola Concerto (1929): written at the suggestion of Beecham for the doyen of violists, Lionel Tertis, who rejected it as too modern. The first performance was given by Hindemith, whose own viola concerto, *Kammermusik* No.5, had influenced Walton to such an extent that 'one or two bars are almost identical'.

Violin Concerto (1938–39): commissioned by the most renowned violinist of the day, Jascha Heifetz, who accepted it 'enthusiastically'; Walton composed it while living in Ravello with Viscountess Alice Wimbourne.

Crown Imperial, coronation march (1937)
Orb and Sceptre, coronation march (1953)
These two pieces are Pomp and Circumstance *à la* Walton; few have conducted them to more electrifying effect than the composer himself.

Film music
'Spitfire' Prelude and Fugue from *The First of the Few* (1942)
Henry V (1944), **Hamlet** (1947) and **Richard III** (1955): the soundtrack recordings are the ones to have.

Also worth investigating
String Quartet (1947)
Five Bagatelles for solo guitar (1972)

Carl Maria von WEBER

'Without Weber, Wagner would have been impossible'
(R.A. Streatfeild)

Born: 18 November 1786, Eutin, Oldenburg
Died: 5 June 1826, London
Full name: Carl Maria Friedrich Ernst von Weber
Type of music: opera, theatre, choral, symphony, concerto, chamber, instrumental (especially clarinet and piano)
Influences: Michael Haydn, Mozart, Abbé Vogler, German folksong and dance
Contemporaries: HUMMEL, FIELD, PAGANINI, AUBER, Louis Spohr, **WEBER**, Henry Bishop, HÉROLD, Carl Czerny, MEYERBEER, ROSSINI, Ignaz Moscheles

HIS LIFE

Weber's father was a keen amateur violinist and dreamed of his children becoming great musicians; his niece Constanza had married Mozart. Carl Maria did not, on the face of it, seem cut out for music – born with a diseased hip, he walked with a limp, and was a sickly consumptive – but he *was* a precociously talented musician. His first teacher was his stepbrother, a pupil of Joseph Haydn; his next was Haydn's brother Michael.

By the age of fourteen, Weber had composed his first opera, *Das Waldmädchen*. By 1811 he had had a further three produced. Simultaneously he established himself as a piano virtuoso and, two years later, was made conductor of the German Opera in Prague. The King of Saxony invited him to take charge of the German Opera Theatre in Dresden, and Weber opened his first season there in 1817. It was a position he held for the remaining years of his life. Here he befriended a lawyer and writer, Friedrich Kind, who suggested the idea of writing a libretto on a German subject. This was to become Weber's masterpiece *Der Freischütz*. Its composition occupied him for three years. Gaspare Spontini was the ruling master of opera in Germany, dictating the Italian–French musical tradition from the Berlin Opera against a rising German nationalism. When *Der Freischütz* received its triumphant premiere in 1821, the curtain had been finally raised on the new Romantic movement.

After the moderate success of his next venture *Euryanthe*, Weber went to Marienbad to seek a cure for his tuberculosis, returning to write *Oberon*, commissioned by London's Covent Garden. He was well enough to travel to England for the premiere in April 1826, where it met with huge success. He knew he was a doomed man and died a few months later. He was buried in London, his remains later transferred to Dresden in 1844. The graveside oration was delivered by Richard Wagner, his successor at Dresden.

HIS MUSIC

Weber was forty when he died, one year before Beethoven and two years before Schubert. His importance in musical history is immense, although few could tell you anything about the man who changed the face of opera in Germany. What Schubert was to song and Beethoven was to the symphony, Weber was to opera. Even now his music is undervalued.

First, there is Weber the pianist. Although a slim and weak man, he had unusually large hands able to cover an interval of a twelfth on the keyboard, and the music he wrote was tailored to his own abilities. The enormous stretches involved put many pages beyond the bounds of the average pianist.

He was also a virtuoso on the guitar; he was even a good singer, until one day in 1806 when he ruined his voice by accidentally drinking a glass of nitric acid – he and his father dabbled in lithography and the glass had been left lying around.

As a conductor appointed to important posts when an extremely young man, Weber had exactly the right personality and natural musicianship to know what he wanted and how to go about getting it; he was fiercely demanding of his singers and musicians, and he ordered German translations to be made of all the important operas, correcting errors in scores and raising standards of work to a new level – a latterday Gluck. But it is *Der Freischütz* that is his lasting memorial.

Before Weber, there had been very little German opera, Mozart's *The Magic Flute* was the only major success in the language and Beethoven's *Fidelio* had not led to any new German School to rival the current French–Italian craze. With this one opera, Weber established the Romantic movement in music. Its highly dramatic, allegorical subject was concerned with a home-grown (i.e. German) subject, which greatly appealed to the public. His melodic genius and mastery of the orchestra made him able to break with the traditions of the past, and many of his ideas anticipate some of Wagner's by thirty years. For example, the Overture to *Euryanthe* has new harmonies that can be heard in *The Ring*; he was among the first composers to insist on control of all aspects of his work; in 1817 he wrote of wanting to create pieces that would fuse every branch of art into one great new art form. Wagner achieved this – forty years later.

Essential works

Der Freischütz, opera (1821): the Overture was the first of its kind to include not only thematic material from the opera but to quote complete melodies. Act 2 has the lovely aria 'Leise, leise fromme Weise' ('Gently, gently lift my song') known as *Agathe's Prayer*; recommended is a haunting record of this by Ljuba Welitsch.

Euryanthe, opera (1823) and **Oberon**, opera (1826): the rousing Overtures are often played separately in concerts. Written the same year, Mendelssohn's *A Midsummer Night's Dream* also portrayed the fairy world of Oberon.

Clarinet Concerto No.1 in F minor, Op.73
Clarinet Concerto No.2 in E flat, Op.74
Both works were written for Weber's friend, the magnificent clarinettist Heinrich Bärmann – he must have been quite a player. In these and his other pieces for the instrument, notably the *Clarinet Quintet* (1814) and the *Grand Duo Concertant* (1816), Weber emphasised its lyrical, vocal qualities, and, in his sparkling finales, transformed the instrument into a brilliant operatic soloist.

Konzertstück in F minor, Op.79 (1821): a pioneering one-movement piano concerto in effect, full of virtuoso athletics for the soloist, portraying medieval knights and crusaders. It is one of the first large concert works to have a programme, preceding Berlioz's *Symphonie fantastique* by seven years.

Piano Sonata No.1 in C, Op.24 (1812): the finale is a fantastic note-spinning study in perpetual motion.

Aufforderung zum Tanz (Invitation to the Dance), Op.65 (1819): Weber's best-known work, a waltz rondo for the piano, now usually heard in Berlioz's orchestral arrangement. It established the form in which the 'Waltz-Kings' (Lanner and the Strauss family) would write their works, and was 'played' to Greta Garbo by Henry Daniell in the film *Camille,* while her lover, Robert Taylor, hesitated outside.

Worth investigating

Concertino in E minor for horn, Op.45 (1815)
Concerto in F for bassoon, Op.35 (1811, rev.1822)
Piano Sonata No.2 in A flat, Op.39 (1816)
Piano Sonata No.3 in D minor, Op.49 (1816)
Piano Sonata No.4 in E minor, Op.70 (1822)
Polacca brillante in E, Op.72 'L'Hilarité' (1819): also in an arrangement by Liszt for piano and orchestra.
Rondo brillante in E flat, Op.62 'La Gaieté' (1819)

Anton WEBERN

'In fifty years one will find it obvious, children will understand it and sing it' (Webern, of his own music)

Born: 3 December 1883, Vienna
Died: 15 September 1945, Mittersill, Austria
Full name: Anton Friedrich Wilhelm von Webern
Type of music: orchestral, chamber, choral
Influences: Schoenberg
Contemporaries: Joaquín Turina, GRAINGER, KODÁLY, STRAVINSKY, **WEBERN**, Alfredo Casella, Lord Berners, BAX, Sir George Dyson, Edgard Varèse

HIS LIFE AND MUSIC

Schoenberg, Berg and Webern are the key figures in the Second Viennese School, composers who subscribed to Schoenberg's theories of harmony and tonality. Little of Webern's music was heard during his lifetime as it was overshadowed by the work being produced by his peers. His compositions are threadbare, economical and delicate (though hugely complex), so much so that his music has been described as 'pianissimo espressivo'.

The son of an aristocratic mining engineer (Webern dropped the 'von' in his name when Austria became a republic after the First World War), it was while he was a student at the University of Vienna that he was introduced to Schoenberg. The relationship between the two men was more disciple and friend than master and pupil and, having produced his official Op.1 (Passacaglia for Orchestra written in the conventional German idiom), Webern then turned to atonalism. His *Six Orchestral Pieces*, Op.6 (written in 1909 and premiered 1913) created a scandal when they were first performed in Vienna. Conciseness and logic are emphasized – his *Five Pieces for Orchestra* (1913, first performed in 1969) takes only ten minutes to perform, while the fourth movement lasts a mere nineteen seconds.

Accepting that he was never likely to be able to make a living as a popular composer, Webern, apart from a year in the army, spent the rest of his life conducting, lecturing and in private teaching. In 1911 he married his cousin, Wilhelmine, and they had three daughters and a son; this did not help their somewhat precarious financial situation. Whatever you think of Webern's music, few composers have shown such fortitude and resolve in adhering to their artistic ideals while having to cope with abuse being thrown at them, whatever they produced. When Schoenberg formalized his theories and gave twelve-note music a structure, Webern began writing longer works that were framed in strict classical forms, but the *Anschluss* of 1938 made his position difficult. He was denounced by the Nazi regime as a 'cultural Bolshevik' and his music was banned in Austria and Germany.

Webern was called up during the Second World War when he was nearly sixty years old, and served as an air-raid warden. In the spring of 1945, he learned that his only son had been killed on the Yugoslav front. Not long afterwards, at Easter, he left his apartment in Mödling, Vienna and travelled to Mittersill near Salzburg, where he had heard that his son-in-law had been involved in the black market. American soldiers arrived to arrest the young man and when Webern stepped outside to smoke a cigar that his son-in-law had given him, an American soldier bumped into him in the dark. Webern was ordered to stop, but he misunderstood the soldier's order and approached him. He was shot dead.

More than Berg and Schoenberg, Webern's music has exercised a profound influence on contemporary composers, particularly on Boulez and Stockhausen. Stravinsky, who had long been an opponent of serial techniques, acknowledged Webern's methods by applying them to the works he wrote during the 1950s. Several jazz composers have adopted Webern's ideas on tone colours. To the public at large, however, Webern's music remains baffling, a closed door.

Essential works

Five Movements, Op.5 (1910, rev.1929): these pieces were originally written for string quartet and revised for string orchestra; they form the best introduction to Webern's fastidious and crystal-clear style of composition. The music ranges from whispered tones to brief, mammoth climaxes within a few seconds, an intense experience that demands concentration and not a few hearings to assimilate.

Symphony for chamber orchestra, Op.21 (1928): its two movements last fifteen minutes, the second one consisting of a theme and seven variations; the music is composed of fragmentary and apparently random notes in which an instrument frequently plays no more than one or two notes before passing on the terse theme to another instrument. This is music stripped to its bare bones.

Kurt WEILL
(1900–50)

The Threepenny Opera, 1928

Having composed a number of modishly modern orchestral works and got nowhere, Weill hit his stride as soon as he began writing for the theatre. In the Berlin of the 1920s he also found an appreciative audience for his short, sharp satirical operas. After composing *Der Protagonist* (1925) and *Royal Palace* (1927), he teamed up with the left-wing writer Bertolt Brecht. Their first success was the 'songspiel' *Mahagonny* (1927), subsequently remodelled as a three-act opera *Rise and Fall of the City of Mahagonny* (1929). But it was Brecht's adaptation of John Gay's *The Beggar's Opera* of 1728 that gave Weill by far his greatest – and most lasting – success. Under the title *Der Dreigroschenoper* it was produced throughout Europe, receiving more than four thousand performances in about 120 German theatres after its premiere in 1928. With the stage peopled by pimps, prostitutes and low-life characters, Weill's haunting, rasping score, and the venomous punch of the libretto, *The Threepenny Opera* retains its vivid association with the decadent years of the Weimar Republic.

Weill was the leading spokesman for the aesthetic inter-war vogue of *Zeitkunst* (vibrantly contemporary art), determined that his music should reflect current experience, that it should be accessible and that his theatre work should be unhampered by the restrictions of an opera house. His two-act opera *Der Jasager* (*The Yes-man*, 1930), written for schools to perform, has some claim to creating the educational genre of opera later taken up by Carl Orff and Benjamin Britten. But whatever his long-term aims, the Jewish-born Weill and his actress wife Lotte Lenya were forced to flee Nazi Germany in 1933. After a final collaboration with Brecht in Paris (*The Seven Deadly Sins*, 1933), Weill left for America and thereafter made his career on Broadway with a string of musicals and attempts at 'American opera', none of which has lasted the course. One of the first, however, *Knickerbocker Holiday* (1936), written with Maxwell Anderson, contains the unforgettable 'September Song' ('Oh it's a long, long time / From May to September...') which, as sung by Walter Huston, became almost as popular as 'Mack the Knife' from *The Threepenny Opera*.

Charles-Marie WIDOR
(1844–1937)

Toccata in F, 1878

This thrilling showpiece for organ is the fifth and final movement of Widor's Organ Symphony No.5 in F minor, Op.42 No.1, a relentless whirlwind of semiquavers with the pedals booming out the magisterial theme. It has eclipsed everything else Widor wrote, even though its musical content is really quite slight. It requires a big organ to makes its full effect felt, a consideration rarely borne in mind by the hundreds of couples who have wanted to walk up the aisle to it ever since it was brought back into fashion in 1961 by the wedding of the Duke and Duchess of Kent.

Widor, who became the doyen of French organists after the death of César Franck, recorded the Toccata himself at the age of eighty-seven on the organ of Saint-Sulpice in Paris, where he had been organist for sixty years. He wrote ten other organ symphonies, of which No.1 in C minor has the powerful *Marche pontificale*, No.4 has a charming *Andante cantabile* and No.6 is the best of the lot. Try also his thunderous *Sinfonia sacra* for organ and orchestra Op.81.

Malcolm WILLIAMSON

Born: 21 November 1931, Sydney
Full name: Malcolm Benjamin Graham Christopher Williamson
Type of music: symphony, orchestral, concerto, opera, ballet, keyboard
Influences: Lutyens, Messiaen, jazz
Contemporaries: George Crumb, Alun Hoddinott, **WILLIAMSON**,
Alexander Goehr, GÓRECKI, Krzysztof Penderecki, BIRTWISTLE, DAVIES, PÄRT

HIS LIFE AND MUSIC

The current Master of the Queen's Musick (he succeeded Sir Arthur Bliss in 1975), Williamson's music has failed to capture the public imagination since his appointment and many people are still waiting for a memorable or significant work to emerge from the holder of this ancient office. There was a time when inspiration struck frequently; he was able to write at an incredible pace – his Piano Concerto No.2 was completed in the space of only eight days – but Williamson's productivity has slowed down considerably during the past two decades.

Although little of his work is currently available on disc, Williamson has written a great deal of fine music that deserves to be far better known. His highly attractive Easter piece, entitled *Procession of Palms,* is his most performed piece but perhaps the most successful music has been that written for children – his operas *Julius Caesar Jones* and *The Happy Prince,* for instance – and the works that require audience participation. As a pianist and organist Williamson has written several concertos for both instruments. His Organ Concerto is a muscular and thrilling work, in which he has peformed as an eloquent soloist.

Williamson studied with Eugene Goossens before coming to live in Britain in 1953. In London he had lessons with the ardent serialist Elisabeth Lutyens and for some time thereafter he wrote works using advanced methods of composition. An eclectic and cultivated man with a love of jazz and popular song (he was employed as a nightclub pianist at an early stage in his career), Williamson has a fine ear for a catchy tune and bouncy rhythms: his musical style and language is too broad to be confined to twelve-note technique.

Essential works
Organ Concerto (1961)
Piano Concerto No.2 (1960)
Piano Concerto No.3 (1962)
Procession of Palms

Our Man In Havana, opera (1963): based on Graham Greene's novel.
The Happy Prince, children's opera (1965): based on Oscar Wilde's fairy tale.

Hugo WOLF

'Poetry is the true source of my music' (Wolf)

Born: 13 March 1860, Windisch-Gräz, Austria
Died: 22 February 1903, Vienna
Full name: Hugo Filipp Jakob Wolf
Type of music: *Lieder*
Influences: Gluck, Mozart, Beethoven and, especially, Wagner
Contemporaries: Sergei Liapunov, Mikhail Ippolitov-Ivanov, **WOLF**,
MACDOWELL, ALBÉNIZ, MAHLER, Ignacy Paderewski, Emil von Reznicek

HIS LIFE AND MUSIC

Of all the sad lives of great composers, that of Hugo Wolf is the most pitiful. There was no period when, through his own fault or other peoples', he did not suffer. All he ever wanted to do was write music. It was his sole *raison d'être* and no one wanted to listen. His own character made life difficult – he had a violent temper and was highly sensitive, defiant, proud and stubborn. Answering a request for biographical details towards the end of his life, he replied 'My name is Hugo Wolf. I was born on March 13th 1860, and am still alive at the moment. That's biography enough.'

The fourth son of a leather merchant, an amateur musician who discouraged a musical career, Wolf was expelled from three different schools and was eventually thrown out of the Vienna Conservatory, which he had entered in 1875, not because of his argumentative nature, his sullen disposition or the neglect of his studies – though all of these were true. He was the innocent victim of a malicious hoax: someone had sent a threatening letter to the director and signed it from Hugo Wolf.

His life was spent in abject poverty. He had to depend on friends for lodgings and funds, scraping pennies together for a single meal a day of soup and a few slices of bread. He read music constantly and when he went through a Beethoven sonata or read a favourite poet 'his hands trembled ... his eyes lit up, and he appeared transfigured, as if at the sight of higher, brighter regions, the gates of which had suddenly sprung open. He gasped for air,' wrote one contemporary. Another wrote of his thin, undernourished body and his eyes staring out starkly. 'He seemed always on the brink of hysteria.' Wagner was his god – he met the great man once, aged fifteen, and showed him a song he had written. Wagner brushed the young hopeful aside, telling him it was far too early for anyone to make judgments on whether one had talent or not.

When at last Wolf landed a job as assistant conductor to Karl Muck in Salzburg, he arrived with a bundle of clothes under one arm and a bust of Wagner under the other. Inevitably, the job lasted only a few months – he quarrelled with everyone – and he found himself once more back in Vienna. In 1884 he became the music critic of the *Salonblatt* and held on to this for three years. His passionately held views made him many friends, for he was devastatingly honest in his criticism and praise. He also made many powerful enemies: the conductor of the Vienna Philharmonic, Hans Richter, accepted Wolf's tone-poem *Penthesilea*, but at the rehearsal in October 1886 instructed the orchestra to play through the piece as lackadaisically as they pleased. Then came the devastating blow – Richter wound up the music by saying: 'Gentlemen, I would not have had this piece performed to the end were it not that I wanted to see the man who dared to write that way about Brahms.'

But in 1888, Wolf had some encouragement. Some of his songs were issued by a small publishing house. This prompted an amazing outburst of creative energy and in one year he wrote fifty-three songs; shortly afterwards, he set fifty of Goethe's poems to music in only three and a half months. He himself could not believe what was happening – it was as if someone else was composing. He tackled German poems, and Italian and Spanish verses translated into German. 'I work at a thousand horsepower,' he declared. 'What I write now, I write for the future. They are masterpieces. There has been nothing like it since Schubert and Schumann.' The curious thing is, he was right. Wolf had sophisticated literary tastes and was attracted to works of diverse subjects and emotions. He had an innate ability to capture the spirit and character of each poem, combining Schumann's genius for striking exactly the right balance between vocal line and accompaniment with Schubert's grander rhetorical style. Wolf's gloomy life and intense personality is reflected in his music, certainly, but these elements by no means dominate. There is more passion, humour and sunshine than morbidity and Austrian *Weltschmerz*.

In 1891, inspiration suddenly dried up like a stream in a drought. He was beside himself until he was able to write once more towards the end of that year. Again, for two years (1892–94) nothing came; then there was another burst of creativity in 1895. By then, there were some signs of recognition and even the formerly hostile dean of critics, Eduard Hanslick, had some kind things to say. Two Hugo Wolf Societies were formed in Berlin and Vienna. But this success was checked by the failure of Wolf's opera *Der Corregidor* at its premiere in Mannheim in 1896. When the Vienna Opera turned the piece down after initially agreeing to perform it, something snapped and the syphilis he had contracted as a seventeen-year-old began to take hold.

Sleepless nights and horrifying dreams haunted him, he was found wandering the streets of Vienna in a daze one night and he began suffering from delusions, at one time convinced he was the director of the Vienna Opera. He was put in a sanatorium for a rest cure, but on returning to Vienna from Italy, he tried to commit suicide in the Traunsee. From 1898 to the end of his life he was confined in the Lower Austrian Mental Hospital. His body became more paralysed, his mind more confused. In the end, he went completely insane.

The most celebrated musicians of Vienna turned out for his funeral. Strange that they should have waited until his death to pay their respects, but by then, of course, it was safe to acknowledge Wolf as one of the supreme composers of German *Lieder*.

Essential works

Of the 242 songs Wolf wrote for voice and piano, usually contained in a cycle, the most famous are:

Three Harfenspieler Songs: Goethe *Lieder* (1889)

'Auch kleine Dinge', **'Du denkst mit einem Fädchen'** and **'Ich hab' in Penna'**: Italian book (1890–96)

'In dem Schatten meiner Locken' and **'Herz, verzage nicht geschwind'**: Spanish book (1890)

'Auf einer Wanderung', **'Storchenbotschaft'**, **'Fussreise'**, **'Der Gärtner'**, **'Der Feuerreiter'** and **'Verborgenheit'**: Mörike Lieder (1888)

'Heimweh', **'Das Ständchen'**, **'Erwartung'**n and **'Verschwiegene Liebe'**: Eichendorff Lieder (1880–88)

Also worth investigating

Italian Serenade, string quartet (1887): in one bright, sunny movement, lasting less than ten minutes.

THE TEN MOST POPULAR PIECES OF CLASSICAL MUSIC

Results of a BBC Radio 2 poll

1 **Bizet**
'Au fond du temple saint' ('In the depths of the temple') from *The Pearl Fishers*
2 **Bruch**
Adagio from Violin Concerto No.1 in G minor
3 **Verdi**
Chorus of the Hebrew Slaves from *Nabucco*
4 **Elgar**
Nimrod from *Enigma Variations*
5 **Beethoven**
Shepherd's Thanksgiving (final movement from Symphony No.6 'Pastoral')
6 **Sibelius**
Finlandia
7 **Mozart**
Andante from Piano Concerto No.21 in C
8 **Mascagni**
Intermezzo from *Cavalleria rusticana*
9 **Rachmaninov**
Piano Concerto No.2 in C minor
10 **Handel**
Hallelujah Chorus from *Messiah*

THE TOP TEN CLASSICAL COMPOSERS

*The composers whose symphonies are played most frequently
in London's concert halls*

1	Beethoven	6	Shostakovich
2	Mozart	7	Schubert
3	Mahler	8	Tchaikowsky
4	Haydn	9	Mendelssohn
5	Dvořák	10	Brahms

THE TOP FIVE REQUESTS ON CLASSIC fM

Classic fM's five most-requested tracks

1 **Rachmaninov**
First movement of Piano Concerto No.2 in C minor
2 **Mascagni**
Intermezzo from *Cavalleria rusticana*
3 **Rimsky-Korsakov**
The Young Prince and the Young Princess from *Scheherazade*
4 **Puccini**
'Che gelida manina' from *La bohème*
5 **Bruch**
Adagio from Violin Concerto No.1 in G minor

THE TOP 25 TITLES ON CLASSIC fM

Classic fM's twenty-five most frequently-played tracks

Bizet
'Au fond du temple saint' ('In the depths of the temple') from *The Pearl Fishers*

Copland
Hoe-Down from *Rodeo*

Debussy
Gollywog's Cakewalk from *Children's Corner* Suite

Debussy
Clair de Lune from *Suite Bergamasque*

Elgar
Nimrod from *Enigma Variations*

Elgar
Pomp and Circumstance March No.1

Falla
Ritual Fire Dance from *El amor brujo*

Grieg
Morning from *Peer Gynt* Suite No.1

Handel
Arrival of the Queen of Sheba from *Solomon*

Haydn
Finale of Trumpet Concerto in E flat

Kabalevsky
Comedians Galop from *The Comedians*

Kreisler
Tambourin chinois

Mendelssohn
'Hebrides' Overture

Offenbach
Barcarolle from *The Tales of Hoffman*

Orff
'O fortuna' from *Carmina Burana*

Prokofiev
Dance of The Montagues and Capulets from *Romeo and Juliet*

Puccini
'O mio babbino caro' from *Gianni Schicci*

Puccini
'Vissi d'arte' from *Tosca*

Smetana
Vltava from *Má vlast*

Rimsky-Korsakov
Flight of the Bumble Bee from *Tsar Sultan*

Stravinsky
Finale from *The Firebird*

Tchaikowsky
Polonaise from *Eugene Onegin*

Tielman Susato
Fanfare

Verdi
'La donna e mobile' from *Rigoletto*

Verdi
Brindisi (Drinking Song) from *La traviata*

THE GROWTH OF THE ORCHESTRA

America's largest classical audience is invited annually by the radio station WQXR to vote for its forty favourite works. The latest results show that with one exception (No.22: Schubert's Piano Quintet in A 'The Trout') all involve an orchestra of one size or another. The most popular work was Beethoven's Symphony No.9 ('Choral'), followed by his Symphony No.5, Dvořák's New World Symphony, Beethoven's 'Emperor' Concerto, J.S. Bach's Brandenburg Concertos, Beethoven's 'Pastoral' Symphony, Vivaldi's 'The Four Seasons', Mozart's 'Eine Kleine Nachtmusik', Handel's Messiah and, in tenth place, Beethoven's Symphony No.7.

The orchestra is an indispensable instrument to most composers, whether as an accompanist, as a partner (in a concerto, say) or as the vehicle through which a composer chooses to express what are frequently his most profound thoughts. To see how the symphony orchestra developed, and at what rate, is clearly germane to the way in which music developed.

All the figures shown in the table below are average values, except for the Milan 1770 entry, which refers to a specific occasion – the first performance of a Mozart opera. There have been many exceptions: in 1844 Berlioz conducted an ensemble of 1,000 musicians, and Mahler gathered the same number together for a performance of his Eighth Symphony in 1908. This pales into insignificance beside the occasion of the World Peace Jubilee in Boston, Massachusetts on 17 June 1872 when Johann Strauss II conducted a force of 2,000 instrumentalists (including 350 violins) and a choir of 20,000 – with the help of 100 assistant conductors who had been engaged to keep the whole thing in tempo!

City and year	Violins	Violas	Cellos	Double basses	Flutes	Oboes	Clarinets	Bassoons	French horns	Trumpets	Trombones	Timpani (pairs)	Total
Leipzig 1730 (Bach)	5	2	2	–	–	2	–	2	–	3	–	1	17
Mannheim 1756 (Stamitz)	20	4	4	4	2	2	2	2	4	1	–	1	46
Milan 1770 (Mozart)	28	6	2	6	2	2	2	2	4	2	–	1	57
Esterházy 1783 (Haydn)	11	2	2	2	–	2	–	2	2	–	–	1	24
Paris Opéra 1788	28	6	12	5	2	4	2	4	?	?	?	1	64
Vienna 1844	20	10	6	4	2	2	2	2	4	2	3	1	58
Bayreuth 1880 (Wagner)	32	12	12	8	4	4	4	4	8	4	6	2	100
Present day	32	12	10	8	4	4	4	4	8	6	3	2	97

Note: The modern orchestra also makes use of piccolo, cor anglais, bass clarinet, saxophone, contra-bassoon, tuba, harp, celesta, piano and a wide range of percussion instruments.

GLOSSARY

a capella

It. 'In the church style'. Choral music unaccompanied by instruments.

adagio

It. 'At ease', i.e. slow. Used to describe the tempo of a piece of music.

aleatory

Lat. *Alea* meaning 'dice'. Music that is dependent on chance for its creation, a method favoured by Stockhausen and others in the 1960s.

allegro

It. 'Lively'. Used to describe the tempo of a piece of music, often in conjunction with other adjectives or qualifications such as *allegro con brio* or *allegro vivace*.

anthem

The word is an English corruption of Lat. *antiphon* and the form derives from the Latin motet of the Roman Catholic church. An anthem is a choral setting of non-liturgical words used in Anglican church services, but can also be a patriotic vocal work.

aria

It. 'Air, tune'. A song for a solo voice in an opera, with instrumental accompaniment. In other words, the famous bits that stand out from the rest, such as 'Nessun dorma', 'Casta diva' and 'Una voce poco fa'.

atonal / atonality

Not in any key / absence of tonality; avoidance of definite key and scale. Music that rejects traditional tonality (such as was established by masters like Beethoven) and abandons the use of a tonic or key-centre to which all the notes and chords of a piece are related. Twelve-note music is a systematized version of atonal music (*see* BERG, SCHOENBERG and WEBERN).

bagatelle

Fr. 'Trifle'. A short instrumental composition, frequently for the piano.

ballade

Fr. A form closely associated with Chopin, whose Four Ballades for piano are atypical: an instrumental composition, improvized in character, that seems to tell a story even where none is indicated. It is also a form of medieval words and music.

barcarolle

Fr. From the Italian *barca*, 'boat'. Originally a boating-song sung by Venetian gondoliers; a term applied to any vocal or instrumental piece in the same lilting rhythm (6/8 or 12/8). Chopin, Offenbach (in *The Tales of Hoffmann*) and Fauré wrote notable examples.

Baroque

See A CHRONOLOGY OF MUSIC, page 17.

bel canto

It. 'Beautiful singing'. An imprecise yet widely-used term describing the traditional Italian *cantabile* style of singing that emphasizes beauty and evenness of tone, fine *legato* (smooth) phrasing and perfection of technique. This contrasts with the German style of

a more dramatic approach with
increased emotional expression. A *bel
canto* singer is usually associated with
the Bellini, Donizetti, Rossini and
Verdi repertoire; not to be confused
with the loud and unmusical singer
known in the business as a *can belto*.

bitonal

The use of two keys simultaneously,
whether indicated by different key
signatures or not. Stravinsky's *Petrushka*
makes use of bitonality.
See also TONALITY.

cadence

The progression of chords (usually
two) that lead the ear to the close of a
piece of music.

cadenza

It. 'Cadence'. The rounding-off of a
musical phrase or close of a piece.
Cadenza has come to mean the flashy
flourish by a soloist just before the
cadence. It is the opportunity for the
singer or instrumentalist to show his or
her agility in performing difficult
musical feats with the greatest of ease.
Two examples: the brief flourish at the
end of 'La donna è mobile' is a
cadenza, so is the titanic solo passage at
the end of the first movement of
Rachmaninov's Piano Concerto No.1.

canon

Fr. 'A rule, a system of rules'.
A composition in which a theme, or
'subject', begun in one part, is strictly
repeated, after a rest, in another part or
parts. There are various kinds of
musical canon. The simplest is a
Perpetual Canon, which is usually
called a round or catch, something that
begins again like 'Frère Jacques' or
'Three Blind Mice'. Byrd's famous
setting of *Non nobis Domine* is a
Perpetual Canon. Since the fourteenth
century, composers have found the
canon a useful device by which to bind
their compositions together. Canonic
writing is the basis of virtually every
motet or madrigal; in the seventeenth

and eighteenth centuries, a fugue
almost always began with a form of free
canon. In Bach's *Goldberg Variations* for
harpsichord, every third variation is a
canon, each canon a different kind.
Listen to the finale of Franck's Sonata
for violin and piano or the Scherzo
from Beethoven's Eighth Symphony
– both are canons.

cantabile

It. 'Singable'. A performance direction
to play in a singing, melodious, flowing
style.

cantata

It. 'A piece to be sung', as opposed to
a sonata, a piece to be 'sounded' or
played. This has come to mean a
setting, usually of a religious text
intended to be sung in church. It is
generally in several sections, longer
than an anthem but shorter than an
oratorio. J.S. Bach's pieces are the best
to try, such as Cantata No.147,
Herz und Mund, from which comes the
popular 'Jesu, joy of man's desiring',
Cantata No.208, *Was mir behagt* or
Cantata No.80, *Ein feste Burg ist unser
Gott*: (*A Safe Stronghold our God is
Still*) – *see* CHORALE. Bach also wrote
some secular cantatas – the 'Coffee'
cantata, for example.

cantus firmus or canto firmo

Lat. 'Fixed song'. The name given to
the thread of a melody, taken either
from plainsong or popular song,
around which other melodies were
woven to make a choral texture.
Clearly, it was essential in the
development in the art of counterpoint.
After the Middle Ages, it came to mean
any subject taken for contrapuntal
treatment.

chaconne

Fr. A slow dance in 3/4 time, similar to
the passacaglia. This is usually written
as a set of variations on a ground bass
(*see* below) of eight bars length. The
same bass line is repeated again and
again, while the harmonies that the

bass suggests free the composer to invent endless melodic variations. Jazz musicians employ the same sort of process. The most famous example in classical music is the great Chaconne at the end of the Partita No.2 for unaccompanied violin by J.S. Bach. 'Dido's Lament' from Purcell's *Dido and Aeneas* is a moving, sung chaconne.

chamber music

Originally, music suitable for performance in a house rather than in a church or theatre. Now the term describes an instrumental work written for a limited number of players, in which there is only one performer to each part and which is therefore, necessarily, intimate in character.

chorale / choral prelude

The hymns of the German Protestant church, which came into being following the Reformation of the sixteenth century, were introduced by Martin Luther who wanted to encourage the congregation to sing. Luther's own most famous hymn or chorale is 'Ein feste Burg ist unser Gott', a setting of Psalm No.46, frequently used since by composers like J.S. Bach, Mendelssohn ('Reformation' Symphony) and Meyerbeer (*Les Huguenots*). Bach also interpolated chorales into his larger works (cantatas and passions), although he composed only about thirty of the four hundred he harmonized. The chorale prelude is an organ piece based on a chorale, Bach being its most notable exponent.

chromatic harmony

See HARMONY.

classical

See A CHRONOLOGY OF MUSIC, page 18.

clavecin

Fr. Another name for the harpsichord.

clavichord

Like the harpsichord, a precursor of the piano, having metal wedges instead of hammers. It was not too large to be carried and was placed on a table for support; it was the prototype of the later square piano.

coda

It. 'Tail'. The passage at the end of a composition, which forms a satisfying conclusion.

coloratura

Ger. *Koloratur*, 'coloured'. A singer's term meaning the colouring or elaboration of a melody in the form of runs, cadenzas and trills. In practice this has come to mean a vocal part demanding great agility, usually associated with a soprano voice (e.g. Joan Sutherland – 'a coloratura soprano'). Examples of coloratura singing are the two arias sung by the Queen of the Night (from Mozart's *The Magic Flute*), the Mad Scene from *Lucia di Lammermoor* (Donizetti) and the 'Bell Song' from *Lakmé* (Delibes). A mezzo coloratura aria is 'Non più mesta' from Rossini's *La Cenerentola*.

concerto

It. 'A concert' or concerted performance. The term has had several stages of meaning. Nowadays, it is an elaborate work for solo instrument with orchestra, frequently in sonata form. The soloist appears alone at intervals and also in conjunction with the orchestra, which similarly has passages alone. This usage first appears late in the seventeenth century.

concerto grosso

It. One of the most popular instrumental forms of the Baroque era, in which a small group of instrumental soloists (the *concertino*) competes and alternates with a larger group (the *ripieno*). Originating in about 1700, the concerto grosso had from three to five contrasted movements. Corelli, Vivaldi, J.S. Bach and Handel wrote the best examples.

continuo

Abbreviation of *Basso continuo*.
See FIGURED BASS.

counterpoint / contrapuntal

The word is derived from Lat. *punctus contra punctum*, or 'point against point' (i.e. note against note) – the setting of points or notes in one part against those in another. Canon and fugue are aspects of counterpoint. In effect it is the weaving together of two or more melodic lines to make a tightly-knit musical texture. The result is known as polyphony. Musical composition can be divided into the horizontal and the vertical – chord-and-note combinations being the vertical (harmony), the threads of melody that run through these being the horizontal (counterpoint). *See also* A CHRONOLOGY OF MUSIC, page 12.

diatonic

The major and minor scales we use are called the diatonic scales, as distinct from the chromatic scale, which is made up of nothing but semitones.

Dies irae

Lat. 'Day of Wrath'. A sequence from the second part of the Requiem Mass. The words were probably written by Thomas of Celano, a Franciscan monk, in the thirteenth century. Composers throughout the centuries have quoted its plainsong melody. Two well-known examples are Liszt's *Totentanz* and Rachmaninov's Variations on a Theme of Paganini.

dissonance

Meaning 'a jarring sound', but this word is hard to define in practice, one man's consonance being another man's dissonance. Mozart's String Quartet in C (K465), composed in 1785, was nicknamed the 'Dissonance' Quartet because of its 'jarring' opening passage.

étude

Fr. 'Study'. A piece of music, usually a solo instrumental work, designed to give practice in some branch of technique. The best études have some intrinsic musical merit as well, such as those by Chopin, Liszt, Scriabin and Debussy, for piano. The first to write études as we know them today was Muzio Clementi (1752–1832).

Expressionism

Hijacked from the term describing the movements in art, literature and drama, and involving the expression of the artist's state of mind by means of external symbols, 'Expressionism' has a rather vague application in the musical sense. Schoenberg's music (indeed German music of the early twentieth century) can be called 'Expressionist', but the term is more useful in defining the antithesis of Impressionism.

figured bass

A practice prevalent especially during the Baroque period was to score the bass part of a composition with figures and bass notes, the figures indicating how far above the bass note the other notes should be sounded – in other words, it was a shorthand indication of the harmonies required from the continuo player, who would accompany or take part in an ensemble generally on a keyboard instrument.

Formalism

Prokofiev and Shostakovich were denounced for 'Formalism' by the Soviet authorities in 1948, a criticism levelled at others at various times. The state demanded music that paid less attention to form and more to content, which in practical terms meant a ban on discordant, 'intellectual' music.

fugue / fugal

From Lat. *Fuga*, 'a flight'. A fugue is the most elaborate form of polyphonic or contrapuntal composition. It consists of the orderly presentation and treatment of one or more themes, set for three or four parts. The underlying principle is that all the parts are of equal importance, all contributing to the total effect. There are almost no stopping points – once a fugue starts, it keeps on going, building up to a climax and finally coming back to the original theme and key. Fugal writing began in the 1600s and grew out of the madrigals and motets for voices. The art reached its peak with J.S. Bach – try *The Well-tempered Clavier* and the organ works listed in the main entry and the joyful fugue by S.S. Wesley in his *Choral Song and Fugue*. The finale of Mozart's 'Jupiter' Symphony and Beethoven's Piano Sonatas Op.101, 106 & 110 include triumphant examples. Other celebrated fugues are the end of Verdi's *Falstaff* (a vocal fugue) and Britten's *Young Person's Guide to the Orchestra*.

gavotte

An old French dance in 4/4 time, popularized by Lully and occasionally revived in modern times. The gavottes from Thomas's opera *Mignon* and Prokofiev's 'Classical' Symphony are examples.

Gregorian chant

See PLAINSONG; and A CHRONOLOGY OF MUSIC, page 9.

ground bass

The Italians call it *basso ostinato:* a short theme repeated over and over again in the bass, with varied melodic and harmonic accompaniments. In reference to seventeenth-century music, a piece is sometimes described as 'divisions on a ground' – this simply means it is a work in variation form constructed over a ground bass. The chaconne and passacaglia forms are written thus. Pachelbel's famous Canon in D is an example.

harmony / harmonically

Lat. and Gk. *Harmonia*, 'Notes in combination'. The sound that results when more than one note is played or sung at the same time. The study of harmony, a basic element in the art of composition, is the examination of how chords are built and move from one to another. There are no rules as to how chords must be employed, the study of harmony is about *how* they have been used. An important element of a composer's unique style is the way in which he builds and uses chords. These are used in block forms, they can be the main motive for a work or they can serve in all kinds of accompaniment, stretched into many different forms and shapes.

If a chord deviates from the typical major or minor form by a small interval (usually a semitone) then the note (tone) is a chromatic note and the new chord it produces is a chromatic chord. These either help a modulation or evoke a particular emotion or reaction. When a composer uses numerous chromatic chords, the harmony is said to be chromatic harmony. In certain works by Liszt, Franck and Wagner, there are so many chromatic sounds that it is sometimes difficult to identify the original key of the music.

Since the end of the last century, composers have discovered new ways of using the chords of traditional harmony. Old medieval church modes, the pentatonic scale and whole-tone scale, in tandem with conventional and chromatic chords, added another dimension to harmony. With Schoenberg's music we arrive at the point where all these principles are completely abandoned and chords are made from any combination of intervals.

Impressionism

See A CHRONOLOGY OF MUSIC, page 28.

impromptu

A short, song-like instrumental piece (usually for piano) that gives the feeling of spontaneity. Schubert's eight Impromptus are the best-known examples.

intermezzo

It. 'In the middle'. A piece of orchestral music in the middle of an opera to

denote the passage of time
(e.g. Mascagni's *Cavalleria rusticana*).
It is also a term applied to a short
concert piece (e.g. Brahms' Intermezzi
Opp.76, 117 & 118).

interval

The pitch difference between any two
notes. Thus the 'distance' between
C and G is described as an interval of a
fifth, by counting upwards and
including both notes at the extreme
ends. The intervals of the 4th, 5th and
8th, in whatever key they occur, are
called Perfect Intervals. Major Intervals
(2nd, 3rd, 6th and 7th notes above the
key-note) and Minor Intervals (the
same but diminished by a semitone)
are nothing to do with the amount of
time allotted to alcoholic refreshment
half-way through a concert.

Kapellmeister

Ger. Same as MAESTRO DI CAPELLA.

key / key signature

The 'key' of a piece of music is
determined by the set of notes chosen
as the main material for its
composition. The chief note is the
key-note; all the other notes used have
a relation to this one. The term is used
to indicate the precise tonality of the
music, in other words, which major or
minor scale and the chords built on
them will be used as the basis for the
piece. (Music that has no perceptible
key-note is called atonal.)

To show the performer which key
the music is written in, the composer
places sharp or flat signs at the
beginning of each line of music. This is
the key signature. For instance, two
sharps mean the piece will be either in
D major or B minor (both scales have
F sharp and C sharp common to
them); three flats mean it will be in
E flat major or C minor (both scales
have E flat, A flat and B flat). As a
broad generalization, you can tell
the key of a tonal piece of music by
looking at the last and lowest bass note
of the work (usually the key-note)

and the major or minor chord that
accompanies it.

legato

It. 'Bound together'. A musical
direction asking the performer to play
smoothly, not *staccato*.

leitmotiv

Ger. Literally 'leading motif'. The
term was first coined in 1871 in a
discussion on the works of Weber who
made much of the device of *leitmotiv* in
Der Freischütz and *Euryanthe*. It is a
short musical phrase identified with a
person, emotion, event or idea.
Leitmotiv is particularly associated with
Wagner, because he, more than any
other composer, consciously developed
the device as an integral part of a score.
He preferred to call these brief phrases
'remembrance motifs' or 'idea motifs',
using them to create subtle evocations
of mood, events and characters. They
ingeniously contrast with one another,
supplement one other and assume new
shapes, thus lending the music a unity
unlike anything previously heard.
There has hardly been an opera since
that has not featured *leitmotiv,* and
Wagnerites become quite obsessive
about them, compiling catalogues like
train-spotters, pointing out the real or
imagined similarity between, say, the
leitmotiv of the *Liebestod* from *Tristan
und Isolde* with that of the Holy Grail
in *Parsifal*.

libretto

It. 'booklet'. The text of an opera or
oratorio. The quality of the librettist's
work has had an important influence
on the style and character of opera
down the ages – Metastasio on
eighteenth-century opera, for example,
Calzabigi on the operas of Gluck and
Hofmannsthal on Richard Strauss.
Many composers have contributed their
own libretti, most notably Wagner;
Berlioz, Busoni, Rimsky-Korsakov,
Delius, Holst, Hindemith and Tippett
wrote some of their own. Very few great
composers, however, are equally adept

dramatists and poets, despite what they may have believed to the contrary.

Lied / Lieder

Ger. 'song' / 'songs'. This is specifically the type of song composed by German composers such as Schubert, Schumann and Wolf, and the equivalent of the French *chanson*. Strictly speaking, a *Lieder* recital should contain nothing but German song.

linear

As in 'linear writing'. This is when voices or parts move with complete freedom of harmonic relationships.

madrigal

Originally a medieval lyrical poem, hence the musical setting of such a verse normally in an elaborate contrapuntal style, based on medieval modes rather than the modern major and minor modes and designed for several unaccompanied voices. The counterpart of the liturgical motet, it was cultivated particularly in the sixteenth and seventeenth centuries.

maestro di capella

It. Literally 'master of the chapel'. The musical director to a bishop, king or nobleman.

Mass

An elaborate choral setting of the principal ritual of the Roman Catholic Church, originally for unaccompanied chorus (Palestrina's *Missa Papae Marcelli* is a fine example) but later for soloists, chorus and orchestra (Bach's Mass in B minor for instance). It is the 'Ordinary' of the Mass that has been most frequently set and which consists of five sections: 'Kyrie', 'Gloria', 'Credo', 'Sanctus and Benedictus', and 'Agnus Dei'.

mode / modes

Lat. *Modus*, 'key'. The order and arrangement of the steps forming a scale. The notes of a mode can be arranged in scalewise order, thus the

so-called Medieval and Ecclesiastical modes can be represented by scales of white notes on the piano. Modes have names derived from the Greek system of music, although the names have nothing to do with the Greek concept of mode. Some examples are the Dorian Mode (notes D to D on the white notes), Phrygian (E to E), Lydian (F to F) and Aeolian (A to A). Until the end of the sixteenth century, the medieval modal and interval theories were the basis of polyphonic composition. By the end of the seventeenth century, the exclusive use of the two modern modes, our major and minor scales, became established. Modal idioms, mainly derived from folk song, reappeared in music in the nineteenth century and are an important element of the work of Debussy, Ravel, Sibelius and Vaughan Williams.

modulate / modulation

A change of key in the course of a composition while keeping the music in a continuous flow. (To stop the music and start again in another key is simply a change of key, not a modulation.) Usually, this is done by passing from one chord to another where two or more of the notes are common to both.

monody / monodic

From Gk. 'single song'. A solo song with accompaniment generally referring to the style of writing found in early seventeenth-century Italian opera. This contrasts with the earlier polyphonic vocal style when all parts were of equal importance and none acted simply as an accompaniment.

motet

A church choral composition, a setting of a Biblical text (usually Latin) in an elaborate contrapuntal style and designed for three or four to several voices, unaccompanied. The counterpart of the secular madrigal, and the Roman Catholic Church equivalent of the English anthem.

movement

A self-contained division of a large composition, each one having a different tempo, hence the name (e.g. Beethoven's Fifth Symphony has four movements). Extended compositions without any divisions are said to be 'in one movement'.

Nationalism

Music that is derived from the folk music of a particular country and suggests or depicts supposed 'national' characteristics. The Nationalist movement in music developed in the latter half of the nineteenth century, and can be seen as a rejection of the dominating concepts of German and Austrian music. Among notable Nationalist composers are Glinka, Mussorgsky, Smetana, Grieg, Sibelius and Vaughan Williams.

Neo-classicism

A rather inappropriate term for a stylistic trend in the 1920s, in which composers such as Stravinsky and Hindemith, in a reaction to late-Romanticism and 'emotionalism', reverted to the forms and techniques of the Baroque era. Counterpoint, concerto grosso technique and small instrumental forces were characteristic. There are few analogies with the Classical era of Haydn and Mozart: a more apt label for the style would have been 'neo-Baroque'.

opera buffa

It. A term used to describe the light, comic operas of the eighteenth century, the opposite of *opera seria*. *Opéra bouffe* (Fr.) describes the same kind of music, but that written in the mid-nineteenth century, particularly the operettas by composers such as Offenbach.

opéra comique

This French term does not mean 'comic opera' but refers both to the eighteenth-century type of French opera with spoken dialogue and less serious themes than those of the contemporary serious operas, which were, generally, on heroic or mythological subjects, and also to any opera (whether comic or not) that contains spoken dialogue. Thus both Bizet's *Carmen* and Gounod's *Faust* (which, in their original versions, have spoken dialogue) are classified as *opéras comiques*.

opera seria

The Italian term by which serious opera, as opposed to comic opera (or *opéra buffa*), was described until the early nineteenth century. This type has an Italian libretto, a plot based on mythology or legend, little action, formal music and, often, leading roles for a castrato.

opus

Lat. 'A work'. Usually abbreviated to Op. The system by which a composer's work is numbered, supposedly in the order of composition, although this is by no means infallible, viz. Chopin's two piano concertos. Works can be subdivided (e.g. Op.10 No.5) if they contain more than one piece. Beethoven was the first great composer to use opus numbers regularly. Op. Nos. also help identify a piece, especially if a composer has written two or more in a similar key and structure, such as Beethoven's Sonatas in E flat Op.7, Op.31 No.3, and Op.81a.

oratorio

Lat. and Gk. *Oratorium*. A sacred work similar to opera but without action, scenery or costume, in extended form and usually for chorus, soloists and orchestra. The term originated in about 1600 in performances at the Oratory of St Philip Neri in Rome (hence the name) composed by Emilio de Cavalieri. The term is also used for some non-religious works with a lofty theme (e.g. Tippett's *A Child of our Time*). J.S. Bach's settings of the passions are generally termed oratorios. Other famous examples are Handel's *Israel in Egypt*, *Messiah* and *Samson,* Haydn's *Creation*, Mendelssohn's *Elijah* and Elgar's *Dream of Gerontius.*

partita

It. 'Division'. The word is most commonly used to describe a group of court dance forms. The best-known examples are J.S. Bach's six keyboard partitas, which open with a prelude, followed by such dances as the allemande, courante, bourée, sarabande and gigue. Formerly, a partita meant a set of variations on a theme, the 'divisions' referring to divisions of notes into shorter notes – in other words, embellishments. It is unclear why Bach and his contemporaries changed this meaning into 'a suite of dances'.

passacaglia

It. A stately dance in 3/4 time in which a theme is continually repeated and which is generally constructed on a ground bass; unlike in the chaconne (to which it is very similar), however, it is not necessarily the bass that is repeated. J.S. Bach's Passacaglia in C minor for organ is a notable example.

pentatonic scale

Gk. *Pente*, 'five'. Strike all the black notes on the piano from C sharp upwards and you have a pentatonic scale, with five notes to the octave. It features in the traditional music of China, Japan and elsewhere in the Far East, and also in Africa. Scottish folk music uses it, as do American spirituals (e.g. 'Swing low, sweet chariot'). Composers like Debussy and Ravel have employed it for an 'Oriental effect' (try *Pagodes* from Debussy's *Estampes* and *Laideronette, Impératrice des pagodes* from Ravel's *Mother Goose* Suite). The pentatonic scale in the music of Java and Bali and played by the gamelan orchestras cannot be reproduced on the piano.

plainsong / plainchant

Also known as Gregorian chant after Pope Gregory the Great (c.540–604), who not only adjusted the liturgy as practised throughout the Middle Ages, but revised the melodies already in use and standardized them. Associated with the liturgy of the Roman Catholic Church, plainsong consists of melodies for unison singing that have no regular rhythm or definite time structure. The influence of plainsong on the world's music, its quantity and variety, and the fact that it has been in use for nearly 1,500 years, make it unique.

polyphony / polyphonic

From Gk. 'many sounds'. The type or method of composition in which two or more voice parts are combined harmoniously without losing their melodic individuality and their independence. Its most common usage is to imply the presence of counterpoint in music, as opposed to homophony, where musical interest is confined to one line of music. *See also* A CHRONOLOGY OF MUSIC, page 10.

polyrhythm

Where a composer exploits several different rhythms simultaneously. Frequently employed by twentieth-century composers, but Mozart's *Don Giovanni* has an example of three different but concurrent dance rhythms.

polytonality

The use of two or more keys simultaneously, usually by superimposing chords, arpeggios or melodies in a different key to the one that unequivocally defines the tonality of the piece.

prelude

A short piece that prepares the way for a longer work, (e.g. Prelude to *Lohengrin*), or a complete composition in itself. Chopin, Scriabin, Debussy, Rachmaninov and Shostakovich all wrote complete sets of preludes, among which are some of their most popular compositions. Another type of prelude is the self-contained work that can precede an organ or keyboard fugue (for example: the forty-eight preludes and fugues of J.S. Bach's *The Well-tempered Clavier*).

programme music

Music in which sound is used to depict a story or image; music that has a pre-ordained programme. A better, more explanatory term for it is 'illustrative music'. This can include the pictorial and bird song references in, say, French seventeenth-century harpsichord music, but is more generally confined to the Romantics. Beethoven's 'Pastoral', although an 'expression of emotion rather than a tone-painting', as the composer confirmed, is programme music, as are the symphonic poems of Liszt and Richard Strauss, Berlioz's *Harold in Italy* and similar works.

quartet

A piece for four instrumentalists or singers: a *string quartet* is made up of two violins, viola and cello; a *piano quartet* consists of piano, violin, viola and cello.

quintet

A piece for five instrumentalists or singers: a *string quintet* adds an extra viola or cello to the standard string quartet; a *piano quintet* adds a piano (except the most famous piano quintet, Schubert's *The Trout*, which dispenses with the second violin and adds a double-bass); a *wind quintet* consists of a flute, clarinet, oboe, bassoon and French horn.

recitative

Speech-like singing used in the narrative and dialogue of operas and oratorios, and frequently as a preliminary to an aria. It is scored in the normal way but delivered with a rhythmic freedom in performance.

requiem

A choral setting of the Mass for the Dead using the words of the Mass with the omission of the *Gloria* and *Credo* and interpolating other sections such as the *Dies irae*. The greatest Requiem Masses are those by Mozart, Berlioz, Verdi and Fauré.

rhapsody

The Bohemian composer and pianist Václav Jan Tomásek (1774–1850) is said to have been the first composer to use the term for his six rhapsodies for the piano, but it was Franz Liszt who popularized the form with his Hungarian Rhapsodies. 'Rhapsodic' suggests a romantic, epic inspiration, and is particularly associated with the piano (Brahms's rhapsodies, Rachmaninov's *Rhapsody on a theme of Paganini*, Gershwin's *Rhapsody in Blue* are popular examples) but the description is also applied to orchestral works. These are free-ranging fantasies, sometimes using folk melodies and employing a range of sharply-contrasted emotions (Enesco's *Romanian Rhapsodies* and Ravel's *Rapsodie espagnole* fall into this category).

Romanticism

See A CHRONOLOGY OF MUSIC, page 24.

rondo

It. or Fr. *rondeau* or 'round'. A type of composition in which the principal tune occurs at least three times in the same key. It became a standard device for the final movement of a concerto or sonata from Mozart's time, built upon a pattern of A-B-A-C-A-D-A, 'A' being the recurring rondo theme. Famous examples are Mozart's 'Turkish' rondo from his Piano Sonata in A (K331) and the finale of Haydn's Piano Trio in G, known as the 'Gypsy rondo'.

rubato

It. 'Robbed'. A way of playing or singing in which some of the notes are slightly hurried and others slowed down, while the underlying pulse remains steady. Used with discretion, *rubato* gives the effect of flexible, poetic expression as opposed to a mechanical, rigid interpretation. Listen to the recordings of the violinist Fritz Kreisler for a masterclass in this particular art.

scale

It. 'scala' meaning stairway. A scale of notes means a stairway of notes progressing upwards (or downwards) at regular intervals. Thus, for instance, the upward scale of C major (C-D-E-F-G-A-B-C) proceeds in a series of tones and semitones that occur at exactly the same point in all other major scales.

scherzo

It. 'A joke'. The scherzo movement of a symphony was developed by Beethoven from the minuet and trio movements employed by Haydn and Mozart. The rhythm is the same (3/4) and so is the structure (A-A-B-A – the B section of a scherzo is called the trio, as with a minuet) but instead of being stately, it is extremely lively. There are also examples of scherzi as independent works, usually for piano (e.g. by Chopin and Brahms).

Second Viennese school

The name given to the music of Schoenberg and his immediate disciples, Berg and Webern, all of whom lived in Vienna in the early years of the twentieth century. This contrasts with the music of the First Viennese school of Haydn and Mozart just over a century earlier.

Serialism

See the entry on SCHOENBERG.

sonata / sonata form

From It. *suonata*, 'to be sounded', as opposed to *cantata*, a piece 'to be sung'. The sonata is the most important form of classical instrumental music. The term has had many usages and each definition has many exceptions – the

keyboard sonatas of Domenico Scarlatti, for instance, are a long way from the Sonata in B minor by Liszt. However, there are points in common. Generally, a sonata is an extended work for piano or solo instrument with piano accompaniment, in three or four movements and with the same structure as a symphony.

The first movement is in sonata form. That is, it is made up of three distinct sections: **1:** *exposition*, presenting the themes, **2:** *development*, enlarging and varying the themes, and **3:** *recapitulation*, repeating the themes as they first appeared. The exposition features two themes: a) in the home key of the work, followed by b) a contrasted theme, or subject, in a related key and different mood. The second movement is in a slow tempo, more lyrical than the first, sometimes a theme and variations, sometimes in an A-B-A-C-A pattern. In a four-movement sonata, the composer frequently turns to a minuet or scherzo between the slow movements and the finale. The finale is lively, sometimes using sonata-form, a rondo or a theme with variations.

C.P. E. Bach clarified the sonata form, but Haydn and Mozart presented it in the manner with which we mainly identify it today. Other notable exponents – and it is fascinating to see how the sonata developed at the hands of succeeding generations of composers – are Beethoven (thirty-two for the piano, others for cello and violin), Schubert, Chopin, Liszt (whose monumental work in B minor resembles a fantasy more than a formal sonata), Brahms, Fauré, Scriabin and on through Bartók, Prokofiev and Barber.

staccato

It. 'detached'. If a composer wishes a note to be played short – and therefore detached from its predecessor – a dot is put over the note indicating that it should be held for less than its full length. The opposite to *legato*.

subject

Musicologists use the term, when analysing a piece of music, to define the group of notes or theme that form the basis of a composition and which are featured in the subsequent development of the work.

suite

From Fr. 'series' or 'set'. A cycle of pieces, the precursor of the sonata and the symphony, popular between about 1600 and 1750. Typically, a suite consists of contrasted dance movements such as the Allemande, Courante, Sarabande, Gigue, Bourrée, Minuet and Passepied. The most important suites of this kind are by Bach and Handel, who wrote them for both keyboard and orchestra. Since the 1800s, the term has also applied to a number of compositions linked together by a story, mood or idea (Tchaikowsky's *Nutcracker* Suite, Bizet's *L'arlésienne*, Grieg's *Holberg*, Ravel's *Mother Goose* are examples).

symphony

The word, literally, means 'sounding together', hence 'symphony orchestra' and 'symphony concert'. Originally, the term indicated an overture (to an opera, for example) or an instrumental section introducing, or between, sections of a vocal work. Today, it is the most important form of instrumental composition, specifically, since 1780, describing a work for orchestra in the form of an instrumental sonata but generally with fuller breadth of development and treatment. Usually, a symphony is in either three or four movements but can range from one (Sibelius) to seven (Anton Rubinstein); it can be for full orchestra or for strings or woodwind alone.

Haydn was nicknamed 'the father of the symphony', although symphonies had been composed before he gave the form eminence. Composers felt that the symphony was the most challenging and complex of musical structures. Musicologists talk about the merits or otherwise of a composer's 'symphonic argument' – whether the ideas and their handling have gelled into a tightly-knit structure. Rather like a novel, a symphony has to be intricately planned and keep the listener's attention with the equivalent of narrative drive, atmosphere and characterization.

syncopation

Placing the accent on a beat that would not normally be accented. This was a characteristic feature of much dance music of the 1920s and jazz-influenced classical music, although syncopation occurs throughout musical history from as early as the fourteenth century.

toccata

From It. *toccare*, 'to touch'. A description of a piece, usually for a solo performer, requiring a rapid, virtuosic execution. Celebrated examples are J.S. Bach's organ Toccata and Fugue in D minor, Widor's organ Toccata from his Fifth Symphony and Schumann's Toccata in C for piano.

tonal / tonality

The 'tonality of a piece' is the same as saying the 'key of a piece' when used abstractly. Music that observes a single key – and this includes most music before the twentieth century – is said to be tonal, i.e. it is usually built on the accepted major / minor chords / scales tradition and the relationship between them. Tonality is the opposite of polytonality (simultaneous use of several keys) or atonality (absence of key).

tone

A confusing word, thanks to the Americans. What we call a note, they call a tone – as in 'that chord is made up of four tones'; and what we could more clearly refer to as a note-row or twelve-note music, when talking of Serialism, the Americans call a tone-row or twelve-tone. We reserve the word to describe the sound an artist makes ('he plays with a brittle tone') or, musicologically, to describe the interval of, say, a major second (e.g. between C and D), in other words two semitones. From C to D is a whole tone. *See also* WHOLE TONE.

tonic

The first note of a scale, the key-note and centre of its tonality. The key-note of compositions written in that tonality (e.g. F is the tonic of the keys of F major and F minor).

tremolo / tremolando

It. 'Trembling'. The rapid repetition of a single note on the violin made by up- and down-strokes with the bow; also one or more notes on the violin, piano or organ, played as rapidly as possible. The equivalent on the drums of a roll.

triad

A three-note chord, the highest sounding a fifth above the lowest, the second sounding a third above the lowest. For example: C-E-G. The interval of a third can be either major (E) or minor (E flat), resulting in a major or minor triad. Similarly, the interval of a fifth can be perfect (G), diminished (G flat) or augmented (G sharp), hence the augmented triad or the diminished triad.

trio

A work for three performers, usually in sonata form, and having several movements. A *piano trio* is a work for piano, violin and cello; a *string trio* is for violin, viola and cello. A trio is also the name given to the central section of a minuet, so called because it was originally written in three-part harmony.

twelve-note music

See the entry on SCHOENBERG.

verismo

It. 'Realism'. The naturalistic school of opera represented by the works of

Mascagni, Puccini, Giordano and Leoncavallo. *Pagliacci* is often cited as the first of its kind, but Bizet's *Carmen* has a stronger claim. The subjects of *verismo* operas were not drawn from legend or morality tales but from contemporary life, and they typically present scenes of heightened violence in sordid surroundings.

viol

General name for the class of stringed instruments dating far back into European history and current up to about 1700, and superseded after that time by the violin family. The viol is not dissimilar to a bowed lute, although with fewer strings. The three principal viols are the treble, tenor and bass viol; all were rested on or between the legs, hence their proper name *viol da gamba*, meaning 'for the leg'.

virginal

Keyboard instrument of the sixteenth and seventeenth centuries resembling a smaller, oblong-shaped harpsichord, with its keyboard along the longer side of the soundboard (unlike the harpsichord). English composers of the period were particularly active in writing for the virginal – Bull, Gibbons and Byrd in particular. *The Fitzwilliam Virginal Book* and *My Ladye Nevells Booke* are two famous collections of pieces for the instrument.

whole tone

A whole-tone scale is one consisting of a series of intervals of a tone. It may begin on any note. There is no tonic or any other implied relationship between the notes of the series. This contrasts with the traditional scale made up of whole tones and semitones. To play a whole-tone scale on the piano you would strike C-D-E-F#-G#-A#-B# (C). Debussy was prominent among those using the whole-tone scale for chords and short passages, as in his *Voiles*, from Book 1 of the *Préludes*.

INDEX

Numbers in **bold** refer to main entries. Numbers in *italics* refer to illustrations.

Songs my Mother taught me (Dvořák) 126
Songs of farewell (Parry) 218
Songs of the Auvergne (Canteloube) 103–04
Songs of the Sea (Stanford) 277
Songs of Travel (Vaughan Williams) 304
Songs without Words (Mendelssohn) 23, 198
Sonnambula, La (Bellini) 75
'Sonnen, Die' String Quartets (Haydn) 158
Sorabji, Kaikhosru 46
Sorcerer, The (Sullivan) 289
Sorcerer's Apprentice, The (Dukas) 122, 243
Sospiro, Un (Liszt) 183
Sound an alarm (Handel) 155
Sound Barrier, The (film) 56
Source, La (Delibes) 117
Sousa, John Philip 275–76
South Bank Show (television) 217
Southern Concerto (Ponce) 45
Souvenir de Moscou (Wieniawski) 41
Souvenir de Porto Rico (Gottschalk) 145
Spanish Dances (Moszkowski) 203, 204
Spanish Overture (Glinka) 141
Sparky's Magic Piano 108
Spartacus (Khachaturian) 172
Spells (Bennett) 76
Spem in alium (Tallis) 293
Spinning Chorus (Wagner) 317
Spinning Song (Mendelssohn) 198
'Spitfire' Prelude and Fugue (Walton) 321
Spleen (Fauré) 133
Spohr, Louis 38
Spontini, Gaspare 38
Skating Rink (Honegger) 164
Sprechstimme 254
'Spring' Sonata (Beethoven) 73
Spring Song (Mendelssohn) 198
Spring Symphony (Britten) 96, 97
'Spring' Symphony (Schumann) 262, 263
Spring Waters (Rachmaninov) 235
Stabat mater
  (Dvořák) 126
  (Palestrina) 12, 218
  (Pergolesi) 37, 74
  (Poulenc) 221, 222
  (Rossini) 245, 246
  (Szymanowski) 291
staccato 343
Stainer, John 41
Stamitz, Carl 19
Stamitz, Johann 18, 19, 37
Ständchen (Brahms) 94
Ständchen (Schubert) 260
Ständchen (R. Strauss) 283
Ständchen, Das (Wolf) 328
Stanford, Charles Villiers 276–77
Stanford in B flat (Stanford) 276, 277
Stanley, John 37
Star of Bethlehem, The (Adams) 41
Star-spangled Banner 145
Stars and Stripes Forever, The (Sousa) 276
Steffani, Agostino 36
Stenka Razin (Glazunov) 139
Sting, The (film) 43
Stockhausen, Karlheinz 32, 49

Stokowski, Leopold 62, 63
Stone Guest, The (Dargomizhsky) 40, 241
Storchenbotschaft (Wolf) 328
Story of Three Loves (film) 235
Stradella, Alessandro 35
Stranger in Paradise (cf. Borodin) 88
Strauss I, Johann 279
Strauss II, Johann 90, 91, 277–79, 278
Strauss, Richard 28–29, 56, 279, 280–81, 281
'Stravaganza, La', violin concertos (Vivaldi) 311
Stravinsky, Igor 29, 130, 136, 284–88, 285
Street Corner Overture (Rawsthorne) 47
Streghe, Le (Paganini) 217
string quartet 342
string quartets 7
  (Bartók) 66–67
  (Beethoven) 21, 69, 73
  (Borodin) 87, 88
  (Carter) 48
  (Debussy) 115, 116
  (Dvořák) 116
  (Elgar) 128
  (Franck) 134–35
  (Haydn) 19–20, 158–59
  (Janáček) 168, 169
  (Milhaud) 201
  (Mozart) 208–09, 336
  (Raff) 40
  (Ravel) 237, 240
  (Schubert) 259
  (Shostakovich) 268, 269
  (Smetana) 274, 275
  (Tchaikowsky) 299
  (Tippett) 301, 302
  (Walton) 321
string quintet 342
string quintets
  (Boccherini) 87
  (Mozart) 206, 208, 209
  (Schubert) 257, 259
string trio 345
Stronghold Sure, A (Luther) 34
subject 344
Suicidio! (Ponchielli) 220
suite 344
Suite Algérienne (Saint-Saëns) 251
Suite 'Bergamasque' (Debussy) 117, 331
Suite de ballet (Ketèlbey) 44
Suite 'Española' (Albéniz) 52
Suite for recorder and strings (Telemann) 301
Suite for two pianos (Arensky) 55
Suite for violin and orchestra (Sinding) 273
Suite Gothique (Boëllmann) 42
Suite in B (Handel) 93
Suite in F sharp minor (Dohnányi) 121
Suite Italienne (Stravinsky) 288
suites 7, 16
  (J.S. Bach) 63, 344
Sullivan, Arthur 214, 288–89, 289
Summa (Pärt) 219
Summer Days (Coates) 45
Summer Evening (Kodály) 173
Summer Morning by a Lake (Schoenberg) 255
Summer Night on the River (Delius) 120